STATISTICAL REASONING
for the
BEHAVIORAL SCIENCES

Richard J. Shavelson

University of California at Los Angeles

Allyn and Bacon, Inc.

Boston, London, Sydney, Toronto

To Patti, Karin, and Amy

Library of Congress Cataloging in Publication Data

Shavelson, Richard J
  Statistical reasoning for the behavioral sciences.

  Bibliography: p.
  Includes index.
  1. Psychometrics. I. Title.
BF39.S43   150'.72   80-17678
ISBN 0-205-06933-9
ISBN 0-205-07739-0 (International)
Printed in the United States of America.
10 9 8 7 6 5 4 3   85 84 83

◆ Contents ◆

SECTION IV

Reasoning Behind Statistical Inference 261

♦ 9 ♦

Statistical Inference: By Intuition 263

♦ 10 ♦

Probability Theory and Mathematical Distributions 283

♦ 11 ♦

Inferences about a Population Mean from Sample Means 299

♦ 12 ♦

Inferences about Differences between Means 333

♦ 18 ♦

Chi-Square Tests 516

SECTION VI

Within-Subjects Designs and Mixed Designs 549

♦ 19 ♦

The t Test for Dependent Samples 554

◆ Preface ◆

The job of a statistics textbook is to communicate the structure of the subject matter to the readers so that they understand the meaning of the statistical concepts and can use those concepts to solve problems. In order to communicate meaning, I have used somewhat extensive verbal and visual exposition, seldom found in statistics or mathematics texts. Knowing that concepts have certain meanings does not guarantee, however, that you know *how* to use them to solve problems. The *procedural knowledge* of statistics—required information and computations—may be just as important as the meaning of the concepts. This text, then, stresses conceptual *and* procedural knowledge of statistics, and the link between them. Typically, in each section of a chapter, one or more concepts are presented verbally and in figures. Then, the link between the concepts and the procedures for applying them is set forth.

Several pedagogical devices have been developed for the text in order to communicate procedural and conceptual knowledge. With respect to procedural knowledge, I have developed something like a computational algorithm, called a *Procedure*. Step by step, the Procedure identifies the information and computations needed to solve a well-defined class of problems. Moreover, Procedures are used to link the verbal and figural exposition of concepts to the working formulas of statistics. Finally, example problems have been inserted in the text and readers are encouraged to work through them to check their knowledge as they study. Detailed solutions to these problems are provided. And extensive sets of problems have been provided at the end of each chapter.

This treatment of procedural knowledge amounts to incorporating a student guide and workbook within the text. Rather than treat procedural knowledge as supplemental, I prefer to treat it as central and integrate it with conceptual knowledge. Together, they define the structure of the subject matter.

With respect to conceptual knowledge, figures have been used to a greater extent than is usual in statistics texts. This has been done to provide visual representations of the concepts that parallel and enhance verbal exposition. Moreover, sequences of pictures are used to represent concepts involving a sequence of processes. These pictorial sequences are as close as I could come to what I wanted—a motion picture of the concepts at work.

In summary, this text stresses both statistical reasoning and procedures in communicating the structure of the subject matter. Statistical concepts are communicated verbally, pictorially, and procedurally. Few texts have attempted an integration of conceptual and procedural knowledge within their covers, as this one does.

The book also *integrates statistics with the design of research* in the behavioral sciences. This has been done for three reasons: 1) to clarify the meaning of statistical concepts as well as to provide realistic problem applications from psychology, sociology, and education; 2) to familiarize the reader with well-defined classes of problems that arise in behavioral research and can be solved by applying the concepts and procedures in this text; and 3) to motivate students by providing a *raison d'etre* for statistics in their behavioral science curriculum. Nevertheless, the material on research design may be omitted by the instructor who prefers a more traditional, statistical approach.

The book is divided into six sections. Section I—Research and the Role of Statistics—contains a chapter on the design of behavioral research and the role of statistics in this research, and a chapter presenting five studies of substantive importance which are then used to exemplify concepts and procedures presented in subsequent chapters. Section II—Descriptive Statistics for Univariate Distributions—contains chapters on frequency distributions, measures of central tendency and variability, and the normal distribution. Section III—Joint Distributions—contains chapters on joint distributions, correlation, and regression. Section IV—Reasoning Behind Statistical Inference—contains five chapters. The first chapter in this section, Chapter 9, provides a conceptual introduction to statistical inference leading to the need for probability theory. The next chapter, Chapter 10, presents those aspects of probability theory needed to understand the inferential statistics contained in the remainder of the book. The next two chapters, Chapters 11 and 12, systematically develop the concept of a sampling distribution of means for one and two sample cases. Both chapters contain procedures for conducting statistical tests and constructing confidence intervals based on the normal sampling distribution. The last chapter in the section, Chapter 13, deals with power and sample size. The last two sections—Between-Subjects, and Within-Subjects and Mixed Designs—contain chapters that present statistical tests such as the t test, simple and factorial analysis of variance, and chi square goodness-of-fit and contingency table tests.

Chapters 3 through 19 are built around the major features of the book. Each chapter has the following general framework: 1) outline of key topics covered in the chapter; 2) conceptual overview of the major concepts presented in the chapter, usually couched in one or more examples of research, one's intuition, or both; 3) presentation of concepts verbally and pictorially; 4) presentation of procedures involved in using the concepts; 5) summary of the concept/procedure in the form of a computational procedure; 6) presentation of example research problems with detailed solutions; 7) brief summary of the chapter; 8) list of key words; and 9) exercises. In order to complete the development of a general topic, steps 3 through 6 are repeated throughout each chapter.

Many different people have been involved in the development of this text and so deserve acknowledgment. I would like to express my thanks to the hundreds of students who, over a period of four years, have participated in the pilot work on the text both at UCLA and at other universities throughout the country. Students have pointed out errors in the text and in the problems. They also helped work on rewording of sections that were unclear. As a consequence, these errors and ambiguities have been eliminated from the text to the extent that is humanly possible.

Three national panels of anonymous reviewers, over the four years, have critiqued the book for its technical accuracy and its utility in teaching introductory statistics. Special thanks go to Andy Porter and Teri Kuhs of Michigan State University, and Larry Hubert of the University of California, Santa Barbara. They patiently and thoroughly provided page-by-page critiques of different versions of the text. I also want to acknowledge the great help of my colleagues who commented on various chapters of the text: Leigh Burstein, Joel Cadwell, Phil Ender, Nancy Russo, Noreen Webb, Hilda Borko, Marsha Brown, Steve Klein, Harold Levine, Miles Rogers, Rod Skager, Ian Smith, and Don Witske.

Linda Powell typed the many drafts of the book over its five-year evolution. She also served as both editorial and mathematical critic. Did you ever work with a colleague with a joint major in English and mathematics? All told, Linda was my toughest critic and whatever benefit students get from the book is due, in large part, to Linda's sometimes relentless "help" on every word, number, symbol, and punctuation mark in the book.

Finally, if it were not for Curt Whitesel, the book would never have come into being. It was Curt's cajoling, as editor for Allyn and Bacon, that led to my writing the book. Curt, then, should share some of the credit for the book. As happens, Curt left Allyn and Bacon before the book was completed. He left me in the very able hands of Gary Folven, Allen Workman, and Margaret Pinette who admirably carried the project through to completion.

SECTION I

Research
and the
Role of Statistics

F ROM the behavioral scientist's perspective, statistics are tools which can be used to unravel the mysteries of the data collected in a research study. In particular, they allow the researcher to summarize the data and to distinguish between chance and systematic effects. While the behavioral scientist's main interest is in the substance of the study, there is an interplay between the substance, the design of the study, and the analysis of the data. This being so, it seems appropriate to begin a text on statistics with issues of substance, design, and statistics.

Substantive issues are the questions behavioral scientists are studying. For example, psychologists are examining the utility of concepts such as memory, thinking, and problem-solving in explaining behavior. Educators are examining the effects of information about students on teachers' expectations and on their instructional decisions. And sociologists are examining the effects of institutional demands on the role of women in society.

The design issue is one of matching the research design to the substantive problem without distorting the problem. This means that the behavioral scientist must have a firm grasp of a variety of research designs along with the logical and statistical rationale underlying them, and build the one most appropriate for the phenomenon being studied.

Once they have a research problem, an appropriate research design, the study run, and data, behavioral scientists rely heavily on statistical tools to unravel answers to their questions. These tools help to describe what happened in the study and to generalize the results from the people observed in the study to the larger group of people of interest to the researcher.

For most students studying in the behavioral sciences, the study of statistics becomes relevant when (and perhaps only when) something about a substantive area is understood, and something about the design of research is understood. It is at this point that you are ready for answers to the question, "How do I make sense out of all the information I have collected?"

The purposes of the two chapters in this section (ambitiously stated) are to get you interested in doing behavioral research, to give you a review of topics on the design of research so that you become confident in designing research, and to provide you with some examples of research that will arouse your interest in statistical methods. More humbly, the purpose here is to get you to a point where you can see the relevance of statistics to research in the behavioral sciences.

Chapter 1 presents material on designing and conducting research, along with some examples to provide a taste of some central concerns in the behavioral sciences. This is done because the use of statistics in analyzing and interpreting data—the major topic of this textbook—depends on the type of research design used. Chapter 2 presents five areas of research currently being explored by behavioral scientists. Then some studies and data are presented. It's up to you to decide what happened in the studies. The remaining chapters of this book provide the statistical tools needed to unravel the results of these studies. These data (as well as data from other studies) will be used throughout the text to demonstrate the use of statistics in answering research questions.

1 ♦

Design of Research
in the
Behavioral Sciences

The Role of Research in the Behavioral Sciences

Purposes of Empirical Research in the Behavioral Sciences

♦ The Process of Empirical Research ♦

The Role of Statistics in Behavioral Research

♦ Descriptive Statistics ♦

♦ Inferential Statistics ♦

♦ Random Sampling ♦

♦ Relation between Descriptive and Inferential Statistics ♦

Some Basic Elements in Designing Research

♦ Variables and Hypotheses ♦

♦ Quantification of Variables ♦

♦ Classification of Variables for Designing Research ♦

Threats to the Validity of Research Studies

♦ Threats to Internal Validity ♦

♦ Threats to External Validity ♦

♦ Relationship between Internal and External Validity ♦

Designs for Behavioral Research

♦ Preexperimental Designs ♦

♦ Experimental Designs ♦

♦ Quasiexperimental Designs ♦

♦ Ex Post Facto Designs ♦

Summary

♦ Key Words ♦

♦ Exercises ♦

Research has been described as "doing one's damnedest to find answers to perplexing questions." This is not the usual textbook definition, but it is the definition used by most of us who are intimately involved in doing research. A more sober definition is that *research* is a systematic approach to finding answers to questions. This is a pretty wide-open definition, as it should be.

THE ROLE OF RESEARCH IN THE BEHAVIORAL SCIENCES

There are many ways to attempt, systematically, to find answers to questions about human behavior. We might, for example, be interested in the nature of human emotion and whether different emotions (euphoria, anger) are due solely to different physiological states of a person or due to a general physiological arousal plus a cognitive component for interpreting the arousal. Or we might investigate the influence of humanistic and behavioristic views of education on the way children are taught, by systematically examining historical events such as the progressive education movement in the 1940s or the emphasis on math and science curricula following the launching of Sputnik in the late 1950s. Or we might proceed quite formally and logically by setting forth some assumptions about, for example, the nature of learning, and then work deductively from them to arrive at answers to our questions about how people learn. Or we might examine ordinary language systematically to find out how people view the world.

However, these are probably not the kinds of research that commonly come to mind for most of us. For some, "research" conjures up an image of a laboratory (perhaps Frankenstein's) with microscopes, glass tubes, flasks, electrical discharges jumping from one pole to another, and smoke rising up from some "experiment." Others think of rats running mazes, monkeys communicating with experimenters, or college sophomores memorizing nonsense syllables. Still others think of experiments in natural settings such as classrooms, or surveys such as the Kinsey Report. In other words, when most of us think of research, we think of one possible type of research, exemplified by the scientific method. With this method, questions (problems) are reduced to their component parts, alternative answers to the questions are identified using some theory, some direct observation, or both, and then the alternative answers are tested empirically. That is, alternative answers are tested by trying out each of them and seeing which ones work. The major characteristics of the scientific method, then, are (1) reducing a question to its observable component parts and (2) testing possible answers to the questions. This book focuses on the scientific method, only one of several approaches to research. It provides basic

4

tools for helping to decide which of the possible alternative answers to questions are best (in some sense) on the basis of empirical tests.

In some ways researchers are like kids, though most of them won't admit it. Research questions are, for researchers, what puzzles or games are for kids (cf. Kuhn, 1970). Researchers attempt to solve puzzles or win games by designing experiments and finding out the best answers. And most researchers have as much fun doing research as kids do playing games. Since the work ethic tells us that if we are having fun, we are not "working," and since some researchers are afraid of being seen to be kids at heart, books and lectures on the topic tend to be quite formal. This is not to say that the questions addressed by researchers are no more than games and that the answers provided by research are no more important than winning at Monopoly. Questions of the effects of schools on students' learning and self-concepts are indeed serious, and the answers must be as accurate as possible. Likewise, questions about the nature of human memory and information processing are important, and the researchers are and should be held responsible for their answers to these questions. So also, questions about the influence of private and public institutions on the behavior of people who work within these institutions are serious and demand accurate answers. Such questions demand care, wisdom, accuracy, and doing one's damnedest in conducting research, but they do not preclude having fun too. The purpose of this book is to let you in on the importance, excitement, and fun of research by providing some of the skills needed to begin to answer research questions. These skills have to do with the analysis and interpretation of data collected in behavioral research in areas such as psychology, sociology, and education.

The purpose of empirical research in the behavioral sciences, in broad terms, is to provide answers to questions about behavior using the scientific method. Throughout this book, the focus will be on examples which provide answers to questions about *human* behavior. Nevertheless, the methods presented apply also to studying the behavior of nonhumans.

PURPOSES OF EMPIRICAL RESEARCH IN THE BEHAVIORAL SCIENCES

Perhaps the best way to give you a flavor of this research is to describe some of it. A central question in psychology has concerned whether or not concepts of "mind" such as memory, thinking, and problem solving are needed to explain behavior. Hull argued that such concepts were unnecessary in a theory of behavior and that behavior depended on habit strength, drive, and incentive. Tolman took the opposite position and argued that concepts involving the mind, such as "cognitive maps," were necessary to explain the behavior of rats running a maze. Watson argued that the concept of mind was unnecessary in explaining human behavior; behavior could be controlled by controlling the environment in which a person was placed. Skinner followed the same lines of reasoning and conducted experiments showing how behavior could be controlled by manipulating schedules of reinforcement (see Hilgard and Bower,

1966, for references to these studies). More recently, concepts such as memory, thinking, and problem solving have come to play an important role in psychological theories which view man as an information-processing system (e.g., Newell & Simon, 1972). Research on human information processing has shown that both the nature of the environment and the information-processing capabilities of the mind affect human behavior. In fact, the question is no longer mind versus no mind. That has been replaced by the more sensible question of how environmental variables and information-processing capabilities of humans, taken together, affect behavior.

In education, a central question today is whether schools in general, or teachers in particular, are responsible for students' achievement. The Coleman (1966) study and most of the reanalyses of Coleman's data suggest that teachers and schools have little impact on students' achievement. Illich (1971) has even gone so far as to recommend deschooling society (not on the basis of Coleman's data). However, Wiley and Harnischfeger (1974) and others have used Coleman's data to show, after some legitimate reconceptualization, that schools and teachers do have an effect on students' achievement. This effect seems to depend on the teacher's ability to keep students actively engaged in learning tasks. Bennett's (1976) study of the effects of progressive and traditional teachers on students' achievement has stirred the controversy over whether progressive or traditional education is more effective in educating students. And the research of Rosenthal and Jacobsen (1968) has raised the controversial question of whether students' achievement is influenced by teachers' expectations.

There is no limit to the examples that could be given. And I apologize to those of you in other fields who feel that our examples should have been drawn from them instead of education and psychology. In any case, you now have some idea of the kinds of questions behavioral researchers attempt to answer.

Regardless of the field in which the question is posed, the purposes of behavioral research, in more specific terms, are to *describe*, *predict*, and *control behavior*. Some questions call for *description of behavior*. For example, a politician might be interested in the preferences of voters in his or her district. A researcher might provide an answer to this question by describing past voting trends or by conducting a survey of voter preferences.

Some questions call for *prediction of behavior*. For example, college administrators would like to predict the behavior (e.g., achievement) of students in order to decide whether or not to admit them to college. College entrance examination scores are collected for the purposes of predicting students' performance in college and, in this way, improving the accuracy of admissions decisions. With this information, the administrator admits those students who are predicted to be successful in that college.

Finally, some questions call for *control of behavior*. That is, they ask about a cause-and-effect relationship. For example, does the organization of a list of words affect the ways in which the words are remembered? In order to answer this question, a researcher might randomly assign college sophomores in introductory psychology to an experimental group that studies a list of words arranged in a logically ordered hierarchy or to a control group that studies the words arranged in a scrambled order. After some period of time, both groups of "subjects" would be asked to recall the words. The average numbers of words recalled by the two groups might then be compared to answer the question.

♦   ♦   ♦   ♦   ♦

Research is a *process* of finding answers to questions. Whenever a process is described in writing (as opposed to doing it), it becomes static and idealized. In an attempt to overcome this problem, the interplay between the steps will be described, and a concrete example—research into the effects of organization on remembering a list of words—will be used. However, it should be noted at the outset that the following is a deliberately simplified outline of what happens. In reality, the process is not so neat, and the researcher must have all of the steps in mind at once and plan ahead.

The Process of Empirical Research

The first step is to *ask a question*. This question will identify a problem and, with some hard thinking, the problem will become adequately defined so that it can be researched. In the example, we ask "What is the effect of organization on remembering a list of words?" This question identified a problem. The selection of a list of words that could be arranged either hierarchically or in a scrambled fashion helped define the problem more precisely, as did the decision to have the subjects recall the words once a period of time had elapsed after studying them.

The next step is to *review theories and past research* which might suggest hypotheses about the solutions to the problem, i.e., answers to the question. For the example study, both past research and theory (Bower et al., 1969; Miller, 1956) suggested that words arranged in a logically ordered hierarchy would be remembered better than words not organized in any way. This work led to the *hypothesis* that subjects studying a hierarchically organized list of words would recall more of the words than subjects studying an unorganized (scrambled) list of words. In general terms, a hypothesis is a statement about what you expect to happen in the experiment.

Actually, the process is not quite so neat. There is an interplay between these two steps. Reading some theory or research may suggest a problem to be researched. Or, having identified a general problem, reviewing theories and past research may help define the problem more precisely. Or reviewing past theory and research may lead to questions that challenge a presumed theory and result in research which attempts to disconfirm the existing theory and provide a basis for an alternative theory.

With a problem and one or more hypotheses in hand, the next step is to *design a study* in order to collect data (information) bearing on your hypotheses. In designing the study, decisions are made about the "subjects" (people, students, groups of people, etc.) to be observed, the factors which are expected to influence the behavior of the "subjects," the ways in which these factors will be observed or manipulated, the ways in which extraneous factors will be controlled, and the ways in which the behavior of the subjects will be systematically observed (measured).

In the example study, the subjects were to be college sophomores enrolled in introductory psychology. One factor was to be manipulated: the organization of the list of words (hierarchical or scrambled). Extraneous factors were to be controlled by flipping a coin to (randomly) assign subjects to either the organized list of words or the scrambled list. And the behavior of the subjects was to be observed (measured) by counting the number of words correctly recalled from the list.

Of course, the way in which the research question is defined will influence the design of the research, as will prior research and theory. Again, there is an interplay between the steps in the research process.

Next, the design is implemented by *conducting* the study. In conducting the study, the actual behavior of the subjects is measured under each of the conditions of the study. The measures of behavior constitute the **data** collected in the study. In the example study, this means that some college sophomores were randomly assigned to the scrambled list of words and some to the organized list. They read and studied a list of words either organized hierarchically or in a scrambled order. Then they were asked to recall these words, say, ten minutes after studying them. This step in conducting the study produces the data of interest.

With the data in hand, the next step is to summarize them in such a way that the summary helps answer the question that started this whole process in motion. This is where statistics come in. Statistics provide methods for summarizing and describing data. In the example study, the data—the number of words recalled by each subject in the control and experimental groups— might be summarized by a statistic called the *mean*. The mean (or average) number of words recalled correctly by subjects in the experimental group and control group might be used to describe the behavior of subjects in each group.

Finally, the data are interpreted so that they bear on the original research question. Here, too, statistics come in handy. At this step, statistics are used to help decide whether the differences in the data may have been due to chance or to the treatments manipulated in the study. In the example study, statistics could be used to determine whether the difference between the means of the experimental and control groups may have been due to chance or caused by the difference in the organization of the lists of words.

To summarize, there are six general steps in conducting research:

1. Identification and definition of a research problem
2. Formulation of hypotheses on the basis of theory, research, or both
3. Design of the research
4. Conduct of the research
5. Analysis of the data from the research
6. Interpretation of the data as they bear on the research problem

Of course, this is an idealization and a gross oversimplification of the steps in the research process. Remember that there is interplay among all of the steps along the way.

The concepts and tools of statistics are involved either implicitly or explicitly throughout most of the research process. They are involved in decisions about selecting subjects for a study, assigning subjects to different groups (if the design calls for this), describing the data collected in the study, and generalizing from the findings in the study. For example, in the study of the effect of organization on remembering a list of words, a decision was made to select college sophomores and *randomly* assign them (by flipping a coin) to either an organized or scrambled list of words. Moreover, once the study was conducted, the two groups of subjects were described and compared with regard to the average number of words recalled. Finally, attention was paid to the particular subjects in the study because, on the basis of their behavior, the researcher could draw inferences about the effect of the organization of the words on other people like them.

THE ROLE OF STATISTICS IN BEHAVIORAL RESEARCH

    Statistics, then, play a number of major, interrelated roles in behavioral research. They set forth guidelines for summarizing and describing data. They also provide methods for drawing inferences from groups of subjects to larger groups of people. And they set forth guidelines for selecting subjects for a study, assigning them to groups (if called for in the design), and collecting data.

◆   ◆   ◆   ◆   ◆

The term **descriptive statistics** refers to a set of concepts and methods used in organizing, summarizing, tabulating, depicting, and describing collections of data. The data can be test scores, reaction times, or ratings; they can be ranks; or they can be indications of group membership (e.g., political party affiliation, personality type, sex). The goal of descriptive statistics is to provide a representation of the data which describes, in tabular, graphical, or numerical form, the results of research. For example, by summarizing the number of words recalled by subjects in the scrambled-word group and in the organized-word group with a mean score for each group, one possible description of the performance of the subjects within each group is achieved. In order to ascertain the effects of organizing a list of words on recall, the means of the two groups can be compared. If organization has a facilitating effect on memory, the mean number of words recalled by subjects in the organized-word group should be greater than that in the scrambled-word group. In other words, descriptive statistics provide a picture of what happened in a study. Without descriptive statistics, data in the researcher's office would be overwhelming and uninterpretable. (Chapters 3–8 present the concepts and skills for describing collections of data.)

Descriptive Statistics

♦   ♦   ♦   ♦   ♦

Inferential Statistics   The term **inferential statistics** refers to a set of methods used to draw inferences about a large group of people from data available on only a representative subset of the group. In statistics, the large group of people is called a **population**. The subset of the large group is called a **sample**. The term inferential statistics, then, refers to a set of methods used to draw inferences about a population from data available on a sample from the population.

Since the purpose of behavioral research is to provide answers to questions about human behavior, the researcher is interested in answers that are true for populations, not just true for samples of (say) 30 people. However, in behavioral research, it is usually impossible to observe an entire population (the population may be indefinitely large) or impractical to do so (the cost may be too great). Thus, the researcher must work inductively and infer the characteristics of populations from data gathered on samples from these populations. Thus, a sample of college sophomores was observed in the study of the effect of organization on remembering, not because the researcher was interested in those students per se, but because, by observing their performance, she could infer something about the effects of organization on the memories of people who were not observed (i.e., in the population).

The validity of the inference from sample to population rests on the degree to which the subjects in the sample are representative of the people in the population. If you were interested in whether the voters in the United States wanted government to set controls on the price of gasoline, common sense would tell you not to limit your sample to the top executives of the major oil companies. Clearly, executives are not representative of voters in the United States. The representativeness of a sample is an important question, and it is addressed in statistics, as we shall see below, by drawing a sample such that every person in the population has an equal chance of being included in the sample.

♦   ♦   ♦   ♦   ♦

Random Sampling   In making inferences from the behavior of the subjects in a sample to the behavior of people in the population, logic demands that the sample be representative of the population. Here the concept of random sampling plays an important role. **Random sampling** is the process of selecting subjects from a population such that each person in the population has an equal chance of being selected. Moreover, random sampling implies that the appearance of one subject in the sample is in no way affected by the appearance of any other subject. That is, random sampling implies the independence of the selection of subjects in the sample.

The concept of random sampling is theoretical. It can be approximated in reality by rolling dice, flipping coins, spinning roulette wheels, or drawing names from a hat. However, these methods are time consuming and limited in their practical application to fairly small samples. For this reason, tables of random numbers have been generated that approximate randomness quite closely. They are tables of digits, 0 through 9, that are generated by a mechanical process with the criterion that each of the digits (0–9) has an equal chance of occurring at any one point in the table.

As an example of how the table of random numbers can be used to draw a

Steps in drawing a random sample of subjects ♦ Procedure 1-1

Operation	Example
1 Assign an identification number to each subject.	Name ID Number Sally 01 Tom 02 ⋮ ⋮ Linda 79 Debbie 80
2 Turn to the table of random numbers (Table A), place your finger anywhere on any page of the table, and locate any two-digit number.	Suppose you placed your finger on 33.
3 Find the number on the same page in the row represented by the first digit of the number located in step 2 and the column represented by the second digit of this number.	33—third row, third column. Find the number located in the third row and the third column on the same page.
4 Beginning with the place in the table found in step 3, group the digits into sets corresponding to the largest identification number.	Since 80 is the largest identification number, two columns are needed to select numbers from the table.

5 Begin reading across the row until you locate a number falling in the range of numbers assigned in step 1. (Ignore all numbers which are outside this range.)
  a If a number has not been selected already, include the subject corresponding to that number in the sample.
  b If a number has already been selected, ignore it and continue.
	Suppose that six subjects are to be included in the sample. Beginning at the third row, third column, we identify the following two-digit numbers:
	
	77
	23
	02
	77 (ignore)
	09
	61
	87 (ignore)
	25

6 Continue the procedure in step 5 until the desired sample size has been reached.	The random sample will consist of individuals with the assigned identification numbers of 77, 23, 2, 9, 61, 25.

random sample, consider the selection of subjects for the study of the effects of organization on memory. Suppose 40 subjects were to be selected randomly from a sophomore class of 800 students. To each student in the class, a different three-digit number (ranging from 001 to 800) would be assigned. Next, a table of random numbers such as Table A at the end of this book would be used to select the 40 subjects as follows. With Table A open to (say) the first page, put your finger on the page with your eyes closed. Suppose you pointed to the number 47. This tells you to begin selecting numbers from the table at row 4 and column 7. Moving along row 4, beginning at column 7, you encounter the following numbers: 716120449032 (and so on). By grouping these digits into sets of three digits, the following numbers are obtained: 716, 120, 449, 032, ... Include in the sample those subjects with the identification numbers 716, 120, 449, 032, etc., until 40 subjects are selected. Suppose you come across the number 801. Since there are only 800 students in the sophomore class, no one has this identification number. So it is disregarded. Now suppose that the number 716 (or any other number of a person who has already been included in the sample) comes up again. That number is also ignored.

The steps in using a table of random numbers (e.g., Table A) to draw a sample are summarized in Procedure 1-1. Throughout this text, "Procedures" are used to summarize step-by-step operations involved in applying concepts and tools in statistics. They may be used for quick reference, as a check of your understanding of the ideas and tools, or both.

♦   ♦   ♦   ♦   ♦

Relationship between Descriptive and Inferential Statistics

Descriptions of both samples and populations are taken from descriptive statistics. When an index such as the mean is used to describe a characteristic of the sample, it is called a **statistic**. When an index such as the mean is used to describe a characteristic of a population, it is called a **parameter**. Thus, a parameter describes a population, whereas a statistic describes a sample.

In behavioral research, we are interested in learning something about the population by means of an inference from the sample. After all, if we could thoroughly describe the population, there would be no need to draw the sample in the first place. When a statistic, computed for a sample, is used to estimate a population parameter, it is called an **estimator**. For example, the mean of a sample may be used to estimate the mean of the population. By using statistics as estimators of parameters, behavioral scientists draw inferences from sample data about the population.

Unfortunately, the value of a sample estimate of a parameter need not exactly equal the value of the parameter. This should come as no surprise, since the sample estimate is based only on a subset of subjects in the population. Likewise, from one sample to the next, the values of the estimators probably will vary. So errors may arise in estimating a parameter with a statistic. One very desirable characteristic of a sample statistic used as an estimator, then, is that over many random samples from a population, the average value of the sample statistic converges on the value of the population parameter it is used to estimate. This characteristic of an estimator is called its unbiasedness. An estimator is *unbiased* if, for an indefinitely large number of random samples from a population, the mean of the sample estimates equals the value of the population parameter being estimated.

In sum, descriptive and inferential statistics are linked by the use of the sample statistic as an estimate of a population parameter. Estimators, then, are the cornerstone of the inferences made by behavioral scientists from sample to population. While this may seem like a lot of unnecessary terminology, the terminology is essential to your ability to understand and apply concepts and principles in statistics. It is also essential to your ability to communicate with others doing research. And, finally, it is the only economical means for me to communicate with you. Without these terms and concepts, the writing would be (even more?) convoluted with long descriptions and distinctions. As you progress through this book, the terms will become familiar parts of your vocabulary, so do not worry about memorizing them now. (Just remember the location of this part of the chapter so you can refer back when needed.)

Two major elements in the design of research are the researcher's hypotheses and the variables used to test them. The hypotheses follow from theory and past research, and motivate the design of the present study. The variables represent the embodiment of the hypotheses in terms of what the behavioral researcher can observe. These two elements are considered in this section. **SOME BASIC ELEMENTS IN DESIGNING RESEARCH**

♦   ♦   ♦   ♦   ♦

A **variable** is an attribute (characteristic, property) of an object or person that can change from object to object or from person to person. Some examples of variables referring to objects are the *length* of a car, since cars differ in length; the *pronounceability* of a nonsense syllable, since some are easy to pronounce (e.g., "zeb"), while others are not (e.g., "zxv"); the *organizational structure* of an institution, since some have rigid hierarchies and some do not; and the *degree of self-pacing* in instruction, since some teachers control the pace, whereas others let students control the pace. Some examples of variables referring to persons are height, sex, and intelligence. Clearly, people differ on each of these variables. Furthermore, from these examples, it is probably obvious that a person or object may be described by any number of variables. **Variables and Hypotheses**

A **constant** is an attribute of an object or person that does not vary from object to object or from person to person. Constants are much more common in the physical sciences than in the behavioral sciences. In Einstein's famous equation for energy, $E = mc^2$, c is a constant (the speed of light). Regardless of the mass of an object (m), or the energy (E), the value of c does not change. Often in the behavioral sciences, the researcher "holds a variable constant." For example, since girls and boys differ in their ability to learn to read, often researchers will observe only boys or only girls in an experiment. The variable sex is held constant.

In attempting to solve theoretical, social, and practical problems through empirical research, an expected solution to the problem is usually set forth for testing. It is based on theory, prior research, or both. This expectation is often called a hypothesis. A **hypothesis** is a tentative statement about the expected relationship between two or more variables. The hypothesis is tentative because its accuracy will be tested empirically. It can be quite formal and backed by a set of established facts; it can be a rough prediction backed by some tentative theory or set of studies; or it can be a best guess in the absence of adequate information.

A hypothesis, then, predicts a relationship between two or more variables. For example, a hypothesis that motivated the study of the effects of organization on the recall of a list of words was: "There is a relationship between the *organization* of a list of words (organized versus scrambled) and the *number of words recalled.*" When people or objects can be ordered on a variable (e.g., lowest to highest score on an achievement test), hypotheses may predict one of three relationships:

1. There is a positive relationship between variable X and variable Y: as X increases, Y also increases.
2. There is a negative relationship between variable X and variable Y: as X increases, Y decreases.
3. There is no relationship between variable X and variable Y: as X increases, Y varies unsystematically.[1]

For example, a hypothesis involving a positive relationship between two variables is: "There is a positive relationship between grade-point average (GPA) and scores on a measure of academic self-concept." That is, as GPA increases, so will scores on academic self-concept. A hypothesis involving a negative relationship is: "There is a negative relationship between scores on a measure of anxiety and scores on the solutions to complex problems." That is, as scores on anxiety increase, scores on problem-solving decrease.

The process of hypothesis formulation can be illustrated with an example from research on teachers' expectations: "What is the effect of teachers' expectations on students' intellectual performance?" The symbolic interactionist theory of Cooley (1902) and Mead (1934) states, roughly, that the expectations of "significant others" affect a person's behavior. Since teachers represent "significant others" to students, the theory predicts that teachers' expectations will influence students' behavior. In addition, past research on experimenter bias in behavioral research (Rosenthal, 1966) supports the theory in that experimenters' expectations influenced the outcome of their experi-

---

[1]This hypothesis should not be confused with the null hypothesis. The distinction will be discussed in Chapter 9.

ments. So both theory and prior research suggest, by inference, a relationship between teachers' expectations and student performance. Stated as a hypothesis, we have:

> There is a relationship between a teacher's expectation concerning a student's intellectual performance and the student's actual intellectual performance.

Once the hypothesis has been developed deductively from a theory, inductively from a set of research studies, or both, several guidelines can be used to sharpen the focus of the hypothesis. They can be stated, briefly, as follows:

1. A hypothesis should predict a particular relationship between two or more variables.
2. A hypothesis should be stated clearly and unambiguously, usually in the form of a declarative sentence.
3. A hypothesis should be testable. That is, the hypothesis should be stated so that data could be collected to test it.

Which of the following represent adequate hypotheses? For those that do not, tell why.

EXAMPLE PROBLEM 1

a. There is a positive relationship between a measure of hyperactivity in children and academic performance as measured by GPA.
b. Positive attitudes about others are important in life.
c. The number of hours in counseling is positively related to the client's improvement in scores on a measure of self-concept.
d. Mental ability may be related to personality.
e. There is a relationship between sex and a measure of preference for type of reading material.

Compare your answers with the ones at the end of the book.

♦   ♦   ♦   ♦   ♦

Numbers can be used to represent the levels of an attribute of an object or person. For example, the length of a car can be expressed in inches. The degree of self-pacing in instruction can also be expressed numerically: most simply a 1 might be assigned to teacher-paced instruction and a 2 to student-paced instruction. Likewise, the level of anxiety while taking a test might be expressed by the student's heart rate—the number of beats per minute—or by a score on an anxiety scale. And the sex of a person might be expressed numerically by assigning a 1 to males and a 2 to females.

From these examples it is clear that the rules used to assign numbers to variables such as length or anxiety differ from those used to assign numbers to self-pacing and sex. In the former case, the numbers represent an underlying

Quantification of Variables

continuum from zero length upward or from slow to fast heart rate. In the latter case, the numbers merely "stand for," "name," or "label categories of" differences on these variables.

Measurement is defined as the assignment of numbers to attributes of objects, events, or persons according to logically acceptable rules. Different kinds of variables (attributes) require different rules for assigning numbers in order to express differences on those variables. There are some well-known rules for assigning numbers to variables. A particular set of rules defines a **scale of measurement**, and different sets of rules define different scales of measurement. Four kinds of scales of measurement are particularly important for quantifying variables in the behavioral sciences: nominal scales, ordinal scales, interval scales, and ratio scales. Each is described briefly below.

Nominal scales A **nominal scale** uses numbers to stand for names or categories representing the way objects or persons differ. *Nominal measurement*, then, is a process of grouping objects or persons into classes and treating the members of each class as if they were the same with respect to some attribute. The particular number assigned to a class is completely arbitrary (see Figure 1-1). For example, numbers are used to identify different players on a football team, to identify differences in the sex of subjects in an experiment (e.g., 1 = male; 2 = female), make of car (1 = Chevrolet, 2 = Ford, 3 = Plymouth), pacing of instruction (1 = teacher-paced, 2 = student-paced), or group (1 = control, 2 = experimental). Since the numbers are no more than labels, arithmetic operations such as addition and subtraction with these numbers imply nothing about the objects or persons themselves because the numbers were not assigned to reflect the order or size of the objects.

Ordinal scales An ordinal measurement is possible when degrees of an attribute can be identified. An **ordinal scale** uses numbers to *order* objects or

Figure 1-1 ◆ Visual representation of the four kinds of measurement scale

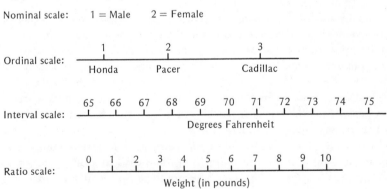

Nominal scale: 1 = Male   2 = Female

Ordinal scale:
1 — Honda   2 — Pacer   3 — Cadillac

Interval scale:
65 66 67 68 69 70 71 72 73 74 75
Degrees Fahrenheit

Ratio scale:
0 1 2 3 4 5 6 7 8 9 10
Weight (in pounds)

persons on some continuum of (say) high to low. Thus, a teacher might order his students on an achievement continuum. The student who is highest in achievement would be assigned a 1, and the student who is lowest in a class of 30 would be assigned a rank of 30. Cars might be ordered as to their length, so that the shortest car was assigned the number 1, and the longest car was assigned the highest rank (see Figure 1-1).

An ordinal scale, then, provides information about the rank order of objects or persons on a variable. Its limitations can be shown by an example. Suppose three cars were ordered according to length: Honda Civic (1), Pacer (2), and Cadillac El Dorado (3). Even though the numbers assigned to these three cars are equally spaced—1, 2, and 3—we cannot say that the Cadillac is as much longer than the Pacer as the Pacer is longer than the Honda. The rank ordering may indicate length intervals that are erratic or unequal. Although numbers standing for ranks can be manipulated arithmetically, the result of these operations cannot necessarily be interpreted as representing the amounts of some attribute that the objects corresponding to the numbers possess. For example, the difference between the rank scores for a Cadillac and a Honda is $3 - 1 = 2$. Does this mean that a Cadillac is twice as long as a Honda? No, it does not, because the result of the arithmetic does not reflect anything quantitative about the length of the two cars. In performing arithmetic operations on data measured on an ordinal scale, the question must always be asked, "Does the result have meaning with respect to the attribute measured?" (See Jones, 1971.)

Interval scales Interval measurement is possible when the differing levels of an attribute can be identified, and *equal distances* between the levels of the attribute can also be identified. For interval measurement, a unit of measurement such as the inch, pound, or degree has been defined. An **interval scale** assigns a number to an object or person such that the number of units of measurement is equal to the amount of the attribute possessed. An interval scale, then, is one for which the intervals between units (numbers) are equal. For example, if temperature is measured in degrees Fahrenheit (equal units), an interval measurement is achieved (see Figure 1-1).

There are many examples of interval scales for physical attributes of objects (e.g., temperature). There are far fewer examples of interval measurements of attributes of people. Of course, temperature is one such measurement. However, many measures in the behavioral sciences involve paper-and-pencil tests such as tests of spatial ability and intelligence. The scores on these tests are the numbers of correct responses. While we are not always sure that these measurements have equal intervals, we proceed *as if* they did.

Interval measurement entails assigning numbers to levels of an attribute (e.g., temperature) such that equal differences in the numbers correspond to equal differences in the amount of an attribute measured. Thus, addition and subtraction of those numbers produces a result that is interpretable with respect to the actual amounts of the attribute. For example, yesterday the maximum temperature was 82 degrees, and the minimum was 60 degrees. The difference between the maximum and minimum temperatures, 22 degrees, is meaningful.

Ratio scales   It is also possible to form a scale such that the numbers represent equal intervals *and* there is a meaningful zero point on it. A **ratio scale** is an interval scale with a zero point that indicates the absence of the attribute measured. Some familiar examples of ratio scales are length, height, and weight (see Figure 1-1). Furthermore, a scale formed by counting, such as counting the number of students in a statistics class, provides values on a ratio scale.

Arithmetic operations with the numbers on a ratio scale produce results that are interpretable with respect to the actual amounts of an attribute. For example, a person weighing 250 pounds weighs 125 pounds more than a person weighing 125 pounds. Moreover, the former person weighs twice as much as the latter person.

In this text, the distinction between interval and ratio scales will not be maintained. Rather, for simplicity, we will speak of both types of scales as having, at least, interval properties.

Levels of measurement and statistical analysis   There has been considerable debate about the application of statistical methods to the different scales on which data can be measured. Some statistics books are even organized according to the scale of measurement. The view taken in this textbook is similar to that taken by Jones (1971) and Hays (1971):

> Statistics is quite neutral on this issue. In developing procedures, mathematical statisticians have assumed that techniques involving numerical scores [etc.] . . . are to be applied where these numbers . . . are appropriate and meaningful within the experimenter's problem. If the statistical method involves the procedures of arithmetic used on numerical scores, then the numerical answer is formally correct. Even if the numbers are the purest nonsense, having no relation to real magnitudes or the properties of real things, the answers are still right *as numbers* [italics in original]. *The difficulty comes with the interpretation of those numbers back into statements about the real world* [italics ours]. If nonsense is put into the mathematical system, nonsense is sure to come out. [Hays, 1971, p. 88]

The problem, then, is not so much the match of statistical method and measurement scales. Rather, the problem is one of interpreting the results of a statistical analysis with respect to the attributes of people or objects measured in the study. "The experimenting psychologist [sociologist, educational researcher] must face the problem of the interpretation of statistical results *within psychology* and on *extramathematical* grounds" (Hays, 1971, p. 89; italics in original). For this reason, little additional attention will be paid to the levels of measurement in this textbook.

Indicate whether the variables below are measured on a nominal, ordinal, or (at least) interval scale:

a. Score on a measure of introversion-extroversion
b. Amount of annual income in dollars
c. Ranking of teachers on enthusiasm
d. Score on a law-school admissions test
e. Type of counseling technique.

EXAMPLE PROBLEM 2

♦   ♦   ♦   ♦   ♦

Behavioral research focuses on the relationship between variables. Studies are designed, in part, for the purpose of observing the effects of certain variables (e.g., different instructional methods) on other variables (e.g., achievement), or of describing the relationship of certain variables (e.g., verbal ability, anxiety) with some other variables (e.g., school grades), or of predicting one variable (e.g., college GPA) from another variable (e.g., College Board scores). As a detailed example, consider the study of the effects of organization on recalling a list of words. The organization of a list of words was systematically varied (viz., hierarchical versus scrambled organization) in order to observe the effects of organization on the number of words recalled correctly from the list. Both *organization* and *number of words recalled* are variables; the former variable is measured on a nominal scale, while the latter is measured on at least an interval scale. Furthermore, we are interested in the effect of the first variable, the "stimulus" of organization, on the second variable or "response" (number of words recalled). Put another way, we are interested in the effect of the "independent variable" or stimulus on the "dependent variable" or response.

This brief introduction demands some additional explanation. What follows is the definition of some concepts and terms that are essential in communicating about the design of research as well as interpreting the findings of research.

Classification of Variables for Designing Research

Independent variables An **independent variable** is a variable which is manipulated, measured, or selected by the researcher in order to observe its relation to the subject's "response" or some other observed variable (i.e., dependent variable). An independent variable, then, is a variable that is employed to influence some other variable; it is an antecedent condition to observed behavior. In the study of the effect of organization on recall of words, the independent variable—organization (hierarchical versus scrambled)—was systematically manipulated by the experimenter to see its effect on recall of words. Specifically, a set of conceptually related words was organized hierarchically by the experimenter and also was scrambled into a random order. An independent variable can also be measured and its relation to some other variable determined. For example, a measure of anxiety might be obtained on a group of white-collar workers and the relation of anxiety to some other variable, such as job satisfaction, determined. Independent variables are often **individual-difference variables** (or *organismic* variables) in that they reflect differences between people. Finally, an independent variable can be selected by the researcher. For example, classrooms might be selected for study because their organizational structures differ in some important way. This would permit the researcher to examine the relationship between classroom organization and, say, behavior problems.

Control variables   A **control variable** is any variable which is held constant in a research study by observing only one of its levels. Control variables are used in research to neutralize the effects of variables which are not of central focus to the study but which may affect the observed behavior. For example, in a study of reading, sex might be controlled, since it is known to be related to reading performance. In this case, only girls (one level of the sex variable) might be used.

Dependent variables   So far this term has been defined informally in these hypothetical experiments as the "response" to the independent variable (stimulus). More formally, a **dependent variable** may be defined as that variable which is observed and measured in response to an independent variable. This variable is expected to increase, decrease, or vary in some systematic fashion as the levels of the independent variable change. In the hypothetical study of the effects of organization, the dependent variable was the recall of a list of words. The words correctly recalled were observed and counted (measured). Like any other variable, dependent variables can be measured on different scales.

Intervening variables   An **intervening variable** is a hypothetical variable which is not observed directly in a research study, but rather is inferred from the relationship between the independent variable and dependent variable. Its importance lies in its ability to explain the relationship between the independent and dependent variables under the conditions of the study *and* under conditions somewhat different from those set up in the study. In all types of behavioral research, intervening variables represent the foundation of theory. In psychological research, for example, a theory might posit that words are arranged in associative networks which are hierarchical. While an associative network in a person's memory cannot be observed and measured directly (it is a hypothetical variable posited by a theory), experiments can be conducted to determine whether people respond (dependent variable) under different conditions of learning words (independent variable) in ways predicted by the existence of an associative network. One of many possible experiments testing this intervening variable is the hypothetical experiment on the effects of the organization of a list of words on subjects' ability to recall words from that list correctly. Intervening variables are as numerous as there are theories. Some intervening variables which are familiar to most of us are: learning, expectancy, cognitive structure, group cohesiveness, intelligence, stages of cognitive and moral development, and attitudes.

Identify the following variables (if specified) in the studies described below:

EXAMPLE PROBLEM 3

a. Independent variable
b. Control variable
c. Intervening variable
d. Dependent variable.

Study 1: In a study of the effects of different types of legal arguments on jurors' perceptions of the guilt or innocence of a defendant, subjects were randomly assigned to hear an argument which related to their daily experiences or to an argument of a more abstract and idealistic nature. Since the researcher felt that subjects with different amounts of education might react differently to these arguments, half of the subjects hearing each argument were college graduates and half were not. After listening to one of these legal arguments, subjects were asked to rate the guilt or innocence of the defendant on a twelve-point scale.

Study 2: A researcher studying child development hypothesized that breast feeding leads to a close mother-child relationship by increasing the warmth and intimacy between mother and child. To test this hypothesis, three-year-old children who had been breast fed for 0, 1–3, or more than 3 months were identified. Then these children and their mothers were observed in an unstructured play situation for two hours. Observers rated the closeness of the relationship between mother and child.

As an answer to the question "Does violence on television lead to aggressive behavior in children?" a researcher might examine the effects of televised violence, an independent variable with (say) three levels (none, some, much) on a measure of the aggressive behavior of children, the dependent variable. At the end of the study, the researcher would like to interpret the results as

THREATS TO THE VALIDITY OF RESEARCH STUDIES[2]

[2]This section and the next draw heavily from the work of Campbell and Stanley (1963, 1966). You may want to refer to this work for additional information.

providing an answer, though not a complete one, to the question of televised violence and aggressive behavior. But suppose, indeed, the most aggressive children viewed the most violent TV program, whereas the least aggressive children viewed the program with no violence. While the researcher might conclude that televised violence leads to aggressive behavior, an alternative, equally plausible explanation is that the children differed in aggressive behavior before viewing the programs. Put another way, it was not the independent variable that led to differences in the dependent variable. Rather, a third variable was responsible. In designing research, then, it is crucial that alternative explanations be ruled out, as best as possible, so that the intended interpretation is the most plausible one or even the only possible interpretation.

The question of the interpretation of the results of a study is one of the most critical questions that can be asked. This is a question of the *validity of a research study*. The **validity** of a research study means the extent to which the interpretation of the results of the study follows from the study itself and the extent to which the results may be generalized to other situations with other people.

Some examples may bring home this notion of validity. Most of you have seen television commercials for deodorants. The commercial for one brand of deodorant challenges viewers to conduct their own experiment. The instruction is to put your old brand under your right arm and the new brand under your left arm in order to see which is better. The implication is that the new brand will work better because it is the better brand. However, there are several possible counterinterpretations. One possible interpretation is that, since most people are right handed and therefore the right arm sees more action than the left arm, the old and new brands are not tested under equivalent conditions. Another possible explanation is that an expectancy is set up—that the new brand will work. Thus, the expectancy and not the new brand caused the outcome. In short, there is a threat to the validity of this proposed study due to the design of the study itself.

A second example is provided by Neisser (1976) in a review of research on human perception. Most such research is conducted in a laboratory. A subject is placed in a darkened room, her head is held steady, and she is instructed to focus on a point directly in front of her. Then a stimulus is presented for a brief period of time (e.g., 200 msec), and the subject is asked to report what she saw in the stimulus. The research design itself rules out virtually all possible counterinterpretations for the proposed interpretation of the experiment. But, as Neisser [and Brunswik (1955) long before him] pointed out, people do not normally perceive under these laboratory conditions. They usually are moving their bodies, their heads, or at the very least their eyes. Furthermore, the stimuli that they observe are much more complex than those in the laboratory. In other words, Neisser has raised questions about the validity of these findings in the laboratory in the sense of their generalizability to human behavior outside.

The concept of the validity of a research study can be divided into two subconcepts: the validity of the interpretation of the results (as in the deodorant example) and the generalizability of the findings to other settings and people (as in the perceptual-laboratory example). The former is termed **internal validity**, and the latter is termed **external validity**. They are discussed in somewhat more detail below.

◆   ◆   ◆   ◆   ◆

The **internal validity** of a research study is the extent to which the outcomes of a study result from the variables which were manipulated, measured, or selected in the study rather than from other variables not systematically treated. In the study of the effect of televised violence on aggressive behavior in children, the threat to its internal validity was that the children in the three groups differed as to their aggressive behavior *before* the study was begun. In the proposed deodorant study, two threats to the internal validity were identified: (1) the two brands of deodorant were not tested under equivalent conditions and (2) an expectancy effect, not the effect of the deodorant, might have been the critical factor.

Threats to Internal Validity

A number of factors which may threaten the internal validity of a research study are now briefly described.

History   By **history** we mean the events that occur at the time the research study is being conducted. These events represent potential counterinterpretations to the interpretation that the independent variable caused the outcomes in the study as measured by the dependent variable.

History may be *external* to the experiment, something that occurs parallel to it but outside. For example, suppose that students' scores on a reading test showed a large increase after they took a special three-month reading course. One possible interpretation is that the instruction caused this increase. But a counterinterpretation might be that the students' parents got interested in the new course and spent time with their children teaching them to read better. The parents, then, represent external history which threatens the proposed interpretation of the results of the study.

History may also be *internal* to the conduct of the study. For example, the experiences of subjects in different groups may differ in ways other than those manipulated by the independent variable. That is, procedures, materials, or conditions may differ for different groups of subjects in ways other than those intended by the manipulation of the independent variable. For example, consider a study in which the experimental and control groups were placed in separate rooms. During the study, men began washing the windows of the room housing the control group. If the experimental group performed better than the control group, a counterinterpretation to the results is that the subjects in the control group were distracted and this led to the observed differences. A second example is the deodorant study, where the "environments" of the right and left underarms were not considered equivalent.

Maturation By **maturation** we mean developmental changes in subjects during the course of a study. This threat to internal validity is especially crucial in studies with young children which are carried out over a period of months or more. For example, suppose a study investigating methods of teaching reading to first-graders showed significant increases in reading scores from pretest (prior to instruction) to posttest (after instruction). These increases may have been due to the treatment, to the maturation of the students, or to some combination of the two. (History is also a possible threat here.)

Testing By **testing** we mean the use of a pretest in a research study. In some studies, subjects receive a pretest, then they are assigned to and receive treatments, and then they receive a posttest. Changes in performance may be due to the treatments. But they also might have come about because students learned something from the pretest itself, or because the pretest cued them to what to look for in the treatments. Since a reading pretest was used in the previous example illustrating threats due to maturation, testing might also be a threat to the interpretation of the results of that study.

Instrumentation By **instrumentation** we mean inconsistencies or changes in the measuring instruments used in a study (e.g., tests or observers producing ratings). For example, in a study examining the effects of a commercially produced program for training listening skills, a pretest and a posttest were given to subjects. The two tests of listening skills were purported to be equivalent. At the end of the study, listening skills had improved. One possible interpretation was that the training caused this change. But another (later verified) was that the pretest was more difficult than the posttest.

Selection By **selection** we mean differences existing between groups of subjects before the study is begun. In such a case, differences between groups need not be due to differences in treatment. Rather, they may be due to preexisting differences. Selection was raised as a threat to the interpretation of the hypothetical study of the influence of televised violence on children's aggressive behavior.

Mortality By **mortality** we mean the loss of subjects from certain groups in a research study. It is an unfortunate term for use in behavioral research with humans, but the term originated in a long tradition of biological research with animals. In most behavioral research, mortality refers to subjects' dropping out of the study because of the treatment they receive. For example, a study comparing a new physics curriculum with a traditional one might show the new curriculum to be superior. One possible interpretation of these results is that the new curriculum is pedagogically superior to the traditional one. But another is that the new curriculum is so much more difficult than the traditional one that all but the brightest students dropped out of the study. This latter interpretation raises the possibility of mortality as a threat to the internal validity of the study.

◆　　◆　　◆　　◆　　◆

The **external validity** of a research study is the extent to which the findings of a particular study can be generalized to people or situations other than those observed in the study. In other words, external validity means the extent to which the findings of research can be generalized to the real world. An example of a threat to the external validity of laboratory studies was given in the description of some typical research on human perception.

Threats to External Validity[3]

There are several factors which may threaten the external validity of a study. One factor is the absence of internal validity. If a study is not internally valid (i.e., the interpretation of the results of the study itself is questionable), it cannot be externally valid. Some of the other common threats to the external validity will now be presented and described briefly.

Selection of subjects　If the subjects observed in the study are not representative of the larger population, the generalization of the results of the study will be hazardous at best. For example, many studies in the behavioral sciences (including psychology, sociology, education, and statistics) use college students who happen to be available to the researcher. They are not necessarily representative of students on that campus, let alone students on other campuses or people in general. The question of whether the results of studies conducted with this selected group of subjects generalize to other students or other populations is one of external validity.

Selection of treatments　If the treatments used in a study are not representative of the kinds of treatments that occur or may be given in the real world, the generalizability of the results is questionable. For example, Neisser (1976) argued that the types of treatments used in laboratory experiments on perception were not representative of the kinds of perception humans carry out in the real world.

Selection of dependent variables　If the dependent variables are not representative of the possible outcomes of a research study, generalizations about the outcomes may be incomplete and in some cases misleading. For example, research on learning and instruction often uses a single dependent variable which is designed to measure the content of what is taught during instruction. However, often the purpose of instruction is more than the acquisition of specific content. Some measure of the subject's ability to generalize on the basis of the content taught might provide important information about the treatment

[3]For additional material on the topic of external validity, see Bracht & Glass (1968) and Snow (1974).

effects. Or some measure of the subject's ability to learn new, related content might provide other, important information. Finally, a measure of the subject's attitude toward the instructional process might shed light on whether the subject would continue to study under the instructional approach if he were given a choice.

♦   ♦   ♦   ♦   ♦

Relationship between Internal and External Validity

As might be expected, there is a tradeoff between optimizing internal validity and optimizing external validity. In order to optimize internal validity, the researcher retreats to the laboratory, where all of the factors threatening internal validity can be controlled as well as is humanly possible. This research often produces interpretations of the results that are valid but do not generalize beyond the laboratory. In order to optimize external validity, the researcher travels into the real world. There he selects existing variations, such as open and traditional classrooms, and observes their effects, for example, on students, teachers, parents, and administrators. While the treatments and subjects may be representative of the real world, the conclusions drawn are often open to counterinterpretations due to threats to internal validity.

There is considerable disagreement on how to resolve this problem. Clearly, there is some middle ground between the two extremes described above. This middle ground depends upon the researcher's knowledge and choice of a research design that is appropriate for the problem under consideration. Some laboratory studies generalize even under restrictive conditions, some can be conducted under realistic conditions, and some field studies can control for threats to internal validity. In the next section, different types of designs are reviewed. These designs represent the tools the researcher has available in attempting to resolve this tradeoff between internal and external validity.

EXAMPLE PROBLEM 4

What threats are there to the internal and external validity of the studies described below?

Study 1: In an attempt to increase the self-concept of children enrolled in a Headstart program, all children were given a self-concept measure. Children with very low scores on this measure were selected to participate in an intensive five-month program designed to provide positive reinforcement, success experiences, and warm interpersonal relationships with others. At the end of the program, these children were administered the same self-concept measure again.

Study 2: In a prose learning study, psychology sophomores at XYZ University were randomly assigned to one of two instructional treatments: textbook, or textbook with questions inserted in the prose. These instructional treatments were administered within the context of a regular psychology course. Subjects were unaware that there were differences in instructional treatments or that they were participating in an experiment. After completing the reading, students were administered a test on the material; this test was a requirement of the course, established with other course requirements on the first day of class.

Different types of research designs control for none, some, or almost all of the threats to internal and external validity; some represent alternative means for resolving the tradeoff between internal and external validity. Many of the designs use one or more of the following methods to counteract threats to internal validity: (1) one or more appropriate control groups, (2) random assignment of subjects to groups, and (3) pretests in order to equate groups statistically.

A **control group** is a group of subjects whose selection and treatment is exactly the same as that of the experimental group except that the control group does not receive the experimental treatment (i.e., the control group receives the neutral or null level of the independent variable). This does not mean that the control group receives "no treatment." It is provided an identical experience to the experimental group except for the particular level of the independent variable. For example, research on the effects of drugs employs a control group that is treated in exactly the same way as the experimental group except that the control group receives a **placebo** or neutral treatment (e.g., a sugar pill) instead of the drug. Research on the effects of "advance organizers" on learning from prose material uses a control group that reads the material and is in all other ways treated exactly as the experimental group, except that the control group receives a placebo or neutral passage rather than an advance organizer passage prior to reading the material.

The control group is very important in dealing with threats to internal validity. Since, for example, control and experimental groups can be treated in exactly the same way, both groups experience the same internal and external history. If the experimental group performs better than the control group, history cannot be used to explain the difference. Similarly, if the experiences of young subjects in the control and experimental groups are equated over a period of months, maturation cannot be used to explain the differences in performance between the groups, since subjects in both groups were maturing and had the same experiences except for the manipulation of the independent variable. As a final example of the potential benefits of using a control group, consider a study in which subjects drop out of the two groups at about the same rate. Mortality then cannot be a factor. On the other hand, if there is a differential dropout rate, the existence of the control group will readily verify, but not remedy, this state of affairs.

Random assignment is a method for assigning subjects to control and

DESIGNS FOR BEHAVIORAL RESEARCH

experimental groups. With this procedure, each subject has an equal and independent chance of being assigned to any of the groups in the study (assuming equal group sizes). By randomly assigning subjects to groups, we are able, in the long run, to control for all factors not systematically varied or controlled in the experiment. The groups differ only by chance on all possible individual difference variables prior to the initiation of the study. This is a particularly potent method for negating threats due to selection.

Random assignment of subjects to groups can be accomplished by assigning a different number to each subject in the study and using a table of random numbers. For example, suppose we wanted to place ten subjects randomly in a control group and an experimental group so that there are five subjects in each group. Table A at the back of this book can be used for this purpose. The steps involved in randomly assigning subjects to groups are enumerated in Procedure 1-2.

When random assignment of subjects to groups is impossible or undesirable,

Procedure 1-2 ♦ Steps in randomly assigning subjects to groups.

Operation	Example
1 Assign an identification number to each subject.	**Name** **ID Number** Sally 01 Mary 02 Tom 03 Richard 04 Linda 05 Debbie 06 Cathy 07 David 08 Jon 09 Roger 10
2 Designate a number to represent each group in the study. A different number is used to represent each group. If there are k groups, k numbers will be used to "name" the groups.	Let 1 = experimental group 2 = control group
3 Turn to the table of random numbers (Table A), place your finger anywhere on any page, and locate any two-digit number.	Suppose you placed your finger on 48.
4 Find the number on the same page in the row represented by the first digit of the number located in step 3 and the column represented by the second digit of this number.	48—4th row, 8th column. Find the number located in the fourth row and the eighth column on the same page.

5 Begin reading down the column until you locate a 1 or 2, and assign the first subject to the group designated by that number.

6 Continue step 5 until 1/k of the subjects have been assigned to one group (1/2 of the subjects if there are two groups, 1/3 of the subjects if there are 3 groups, etc.). Then continue assigning subjects to the remaining groups using this process until all groups except one have been assigned 1/k subjects. Then assign the remaining subjects to the last group. (This process insures that the groups will be of equal size.)

If the first number located is a 1, assign subject 01 to the experimental group.

Subject	Group
01	1
02	1
03	2
04	2
05	2
06	2
07	1
08	2[a]
09	1
10	1

[a]At this point, 1/k or, in this case, 1/2 of the subjects were assigned to the control group. The remaining subjects were assigned to the experimental group.

pretests can be used to examine the possibility of prior existing differences between groups and to statistically adjust for these differences. When pretests are used for this purpose, the following procedures should be followed: (1) several different pretests should be used, (2) one of the pretests should be the same as or parallel to the posttest (Porter, 1973), and (3) the pretests selected should be related to the dependent variable.

Some words of warning are needed in using statistical adjustments for equating groups in a research study. Researchers, statisticians, and philosophers are by no means in agreement on the value of using statistical adjustments to equate groups which have not been formed randomly. The disagreement arises over the assumption that the variables used to make the statistical adjustment account for all the prior relevant differences between the groups. This is often hard to swallow. We will not jump into this controversy (see, for example, Elashoff, 1969; Lord, 1967; Porter, 1973); suffice it to say that some very important studies are conducted without random assignment (e.g., some evaluations of federally funded educational programs)—that may provide critical data for national policy decisions. To ignore such data because statistical adjustments are required to equate groups would not be "doing one's damnedest to provide answers to perplexing problems." If statistical adjustments are used with appropriate caution and if the interpretations of the results of these studies reflect this uncertainty, the use of these adjustments seems warranted.

With these preliminary considerations about design covered, four major categories of designs are reviewed: (1) preexperimental designs, (2) experimental designs, (3) quasiexperimental designs, and (4) ex post facto designs.

◆   ◆   ◆   ◆   ◆

Preexperimental Designs

Preexperimental designs are so named because they represent pieces of the ideal model, true experimental designs. They do not provide results that are amenable to a single, most plausible interpretation. Preexperimental designs, then, are loaded with threats to their internal validity.

Preexperimental designs lack two fundamental elements needed to ward off threats to internal validity. They lack an appropriate control group and they lack random assignment. Our reasons for discussing them are three. First, as a "quick and dirty" method for collecting data, they may provide useful insights which can be incorporated into other research designs. Second, they provide good examples of what *not* to do if you want to obtain interpretable results from your research. And third, these designs are commonly used in behavioral research, and perhaps, by "exposing" them, their use will be decreased in the long run.

One-shot case study In the **one-shot case study**, a treatment (X) is administered to a subject or group of subjects, and then an observation (O) is made in order to measure the effect of the treatment. This design can be diagrammed schematically as:

	Treatment	Observation/Measure
Group (1)	X	O

For example, a teacher might try a new teaching technique and, on the basis of a test, conclude that this new method resulted in the students' learning the material. Since there is no control group, this design is open to almost all the possible threats to internal validity (e.g., the students already knew the material; see Table 1-1). And since there are so many plausible counterinterpretations to the one proposed, it is impossible to conclude that X caused O.

One-group pretest-posttest design In the **one-group pretest-posttest design**, a group of subjects receives a pretest (O_1), then the treatment (X), and then the posttest (O_2):

	Measure	Treatment	Measure
Group (1)	O_1	X	O_2

30

Table 1-1 ◆ Threats to the internal validity of preexperimental designs.

Design	Schematic diagram of the design[a]			Threats to internal validity[b]					
	Measure	Treatment	Measure	History	Maturation	Testing	Instrumentation	Selection	Mortality
One-shot case study		X	O	*	*			*	*
One-group, pretest, posttest design	O	X	O	*	*	*	*	+	+
Intact group comparison		X	O	+	?	+	±	*	*
			O						

[a] Blanks indicate an absence of a measure or a treatment, and a broken line indicates a separation of two groups which were *not* formed by random assignment.
[b] * indicates a definite threat; + indicates that the threat is controlled; ? indicates a possible source of concern; and a blank indicates that the threat is not relevant.

For example, in an evaluation of a program designed to improve salespersons' listening ability, the salespersons received a pretest on listening skills. Then they received a two-hour audio-recorded training program designed to improve their listening skills. At the end of training, they received the posttest. Since this study does not employ an appropriate control group, it is open to a number of threats to internal validity (see Table 1-1). One possible counterinterpretation to the interpretation that the treatment improved listening skills is that the posttest was easier than the pretest.

Intact-group comparison   In the **intact-group comparison** study, two existing groups are used: one group serves as the "control" group, while the other serves as the experimental group which receives the treatment (X). At the end of the study, both groups are observed (O):

	Treatment	Observation/Measure
Intact "experimental" group	X	O
Intact "control" group		O

(The broken line indicates that subjects were not randomly assigned to the groups, and the blank space below the X indicates that the lower group is a control.)

Without random assignment and a pretest to determine the equivalence of the two groups, the validity of this design is threatened, especially by selection (see Table 1-1). As an example, suppose that an instructor for two sections of an introductory psychology class taught in a traditional way to the "control" class and used an individualized approach in the "experimental" class. A counterinterpretation to the interpretation that the treatment caused the observed effects is that the ability of one group was superior to that of the other group prior to the study.

EXAMPLE PROBLEM 5

Identify the type of design and threats to internal validity of the studies described below:

a. Ms. Marple decides to use a programmed instruction method for teaching algebra to her third-period class. She gives the class an achievement test before using the new method. After using the programmed instruction method for three weeks, she administers an alternate form of the achievement test to determine the effectiveness of the new program.

b. Suppose Ms. Marple decided to omit the pretest and use the posttest alone to determine the effectiveness of the programmed instruction method.

c. Suppose Ms. Marple decided to omit the pretest and compare the performance of her third-period class receiving the programmed instruction with that of her fourth-period class receiving a more traditional lecture approach to see if the programmed instruction method was effective.

♦ ♦ ♦ ♦ ♦

Experimental Designs

Experimental designs represent ideal models for the design of behavioral research. They are ideal in the sense that actual research designs, including actual experimental designs, only approximate the ideal; they never duplicate the ideal model in all respects. For example, true experiments use randomization to control for threats due to selection. Experimental designs serve as models against which other designs may be compared, because they rule out virtually all of the threats to internal validity. This means that these designs permit the researcher to make causal inferences about the effect of the independent variable on the dependent variable.

True experiments have two distinguishing characteristics. First, all true experiments employ one or more control groups in addition to one or more treatment groups. Second, they use random assignment to place subjects in control and experimental groups. These characteristics, along with appropriate instrumentation (e.g., use of the same measures on the control and experimental groups; use of reliable and valid measures) and procedures (e.g., identical experiences for control and experimental groups except for the manipulation of the independent variable), allow the researcher to rule out all or almost all counterinterpretations to the interpretation that the independent variable caused the differences observed on the dependent variable.

There are three prototypical experimental designs—blocks out of which many other experimental designs can be built. They are the posttest-only control-group design, the pretest-posttest control-group design, and the factorial experimental design.

Posttest-only control-group design   With the **posttest-only control-group design**, subjects are randomly (R) assigned to a control group or to an experimental group. The subjects in both groups then receive identical treatments except for differences defined by the manipulation of the independent variable. At the conclusion of the treatments, both groups receive identical posttests (O):

	Assignment	Treatment	Observation/Measurement
Experimental group	R	X	O
Control group	R		O

An example of this design would be randomly assigning subjects to receive either traditional or individualized instruction in introductory psychology, and then using their scores on the (same) final examination as the posttest (dependent) variable.

Pretest-posttest control-group design   With the **pretest-posttest control-group design**, subjects are randomly assigned to a control group or an experimental group and receive a pretest (O_1). After they receive their respective treatments, subjects receive the posttest:

	Assignment	Pretest	Treatment	Posttest
Experimental group	R	O_1	X	O_2
Control group	R	O_1		O_2

As an example of this design, suppose that students were being trained to improve their note-taking during lectures. They receive a pretest; are randomly assigned to, and receive, either note-taking training or a control treatment; and then receive a posttest in the form of, say, a test using notes taken during a lecture.

Factorial experimental design In a **factorial experimental design**, two or more independent variables are manipulated at the same time. Each level of the first variable is combined with each level of the second variable in the study. For example, suppose a study is conducted to explore the effects of listening training and note-taking training on students' learning from lectures. If there are two levels of listening training (control and training) and two levels of the note-taking training (control and training), there are four possible combinations of the two variables: (1) listening control + note-taking control; (2) listening control + note-taking training; (3) listening training + note-taking control; and (4) listening training + note-taking training (see Table 1-2).

In order to have a factorial experimental design, subjects must be randomly assigned to the levels of at least one of the two or more independent variables in the design. In the listening and note-taking study, subjects could be randomly assigned to both independent variables. In this case, a subject would be randomly assigned to one of the four groups in the design.

Despite their complexity, it's worth the trouble to conduct factorial experiments. In the study of listening and note-taking training, two posttest-only control-group designs were combined: a listening-training study with subjects randomly assigned to control and experimental groups, and a note-taking study with subjects randomly assigned to control and experimental groups. If these two studies were run separately, conclusions would be reached about the effects of listening training and note-taking training. If a factorial experiment were run, the same information would be obtained, and some additional information as well. We would learn whether combined listening and note-taking training causes greater learning from lectures than does either listening or note-taking

Table 1-2 ◆ Schematic diagram of the listening × note-taking factorial design

| Group | Assignment | Treatment | | Observation/measurement of dependent variable |
		First variable (Note-taking training)	Second variable (Listening training)	
Control group	R			O
Note-taking only	R	X_1		O
Listening only	R		X_2	O
Listening and note-taking	R	X_1	X_2	O

training alone. It might even be that listening training alone or note-taking training alone does not improve learning from lectures, but the combination does.

Identify the design of each study described below:

EXAMPLE PROBLEM 6

a. In a study of the effects of marijuana use on driving skills, college students were randomly assigned to smoke two marijuana cigarettes in the laboratory or to smoke two "placebo" cigarettes which taste and smell like marijuana but do not contain the drug. A short time later, subjects were given a driving test in a simulator.
b. Another researcher investigating the effects of marijuana hypothesized that the effects of marijuana on driving skills may differ for regular users and nonusers. He replicated the study. However, half of the subjects in each condition (marijuana versus placebo) were regular users and half were nonusers.

♦   ♦   ♦   ♦   ♦

Often behavioral researchers are interested in studying human behavior in naturally occurring social settings such as classrooms, businesses, and homes. If at all possible, true experiments should be used. In some situations, it is either unfeasible or undesirable to assign subjects randomly (Thistlethwaite & Campbell, 1969). In these cases, **quasiexperimental designs**, which include one or more control groups but do not employ random assignment, provide an important alternative to true experiments. They attempt to rule out, as well as possible, threats to internal validity by collecting data which can be used to examine these threats. For example, with the nonequivalent-group design, subjects are not randomly assigned to the control and experimental groups but receive a pretest, their respective treatments, and then a posttest. The pretest data are used to deal with the counterinterpretation that the differences between groups at posttest were due to differences at pretest and not to the treatment effect. Causal interpretations of the results of quasiexperiments are more tenuous than causal interpretations of the results of true experiments. But they are certainly much more tenable than causal interpretations from preexperimental designs.

There are a large number of quasiexperimental designs (see, for example, Campbell and Stanley, 1963). Rather than review all of them, two representative designs have been selected. One quasiexperimental design, the time-series design, builds upon and improves upon the one-group pretest-posttest design (a preexperimental design). The other design, the nonequivalent-control-group design, is an approximation of a true experimental design.

Quasiexperimental Designs

Time-series design   With the **time-series design**, multiple observations are taken at different points in time before the treatment is implemented. Then the treatment is given. Finally another series of observations is taken over additional points in time:

	Pt. 1	Pt. 2	Pt. 3	Treat-ment	Pt. 4	Pt. 5	Pt. 6
Group (1)	O_1	O_2	O_3	X	O_4	O_5	O_6

where observations O_1–O_3 are taken at different points in time prior to treatment (the *control* condition), and observations O_4–O_6 are taken at different points in time following treatment (the *experimental* condition).

The subjects in this design serve both as a control group and as an experimental group. Prior to receiving the treatment, they are in a control condition. After receiving the treatment, the subjects are in the experimental condition. As an example of a time-series design, consider a study on the effectiveness of certain behavior modification techniques (e.g., self-reinforcement) on weight reduction. Prior to implementing the treatment, the calorie intake of subjects is measured daily over a two-week period. Then the treatment is implemented for a period of, say, a month, and then caloric intake is measured for another two weeks. If the treatment is successful, caloric intake should decrease after the treatment, compared to intake before the treatment. Some hypothetical data are presented in Figure 1-2. From this figure, it is clear

Figure 1-2 ♦ Time series design using hypothetical data from a study of the effects of behavior modification on reduction of caloric intake.

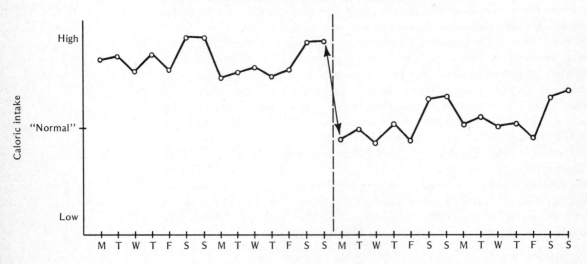

that the behavior modification treatment affected the caloric intake of weight watchers. Prior to treatment, the caloric intake of subjects was *consistently* above normal, especially on weekends (as we all know). After treatment, caloric intake was *consistently* at normal (except for slight lapses on weekends, as might be expected).

Now there is no way to be absolutely sure that the treatment caused the reduction in caloric intake. For example, the control observations occurred only before the treatment was initiated; the observations on a control group were not made at exactly the same time as the observations on an experimental group. It is possible that the causal interpretation is threatened by a counterinterpretation such as history. For example, it might be that, just as the treatment was initiated, the price of sugar increased 100 percent; thus the reduction in caloric intake was due to the increased price of sugar and not to the treatment effect. (For this and other potential threats to validity, see Table 1-3.) This is, of course, an unlikely possibility that could be readily documented. The most plausible interpretation, given the consistency in the data, is that the behavior modification treatment caused the decrease in caloric intake.

Nonequivalent-control-group design   With the **nonequivalent-control-group design**, subjects in a control group and an experimental group receive a pretest (or several pretests, see above), their respective treatments (placebo or actual treatment), and then a posttest. However, in contrast to the pretest-posttest control-group design (see above under "Experimental Designs"), subjects are not randomly assigned to control or experimental groups. Rather, the assignment may have been made on the basis of their choice of group (e.g., choice of class), on the basis of the researchers' knowledge of individual differences between subjects (e.g., low and high ability), or on the basis of some unknown assignment process. This design can be represented schematically as:

	Assignment	Pretest	Treatment	Posttest
Experimental group	(?)	O_1	X	O_2
Control group	(?)	O_1		O_2

As an example of this type of design, suppose a computer-science instructor taught four sections of a computer programming course. Since he has no control over the assignment of students to sections, the allocation of students to classes represents an unknown, nonrandom assignment process. (The best the instructor can do is randomly assign two classes to the control group and two classes to the experimental group.) Subjects in the control group receive large-group lectures on programming and work individually on their assignments. Subjects in the experimental group receive individualized instruction using an interactive computer program. If subjects are equivalent on the pretest

Table 1-3 ◆ Threats to the internal validity of quasiexperimental designs.

	Schematic diagram of the design[a]			Threats to internal validity[b]					
Design	Measure(s)	Treatment	Measure(s)	History	Maturation	Testing	Instrumentation	Selection	Mortality
Time-series	O_1 O_2 O_3	X	O_4 O_5 O_6	*	+	+	?	+	+
Nonequivalent-control-group	O_1	X	O_2	+	+	+	+	*	+
	O_1		O_2						

[a] Blanks indicate an absence of a measure or a treatment, and a broken line indicates a separation of two groups which were *not* formed by random assignment.

[b] * indicates a definite threat; + indicates that the threat is controlled; ? indicates a possible source of concern.

(or pretests) but differ on the posttest, the most plausible explanation is that there was an effect due to instructional method. If they differ at pretest, statistical adjustments can be made to compare them at posttest. If, after adjustment, there is still a difference between groups, again the most plausible explanation is that the treatment caused the effect (see introduction to "Designs for Behavioral Research").

Of course, this design does not rule out all possible counterinterpretations (see Table 1-3). For example, someone could always argue that *selection* is a threat. Some variable not observed at pretest might account for the differences. But as the number of pretests increases, this counterinterpretation becomes increasingly implausible.

EXAMPLE PROBLEM 7

Identify the type of design and threats to internal validity of the studies described below.

a. In a study of the effects of human-relations programs designed to improve relations between different social and ethnic groups, two groups of students were identified: those who participated in such programs and those who did not. A measure of racial attitudes was administered to all students.

b. In an attempt to improve production of assembly-line workers, a policy was implemented in which workers performed a variety of jobs along the assembly line rather than a single job on the line. Weekly production was measured for four weeks before the new policy had been implemented and four weeks after.

38

♦   ♦   ♦   ♦   ♦

Ex post facto designs are most commonly used to describe relationships between two or more variables. For example, a study of the relationship between Scholastic Aptitude Test (SAT) scores and GPAs is an ex post facto design. So is a design that compares the achievement-test scores of children from low, middle, and high socioeconomic status (SES). In either case, interpretations that SAT caused GPA or that SES caused achievement *are not warranted*. Did SES cause achievement or did achievement cause SES? Or did some other variable cause the observed relationship? In general, ex post facto designs, then, examine the degree of association between two or more variables; they do not examine the causal relationship. (For an exception to this rule, see the section "Correlation and Causality" in Chapter 7.)

These designs are called ex post facto designs because when the researcher comes on the scene, nature has already implemented a treatment, either through differences in environments in which subjects find themselves, through differences in inheritance, or through some combination of these two factors. Thus, the researcher arrives after the fact (ex post facto) that the treatments have been imposed on the subjects.

Correlational design With a **correlational design**, one group of subjects is measured on two continuous individual-difference variables such as aptitude (SAT) and achievement (GPA). The correlational design can be represented schematically as follows:

	Measurement (Test 1)	Measurement (Test 2)
Group (1)	O_1	O_2

The subscripts are arbitrary; they simply designate different variables (see below).

Since a causal ordering between the two variables is not posited in a correlational design, the distinction between independent variables and dependent variables is not an important one in these designs. However, by convention, if one variable is measured prior in time to another variable, the first variable is often called the independent variable and the second the dependent variable. Thus, in the example, SAT scores might be labeled the independent variable (X) and GPAs might be labeled the dependent variable (Y).

Criterion-group designs With **criterion-group designs**, subjects falling into discrete groups (the independent variable) are compared on a dependent variable. For example, normal and neurotic subjects might be compared on a

Ex Post Facto Designs

measure of self-concept. The expectation is that there should be differences between these two "criterion" groups in their views and evaluations of themselves; normals would be expected to have higher self-concepts than neurotics.

The simplest criterion-group design can be represented schematically as:

	Assignment	Measurement/Observation
Group (1)	C_1	O
Group (2)	C_2	O

In this case, the levels of the criterion-group variable represent a discrete independent variable. The dependent variable is usually a continuous variable.

Factorial criterion-group designs can also be formulated. In this case, two or more discrete independent variables can be combined factorially. For example, male (M) and female (F), normal (No) and neurotic (Ne) subjects can be compared on a measure of self-concept (S-C). A schematic representation of this design would be:

	Assignment criteria	Measurement/Observation
Group (1)	C_M, C_{No}	O
Group (2)	C_M, C_{Ne}	O
Group (3)	C_F, C_{No}	O
Group (4)	C_F, C_{Ne}	O

or

		Mental health	
		Normal	Neurotic
Sex	Male	Normal males' S-C	Neurotic males' S-C
	Female	Normal females' S-C	Neurotic females' S-C

Data from criterion group designs show relationships between independent variables and a dependent variable; they *do not* show cause-effect relationships.

Identify the designs of the studies described below.

a. In a study of the relationship between student achievement in mathematics and attitudes toward mathematics, a researcher collected two measures on all freshmen enrolled at a major university. All subjects completed a scale measuring attitudes toward math during an orientation meeting. In addition, the scores of these students on the quantitative section of the SAT were collected.

b. A researcher interested in comparing the empathy of psychologists in different areas of specialization administered a measure of empathy to clinical psychologists and experimental psychologists. Since there is some evidence that men and women differ in empathy, the researcher was careful to recruit both males and females in each of these areas of specialization.

◆　　◆　　◆　　◆　　◆

Summary

This chapter presents basic concepts related to conducting research studies in the behavioral sciences. The *steps* in conducting empirical research are presented. The role of *descriptive* and *inferential statistics* in describing, and interpreting the outcome of research studies is discussed. Different *scales of measurement* and classification of *variables* for designing research are also covered. Finally, threats to the *internal* and *external validity* of research studies and *designs* for conducting behavioral research are discussed.

◆　　◆　　◆　　◆　　◆

Key Words

constant	history
control group	hypothesis
control variable	independent variable
correlational design	individual-difference variable
criterion group design	inferential statistics
data	instrumentation
dependent variable	intact-group comparison
descriptive statistics	internal validity
estimator	interval scale
ex post facto design	intervening variable
experimental design	maturation
external validity	measurement
factorial experimental design	mortality

nominal scale	quasiexperimental design
nonequivalent control-group design	random assignment
one-group pretest-posttest design	ratio scale
one-shot case study	sample
ordinal scale	scale of measurement
parameter	selection
placebo	statistic
population	testing
posttest-only control group design	time-series design
preexperimental design	validity
pretest-posttest control-group design	variable

◆　　◆　　◆　　◆　　◆

Exercises　　1–8 For each of the studies described, identify the following. If the information does not apply to the study, write N/A.

a. Design of the study
b. Independent variable(s)
c. Dependent variable
d. Control variable
e. Intervening variable
f. Threats to the internal validity of the study
g. Threats to the external validity of the study

1. Ms. Robbins was interested in increasing the number of students who voluntarily participated in class discussions in her sixth-grade class. She felt that many students were not participating because speaking in front of the entire class was frightening to them. So she rearranged the desks in the classroom into small groups during the discussion period to see if this might encourage a greater number of students to participate. She had kept a daily record of the number of times each student volunteered in class discussions for three weeks prior to the rearrangement of the desks. For three weeks after the change she continued to record the amount of participation of students. She found that the number of students volunteering in class discussions was significantly increased using the new arrangement.

2. Suppose that instead of recording the amount of participation before and after changing the seating arrangement, Ms. Robbins simply observed the amount of class participation after the change. How would your answers to a–g change?

3. In a study of achievement motivation (i.e., motivation to succeed in intellectual or academic tasks), all students in a particular high school were administered the Thematic Apperception Test (TAT). The TAT is a projective measure in which students write a story after being shown a picture. Stories are scored for achievement-related content. This score is considered an indication of achievement motivation. All students were then randomly assigned to an experimental or a control group. The experimental group was given practice in achievement-related activities, such as learning how to define appropriate goals for themselves. The control group spent the same amount of time on an activity of their own choice. After the session, all students completed the TAT again.

4. Suppose a control group had not been used in this study. How would your answers to a–g change?

5. Suppose the researcher had simply wanted to find if there was a relationship between the TAT scores and the grades these students earned at the end of the semester. How would your answers to a–g change?

6. Forty undergraduate psychology students who volunteered for assertion training were randomly assigned to two groups. The experimental group completed a set of exercises that were designed to increase assertive behavior. The control group spent the same amount of time discussing why they have volunteered for the assertion training. Following these sessions, both groups were asked to complete a questionnaire that sought to obtain the degree of assertiveness that they felt they would show in a series of situations.

7. Suppose that the two groups in the previous study were composed of two undergraduate psychology classes instead of volunteers who were randomly assigned to the two groups. How would your answers to a–g change?

8. A researcher was interested in the effects of two different types of preparation for the Doppelt Mathematical Reasoning Test. He also suspected that field-independent and field-dependent subjects might perform differently on the test, depending on the preparation they received. Therefore, he randomly assigned field-independent and field-dependent subjects to one of two types of preparation. One type consisted of practice on the construction and analysis of geometric shapes. The second type involved the construction and analysis of algebraic equations. After receiving the training, subjects were given the Doppelt Mathematical Reasoning Test.

9–13. Indicate the type of measurement scale on which each of the variables listed below is measured.

9. The ethnic groups represented in the classroom.

10. The level of anxiety of students taking a test, where anxiety is classified as high, medium, low.

11. The score on a college aptitude test, such as the SAT.

12. The amount of class participation by a student in a discussion group.

13. The amount of rainfall in the month of August in California.

14. Listed below are four alternative sequences of some of the activities involved in conducting research. Which of the sequences generally represents the ideal model of research?

a. Design of the research
   Conduct of the research
   Definition of the problem
   Analysis of the data

b. Definition of the problem
   Design of the research
   Conduct of the research
   Analysis of the data

c. Definition of the problem
   Formulation of hypotheses
   Design of the research
   Conduct of the research

d. Formulation of hypothesis
   Design of the research
   Analysis of the data
   Interpretation of the data

15–19 Identify which are constants and which are variables.

15. All sixth grade students.
16. The style of dress of college students.
17. People's estimates of their self-esteem.
18. The sex of the students in an all-girl school.
19. The average annual income of a family of four.

20. Describe three common methods for counteracting threats to internal validity.

2.

Statistics in Context:
Some Behavioral Research

Research on Teacher Expectancy: Pygmalion in
the Classroom

Development of Moral Judgment

Student Achievement and Congruence between Students'
and Instructors' Beliefs

The Disparity in College Grades Earned by Men and Women

Determinants of Emotion

Summary

For most researchers, statistics are not ends in themselves but means to an end such as theory building or policy analysis. Thus the subject of statistics, when taught out of the context of the research it serves, is like an answer to a question you didn't ask and don't care about. Consequently this chapter provides a research context for studying statistics and indicates, by example, the role statistics can play in research in the behavioral sciences.

Five studies are described here.[1] Some of them bear on theory building, while others bear on policy; some are drawn from psychology, some from sociology, and some from education. In each study, attention is given to (1) the theory and/or practical problem that generated it, (2) its design, (3) its results, and (4) its possible interpretations (and misinterpretations).

The role that statistics play in research is shown by giving particular emphasis to the fact that, once the data are collected, the researcher is confronted with stacks of biographical information, tests or physiological indices, notes about what happened, and so on. At this point an uninformed, head-on attack on the unorganized data can result in little but frustration and fatigue. The need for knowledge and skills in statistics becomes readily apparent. This is because statistical tools help to organize, describe, and interpret the data.

Throughout this chapter, then, emphasis is placed on the two major roles played by statistics: *description* and *inference* (see the section on "The Role of Statistics in Behavioral Research" in Chapter 1). That is, statistics provide ways of organizing, summarizing, tabulating, depicting, and describing collections of data (cf. "Descriptive Statistics" in the same section in Chapter 1). And they provide ways of systematically drawing inferences about the possibility of differences between larger groups of people (*populations*) than just those observed in the study (*samples*; cf. "Inferential Statistics" in the same section of Chapter 1). Without statistics, the researcher would have difficulty making sense out of her data. When you see statistics at work organizing, clarifying, and helping you to interpret previously incomprehensible pieces of information, the mystery of the formulas will fall away to reveal useful research tools.

---

[1]For pedagogical reasons, we have chosen to use hypothetical data which preserve the characteristics of the original data, rather than the actual data. This permitted us to present data on fewer subjects than were used in the original studies and so reduce the time needed for computation of statistics. And it allowed us to simplify the numbers in order to make computations easier.

Do teachers' expectations of students' intellectual abilities influence students' behavior? Some say that one person's perception of another influences the way the other person behaves. To put the question more personally: Have you ever found yourself in a classroom where the teacher expects you to make mistakes? You *feel* that's what the teacher expects—and you do just what is expected. This is called an "expectancy effect." Intuition, at least for many of us, suggests a teacher-expectancy effect: the way a teacher perceives a student influences the student's behavior. There is also some theory in sociology and social psychology which says that perceptions of "significant others" (e.g., teachers) influence people's behavior (e.g., students).

While intuition and theory suggest this expectancy effect, the issue is not resolved. We still need to answer the question, "Does the expectancy effect operate in classrooms?" In other words, if teachers are led to expect certain behavior from a student chosen randomly, does the student behave in the ways the teacher expects? To answer this question, suppose you decide to do a study on teacher expectancy. You select some classrooms, grades 1–6, at random and tell the teachers that based on pretest information, 20 percent of the students in each class are expected to show tremendous academic and intellectual gains during the school year. Actually, the students you identified in each class as "bloomers" are selected at random; they wouldn't be expected to gain any more than the other students in the class. In order to determine whether the expectancy effect operated, you give all of the students in the classes a posttest at the end of the school year.

If there was an expectancy effect, students who were designated as "bloomers" should receive higher posttest scores—or higher gain scores (post-test minus pretest scores)—than the other students. If the expectancy effect did not occur, test scores for the two groups should be approximately the same. Suppose the test scores from your study look like those presented in Table 2-1. What can you conclude about the expectancy effect from your data? Should you summarize the data in the form of gain scores (posttest minus pretest scores)? How about a summary by grade level? By experimental (bloomers) and control group? By both grade and group? Would you look at some average score on the pretest and posttest for first- and second-graders in the experimental group? Would you be interested in how much the scores of third- and fourth-graders in the control group differ from each other? Suppose you found that the average gain score for fifth- and sixth-graders was 13.33 in the experimental group and 13.20 in the control group. Could you be sure that this slight difference represents a true difference between groups? Could you conclude that teacher expectancy influences students' intellectual performance? In attempting to answer questions such as these, *descriptive statistical techniques will help you to* **describe** *your data, and inferential statistical techniques will help you to* **infer** *whether differences in means may have arisen from true differences or from chance.*

RESEARCH ON
TEACHER EXPECTANCY:
PYGMALION IN THE
CLASSROOM

Table 2-1 ♦ Hypothetical IQ data for the teacher-expectancy study

Grade level	Experimental group ("bloomers")			Control group		
	Student	Pretest	Posttest	Student	Pretest	Posttest
1	1	60	107	31	60	90
	2	85	111	32	75	99
	3	90	117	33	90	102
	4	110	125	34	105	114
	5	115	122	35	120	121
2	6	65	118	36	80	99
	7	79	115	37	85	95
	8	80	115	38	95	104
	9	95	116	39	99	108
	10	110	122	40	120	123
3	11	90	98	41	80	102
	12	93	103	42	100	106
	13	104	107	43	105	107
	14	108	100	44	110	111
	15	125	125	45	119	119

Your hypothetical study and the patterns in the hypothetical data parallel a study and data reported by Rosenthal and Jacobson (1968) in *Pygmalion in the Classroom*. Actual studies will often be paraphrased in this book, and hypothetical data will be created which parallel the actual data but which will use smaller numbers and fewer cases (students, subjects) to make computations as easy as possible. For example, the data in Table 2-1 will be used throughout the book to exemplify different descriptive and inferential statistical techniques. However, for those of you who are interested in what the data say about teacher expectancy, one summary of data used by Rosenthal and Jacobson is presented in Table 2-2.

Rosenthal and Jacobson (1968, p. 121) concluded that "The evidence presented . . . suggests rather strongly that children who are expected by their teachers to gain intellectually in fact do show greater intellectual gains after one year than do children of whom gains are not expected." "Teachers' favorable expectations can be responsible for gains in their pupils' IQs and, for the lower grades, these gains can be quite dramatic" (p. 98).

Table 2-1 ♦ (Continued)

Grade level	Experimental group ("bloomers")			Control group		
	Student	Pretest	Posttest	Student	Pretest	Posttest
4	16	95	95	46	95	102
	17	100	108	47	99	102
	18	104	108	48	104	107
	19	106	104	49	110	116
	20	110	116	50	120	120
5	21	75	106	51	85	112
	22	88	106	52	90	110
	23	90	95	53	100	115
	24	105	115	54	110	119
	25	120	124	55	115	125
6	26	80	97	56	79	96
	27	95	102	57	100	120
	28	100	110	58	105	117
	29	110	98	59	106	110
	30	120	122	60	110	116

Due to the important social and educational implications of the phenomenon of teacher expectancy, results of Rosenthal and Jacobson's study were widely distributed by the news media. Some example of reactions in the popular press are the following: "Here may lie the explanation of the effects of socio-economic status on schooling. Teachers of a higher socio-economic status expect pupils of a lower socio-economic status to fail" (Hutchins, *San Francisco Chronicle*, August 11, 1968). "The findings raise some fundamental questions about teacher training. They also cast doubt on the wisdom of assigning children to classes according to presumed ability, which may only mire the lowest groups into self-confining ruts" (*Time*, September 20, 1968).

Before you reach these same conclusions, consider the following. In the actual study, the gain in the experimental group is due almost completely to a total of 19 first- and second-graders (see Table 2-2). Data for grades 3 and 5 do not show the expectancy effect. Data for grade 4 show a slight expectancy effect, while data for grade 6 show a slight disadvantage. Furthermore, there are good reasons to doubt the validity of these data, especially for grades 1 and

Table 2-2 ♦ Average gain scores from the Pygmalion study (adapted from Rosenthal and Jacobson, 1968)

Grade level	Experimental group		Control group		Difference in gain (experimental gain minus control gain)	Do differences represent true differences between groups?[b]
	N [a]	Gain	N	Gain		
1	7	+27.40	48	+12.00	+15.40	Yes
2	12	+16.50	47	+ 7.00	+ 9.50	Yes
3	14	+ 5.00	40	+ 5.00	0.00	No
4	12	+ 5.60	49	+ 2.20	+ 3.40	No
5	9	+17.40	26	+17.50	0.00	No
6	11	+10.00	45	+10.70	− 0.70	No
Grades 1–6 combined	65	+12.22	255	+ 8.42	+ 3.80	Yes

[a] N denotes the number of students' scores entering into the average score.
[b] Much of this textbook deals with deciding whether or not the differences may have arisen by chance or by a treatment's effect.

2 where the expectancy effect is the greatest. For example, the test used does not have adequate norms for the youngest children. Examination of scores for individual students suggests that the test may have been invalid at these younger age levels. For example, one subject had a pretest reasoning IQ of 17 and a posttest IQ of 148. In addition, when interviewed, teachers could not remember the names on the original list of "bloomers," and reported hardly having glanced at them. (For an excellent, thorough critique of *Pygmalion*, see Elashoff & Snow, 1971.)

DEVELOPMENT OF MORAL JUDGMENT

Much of behavioral research has, as its aim, theory building. From a theory, predictions are made about how people will behave under certain situations. These predictions are then tested empirically, that is, by observation and experiment. The data obtained bear directly on the accuracy of the predictions, and thus indirectly on the validity of the theory. Although the Pygmalion study was based on social-psychological theory and empirical evidence (Rosenthal, 1966), its major impact was *not on conclusions* about the theory. Rather its major impact was on *decisions* about socioeducational policy. For example, many school districts abandoned the use of intelligence tests partly in response to the Pygmalion findings.

Other research—for example research on the development of moral judgment—has had major impact on conclusions about a theory. For example,

Piaget's (1966) theory about the development of moral judgment, somewhat parallel to his theory of cognitive development, postulates two distinct stages. In the first stage—early childhood—moral judgments are thought to be based solely on the *outcome* of a moral act—e.g., did the moral act of the "actor" produce benefit or harm to another person? In the second stage—late childhood, adolescence, and adulthood—moral judgments are thought to be based solely on the actor's *intent*. For example, did the actor intend to cause benefit or harm to another person? The theory does allow for a transition period where moral judgments may be based on either outcome or intent; but this period is deemphasized. The theory, then, predicts that young children will base their moral judgments solely on information about outcome, while adolescents and adults will base their judgments solely on information about intent.

One way to test this theory empirically is to present stories to children and adults which depict a moral situation and systematically vary information about *outcome* (positive and negative) and *intent* (positive and negative). For example, a story used to test the theory depicts a lost child seeking help to get home in time for dinner. An older child either does or does not want to help the younger child (positive or negative intent) and the younger child either does or does not arrive home in time for dinner (positive or negative outcome).

Suppose you decide to do a study to test Piaget's theory. You select subjects at random from the ages of 4 to 18, present moral stories to them in which both outcome and intent differ, and ask these subjects to judge the older child. If the judgment is positive—the older child is judged to be morally good—the subject assigns the older child a reward ranging from +1 to +5, depending on how "morally good" he or she has been. If the judgment is negative, the subject punishes the older child by assigning an evaluation of −1 to −5 depending on how "morally bad" he or she has been. If the judgment is neutral, a zero is assigned.

A listing of hypothetical data from your study is presented in Table 2-3. Do the data support the predictions from Piaget's theory? Do young children (ages 4–6) make moral judgments solely on the basis of outcome information while young adults (ages 16–18) make judgments solely on the basis of information about intent? How might you summarize these data to help reach this conclusion? Should you take average scores for outcome and intent, ignoring whether the data represent positive or negative outcomes? Or should you be more precise and look at evaluations separately for each age level, for example, under the condition of negative outcome and negative intent? Would you be interested in how much the subjects under this condition varied in evaluating the older child? Would you be interested in the relationship between age and evaluation under the condition of negative outcome and positive intent? Suppose you found that subjects 4–6 years old gave an average rating of 0.80 to positive intent. Could this have arisen by chance when the true rating is zero as suggested by Piaget's theory? In attempting to answer questions such as these, *descriptive statistical techniques can help you to* **summarize** *or* **describe** *your data, and*

Table 2-3 ◆ Computer listing of hypothetical data from a study on the effects of outcome and intent information on children's and adults' moral judgments

Subject	Age	Story conditions[b]			
ID No.	Group[a]	O+ I+	O+ I−	O− I+	O− I−
01	1	+2	+1	−2	−3
02	1	+2	−1	−3	−3
03	1	+3	−1	+1	−2
04	1	+3	+1	−1	−4
05	1	+4	+2	−2	−1
06	2	+2	−2	+2	−3
07	2	+3	−2	−1	−4
08	2	+3	−3	+2	−4
09	2	+4	−4	+1	−2
10	2	+4	+1	+3	−5
11	3	+3	−2	+4	−5
12	3	+3	−3	+3	−3
13	3	+4	+1	−1	−4
14	3	+2	−3	+1	−3
15	3	+4	−4	+3	−3
16	4	+3	−3	+2	−3
17	4	+4	−2	+3	−4
18	4	+4	−4	+1	−2
19	4	+3	−1	+4	−3
20	4	+4	−5	+3	−5
21	5	+3	−5	+2	−3
22	5	+4	−2	+4	−3
23	5	+2	−2	+3	−4
24	5	+3	−2	+3	−2
25	5	+4	−3	+3	−3

[a] 1, 4–6 years; 2, 7–9 years; 3, 10–12 years; 4, 13–15 years; 5, 16–18 years.
[b] O = outcome; I = intent; + = positive; − = negative.

*inferential statistical techniques can help you to **infer** whether observed differences between average values are likely to reflect true or chance differences in reality.*

Your study and the patterns in the hypothetical data (if you can find them!) parallel a study and data reported by Weiner and Peter (1973). For those of

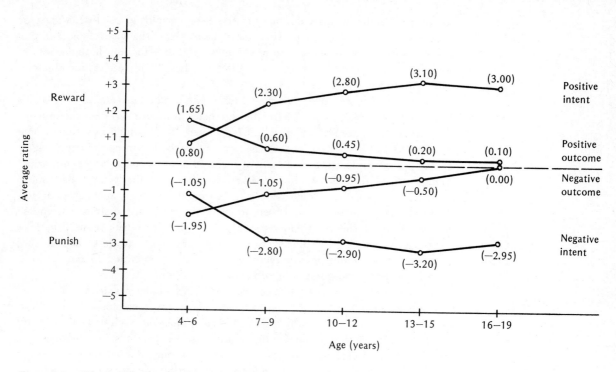

Figure 2-1 ♦ Effect of outcome and intent information on moral judgments of children, adolescents, and young adults. (Adapted from Weiner & Peter, 1973.)

you interested in the results of the actual study, Figure 2-1 summarizes the findings. For each of five age groups (4–6, 7–9, . . . , 16–18) the average of the subjects' moral judgments for stories with positive and negative outcomes and positive and negative intents is shown. For example, the average moral judgment for a story with a positive outcome for children 4–6 years of age is 1.65. The average judgment on a story with negative intent is −3.20 for adolescents aged 13–15. If you read this figure carefully, you will see that, as age increases, less importance is given to outcomes in the subjects' moral judgments and more importance is given to positive and negative intent. From these and other data, Weiner and Peter (1973, p. 299) concluded that: " . . . a progressive decline in use of objective outcome information and an increment in the use of subjective intent information [occurs], given both positive and negative outcomes and intents, until the age of 18." These data, then, are what Piaget's theory predicts. Such findings have been interpreted as supporting the theory.

It is unfair to leave you with the impression that Piaget's theory is the only one that predicts the data in Figure 2-1 or that the data in this figure are entirely consistent with Piaget's theory. First, are the data in Figure 2-1 entirely consistent with Piaget's two-stage theory? Piaget's theory predicts that young children (e.g., our 4–6-year-olds) do not use information about intent. We should expect the average judgment of the 4–6-year-olds to be close to zero for stories with positive or negative intent. This is not the case. For example, information about negative intent led these children to punish the actor by assigning an average judgment of −1.05. Further discrepancies like this one can be found in the data.

Second, there are other theories which make predictions similar to Piaget's but which can also account for the discrepancies in Figure 2-1. One such theory is attribution theory (e.g., Kelley, 1967; Weiner, 1972), which says that people attempt to make sense out of the world by trying to determine the causes of an event. For example, suppose a student received a low score on an examination. What caused this? Low ability? Lack of effort? Difficult test? Bad luck? Attribution theory says that people try to explain events, such as poor test performance, from their own observations of the student, the situation, and so on. Attribution theory, then, examines how people ascribe causality, how people judge why a particular event occurred. The theory suggests that once we attribute responsibility for an event to someone or something in the environment, this ascription guides our subsequent behavior.

In determining causality, two categories of causes of events can be identified: (1) causes which lie *within the actor* in the event, such as the actor's ability, effort, and/or intent; (2) causes which lie *within the environment*, such as task difficulty or chance. In making a moral judgment about the "goodness" or "badness" of an action, the judge must first attribute responsibility for an outcome to the actor or the environment. If the actor is perceived as the cause of the event, he is held responsible for the outcomes and judged morally responsible. In this case, *both outcome and intent* information are used. If the environment is seen as the cause of the event, the actor is not held responsible and neither outcome nor intent information influences moral judgment. Several studies have shown that although both children and adults use outcome and intent information to some degree, children give greater weight to outcome information, while adults give greater weight to intent information (e.g., Hebble, 1971). In terms of attribution theory, these findings suggest that while the actor is perceived as the cause of the event by both children and adults, information about the environment (i.e., outcome) is generally more salient to children, while information about the actor (i.e., intent) is more salient to adults. However, this does not mean that children do not use information about intent or that adults do not use information about outcomes. In some cases, adults may actually attend to outcome information more than information about intent if the information about the environment is very salient, as when an outcome is extreme (e.g., death results from an act).

In sum, attribution theory predicts that when the actor is seen as the cause of the event, both outcome and intent information will be used in making moral judgments. However, greater emphasis will be placed on outcome if information about the environment is more salient, as is the case with children. Greater emphasis will be placed on intent if information about the actor is more salient, as is the case with adults. The data from Weiner and Peter's study are entirely consistent with these predictions. For example, the data show that, although outcome information is more salient to young children, they do use intent information to some degree. Since the outcomes used in this study were not extreme ("being late for dinner"), we cannot test the prediction that adults will use outcome when information about the environment is particularly salient as with extreme outcomes.

Intuition and perhaps prior experience suggest that it is easier to learn from teachers who have the same beliefs as we do than from teachers with opposing beliefs. At least, we have earned higher grades in classes with instructors who share our beliefs than in classes with instructors who do not. For example, if your beliefs tend toward humanism, you might do better in an introductory psychology class with an instructor who shares this belief than in a class taught by a behaviorist, and vice versa.

STUDENT ACHIEVEMENT AND CONGRUENCE BETWEEN STUDENTS' AND INSTRUCTORS' BELIEFS

In order to test these predictions (intuitions), suppose you develop a short "Psychological Belief Scale" and give it to instructors and students on the first meeting of introductory psychology classes. At the end of the semester you collect the students' scores on course examinations. Intuition leads you to predict that those students whose beliefs are closest to their instructor's beliefs will earn the highest examination scores. You also predict that exam scores should decrease as the difference between the students' and their instructor's beliefs increases. Hypothetical data bearing on these predictions are presented in Table 2-4 for three introductory psychology classes at three different colleges. Are these data consistent with your predictions? Should you combine the data for all three classes and compare the average belief score and average achievement score? Or should your analysis be more specific and compare students' beliefs and final-examination scores in each class separately? Suppose you find that the relationship between students' beliefs and examination scores differs somewhat from one class to another. How likely are the differences in these observed relationships to arise by chance? How do these differences correspond to differences in the beliefs of the instructors for the three courses?

In attempting to answer questions such as these, *descriptive statistical techniques will help you to* **describe the relationship** *between two (or more) variables such as beliefs and examination scores, and inferential statistical techniques will aid in* **making inferences** *about whether the relationship between two variables in one group differs from the relationship between these variables in another group. (Are these differences likely to have arisen because of true differences between the groups, or because of chance fluctuations in the particular classes chosen?)*

This hypothetical study and the patterns in the hypothetical data parallel a study and data reported by Majasan (1972; for a concise, accessible overview, see Cronbach, 1975). In order to measure beliefs about the study of psychology, he developed a scale in which each item offered a "humanistic" (H) or

Table 2-4 ♦ Hypothetical data from a study on the relationship between student belief and achievement in three classes ($N = 7$ per class)

Instructor 1's score on belief scale: 6		Instructor 2's score on belief scale: 7		Instructor 3's score on belief scale: 8	
Belief score	Ach. score	Belief score	Ach. score	Belief score	Ach. score
3	7	2	1	8	10
4	6	5	7	7	8
6	9	7	10	3	2
5	10	6	9	5	6
8	2	9	3	7	9
9	3	3	4	2	2
6	10	7	9	4	5

"behavioristic" (B) alternative. For example: "The central focus of the study of human behavior should be: (a) the specific principles that apply to unique individuals (H); (b) the general principles that apply to all individuals (B)." Instructors in introductory psychology classes and their students received the scale at the beginning of the course. A high score on the belief scale indicated a behavioristic orientation, while a low score indicated a humanistic orientation. The achievement score was the students' total scores earned on all class examinations. Actual data from 3 of the 12 classes in the study are presented in Figure 2-2. The lines in the figure ("regression lines"; see Chapter 8) represent the relationship between scores on the belief scale and classroom achievement scores. Since each instructor gave a different examination, the number of items, and thus the magnitude of students' scores, differed from one class to the next. Therefore, all examination scores have been converted to "standard scores" which show how far above ($+$) or below ($-$) the class average a particular examination score falls.

In eleven of the twelve classes, Majasan found that examination scores were highest for students whose beliefs corresponded closely with their instructors. In the one class which did not support his prediction, examinations were not used. Rather, the only available measure of achievement in this class, taught by a humanist, was the student's grade on an independent project.

What might account for the higher achievement of students whose beliefs corresponded closely to those of their instructors? One theory is that teachers and students with similar beliefs about psychology have similar cognitive structures (i.e., similar organizations of concepts and ideas). Teachers may be

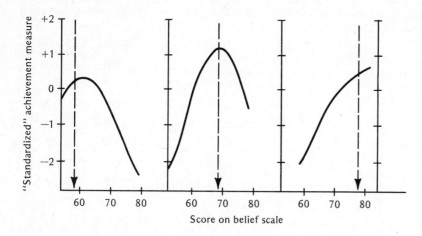

Figure 2-2 ♦ Relationship between student achievement and belief in three representative classes (data from Cronbach, 1975). (Arrow denotes instructor's score on Belief Scale.)

able to communicate the subject matter more effectively to students with cognitive structures similar to their own. The higher achievement of these students may be a result of this increased effectiveness of communication (see Runkel, 1956). Further research studies are needed, however, to test this speculation.

Did you know that when college grades of men and women of equivalent aptitude are compared, the women tend to earn higher grades than the men? In the literature on sex differences in higher education, there have been several "explanations" of this finding. One proposed explanation has been that women's achievement might be due to a difference in standards used for grading men and women; perhaps men are graded harder than women. A second explanation has been that the same grading standard is used for men and women and that the differences in grades are due to "typically feminine" traits. For example, in its most pejorative form, the reasoning has been that women, being more docile, may follow their instructor's directions more closely than men. Hence, they attend class more regularly, turn in assignments on time more often, and are more responsive to the instructor's criticisms of their work. Still another proposed explanation has been that the difference in grades may stem from women's highly developed "clerical traits." In this view, their work may be neater than the men's, it may be more artistic, or it may be more tedious in detail. Regardless of the exact nature of the explanation, it has "typically female," non-academic-related characteristics.

A plausible, but often overlooked, alternative explanation is that the appar-

THE DISPARITY IN COLLEGE GRADES EARNED BY MEN AND WOMEN

Table 2-5 ♦ Hypothetical data from a study on college GPA

College[a]	Student	Sex	Major	GPA[a]	SAT[a]
UCLA	1	M	Physics	2.90	1050
	2	M	Physics	2.00	1200
	3	M	Anthropology	3.50	1100
	4	M	English	3.20	1130
	5	M	Chemistry	2.50	1160
	6	F	English	2.90	1075
	7	F	English	3.60	1100
	8	F	Engineering	2.30	1025
	9	F	Design	3.00	1000
	10	F	Biology	2.50	1000
UCD	11	M	Physics	2.90	1175
	12	M	Engineering	3.20	1125
	13	M	Biology	3.00	1100
	14	M	Engineering	2.70	1150
	15	M	Biology	2.50	1200
	16	F	Chemistry	2.50	1120
	17	F	Sociology	3.30	1090
	18	F	Sociology	3.00	1100
	19	F	English	2.90	1085
	20	F	Anthropology	3.20	1125
UCI	21	M	Physics	2.70	1125
	22	M	Biology	2.90	1175
	23	M	Chemistry	3.20	1200
	24	M	Biology	2.90	1100
	25	M	Engineering	3.00	1150
	26	F	Sociology	3.10	1090
	27	F	Design	2.90	1060
	28	F	English	2.70	1050
	29	F	Anthropology	3.00	1175
	30	F	English	3.20	1100

[a] UCLA = University of California, Los Angeles; UCD = University of California, Davis; UCI = University of California, Irvine; UCSD = University of California, San Diego; GPA = grade-point average; SAT = Scholastic Aptitude Test (verbal and mathematics combined).

Table 2-5 ♦ (Continued)

College[a]	Student	Sex	Major	GPA[a]	SAT[a]
UCSD	31	M	Physics	2.70	1150
	32	M	Chemistry	2.80	1185
	33	M	Engineering	3.10	1200
	34	M	Biology	3.00	1160
	35	M	English	3.40	1200
	36	F	Biology	2.50	1150
	37	F	Sociology	3.00	1100
	38	F	Anthropology	3.10	1120
	39	F	Anthropology	2.90	1080
	40	F	Design	3.50	1150

ent disparity in grades between men and women of equal ability is due to differences in the grading practices in different fields of study and not due to some inherent or learned characteristics of women. Goldman, Schmidt, Hewett, and Fisher (1974) have found that grading standards are more stringent in the biological and physical sciences than in the humanities and social sciences. It may simply be that a greater percentage of women than men enroll in the humanities and social sciences, while a greater percentage of men than women enroll in biology and the physical sciences.

In order to check out this explanation, suppose you collect information on men's and women's choices of academic majors, grade-point averages, and aptitude-test scores. If your hunch is correct, these data should show that men and women tend to choose different academic majors, that women tend to major in the humanities and social sciences while men tend to major in the biological and physical sciences, and that men and women of similar ability have similar grade-point averages when major field is taken into account.

Data from your hypothetical study are presented in Table 2-5 for male and female undergraduates from four campuses of the University of California. Do these data support your hypothesis that men and women choose different major fields? Do they support your hypothesis that men and women of similar aptitudes have similar grade-point averages when major field is taken into account? Should the data be combined for students from different universities, or should they be examined separately? Suppose your data show 15 men majoring in the physical sciences and only 5 women. Does this reflect a systematic difference between men and women in their choice of a major, or is it likely to have occurred by chance? In attempting to answer questions such as these, *descriptive statistical techniques can be used to **summarize** the data in your study and*

Table 2-6 ♦ Major-field choices of male and female undergraduates at UCLA (data from Hewitt and Goldman, 1975)

		Major field			
		Physics	Engineering	English	Design
Sex	Male	108	345	94	17
	Female	8	12	253	60

*to **describe the relationship** between two (or more) variables, such as sex and major field. Furthermore, inferential statistical techniques provide ways to **infer** whether or not the relationship between sex and academic major may have arisen by chance.*

This hypothetical study and the patterns in the hypothetical data parallel a study and data reported by Hewitt and Goldman (1975). They collected data on all undergraduates enrolled at four campuses of the University of California for whom complete data on the following measures were available: major, GPA, and SAT scores. The final sample numbered over 13,000 students.

Hewitt and Goldman sought answers to two major questions. First, "Do men and women tend to choose different majors?" Actual data showing the numbers of men and women choosing four majors at UCLA are presented in Table 2-6. A similar pattern occurred at the three other universities. From these and other data, Hewitt and Goldman concluded that sex and major field were significantly related at all four schools.

The second question was whether or not men and women showed differences in academic achievement when their major field was taken into account. They found that, in general, women did tend to have higher grade-point averages than men of similar ability. However, these differences were drastically reduced or entirely eliminated when major field was considered. The authors concluded that: "It seems very clear that men and women tend to major in different college fields. This difference in major field is sufficient to account for much, if not most, of the apparent 'overachievement' of college women" (Hewitt & Goldman, 1975, p. 329). The question of why certain fields grade more leniently, however, cannot be answered from this study.

DETERMINANTS OF EMOTION

Love, euphoria, fear, anger, happiness, are all psychological states called emotions. While most, if not all, of us have felt them at one time, probably few of us have given much thought to their origin. However, psychologists have been studying emotions for about a century. Initially, they believed that emotions were based primarily on changes in physiological states such as rapid heart or respiration rate, trembling hands, flushed face, or numbness. This is the hypothesis William James put forth in 1890: "the bodily changes [physiological states] follow directly the perception of the exciting fact [stimulus], and . . . our feeling of the same changes as they occur *is* the emotion" (p. 449). Following James's hypothesis, an awesome number of studies sought to show that certain physiological indices (e.g., rapid heart and respiration rate) were associated with particular emotions (e.g., anger). What they found, however, was that "the same visceral changes occur in very different emotional states and in non-emotional states" (Cannon, 1929, p. 351).

While particular physiological states do not explain emotions adequately, at least a generalized state of arousal accompanies emotions. What other factors might be involved in determining particular emotions? Attribution theory provides one possible answer to this question. Recall from the section on "Development of Moral Judgment" that attribution theory assumes that people attempt to make sense out of events such as perceived physiological arousal by determining the causes of the events. Thus, given a state of arousal, a person attempts to explain it by searching for causes in the environment or within himself. For example, given a heightened state of arousal and a stranger pointing a gun at me, I would probably label my emotional state as fear and feel fearful. In contrast, I would attribute my heightened state of arousal at a UCLA basketball game to anxiety or euphoria, depending on the score. Attribution theory, then, suggests that given a readily available cause for a person's state of physiological arousal, the emotion will be attributed to that cause (fear in the first example). However, given arousal and several possible attributions (labels) for it (euphoria or anxiety), situational factors (e.g., the score of the game) will influence the labeling of the emotion. Precisely the same state of physiological arousal experienced in two different situations could be labeled and felt as euphoria or anxiety (etc.).

To recap, two possible "theories" of emotion have been put forth. The first theory asserts that emotion is the feeling accompanying a physiological state of arousal and that different indicators (e.g., heart rate, numbness) lead to the feeling of different emotional states. The second theory asserts that there are two components involved in producing emotion: (1) physiological arousal ("a general pattern of excitation of the sympathetic nervous system"—Schacter & Singer, 1962), and (2) cognitive factors involved in identifying, labeling, and interpreting this stirred-up state.

The two-component theory makes the following predictions about a person's emotional state: (1) given a state of *arousal* and a readily available, plausible *explanation* for it, the person will label and describe his feelings according to the explanation; (2) given a state of arousal and no immediate explanation, the person will label and describe his feelings according to the situation in which he finds himself; and (3) given the same explanation or situation, a person will react emotionally or describe his feelings as emotional only if he experiences arousal. The physiological theory predicts that a person will react emotionally or describe his feelings as emotional in the presence of a state of arousal and the particular physiological symptoms will determine the nature of the emotion.

While past research suggests that the two-component theory is the more plausible, suppose you decided to do a study that extends past research in testing the two competing theories. In designing the study, you have three variables to consider. First, you have to vary the level of *physiological arousal* (presence or absence). This might be done by giving some subjects a drug such as epinephrine (adrenalin) and giving the other subjects a placebo such as a saline solution.[2] Epinephrine leads to heightened arousal with the following symptoms: palpitation, tremor, and sometimes flushing and accelerated breathing. So that subjects are unaware of whether or not they received epinephrine, let's set up the experiment so that subjects are asked to drink orange juice which either does or does not contain the tasteless drug, while they wait to participate in an experiment on visual perception.

A second variable that needs to be considered is whether or not subjects have a readily available, accurate *explanation* for their physiological states. This can be accomplished by telling a subject that the orange juice contains a vitamin compound, "Suproxin," that may have side effects such that: (1) your heart and respiration rate may increase and your face may get warm and flushed (*accurate explanation*), or (2) your feet may feel numb and you may itch over parts of your body (*inaccurate explanation*). In addition, some subjects would not be told anything about their possible state of physiological arousal after drinking the orange juice (*ignorance of explanation*).

Finally, the third variable is the *situation* in which the subject is placed. Suppose the subject is joined in drinking orange juice by a confederate ("stooge") of the experimenter who, after a period of time, acts either "euphoric" or "angry." In the euphoric condition, the stooge chats with the subject, jokes, and takes paper lying around the room, wads it up, and shoots "baskets" in the paper basket, all the time imploring the subject to join him. In the angry condition, the experimenter asks both the subject and the stooge to fill out a tedious and insulting questionnaire. As the stooge proceeds through the questionnaire, he becomes increasingly angry and finally yells, "To hell with it! I don't have to do this crap!" He then rips up the questionnaire and throws it away.

In designing a study, then, these three variables must be taken into account.

---

[2]Clearly, ethical issues arise when drugs are given to human subjects in experiments. We assume that: (1) all subjects gave their informed consent prior to the study; (2) the potential benefits of this study far outweigh the potential harm to a subject; and (3) subjects were screened by a physician before being permitted to participate. In addition, we assume that subjects are not necessarily aware that this particular study is the one in which, with their informed consent, their state of physiological arousal is being influenced. Again, we assume that the potential benefits of the study outweigh this risk of deception.

One possible design is a $2 \times 3 \times 2$ (arousal $\times$ explanation $\times$ situation) design. The problem with this design, however, is that it combines the placebo condition of the arousal variable with an explanation variable that refers only to drugs. For example, a subject receiving the placebo would be told that his heart rate etc. would increase—an "accurate" explanation, but only for the drug condition. An alternative design avoids this problem by combining the arousal variable with the explanation variable as follows: drug + accurate explanation, drug + inaccurate explanation, drug + no explanation, and placebo. The result is a 2×4 design with two levels of the situation variable (euphoria, anger) and four levels of the arousal and explanation variables combined. Each subject would be randomly assigned to one of the eight cells of the design. A subject would enter a waiting room, be joined by a stooge, drink the orange juice, and then either be told about the effects of "Suproxin" or not, depending on the cell of the 2×4 design. Finally, the subject would experience, with the stooge, "euphoria" or "anger." At the end of the session, the subject would be asked to check the following rating scale:

How would you say you feel at present?

0	1	2	3	4	5	6	7	8
I feel extremely angry	I feel very angry	I feel somewhat angry	I feel slightly angry	I don't feel angry or happy	I feel slightly happy	I feel somewhat happy	I feel very happy	I feel extremely happy

The results of this hypothetical study are presented in Table 2-7 for each cell of the 2×4 design. The scores in each cell are the subjects' ratings of their feelings. What can you conclude about the validity of the two theories? Is physiological arousal sufficient to account for the results? Is a two-component model—arousal and cognition—sufficient to explain the results? Is it possible that a cognitive theory without a physiological component provides the most parsimonious explanation of the data in Table 2-7? In attempting to answer questions such as these, *descriptive statistical techniques will help you to* **describe** *your data. Inferential statistical techniques will help you to* **infer** *whether differences in combinations of the means of the eight groups may have arisen from true differences or from chance.*

This hypothetical study and the patterns in the hypothetical data parallel a study and data reported by Schacter and Singer (1962). For those of you interested in what happened in that study, Table 2-8 shows the data reported by Schacter and Singer. (Note: They did not have a group of subjects who received drug + inaccurate explanation in the anger situation. This condition is included in the hypothetical study; see Table 2-7.) In general, the data from this and other studies (such as Schacter & Wheeler, 1962) supported the

Table 2-7 ♦ Hypothetical data for the study on the determinants of emotion[a]

| Treatment | Situation | |
	Euphoria	Anger
Drug + accurate explanation	5	2
	4	3
	6	2
	5	1
Drug + inaccurate explanation	6	1
	7	1
	5	0
	6	2
Drug + no explanation	6	2
	7	3
	5	2
	5	3
Placebo	4	4
	4	4
	4	3
	6	3

[a] Scores refer to subjects' ratings of their feelings on a scale from 0 (angry) to 8 (happy). See text.

two-component model of emotion. That is, the attribution of an emotional state to oneself depends on physiological arousal and cognition. Moreover, the importance of the cognitive component is considerable. In fact, subjects can be fooled into attributing their own naturally occurring physiological states to the effects of a drug and consequently feel less emotion. For example, Nisbett and Schacter (1966) found that subjects who perceived their normal reactions to electric shocks (see footnote 2) as being drug induced (e.g., rapid heart rate and breathing) were able to tolerate stronger shocks than subjects who could not attribute their symptoms to a drug, and they reported less fear and pain. (For other studies on the importance of cognition in determining emotional states, see London & Nesbitt, 1974; Valins, 1966.)

Table 2-8 ◆ Self-report of emotional states: mean ratings[a]

	Situation	
Treatment	Euphoria	Anger
Drug + accurate explanation	4.98	2.09
Drug + inaccurate explanation	5.90	Not included in design
Drug + no explanation	5.78	2.61
Placebo	5.61 [b]	2.37 [b]

[a] Adapted from S. Schacter and J. E. Singer, "Cognitive, social, and physiological determinants of emotional state." *Psychological Review*, 1962, *9*, 379–399. Copyright 1962 by the American Psychological Association. Reprinted by permission. Data adjusted to fit dependent variable as described in text.

[b] Notice that subjects receiving the placebo did not report the lowest amount of emotion as theory predicted (i.e., a score of 4 on our scale; see text). In Schacter and Singer's study, they received injections of either epinephrine or saline solution. So, even the placebo subjects could attribute their feelings to an "injection." For this reason, we used orange juice in our study as a vehicle for receiving the drug.

◆   ◆   ◆   ◆   ◆

Summary

Five studies have been described to try to arouse your interest in behavioral research. The hypothetical data from these five studies, as well as data from other studies, will be used throughout this book to illustrate how statistical techniques can be used to help answer questions that we want to investigate. You will see how *descriptive statistics* can be used to present and organize data in a convenient, usable, and communicable form. Then you will also see how *inferential statistics* can be used to make generalizations from these data.

SECTION II

Descriptive Statistics
for
Univariate Distributions

In this section, statistical methods are presented for summarizing and describing what has happened in a research study. More specifically, these methods summarize and describe data for each of the variables in a study.

Measures for each variable in a study, such as test scores, reaction times, and ratings, are first summarized in the form of a *data matrix*. This matrix is a table showing the scores for each subject on each variable.

From the data matrix, a *frequency distribution* can be constructed for each variable. This distribution tells us how many subjects earned each of the possible scores on the variable. When this distribution is graphed, a pictorial summary of the patterns in the data is obtained. Often data summarized this way look like a bell-shaped curve, sometimes called a normal distribution.

The data in the frequency distribution can be summarized even further in order to provide a clearer picture of what happened in a study. The average score (mean, mode, or median), for example, can be used to tell us where the center of the frequency distribution is. This average, then, provides a measure of the *central tendency* of the distribution. And a measure of the spread of the distribution (e.g., range, standard deviation) can be used to describe the variability of scores from subject to subject.

Since these statistical methods for summarizing data deal with one variable at a time, they are sometimes called univariate, descriptive statistics. And since all of the methods provide descriptions of a distribution of data, these statistical methods are applied to univariate distributions.

3.

Frequency Distributions

The Data Matrix

Frequency Distributions

Class Intervals: A Method for Grouping Data
♦ Limits of Class Intervals ♦
♦ Midpoints of Class Intervals ♦

Graphical Representations of Frequency Distributions
♦ Shapes of Frequency Distributions ♦
♦ The Relative Frequency Distribution ♦
♦ Relative Frequency Polygons ♦
♦ The Cumulative Frequency Distribution ♦
♦ The Cumulative Frequency Polygon ♦
♦ Cumulative Proportions and Percentages ♦

Percentile Scales
♦ Computing Percentile Scores Directly ♦
♦ Computing a Score Corresponding to a Given Percentile Rank ♦

Summary
♦ Key Words ♦
♦ Exercises ♦

THE OBVIOUS first step in dealing with a mass of data is, somehow, to organize them. The next step is to summarize the data in such a way that the important information is preserved while the unimportant information is discarded. In this chapter, you will discover how statistics can help you put together a picture which focuses on those aspects of the data which bear on research questions. For example, data can be organized by placing them in a data matrix. A *data matrix* is a table identifying each subject and showing his or her score on each variable in the study. Data from the matrix can then be readily summarized by a frequency distribution. A *frequency distribution* orders score values from lowest to highest and gives the number (frequency) of subjects earning each score value.

The purpose of this chapter is to teach you how to organize the information collected in a research study using a data matrix and to build, display, and interpret different types of frequency distributions. Data in frequency distributions can be presented in tabular form or graphically as a *histogram* (a form of the familiar bar graph) or as a *frequency polygon* (a smoothline curve). They can also be represented by a *relative frequency distribution*, which gives the proportion of subjects earning each score value. Such distributions allow comparison of data from two or more samples of different sizes. Finally, the data can be represented as percentile scores, which are score values below which a certain percentage of scores fall. They can be presented graphically as a *cumulative relative frequency distribution*.

To make the presentation on distributions more relevant, the hypothetical data from the teacher-expectancy study—*Pygmalion in the Classroom*—will be used. Remember, Rosenthal and Jacobson (1968) wanted to find out whether teachers' perceptions of students' intellectual abilities actually influenced those students' intellectual performance. Several classrooms at grades one through six were selected at random. Teachers were told that several students in their class were expected to show tremendous academic and intellectual gains during the school year. Actually, these "bloomers" were selected at random; so they should not have gained any more than the other students in the class. At the end of the school year, students were tested to see if there were differences in intellectual performance between the "bloomers" and the other children. (See the beginning of Chapter 2 for a more complete description.)

THE DATA MATRIX   The process of examining data begins seriously when the data have been collected and your desk (or floor) is inundated with piles of tests and stacks of hastily scribbled notes about subjects. Somehow this flood of information must be organized before you can make sense out of it. The data matrix provides a method. A **matrix** is defined as a rectangular arrangement of elements (e.g., persons, variables) into horizontal lines called rows and vertical lines called columns. These horizontal and vertical lines meet to form the *cells* of the matrix. A **data matrix** is a table or matrix of scores in which persons or subjects or cases are listed on the rows of the table and the information collected on each subject (the variables) is listed along the columns of the table (see Table 3-1). Scores and other data for each individual are entered in the appropriate cells of the matrix. In this way, a convenient and easily read layout of the data is provided.

A data matrix for the experimental group in the teacher-expectancy study is shown in Table 3-1. Notice that an identification number is assigned to each

Table 3-1 ♦ Data matrix for the data from the hypothetical study of teacher expectancy (experimental group)

Cell	Column		
		Variables	
Persons	Treatment group[a]	Grade level	Posttest
Row ⟶ 01	1	1	107
02	1	1	111
03	1	1	117
04	1	1	125
05	1	1	122
06	1	2	118
07	1	2	115
08	1	2	115
09	1	2	116
10	1	2	122
11	1	3	98
12	1	3	103
13	1	3	107
14	1	3	100
15	1	3	125
16	1	4	95

(continued on p. 72)

Table 3-1 ◆ (continued)

Cell	Column		
		Variables	
Persons	Treatment group[a]	Grade level	Posttest
17	1	4	108
18	1	4	108
19	1	4	104
20	1	4	116
21	1	5	106
22	1	5	106
23	1	5	95
24	1	5	115
25	1	5	124
26	1	6	97
27	1	6	102
28	1	6	110
29	1	6	98
30	1	6	122

[a] 1 = experimental group.

Procedure 3-1 ◆ Construction of a data matrix using all of the data from the hypothetical study of teacher expectancy (Table 2-1)

Operation	Example
1 List persons by subject number in rows of matrix. *Begin with lowest subject number and list in numerical order to highest subject number*	Persons
	1
	2
	3
	.
	.
	.
	58
	59
	60

2 Label variables in columns of matrix.

Persons	Variables		
	Treat-ment	Grade level	Post-test
1			
2			
3			
.			
.			
.			
58			
59			
60			

3 Assign numerical values to nonnumerical variables and enter the appropriate value for each person in the appropriate column.

Often 0 and 1 or 1 and 2 are used when there are two levels of a variable (e.g., experimental group = 1; control group = 2). This procedure is often referred to as "coding."

Persons	Variables		
	Treat-ment	Grade level	Post-test
1	1		
2	1		
3	1		
.	.		
.	.		
.	.		
58	2		
59	2		
60	2		

4 For numerical variables, enter the value for each person in the appropriate column.

Persons	Variables		
	Treat-ment	Grade level	Post-test
1	1	1	107
2	1	1	111
3	1	1	117
.	.	.	.
.	.	.	.
.	.	.	.
58	2	6	117
59	2	6	110
60	2	6	116

subject, beginning with 1 and ending with the number corresponding to the last subject. Also, notice that a number is used to designate treatment-group membership (1 = experimental group, in Table 3-1) instead of a letter (e.g., E) or a label. In general, numerical designation of nominal variables should be used in constructing a data matrix. This makes for easy transfer of the data to data cards for computer analysis. The steps for constructing a data matrix are summarized in Procedure 3-1. Note that the operation, any special comment about the operation, and an example using all data from the teacher-expectancy study (cf. Table 2-1) are presented for each step. This and any subsequent Procedure can be skipped if you are sure you can accurately carry out the steps involved.

EXAMPLE PROBLEM 1

Construct a data matrix for the control group in the teacher-expectancy study using the posttest data in Table 2-1 near the beginning of Chapter 2. (Hint: Be sure to code treatment level.)

FREQUENCY DISTRIBUTIONS

The frequency distribution provides a means of summarizing and highlighting important aspects of the data in the data matrix. By summarizing the critical features of the data, it presents the mass of data in a more interpretable form.

A **frequency distribution** is a tabular arrangement of score values showing the frequency with which each value occurs. In this definition, probably the only unfamiliar term is **score value**. It refers to any possible value (number) on a scale of numbers. For example, on a ten-item test, score values can range from 0 to 10. "Score" refers to a score value earned by a particular individual. Score values are usually arranged from lowest to highest in a frequency distribution (see Table 3-2).

A frequency distribution, then, summarizes the data collected on a particular variable by arranging the score values in order of size or magnitude and indicating how often each is obtained. Notice that some information is lost in this process. Although we know how often a particular score value was earned, we lose information about the scores of specific individuals. The link, then, between subjects and their scores is lost.

Table 3-2 shows a frequency distribution using posttest scores for subjects ("bloomers") in the experimental group of the teacher-expectancy study.[1] Notice that the frequency distribution quickly supplies some information about the performance of these subjects that is difficult to find in the data matrix. For example, posttest performance varied greatly among individual subjects; scores ranged from 95 to 125. The most frequently earned scores were 115 and 122.

In constructing a frequency distribution, begin with the lowest score value at

---

[1]Notice that posttest scores were chosen for examination in the frequency distribution. These data are sufficient to investigate the teacher-expectancy effect; pretest data are helpful but not necessary. Since subjects were randomly assigned to either the experimental or the control group, we assume that any differences between the groups are due to chance. *Pretest information may be used to verify this reasoning.* If the random assignment worked and there is no systematic difference between the groups initially in intellectual performance, their average pretest scores should be approximately equal. Indeed, this was found to be the case when average pretest scores were computed: they were 96.90 for the experimental group and 99.03 for the control group.

Table 3-2 ♦ Frequency distribution of posttest scores from
the hypothetical study of teacher expectancy (experimental group)

Score value X	Tally	Frequency f
125	//	2
124	/	1
123		0
122	///	3
121		0
120		0
119		0
118	/	1
117	/	1
116	//	2
115	///	3
114		0
113		0
112		0
111	/	1
110	/	1
109		0
108	//	2
107	//	2
106	//	2
105		0
104	/	1
103	/	1
102	/	1
101		0
100	/	1
99		0
98	//	2
97	/	1
96		0
95	//	2

the bottom of the table and list the score values upward until you reach the highest score received by a subject. Then, for each subject, tally his score against the appropriate score value. Finally, count the tallies associated with each score value to obtain the frequency with which it occurs. For reference, the steps in constructing a frequency distribution are summarized in Procedure 3-2.

Procedure 3-2 ◆ Construction of a frequency distribution using data from the experimental group in Table 3-1

Operation	Example		
1 List score values in descending numerical order from the highest at the top to the lowest at the bottom. *Highest score value at top; lowest at bottom.*	Score value	Tally	Frequency
	125		
	124		
	123		
	.		
	.		
	97		
	96		
	95		
2 Working from the data matrix, count (tally) the number of times each score value occurs in the set of data.	Score value	Tally	Frequency
	125	//	
	124	/	
	123		
	.	.	
	.	.	
	97	/	
	96		
	95	//	
3 Convert the number of tallies to Arabic numerals in the column labeled "frequency."	Score value	Tally	Frequency
	125	//	2
	124	/	1
	123		0
	.	.	.
	.	.	.
	97	/	1
	96		0
	95	//	2

	Score value	Tally	Frequency
4 Check the accuracy of your counting by adding up the numbers in the frequency columns. The sum should equal the total number of scores you began with.	125	//	2
	124	/	1
	123		0
	⋮	⋮	⋮
	97	/	1
	96		0
	95	//	2
			Sum = 30

EXAMPLE PROBLEM 2

a. Using the data matrix from Example Problem 1, construct a frequency distribution of posttest scores for the control group in the teacher-expectancy study.

b. Compare this distribution with the frequency distribution for the experimental group in Table 3-2. Are the scores equally spread out for both groups? Are the same or different score values most frequently earned in the experimental and in the control group?

CLASS INTERVALS: A METHOD FOR GROUPING DATA

With a wide range of score values, as in Table 3-2, it is difficult to see whatever patterns may exist in the data. A common solution to this problem is to group score values together. For example, the IQ scores in Table 3-2 have been grouped together in Table 3-3 so that three score values are placed in each group [e.g., (93, 94, 95); (96, 97, 98); (123, 124, 125)]. By squeezing score values together, the distribution becomes more compact and often patterns emerge more clearly. Notice that Table 3-3 is more economical, both in the time it takes to read the data and in the space it occupies, than Table 3-2. We can see at a glance a pattern in the data: the most frequently earned scores fall in the interval 114–116, and other scores are spread out both above and below. Such information is more difficult to extract from Table 3-2.

The term given to the grouping of score values is **class interval**. Class intervals may be characterized by their size. The *size* of a class interval is simply the number of score values within it. The size of the class intervals in Table 3-3 is 3, since three score values are contained within each interval (e.g., the highest interval contains three score values: 123, 124, 125). (Notice that the size of the class intervals in Table 3-2 is 1. Thus the score value and the class interval are the same. Regrouping has not been done.)

Table 3-3 ◆ Frequency distribution using class intervals of posttest scores from the hypothetical study of teacher expectancy (experimental group)

(1) Class interval	(2) f	(3) Real limits	(4) Midpoint
123–125	3	122.5–125.5	124
120–122	3	119.5–122.5	121
117–119	2	116.5–119.5	118
114–116	5	113.5–116.5	115
111–113	1	110.5–113.5	112
108–110	3	107.5–110.5	109
105–107	4	104.5–107.5	106
102–104	3	101.5–104.5	103
99–101	1	98.5–101.5	100
96– 98	3	95.5– 98.5	97
93– 95	2	92.5– 95.5	94

In constructing class intervals, first decide on the number of intervals to be used. As a rule of thumb, between 10 and 20 intervals are recommended. This recommendation represents a reasonable tradeoff between having very few wide intervals (*economy*) and having intervals so wide that the data may be misrepresented (*error*). Next, determine the size of the intervals, i. This is done by first finding the *range* of scores—highest score minus lowest score—and dividing this range by the number of intervals:

$$i = \frac{\text{highest score} - \text{lowest score}}{\text{number of class intervals}}.$$

For example, in Table 3-2, the scores go from 95 to 125 so the range is 30 ($125 - 95 = 30$). If ten class intervals are to be used as in Table 3-3, then the size of each interval will be $30 \div 10 = 3$. Notice that in Table 3-3 the lowest interval begins with the score value of 93 even though the lowest score in Table 3-2 is 95. By convention, the lowest class interval is usually started at a score value evenly divisible by the size of the interval ($93 \div 3 = 31$). For reference, the steps in constructing class intervals are presented in Procedure 3-3.

Once class intervals have been formed for a set of data, a frequency distribution can be constructed with class intervals in the same way the distribution was constructed with individual score values (see Procedure 3-2). The only difference is that, instead of counting the frequency of each score value (step 2 in Procedure 3-2), the frequency with which scores fall within each *class interval* is determined.

Operation	Example
1 Choose the number of class intervals to be used. *10–20 intervals.*	Use 10 intervals
2 Find the range of the scores obtained by subtracting the lowest score value from the highest.	$125 - 95 = 30$
3 Divide the range (step 2) by the number of intervals (step 1) to find the size of the interval. Round off if a whole number is not obtained. *Interval sizes of 2, 3, 5, 10 or 20 points are preferred.*	$30 \div 10 = 3$
4 Begin with the lowest score divisible by the interval size. (If the lowest score obtained in the set of data is not divisible by the interval size, begin with the first number below the lowest score which is divisible by the interval size.) To obtain the highest score in any given interval, add the interval size minus 1 to the lower score of that interval. For example, if the interval size is 3, $3 - 1$, or 2 can be added to the lower score of the interval to obtain the highest score of the interval (e.g., interval beginning with 93 ends with $93 + 2$ which equals 95). *An interval is usually started with the lowest score divisible by the interval size.*	123–125 (123, 124, 125) 120–122 (120, 121, 122) ⋮ 96– 98 (96, 97, 98) 93– 95 (93, 94, 95)

Steps in calculating the class interval using data from Table 3-2 ◆ Procedure 3-3

---

a. Using the posttest scores for the control group in the teacher-expectancy study (see Problem 1), construct a frequency distribution with 12 class intervals.

b. Are there any major differences in overall performance between the experimental and control groups?

EXAMPLE PROBLEM 3

◆   ◆   ◆   ◆   ◆

The next step in summarizing data is to construct a graph or pictorial representation of the frequency distribution. In order to do this, the limits (boundaries) of each class interval must be established. A class interval has two different types of limits: the score limits and the real limits. Both of these

Limits of Class Intervals

concepts will become important in the next section when methods for graphing frequency distributions are discussed.

Score limits   The **score limits** are defined as the highest score and the lowest score used in setting up a class interval. An illustration of the score limits for intervals of three points is shown in Figure 3-1a. Notice that the upper and lower score values mark the boundaries of each interval. For example, the lower score limit of the interval 93–95 is 93, while the upper score limit is 95.

Real limits   The intervals as defined by their score limits in Figure 3-1a do not meet. For example, the upper score limit of the first interval is 95, while the lower score limit of the second interval is 96. Nevertheless, scores of 95.1 and 95.4 would fall in the lowest interval, 93–95, while scores of 95.5 and 95.8 would fall in the next interval, 96–98. Thus the real limits of these two intervals are: 92.5–95.5 and 95.5–98.5. The **real limits** of a class interval are defined as the point falling exactly halfway between the two score values indicating the upper boundary of one interval and the lower boundary of the other interval. The real limits of an interval, then, are:

$$\text{real lower limit} = \text{score limit} - 0.5(\text{unit}),$$

$$\text{real upper limit} = \text{score limit} + 0.5(\text{unit}).$$

Figure 3-1 ♦ Illustration of score limits, real limits, and midpoints of class intervals used for teacher expectancy data

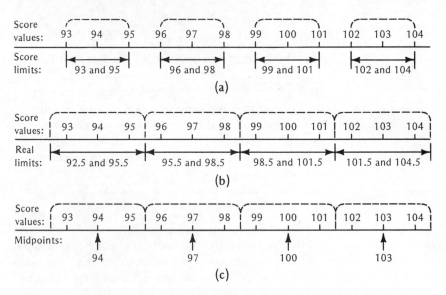

The term 0.5(unit) needs some explanation. Measurements in the behavioral sciences are not perfect, and so they are rounded either when the measurement is taken or afterwards. In measuring IQ, for example, scores are rounded to whole numbers, although in theory a person's score could be 105.3. In this example, then, the *unit* used for the measurement is 1; viz., one IQ point. Hence 0.5(unit) would be $0.5(1) = 0.5$. In contrast, suppose a measure of subjects' reaction times was accurate to one-tenth of a second and all reaction time scores were rounded to tenths (e.g., 2.1). In this case, the unit would be tenths or 0.1. Thus $0.5(0.1) = 0.05$, and so the real limits of a class interval such as 1.0–2.0 would be 0.95–2.05 (i.e., $1.00 - 0.05 = 0.95$ and $2.00 + 0.05 = 2.05$).

Figure 3-1b shows the real limits for class intervals used in the teacher-expectancy study. Notice that adjacent intervals meet, so that all possible score values are included in the intervals. For example, the lower real limit of the class interval 93–95 is 92.5, while the upper real limit is 95.5.

For reference, the steps in finding score limits and calculating real limits are summarized in Procedure 3-4. The data are taken from the experimental group in the teacher-expectancy study.

Steps in calculating the limits of a class interval using data from Table 3-3 ♦ Procedure 3-4

Operation	Example
1 Find *score limits* by identifying the lowest and highest score value of each interval.	Class interval — Score limits
	123–125 123, 125
	120–122 120, 122
	⋮ ⋮
	96– 98 96, 98
	93– 95 93, 95

Operation	Example
2 Calculate *real limits* by identifying the point halfway between the upper score limit of a particular interval and the lower score limit of the next higher interval:	Class interval — Score limits — Real limits
Real lower limit = score limit − 0.5(unit) Real upper limit = score limit + 0.5(unit)	123–125 123, 125 122.5, 125.5 120–122 120, 122 119.5, 122.5 ⋮ ⋮ ⋮ 96– 98 96, 98 95.5, 98.5 93– 95 93, 95 92.5, 95.5
Notice that IQ scores are rounded to the nearest whole number, so the unit is 1. See text for a discussion of unit.	(Upper real limit of the interval 93–95) $= 95 + 0.5(1)$ $= 95 + 0.5 = 95.5$

EXAMPLE PROBLEM 4

Using the frequency distribution with class intervals constructed in Example Problem 3, add a column labeled "real limits." Calculate the real limits of each interval.

♦   ♦   ♦   ♦   ♦

Midpoints of Class Intervals

In graphing frequency distributions, it is also necessary to select a value that represents all of the scores falling within each class interval. Most often the score that best characterizes the interval is the midpoint. The **midpoint** of a class interval is defined as the score falling exactly midway between the possible numbers in the interval. To get a picture of the relationship between the midpoint and the class interval, see Figure 3-1c. The midpoint for the class interval with score limits 93–95 or real limits 92.5–95.5 is 94, the value falling exactly in the middle of the class interval.

The midpoint of a class interval can be found by dividing the size of the interval in half ($i \div 2$) and adding this value to the real lower limit of the interval. For example, the class interval 93–95 has a size of 3 and a real lower limit of 92.5. The midpoint of this interval, then, is

$$92.5 + \frac{3}{2} = 92.5 + 1.5 = 94.$$

Clearly, 94 falls exactly halfway between 93 and 95. For reference, steps in calculating the midpoint are summarized in Procedure 3-5 using examples from the data for the experimental group. (Midpoints for each class interval are shown in column 4 of Table 3-3.)

Procedure 3-5 ♦ Steps in calculating the midpoint of a class interval using data from Table 3-3

Operation	Example
1 Divide the *interval size* in half.	Since interval size is 3, $3 \div 2 = 1.5$
2 Add this value to the lower real limit of the interval.	For interval 93–95: $92.5 + 1.5 = 94$
3 Continue this process until a midpoint is computed for each interval.	

Class interval	Real limits	Mid-points
123–125	122.5–125.5	124
120–122	119.5–122.5	121
⋮	⋮	⋮
96– 98	95.5– 98.5	97
93– 95	92.5– 95.5	94

Table 3-4 ♦ Frequency distribution of data from Table 3-2
with class intervals of 10 points

Class interval	f	Midpoint
120–129	6	124.5
110–119	9	114.5
100–109	10	104.5
90– 99	5	94.5

The midpoint is a single number used to describe a class interval. For example, 94, the midpoint of the interval 93–95, is used to describe all of the frequency data falling within that interval. This use of the midpoint seems reasonable, for what better number could be used to represent the class interval than the one falling exactly in the middle of it? However, if the interval is too wide (i.e., too economical), the midpoint may not accurately describe where most scores are in the interval. Table 3-4 shows the frequency distribution and midpoints for the teacher-expectancy data using only three class intervals of size 10. Notice that the interval 120–129 is characterized by the midpoint 124.5. This value, however, is misleading, since the scores within this interval were actually somewhat lower (see Table 3-3). In general, as the interval size increases (i.e., as economy increases), the midpoint becomes less representative of the data (i.e., error increases).

Using the frequency distribution for the control group data constructed in Example Problem 3, add another column labeled "midpoint." Compute the midpoint for each class interval.

EXAMPLE PROBLEM 5

Graphs are often used to present frequency distributions so that the shape of the distribution is easily seen. Two types of graphs are commonly used for picturing data from a frequency distribution: the histogram, a version of the common bar graph (see Figure 3-2a); and the frequency polygon, a smoothline curve (see Figure 3-4a).

GRAPHICAL REPRESENTATIONS OF FREQUENCY DISTRIBUTIONS

In constructing graphs, several general principles apply: (1) The two axes of the graph are constructed at right angles to each other. The vertical axis of a graph is called the **ordinate**, and the horizontal axis is called the **abscissa**. (2) The values of a dependent variable are listed along the abscissa, and the frequencies are listed along the ordinate (e.g., Figure 3-2). (3) The figure is constructed so that it begins and ends with zero frequency (e.g., Figure 3-2a).

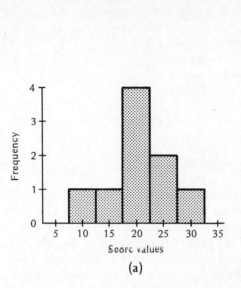
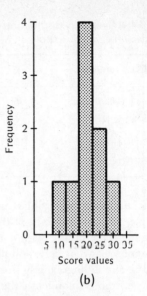

Figure 3-2 ♦ Two histograms: (a) drawn to scale of ordinate two-thirds as long as abscissa; (b) drawn to misrepresent scale; ordinate is longer than abscissa

(4) Finally, the ordinate is drawn about two-thirds as long as the abscissa. The value of this principle is illustrated in Figure 3-2. Figure 3-2a is drawn to scale and presents an accurate picture of the relation between score values and their frequencies. Figure 3-2b is drawn with the ordinate longer than the abscissa. It distorts the relation between scale values and their frequencies by (a) squeezing the score values together and (b) emphasizing small differences between frequencies (one or two subjects).

Histogram   The histogram is a version of the familiar **bar graph** (see Figure 3-3). A **histogram**, then, is a graph in which each class interval is represented on the abscissa and the frequency of each class interval is represented by the height of the bar.

Figure 3-3 shows a histogram of the data for the experimental group in the teacher-expectancy study. Notice that a rectangular bar is drawn such that the height of the bar denotes the frequency with which the class interval occurs. The width of each bar is the same, since all class intervals are of the same size. Finally, notice that class intervals with zero frequency immediately precede and follow the bars.

In constructing a histogram, list the frequencies on the ordinate and the class intervals (or score values if $i = 1$) on the abscissa. Be sure to label the abscissa

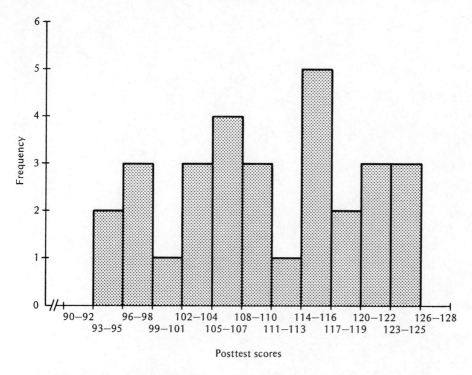

Figure 3-3 ◆ Histogram of posttest scores for the experimental group in the hypothetical study of teacher expectancy. (Data from Table 3-3.)

and ordinate so that the reader knows the variable to which the data refer (abscissa) and the meaning of the values on the ordinate. In listing class intervals on the abscissa, use the *score limits* (cf. Figure 3-3). Then, erect a bar over each class interval to a height corresponding to the frequency of the class interval. Thus, in Figure 3-3, the bar constructed over the interval 93–95 indicates that the frequency associated with the interval is 2. In drawing the bars, use the lower and upper *real limits*. Then the bars touch one another. For reference, the steps in constructing a histogram are given in Procedure 3-6.

Using the frequency distribution constructed in Example Problem 3, construct a histogram for the control-group data from the study of teacher expectancy.

EXAMPLE PROBLEM 6

Frequency polygon A **frequency polygon** is a graph in which each midpoint of each class interval (score values if $i = 1$) is represented on the abscissa, the

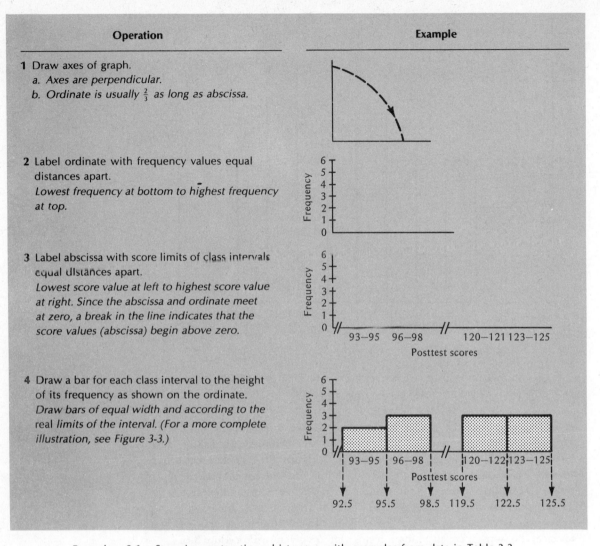

Operation	Example
1 Draw axes of graph. a. *Axes are perpendicular.* b. *Ordinate is usually $\frac{2}{3}$ as long as abscissa.*	
2 Label ordinate with frequency values equal distances apart. *Lowest frequency at bottom to highest frequency at top.*	
3 Label abscissa with score limits of class intervals equal distances apart. *Lowest score value at left to highest score value at right. Since the abscissa and ordinate meet at zero, a break in the line indicates that the score values (abscissa) begin above zero.*	
4 Draw a bar for each class interval to the height of its frequency as shown on the ordinate. *Draw bars of equal width and according to the real limits of the interval. (For a more complete illustration, see Figure 3-3.)*	

Procedure 3-6 ♦ Steps in constructing a histogram with examples from data in Table 3-3

frequency of each midpoint is represented by the height of a point above it, and the points are joined by straight lines. Frequency polygons, like histograms, are used to graph frequency distributions. They differ from histograms in that straight lines are used to show the relation between the levels of a variable and their frequencies instead of a series of connected bars. Often the decision to use a histogram or a frequency polygon is arbitrary; they can be used interchangeably. In experiments with two groups (e.g., an experimental group and a control group), however, it is often desirable to portray the frequency distribu-

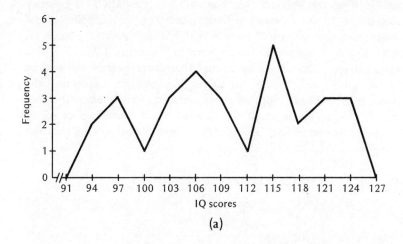

(a)

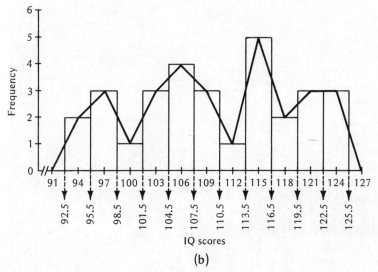

(b)

Figure 3-4 ◆ Frequency polygon and histogram of posttest scores for the experimental group in the hypothetical study of teacher expectancy. (Data from Table 3-3.)

tions of both groups on one graph. In this case, the frequency polygon is preferred because it is easier to read.

In constructing a frequency polygon, list the frequency values on the ordinate and the *midpoints* of class intervals on the abscissa. Plot the frequency of each class interval at the appropriate height as a *point* above the midpoint of the interval. Then connect these points with straight lines. Like the histogram, the frequency polygon begins and ends with zero frequencies, indicated by the straight lines touching the abscissa (see Figure 3-4a). Actually, a frequency polygon is nothing more than a series of lines connecting the midpoints of the bars of a histogram (see Figure 3-3a and b). For reference the steps in constructing a frequency polygon are summarized in Procedure 3-7.

One last point deserves brief mention. Notice that the frequency polygons in Figure 3-4 have "dips" and "peaks" in them. The polygon connecting the various frequencies in each distribution is not smooth. This is often the case when the number of scores is small. In general, as the number of scores increases, the polygon connecting the midpoints in the distribution becomes

Procedure 3-7 ♦ Steps in constructing a frequency polygon from data in Table 3-3

Operation	Example

1 Draw axes of graph.
  a. Axes are perpendicular.
  b. Ordinate $\frac{2}{3}$ as long as abscissa.	

2 Label ordinate or vertical axis with frequency value. *Lowest frequency at bottom to highest frequency at top.*	
3 Label abscissa or horizontal axis with *midpoints* of class intervals. *Begin with the midpoint of the class interval just below the lowest class interval with a frequency of 1 or more, and end with the midpoint of the class interval just above the highest class interval with a frequency of 1 or more. Indicate a break in the scale of values as shown in the example.*	
4 Plot a point over each midpoint at the height of the appropriate frequency as indicated on the ordinate.	

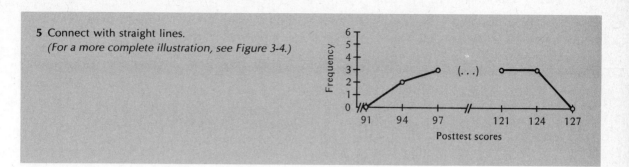

5 Connect with straight lines.
(For a more complete illustration, see Figure 3-4.)

smoother. When the purpose of presenting a frequency distribution is only to show the general nature of the distribution, the polygon may be smoothed. (There are statistical methods for doing this; for an elementary presentation, see Clarke et al., 1965, pp. 19–21.)

Using the frequency distribution constructed in Example Problem 1, draw a frequency polygon for the control-group data.

EXAMPLE PROBLEM 7

◆　　◆　　◆　　◆　　◆

Frequency distributions can have a variety of shapes. The shape of any particular graph depends on the frequencies of class intervals being examined. Examples of several common types of distributions are shown in Figure 3-5.

Shapes of Frequency Distributions

One characteristic of a distribution is symmetry. A distribution is **symmetric** when the two halves of the distribution are mirror images of each other. Figure 3-5a–c shows examples of symmetric distributions. Nonsymmetric distributions (e.g., Figure 3-5d, e) are sometimes described as skewed. A **skewed** distribution is a distribution in which one of its tails is longer than its other tail, relative to its central portion. In skewed distributions, then, most scores fall at one end of the scale and only a few scores at the opposite end. The distribution shown in Figure 3-4d is called a *positively skewed* distribution because the tail extends in the direction of the positive or higher end of the scale. This distribution indicates that most scores were low; however, a few scores were very high. Figure 3-4e shows a *negatively skewed* distribution; that is, the tail extends toward the negative or lower end of the scale. This distribution shows that while most scores were high, a few scores were quite low.

Another characteristic of a distribution is its *modality*—the number of relative peaks it exhibits. (By relative we mean that the peaks must be higher than the neighboring values but not necessarily the same height.) For example, the flat

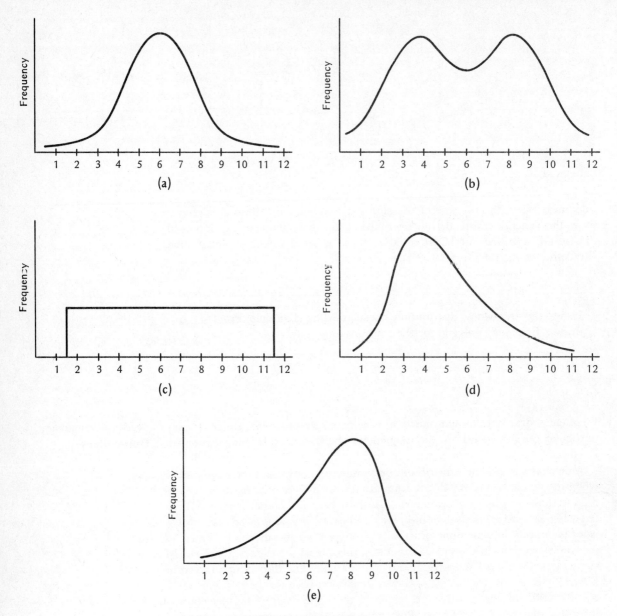

Figure 3-5 ◆ Common shapes of frequency polygons

distribution in Figure 3-5c has no peaks and is therefore often called a *rectangular* distribution. The bell-shaped curve in Figure 3-5a has one peak, and so it is called a **unimodal distribution**. The distribution in Figure 3-5b has two relative peaks, and so it is called a **bimodal distribution**.

◆   ◆   ◆   ◆   ◆

In some experiments, it is necessary to compare the distributions of scores of two (or more) groups which differ in size. A direct comparison of frequencies using a tabular frequency distribution or a frequency polygon is difficult to make. For example, a frequency of 5 in a group of 10 represents 50 percent of the subjects, while in a group of 20 it represents 25 percent of the subjects. The relative frequency distribution provides a means for comparing frequencies based on different group sizes. A **relative frequency distribution** is a frequency distribution in which the frequency of each score value or class interval is converted to a proportion by dividing the frequency by the total number of cases in the sample. (Either ungrouped score values or data grouped by class intervals may be used in relative frequency distributions; however, class intervals are preferred and will be used here.) *Relative frequencies*, then, are proportions; they can vary from 0 to 1. As will be shown in later chapters, relative frequency distributions can also be interpreted as probability distributions. Since probability distributions stand at the heart of inferential statistics, we will continually return to these distributions throughout the book.

The Pygmalion study illustrates a case where relative frequency distributions are useful in examining the data. It may be that, since younger children are

The Relative Frequency Distribution

Table 3-5 ◆ Relative frequency distributions of posttest scores for experimental-group students in grades 1–2 and grades 3–6 (teacher-expectancy study)

Posttest scores	Primary grades (1–2)		Upper grades (3–6)	
	f	Rel. f	f	Rel. f
123–125	1	.10	2	.10
120–122	2	.20	1	.05
117–119	2	.20	0	.00
114–116	3	.30	2	.10
111–113	1	.10	0	.00
108–110	0	.00	3	.15
105–107	1	.10	3	.15
102–104	0	.00	3	.15
99–101	0	.00	1	.05
96– 98	0	.00	3	.15
93– 95	0	.00	2	.10

often more impressionable and eager to please than older children, they might be more affected by their teachers' expectations of them. This hunch could be explored by constructing frequency distributions of posttest scores for subjects in the experimental and control groups at the primary grades (grades 1–2) and at the upper grades (grades 3–6). Since, in the hypothetical study, the number of students in grades 1 and 2 is less than the number in grades 3–6, the data must be compared using a relative frequency distribution.

Relative frequencies for the experimental group ("bloomers") in primary grades and upper grades are presented in Table 3-5. The relative frequencies show that in grades 1 and 2, most of the experimental "bloomers" tended to score relatively high (i.e., above 111). In grades 3–6, however, the majority of subjects tended to have somewhat lower scores (i.e., below 111). If only frequencies had been used, this difference in the distributions of scores would not have been so apparent.

The steps in constructing a relative frequency distribution are the same as those in constructing a frequency distribution except that relative frequencies are used instead of the original frequencies. Relative frequencies or proportions may be obtained by dividing the frequencies by the total number of subjects in the sample:

$$\text{relative frequency} = \frac{\text{frequency}}{\text{total number of subjects}}.$$

For example, one out of the ten first- and second-graders earned an IQ score falling in the class interval 123–125 (Table 3-5). The relative frequency of the interval, then, is

$$\text{relative frequency} = \frac{1}{10} = .10.$$

For reference, the steps in constructing a frequency distribution can also be used to construct a relative frequency distribution. Just divide the frequencies in Procedure 3-2 by the total number of subjects.

EXAMPLE PROBLEM 8
    a. Construct a relative frequency distribution for control-group subjects in primary grades (1–2) and upper grades (3–6). (Hint: These data are shown in your data matrix constructed in Example Problem 1. Use the same class intervals as used in Example Problem 3.)

    b. Compare the relative frequency distributions for grades 1–2 and grades 3–6 in the experimental and control groups. Is the pattern of posttest scores the same in the experimental and control groups at the primary and upper grades?

◆   ◆   ◆   ◆   ◆

In order to compare relative frequency distributions more easily, **relative frequency polygons** can be constructed. These graphs are constructed exactly like frequency polygons except that relative frequencies are listed on the ordinate. Figure 3-6 shows the relative frequency polygons for the experimental group in grades 1–2 and grades 3–6. It is clear from this figure that younger children tended to earn higher scores while older children tended to earn somewhat lower scores. The steps for constructing a relative frequency polygon are the same as those for constructing a frequency polygon except that relative frequencies are listed on the ordinate. Hence, the steps are as summarized in Procedure 3-2. Just remember to use relative frequencies on the ordinate and not frequencies.

Relative Frequency Polygons

Using the relative frequency distributions constructed in Example Problem 8, construct relative frequency polygons in one graph for control-group data at primary and upper grades.

EXAMPLE PROBLEM 9

◆   ◆   ◆   ◆   ◆

A **cumulative frequency distribution** is a distribution which shows the number of scores falling below a certain point on the scale of scores. It provides a basis for computing certain statistics, such as percentiles, which indicate the per-

The Cumulative Frequency Distribution

Figure 3-6 ◆ Relative frequency polygons for IQ data from Table 3-5

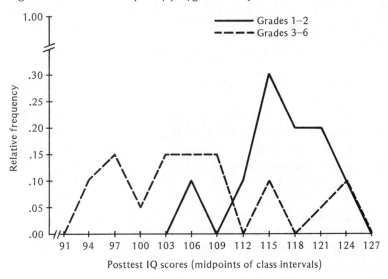

Table 3-6 ♦ Cumulative frequency distributions for the experimental group ("bloomers") in the hypothetical study of teacher expectancy

(1) Class interval	(2) f	(3) Upper real limit	(4) cf	(5) Cum. prop.	(6) Cum. %
123–125	3	125.5	27 + 3 = 30	1.00	100
120–122	3	122.5	24 + 3 = 27	.90	90
117–119	2	119.5	22 + 2 = 24	.80	80
114–116	5	116.5	17 + 5 = 22	.73	73
111–113	1	113.5	16 + 1 = 17	.57	57
108–110	3	110.5	13 + 3 = 16	.53	53
105–107	4	107.5	9 + 4 = 13	.43	43
102–104	3	104.5	6 + 3 = 9	.30	30
99–101	1	101.5	5 + 1 = 6	.20	20
96– 98	3	98.5	2 + 3 = 5	.17	17
93– 95	2	95.5	0 + 2 = 2	.07	7

centage of subjects scoring *below* a particular score. And it provides another method for comparing the scores in two or more groups.

The **cumulative frequency** of a score value or class interval is defined as the number of cases falling *below the upper real limit* of that class interval. The cumulative frequency distribution of posttest scores for the experimental group in the teacher-expectancy study is shown in Table 3-6. (Ignore columns 5 and 6 for the moment.)

A cumulative frequency distribution is usually constructed from a frequency distribution as in Table 3-6, column 2. From this, cumulative frequencies are readily calculated by a process of successive addition of entries in the frequency column (as in Table 3-6, column 4). For reference, the steps in constructing a cumulative frequency distribution are summarized in Procedure 3-8 using the experimental-group data in the Pygmalion study.

EXAMPLE PROBLEM 10   Construct a cumulative frequency distribution for the control group in the Pygmalion study from the frequency distribution constructed in Example Problem 3. Identify the upper real limit and cumulative frequency of each class interval.

◆   ◆   ◆   ◆   ◆

The cumulative frequency distribution is commonly graphed in the form of a cumulative frequency polygon. The **cumulative frequency polygon** is a graph with *cumulative frequencies* listed on the ordinate and the *upper real limits* of class intervals listed on the abscissa (see Figure 3-7).

The Cumulative Frequency Polygon

Steps in constructing a cumulative frequency distribution (data from Table 3-6) ◆ Procedure 3-8

Operation	Example

1 Identify the real upper limit of each score value or class interval.
Construct cumulative frequency distribution from a tabular frequency distribution.

Class Interval	f	Upper real limit
123–125	3	125.5
120–122	3	122.5
117–119	2	119.5
⋮	⋮	⋮
99–101	1	101.5
96– 98	3	98.5
93– 95	2	95.5

2 Calculate the cumulative frequencies by *successive* addition. Begin with the observed frequency of the lowest score or interval.

Class Interval	f	Upper real limit	cf
123–125	3	125.5	
120–122	3	122.5	
117–119	2	119.5	
⋮	⋮	⋮	
99–101	1	101.5	
96– 98	3	98.5	
93– 95	2	95.5	2

3 Add the frequency of the bottom interval to the frequency of the second to find the cumulative frequency of the second interval.

Class Interval	f	Upper real limit	cf
123–125	3	125.5	
120–122	3	122.5	
117–119	2	119.5	
⋮	⋮	⋮	
99–101	1	101.5	
96– 98	3	98.5	5
93– 95	2	95.5	2

(continued on p. 96)

4 Add the cumulative frequency of the second class interval to the frequency of the third interval to find the cumulative frequency of the third interval.

Class Interval	f	Upper real limit	cf
123–125	3	125.5	
120–122	3	122.5	
117–119	2	119.5	
⋮	⋮	⋮	
99–101	1	101.5	6
96– 98	3	98.5	5
93– 95	2	95.5	3

5 Continue this process of successive addition to the highest score or class interval.

Class Interval	f	Upper real limit	cf
123–125	3	125.5	30
120–122	3	122.5	27
117–119	2	119.5	24
⋮	⋮	⋮	⋮
99–101	1	101.5	6
96– 98	3	98.5	5
93– 95	2	95.5	2

6 Check the accuracy of the successive addition by noting the cumulative frequency of the highest interval. This value should equal the total number of cases (N).

The trend of the cumulative frequency curve is always rising. It never drops down, since cumulative frequencies are formed by successive addition and can never be less than the cumulative frequency of the preceding interval. The form of the curve is generally not a straight line but is S-shaped. These properties are illustrated in Figure 3-7, which shows the cumulative frequency curve for the experimental group in the expectancy study.

This graphical representation is also useful in comparing the cumulative frequency distributions of two or more groups which are equal in size. For example, plotting the cumulative frequency curves of two groups, such as an experimental and control group, on the same set of axes provides a unique way of comparing differences between the groups. The closer together the two curves, the more similar the performance of the two groups.

For reference, the steps for constructing a cumulative frequency polygon are summarized in Procedure 3-9. Data in Table 3-6 serve as an example.

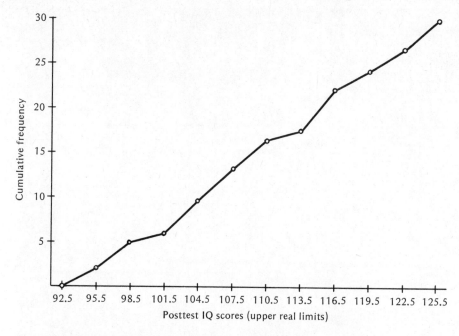

Figure 3-7 ◆ Cumulative frequency polygon of posttest IQ scores for the experimental group in teacher expectancy study. (Data from Table 3-6.)

Steps in constructing a cumulative frequency polygon using data from Table 3-6. ◆ Procedure 3-9

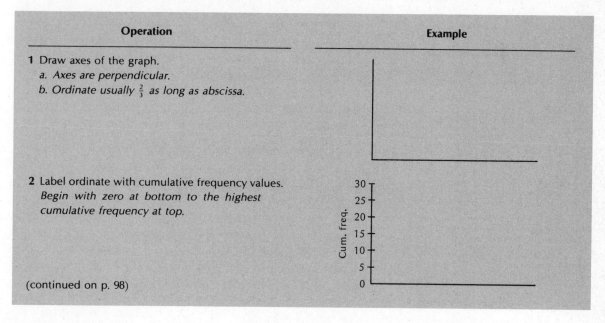

Operation	Example
1 Draw axes of the graph. a. *Axes are perpendicular.* b. *Ordinate usually $\frac{2}{3}$ as long as abscissa.*	
2 Label ordinate with cumulative frequency values. *Begin with zero at bottom to the highest cumulative frequency at top.*	

(continued on p. 98)

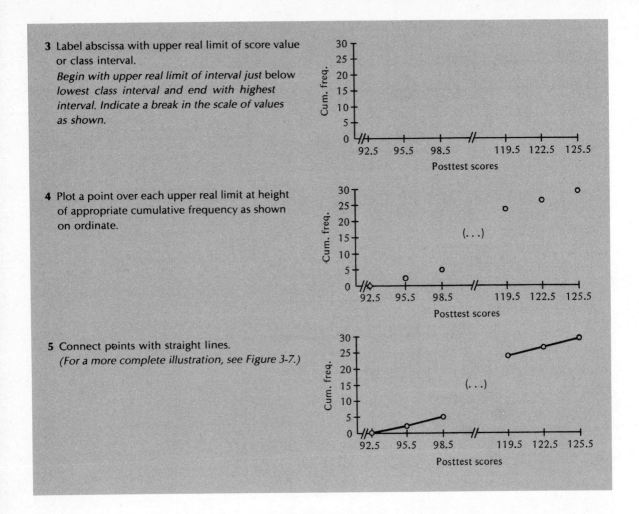

3 Label abscissa with upper real limit of score value or class interval.
Begin with upper real limit of interval just below lowest class interval and end with highest interval. Indicate a break in the scale of values as shown.

4 Plot a point over each upper real limit at height of appropriate cumulative frequency as shown on ordinate.

5 Connect points with straight lines.
(For a more complete illustration, see Figure 3-7.)

EXAMPLE PROBLEM 11   Using the cumulative frequency distribution constructed in Example Problem 10, construct a cumulative frequency polygon with the control-group data.

◆   ◆   ◆   ◆   ◆

Cumulative Proportions and Percentages   It is easier to interpret the statement that 80 percent of the subjects in the experimental group of the expectancy study received a posttest score below 119.5 than the statement that the cumulative frequency for a score of 119.5 is 24. So it is often useful to convert cumulative frequency distributions to cumulative proportions or percentages in order to interpret the cumulative frequencies more easily. A **cumulative proportion** is defined as the cumulative frequency divided by the total number of subjects in the group. A **cumulative percentage** is defined as a cumulative proportion multiplied by 100:

$$\text{cumulative proportion} = \frac{\text{cumulative frequency}}{\text{total number of subjects}},$$

$$\text{cumulative percentage} = \frac{\text{cumulative frequency}}{\text{total number of subjects}} \times 100.$$

A cumulative proportion indicates the proportion of subjects with scores below a particular value, while a cumulative percentage or **percentile score** indicates the percentage of subjects falling below a particular value. For example, a percentile score of 75 indicates that 75 percent of the subjects received lower scores. Finally, just like relative frequencies, cumulative proportions or percentage distributions can be used to compare cumulative frequency distributions based on different sample sizes.

Cumulative proportions and percentages are shown in columns 5 and 6 of Table 3-6. They can be calculated directly from the cumulative frequencies in the table. The cumulative proportion of the class interval 117–119 is the cumulative frequency of the interval (24) divided by the total number of subjects (30): $24 \div 30 = .80$. The cumulative percentage of this class interval is simply the cumulative proportion multiplied by 100: $.80 \times 100 = 80$. In this way, cumulative proportions and percentages can be found from cumulative frequencies for all class intervals. Thus cumulative proportion and percentage distributions can be constructed.

Using the cumulative frequency distributions which you constructed in Example Problem 10, calculate the cumulative proportions and cumulative percentages of each class interval.

EXAMPLE PROBLEM 12

Percentile scores or ranks are familiar to probably every college student, since these scores are often reported to indicate the student's relative standing on a test. The popularity of percentile ranks lies in their interpretability. Jane's percentile score of 95, for example, means that she scored higher than 95 percent of her peers on the test. Because of the wide use of percentile scores in educational and psychological testing, you may want to pay particularly close attention to how they are obtained.

Percentile scores can be read directly from a graph of a cumulative percentage distribution. This distribution is plotted just like the cumulative

PERCENTILE SCALES

frequency polygon except that cumulative percentages, rather than cumulative frequencies, are listed on the ordinate.

A percentile scale for the experimental group of the expectancy study is shown in Figure 3-8. This curve provides a means for easily converting any test score in this group to its percentile rank. For example, in order to determine the percentile rank of a posttest score of, say, 113.5, the score value of 113.5 is located on the abscissa and a perpendicular line is extended until it intersects the curve. The percentile is then obtained from the scale on the ordinate by reading directly across to the left. From Figure 3-8, a raw score of 113.5 has a percentile rank of 57.

Notice that this procedure can be reversed. A percentile scale can also be used to obtain the raw score corresponding to any percentile score. This value is obtained by locating the particular percentile score on the ordinate, reading directly to the right until the curve is intersected, constructing a line perpendicular to the abscissa, and reading the raw score value on the scale of scores. For example, Figure 3-8 indicates that the posttest score corresponding to the 90th percentile was 122.5.

The steps for constructing a percentile scale are the same as the steps in constructing a cumulative frequency polygon except that cumulative per-

Figure 3-8 ◆ Percentile scale for the experimental group in the teacher expectancy study

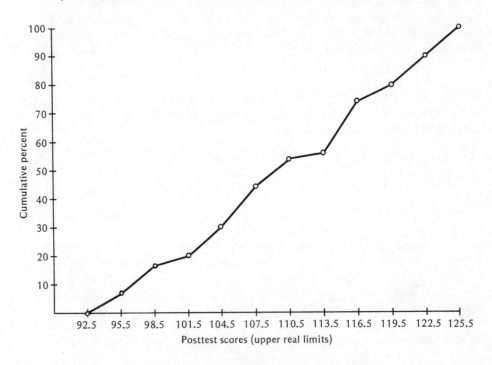

centages are listed on the ordinate. For reference, Procedure 3-9 provides these steps. Just remember to use cumulative percentages and not cumulative frequencies.

Construct a graph using percentiles for the control group. (You will need to refer to the cumulative percentage distribution constructed for these data in Example Problem 12.)

EXAMPLE PROBLEM 13

♦   ♦   ♦   ♦   ♦

It is sometimes useful to determine the percentile score more precisely than is possible using a graph. In this case, the following formula may be used:

Computing Percentile Scores Directly

$$\text{Percentile rank} = \frac{cf_{ul} + \left(\dfrac{X - X_{ll}}{i}\right)f_i}{N} \times 100, \qquad [\text{3-1}]$$

where cf_{ul} = cumulative frequency at the upper real limit of the class interval *below* the interval containing the score of interest (X),

X = score of interest,

X_{ll} = lower real limit of the interval containing X,

i = width of the interval,

f_i = frequency within the interval containing X,

N = total number of cases.

That is a messy formula, especially for the first one. However, it looks much tougher than it is. It tells you to:

1. Find the cumulative frequency of the interval just below the interval containing X.
2. Calculate the number of scores in the interval of interest that fall below X,

$$\left(\frac{X - X_{ll}}{i}\right)f_i.$$

 (An implicit assumption here is that the frequencies of the scores within the interval are equal.)
3. Add (1) and (2) to get a cumulative frequency (cf) and then convert it to a percentile: $(cf \div N) \times 100$.

For example, suppose we wish to find the percentile rank for an IQ score of 115 using the data in Table 3-6: $cf_{ul} = 17$, $X = 115$, $X_{ll} = 113.5$, $i = 3$, $f_i = 5$, and

$N = 30$. Inserting these values into Formula 3-1, we find

$$\text{percentile rank} = \frac{17 + \left(\dfrac{115 - 113.5}{3}\right)5}{30} \times 100$$

$$= \frac{17 + (0.5)5}{30} \times 100$$

$$= \frac{19.5}{30} \times 100$$

$$= 65.$$

An IQ score of 115 has a percentile rank of 65 in the experimental group of the teacher-expectancy study. If you are unsure as to how to find the exact value of the percentile rank given a score, Procedure 3-10 may be of assistance.

Procedure 3-10 ◆ Steps in calculating percentile score directly using data from Table 3-6 as an example

Operation	Example
1 Construct a cumulative frequency distribution (see Procedure 3-8).	

Class interval	f	Upper real limit	cf
123–125	3	125.5	30
120–122	3	122.5	27
117–119	2	119.5	24
114–116	5	116.5	22
111–113	1	113.5	17
⋮	⋮	⋮	⋮
99–101	1	101.5	6
96– 98	3	98.5	5
93– 95	2	95.5	2

2 Use Formula 3-1 to compute

$$\boxed{\text{Percentile rank} = \frac{cf_{ul} + \left(\dfrac{X - X_{ll}}{i}\right)f_i}{N} \times 100}$$

Suppose we wish to determine the percentile rank of a score of 115. Then:

where cf_{ul} = cumulative frequency at upper real limit of interval *below* the interval containing score of interest (X),

X = score of interest,

X_{ll} = lower real limit of interval containing X,

$cf_{ul} = 17$,

$X = 115$,

$X_{ll} = 113.5$,

$i =$ width of interval, $i = 3,$

$f_i =$ frequency within interval containing $f_i = 5,$

    $X,$

$N =$ total number of cases. $N = 30.$

3 Insert appropriate values into Formula 3-1 and compute.

Percentile rank

$$= \frac{17 + \left(\dfrac{115 - 113.5}{3} \right) 5}{30} \times 100$$

$$= 65.$$

Using the cumulative frequency distribution constructed in Example Problem 10, calculate the percentile score corresponding to a raw score of 106 in the control group of the teacher-expectancy study.

EXAMPLE PROBLEM 14

◆　　◆　　◆　　◆　　◆

It is also possible to compute directly the score which corresponds to a particular percentile. The formula for finding a particular score X from a percentile score is

Computing a Score Corresponding to a Given Percentile Rank

$$X = X_{ll} + \frac{i(cf - cf_{ul})}{f_i} \qquad [\textbf{3-2}]$$

where $cf =$ cumulative frequency corresponding to the percentile score of interest:

$$cf = \frac{\text{percentile rank} \times N}{100}, \qquad [\textbf{3-3}]$$

$f_i =$ frequency in interval of interest,
$X_{ll} =$ lower real limit of interval containing cf,
$i =$ width of the interval,
$cf_{ul} =$ cumulative frequency at upper real limit of interval below interval containing cf of interest.

Suppose we wished to find the score X having a percentile rank of 95 in the experimental group. In this case, $cf = (95 \times 30) \div 100 = 28.5$, $X_{ll} = 122.5$ (see table in Procedure 3-10), $i = 3$, $cf_{ul} = 27$, and $f_i = 3$:

$$X = 122.5 + \frac{3(28.5 - 27)}{3}$$

$$= 122.5 + 1.5$$

$$= 124.$$

The score at the 95th percentile, then, is 124. That is, 95 percent of the subjects in the experimental group received a score below 124. Note that this computation corresponds approximately to the score which would be identified using the percentile scale for these data shown in Figure 3-7. For reference, the steps in using Formula 3-2 are given in Procedure 3-11.

Procedure 3-11 ◆ Steps in computing the score corresponding to a percentile rank using data from Table 3-6 as an example

Operation	Example			
1 Construct a cumulative frequency distribution (see Procedure 3-9).	Class interval	f	Upper real limit	cf
	123–125	3	125.5	30
	120–122	3	122.5	27
	117–119	2	119.5	24
	⋮	⋮	⋮	⋮
	99–101	1	101.5	6
	96– 98	3	98.5	5
	93– 95	2	95.5	2

2 Use Formula 3-2 for computing score at a given percentile rank:

Suppose we wished to compute the score corresponding to a percentile of 95.

$$\boxed{\text{Score at given percentile rank} = X_{ll} + \frac{i(cf - cf_{ul})}{f_i}}$$

where cf = cumulative frequency corresponding to percentile of interest computed by:

$$cf = \frac{95 \times 30}{100} = 28.5$$

$$\boxed{cf = \frac{\text{percentile rank} \times N}{100}} \quad [3\text{-}3]$$

This cf is required to obtain the values of X_{ll} and cf_{ul} (see below).

X_{ll} = lower real limit of interval containing cf computed above,

i = width of interval,

cf_{ul} = cumulative frequency at the upper real limit of the interval just *below* the interval of interest,

f_i = frequency within the interval containing the cumulative frequency of interest.

$X_{ll} = 122.5,$

$i = 3,$

$cf_{ul} = 27,$

$f_i = 3,$

3 Insert appropriate values into Formula 3-2 and compute.

Score at 95th percentile rank

$$= 122.5 + \frac{3(28.5 - 27)}{3}$$

$$= 122.5 + 1.5$$

$$= 124.$$

Using the cumulative frequency distribution constructed in Example Problem 10, compute the raw score corresponding to a percentile score of 70 in the control group of the teacher-expectancy study.

EXAMPLE PROBLEM 15

◆   ◆   ◆   ◆   ◆

This chapter provides procedures for beginning to describe and summarize a set of data. First, data are entered into a *data matrix*. Then a *tabular frequency distribution* is constructed to summarize the frequency with which each score value (for ungrouped data) or class interval (for grouped data) occurs. In addition, a *relative frequency distribution* may be constructed if data from two or more groups of unequal size are to be compared. Or a *cumulative frequency distribution* may be constructed if cumulative frequencies, proportions, or percentages are of interest. These frequency distributions can then be represented graphically to highlight the shape of the distribution, using a *histogram*, a *frequency polygon*, a *relative frequency polygon* (if a relative frequency distribution has been constructed), a *cumulative frequency polygon* (if a cumulative frequency distribution has been constructed), or a *cumulative percentage polygon* (if cumulative percentages are of interest). It should be noted, however, that in many cases firm conclusions about research questions cannot be drawn until further statistical analyses are made on the data.

Summary

♦   ♦   ♦   ♦   ♦

Key Words

abscissa	matrix
bar graph	midpoint
bimodal distribution	ordinate
class interval	percentile scale
cumulative frequency	percentile score
cumulative frequency distribution	real limits
cumulative frequency polygon	relative frequency distribution
cumulative percentage	relative frequency polygon
cumulative proportion	score limits
data matrix	score value
frequency distribution	skewed distribution
frequency polygon	symmetric distribution
histogram	unimodal distribution

♦   ♦   ♦   ♦   ♦

Exercises

1–5 Below are a set of scores on a measure of academic self-concept collected from a sample of third-graders enrolled in two schools. Scores on the self-concept scale could range from 1 to 14, where higher scores indicate more positive self-regard in achievement situations.

Maple School		Banyan School	
Boys	Girls	Boys	Girls
7	9	8	10
4	4	7	7
6	7	10	8
5	5	6	9
8	5	9	7

1. Construct a data matrix for these data. Make sure that all relevant variables are included and coded, if necessary.

2. Using your data matrix, construct a frequency distribution, histogram, and frequency polygon for the total sample of self-concept scores.

3. Construct a relative frequency distribution and a relative frequency polygon from your frequency distribution of self-concept scores. (For convenience, columns may be added to the frequency distribution to construct distributions in Exercises 3–5.)

4. Construct a cumulative frequency distribution and a cumulative frequency polygon from your frequency distribution of self-concept scores. Be sure to indicate the upper real limit of each score value on your cumulative frequency distribution.

5. Calculate cumulative proportions and cumulative percentages for each score value in Exercise 4, and construct a cumulative percentage polygon.

6–12 The following set of scores on a measure of mathematical creativity were collected after students completed a course in creative problem-solving. Scores on this test could range from 0 to 50, where higher scores indicate a greater degree of mathematical creativity: 8, 21, 5, 17, 20, 20, 22, 25, 26, 27, 26, 27, 30, 28, 34, 30, 30, 35, 34, 37, 37, 43, 41, 29, 40.

6. Construct a frequency distribution with ten class intervals. Indicate the real limits and midpoint of each class interval.

7. Construct a histogram and frequency polygon from your frequency distribution of mathematical creativity scores.

8. Construct a relative frequency distribution and relative frequency polygon from your frequency distribution of mathematical creativity scores. (For convenience, columns may be added to the tabular frequency distribution to construct distributions in Exercises 8–10.)

9. Construct a cumulative frequency distribution and a cumulative frequency polygon from the frequency distribution of mathematical creativity scores constructed in Exercise 6.

10. Calculate cumulative proportions and cumulative percentages for each class interval in Exercise 9, and construct a percentage polygon.

11. Compute the percentile rank of a score of 21 and of a score of 38.

12. Compute the score corresponding to a percentile rank of 75 and to one of 25.

13–15 The scores on a social-science test have been grouped into class intervals with the following score limits: 1–7, 8–14, 15–21, 22–28, 29–35, 36–42, and 43–49.

13. What are the real limits for each class interval?
14. What are the midpoints for each class interval?
15. What is the interval size?

16–19 Give a name describing the distributions whose polygons have the shapes shown schematically below.

16.

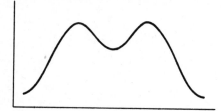

17.

107

18.

19.

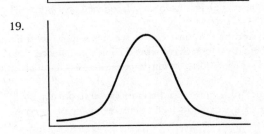

20–25 Define the following terms:

20. Histogram.
21. Real limits.
22. Abscissa.
23. Frequency polygon.
24. Relative frequency distribution.
25. Cumulative frequency of score value.

4.

Measures of Central Tendency
and
Variability

A Research Example: Development of Moral Judgment
Measures of Central Tendency
♦ The Mode ♦
♦ The Median ♦
♦ The Mean ♦
♦ Averaging Means ♦
♦ Relationship between Measures of Central Tendency ♦
Measures of Variability
♦ The Range ♦
♦ The Semi-Interquartile Range ♦
♦ The Standard Deviation ♦
♦ The Raw-Score Formula ♦
♦ The Variance ♦
♦ Comparison of Measures of Variability ♦
Summary
♦ Key Words ♦
♦ Exercises ♦

F REQUENCY DISTRIBUTIONS provide an important picture of the data bearing on a research question. However, distributions, like raw data, provide too much information to interpret easily. What is needed, in addition to a distributional representation of the data, is ways of describing the important features of the distribution more precisely. This chapter presents two important concepts for this purpose—central tendency and variability—and provides the skills necessary to calculate and interpret measures of these concepts.

The *central tendency* of a distribution is an "average" or "typical" score value in the distribution. Or, put another way, the central tendency of a distribution describes the location of the center of the distribution by indicating one score value which represents the "average" score for a sample. Three measures of central tendency are commonly used: (1) the *mode*—the score value that occurs most frequently in the distribution; (2) the *median*—the score value that divides the distribution into the lower and upper 50 percent of the scores; and (3) the *mean*—the "center of gravity" of the distribution, such that the scores above the mean exactly balance the scores below it.

The *variability* of a distribution describes the spread or range of scores in the distribution. Four measures are commonly used to describe the variability of a distribution: (1) the *range*—the highest score minus the lowest score; (2) the *semi-interquartile range*—one-half the difference between the score values at the 75th and 25th percentiles; (3) the *standard deviation*—an average variability of scores in the distribution measured in units of the original score scale; and (4) the *variance*—an average variability of scores in the distribution measured in squared units of the original score scale.[1]

A RESEARCH EXAMPLE: DEVELOPMENT OF MORAL JUDGMENT	The hypothetical data from the study of the development of moral judgment (Chapter 2) will be used in order to illustrate how measures of central tendency and variability describe the data more economically than a frequency distribution. Recall that Weiner and Peter (1973) wanted to test the prediction from Piaget's theory that young children make moral judgments solely on the basis of information about the *outcome* of an act (e.g., did the act produce benefit or

[1] These measures are sample statistics; they describe the central tendency and variability of a set of scores collected on a *sample* of subjects. However, as mentioned in Chapter 1, researchers are usually interested in generalizing to the population from which the sample was drawn. Since it is usually not feasible to collect information about an entire population and calculate the population parameters directly, these sample statistics are used as estimates of population parameters. This point will become clearer in Chapter 9.

harm to another person?), whereas young adults make moral judgments solely on the basis of information about the *intent* of the actor (e.g., did the actor intend to cause benefit or harm to another person?).

A frequency distribution of hypothetical moral judgments of the young adults (16–18-year-olds) is shown in Table 4-1 under the following four conditions of the story: positive outcome, positive intent, negative outcome, and negative intent. Notice that the data concerning the outcome of the act ignore the intent of the actor. For example, data listed under *positive outcome* include judgments from stories in which the outcome was positive (e.g., the child arrived in time for dinner) regardless of whether the intent of the actor was positive or negative (e.g., the older child did or did not want to help the younger child). Similarly, data concerning intent of the actor ignore the outcome of the act. For example, data listed under *positive intent* include judgments from stories in which the actor's intent was positive (e.g., the older child wanted to help the younger child), regardless of whether the outcome was positive or negative (e.g., the child did or did not arrive home in time for dinner). Actually, this way of examining the data does make sense. The frequency distribution for negative outcomes includes data from subjects in

Table 4-1 ♦ Frequency distribution of moral judgments using the data in Table 2-3 for 16–18-year-olds

Moral judgment[a]	Frequency			
	Positive outcome	Positive intent	Negative outcome	Negative intent
+ 5	0	0	0	0
+ 4	2	3	1	0
+ 3	2	5	3	0
+ 2	1	2	1	0
+ 1	0	0	0	0
0	0	0	0	0
− 1	0	0	0	0
− 2	3	0	1	4
− 3	1	0	3	4
− 4	0	0	1	1
− 5	1	0	0	1

[a] Positive numbers correspond to recommended rewards; negative, to recommended punishments.

both the negative and positive intent conditions, as does the frequency distribution for positive outcomes. So, in comparing the effects of negative and positive outcomes on moral judgments, the effect of intent is averaged over both outcome conditions (assuming equal numbers of subjects, as is the case here). In this way we can test the prediction that young children make moral judgments solely on the basis of *outcome* information, while young adults make moral judgments solely on the basis of intent information.[2]

What can you conclude about the development of moral judgment from these data? Are the predictions from Piaget's theory supported? The frequency distributions in Table 4-1 provide too much information to answer this question. We need a description that will focus our attention on important ways in which the distributions differ. Measures of central tendency provide one such description. They provide a single value which describes the "typical" or "average" score in the distribution.

MEASURES OF CENTRAL TENDENCY

The **central tendency** of a distribution is an "average" or "typical" score value in the distribution. Measures of central tendency describe a frequency distribution by indicating one score value which represents the center of the distribution or the "average" score in a group of persons. This value can also be thought of as representing the *location* of a distribution on a scale of score values. This location can then be used to compare different distributions. For example, frequency polygons varying in central tendency (and variability) are shown in Figure 4-1.[3] Notice that distributions *A* and *B* have about the same location since they center at approximately the same point on the scale. Distribution *C* centers on a somewhat lower point on the score scale and thus differs in location. The location of these distributions can be compared using measures of central tendency.

The Mode

The **mode** is defined as that score value which is obtained most often. When data are grouped into class intervals, the mode is taken to be the midpoint of the interval which contains the most cases. This measure is referred to as the **crude mode**.

The modes for hypothetical moral judgments of 16–18-year-olds are shown in the first row of Table 4-2 (ignore the last two rows for now). The modal values under conditions of positive and negative intent tend to support the predictions from Piaget's theory. The young adults seemed to consider intent

---

[2]Note that a rating of 0 has a zero frequency. This occurred because, for all versions of the moral stories, no subjects gave neutral moral judgments.

[3]Throughout the remainder of this text, many of the figures will be smoothed even if they represent data from a sample, in order to make concepts as clear as possible.

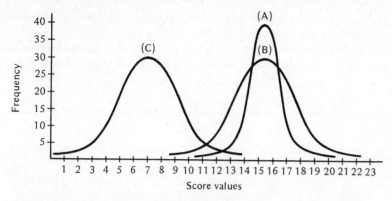

Figure 4-1 ◆ Three frequency polygons differing in central tendency, variability, or both

information in making moral judgments by rewarding the older child if the intent was positive and punishing the child if the intent was negative.

The data under negative outcome also seem to support this prediction. When the outcome of the story was negative, the most frequently made judgment was either +3.00 or −3.00. This is a *bimodal distribution* (see Chapter 3 and Figure 3-4b), which occurs because the category of negative outcome includes both stories in which the intent was positive and stories in which it was negative. Regardless of the negative outcome, subjects 16–18 years old gave rewards if the intent was positive and punishment if the intent was negative (see Table 2-3).

In order to find the mode, scores are placed in a frequency distribution; the mode is simply the score value that occurs most frequently in the distribution. For reference, the steps in finding the mode of a frequency distribution are given in Procedure 4-1, where the data in Table 4-1 are used as an example. (If

Table 4-2 ◆ Measures of central tendency for moral judgments of 16–18-year-olds using data from Table 4-1

Measure of central tendency	Story condition			
	Positive outcome	Positive intent	Negative outcome	Negative intent
Mode	−2.00	+3.00	+3.00 and −3.00	−2.50
Median	0.00	+3.00	0.00	−3.00
Mean	+0.20	+3.10	0.00	−2.90

necessary, refer to Procedures 3-4 and 3-5 to review calculation of the real limits and the midpoint of a class interval.)

While the mode can be useful when a quick estimate of central tendency is needed, it has several serious limitations. First, the mode is unduly affected by

Procedure 4-1 ♦ Steps in calculating the mode with examples from moral judgments of 16–18-year-olds (data from Table 4-1)

Operation	Example
1 Construct a frequency distribution with score values or class intervals.	Moral judgment with positive intent
2 If scores are used (data *not grouped* into class intervals), the mode is the score value most frequently observed.	

intent	f
+5	0
+4	3
+3	5
+2	2
+1	0
0	0
−1	0
−2	0
−3	0
−4	0
−5	0

3 If data are grouped into class intervals, find the midpoint of the interval with the maximum frequency. The value of the midpoint is the crude mode.

(See Procedure 3-5.)

4 When there are two score values or class intervals containing the most cases, then:
  a If the values or intervals are *adjacent*, locate the real limit separating the two values or intervals (cf. Procedure 3-4). For score values, the value of the real limit is the mode; for class intervals, this value is the crude mode.

Moral judgment with negative intent

intent	f
+5	0
+4	0
+3	0
+2	0
+1	0
0	0
−1	0
−2	4
−3	4
−4	1
−5	1

b If the values *are not adjacent* (bimodal distribution), locate the two score values most frequently earned; these are the modes. If the intervals are not adjacent, locate the midpoints of the two intervals with greatest frequency; these are the crude modes.

Moral judgment with negative outcome	f
+5	0
+4	1
+3 ←	3
+2	1
+1	0
0	0
−1	0
−2	1
−3 ←	3
−4	1
−5	0

chance factors unless the number of subjects (N) in the sample is very large. When N is small, a shift in the scores of one or two subjects may move the mode several points on the score scale. For example, recall that each condition in the moral-judgment study had $N = 10$. The mode for the moral judgments of 16–18-year-olds in the positive outcome condition was negative (-2.00). But this judgment was only made three times, while judgments of $+4.00$ and $+3.00$ were each made two times (see column 1 of Table 4-1). So the mode may not accurately represent the central tendency of this distribution, because of the small sample size.

Secondly, when data are grouped into class intervals, the crude mode can only fall at the midpoint of the interval. Thus, the value of the crude mode will depend upon the particular size of the intervals used, even though the data set is the same.

Finally, the mode is an especially poor representation of frequency distributions in which the frequencies for the intervals containing the most cases are nearly the same. For such "flat" or rectangular distributions (see Figure 3-4c), a shift of just one or two cases moves the crude mode very considerably.

The frequency distribution of moral judgments of 4–6-year-olds is shown in Table 4-3.

a. Calculate the mode for each condition.
b. Do young children appear to use information about outcome when making moral judgments, as Piaget predicts? Do they appear to use information about intent?

EXAMPLE PROBLEM 1

Table 4-3 ◆ Frequency distribution of moral judgments using the data in Table 2-3 for 4–6-year-olds

Moral judgment[a]	Frequency			
	Positive outcome	Positive intent	Negative outcome	Negative intent
+ 5	0	0	0	0
+ 4	1	1	0	0
+ 3	2	2	0	0
+ 2	3	2	0	1
+ 1	2	1	1	2
0	0	0	0	0
− 1	2	1	2	3
− 2	0	2	3	1
− 3	0	1	3	2
− 4	0	0	1	1
− 5	0	0	0	0

[a] Positive numbers correspond to recommended rewards; negative, to recommended punishments.

◆   ◆   ◆   ◆   ◆

The Median The median is a more useful and informative measure of the central tendency of a frequency distribution than the mode. The **median** is defined as the point or score value below which 50 percent of the scores fall. Notice that, according to this definition, the median coincides with the 50th percentile of a distribution. Figure 4-2 shows the medians of several distributions with different shapes.

The median is generally used as a measure of the central tendency of distributions which are drastically *asymmetric* (skewed). These distributions often contain extreme scores (see Figure 4-2b, c). The median is particularly useful as a measure of central tendency for such distributions because it is less sensitive to extreme scores. (This point will be elaborated when the relationships between the three measures of central tendency are discussed).[4]

The medians for the hypothetical data on moral judgments of 16–18-year-olds are shown in the second row of Table 4-2. Notice that the medians are equal or quite similar to the corresponding modes in the positive and negative

[4]The median is also sometimes used as the dividing point in experiments in which the researcher wants to divide a sample of subjects into two groups on the basis of some individual-difference

116

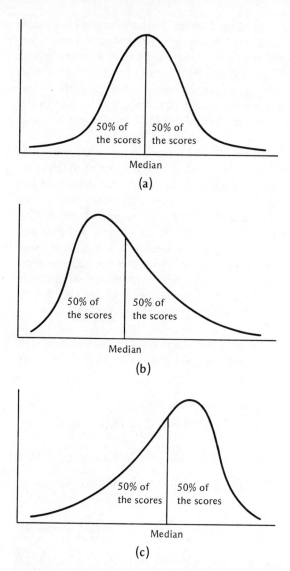

Figure 4-2 ♦ Medians of several distributions with different shapes:
(a) Symmetric distribution; (b) Positively skewed distribution;
(c) Negatively skewed distribution

variable, such as high and low self-concept or high and low verbal ability. However, this "median split" procedure has several drawbacks and is usually not recommended. For example, it treats a subject whose score is just below the median as more similar to a subject whose score is far below the median than to a subject whose score is just above the median. Other statistical procedures presented later in this book, such as regression, permit analysis of the effects of an individual-difference variable without these limitations.

intent conditions. However, they are quite different in the outcome conditions. Piaget's predictions are entirely supported in this age group when the median is taken as the measure of central tendency. Subjects appear to make moral judgments solely on the basis of information about intent. Judgments tended to be strongly positive when the intent was positive and strongly negative when the intent was negative. Outcome information does not seem to be considered by this age group, as evidenced by a median of 0.00 in both the positive and negative outcome conditions.[5]

In calculating the median, recall that it is the score value below which 50 percent of the cases fall. When the scores are arranged in order of magnitude, the median is the score value which corresponds to the middle subject, or the score value that divides the subjects into two groups with equal numbers in either group. If there are an odd number of subjects, the median corresponds to the score value of the subject exactly in the middle of the range of score values. For example, in the set of scores 2, 3, 4, 5, 6, the median is 4, the score value earned by the subject in the middle of the range of scores. If there are an even number of subjects, the median is the score value halfway between the scores of the two middle subjects. For example, in the following set of scores 1, 2, 3, 4, 5, 6, the median is 3.5, the score value halfway between the two middle scores (3 and 4).

When the median is calculated from scores grouped into class intervals, or from individual scores (where the class interval equals size 1), the following general formula can be used:

$$\text{Median} = X_{ll} + \frac{i(N/2 - cf_{ll})}{f_i} \qquad [\textbf{4-1}]$$

where X_{ll} = lower real limit of the interval which contains the median,
        i = interval size,
        N = total number of scores,
        cf_{ll} = cumulative frequency of interval below the interval containing the median (cf. Procedure 3-8),
        f_i = frequency of the interval containing the median.

While this formula may look ominous, it does just what the easier counting procedure does. It says to identify the interval which contains the median. This is not hard to do, since the median lies in the interval below which half the scores fall. X_{ll}, then, refers to the lower real limit of that critical interval. Next,

[5]More precisely, a median of 0.00 for the positive and negative outcome conditions indicates that half of the moral judgments in each condition were positive (i.e., reward) and half were negative (i.e., punishment). This probably occurred because each outcome condition contained stories with both positive and negative intent. It seems that subjects were rewarded when intent was positive and punished when intent was negative, which resulted in an overall median of 0.00 when the two types of stories were combined.

it says to find the number of scores in the critical interval below the median $(N/2 - cf_{ll})$. Here $N/2$ is (roughly) the rank of the middle person in the distribution, and cf_{ll} is the total number of persons below the interval containing the median. Finally, $i \div f_i$ simply distributes the frequency of scores evenly over each score value in the interval. Put another way, in calculating a median from grouped data, the formula *assumes* that the frequency with which each score value appears in the interval is the same for all score values within the interval. If this assumption is not true, the median may not fall exactly at the point below which 50% of the scores fall. But the difference will be negligible.

As an example of how to use this formula, suppose you have the following frequency distribution ($N = 20$; only a few intervals are used to simplify the example):

Class interval	f	cf
45–49	3	20
40–44	5	17
35–39	7	12
30–34	3	5
25–29	2	2

With an even number of subjects (20), the median will lie between the score values of the middle two (tenth and eleventh) subjects. So it will lie in the interval 35–39, since the tenth and eleventh subjects lie in this interval. The lower real limit of this interval, X_{ll}, is 34.5. The size of the interval is 5 and the frequency is 7, so $i \div f_i = \frac{5}{7} = .71$. Finally the cumulative frequency of the interval below (i.e., the interval 30–34) is 5. Inserting these values into Formula 4-1 we have:

$$\text{Median} = 34.5 + \frac{5(20/2 - 5)}{7}$$

$$= 34.5 + (5)(.71)$$

$$= 38.05.$$

For reference, the steps in calculating the median for a set of ungrouped scores ($i = 1$) or scores grouped by class intervals ($i > 1$), are summarized in Procedure 4-2.

---

a. Calculate the median for the moral judgments of 4–6-year-olds under each of the four conditions. (See Example Problem 1 for data.)

b. With the median as a measure of central tendency, do your conclusions about the use of outcome and intent information for this age group change?

EXAMPLE PROBLEM 2

Operation	**Example**
1 Determine the value of the frequency below which 50% of the cases fall by dividing N by 2: $$f_{50th} = N \div 2.$$ *Begin with data arranged in a frequency distribution.*	If $N = 20$, $$f_{50th} = 20 \div 2$$ $$= 10.$$

2 Beginning at the bottom of the distribution, add the values in the frequency column until the halfway point (f_{50th}) is reached.

Test scores	Frequency
65–69	1
60–64	4
55–59	8
50–54	4
45–49	3
	20

3 Use Formula 4-1 for calculating the median:

$$\text{Median} = X_{ll} + \frac{i(N/2 - cf_{ll})}{f_i}$$

where X_{ll} = lower exact limit of interval which contains the median,
   i = interval size,
   N = total number of scores,
   cf_{ll} = cumulative frequency of interval *below* interval containing the median (cf. Procedure 3-8),
   f_i = frequency of interval containing the median.

$X_{ll} = 54.5$

$i = 5$
$N = 20$
$cf_{ll} = 7$

$f_i = 8$

4 Insert appropriate values into Formula 4-1 and solve.

$$\text{Median} = 54.5 + \frac{5(20/2 - 7)}{8}$$
$$= 54.5 + 1.88$$
$$= 56.38$$

Procedure 4-2 ◆ Steps in calculating the median

◆   ◆   ◆   ◆   ◆

The Mean   The most basic and frequently used measure of central tendency is the arithmetic mean. It is also the measure of central tendency most familiar to you, since it is the same as the "average" you learned to calculate in elementary school. The arithmetic **mean** is defined as the sum of the scores divided by the number of scores that entered that sum. In expressing this definition as a formula, special notation—summation notation—is used. The symbol, Σ (an oversized Greek capital letter sigma) is used to denote the operation of summing or adding up a group of numbers. And the capital letter X is used to represent any score on a particular variable. Thus, ΣX means the sum of the values of X. If N is used to denote the number of scores entering the sum, then ΣX can be written as

$$\Sigma X = X_1 + X_2 + \cdots + X_N.$$

The notation ΣX, then, is simply the notation for the verbal statement: "add up all of the (N) scores." With this notation, the formula for the mean can be written as

$$\overline{X} = \frac{\Sigma X}{N}, \qquad [\text{4-2}]$$

where $\overline{X} =$ the mean of a set of scores on variable X (read "X-bar"),
$N =$ the total number of scores entering the sum.

This formula, read in verbal form, says that the mean ($\overline{X}$) equals the sum (Σ) of the scores (X) divided by the number of scores entering the sum (N). Often summation notation is written even more precisely to indicate exactly what persons' scores enter the sum. In this case, p stands for any person from the first person up to the Nth person, and we write

$$\sum_{p=1}^{N} X_p = X_{p=1} + X_{p=2} + \cdots + X_{p=N}$$

$$= X_1 + X_2 + \cdots + X_N$$

The embellished summation symbol is read as "the sum of X sub p from $p = 1$ to N." In this more detailed notation, the formula for the mean is

$$\overline{X} = \frac{\sum_{p=1}^{N} X_p}{N}$$

Throughout this book, summation notation will be used to express formulas. In order to be able to read and use these formulas, you should review the presentation of summation notation in Appendix A if you are not already familiar with the notation.

If scores are ordered along a scale of score values, the mean will fall directly at the "balance point" or "center of gravity" of the distribution, as shown in Figure 4-3. This figure looks like a seesaw with the mean as the point of

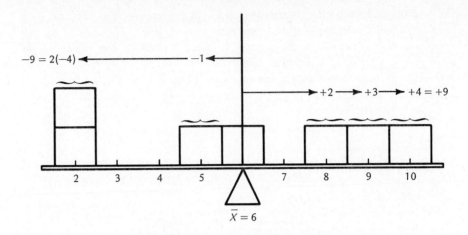

$$-9 = 2(-4) \qquad -1$$

$$+2 \rightarrow +3 \rightarrow +4 = +9$$

$$\bar{X} = 6$$

Figure 4-3 ♦ An illustration of the mean as the point of balance of a see saw

balance for all scores on either side of it. If the mean were subtracted from each score in the distribution, some of the differences $(X - \bar{X})$ would be positive, some zero, and some negative, with the positive scores exactly cancelling out the negative scores. So the mean can be described more formally as *that point in a distribution such that the algebraic sum of the differences of all scores from the point is zero.*

Figure 4-3 shows hypothetical scores for seven subjects on a test. The mean of this distribution is 6. Notice that the sum of the differences of all scores from

Table 4-4 ♦ Comparison of means of two distributions, one of which contains an extreme score

X	X^*
10	38
9	9
8	8
6	6
5	5
2	2
2	2
$\Sigma X = 42$	$\Sigma X^* = 70$
$\bar{X} = 6$	$\bar{X} = 10$

this mean on the right is $+9$, and on the left it is -9. These values sum to 0, as expected.

The analogy between the mean and the balance point of a seesaw illustrates another important characteristics of the mean: It is very sensitive to extreme scores at one or the other end of the range. The hypothetical test scores from Figure 4-3 are shown in the first column (labeled "X") of Table 4-4. The mean of this distribution is 6. Column 2 (labeled "$X*$") contains the same set of scores except for one extremely large score, 38. This one extreme score is sufficient to shift the mean from 6 to 10. Thus, by adding one extreme score, or more weight to one end of the seesaw, the balance is shifted radically. The balance point must be moved toward the extreme score, or toward the end with the new weight, to achieve a new balance.

The means for the hypothetical moral judgments of young adults are shown in the third row of Table 4-2. Notice that means in this group closely parallel the other measures of central tendency in each condition. Again, Piaget's predictions appear to be supported. Young adults seem to base moral judgments on information about intent rather than outcome.

The steps for calculating a mean from raw scores is summarized in Procedure 4-3 using moral judgments of 16–18-year-olds under the positive intent condition.

Steps in calculating the mean from raw scores: moral judgments of 16–18-year-olds ◆ Procedure 4-3 (data from Table 2-3)

Operation	Example
1 Obtain data for Formula 4-2: $$\bar{X} = \frac{\Sigma X}{N}$$	Data from stories with positive intent:

Subject	Judgment
1	4
2	4
3	4
4	3
5	3
6	3
7	3
8	3
9	2
10	2

Operation	Example
2 Find ΣX by adding all raw scores: $$\Sigma X = X_1 + X_2 + \cdots + X_N$$	$\Sigma X = 4 + 4 + \cdots + 2$ $= 31$
3 Divide ΣX (step 2) by N to find $\Sigma X / N$.	$\bar{X} = 31 \div 10 = 3.10$

EXAMPLE PROBLEM 3

a. Calculate the mean of the moral judgments of 4–6-year-olds under each condition (see Table 2-3 for data).

b. Do your conclusions from Example Problem 2 change?

♦   ♦   ♦   ♦   ♦

Averaging Means   Suppose a teaching assistant gives his instructor the mean final exam scores for each of her two statistics classes. Suppose further that the instructor wishes to obtain a measure of the average performance of all her students, regardless of class. She could, of course, obtain the final examination scores for students in both classes and calculate a mean over all these scores. Suppose, however, that she is looking for a simpler way or that she doesn't have all the scores handy. Could she use the mean of the two means to obtain a measure of the average performance of her students? This procedure is only appropriate when the means are based on samples of equal size. In that case, the means have equal weights, since they are based on the same sample size (N). Suppose, for instance, that the mean final examination score was 77 in class 1 and 83 in class 2, and that each class had the same number of students (say, 25). In this case, the mean for all students in both classes is simply the mean of the two separate class means:

$$\frac{77 + 83}{2} = 80.$$

In writing the formula for the average of two or more means based on samples of equal size, some additional notation needs to be introduced. Notice that, in taking the average of the group means, the summation is over different groups and not over persons (p). So, let i refer to any group and k refer to the last group: $i = 1, 2, \ldots, k$. Then, the formula for the average of two or more means based on equal sample sizes is

$$\text{Ave. } \overline{X} = \frac{\sum_{i=1}^{k} \overline{X}_i}{k}$$

$$= \frac{\overline{X}_1 + \overline{X}_2 + \cdots + \overline{X}_k}{k}. \quad [4\text{-}3]$$

In words, this notation says: "take the sum of the means over all of the (k) groups and divide that sum by the number of groups entering it." Notice that now the precise notation on the summation symbol is essential. It says that this is a sum over groups (and not persons). Again, you should consult the Review of Summation Notation so that you can read and use the formulas in this book. The steps in computing the average of two or more means based on samples of *equal* size are summarized in Procedure 4-4.

Suppose, however, that this instructor's classes were *unequal* in size. In this more common case, a *weighted mean* must be computed—that is, means based on a larger sample are weighted more heavily than those based on a smaller number of cases. Because the instructor knows the mean and number of students for each class, she can easily discover the sum of all the individual scores in each class (even if they are not readily available). Here's how: Recall from Formula 4-2 that

$$\overline{X} = \frac{\Sigma X}{N}.$$

Using the standard algebraic device of multiplying both sides of the equation by N, we find that $\Sigma X = N\overline{X}$. If, in this way, the instructor calculates the sum of individual scores (ΣX) for each of the two classes and adds these sums together, she will obtain the sum of scores for all students in both classes. Now, if this total sum is divided by the total number of students in the two classes, the mean score for all students will be obtained.

For example, suppose that the mean final-examination score was 77 in class 1 and 83 in class 2, but this time there were 30 students in class 1 and 20 in class 2. Because the classes are unequal in size, a weighted mean must be

Steps for averaging means based on samples of equal size ◆ Procedure 4-4

Operation	Example
1 Look up Formula 4-3: $$\text{Ave. } \overline{X} = \frac{\sum_{i=1}^{k} X_i}{k}.$$	
2 Add the k means ($\overline{X}$'s) together to obtain $\sum_{i=1}^{k} \overline{X}_i$: $$\overline{X}_1 + \overline{X}_2 + \cdots + \overline{X}_k$$	Mean final exam scores ($k = 2$) 77 $+83$ 160
3 Divide $\sum_{i=1}^{k} \overline{X}_i$ (step 2) by the number of means (k).	$160 \div 2 = 80$

computed. First, the instructor could calculate the sum of all scores for class 1 ($\Sigma X = N\overline{X} = 30 \times 77 = 2310$) and for class 2 ($\Sigma X = N\overline{X} = 20 \times 83 = 1660$). Then, the mean for all students in both classes can be obtained by adding these two sums and dividing by the total number of students:

$$\frac{2310 + 1660}{30 + 20} = \frac{3970}{50} = 79.4.$$

The weighted mean for these two classes of unequal size is somewhat lower than the mean for the two classes of equal size. This makes sense, since the larger class received a lower mean score. This procedure for calculating a **weighted mean** can be summarized by the following formula:

$$\overline{X}_w = \frac{\displaystyle\sum_{i=1}^{k} N_i \overline{X}_i}{\displaystyle\sum_{i=1}^{k} N_i}$$

$$= \frac{N_1 \overline{X}_1 + N_2 \overline{X}_2 + \cdots + N_k \overline{X}_k}{N_1 + N_2 + \cdots + N_k}, \qquad [4\text{-}4]$$

where $\overline{X}_w$ = weighted mean,
k = number of means being combined,
N = number of scores (cases) entering into a mean,
$\overline{X}_i$ = sample mean for group i.

The steps in computing the weighted mean are summarized in Procedure 4-5.

Procedure 4-5 ◆ Steps for averaging k means based on samples of *unequal* size (weighted mean)

Operation	Example
1 Look up the general formula for the weighted mean: $$\overline{X}_w = \frac{\displaystyle\sum_{i=1}^{k} N_i \overline{X}_i}{\displaystyle\sum_{i=1}^{k} N_i}$$	

2 Multiply each mean ($\bar{X}$) by its sample size (N) to obtain $N_1\bar{X}_1, N_2\bar{X}_2, \ldots, N_k\bar{X}_k$.

Mean exam scores for three classes ($k = 3$)

N	$\bar{X}$	$N\bar{X}$
30	77	2310
20	83	1660
25	80	2000

3 Add $N_1\bar{X}_1, N_2\bar{X}_2, \ldots, N_k\bar{X}_k$:

$$N_1\bar{X}_1 + N_2\bar{X}_2 + \cdots + N_k\bar{X}_k$$

$$2310 + 1660 + 2000 = 5970$$

4 Add $N_1, N_2, \ldots, N_k$ to find the total N:

$$N_1 + N_2 + \cdots + N_k$$

$$30 + 20 + 25 = 75$$

5 Divide the result of step 2 by the result of step 3:

$$\frac{N_1\bar{X}_1 + N_2\bar{X}_2 + \cdots + N_k\bar{X}_k}{N_1 + N_2 + \cdots + N_k}$$

$$\frac{5970}{75} = 79.6$$

An instructor taught four introductory psychology classes one year. The mean scores of these classes on the final examination were: (a) 71, (b) 76, (c) 79, and (d) 81. The number of students enrolled in these classes were: (a) 22, (b) 30, (c) 35, and (d) 28. Find the mean of the final examination scores for all students enrolled in this instructor's classes.

EXAMPLE PROBLEM 4

◆   ◆   ◆   ◆   ◆

There is no one best measure of the central tendency of a distribution. The preferred measure depends on the shape of the distribution and on what you are trying to communicate about the distribution. For example, if the distribution is symmetric, as in Figure 4-4a, the values of the mean, mode, and median are equal, so any one of the three will tell the same story. With symmetric or nearly symmetric distributions, often the mean or median is preferred to the mode since the mode is the least stable measure of central tendency (see section on "The Mode" above). Most often, in practice, the mean is used, because the researcher not only wants to describe the distribution of scores in the sample but also wants to draw inferences from the sample to the population. In this case, "the median has mathematical properties making it difficult to work with, whereas the mean is mathematically tractable. For this and other reasons, mathematical statistics has taken the mean as the focus of most of its inferential

Relationship between Measures of Central Tendency

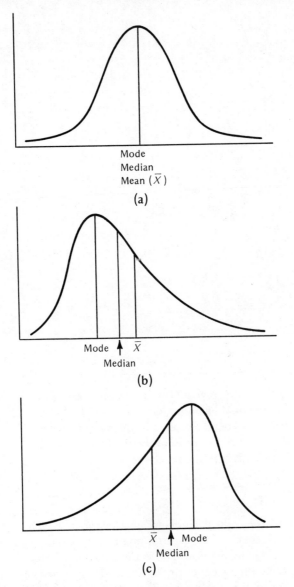

Figure 4-4 ◆ Relative position of measures of central tendency in three distributions: (a) Symmetric (bell-shaped) distribution; (b) Distribution with a few extremely high scores ("positively skewed"); (c) Distribution with a few extremely low scores ("negatively skewed")

methods, and the median is relatively unimportant in inferential statistics" (Hays, 1973, p. 224).

However, in some cases the median or mode may be preferred to the mean as a measure of central tendency. In distributions with a few extremely high scores ("positively skewed" distributions) such as that shown in Figure 4-3b, the mode, the median, and the mean have very different values. Extreme scores usually have their greatest effect on the mean, a smaller effect on the median, and the least effect on the mode. Because the mean has to balance the distribution, it is pulled out toward the extreme scores of the tail. Thus, in a distribution with a few extremely high scores, the mean has the highest value of all the measures of central tendency. The median has an intermediate value. The mode, or most frequently earned score, has a somewhat lower value than the median. Similarly, in distributions with a few extremely low scores (negatively skewed distributions) such as that shown in Figure 4-3c, the mean is pulled out toward the extreme scores and has the lowest value of all the measures of central tendency. The median has a somewhat higher value, and the mode has the highest value of all the measures of central tendency. Thus, in asymmetric distributions in which there are very high or very low scores, the mean is less representative of most scores than the other measures of central tendency and so the median is usually preferred. The mode is appropriate when a quick, approximate estimate of central tendency is desired; however, as already mentioned, it is rarely used in drawing conclusions from behavioral research, due to its instability.

MEASURES OF VARIABILITY

Another way to characterize a frequency distribution is by the *spread* of scores in the distribution. The greater the differences between scores earned by different people, the more spread out (or scattered) the scores are in a distribution. The more tightly the scores cluster together, the smaller the spread of scores in the distribution. The **variability** of a distribution is the general term for the spread of scores in it.

Distributions may be the same with respect to central tendency (location on a score scale) but differ considerably with respect to variability. Three hypothetical distributions of test scores are shown in Figure 4-1 above. Notice that scores in classes A and B have the same central tendency but differ in variability. How do classes B and C compare on central tendency and variability?

♦　　♦　　♦　　♦　　♦

The Range

In developing measures of variability, an index is needed which indicates the spread or distance of scores along the score scale. The range is one such measure of spread. It is the easiest to compute and, probably, to understand. It is simply the difference between the highest and the lowest score in the distribution. Formally, the **range** is defined as the highest score in the distribution minus the lowest score:

$$\text{Range} = X_{\text{highest}} - X_{\text{lowest}}. \qquad [4\text{-}5]$$

Table 4-5 ♦ Measures of variability for moral judgments of 16–18-year-olds using data from Table 4-1

Measure of variability	Story condition			
	Positive outcome	Positive intent	Negative outcome	Negative intent
Range	9	2	8	3
SIQR	2.79	.54	3.00	.63
S.D.	3.33	.74	3.23	.99
Variance	11.07	.54	10.44	.98

The range of moral judgments of young adults is presented in the first row of Table 4-5 for each of the four conditions in the experiment. (Ignore the other rows for the moment.) Notice that the range is considerably smaller in the intent conditions than in the outcome conditions. This occurs because adults use intent information as a basis for their judgments and ignore outcome. So the data about intent do not greatly depend on the negative or positive outcome, which is ignored. Hence the small range, indicating agreement among subjects' judgments. The data about outcome, on the other hand, depend on negative or positive intent—for example, a positive outcome is punished if the intent is negative and rewarded if the intent is positive. Hence the bimodal distribution and greater range of judgments.

Although the range is easy to compute, it is seldom used as the only measure of variability, for several reasons. First, it is based only on the two most extreme scores in the distribution. This makes it highly unstable. For example, the range might differ greatly in two groups of subjects just because one subject in one of the groups earned an extremely high score. Second, the range does not fully reflect the pattern of variation in the distribution. For example, if there is one extreme score in a distribution, the range of scores will be very large when, in fact, all of the other scores might cluster together.

EXAMPLE PROBLEM 5

a. Calculate the range of moral judgments of 4–6-year-olds under each of the four conditions. (See Example Problem 1 for data.)
b. Are the ranges for this age group similar to those of the 16–18-year-olds?

♦   ♦   ♦   ♦   ♦

The Semi-Interquartile Range   The semi-interquartile range (SIQR) also provides a measure of the spread of scores along a score scale. More specifically, the SIQR provides a measure of the spread of the middle 50 percent of the scores. Formally, the **semi-inter-quartile range** is defined as half the difference between the scores at the 75th and 25th percentiles:

$$SIQR = \frac{Q_3 - Q_1}{2} \qquad [4\text{-}6]$$

where Q_3 = score at 75th percentile (i.e., top of third quarter),
   Q_1 = score at 25th percentile (i.e., top of first quarter).

Figure 4-5 shows the SIQR for a symmetric and an asymmetric distribution. Notice that the extreme scores in Figure 4-5b have much less of an influence on the SIQR than they do on the range.

In calculating the SIQR, the score values corresponding to the 25th and 75th percentiles have to be calculated. As an example of how this is done,

Figure 4-5 ♦ Symmetric and asymmetric distributions with the spread for determining the semi-interquartile range (SIQR) indicated

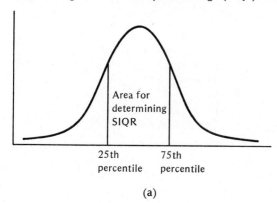

Area for
determining
SIQR

25th   75th
percentile   percentile

(a)

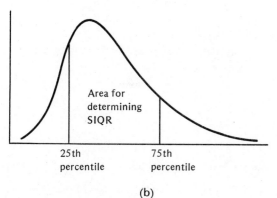

Area for
determining
SIQR

25th   75th
percentile   percentile

(b)

suppose the following data were collected on a sample of 20 subjects (only a few class intervals are used to simplify the example):

Class interval	f	cf
35–39	1	20
30–34	2	19
25–29	9	17
20–24	6	8
15–19	2	2

In order to find the score values corresponding to the 25th and 75th percentiles, first the cumulative frequencies corresponding to these percentiles have to be found. Then the score values corresponding to these cumulative frequencies can be calculated (see the last section in Chapter 3 for the details):

(1)

$$cf = \frac{(\text{percentile rank}) \times N}{100};$$ [3-3]

thus

$$cf_{25} = \frac{25 \times 20}{100} = 5,$$

$$cf_{75} = \frac{75 \times 20}{100} = 15.$$

(2)

$$\text{Score at percentile} = X_{ll} + \frac{i(cf - cf_{ll})}{f_i}$$ [3-1]

where X_{ll} = score at lower real limit of the interval containing cf of interest,
i = width of the interval,
cf = cumulative frequency corresponding to percentile,
cf_{ll} = cumulative frequency of interval below interval containing cf,
f_i = frequency of the interval containing cf;

thus

$$Q_1 = 19.5 + \frac{5(5 - 2)}{6} = 22,$$

$$Q_3 = 24.5 + \frac{5(15 - 8)}{9} = 28.39.$$

Once Q_1 and Q_3 are known, the semi-interquartile range can be calculated:

$$\text{SIQR} = \frac{Q_3 - Q_1}{2}$$

$$= \frac{28.39 - 22}{2}$$

$$= 3.20. \hspace{3cm} [4\text{-}6]$$

The steps in calculating the SIQR are reviewed in Procedure 4-6. In reviewing these steps, note that, in finding Q_1 and Q_3 with data in class intervals, we assume that the frequency of each score value is equal to the frequency of every other score value within the interval. If this assumption does not hold, Q_1 and Q_3 may be slightly in error. But this error is negligible.

The semi-interquartile range for the moral judgments of 16–18-year-olds in each of the four conditions is shown in Table 4-5. Notice that the pattern of variability in the semi-interquartile range is like that in the range. The semi-interquartile range is much smaller in the intent conditions than in the outcome conditions, for reasons explained above (see section on "The Range"). However, as a measure of spread, the magnitude of the SIQR is considerably smaller than the range. Because the SIQR focuses on the middle 50 percent of the scores, it is much less affected by extreme scores than is the range.

For this reason, the semi-interquartile range is often preferred to the range. For this reason also, the SIQR is often used as a measure of variability in "skewed" distributions which have a few extremely high or extremely low scores (see Figure 4-5b). Given a skewed distribution, then, the median is often used to measure its central tendency and the semi-interquartile range is often used to describe and measure its variability.

EXAMPLE PROBLEM 6

a. Calculate the semi-interquartile range for the moral judgments of 4–6-year-olds under each of the four conditions. (See Example Problem 1 for data.)
b. Does the pattern of variability change when the SIQR is used rather than the range? If so, how?

◆   ◆   ◆   ◆   ◆

The Standard Deviation

The most commonly used measure of the variability of scores in a distribution is the standard deviation. It is an index of the variability (spread) of scores about the mean of a distribution, something like the average dispersion or deviation of the scores (X) about their mean $(\overline{X})$. The greater the spread of scores, the greater is the standard deviation. For example, in Figure 4-1, the scores in distribution A cluster about the mean of the distribution, while the scores in

Procedure 4-6 ◆ Steps in computing the semi-interquartile range (example taken from Table 4-1: positive outcome condition)

Operation	Example

1 Look up Formula 4-6 for calculating the SIQR:

$$\boxed{\text{SIQR} = \frac{Q_3 - Q_1}{2}}$$

where Q_3 = score value corresponding to 75th percentile,

Q_1 = score value corresponding to 25th percentile.

2 Construct a cumulative frequency distribution. (See Procedure 3-8 for the steps.)

Score value	f	Upper real limit	cf
+5	0	5.5	10
+4	2	4.5	10
+3	2	3.5	8
+2	1	2.5	6
+1	0	1.5	5
0	0	0.5	5
−1	0	−0.5	5
−2	3	−1.5	5
−3	1	−2.5	2
−4	0	−3.5	1
−5	1	−4.5	1

3 Calculate the cumulative frequency corresponding to Q_3 (score at 75th percentile) using Formula 3-3:

$$cf = \frac{(\text{percentile rank}) \times N}{100}$$

$$cf = \frac{75 \times 10}{100} = 7.5.$$

4 Compute Q_3 (the score value at the 75th percentile) by inserting the appropriate values into Formula 3-2. (See Procedure 3-11 for the steps.)

Score at given percentile $= X_{ll} + \dfrac{i(cf - cf_{ll})}{f_i}$

where X_{ll} = score at lower real limit of the interval containing the cf of interest,

i = the width of the interval,

cf = cumulative frequency corresponding to percentile of interest,

$X_{ll} = 2.5,$

$i = 1,$

$cf = 7.5$ (computed in step 3),

cf_{ll} = cumulative frequency of interval *below* interval containing cf,

f_i = frequency of interval containing cf,

cf_{ll} = 6,

f_i = 2.

Hence

$$Q_3 = 2.5 + \frac{1(7.5 - 6)}{2}$$

$$= 2.5 + \frac{1.5}{2}$$

$$= 3.25.$$

5 Calculate the cumulative frequency corresponding to Q_1 (score value at 25th percentile) using Formula 3-3 (see step 3 above).

$$cf = \frac{25 \times 10}{100}$$

$$= 2.5,$$

6 Compute Q_1 (the score value at the 25th percentile) by inserting the appropriate values into Formula 3-2 (see step 4).

X_{ll} = −2.5,

i = 1,

cf = 2.5 (see step 5),

cf_{ll} = 2,

f_i = 3.

Hence

$$Q_1 = -2.5 + \frac{1(2.5 - 2)}{3}$$

$$= -2.33.$$

7 Insert the appropriate values in Formula 4-6 (see step 1 above) and solve.

$$SIQR = \frac{3.25 - (-2.33)}{2}$$

$$= \frac{5.58}{2}$$

$$= 2.79$$

distribution B are spread out. The standard deviation for distribution A, then, would be less than the standard deviation for distribution B.

More formally, the **standard deviation** may be defined as the square root of the average squared deviation of scores from the mean of the distribution, measured in units of the original score scale. This definition is reflected in the **deviation-score formula** for the standard deviation:

$$s = \sqrt{\frac{\Sigma(X - \bar{X})^2}{N - 1}} \, . \qquad [4\text{-}7]$$

135

In this formula, $\Sigma(X - \bar{X})^2$ represents the sum of the squared deviations of each person's score from the mean. By dividing $\Sigma(X - \bar{X})^2$ by $N - 1$, we get (approximately) an average of the squared deviations. Finally, by taking the square root of this average, we get a measure of variability in the original measurement units. That is, since we squared $X - \bar{X}$, we have to take the square root to get back to the original measurement units.

At first glance, this formula is somewhat awesome. In order to give you a feeling about how it works, we will start from the beginning and build the formula. Don't be alarmed—no sophisticated mathematical concepts are needed.

To begin, recall that the major limitation of the range as a measure of the variability of scores in a distribution is that it is based on two extreme, often unstable scores. Another way to measure the spread of scores in a distribution might be to consider the variability of each of the scores in the distribution about the central tendency of the distribution. More specifically, then, we might begin to develop this measure of variability, the standard deviation, by subtracting the mean—the most stable measure of central tendency—from each of the scores in the distribution. This process will give us deviation scores which can be represented as $x = X - \bar{X}$. These deviation scores provide a measure of the *distance* of each raw score from the mean of the distribution.

Since we want a measure which takes all deviation scores into account, the most obvious next step would be to sum up the deviation scores. This process gives us Σx, or $\Sigma(X - \bar{X})$. However, since the mean is the balance point of the distribution, we know that this attempt is doomed to failure: $\Sigma(X - \bar{X}) = \Sigma x = 0$. Back to the drawing board! The difficulty in summing deviation scores is due to the fact that the ones with positive $(+)$ signs cancel out the ones with negative $(-)$ signs, leaving us with zero.

One possible way around this problem is to simply ignore the sign of the deviation scores. In this case, we would be summing the absolute values of the deviation scores. This procedure provides a measure of variability called the *average deviation*. The average deviation has some history as a measure of variability; however, it is seldom used today because it is unsuitable for use in other statistical analyses.

Another way to do away with the nuisance of the signs of the deviation scores canceling each other is to square each deviation score. This will work because the square of a negative number is positive, as is the square of a positive number. We now have the sum of the squared deviation scores: $\Sigma(X - \bar{X})^2 = \Sigma x^2 \neq 0$ unless all of the scores are exactly equal to the mean. This procedure turns out to be useful for our own purposes as well as applicable to other statistical analyses.

We now have a measure of variability that takes all of the deviation scores into account. The next problem is to get some measure of the "average" amount of variability about the mean of the distribution. This can be obtained by dividing the sum of squared deviation scores, $\Sigma(X - \bar{X})^2 = \Sigma x^2$, by $N - 1$:

$$\frac{\Sigma(X - \bar{X})^2}{N - 1} = \frac{\Sigma x^2}{N - 1}$$

This will give us something like the average dispersion of scores in the distribution about the mean; it is defined as the variance (see "The Variance" below).[6] The last problem is to return the measure of variability back to the original score scale. (Remember each deviation score was squared.) This problem can be solved by taking the square root. Thus, we have

$$s = \sqrt{\frac{\Sigma(X - \bar{X})^2}{N - 1}} \qquad [\textbf{4-7}]$$

$$= \sqrt{\frac{\Sigma x^2}{N - 1}} \qquad [\textbf{4-7a}]$$

The result matches the formula for the standard deviation given at the beginning of this section.

In order to show how to calculate a standard deviation and to keep things simple, assume that we are interested in the standard deviation of a sample of three scores—1, 2, 3. Two preliminary calculations have to be made:

$$\bar{X} = \frac{1 + 2 + 3}{3} = 2,$$

---

[6]This text assumes that its audience, by and large, is interested in learning statistics as tools which can be used to answer research questions. As a consequence, it sidesteps certain statistical developments which are not directly germane to the audience. The use of $N - 1$ in the denominator of the expression $\Sigma(X - \bar{X})^2 \div (N - 1)$ is a case in point. Formally, this term, called the variance, is defined as the mean of the squared deviation of scores about $\bar{X}$: $\Sigma(X - \bar{X})^2 \div N$. Thus, it is an average of the squared deviations of scores about the sample mean. However, in answering research questions, we are seldom interested in describing the sample as an end in itself. Rather, we are interested in the sample because it gives us some insight into the nature of the population. That is, we typically use sample statistics as estimators of population parameters (see Chapter 1). Thus, the sample mean is used to estimate the population mean, and the sample variance is used to estimate the spread of scores in the population—the population variance. When the sample variance is used to estimate the population variance, it is defined as $\Sigma(X - \bar{X})^2 \div (N - 1)$. This definition produces an unbiased estimate of the population variance, whereas $\Sigma(X - \bar{X})^2 \div N$ produces a biased estimate (see Chapter 1; see Hays, 1973, pp. 283–284, for the derivation). So, we have opted to define the sample variance as $\Sigma(X - \bar{X})^2 \div (N - 1)$. This provides for a simplification of notation and presentation of new concepts when we take up material on inferential statistics. It also allows the reader to focus on those aspects of statistics which provide tools for answering research questions.

$$\Sigma(X - \bar{X})^2 = \left(X_1 - \bar{X}\right)^2 + \left(X_2 - \bar{X}\right)^2 + \left(X_3 - \bar{X}\right)^2$$
$$= (1 - 2)^2 + (2 - 2)^2 + (3 - 2)^2$$
$$= 1 + 0 + 1$$
$$= 2$$
$$= \Sigma x^2.$$

With these preliminary calculations made, the appropriate values can be entered into the formula for the standard deviation with the following result:

$$s = \sqrt{\frac{\Sigma x^2}{N - 1}}$$
$$= \sqrt{\frac{2}{3 - 1}}$$
$$= \sqrt{1}$$
$$= 1.$$

The average squared deviation of the set of scores about their mean is 1 score point.

For reference, the steps in calculating a standard deviation are given in Procedure 4-7.

As mentioned earlier, the greater the variability of scores in the distribution, the larger the standard deviation of the distribution. The standard deviations of young adults' moral judgments are presented in Table 4-5. They are much

Procedure 4-7 ♦ Steps in calculating the standard deviation using deviation scores

Operation	Example
1 Look up Formula 4-7 for calculating the standard deviation from deviation scores: $$s = \sqrt{\frac{\Sigma(X - \bar{X})^2}{N - 1}}$$ $$= \sqrt{\frac{\Sigma x^2}{N - 1}}$$	
2 Set up a table with the following four columns: $X, \bar{X}, x, x^2$.	$\quad X \qquad \bar{X} \qquad x \qquad x^2$

3 List all raw scores in the column labeled X.

X	$\bar{X}$	x	x^2
2			
4			
6			

4 Calculate the mean and list it in the column labeled $\bar{X}$.

X	$\bar{X}$	x	x^2
2	4		
4	4		
6	4		

5 Subtract the mean $(\bar{X})$ from each raw score (X) to obtain the deviation score (x): $x = X - \bar{X}$. List each deviation score in the column labeled x.

X	$\bar{X}$	x	x^2
2	4	-2	
4	4	0	
6	4	2	

6 Square each deviation score (x). List values of squared deviation scores in the column labeled x^2.

X	$\bar{X}$	x	x^2
2	4	-2	4
4	4	0	0
6	4	2	4

7 Sum the squared deviation scores to obtain Σx^2.

X	$\bar{X}$	x	x^2
2	4	-2	4
4	4	0	0
6	4	2	4
			$\Sigma x^2 = 8$

8 Divide Σx^2 by $N - 1$.
This value is defined as the variance.

$$8 \div 2 = 4.00.$$

9 Take the square root of the value obtained in step 8.

$$\sqrt{4.00} = 2.00.$$

larger under the outcome conditions than under the intent conditions. This pattern was also reflected in the corresponding ranges and SIQRs for these conditions. These data suggest that subjects of this age vary little in their use of intent information. The variation in their use of outcome information is due to the fact that outcome data are summed over positive and negative intent judgments.

The standard deviation has several advantages over the range and SIQR as a measure of variability. While both the range and SIQR are defined relative to the total distribution of scores, the former focuses on only two scores, while the latter focuses on 50 percent of the scores. In contrast, the standard deviation uses each score in the distribution in providing a measure of variation among scores. It is a more *stable* measure of variation than the range or the SIQR. Furthermore, when referred to the normal distribution, the standard deviation permits a precise interpretation of scores in the distribution. This point is the focus of the next chapter. Lastly, many statistical tests rely on the standard deviation to represent the variability of a set of data.

EXAMPLE PROBLEM 7   a. Use the deviation-score formula to calculate the standard deviation of the moral judgments of 4–6-year-olds in the positive and negative outcome conditions.

b. Are the standard deviations of this group similar to those of the 16–18-year-olds in these conditions?

♦   ♦   ♦   ♦   ♦

The Raw-Score Formula   Calculating the standard deviation using deviation scores may be a long and tedious process, particularly when there are a large number of scores. Fortunately, it is possible to compute the standard deviation directly from the original (raw) scores without calculating deviation scores. This calculation can be quickly made, particularly if a desk or pocket calculator is available. This procedure is represented by the following **raw-score formula**:

$$s = \sqrt{\dfrac{\Sigma X^2 - \dfrac{(\Sigma X)^2}{N}}{N-1}} \qquad [4\text{-}8]$$

The raw score formula can be shown to be equivalent to the deviation-score formula for calculating a standard deviation.[7] The steps in the resulting

---

[7]The following proof demonstrates the equivalence of the deviation-score formula and raw-score formula for calculating the standard deviation s of a distribution:

$$\sqrt{\dfrac{\Sigma x^2}{N-1}} = \sqrt{\dfrac{\Sigma X^2 - \dfrac{(\Sigma X)^2}{N}}{N-1}}$$

In the proof, we deal only with the equivalence of Σx^2 and $\Sigma X^2 - (\Sigma X)^2/N$, since the two formulas are otherwise the same.

Step	Reason
$\Sigma x^2 = \Sigma(X - \bar{X})^2$	Definition of a deviation score
$= \Sigma(X^2 - 2X\bar{X} + \bar{X}^2)$	Expansion of a polynomial

140

calculation are summarized in Procedure 4-8.[8] The same set of scores are used as used in Procedure 4-7, so that these data may be used to verify that the deviation-score and raw-score formulas are equivalent.

---

a. Use the raw-score formula to compute the standard deviation of 4–6-year-olds in the positive and negative intent conditions.
b. Are the standard deviations of this age group similar to those of the 16–18-year-olds in these conditions?

EXAMPLE PROBLEM 8

◆   ◆   ◆   ◆   ◆

Another commonly used measure of variability is the variance. The **variance** is defined as the average squared deviation of scores about their mean. It is denoted as s^2, since it is equal to the square of the standard deviation s. The deviation-score formula for the variance is

The Variance

$$s^2 = \frac{\Sigma(X - \bar{X})^2}{N - 1} \qquad [4\text{-}9]$$

$$= \frac{\Sigma x^2}{N - 1}. \qquad [4\text{-}9a]$$

Step	Reason
$= \Sigma X^2 - 2\Sigma X\bar{X} + \Sigma \bar{X}^2$	Distribution of summation sign
$= \Sigma X^2 - 2N\bar{X}^2 + \Sigma \bar{X}^2$	Substitution, since $\Sigma X = N\bar{X}$. Thus,
	$2\Sigma X\bar{X} = 2(N\bar{X})\bar{X} = 2N\bar{X}^2$
$= \Sigma X^2 - 2N\bar{X}^2 + N\bar{X}^2$	Effects of summation over a constant
$= \Sigma X^2 - N\bar{X}^2$	Combination of terms
$= \Sigma X^2 - N(\Sigma X)^2/N^2$	Definition of a mean
$= \Sigma X^2 - (\Sigma X)^2/N$	Combination of terms
$s = \sqrt{\dfrac{\Sigma x^2}{N - 1}}$	Definition
$= \sqrt{\dfrac{\Sigma X^2 - \dfrac{(\Sigma X)^2}{N}}{N - 1}}$	Substitution

[8]In calculating the standard deviation using the raw-score method, the terms ΣX^2 and $(\Sigma X)^2$ are sometimes confused. It is important to remember that ΣX^2 represents the sum of the squares of all the raw scores. In contrast, $(\Sigma X)^2$ represents the square of the sum of the raw scores.

The raw-score formula for the variance is

$$s^2 = \frac{\sum X^2 - \frac{(\sum X)^2}{N}}{N-1}. \qquad [\textbf{4-10}]$$

The variance is mentioned here because it is frequently used in more advanced statistical tests, such as the analysis of variance, and will be referred to in later sections of this book.

　　　The variances of moral judgments are shown in Table 4-5 for young adults. To calculate the variance simply square the standard deviation. Or, to calcu-

Procedure 4-0 ▾ Steps in calculating the standard deviation using the raw-score formula (example data from Procedure 4-7)

Operation	Example
1 Look up Formula 4-8 for calculating the standard deviation from raw scores: $$s = \sqrt{\frac{\sum X^2 - \frac{(\sum X)^2}{N}}{N-1}}$$	
2 Set up a table with two columns labeled X and X^2, and list raw scores in the column labeled X.	X　X^2 2 4 6
3 Sum the raw scores to obtain $\sum X$.	X　X^2 2 4 6 $\sum X = \overline{12}$
4 Square each raw score (X) to obtain X^2.	X　X^2 2　　4 4　　16 6　　36 $\overline{12}$

5 Sum values of X^2 (step 4) to obtain ΣX^2.

X	X^2
2	4
4	16
6	36
$\overline{12}$ $\Sigma X^2 =$	$\overline{56}$

6 Square ΣX (step 3) to obtain $(\Sigma X)^2$.

$(\Sigma X)^2 = 12^2 = 144.$

7 Divide $(\Sigma X)^2$ (step 6) by N, to obtain $(\Sigma X)^2/N$.

$144 \div 3 = 48.$

8 Subtract $(\Sigma X)^2/N$ (step 7) from ΣX^2 (step 5) to obtain

$56 - 48 = 8.0$

$$\Sigma X^2 - (\Sigma X)^2/N$$

9 Divide $\Sigma X^2 - (\Sigma X)^2/N$ (step 8) by $N-1$ to obtain

$\dfrac{8.0}{2} = 4.00$

$$\frac{\Sigma X^2 - (\Sigma X)^2/N}{N-1}$$

This value is defined as the variance.

10 Take the square root of

$\sqrt{4.00} = 2.00$

$$\frac{\Sigma X^2 - \dfrac{(\Sigma X)^2}{N}}{N-1} \quad \text{(step 8)}$$

to obtain

$$s = \sqrt{\frac{\Sigma X^2 - \dfrac{(\Sigma X)^2}{N}}{N-1}}$$

late it directly, compute steps 1–8 in Procedure 4-7 or steps 1–9 in Procedure 4-8.

Calculate the variances of moral judgments of 4–6-year-olds in each condition.

EXAMPLE PROBLEM 9

♦ ♦ ♦ ♦ ♦

In general, the standard deviation is the most commonly used measure of variability. It has several desirable characteristics. First, it is as stable (reliable) as the variance, and more so than the range. Furthermore, the standard

Comparison of Measures of Variability

deviation, unlike the variance, is directly interpretable in terms of actual score units. Finally, the standard deviation (like the variance) is used in inferential statistics, while the range and semi-interquartile range are not. The virtue of the range is that it provides a quick, rough estimate of the variability of a distribution. The major advantage of the semi-interquartile range is that it is relatively unaffected by extreme scores. Thus, the SIQR is often used with skewed distributions.

♦   ♦   ♦   ♦   ♦

Summary

This chapter describes measures which can be used to describe the *central tendency* and *variability* of a distribution of scores. Measures of central tendency —the *mode*, the *median*, and the *mean*—describe the location of a distribution on a score scale. Indexes of variability—the *range*, the *semi-interquartile range*, the *standard deviation*, and the *variance*—describe the spread of scores in the distribution.

♦   ♦   ♦   ♦   ♦

Key Words

central tendency	raw-score formula
crude mode	semi-interquartile range
deviation-score formula	standard deviation
mean	variability
median	variance
mode	weighted mean
range	

♦   ♦   ♦   ♦   ♦

Exercises

1–5 In a study of the effects of imagery on memory, a researcher administered a spatial manipulation test to all subjects in order to measure their ability to create vivid mental images of objects. Subjects were then divided into two groups: a group of subjects who exhibited low imaging ability (Lo I) and a group of subjects who exhibited high imaging ability (Hi I). Each subject was then randomly assigned to one of two paired associate learning tasks: a task using pairs of pictures as stimuli and a task using pairs of words as stimuli. After one presentation of the series of pairs, subjects made the numbers of correct responses given in Table 4-6.

1. Calculate the mode for each of the four groups in Table 4-6.. Based on this information, what can you conclude about the effect of imagery on memory for these two types of paired-associate tasks?

2. Calculate the median for each of the four groups. Using the median as a measure of central tendency, what would you conclude about the effects of imagery on memory? How similar is the median to the mode of each distribution?

3. Calculate the mean number of correct responses for each experimental group. How similar is the mean to the median and mode of each group? Using the mean as a measure of central tendency, do your conclusions change? If so, how?

4. Using the means computed in Exercise 3, calculate a *weighted* mean for subjects

Table 4-6

Hi I		Lo I	
Words	Pictures	Words	Pictures
6	16	6	7
5	13	18	7
5	13	14	10
4	13	13	9
6	19	12	14
6	15	13	7
9	17	12	11
10	11	17	11
12	20	15	5
11			11

receiving the word task and subjects receiving the picture task. What can you conclude about performance on these two tasks?

5. Which measure (mean, median, or mode) best describes the central tendency of each of the four groups? Explain your answers briefly.

6. Using the data in Exercise 1, compute the range of scores for each group.

7. Compute the SIQR for each group.

8. Calculate the standard deviation for each of the two groups receiving word pairs, using the deviation-score formula.

9. Calculate the standard deviation for each of the two groups receiving picture pairs using the raw-score formula.

10. Compute the variance for each of the four experimental groups.

11. What information about a distribution of scores do measures of *central tendency* and *variability* provide?

12–14 Explain the limitation(s) of the mode as a measure of central tendency in each of the following distributions:

12.

Stanine scores on reading achievement test	f
8	1
7	3
6	2
5	1
4	2

13.

Score on introversion-extroversion scale	f
15–17	1
12–14	1
9–11	4
6–8	5
3–5	3

14.

Price of movie ticket at theatres in Los Angeles	f
$4.00	7
3.50	8
3.00	7
2.50	1

15–17 Indicate whether the mean, median, or mode best characterizes the central tendency of each of the following distributions:

15.

Heights (in.)	f
76–79	3
72–75	5
68–71	6
64–67	6
60–63	4
56–59	2

16.

Number of words recalled in memory experiment	f
24–25	1
22–23	0
20–21	1
18–19	0
16–17	0
14–15	3
12–13	4
10–11	7
8–9	6
6–7	5

17.

Rating of work satisfaction	f
10	1
9	2
8	2
7	4
6	3
5	6
4	5
3	2
2	3
1	1

18. Why was the mean described as the "balance point" in the distribution? What does this analogy imply?

19–21 Draw the following types of distributions and indicate the location of the mean, median and mode:

19. Symmetric, bell-shaped.
20. Positively skewed (i.e., few extremely high scores).
21. Negatively skewed (i.e., few extremely low scores).
22. Why is the range an inadequate measure of the variability of this distribution?

Score on dogmatism scale	f
8	1
7	0
6	0
5	0
4	7
3	10
2	8
1	6

23. What advantages does the standard deviation have over the range as a measure of variability?

24. One group of ten scores has a mean of 15, and another group of twenty scores has a mean of 25. What is the mean of all the scores?

5.

The Normal Distribution

A CURIOUS thing happens when data are summarized in a frequency polygon. Regardless of the characteristic being measured (e.g., achievement, personality, height), often this distribution looks like a bell (as in Figure 5-1) and so is described as a *bell-shaped curve*. The curve is roughly symmetric with the most frequently earned scores at the middle of the distribution. The mean, mode, and median provide about the same numerical values as measures of the central tendency of the distribution. Often this bell-shaped curve can be described as a normal distribution. The **normal distribution** is a mathematical idealization of a particular type of symmetric distribution. In other words, it is a mathematical curve that provides a good model of relative frequency distributions found in behavioral research. Since the normal distribution serves as a model for much of the data collected in behavioral research, it plays a critical role in statistics.

This chapter examines the normal distribution and its properties in some detail. In particular, the purposes of this chapter are: (1) to introduce you to the properties of the normal distribution and (2) to provide you with the concepts and skills to identify areas under the normal curve corresponding to particular scores.

Figure 5-1 ◆ The normal distribution or "bell-shaped curve"

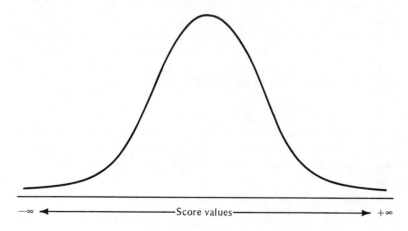

−∞ ◄──────────Score values──────────► +∞

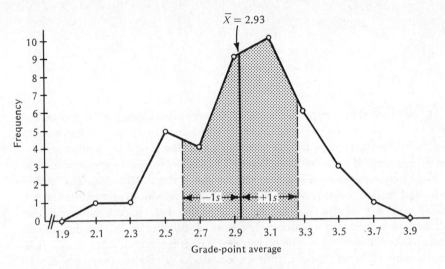

Figure 5-2 ♦ Distribution of hypothetical grade point averages where $\bar{X} = 2.93$ and $s = .33$ (data from Table 2-5)

A RESEARCH EXAMPLE: WOMEN'S AND MEN'S GRADE-POINT AVERAGES

As an example, consider the data from the study of women's and men's grade-point averages. The researchers were interested in whether men and women choose different major fields of study in college and whether men and women of similar aptitudes have similar grade-point averages when major field is taken into account. The following measures were collected on a large sample of undergraduates from four campuses of the University of California: major, grade-point average (GPA), and Scholastic Aptitude Test (SAT) scores. (See Chapter 2 for a more complete description.)

A frequency polygon summarizing the distribution of hypothetical GPAs is shown in Figure 5-2. About half the GPAs fall above the mean, and about half fall below (give or take a few). This distribution resembles the bell-shaped curve in Figure 5-1. About two-thirds of the GPAs in this sample fall between one standard deviation above and one standard deviation below the mean. Few GPAs fall at the extremely high or extremely low ends of the scale.

THE NORMAL DISTRIBUTION: AN OVERVIEW

The normal distribution does not actually exist. It is not a fact of nature. Rather, it is a mathematical model—an idealization—which can be used to represent data collected in behavioral research.[1] For example, the distribution

---

[1]The normal distribution is defined by the somewhat forbidding equation

$$y = \frac{1}{\sqrt{2\pi\sigma^2}} e^{-(X-\mu)^2/2\sigma^2}, \qquad \text{[5-1*]}$$

of heights of people in a population can be modeled reasonably well with the normal distribution. Most people are about average in height, while a few are quite short and a few are quite tall. Likewise, the normal distribution serves as a reasonably accurate model of the frequency distribution of IQ scores. However, as is often the case in science, the observed data and the abstract mathematical model almost never fit exactly.

The major value of the normal distribution lies in its ability to serve as a reasonably good model of many natural phenomena. In fact, scores on many measures used in the behavioral sciences are distributed so that the normal distribution provides a good model of their frequency distributions.

The normal distribution has particular importance in inferential statistics as a probability distribution. (For a discussion of terms such as inferential statistics, samples, and populations, see Chapter 1.) One reason is that when measures on large samples of natural phenomena such as height, weight, and

---

where y = the ordinate on the graph,
  X = an observed score,
  μ = the mean of the distribution in the population,
  σ^2 = the variance of the distribution in the population,
  π = 3.1416 (rounded),
  e = 2.7183 (rounded).

(Note: in using the normal distribution as an idealized representation of data, μ and σ will be used instead of $\overline{X}$ and s. The rationale for this is explained in Chapter 9 ff.) This equation defines the relative frequency with which particular values of X occur in a normal distribution. It says that these frequencies depend on two parameters—the mean (μ) and the variance (σ^2) of the distribution in the population—and two constants—pi (π = 3.1416) and the base of the natural system of logarithms (e = 2.7183).

In all this, it turns out that X is the only term in this equation that takes on different values once μ and σ^2 are specified. Thus, the working part of this equation is the exponent where X appears:

$$e^{-(X-\mu)^2/2\sigma^2}. \qquad\qquad\qquad [5\text{-}2^*]$$

As the distance between X and μ becomes increasingly large, the value of Formula 5-2, which is less than 1, becomes increasingly small, since

$$e^{-(X-\mu)^2/2\sigma^2} = \frac{1}{e^{(X-\mu)^2/2\sigma^2}}. \qquad\qquad\qquad [5\text{-}2a^*]$$

Thus, the greater the distance between particular values of X and the mean of the distribution, μ, the lower the relative frequencies with which these values of X occur:

$$y = \frac{1}{\sqrt{2\pi\sigma^2}} \cdot \frac{1}{e^{(X-\mu)^2/2\sigma^2}}. \qquad\qquad\qquad [5\text{-}1a^*]$$

When the score value X equals the mean μ, the exponent (Formula 5-2) becomes zero and

$$e^{-(X-\mu)^2/2\sigma^2} = e^{-0} = \frac{1}{e^0} = \frac{1}{1} = 1. \qquad\qquad\qquad [5\text{-}3^*]$$

In this case, the curve is at the maximum since

$$y = \frac{1}{\sqrt{2\pi\sigma^2}} \cdot 1. \qquad\qquad\qquad [5\text{-}4^*]$$

IQ are represented as a frequency distribution, the normal distribution provides a reasonably good model of the frequency distribution. Hence, the distribution of the true magnitudes of a trait such as intelligence may be thought of as being normally distributed in the *population*. A second reason is that there is a close connection between the sample size and the distribution of means calculated for many samples of subjects drawn from the same population. As the sample size increases, the distribution of sample means can be approximated by the normal distribution even though the distribution of scores in the population is not normal. And a third reason is that the normal distribution may provide a good approximation of other theoretical distributions that are more difficult to work with in determining probabilities.

PROPERTIES OF THE
NORMAL
DISTRIBUTION

The mathematical model for the normal distribution implies that the normal distribution will have a set of properties which characterize it. Other nonnormal distributions may have some of these properties. However, only those distributions following the mathematical rule for the normal distribution are normal distributions.

One property of the normal distribution is that it is *unimodal*. In a large frequency distribution, the most frequently observed value of X is that value of X falling exactly at the mean of the distribution. The greater the distance between X and the mean, the smaller the frequency with which X occurs. This fact results in the characteristic bell shape.

A second property of the normal distribution is that it is *symmetric* about its mean; that is, if you folded the distribution along its mean, the two sides of the distribution would coincide exactly. The distribution of scores above the mean, then, is a mirror image of the distribution of scores below the mean.[2]

Since the normal distribution is unimodal and symmetric about its mean, a third property of the normal distribution is that *the mean, mode, and median of the distribution are all equal*. Since the mode is the most frequent value of X, the mean and the mode are the same. Since the distribution is symmetric, half the scores fall above the mean and half below. Thus, the median equals the mean, which equals the mode.

A fourth property of the normal distribution is that it is *asymptotic*. That is, the curve never touches the abscissa.[3] This property arises from the fact that the

---

[2]This property is also implied by the working part of Formula 5-1: $(X - \mu)^2/2\sigma^2$. Since the difference between X and μ is squared, a score below the mean ($X - \mu$ negative) has exactly the same effect on Formula 5-1 as its counterpart above the mean ($X - \mu$ positive). For example, suppose $\mu = 5$ and that scores one unit below and above μ (4 and 6, respectively) are considered. Then $(4 - 5)^2 = (-1)^2 = 1$ and $(6 - 5)^2 = 1$. Both scores will produce the same value, so that the distribution is symmetric. One caution here is in order. While the normal distribution is symmetric, there are also many other mathematical rules that can form symmetric distributions.

[3]Even if the distance between X and μ is infinite, the working part of the equation, $e^{-(X - \mu)^2/2\sigma^2}$, will never be zero.

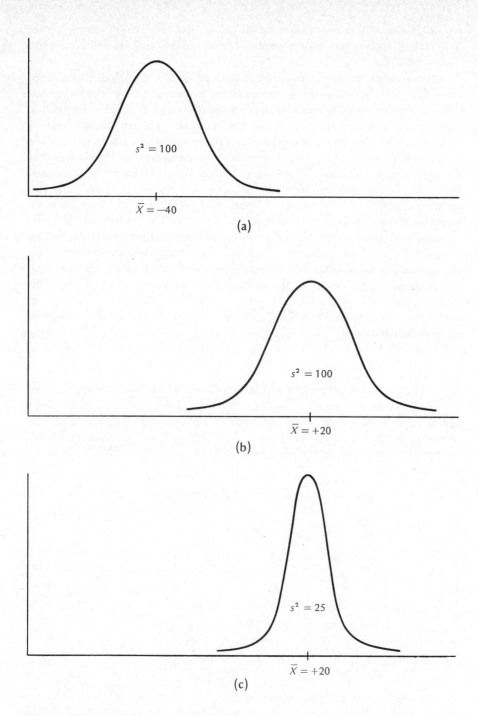

$s^2 = 100$

$\overline{X} = -40$

(a)

$s^2 = 100$

$\overline{X} = +20$

(b)

$s^2 = 25$

$\overline{X} = +20$

(c)

Figure 5-3 ◆ Normal distributions based on sample data with different means (a and b) and different variances (b and c)

normal distribution is continuous for all values of a variable (X) from $-\infty$ to $+\infty$. Thus, each conceivable nonzero interval of real numbers will occur with some probability.

All normal distributions possess the four properties discussed above, since these properties all follow from the mathematical model on which the normal distribution is based. A closer look at the mathematical rule for the normal distribution indicates that its mean and variance are not fixed. That is, different normal distributions can be obtained by applying the rule defining the normal distribution to distributions with different means and variances. For example, Figure 5-3 shows three normal distributions based on sample data. Distributions (a) and (b) have the same variance ($s^2 = 100$) and different means ($\overline{X}_{(a)} = -40$; $\overline{X}_{(b)} = +20$). Distributions (b) and (c) have the same mean ($+20$) and different variances ($s^2_{(b)} = 100$; $s^2_{(c)} = 25$). Finally, distributions (a) and (c) have different means and variances. Despite these differences, however, they are all normal distributions. Thus, the mathematical model for the normal distribution actually defines a family of distributions. These normal distributions may differ in their means and variances, but they all have the properties of the normal distribution in common. Since these distributions resemble each other in this way, they are often referred to as a **family of normal distributions.**

AREAS UNDER THE NORMAL DISTRIBUTION CURVE

Since 100 percent (a proportion of 1.00) represents an entire quantity, the total area underneath the curve of any distribution is 100 percent, or 1.00. When this area is divided into parts, the relative frequency or proportion or percentage of scores falling in some part of the distribution can be determined. For example, as shown in Figure 5-4, approximately one-third (.3413) of the scores

Figure 5-4 ♦ Areas under the curve of a normal distribution

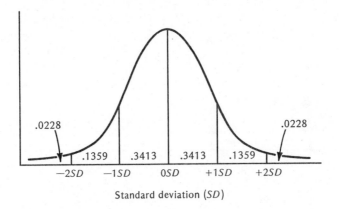

Standard deviation (*SD*)

in the normal distribution fall between the mean and one standard deviation above the mean. Since the normal distribution is symmetric, approximately one-third of the scores fall between the mean and one standard deviation below the mean. Thus, approximately two-thirds (or approximately 68 percent) of the scores in a normal distribution fall in the interval ranging from one standard deviation below the mean to one standard deviation above the mean: .3413 + .3413 = .6826 or 68.26 percent (see Figure 5-4).

In order to illustrate the importance of the normal distribution in interpreting score values, suppose you earned a score of 20 correct out of 32 on a statistics examination. Your first feeling might be panic, since this score is not close to 32. After calming down, your next thought might be that the test was difficult for everyone else, so you might try peeking at test scores earned by your fellow students. However, not until the instructor puts the distribution of scores on the board will you know exactly where your score stands with respect to other students' scores. Suppose, instead, the teacher returned your test with a note that a score of 20 fell 2 standard deviations above the mean of the class. *Assuming that the distribution of scores on the test can be represented by the normal distribution*, this information will tell you exactly where you stand with respect to other students. Since a score of two standard deviations above the mean is greater than 98 percent of the scores earned by other students (see Figure 5-4: .0228 + .1359 + .3413 + .3413 + .1359 = .9772 or 97.72 percent), now you know that you actually did extremely well on the exam.

One important feature of the normal distribution, then, is that when it is used appropriately as a model of the distribution of test scores, it permits us to interpret these scores and other measures (dependent variables in our research) with reference to the part of the distribution in which a particular score falls. For example, Scholastic Aptitude Test (SAT) scores have a mean of 500 and a standard deviation of 100. A person with a score of 700 has earned a score 2 standard deviations above the mean and hence has scored higher than 98 percent of the students who have taken the examination.

A second feature of the normal distribution, one which will become quite important later in this book, is that it is a probability distribution. Thus, the area under the normal curve can be used to determine probabilities. Since the normal distribution is so commonly used in measurement and statistics and since skills in working with the normal distribution as well as other distributions are needed throughout this text, methods for finding areas under the normal curve will be covered in some detail.

STANDARD SCORES

Introduction

In behavioral research, many different scales of measurement are used to measure the outcome of a study. For example, scholastic aptitude is often measured on a scale with a mean of 500 and a standard deviation of 100; reaction time may be measured in seconds or even milliseconds; and tests developed for specific research purposes usually contain 50 questions or less and may have means of 20 or 30 with standard deviations of less than 10 points. In order to interpret scores from these measures, it is helpful to transform the raw scores into a standard type of score that shows a person's *relative* status in a distribution of scores. Remember that we were able to tell how well you did on a hypothetical statistics examination, relative to your classmates, by knowing that your score of 20 fell two standard deviations above the mean. This suggests that we need only a method for determining how far a score falls above or below the mean in terms of standard deviations in order to render interpretable a score from any one of many measurements made in behavioral research.

This reasoning suggests that we need to determine the distance of a score from its mean and then convert that distance into the number of standard deviations which the score falls above or below the mean. In short, we need to get a **standard score**, a score indicating the *relative standing* of the raw score in a distribution. Put another way, a standard score tells how many standard deviations a raw score falls above or below the mean of the distribution.

♦   ♦   ♦   ♦   ♦

Formula for a Standard Score

In developing the logic behind a formula for calculating a standard score, a simple example is helpful. Suppose that Charlie received a score of 70 on a test which has a mean of 50 and a standard deviation of 10. How many standard-deviation units is this GPA above the mean? You have probably figured it out already, but let's follow the reasoning behind the standard score. First, find the distance between Charlie's score and the mean:

$$70 - 50 = +20 \quad \text{or} \quad 20 \text{ points above the mean.}$$

The next step is to convert this measure of distance into the number of standard deviations that this distance covers, i.e., into standard-deviation units. How many standard deviations does 20 points above the mean cover? Since the standard deviation is 10, the distance can be divided by 10 in order to find the number of standard-deviation units that the score of 70 lies above the mean of 50:

$$20 \div 10 = 2.00.$$

This procedure tells us that the score of 70 lies 2.00 standard deviations above the mean.

This procedure for computing a standard score, usually referred to as a *z* score, can be summarized by the following formula:

$$z = \frac{X - \overline{X}}{s} = \frac{x}{s}. \qquad [\textbf{5-1}]$$

Charlie's z score, corresponding to a raw score of 70 on a test with a mean of 50 and a standard deviation of 10, is

$$z = \frac{70 - 50}{10}$$

$$= \frac{20}{10}$$

$$= 2.$$

For reference, the steps in computing a z score are summarized in Procedure 5-1 using the hypothetical GPA data from the study of men's and women's achievement in college.

A z score contains two important pieces of information about the corresponding observed score. The *magnitude* of the z score tells how many standard deviations the observed score lies from the mean. The *sign* of the z score indicates whether the observed score lies above the mean (z is positive) or below the mean (z is negative).

Steps in computing a z score (example data taken from Figure 5-2) ♦ Procedure 5-1

Operation	Example
1 Use Formula 5-1: $$z = \frac{X - \bar{X}}{s},$$ $$= \frac{x}{s}.$$	To find the z score for a GPA of 3.50
2 Compute $\bar{X}$ and s if not given. (See Procedures 4-3 and 4-8.)	$\bar{X} = 2.93,$ $s = .33.$
3 Insert appropriate values into Formula 5-1 and solve for z.	(a) Insert 3.50 for X. (b) Insert 2.93 for $\bar{X}$. (c) Insert 0.33 for s. $$z = \frac{3.50 - 2.93}{.33}$$ $$= \frac{.57}{.33}$$ $$= 1.73.$$ Interpretation: A GPA of 3.50 lies 1.73 standard deviations above the mean.

The z scores also have some other important characteristics. First, the mean of the distribution of z scores will always be zero regardless of the value of the mean of the original score distribution:

$$\bar{z} = \frac{\Sigma z}{N}$$

$$= \frac{1}{N}\Sigma\frac{X - \bar{X}}{s}$$

$$= \frac{1}{Ns}\Sigma(X - \bar{X})$$

$$= 0.$$

This happens because, as you know, the mean is that point in a distribution at which the algebraic sum of the difference of each score (X) from the mean $(\bar{X})$ is zero [i.e., $\Sigma(X - \bar{X}) = 0$]. Second, the variance of z scores, s_z^2, always equals 1. Therefore, the standard deviation of z scores, s_z, also equals 1. This characteristic is not obvious; the proof is given in footnote 4.[4] The upshot of these characteristics is that, regardless of the scale of measurement, z scores always refer to a distribution with a mean of 0 and a standard deviation of 1.

While transforming raw scores to z scores changes the mean and standard deviation of the frequency distribution, this transformation does not alter the shape of it. The frequency of a particular z score is exactly equal to the frequency of its corresponding raw (X) score. If the shape of the original frequency distribution is symmetric, the shape of the distribution of z scores will be as well. Likewise, if the original distribution is skewed, so will be the distribution of z scores. Finally, if scores in a theoretical distribution such as the normal distribution are transformed to z scores, the exact shape given by the mathematical rule for the theoretical distribution will not be changed. Only the mean and standard deviation of the theoretical distribution will be changed to 0 and 1, respectively.

[4]The proof below shows that the variance (and standard deviation) of z score always equals one:

$$s_z^2 = \frac{\Sigma(z - \bar{z})^2}{n - 1} \qquad \text{by definition}$$

$$= \frac{\Sigma z^2}{n - 1} \qquad \text{since } \bar{z} = 0$$

$$= \frac{\Sigma(X - \bar{X})^2/s^2}{n - 1} \qquad \text{by substitution}$$

$$= \frac{1}{s^2}\left[\frac{\Sigma(X - \bar{X})^2}{n - 1}\right] \qquad \text{by rearranging terms}$$

$$= \left(\frac{1}{s^2}\right)s^2 \qquad \text{by definition of } s^2$$

$$= 1.$$

♦   ♦   ♦   ♦   ♦

As pointed out in the section on "Areas under the Normal Distribution Curve," when the sample frequency distribution can be modeled accurately by the normal distribution, the relative frequency, or proportion of scores falling in some area of the distribution, can be determined. In order to use the normal distribution for this purpose (and others), it might seem that a different normal distribution would be needed for every frequency distribution with a different mean and standard deviation, since the normal distribution is a family of distributions, each member defined by its mean and standard deviation. Fortunately, this is not the case. If raw scores are converted to z scores, then, regardless of the original score scale and its mean and standard deviation, the distribution of z scores will have a mean of 0 and a standard deviation of 1. Thus, by converting raw scores to z scores, the z scores can be referred to just one member of the family of normal distributions—the member with mean equal to 0 and standard deviation equal to 1. The normal distribution with a mean of 0 and a standard deviation of 1 is called the **standard normal distribution**.

The standard normal distribution can be used as follows. Remember that Charlie earned a score of 70 on a test with a mean of 50 and a standard deviation of 10. By converting Charlie's score of 70 to a z score of $+2$, the standard normal distribution can be used to determine, say, the percentage of scores falling below Charlie's score of 70 (assuming the scores are accurately modeled by the normal distribution). From Figure 5-4, we find that Charlie's score is greater than 97.72 percent of the scores in the distribution (i.e., $.0228 + .1359 + .3413 + .3413 + .1359 = .9772$, and $.9772 \times 100 = 97.72$ percent).

Standard Scores and the Standard Normal Distribution

What is the z score corresponding to a GPA of 2.65 in Figure 5-2?

EXAMPLE PROBLEM 1

The normal distribution permits interpretation of scores with reference to where they fall in the distribution. For example, Figure 5-4 shows that when the standard normal distribution is divided into standard-deviation units, the proportion (percentage) of scores falling in each area of the distribution can be determined: approximately 34 percent of the scores fall between the mean and one standard deviation above the mean, and so on. However, in interpreting scores, Figure 5-4 is of limited usefulness because z scores may take on values other than just whole numbers. For this reason, Table B at the end of the book gives proportions of area under the standard normal distribution that correspond to each possible z score (rounded to two decimal places). In examining Table B, notice that the first column lists z scores. Columns 2–4 give areas

USING THE STANDARD NORMAL DISTRIBUTION

corresponding to particular areas under the normal distribution. For example, column 2 identifies the area between the mean and the z score listed in column 1. Thus, the area between a z score of 1.00 and the mean is .3413. (Note that this agrees with Figure 5-4.)

Several types of questions can be answered using z scores and Table B. These questions are:

1. What proportion of scores fall between the mean and a given raw score?
2. What proportion of scores fall above (or below) a given raw score?
3. What proportion of scores fall between two raw scores?
4. What raw score falls above (or below) a given percentage of scores?

Each of these questions is discussed in turn, along with the step-by-step procedure for answering them. The main reason for the following "exercise" is that an understanding of subsequent chapters will depend on your skill in finding areas under the normal curve.

♦   ♦   ♦   ♦   ♦

What Proportion of Scores Fall between the Mean and a Given Raw Score? In answering this question, first convert the raw score to a z score and then refer to column 2 of Table B (Area from Mean to z) to find the proportion of scores. For example, Charlie's score of 70 in a distribution with a mean of 50 and a standard deviation of 10 corresponds to a z score of

$$z = \frac{70 - 50}{10} = 2.$$

From Column 2 in Table B, the proportion of cases falling between Charlie's z score of 2 and the mean is .4772.

Suppose Bart, a fellow student of Charlie's, earned a score of 42. What proportion of the scores fall between 42 and the mean of 50? First, calculate a z score for Bart:

$$z = \frac{42 - 50}{10}$$

$$= \frac{-8}{10}$$

$$= -.80.$$

Next, find a z score in Table B corresponding to .80. (Note that you ignore the sign of z in using Table B, since the normal distribution is symmetric. So the proportion of scores between the mean and a positive score will also be the proportion of scores between the mean and a negative score of the same magnitude.) Then refer to column 2 of the table to find the proportion of scores between $-.80$ and the mean; this value is .2881.

For reference, the steps in finding the proportion of scores between a raw score and the mean are given in Procedure 5-2. The data used as examples are taken from the study of college GPAs. Note that throughout the remainder of this chapter we assume that the normal distribution is a valid model of the frequency distributions providing the data for examples.

Identify the proportion of scores in Figure 5-2 falling between the mean and a GPA of 2.25.

EXAMPLE PROBLEM 2

Steps for identifying the proportion of scores falling between the mean and a given observed score (example GPA data taken from Figure 5-2). *Overview: Basically, these procedures involve converting X scores to z scores and using column 2 of Table B in the Appendix to locate this area in the standard normal distribution. The use of Table B rests on the assumption that the normal distribution is a valid model of the frequency distribution.*

◆ Procedure 5-2

Operation	Example
1 Convert the observed score to a z score using Formula 5-1: $$z = \frac{X - \bar{X}}{s}$$ *The observed score must be converted to a z score in order to use the standard normal distribution.*	To identify the proportion of scores falling between the mean and a GPA of 3.70, first compute z: $$z = \frac{3.70 - 2.93}{.33}$$ $$= 2.33.$$
2 Draw a picture of the normal distribution and block out area to be identified. *This figure helps define the problem and determine the column in Table B-2 which provides the needed information.*	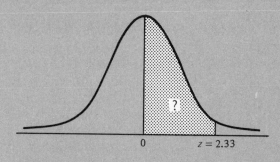 0 z = 2.33 Area = .4901

3 Turn to Table B in the Appendix.
  a If z is *positive*, locate z in column 1 and read across to column 2.
  Note that the area blocked off in the figure
	The proportion of cases falling between the mean and a z score of 2.33 is approximately .49 (or 49%).
	(continued on p. 162)

above column 1 corresponds to the area blocked off in step 2 above.

b *If z is negative, ignore the sign of z and follow (a).*
This procedure is possible because the normal distribution is symmetric. The area between the mean and a particular positive z score (e.g., 1.50) is equal to the area between the mean and the same z score with a negative sign.

If $z = -2.33$, area $= .4901$, since the area between $\bar{X}$ and -2.33 is the same as the area between $\bar{X}$ and $+2.33$

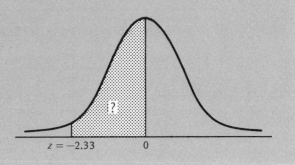

$z = -2.33 \qquad 0$

◆　◆　◆　◆　◆

What Proportion of Scores Fall above (or below) a Given Raw Score? In answering this question, first convert the raw score to a z score. Next, draw a picture of a normal distribution and shade in the area you are looking for. Then use column 4 to find the area in the smaller tail of the distribution if that is the area you shaded, or column 3 to find the area in the larger tail if that is what you have shaded.

For example, what is the proportion of scores falling above Charlie's score of 70? First, calculate Charlie's z score; we have already done so and it is 2. Next, draw a picture of the normal distribution and shade in the area of interest. Since Charlie's score is way above the mean and we are interested in scores above Charlie's, we draw the following diagram:

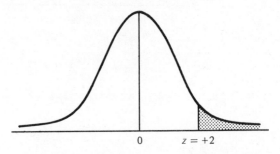

$0 \qquad z = +2$

Since the area of the smaller tail is shaded, column 4 of Table B is used to find the proportion, which is .0228.

What is the proportion of cases falling above Bart's score of 42? The z score corresponding to Bart's score of 42 has been calculated: $z = -.80$. Next, draw a picture representing the answer to the question. Since Bart's score falls below the mean and we are interested in scores above Bart's, we have

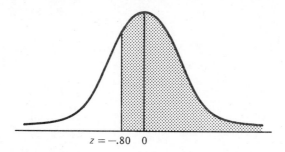

$$z = -.80 \quad 0$$

(Note that, as explained above, the sign of z is ignored when using Table B. But it is *not* ignored in drawing the figure above.) With the area of the larger tail shaded, column 3 is used to find the proportion, which is in this case .7881. For

Steps for identifying the proportion of scores falling above (or below) a given observed ♦ Procedure 5-3
score (example data from Figure 5-2).   *Overview: Basically, these procedures involve converting X to z and using the appropriate column of Table B to locate this area in the standard normal distribution. The use of Table B rests on the assumption that the normal distribution is a valid model of the frequency distribution.*

Operation	Example
Procedures for Scores above the Mean:	
1 Convert the observed score to a z score using Formula 5-1:	To identify the proportion of scores falling above (or below) a GPA of 3.50, first compute z:
$$z = \frac{X - \bar{X}}{s}.$$	$$z = \frac{3.50 - 2.93}{.33}$$
	$$= 1.73.$$
The observed score must be converted to a z score in order to use the standard normal distribution.	
2 Draw a figure of the normal distribution and block out the area to be identified. *This picture helps define the problem and determine the column in Table B which provides the needed information.*	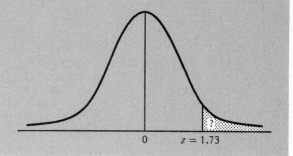
(continued on p. 164)	$$0 \qquad z = 1.73$$

3 Turn to Table B.

a If the area to be identified represents the *smaller* tail of the curve, locate z in column 1 and read across to column 4.

Note that the area blocked off in the figure above column 4 corresponds to the shaded area in step 2.

b If the area to be identified represents the *larger* tail of the curve, locate z in column 1 and read across to column 3.

Note that the area blocked off in the figure above column 3 corresponds to the shaded area in the example to the right.

Area = .0418. The proportion of scores falling above a z score of 1.73 is approximately .04 or 4%.

The proportion of scores falling below $z = 1.73$ is .9582—the area in the larger tail of the curve.

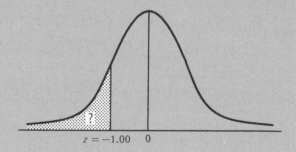

Procedures for Scores below the Mean:

1 Convert the observed score to a z score using Formula 5-1:

$$z = \frac{X - \bar{X}}{s}$$

The observed score must be converted to a z score in order to use the standardized normal distribution.

2 Draw a figure of the normal distribution and block out the area to be identified.

The picture helps to define the problem and determine the column in Table B which provides the needed information.

To identify the proportion of cases falling below (or above) a GPA of 2.60, first compute z:

$$z = \frac{2.60 - 2.93}{.33}$$

$$= \frac{-.33}{.33} = -1.$$

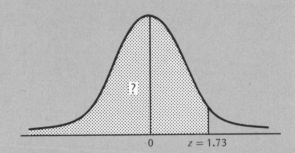

3 Turn to Table B.

a If the area to be *identified represents the smaller* portion of the curve, locate |z| (i.e., the value of z ignoring the sign) in column 1 and read across to column 4.

Note that, since the normal distribution is symmetric, the area below a z score of −1.00 is equal to the area above a z score of 1.00.

Area = .1587. The proportion of scores falling below $z = -1.00$ is .1587—the area in the smaller portion of the curve.

b If the area to be identified represents the *greater* portion of the curve, locate $|z|$ (i.e., the value of z ignoring the sign) in column 1 and read across to column 3.
Note that, since the normal distribution is symmetric, the area above a z score of −1.00 is equal to the area below a z score of 1.00.

Area = .8413. The proportion of scores falling above $z = -1.00$ is .8413—the area in the greater portion of the curve.

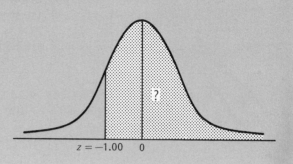

reference, the steps in finding the proportion of scores above (or below) a given raw score are summarized in Procedure 5-3.

Using the data given in Figure 5-2, identify the proportion of cases falling above a GPA of 2.75.

EXAMPLE PROBLEM 3

◆   ◆   ◆   ◆   ◆

In answering this question, first transform the two raw scores into z scores. Second, draw a normal distribution, locate the two z scores on the abscissa, and shade in the area between them. Finally, find the proportion of scores falling below each of the z scores and subtract the smaller area from the larger area to find the proportion of scores.

For example, what proportion of scores fall between Bart's and Charlie's scores of 42 and 70, respectively? The first step is to convert these raw scores to z scores. This has been done: $-.80$ and $+2.00$. Next, draw a normal distribution and shade in the area between the two scores:

What Proportion of Scores Fall between Two Raw Scores?

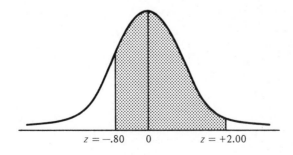

165

Now, find the area below both z scores. The area to the left of $z = 2.00$ is the area in the larger tail. So column 3 in Table B can be used to find this area: .9772. The area to the left of $z = -.80$ is the area in the smaller tail. So column 4 in Table B can be used to find this area: .2119. Finally, subtract the smaller area from the larger area in the distribution: $.9772 - .2119 = .7653$. For reference, the steps in finding the proportion of scores between two raw scores are summarized in Procedure 5-4.

EXAMPLE PROBLEM 4

Using the data given in Figure 5-2, identify the proportion of scores falling between a GPA of 3.00 and 3.35.

Procedure 5-4 ♦ Steps for identifying the proportion of scores falling between two observed scores (example GPA data from Figure 5-2). *Overview: These procedures are somewhat more complicated than those in Procedures 5-2 and 5-3, since these areas are not given directly in Table B. Basically, these procedures involve converting each X score to a z score and using areas given in Table B to compute the area to be identified. The use of Table B rests on the assumption that the normal distribution is a valid model of the frequency distribution.*

Operation	Example
1 Convert each observed score to a z score using Formula 5-1: $$z = \frac{X - \bar{X}}{s}.$$ *Observed scores must be converted to z scores in order to use the standard normal distribution.*	To identify the proportion of scores falling between a GPA of 2.40 and a GPA of 3.20, first compute z for each GPA: $$z_{GPA = 2.40} = \frac{2.40 - 2.93}{.33}$$ $$= -1.61,$$ $$z_{GPA = 3.20} = \frac{3.20 - 2.93}{.33}$$ $$= .82.$$
2 Draw a graph of the normal distribution and block out the area to be identified. Note that the area to be identified is not directly given in Table B. *This graph helps define the problem and determine the column(s) in Table B which provide the needed information.*	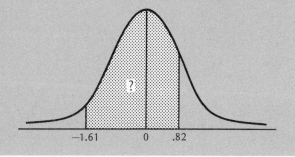

3 If at least *one* of the z scores is positive, locate the area of interest as follows:

a Identify the area below the highest z score, using column 3 of Table B.
This area contains the area to be identified as well as some area to the left which is not of interest.

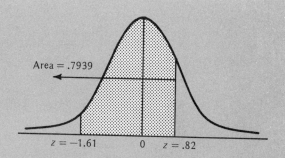

Since the area to the left of a positive z score always constitutes the greater portion of the curve, it is found in column 3 of Table B.

b Identify the area to the left of the lower z score, using the appropriate column of Table B (see step 3 of Procedure 5-3 to identify the appropriate column).
This area represents the area not *of interest contained in* (a).

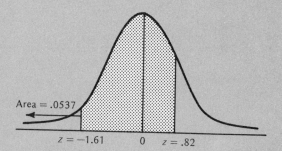

Since this area in this example constitutes the smaller portion of the curve, it is found in column 4 of Table B.

c Subtract the area located in (b) from that located in (a).
This difference represents the area to be identified.

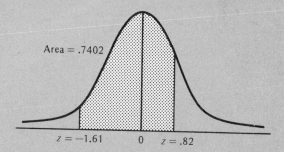

Area = .7939 − .0537
= .7402.

The proportion of cases falling between a z score of −1.61 and 0.82 is approximately .74 or 74%.

4 If *both* z scores are *negative*, locate the area of interest by the following:

(continued on p. 168)

Suppose we wish to identify the proportion of scores falling between z scores of −1.00 and −2.30.

a Identify the area to the left of the *z* score with the lowest negative value (i.e., the value closest to zero) by locating $|z|$ (value of *z* ignoring the sign) in column 1 and reading across to column 4.

This area contains the area to be identified as well as some area to the left which is not of interest.

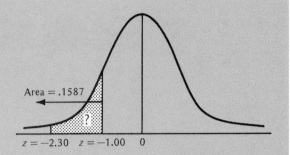

Since the area below a negative *z* score always constitutes the smaller portion of the curve and since the normal curve is symmetric, this area can be found by locating the area in column 4 corresponding to $|z|$.

b Identify the area to the left of the *z* score with the highest negative value (i.e., value farthest from zero) by locating $|z|$ in column 1 and reading across to column 4 of Table B.

This area represents the area not *of interest contained in* (a).

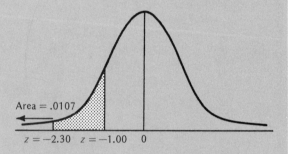

Since the area below a negative *z* score always constitutes the smaller portion of the curve and since the normal curve is symmetric, this area is found in column 4 of Table B corresponding to $|z|$.

c Subtract the area located in (b) from that located in (a).

This difference represents the area to be identified.

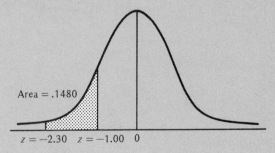

Area = .1587 − .0107
    = .1480

The proportion of cases falling between a *z* score of −1.00 and −2.30 is approximately .15 or 15%.

♦   ♦   ♦   ♦   ♦

In answering this question, first draw a picture of a normal distribution and shade in the area (percentage of scores) to be found. Next, convert the given percentage to a proportion by dividing it by 100. Then, turn to Table B and find the column corresponding to the shaded area of your diagram. Read down this column to find the proportion of scores corresponding to the shaded area, and then read to the left to column 1 to find the z score corresponding to this area. Now you know the values of z, $\overline{X}$, and s. Since $z = (X - \overline{X}) \div s$, you need to find X, the score above (or below) a given percentage of scores. In order to find X, the following formula[5] can be used:

What Raw Score Falls above (or below) a Given Percentage of Scores?

$$X = s \cdot z + \overline{X}. \qquad [\text{5-1a}]$$

For example, what raw score falls above 38 percent of the scores in Charlie's class? To answer this question, first draw a picture. In doing so, note that 50 percent of the scores fall below the mean of the normal distribution (mean = median), so the shaded area of the distribution will be in the small tail below the mean:

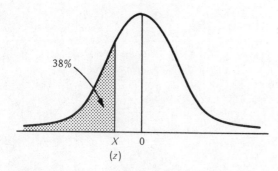

Next, convert 38 percent to a proportion by dividing by 100: $38 \div 100 = .38$. Then, turn to column 4 in Table B, the column providing proportions in the smaller tail, and read down to .3783 (as close as we can get to .3800 in the column). Now read the z score in column 1 corresponding to .3783: $z = .31$. Since this z score corresponds to the lower tail of the distribution, it is negative:

[5]We have

$$\frac{X - \overline{X}}{s} = z \qquad [\text{5-1}] \qquad \text{(definition of a } z \text{ score)}$$

$$X - \overline{X} = sz \qquad \qquad \text{(multiply both sides of the equation by } s\text{)}$$

$$X = sz + \overline{X} \qquad [\text{5-1a}] \qquad \text{(add } \overline{X} \text{ to both sides of the equation).}$$

$z = -.31$. With the following information available—$z = -.31$, $\overline{X} = 50$, $s = 10$—the raw score falling above 38 percent of the scores in Charlie's class can be found with Formula 5-1a:

$$X = (10)(-.31) + 50$$
$$= -3.1 + 50$$
$$= 46.9.$$

A raw score of 46.9 falls above 38 percent of the scores in Charlie's class. For reference, the steps in finding a raw score falling above (or below) a given percentage of scores in a normal distribution are given in Procedure 5-5.

Procedure 5-5 ♦ Steps for identifying the raw score which falls above (or below) a given percentage of scores (example data taken from Figure 5-2). *Overview: The problem of finding a raw score corresponding to a certain percentage of scores in the normal distribution is the reverse of previous ones. In this case, the proportion of area under the normal distribution is given and the problem is to find the corresponding raw score. Basically, this type of problem is solved by finding the z score in Table B that corresponds to the percentage of cases under the curve and then converting that z score to the corresponding X score. The use of Table B rests on the assumption that the normal distribution is a valid model of the frequency distribution.*

Operation	Example
1 Draw a graph of the normal distribution, blocking out the area to be identified. *This helps define the problem and determine the column of Table B which provides the needed information.*	To identify the observed GPA which falls above 85% of the GPAs in this sample: 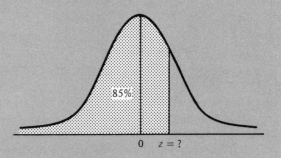
2 Convert the given percentage to a proportion by dividing by 100.	Proportion = 85 ÷ 100 = .85
3 Read down the appropriate column in Table B, locate the nearest proportion to that identified in step 2, and locate z by reading across to column 1. *This procedure locates the z score corresponding to the proportion of interest.*	

a If the area represents the *greater* portion of the curve, read down column 3.

b If the area represents the *smaller* portion of the curve, read down column 4.

Reading down column 3 of Table B, the closest figure to .85 is .8508. This area corresponds to a z score of 1.04.

4 Check the graph constructed in step 1 to determine whether z is positive or negative. *z will be positive if z is above $\bar{X}$, negative if z is below $\bar{X}$.*

In this case, z is positive.

$$z = 1.04$$

5 Convert z to X using Formula 5-1a:

$$X = s \cdot z + \bar{X}.$$

$$X = .33(1.04) + 2.93$$

$$= 3.27.$$

A GPA of 3.27 falls above 85% of the GPAs in this sample.

♦   ♦   ♦   ♦   ♦

Summary

This chapter discusses the *normal distribution* and its properties in some detail. In addition, the concept of a *standard score* (z *score*) is presented, along with procedures for computing z scores. Finally, the *standard normal distribution* is presented along with methods for using z scores to identify areas in this distribution. These concepts and skills will become particularly important in later chapters when inferential statistics are considered.

♦   ♦   ♦   ♦   ♦

Key Words

family of normal distributions
normal distribution
standard normal distribution

standard score
z score

♦   ♦   ♦   ♦   ♦

Exercises

1–3 In a normal distribution, what percentage of scores fall:

1. Above the mean?
2. Below a z score of $+1$?
3. Between a z score of $+1$ and -1?

4. List four important properties of the normal distribution.
5. What information does the magnitude and sign of a z score give?
6. Give two advantages of converting observed scores to standard scores.

7–13 Assume that each section of the Scholastic Aptitude Test has a mean of 500 and a standard deviation of 100. Assume that the frequency distribution of SAT scores can be modeled by the normal distribution.

7. Determine the proportion of scores that fall between the mean and a score of:
   a. 600
   b. 450

    c. 530

    d. 490

8. Determine the proportion of scores that fall *above* a score of:

    a. 500

    b. 650

    c. 375

    d. 590

9. Determine the proportion of scores that fall *below* a score of:

    a. 400

    b. 720

    c. 580

    d. 620

10. Determine the proportion of scores falling between the following scores:

    a. 450 and 550

    b. 375 and 425

    c. 525 and 600

    d. 490 and 640

11. Determine the score below which 90 percent of the scores fall.

12. Determine the score above which 70 percent of the scores fall.

13. Linda received the following scores in each section of the SAT:

Verbal:	660
Quantitative:	590
Psychology:	465

Above what percentage of students taking the SAT did she score on each section?

14–16 Jekyll received the following scores on the midterm and final examination in his introductory psychology course. The mean and standard deviation for each test are also given below. Assume that the normal distribution provides a good model of the frequency distributions.

	X	$\overline{X}$	s
Midterm	40	50	10
Final	90	100	15

14. On which test did Jekyll do better relative to the rest of the class?

15. What percentage of students scored better than Jekyll on the midterm? On the final?

16. What was assumed about these test scores in order to answer these questions?

17–18 Hyde was enrolled in another section of introductory psychology. His scores, along with the mean and standard deviation for his section, are shown below:

	X	$\overline{X}$	s
Midterm	24	30	8
Final	77	65	10

Assume, in answering Exercises 17 and 18, that the normal distribution provides a good model of the frequency distribution.

17. How did Hyde perform on his midterm compared to Jekyll's performance on his midterm? On the final?

18. Above what percentage of the students did Hyde score on the final?

19–23 The following means and standard deviations were obtained on a statistics final examination in four different sections:

	$\bar{X}$	s
Section I	70	10
Section II	80	20
Section III	70	5
Section IV	65	10

Suppose that the frequency distribution of final exam scores can be modeled by the normal distribution. Assuming that the instructor grades on the curve (mostly C's, some B's and D's, and a few A's and F's), in which section would you prefer to be enrolled if you received the following scores? (Don't be surprised if some of your answers are contrary to your first reactions!)

19. 73
20. 68
21. 78
22. 81
23. On what basis did you make your choices?

24. Suppose that several sections of a beginning sociology course ($N = 1000$) are to be graded on the same curve. The final examination for the course resulted in a mean of 75 and a standard deviation of 15. (The frequency distribution can be modeled by the normal distribution.) The instructors decide to give 10 percent A's, 20 percent B's, 40 percent C's, 20 percent D's, and 10 percent F's. Find the minimum score that a student would need to earn in order to receive each of these grades.

SECTION III

Joint Distributions

SECTION II dealt with *univariate distribution*—distributions summarizing one variable at a time (e.g., the frequency distribution of achievement-test scores). Statistics such as means and standard deviations were used to describe these distributions. In this section, attention is focused on *joint distributions*—distributions in which *two variables are considered simultaneously*. These distributions arise from data collected in correlational studies—studies in which the researcher is interested in the relationship between two variables.

Joint distributions are used to summarize the relationship between two variables. Just as univariate distributions could be described by means and standard deviations, joint distributions can be described by a *correlation coefficient*—a single number describing the relationship between two variables—and a *regression equation*— an equation describing a functional relationship between two variables.

In a correlational study, the researcher is interested in the relationship between two continuous variables such as scores on an achievement test and scores on an anxiety inventory. In the study of men's and women's achievement in college, for example, one concern was the relationship between Scholastic Aptitude Test (SAT) scores and college grade-point averages (GPA). In the Majasan study (Chapter 2), the focus was on the relationship between beliefs measured on a humanistic-behavioristic scale and grades in an introductory psychology course. In each of these studies, the relationship between the two variables could be described by a *correlation coefficient*. The correlation coefficient provides a measure of the strength of association between two variables. Or, put another way, the correlation coefficient provides an index of how closely two variables "go together."

In studies of the relationship between two variables, it is also possible to describe the approximate *functional relationship* between two variables. The term functional relationship refers to a statement something like the following: "As scores on the achievement test increase one point (at a time), scores on the anxiety inventory decrease three points (at a time)." Or the functional relationship between SAT scores and GPA in the study of men's and women's achievement might be described as follows: "As scores on the SAT increase by 50 points, GPA increases by .10 point." (Note that the GPA usually ranges from 0 to 4 points, while SAT scores usually range from 200 to 800 points.) Our concern with functional relationships, then, is a concern with predicting how much of a change in one variable is associated with a change in the second variable. This functional relationship is described by an equation called a *regression equation*.

The next three chapters describe how to compute and interpret joint distributions, correlation coefficients, and regression equations, respectively.

6 ♦

Joint Distributions

A Research Example: The Psychological Belief Scale and Student Achievement

Joint Distribution: Tabular Representation

Joint Distribution: Graphical Representation

Summary

♦ Key Words ♦

♦ Exercises ♦

Iₙ CORRELATIONAL studies, the researcher is interested in the question, "What is the relationship between variable X and variable Y?" If X represents scores on the Scholastic Aptitude Test (SAT) and Y represents college grade-point averages (GPAs), the research question can be stated as: "What is the relationship between scores on the SAT and GPAs?" This was one of the research questions posed in the study of men's and women's achievement in college. If X represents scores on a measure of self-concept and Y represents scores on a measure of peer popularity, the research question in this correlational study can be stated as: "What is the relationship between scores on the self-concept measure and scores on the peer popularity measure?"

In all cases, correlational studies focus on answering the question, "How are scores on one measure associated with scores on another measure?" In conducting a correlational study, two measures—representing the two variables of interest—are given to one group of subjects. The subjects' scores on both measures are summarized, and the relationship between the scores on the two measures is examined.

The first step in examining the relationship between scores on two measures is to arrange them in the form of a joint distribution. A **joint distribution** is a distribution in which a pair of scores for each subject is represented. The purpose of this chapter is to develop the concept of joint distribution and to provide you with the skills needed to build a joint distribution from a set of data.

A RESEARCH EXAMPLE: THE PSYCHOLOGICAL BELIEF SCALE AND STUDENT ACHIEVEMENT

Throughout this section of the book, hypothetical data based on Majasan's study of the congruence between students' and instructors' beliefs and student achievement will be used to illustrate the concepts presented. At this point, you may want to return to Chapter 2 to review the study. Briefly, a Psychological Belief Scale was given to students and instructors in three introductory psychology classes at the beginning of the school year. At the end of the course, students' final examination scores were collected. One purpose of the study was to examine the relationship between students' scores on the belief scale and their scores on the final examination in each of the three classes. Data from seven students in each of the three classes are presented in Table 6-1.

JOINT DISTRIBUTION: TABULAR REPRESENTATION

Table 6-1 is a tabular representation of a joint distribution. Consider the data for class 1. The identification number for each student in the class is listed in the first column. In the second column, each student's score on variable X

Table 6-1 ◆ Tabular form of a joint distribution: the relationship between scores on the belief scale and the achievement test in three classes of introductory psychology

Class 1			Class 2			Class 3		
(1) Student's identification (ID)	(2) Score on belief scale (X)	(3) Score on final examination (Y)	(1) ID	(2) X	(3) Y	(1) ID	(2) X	(3) Y
1	3	7	1	2	1	1	8	10
2	4	6	2	5	7	2	7	8
3	6	9	3	7	10	3	3	2
4	5	10	4	6	9	4	5	6
5	8	2	5	9	3	5	7	9
6	9	3	6	3	4	6	2	2
7	6	10	7	7	9	7	4	5

(belief scale) is entered. Finally, in the third column, each subject's score on variable Y (final examination) is entered. In correlational studies, the identification of scores on one measure as variable X and scores on the other measure as variable Y is arbitrary. Often, variable X represents the first measure taken, while variable Y represents the second measure. Or variable X may represent the variable on which predictions are based, and variable Y the outcome or criterion predicted.

Since the arrangement of scores in Table 6-1 is somewhat obvious, this procedure may seem trivial at first glance. However, it is important to note that when subjects' scores are arranged in this manner, it is possible to get an idea of the relationship between the two sets of scores. For example, by examining the X and Y scores for each subject in class 1, it is apparent that the general pattern in the data for class 1 is: (1) low scores on the belief scale are associated with moderately high scores on the final examination (subjects 1 and 2); (2) moderate scores on the belief scale are associated with high scores on the final examination (subjects 3, 4, and 7); and (3) high scores on the belief scale are associated with low scores on the final examination (subjects 5 and 6).

When scores in class 2 are examined, it is clear that as scores on the belief scale increase, so do scores on the achievement test, with one exception: subject 5 received a score of 9 on the belief scale and a score of 3 on the final exam. Finally, comparison of scores in the third class reveals that as scores on the belief scale increase, so do scores on the final exam, without exception.

When the number of subjects is small, the tabular form of the joint distribution can be used with some difficulty to identify relationships between two variables. When the number of subjects is large, this tabular display is almost impossible to use. Regardless of the number of subjects, it would be much easier to find patterns in the data with a graphical representation of the relationship between scores on two variables. This graphical representation would provide a *picture* of how the two variables "go together."

JOINT
DISTRIBUTION:
GRAPHICAL
REPRESENTATION

A graphical representation of a joint distribution is called a **scatterplot**. It provides a picture which shows pairs of scores for each of the subjects in a group. A scatterplot of the scores for subjects in class 1 is presented in Figure 6-1. Each point in the scatterplot represents one subject. There are seven points in Figure 6-1, representing the seven subjects in class 1. In order to show that each point represents one subject, each point is plotted as a circle surrounding the subject's identification number. If a line is drawn from a point in the scatterplot perpendicular to the abscissa (horizontal axis), the score on the belief scale for that particular subject can be read. If a line is drawn from the same point perpendicular to the ordinate (vertical axis), the same subject's achievement test score can be found. For example, the score for subject 3 on the belief scale is 6, and the score for this subject on the achievement test is 9 (broken lines in Figure 6-1). The steps in constructing a scatterplot are summarized in Procedure 6-1. Data from Class 3 are used as an example.

The relationship between scores on two variables such as the belief scale

Figure 6-1 ♦ Scatterplot of scores for subjects in class 1 (data from Table 6-1)

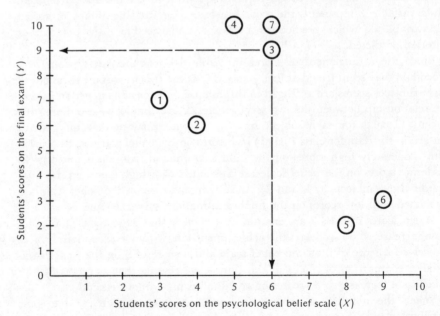

(variable X) and scores on the final exam (variable Y) is revealed by the points in the scatterplot. In addition, scatterplots for different groups of subjects can be compared to see if the relationships between the variables are the same in each group. Scatterplots for classes 1, 2, and 3 are shown in Figure 6-2. Lines are drawn on the scatterplots to highlight the pattern in the data.

For classes 1 and 2, a curved line best describes the relationship between scores on the belief scale and final exam. In other words, as scores on the belief

Steps in constructing a scatterplot (example data taken from class 3 in Table 6-1) ◆ Procedure 6-1

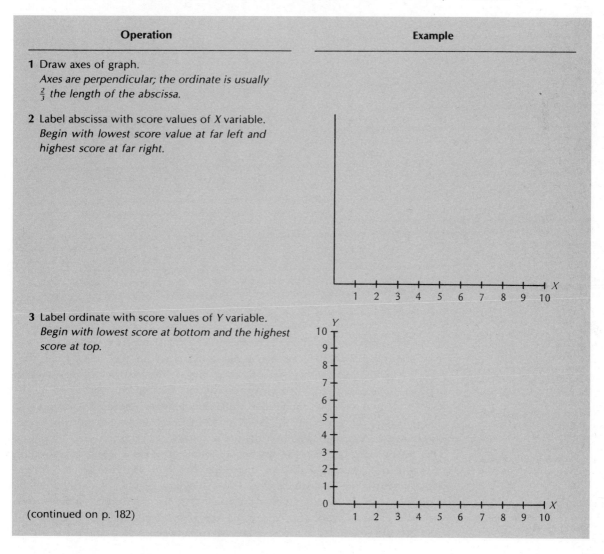

Operation	Example
1 Draw axes of graph. *Axes are perpendicular; the ordinate is usually $\frac{2}{3}$ the length of the abscissa.*	
2 Label abscissa with score values of X variable. *Begin with lowest score value at far left and highest score at far right.*	
3 Label ordinate with score values of Y variable. *Begin with lowest score at bottom and the highest score at top.*	

(continued on p. 182)

4 Plot one point for each subject so that:
  a a line drawn from the point perpendicular to the abscissa crosses the abscissa at the subject's score on the X variable, and
  b a line drawn from the point perpendicular to the ordinate crosses the ordinate at the subject's score on the Y variable.

5 Draw a line to highlight the pattern of the data if there is a systematic trend or pattern.

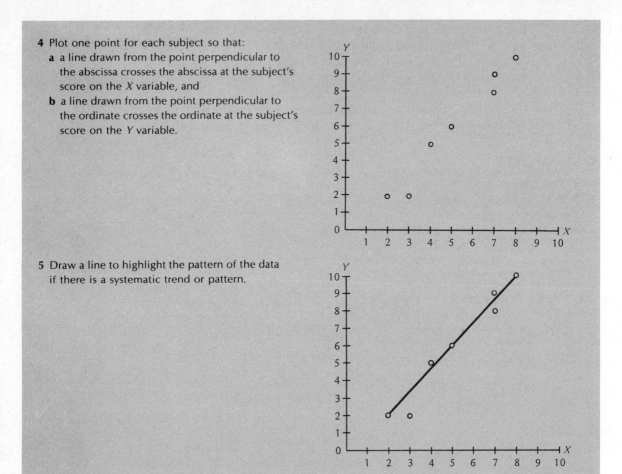

scale increase, so do scores on the exam, up to some point ($X = 6$ for class 1 and $X = 7$ for class 2). Then, as scores increase further on the belief scale, they decrease on the achievement test. Since a curved line best fits the relationship between the scores on the two measures, the relationship between scores on the belief scale and scores on the final exam is called a **curvilinear relationship**.

For class 3, as scores on the belief scale increase, scores on the final exam also increase. A straight line best fits the pattern of scores on the two measures. This relationship between the two sets of scores is called a **linear relationship**.

Figure 6-2 also highlights an important problem which arises in correlational studies. The problem is that a few "deviant points" or **outliers** on the scatterplot can drastically change the pattern of the relationship between two variables. This is especially true when the number of subjects is small. For example, we concluded that the relationship between beliefs and achievement

182

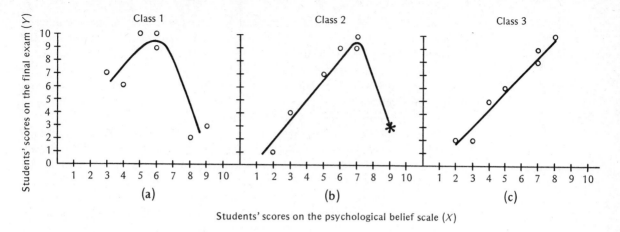

Figure 6-2 ♦ Comparison of scatterplots for each of the three classes in the study (data from Table 6-1)

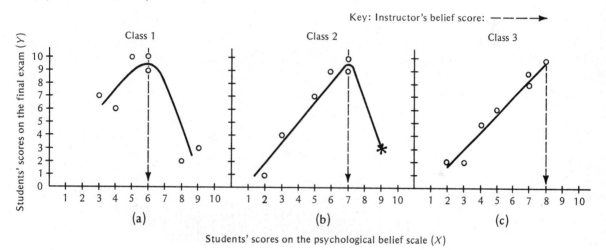

Figure 6-3 ♦ Scatterplots for three classes with instructor's belief score superimposed

was curvilinear in Classes 1 and 2. But suppose the starred point in the scatterplot for Class 2 represents a chance occurrence, e.g., that particular student might have been ill at the time the final exam was given. If that subject is ignored, the relationship between beliefs and achievement in Class 2 is no longer curvilinear, it is linear. The nature of the relationship is drastically changed.

In any correlational study, then, the data should be cast into a scatterplot and the scatterplot should be examined for deviant points in the data. If such outliers are found, the data can first be analyzed with the outliers included in the data and then with them deleted. If the pattern changes drastically, the researcher must decide what to do with the outliers. The decision of whether to include or ignore "outliers" will depend on the questions that the researcher wishes to answer and the information available. If a decision is made to ignore them, the researcher should give a full description—a kind of case study—of each subject representing an outlier.

Figure 6-3 presents the intriguing data in the Majasan study. It is the same as Figure 6-2 except that it contains information about the belief score of each of the three instructors. Notice that those students whose scores on the belief scale tend to agree with their instructor's belief score also tend to earn the highest scores on the final exam. The greater the difference between the student's and the instructor's beliefs, the lower the student's score is on the exam. This relationship between students' and instructors' beliefs and student achievement holds for all instructors even though the instructors obtained different scores on the belief scale.

♦　　♦　　♦　　♦　　♦

Summary　This chapter presents the concept of a *joint distribution* and describes procedures for constructing one in the form of a table or *scatterplot*. The joint distribution provides information about the relationship between two variables. These representations indicate whether the variables are systematically related to one another (changes in variable X are associated with changes in variable Y) or whether they are unrelated (changes in variable X are not systematically associated with changes in variable Y). The following chapter discusses a more precise measure of the relationship between two variables: the correlation coefficient.

♦　　♦　　♦　　♦　　♦

Key Words

curvilinear relationship	outlier
joint distribution	scatterplot
linear relationship	

♦　　♦　　♦　　♦　　♦

Exercises　1–4 A researcher was interested in the relationship between test anxiety and ability to solve complex problems. He administered a measure of test anxiety and a problem-solving measure to ten high-school juniors. Subjects obtained the following scores:

Adolescent Test Anxiety Scale			
Laurie	1	Mary	7
Hilda	2	Tom	8
Mike	4	Melanie	3
Bob	1	Larry	8
Amy	5	Mark	6

Fisher Complex Problems Test			
Mike	5	Tom	2
Amy	5	Mary	4
Laurie	2	Larry	3
Bob	3	Melanie	5
Hilda	4	Mark	4

1. Construct a joint distribution for the data above in tabular form.

2. Construct a scatterplot from the joint distribution in Exercise 1.

3. What can you conclude about the relationship between test anxiety and complex problem-solving from the scatterplot constructed in Exercise 2?

4. Is the relationship shown in the scatterplot constructed in Exercise 2 best described as linear or curvilinear?

5–9 A teacher training center at a large urban university decided to conduct a research program in order to improve their selection procedures. They were primarily interested in the relationship between certain characteristics of potential applicants, such as dogmatism, and student teaching performance. A portion of the data collected is shown below.

Teacher ID	Dogmatism scale (X)	Supervisor rating of student teaching performance (Y)
1	5	4
2	5	5
3	10	3
4	10	4
5	15	2
6	20	2
7	20	1
8	25	1

5. Construct a scatterplot for the data shown above.

6. What can you conclude about the relationship between dogmatism and performance in student teaching from these data?

7. Can this relationship be best described as linear or curvilinear?

8. Suppose that one student teacher who received a score of 25 on the Dogmatism Scale and a rating of 5 from his or her student teaching supervisor was not included in the data set above. How does the pattern of the data change if this teacher is included in the data set?

9. When would it be defensible to delete the teacher in (8) from the data set?

10–14 See Figure 6-4.

10. Is the trend in the data in this scatterplot best described as flat, linear, or curvilinear?

11. Which point on the scatterplot is probably an outlier?

12. Point E in the scatterplot represents what X and Y scores?

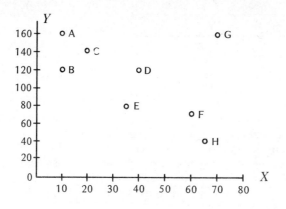

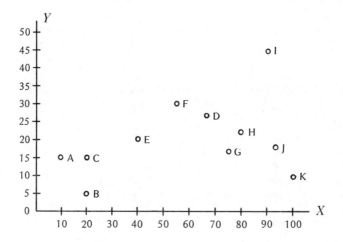

13. Which two points in the scatterplot represent the same score on X but different scores on Y?

14. Which of the points in the scatterplot represent the same score on Y but different scores on X?

15–19 See Figure 6-5.

15. Is the trend in the data best described as flat, linear, or curvilinear?

16. Which point on the scatterplot is probably an outlier?

17. Point A on the scatterplot represents what X and Y scores?

18. Which two points on the scatterplot represent the same score on Y but different scores on X?

19. Which two points on the scatterplot represent the same score on X but different scores on Y?

7.

Correlation

Characteristics of Correlation Coefficients

Development of the Correlation Coefficient: An Intuitive
Approach
♦ Deviation-Score Formula ♦
♦ Raw-Score Formula ♦

The Squared Correlation Coefficient, r_{XY}^2

Spearman Rank Correlation Coefficient

Sources of Misleading Correlation Coefficients
♦ Restriction of Range ♦
♦ Extreme Groups ♦
♦ Combining Groups ♦
♦ Outliers ♦
♦ Curvilinearity ♦

Correlation and Causality

Summary
♦ Key Words ♦
♦ Exercises ♦

THE RELATIONSHIP between two variables can be described numerically, as well as graphically by a scatterplot. The statistic that describes this relationship is called a correlation coefficient. The **correlation coefficient** is a measure of the strength of association between two variables. It reflects how closely scores on two variables go together. The more closely two variables go together, the stronger the association between them and the more extreme the correlation coefficient.

There are many different types of correlation coefficients. Most coefficients have been developed to measure the strength of relationship between two variables which show a *linear relationship* in a scatterplot. (See Figure 7-1 for examples of linear relationships.) In this chapter, the most widely used measure of the strength of relationship between two linearly related variables—the Pearson product-moment correlation coefficient—is presented. Actually, the Pearson correlation coefficient is a family of correlation coefficients; only some of the members of the family are introduced here.

CHARACTERISTICS OF CORRELATION COEFFICIENTS

When a correlation coefficient is used to describe a linear relationship, the coefficient can take on values from -1.00 to $+1.00$. The *sign* of the correlation indicates the *direction* of the relationship between two variables. A **positive relationship** means that low scores on X go with low scores on Y while high scores on X go with high scores on Y. In other words, it indicates that as scores on X increase, scores on Y also increase. A positive relationship is denoted by a $+$ (plus or positive) sign or the absence of a sign in front of the correlation coefficient. A **negative relationship** means that as scores on X increase, scores on Y decrease. That is, low scores on one measure go with high scores on the other measure and vice versa. A negative relationship is always denoted by a $-$ (minus or negative) sign in front of the correlation coefficient.

The absolute *magnitude* or size of the correlation coefficient—that is, ignoring the plus or minus sign—indicates the strength of the relationship between the two variables. A correlation of $+0.95$ reflects a very strong relationship between X and Y. A correlation of -0.95 also reflects a very strong relationship. A correlation coefficient of 0 indicates that there is no linear relationship.

The correlation coefficient is a *descriptive statistic* used to summarize the relationship between two variables represented in a joint distribution. Figure 7-1 shows a series of joint distributions in which each set of variables has a linear relationship. Notice that in Figure 7-1 a–c, the points in the scatterplot rise from left to right. As scores on X increase, scores on Y increase. There is a

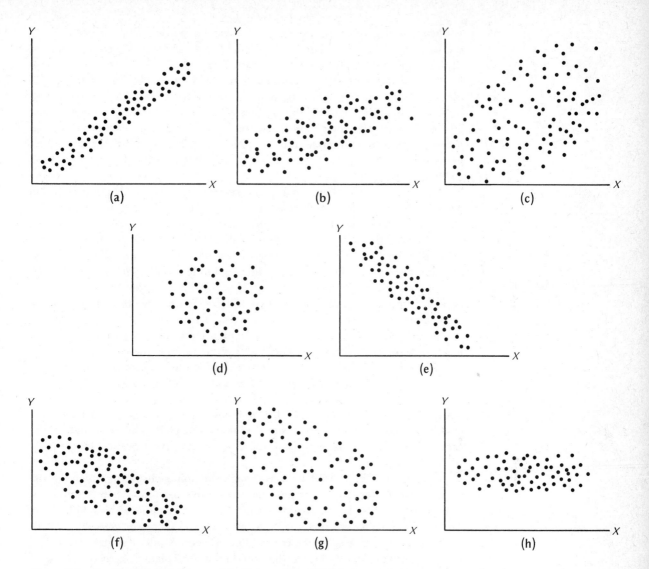

Figure 7-1 ◆ Scatterplots of some possible linear relationships between two variables

positive relationship between X and Y. Therefore, the correlation between X and Y will be positive. The points in Figure 7-1 e–g fall from the upper left of the joint distribution to the lower right. As scores on X increase, scores on Y decrease. There is a negative relationship between X and Y. Therefore, the correlation between X and Y will be negative and the correlation coefficient will always be preceded by a minus sign. Finally, in Figure 7-1 d and h, as scores on X increase, scores on Y may either increase or decrease; there is no relationship between X and Y. The correlation coefficient will be zero.

Two characteristics of a scatterplot provide important clues to determining the magnitude of a correlation coefficient: (1) the slope of the scatterplot and (2) the degree to which the points in the scatterplot cluster about an imaginary line representing the slope. Consider first the slope of the scatterplot. If the scatterplot can be represented by a line drawn either parallel to the abscissa (a horizontal line) or perpendicular to the abscissa (a vertical line), the magnitude of the correlation is zero. Notice that in Figure 7-1 d, a horizontal or vertical line can be used to represent the scatterplot. If the slope of the line *is not* horizontal or vertical to the abscissa, the magnitude of the correlation coefficient is not zero.

If the slope of the scatterplot is not horizontal or vertical, the correlation coefficient is not zero and the magnitude of the coefficient depends upon how closely the points cluster about an imaginary line representing the slope of the scatterplot. If the points cluster tightly about the line, the magnitude of the correlation coefficient is high. If they scatter way out, it is low. This clustering of points around the line and, thus, the magnitude of the correlation coefficient depends on the variability of X and Y as well as the degree of association between the two variables. This point will become clearer in later sections of this chapter.

Figure 7-1 a and e show points tightly clustered about the slope; the magnitude of the correlation coefficient summarizing these two scatterplots would be high (0.80 or above). They would differ only in sign (plus and minus, respectively). The points in Figure 7-1 b and f cluster somewhat more widely about the slope, so the magnitude of the correlation summarizing these two scatterplots would be moderate (0.40 to 0.60). Finally, the points in Figure 7-1 c and g scatter widely about the slopes of the scatterplots. The magnitude of the correlation coefficient summarizing those two scatterplots would be low (0.30 or less).

Notice that in Figure 7-1 h, even though the points cluster tightly about the slope of the scatterplot, the slope is parallel to the abscissa. When a horizontal slope is found, the correlation coefficient is zero regardless of how tightly the scores cluster. What this means is: as scores on X increase, *scores on Y do not systematically change*. Hence, the correlation between X and Y is zero. Similarly, when a vertical slope is found, the correlation coefficient is zero regardless of how tightly the scores cluster. What this means is: as scores on Y increase, *scores on X do not systematically change*. Hence, the correlation between X and Y is zero.

DEVELOPMENT OF THE CORRELATION COEFFICIENT: AN INTUITIVE APPROACH

Up to this point, a scatterplot has been used to get "eyeball" estimates of the magnitude and sign of the correlation coefficient. Now, let's develop a statistic —the correlation coefficient—that describes the relationships shown in Figure 7-1. In order to clarify the ideas presented, the data shown in Table 7-1 will be used as an example.

Table 7-1 ◆ Relationships between Scholastic Aptitude Test scores and grade-point averages at Bart Farguart College

Student	SAT (X)	GPA (Y)	Scatterplot
1	450	2.40	
2	500	3.12	
3	525	3.05	
4	650	3.19	
5	760	3.74	
Σ	2885.00	15.50	
$\overline{X}$	577.00	3.10	
s	126.08	0.48	

First, since a joint distribution or scatterplot shows how two variables *go together*, the measure of the relationship between these variables should show how the scores go together (how they covary). In order to see how scores covary, begin by comparing the SAT score and the GPA for the first student. In making the comparison, a major problem is encountered immediately. The variables are measured on different score scales. GPA is measured on a 4-point scale, while SAT scores can be as high as 800 points. A direct comparison, then, is impossible. The first step toward solving this problem of comparing scores on different measurement scales is to represent each score on each variable as a deviation score. This would provide a measure of how far each score on each measure is from the mean for that variable. For example, subject 1's deviation score on the SAT is

$$x = X - \overline{X} = 450 - 577 = -127.$$

Her deviation score on the GPA is

$$y = Y - \overline{Y} = 2.40 - 3.10 = -0.70.$$

This seems to be a reasonable beginning. We now know that student 1 earned scores below the mean of each variable. This rescaling is completed for the scores of the other four subjects on columns (b)–(g) in Table 7-2.

Table 7-2 ♦ Covariance of Scholastic Aptitude Test scores with grade-point averages at Bart Farguart College

(a) Student	(b) X	(c) $\bar{X}$	(d) x $X - \bar{X}$	(e) Y	(f) $\bar{Y}$	(g) y $Y - \bar{Y}$	(h) xy
1	450	577	−127	2.40	3.10	−.70	88.90
2	500	577	−77	3.12	3.10	.02	−1.54
3	525	577	−52	3.05	3.10	−.05	2.60
4	650	577	73	3.19	3.10	.09	6.57
5	760	577	183	3.74	3.10	.64	117.12
Σ	2885.00	2885.00	0	15.50	15.50	0	213.65

We are now in a position to get a measure of how the two sets of deviation scores go together or covary. By multiplying each student's x score by his y score, a measure of covariation is obtained for each person. This product is called a **cross-product**. The cross-product for each person is shown in column (h) of Table 7-2. Notice that when a subject's scores on both measures deviate markedly from the mean for that measure (i.e., $|x|$ and $|y|$ are large), the cross-products are large. (See subjects 1 and 5 in Table 7-2.) When subjects' scores on both measures are close to their respective means (i.e., $|x|$ and $|y|$ are small), the cross-product is small. (See subjects 2, 3, and 4 in Table 7-2.) Thus, this procedure gives us a measure of the covariation between X and Y for each person.

Ultimately, however, we are interested in describing the relationship between X and Y over the entire group rather than for particular individuals. Thus, we need to obtain a measure of the average covariation between pairs of scores for all students. To obtain a measure of the average covariation between pairs of scores, we then add the cross-products (x, y) and divide by $N - 1$, where N is the number of persons. (See footnote 6 in Chapter 4 for an explanation of why $N - 1$ and not N is used to obtain this average. See also the discussion of degrees of freedom in Chapter 14.) In our example, the sum of the cross-products is 213.65. (In adding the cross-products, be sure to pay attention to the *sign* of each cross-product.) To obtain the average covariation, divide this sum by $N - 1 = 4$:

$$213.65 \div 4 = 53.41.$$

Let's summarize briefly. To get a measure of covariance—how scores covary—raw scores were converted to deviation scores to obtain a measure of how far each score deviated from the mean. Then, to get a measure of the covariation of pairs of scores, the cross-product of each subject's deviation scores was found by multiplying each subject's deviation score on variable X by his deviation score on variable Y. Then to find the average covariation between X and Y over all subjects, the cross-products were summed and divided by $N-1$.

At this point the statistic called the covariance has been obtained. The **covariance** is the sum of the cross-products of the deviation scores divided by $N-1$ or, in other words, the average of the sum of the cross-products of deviation scores on two variables. The formula for the covariance, Cov_{XY}, can be written as

$$Cov_{XY} = \frac{\Sigma(X - \bar{X})(Y - \bar{Y})}{N - 1} = \frac{\Sigma xy}{N - 1}. \qquad [7\text{-}1]$$

In the formula, Cov_{XY} stands for the covariance of variables X and Y. Cov_{XY} is a measure of how two variables go together, or *covary*. The other symbols should be familiar to you. By inserting information from Table 7-2 into the formula, we get

$$Cov_{XY} = \frac{\Sigma xy}{N - 1}$$

$$= \frac{(-127 \times -.70) + (-77 \times .02) + (-52 \times -.05) + (73 \times .09) + (183 \times .64)}{5 - 1}$$

$$= \frac{213.65}{4}$$

$$= 53.41.$$

The covariance measures the direction and magnitude of relationship between two variables. However, the covariance has one severe limitation. Its magnitude depends upon the variability of scores on X and on Y. If the scores are quite spread out on both X and Y, then $X - \bar{X}$ and $Y - \bar{Y}$ will be quite large, and so will be the sum of their cross-products, $\Sigma(X - \bar{X})(Y - \bar{Y})$. In short, the magnitude of the covariance depends upon the standard deviation of X and the standard deviation of Y. Thus, it is impossible, for example, to compare the six possible covariances obtained from a set of four different measures such as achievement, verbal aptitude, self-concept, and anxiety. Differences in covariances may be due to differences in relationships between pairs of variables, differences in standard deviations, or both.

A last step, then, must be taken in order to develop a precise measure of the relationship between X and Y: the correlation coefficient. Variable X and variable Y must be corrected for differences in standard deviation. This can be done by dividing the covariance by the product of the standard deviation of X and the standard deviation of Y:[1]

$$\text{Correlation}(X,\ Y) = r_{XY} = \frac{\text{Cov}_{XY}}{s_X s_Y}. \qquad [7\text{-}2]$$

This value, r_{XY}, is called the **Pearson product-moment correlation coefficient**. It is defined as the covariance of X and Y divided by the product of the standard deviation of X and the standard deviation of Y. It has just those properties of correlation coefficients described in the beginning of the chapter: (1) it provides a measure of the strength of association between two variables, (2) it describes a linear relationship between two variables, and (3) it can take on values from -1.00 to $+1.00$, where the absolute magnitude provides an index of the strength of the relationship between the two variables and the sign indicates the direction of the relationship.

---

[1]This equating of X and Y for standard deviations amounts to converting scores on X to z_X scores and scores on Y to z_Y scores. As you know from Chapter 5, z scores have unit standard deviations: $s_{z_X} = s_{z_Y} = 1$. Therefore, the correlation coefficient can be thought of as a covariance of z_X and z_Y scores, that is, a measure of the average covariation between z_X and z_Y scores over all pairs of scores.

Mathematically, it works like this:

$$r_{XY} = \frac{\text{Cov}_{XY}}{s_X s_Y}$$

$$= \frac{\dfrac{\Sigma xy}{N-1}}{s_X s_Y}$$

$$= \frac{\dfrac{1}{N-1}\Sigma xy}{s_X s_Y}$$

$$= \frac{1}{N-1}\frac{\Sigma x}{s_X s_Y}$$

$$= \frac{1}{N-1}\Sigma\left[\frac{X-\bar{X}}{s_X}\cdot\frac{Y-\bar{Y}}{s_Y}\right]$$

$$= \frac{1}{N-1}\Sigma(z_X z_Y)$$

$$= \frac{\Sigma(z_X z_Y)}{N-1}$$

$$= \text{Cov}_{z_X z_Y}.$$

The correlation between SAT scores and GPAs sampled at Farguart College, then, can be found using information from Tables 7-1 and 7-2. From Table 7-2, the sum of cross-products is 213.65. So $\text{Cov}_{XY} = 213.65 \div (5-1) = 53.41$. From Table 7-1, $s_X = 126.08$ and $s_Y = .48$. Thus,

$$r_{XY} = \frac{\text{Cov}_{XY}}{s_X s_Y} = \frac{53.41}{(126.08)(0.48)} = \frac{53.41}{60.52} = 0.89.$$

The correlation between scores on the SAT and GPAs is 0.89. This statistical finding corresponds to what one might expect from eyeballing the scatterplot in Table 7-1. The points show a linear relationship with a positive slope, indicating that the correlation is positive. (Note: If the covariance had been negative, the correlation coefficient would have been negative also.) Finally, the points cluster closely about an imaginary straight line drawn through them; the magnitude of the correlation coefficient is what we expected from an "eyeball" analysis.

◆ ◆ ◆ ◆ ◆

The formula, 7-2,

Deviation-Score Formula

$$r_{XY} = \frac{\text{Cov}_{XY}}{s_X s_Y}. \qquad [\textbf{7-2}]$$

developed above for r_{XY} is often referred to as the **deviation-score formula** for the Pearson product-moment correlation. The name "deviation-score" reflects the fact that deviation scores, $x = X - \overline{X}$ and $y = Y - \overline{Y}$, must be computed to use Formula 7-2. In computing this correlation, the first step is to make a scatterplot of the two variables of interest. If the scatterplot can be approximated by a straight line, Formula 7-2 can be used to calculate the correlation coefficient.[2]

For reference, the steps in computing this correlation coefficient are shown in Procedure 7-1 using data from class 3 in the Majasan study. The scatterplot in Procedure 7-1 shows a linear relationship between scores on the Psychological Belief Scale and scores on the final exam in class 3. The correlation between these variables is 0.98. This correlation coefficient is consistent with an eyeball analysis of the scatterplot. The slope of the points in the scatterplot is not horizontal; it rises from lower left to upper right. Hence, the correlation should not be zero; it should be positive. The points in the scatterplot cluster closely about the imaginary line, indicating a linear relation. The correlation coefficient, then, should be positive and large in magnitude. This means that there is a very strong relationship between scores on the belief scale and scores

---

[2]If the scatterplot cannot be described as linear, the Pearson product-moment correlation coefficient may not provide the best measure of the relationship between X and Y. For curvilinear relationships, the correlation ratio η (eta) should be used. (See Guilford & Fruchter, 1973, p. 285 ff.)

Procedure 7-1 ♦ Steps in calculating the Pearson product-moment correlation, r_{XY}, using deviation scores (data from class 3 of Majasan study; see Table 6-1)

Operation	Example

1 Look up the *deviation-score formula*:

$$r_{XY} = \frac{Cov_{XY}}{s_X s_Y}$$

2 Draw a scatterplot to check that X and Y are *linearly* related.
See Procedure 6-1 for constructing a scatterplot.

Class 3

Students' scores on the final exam (Y)

Students' scores on the psychological belief scale (X)

3 Set up a table with the following columns: X, $\bar{X}$, x, Y, $\bar{Y}$, y, xy.

X	$\bar{X}$	x	Y	$\bar{Y}$	y	xy

4 For each subject, enter the scores on variables X and Y in the appropriate columns.

X	$\bar{X}$	x	Y	$\bar{Y}$	y	xy
8			10			
7			8			
3			2			
5			6			
7			9			
2			2			
4			5			

5 Calculate the means of X and Y, and enter in the columns labeled $\bar{X}$ and $\bar{Y}$.
See Procedure 4-3 for calculating a mean.

X	$\bar{X}$	x	Y	$\bar{Y}$	y	xy
8	5.14		10	6.00		
7	5.14		8	6.00		
3	5.14		2	6.00		
5	5.14		6	6.00		
7	5.14		9	6.00		
2	5.14		2	6.00		
4	5.14		5	6.00		

6 Calculate deviation scores for the X and Y variables by subtracting the mean from each raw score:

$$x = X - \bar{X},$$
$$y = Y - \bar{Y}.$$

X	$\bar{X}$	x	Y	$\bar{Y}$	y	xy
8	5.14	2.86	10	6.00	4.00	
7	5.14	1.86	8	6.00	2.00	
3	5.14	−2.14	2	6.00	−4.00	
5	5.14	−.14	6	6.00	.00	
7	5.14	1.86	9	6.00	3.00	
2	5.14	−3.14	2	6.00	−4.00	
4	5.14	−1.14	5	6.00	−1.00	

7 Multiply each subject's deviation score x for variable X by his or her deviation score y for variable Y to obtain the cross-product for each subject (xy).
Pay attention to the signs of x and y when multiplying.

X	$\bar{X}$	x	Y	$\bar{Y}$	y	xy
8	5.14	2.86	10	6.00	4.00	11.44
7	5.14	1.86	8	6.00	2.00	3.72
3	5.14	−2.14	2	6.00	−4.00	8.56
5	5.14	−.14	6	6.00	.00	.00
7	5.14	1.86	9	6.00	3.00	5.58
2	5.14	−3.14	2	6.00	−4.00	12.56
4	5.14	−1.14	5	6.00	−1.00	1.14

8 Sum cross-products to obtain Σxy.
Pay attention to the sign of each cross-product when summing.

X	$\bar{X}$	x	Y	$\bar{Y}$	y	xy
8	5.14	2.86	10	6.00	4.00	11.44
7	5.14	1.86	8	6.00	2.00	3.72
3	5.14	−2.14	2	6.00	−4.00	8.56
5	5.14	−.14	6	6.00	.00	.00
7	5.14	1.86	9	6.00	3.00	5.58
2	5.14	−3.14	2	6.00	−4.00	12.56
4	5.14	−1.14	5	6.00	−1.00	1.14
					$\Sigma xy =$	43.00

9 Divide Σxy (found in step 9) by $N - 1$ to obtain

$$\text{Cov}_{XY} = \frac{\Sigma xy}{N-1}.$$

$$\frac{43.00}{6} = 7.17$$

This value is known as the covariance.

10 Calculate the standard deviations (s_X and s_Y) of X and Y.
See Procedures 4-7 and 4-8 for calculating a standard deviation.

$$s_X = 2.27$$
$$s_Y = 3.21$$

11 Multiply s_X by s_Y.

$$(2.27)(3.21) = 7.29$$

12 Divide the Cov_{XY} (found in step 9) by $s_X s_Y$ (found in step 11) to obtain

$$\frac{7.17}{7.29} = .98$$

$$r_{XY} = \frac{\text{Cov}_{XY}}{s_X s_Y}$$

$$= \frac{\frac{\Sigma xy}{N-1}}{s_X s_Y}.$$

Table 7-3 ♦ Hypothetical aptitude and achievement scores at UCLA, collected in the College Achievement Study (data from Table 2-5)

Student	GPA	SAT
1	2.90	1050
2	2.00	1200
3	3.50	1100
4	3.20	1130
5	2.50	1160
6	2.90	1075
7	3.60	1100
8	2.30	1025
9	3.00	1000
10	2.50	1000

on the final exam. Since a high score represents a strong belief in behaviorism, the correlation coefficient tells us that the greater the student's belief in behaviorism, the higher her score on the final exam given in class 3.

EXAMPLE PROBLEM 1   In the study of men's and women's college achievement described in Chapter 2, aptitude and achievement information was collected for a large number of undergraduates at several campuses of the University of California. Table 7-3 shows the hypothetical SAT scores and GPAs collected at one of the campuses (UCLA). Compute the correlation between these measures using the deviation-score formula.

Raw-Score Formula   While the deviation-score formula (7-2) makes sense conceptually, this formula is time consuming and tedious to use. When a calculator is available, the **raw-score formula** provides a less tedious method for calculating the Pearson correlation coefficient:

$$r_{XY} = \frac{N(\Sigma XY) - (\Sigma X)(\Sigma Y)}{\sqrt{\left[N\Sigma X^2 - (\Sigma X)^2\right]\left[N\Sigma Y^2 - (\Sigma Y)^2\right]}} \qquad [7\text{-}3]$$

At first glance, it may not be obvious that this equation provides a less tedious approach to finding the correlation between X and Y. However, it does, because it works directly with raw scores and does not require calculation of means ($\overline{X}$, $\overline{Y}$) and standard deviations (s_X, s_Y) as the deviation-score formula does. First, let's decipher the formula. The numerator turns out to contain a raw-score formula for covariance. The terms in the denominator represent raw-score formulas for s_X and s_Y. Since Cov_{XY}, s_X, and s_Y all are divided by $N-1$, this term has been dropped from the numerator and denominator. (This is an extreme oversimplification; for the derivation of the raw-score formula from the deviation-score formula, see footnote 3.)[3] Procedure 7-2 shows the

[3]The following mathematical proof shows the equivalence of the deviation-score and raw-score formulas for the Pearson correlation coefficient:

$$r_{XY} = \frac{\text{Cov}_{XY}}{s_X s_Y} = \frac{N(\Sigma XY) - (\Sigma X)(\Sigma Y)}{\sqrt{[N\Sigma X^2 - (\Sigma X)^2][N\Sigma Y^2 - (\Sigma Y)^2]}}.$$

$$\frac{\text{Cov}_{XY}}{s_X s_Y} = \frac{\frac{\Sigma xy}{N-1}}{s_X s_Y} \qquad\qquad \text{by definition}$$

$$= \frac{\Sigma xy}{(N-1)s_X s_Y} \qquad\qquad \text{simplifying terms.}$$

Dealing only with the numerator,

$$\Sigma xy = \Sigma(X - \overline{X})(Y - \overline{Y}) \qquad\qquad \text{by definition}$$

$$= \Sigma(XY - X\overline{Y} - \overline{X}Y + \overline{X}\overline{Y}) \qquad\qquad \text{expansion of a polynomial}$$

$$= \Sigma XY - \overline{Y}\Sigma X - \overline{X}\Sigma Y + N\overline{X}\overline{Y} \qquad\qquad \begin{array}{l}\text{distribution of summation}\\ \text{sign and effects of constants}\end{array}$$

$$= \Sigma XY - \frac{(\Sigma Y)(\Sigma X)}{N} - \frac{(\Sigma X)(\Sigma Y)}{N} + \frac{N(\Sigma X)(\Sigma Y)}{(N)(N)} \qquad \begin{array}{l}\text{substitution } (\Sigma X/N \text{ for } \overline{X};\\ \text{and } \Sigma Y/N \text{ for } \overline{Y})\end{array}$$

$$= \Sigma XY - \frac{2(\Sigma X)(\Sigma Y)}{N} + \frac{(\Sigma X)(\Sigma Y)}{N} \qquad\qquad \text{simplifying terms}$$

$$= \Sigma XY - \frac{(\Sigma X)(\Sigma Y)}{N} \qquad\qquad \text{combining terms.}$$

Now, turning to the denominator,

$$s_X = \sqrt{\frac{1}{N-1}\left[\Sigma X^2 - \frac{(\Sigma X)^2}{N}\right]} \qquad\qquad \text{by definition (see Chapter 4)}$$

$$s_Y = \sqrt{\frac{1}{N-1}\left[\Sigma Y^2 - \frac{(\Sigma Y)^2}{N}\right]} \qquad\qquad \text{by definition.}$$

Therefore,

$$(N-1)s_X s_Y = (N-1)\sqrt{\frac{1}{N-1}\left[\Sigma X^2 - \frac{(\Sigma X)^2}{N}\right]}\sqrt{\frac{1}{N-1}\left[\Sigma Y^2 - \frac{(\Sigma Y)^2}{N}\right]} \quad \text{by substitution}$$

$$= \sqrt{\left[\Sigma X^2 - \frac{(\Sigma X)^2}{N}\right]\left[\Sigma Y^2 - \frac{(\Sigma Y)^2}{N}\right]} \qquad\qquad \text{by cancellation, since}$$

Table 7-4 ♦ Hypothetical aptitude and achievement scores at UCD, collected in the College Achievement Study (data from Table 2-5)

Student	GPA	SAT
11	2.90	1175
12	3.20	1125
13	3.00	1100
14	2.70	1150
15	2.50	1200
16	2.50	1120
17	3.30	1090
18	3.00	1100
19	2.90	1085
20	3.20	1125

computational steps in using the raw score formula using data from Procedure 7-1. Again, the correlation between scores in the belief scale and the final exam is 0.98 (not unexpectedly).

EXAMPLE PROBLEM 2 Calculate the correlation between the aptitude and achievement scores for students at UCD shown in Table 7-4, using the raw-score formula.

$$(N-1)\left(\sqrt{\frac{1}{N-1}}\ \sqrt{\frac{1}{N-1}}\ \right) = \frac{N-1}{N-1} = 1.$$

Now, combining the numerator and denominator:

$$r_{XY} = \frac{\Sigma XY - \frac{\Sigma X \Sigma Y}{N}}{\sqrt{\left[\Sigma X^2 - \frac{(\Sigma X)^2}{N}\right]\left[\Sigma Y^2 - \frac{(\Sigma Y)^2}{N}\right]}} \qquad \text{by substitution.}$$

Finally,

$$r_{XY} = \frac{N(\Sigma XY) - (\Sigma X)(\Sigma Y)}{\sqrt{[N\Sigma X^2 - (\Sigma X)^2][N\Sigma Y^2 - (\Sigma Y)^2]}}$$

by multiplying by $N/\sqrt{N^2}$, which equals 1.

Steps in calculating the Pearson product-moment correlation r_{XY} using the raw-score ♦ Procedure 7-2
formula (same example data as Procedure 5-1)

Operation	Example

1 Look up the *raw-score formula* (Formula 7-3):

$$r_{XY} = \frac{N(\Sigma XY) - (\Sigma X)(\Sigma Y)}{\sqrt{[N\Sigma X^2 - (\Sigma X)^2][N\Sigma Y^2 - (\Sigma Y)^2]}}.$$

2 Draw a scatterplot to check that X and Y are
linearly related
See Procedure 6-1 for construction of a scatterplot.

Class 3

Students' scores on the achievement test (Y)

Students' scores on the psychological belief scale (X)

3 Set up a table with the following columns: X, X^2,
Y, Y^2, XY.

X	X^2	Y	Y^2	XY

4 For each student, enter the score on variables X
and Y in their columns.

X	X^2	Y	Y^2	XY
8		10		
7		8		
3		2		
5		6		
7		9		
2		2		
4		5		

5 Square each X score to obtain X^2 and each Y score
to obtain Y^2 for each subject.

X	X^2	Y	Y^2	XY
8	64	10	100	
7	49	8	64	
3	9	2	4	
5	25	6	36	
7	49	9	81	
2	4	2	4	
4	16	5	25	

(continued on p. 202)

6 Multiply each X score by the corresponding Y score to obtain XY for each subject.

X	X^2	Y	Y^2	XY
8	64	10	100	80
7	49	8	64	56
3	9	2	4	6
5	25	6	36	30
7	49	9	81	63
2	4	2	4	4
4	16	5	25	20

7 Sum each column to obtain $\Sigma X, \Sigma X^2, \Sigma Y, \Sigma Y^2, \Sigma XY$.

X	X^2	Y	Y^2	XY
8	64	10	100	80
7	49	8	64	56
3	9	2	4	6
5	25	6	36	30
7	49	9	81	63
2	4	2	4	4
4	16	5	25	20
$\Sigma 36$	216	42	314	259

8 Insert these into the raw-score formula (Formula 7-3) and solve for r_{XY}:

$$r_{XY} = \frac{N(\Sigma XY) - (\Sigma X)(\Sigma Y)}{\sqrt{[N\Sigma X^2 - (\Sigma X)^2][N\Sigma Y^2 - (\Sigma Y)^2]}}$$

Remember that ΣX^2 and ΣY^2 represent the sums of the squares of each of the X and Y scores, respectively. In contrast, $(\Sigma X)^2$ and $(\Sigma Y)^2$ represent the squares of the sums of the X and Y scores, respectively.

$$r_{XY} = \frac{7(259) - (36)(42)}{\sqrt{[7(216) - (36)^2][7(314) - (42)^2]}}$$

$$= \frac{301}{306.18}$$

$$= .98$$

THE SQUARED CORRELATION COEFFICIENT: r_{XY}^2

Recall that the Pearson product-moment correlation coefficient provides a measure of the strength of association between X and Y. The larger the absolute value of r_{XY}, the stronger the relationship between X and Y. When r_{XY} is squared (r_{XY}^2), it can be interpreted as the proportion of variability in Y that can be accounted for by knowing X or the proportion of variability in X that can be accounted for by knowing Y.

In order to give r_{XY}^2 some meaning, the concept of percentage of variance needs to be explained. The scores on the belief scale (X) vary from one subject to another as do scores on the final exam. This variability on each measure can be described by the standard deviation (s_X and s_Y), or the variance (s_X^2 and s_Y^2). The variability in X is due to two factors: (1) predictable differences between subjects (i.e., differences in beliefs) and (2) random error (i.e., unsystematic differences between subjects unrelated to differences in beliefs, such as fatigue, inattention, misunderstanding of instructions, etc.). Similarly, the variability in Y is also affected by these two factors. Thus the correlation coefficient might be thought of as a ratio, with the numerator representing the common variability or covariability between X and Y (covariance), and the denominator representing the total possible variability of X and Y ($s_X \cdot s_Y$). When this coefficient is squared, the result is a ratio of variances, with the **common variance** shared by X and Y in the numerator, and the total variance in the denominator:

$$r_{XY}^2 = \frac{(\text{Cov}_{XY})^2}{s_X^2 s_Y^2} = \frac{\text{shared variance}}{\text{total variance}}.$$

In other words, r_{XY}^2 gives the proportion of the total variance shared by X and Y. Put still another way, r_{XY}^2 is the proportion of variance in Y predictable from X or vice versa. The actual **percentage of variance** in Y **accounted for** by X can be found with the following formula:

> Percentage of variance in Y accounted for by knowing X
> $$= r_{XY}^2 \times 100 \qquad [\textbf{7-4}]$$

Within a correlation of .98, the percentage of variance in Y accounted for by X is:

$$.98^2 \times 100 = .96 \times 100 = 96 \text{ percent.}$$

Figure 7-2 provides a pictorial representation of the concept of percentage of variance accounted for. The circle labeled X represents the variability of scores on X, and the circle labeled Y represents the variability of scores on Y. The

Figure 7-2 ♦ Percent of variance in Y (X) accounted for by knowing X (Y)

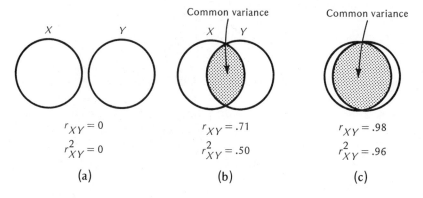

greater the overlap of circles, (1) the greater the common variance shared by X and Y (i.e., the stronger the relationship between X and Y), (2) the greater the percentage of variance in Y that is accounted for by knowing X, and (3) the greater the percentage of variance in X that is accounted for by knowing Y. For example, Figure 7-2a represents the case in which X and Y do not share variability in common; they are independent and $r_{XY}^2 = 0$. Figure 7-2b shows the case in which X and Y share a moderate percentage of variance in common, i.e., X is moderately predictable from Y, and Y is moderately predictable from X. Finally, Figure 7-2c represents the percentage of variance in exam scores accounted for by variability in scores on the belief scale—96 percent. In this case, almost all the variability in Y is accounted for by variability in X and vice versa.

Example Problem 3

What percentage of the variance in grade-point averages reported in Table 7-3 is accounted for by SAT scores?

♦   ♦   ♦   ♦   ♦

Spearman Rank Correlation Coefficient

The Pearson correlation coefficient is a measure of the *linear* relationship between X and Y. However, linearity is not always found for data in the behavioral sciences. As we saw in Chapter 6, the relationship between beliefs and achievement in psychology classes may be curvilinear.

Several cases of curvilinearity can be distinguished. Some examples are provided in Figure 7-3. In Figure 7-3 a and b, the scatterplots "just miss" being linear; they are *weak* examples of curvilinear relationships. (More marked curvilinear relationships are shown in Figure 7-3 c and d.) The scatterplots in Figure 7-3 a and b show Y to be *monotonically* related to X. A **monotonic relationship** is one in which an increase in scores on one variable is always accompanied by an increase in scores on a second variable (monotone increasing) or by a decrease in such scores (monotone decreasing). Put another way, a monotonic relationship is one where the scatterplots (curves) are everywhere increasing or everywhere decreasing. In Figure 7-3a, Y decreases at a faster rate (steeper slope) for low values of X, and continues to decrease, though at a slower rate (less steep slope), for high levels of X. In this case, Y is described as a **monotonically decreasing function** of X. In Figure 7-3b, just the reverse occurs. Initially, Y increases at a slower rate for low values of X and continues to increase, though at a faster rate, for high values of X. In this case, Y is described as a **monotonically increasing function** of X. The Spearman rank correlation can be used when a nonlinear, monotonically increasing or decreasing function describes the relation between X and Y. Furthermore, the Spearman coefficient can be used when the original data are ordinal, as with ranks

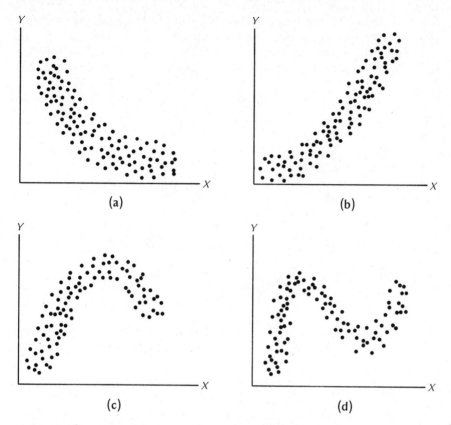

Figure 7-3 ◆ Examples of several curvilinear relationships between two variables

(e.g., a teacher's ranking of students as to their achievement and cooperation in class).

When a monotonic relationship between X and Y exists, scores on continuous variables are converted to scores representing each person's rank on the variables (from lowest = 1, next lowest = 2, . . . , highest = N). By converting scores to ranks, a scatterplot of the monotonic relationship between X and Y is converted to a scatterplot of rank scores which is *linear*. With a linear relationship of rank scores, the **Spearman rank correlation coefficient**, r_S, can be computed. It is the Pearson coefficient for ranks. It reflects the magnitude and direction of the relationship between X and Y.

As an example, consider some hypothetical data on the relationship between scores on an extroversion scale and scores on a humor scale presented in Table 7-5. The scatterplot in this table shows that Y is a monotonically increasing function of X. Hence, the usual product-moment coefficient on the original scores may not be appropriate. The rank-order correlation, then, is an appropriate correlation coefficient for these data.

Ranks on X and Y are shown in Table 7-6 along with the scatterplot of the

Table 7-5 ♦ Data bearing on the relationship between scores on extroversion (X) and humor (Y)

Person	Extroversion (X)	Humor (Y)	Scatterplot of X and Y
1	1	4	
2	1	8	
3	2	10	
4	3	14	
5	4	15	
6	5	16	
7	6	17	
8	7	18	
9	8	18	

Table 7-6 ♦ Rank-order data bearing on the relationship between extroversion (X) and humor (Y)

Person	Extroversion (X)	Humor (Y)	Scatterplot of ranks on X and Y
1	1.5	1	
2	1.5	2	
3	3	3	
4	4	4	
5	5	5	
6	6	6	
7	7	7	
8	8	8.5	
9	9	8.5	

206

ranked data. Notice the difference between the scatterplots in Tables 7-5 and 7-6. The monotonic relation between scores on X and Y in Table 7-5 has been converted to a linear relation between ranks on X and Y in Table 7-6.

With scores on X and Y transformed to rank scores on X and Y, a

Steps in computing the Spearman rank correlation coefficient (r_s) using data from ♦ Procedure 7-3
Table 7-5 as an example

Operation	Example			

Operation	**Example**

1 Set up a table with the following columns: X, Y, Rank on X, Rank on Y.
Note that r_s is appropriate for: a. variables measured on an ordinal scale, or b. continuous variables with a monotonically increasing or decreasing relationship as shown in Figures 7-3a, b.

X	Y	Rank on X	Rank on Y

2 Enter the X and Y scores for each subject.
List X scores in order from smallest to largest.

X	Y	Rank on X	Rank on Y
1	4		
1	8		
2	10		
3	14		
4	15		
5	16		
6	17		
7	18		
8	18		

3 Convert scores on X to ranks. (Then convert scores on Y to ranks.)
a   1 = lowest score,
             2 = next lowest score,
              ⋮
             N = highest score.
b *If 2 scores are tied for a rank, average the ranks and assign the average rank to both scores.*

X	Y	Rank on X	Rank on Y
1	4	1.5	1
1	8	1.5	2
2	10	3	3
3	14	4	4
4	15	5	5
5	16	6	6
6	17	7	7
7	18	8	8.5
8	18	9	8.5

On X, there are 2 scores of 1 which are tied for ranks of 1 and 2. The ranks of 1 and 2 are averaged

(continued on p. 208)

$[\dfrac{(1+2)}{2} = 1.5]$ and this average rank is assigned to both scores of 1 on X.

4 Sum xy. Then calculate the correlation between the ranks on X and Y using the Pearson correlation. Steps are given in Procedure 7-1 (or 7-2):

$$r_S = \dfrac{\text{Cov}_{XY}}{s_X s_Y} \quad [7\text{-}5]$$

where X and Y are ranks. Recall

$$\text{Cov}_{XY} = \dfrac{\Sigma xy}{N-1}, \quad [7\text{-}1]$$

$$s = \dfrac{\Sigma x^2}{N-1}. \quad [4\text{-}7]$$

Rank on X	$\bar{X}$	x	Rank on Y	$\bar{Y}$	y	xy
1.5	5	−3.5	1	5	−4	14
1.5	5	−3.5	2	5	−3	10.5
3	5	−2	3	5	−2	4
4	5	−1	4	5	−1	1
5	5	0	5	5	0	0
6	5	1	6	5	1	1
7	5	2	7	5	2	4
8	5	3	8.5	5	3.5	10.5
9	5	4	8.5	5	3.5	14

$$\Sigma xy = 59$$

$$\text{Cov}_{XY} = \dfrac{\Sigma xy}{N-1} = \dfrac{59}{8} = 7.375,$$

$$s_X = \sqrt{\dfrac{\Sigma x^2}{N-1}} = \sqrt{\dfrac{59.5}{8}} = \sqrt{7.44} = 2.73,$$

$$s_Y = \sqrt{\dfrac{59.5}{8}} = \sqrt{7.44} = 2.73,$$

$$r_S = \dfrac{\text{Cov}_{XY}}{s_X s_Y} = \dfrac{7.375}{(2.73)(2.73)} = .9899.$$

correlation can be computed with the Pearson formula,[4] which, with rank-order data, gives Spearman's rho (r_S):

$$r_S = \dfrac{\text{Cov}_{XY}}{s_X s_Y} \quad [7\text{-}5]$$

where X and Y are ranks.

[4]The common form of the rank-order correlation,

$$r_S = 1 - \dfrac{6\Sigma d_p^2}{N(N^2-1)}$$

Table 7-7 ◆ Hypothetical rankings of teachers on
warmth and enthusiasm

Teacher	Warmth	Enthusiasm
1	3	5
2	4	2
3	1	1
4	6	4
5	5	3
6	2	6

For reference, the steps in calculating r_S are given in Procedure 7-3.

The correlation between ranks on extroversion (X) and humor (Y) is 0.9899. This correlation is consistent with an eyeball analysis of the scatterplot in Table 7-6. First, the slope of the scatterplot goes from the lower left to the upper right. Hence, the correlation coefficient is different from zero and should be positive (+). Second, most of the points in the scatterplot fall on an imaginary straight line. Therefore, the correlation coefficient should be large in magnitude.

Recall that r_S is the appropriate correlation coefficient for variables measured on an ordinal scale or for variables measured on interval scales where a weak curvilinear relationship is found—e.g., monotonically decreasing or monotonically increasing functions as shown in Figure 7-3a and b. (The Spearman rank-order correlation is not appropriate for marked curvilinear relationships as shown in Figure 7-3 c and d; see footnote 2 above.) Rho is interpreted in the same way as the product-moment correlation: the sign of the coefficient indicates the direction of the relationship between the two variables, and the absolute magnitude of the coefficient indicates the strength of association between the two variables.

Table 7-7 reports hypothetical rankings of teachers on warmth and enthusiasm that were obtained in a study of teaching. Compute the correlation between these variables.

EXAMPLE PROBLEM 4

(where d_p^2 is the square of the difference between each person's rank on X and Y), is derived from the product-moment correlation (Equation 7-2). It is the equivalent to the product-moment correlation using rank-order data with untied ranks (i.e., no two subjects have the same rank on X, Y, or both; see Siegal [1956] for the mathematical derivation). Since the common form of the formula assumes no ties in ranks while the Pearson formula used with ranks permits ties, the latter is presented in the text.

SOURCES OF
MISLEADING
CORRELATION
COEFFICIENTS

Sometimes researchers and users of research are all too confident in correlations based on sample data. When low correlations are found, they are tempted to conclude that there is little or no relationship between the variables; when high correlations are obtained, they are tempted to conclude that there is a strong relationship. However, certain characteristics of the sample data may lead to spuriously low or high correlation coefficients and thus distort the true relationship between the variables. In particular, we will show that: (1) *restriction of the range* of values on one of the variables may reduce the magnitude of the correlation coefficient; (2) use of *extreme groups* may inflate the correlation coefficient; (3) *combining groups* with different means on one or both variables may have an unpredictable effect on the correlation coefficient; (4) *extreme scores* may have a marked effect on the correlation coefficient, especially if the sample size is small; and (5) a *curvilinear relationship* between X and Y may account for a near-zero Pearson correlation coefficient.

◆　　◆　　◆　　◆　　◆

Restriction of Range

A low correlation coefficient may result from a **restriction of the range** of values of one of the variables. This effect becomes especially important when interpreting correlations based on *selected* groups of individuals. For example, suppose that a college admissions officer is interested in the relationship between SAT scores and GPA in the first year of college. If students taking the SAT were admitted to college without regard to these scores, a scatterplot of the relationship between SATs and GPAs might resemble the hypothetical scatterplot shown in Figure 7-4a. The correlation is probably about .60; that is, there is a positive, moderately strong relationship between these variables. Now consider the fact that most major colleges and universities only admit students with SAT scores of 1000 or above. The vertical line in Figure 7-4b represents

Figure 7-4 ◆ Illustration of the effect of restricting the range of X (e.g., SAT) scores on the correlation between X and Y (e.g., GPA)

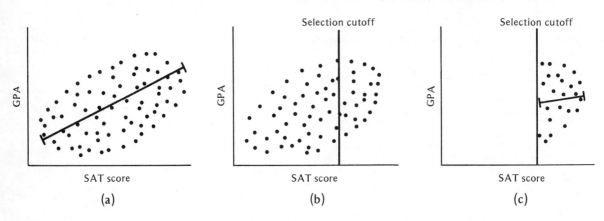

this admission policy, which results in restricting the range of scores as shown in Figure 7-4c. Notice that an imaginary straight line fitted to the circular scatterplot in Figure 7-4c would almost be flat, suggesting a low correlation. Since freshman grades are available only for students admitted to college, the admissions officer might erroneously conclude that there is little relationship between SAT scores and freshman GPAs. Thus, one must be cautious in interpreting correlations based on selected groups. Variances or standard deviations of measures on which a correlation coefficient is calculated should be checked in order to determine if restriction of range has occurred. Small variances or standard deviations for these measures may suggest a restriction of range and signal that caution must be taken in interpreting the correlation coefficient.

♦   ♦   ♦   ♦   ♦

Researchers sometimes use **extreme groups**—that is, they select subjects with extreme scores on a certain variable (X) in order to study whether subjects who differ on this dimension also differ in other ways (Y). For example, a researcher might be interested in whether subjects who differ in need for achievement (X) also show differences in other personality traits, such as anxiety (Y). Thus she might select subjects who scored very high or very low on need for achievement and correlate these scores with their scores on a test of anxiety. This procedure may result in a larger correlation coefficient than would be obtained if subjects with moderate scores on need for achievement had also been included. This occurs because subjects with very extreme scores on one variable may also tend to have very extreme scores on the other variable. Subjects with moderate scores on one variable may also tend to have moderate scores on the other variable. However, the variability of the moderate score on the Y variable may be greater than the variability of the extreme scores on the same variable. Because of the larger spread of scores in the middle of the joint distribution, the points do not cluster as tightly around an imaginary straight line as they do at the extremes. Thus, correlation coefficients based on extremely high and extremely low scores usually tend to be higher than those which also take moderate scores into account.

Extreme Groups

The effect of extreme groups is illustrated in Figure 7-5a. A scatterplot of hypothetical scores for need for achievement and anxiety is shown for a sample which contained only subjects with extreme scores on need for achievement. The points on the scatterplot cluster tightly around an imaginary line representing the slope of the scatterplot. The correlation is negative and strong— about $-.80$. The figure shows that subjects who score extremely low on need for achievement tend to score extremely high on anxiety; subjects who score very high on need for achievement tend to score very low on anxiety. Figure 7-5b shows how the correlation is affected by including scores falling in the intermediate range on need for achievement. In this case, the points cluster less tightly around the imaginary line drawn to represent the slope of the scatter-

211

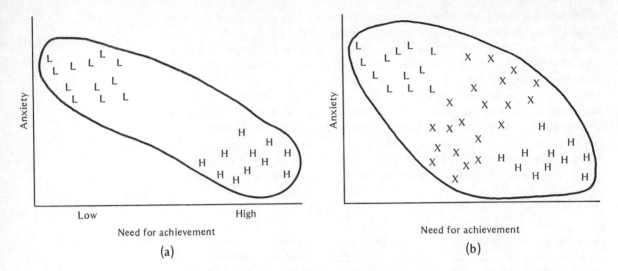

Figure 7-5 ◆ Illustration of the effects of extreme groups on r_{XY}, where H = high need for achievement, X = moderate need for achievement, and L = low need for achievement. In (a), when extreme groups only are used, $r_{XY} = -.80$. In (b), when moderate scores are also included, $r_{XY} = -.60$.

◆ ◆ ◆ ◆ ◆

plot; the coefficient is reduced to about $-.60$. Thus, caution must be used in making general statements about the degree of association between two variables based on correlation coefficients which are computed on subjects with extreme scores on one of the variables.

Combining Groups In general, caution should be taken in interpreting a correlation coefficient based on subjects which represent samples from two or more populations. In such cases, the correlation coefficient for the combined sample may be quite misleading. There are two reasons for this. First, differences in means may produce a misleading correlation coefficient even if the relationship between the variables is the same in each group (see Figure 7-6 a, b, and f). Second, the relationship between variables may differ from group to group (see Figure 7-6 c, d, and e). For example, suppose a school district is interested in the relationship between reading and mathematics achievement. The correlation coefficient will provide a measure of this relationship over all subgroups of students (e.g., boys and girls; native English and Spanish speakers) in the district. Notice, though, that this correlation may be influenced by differences in the means of the subgroups on X, on Y, or both. Or it may be influenced by the fact that the relation between X and Y is not the same for all of the subgroups. Figures 7-6 a through f show the effects of combining groups with different means and/or different relationships between X and Y on the correla-

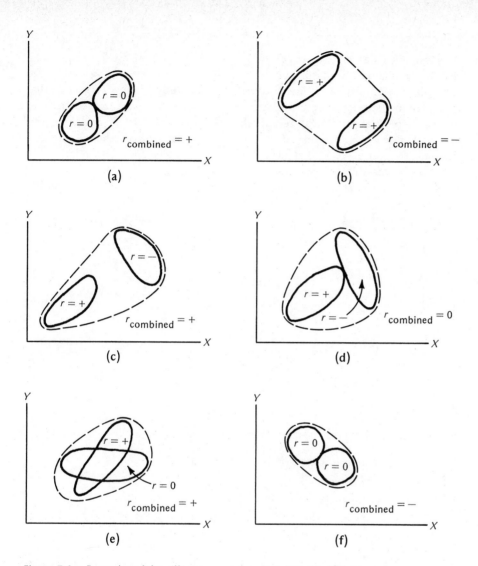

Figure 7-6 ◆ Examples of the effect on r_{XY} when groups with different means and different relationships between X and Y are combined

tion coefficient. Figure 7-6a shows how a positive correlation may be obtained by combining groups with different means when, within each group, there is no systematic relationship between X and Y. Figures 7-6 b through f show the results of some other possible combinations of groups with different means. In general, if a sample consists of subjects whose scores tend to fall into two different groups with different means, correlation coefficients should be computed separately for each group.

♦   ♦   ♦   ♦   ♦

Outliers   As shown in Chapter 6, a few outliers (deviant points) on the scatterplot can drastically change the nature of the relationship between two variables. For example, the scatterplot of class 2 in the Majasan study (Figure 7-7) shows that a curved line best describes the relationship between the two variables. In other words, there is a curvilinear relationship between variables X and Y in this group. However, notice that if the one outlier is ignored, the relationship between the variables is best described by a straight line. The relationship between the variables is linear now.

Not only can extreme scores drastically change the nature of the relationship

Figure 7-7 ♦ Scatterplot for class 2 of Majasan Study (from Figure 6-2)

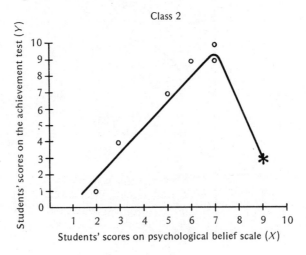

Figure 7-8 ♦ An illustration of the effects of an extreme score on r_{XY}

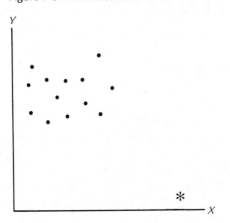

214

between the two variables (linear versus curvilinear), but they may also change the *direction* and *magnitude* of the correlation coefficient, particularly if the sample size is small. For example, the scatterplot in Figure 7-8 shows the relationship between scores on variables X and Y. The correlation between these scores is negative and moderately large ($r = -.48$). However, suppose the one subject who scored extremely high on variable X and extremely low on variable Y (denoted by * in Figure 7-8) is ignored. When this one subject is excluded from the sample, the correlation is low and in the opposite direction ($r = .05$). In general, extreme scores only have such a drastic effect on the correlation coefficient when the number of subjects is small and the extreme scores deviate markedly from the general cluster. With a reasonably large number of subjects (e.g., $N = 100$), the effect of the outlier is unlikely to be dramatic.

If such outliers are found, the researcher must decide whether to include or ignore them in the data analysis. As noted in Chapter 6, this decision will depend on the questions that the researcher wishes to answer and the information that is available. If a decision is made to ignore outliers, a full description — a kind of case study—should be given for each subject representing an outlier.

◆　　◆　　◆　　◆　　◆

When a low or near-zero correlation is obtained between two variables, one is tempted to conclude that there is no relationship between the two variables under study. However, recall that the correlation coefficients calculated in this chapter are meaningful only for a linear relationship between X and Y. Thus, a correlation of zero indicates only that there is no *linear* relationship between the variables. Yet, X and Y may be closely related in a curvilinear fashion and r_{XY}

Curvilinearity

Figure 7-9 ◆ Two examples of an approximately zero Pearson product-moment correlation (after Glass and Stanley, 1970)

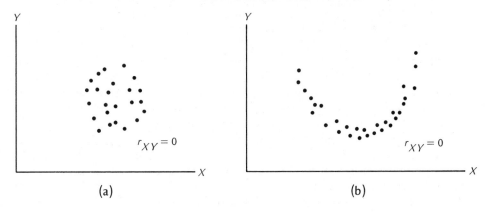

$r_{XY} = 0$

$r_{XY} = 0$

(a)　　　　　　　　　　　　　　(b)

may be low. For example, Figure 7-9 shows two scatterplots which have correlation coefficients of zero. In one case (a), X and Y lack any systematic relationship, but in the other case (b), X and Y are curvilinearly related. Thus, data should be cast into a scatterplot before computing a correlation coefficient. If the relationship to be described is curvilinear, the eta coefficient should be used (see footnote 2).

CORRELATION AND CAUSALITY

A single correlation is a measure of association between two variables. In the absence of additional information, the correlation coefficient cannot tell us anything about the causal relation between the two variables. However, this should not be interpreted to mean that correlations cannot tell us something about causal relationships. The purpose of this last section on correlation is to provide the logic underlying causal interpretations of patterns of correlations. The presentation is conceptual only, and reading it will not give you the skills needed to do the statistical analyses suggested here. Nevertheless, this is an extremely important topic in behavioral research, and so you should at least be familiar with it.

A true experiment is characterized by random assignment of subjects to one or more experimental groups and to one or more control groups; the researcher manipulates one or more independent variables in order to make inferences about the effects of the independent variables on the dependent variable (see Chapter 1). While causality cannot be proved empirically, support for some kind of causal influence can be inferred from true experiments with some degree of certainty. The procedures of the experiment help rule out alternative interpretations to the experimenter's assertion that the independent variable caused the change in the dependent variable.

In correlational studies, the researcher does not systematically manipulate the independent variable to observe its effect on the dependent variable; rather, he *selects* two variables to see how they covary in a group (random sample) of subjects. Subjects cannot be randomly assigned to different levels of the variables; rather, "nature" has already performed the "treatment" at the time of the study and the researcher observes a group of subjects on two variables. For example, in a study of the relationship between sex and self-concept, nature has assigned subjects to the sex variable (male or female) and to the self-concept variable (degree of positive self-concept). Hence, the experimenter cannot randomly assign subjects to the levels of the variables. Finally, since nature has performed the "treatments" prior to the researcher's observation, correlational studies do not have control groups. The procedures of a correlational study, then, make it impossible to verify that the correlation coefficient is a measure of causality between two variables. *A single correlation coefficient cannot be interpreted as a measure of causality. There are too many alternative hypotheses which cannot be ruled out* (cf. Chapter 1).

Indeed, there are three rival hypotheses about the causal relationship

216

between two correlated variables, X and Y: (1) X causes Y, (2) Y causes X, or (3) the relation between X and Y is caused by some third variable, Z. For example, in the Majasan study of the relation between beliefs (X) and achievement (Y), did behavioristic beliefs (X) cause high achievement (Y)? Or did high achievement (Y) cause behavioristic beliefs (X)? Or did some other variable (Z)—such as the knowledge gained from courses with content related to the psychology course—cause the relation between beliefs (X) and achievement (Y) in class 3?[5] The nature of the correlational study does not permit us to decide which is the correct interpretation.

Even though a single correlation coefficient cannot be interpreted as a measure of the causal relationship between X and Y, causal inferences can be made from correlational studies. The key to examining the causal relationship between X and Y is to include in a correlational study a third variable (Z) which challenges the hypothesized causal relationship. In the Majasan study, for example, suppose we wanted to test the hypothesis that beliefs (X) caused achievement in introductory psychology (Y). There are a number of rival hypotheses to the proposed causal interpretation. One such hypothesis is that achievement (Y) caused beliefs (X). However, this hypothesis can be discounted because of the order in which the data were collected; viz., beliefs were measured at the beginning of the semester, before students studied psychology, and achievement in introductory psychology was measured at the end. A second, more plausible rival hypothesis is that knowledge gained from courses with similar content caused the observed correlation between beliefs and achievement. A third variable (Z) representing this rival hypothesis might then be measured in the study. For example, grade-point average in related courses might be used as the third variable, Z.

With three variables in the correlational study, a number of **causal models** (possible causal relationships between X, Y, and Z), might be postulated. Suppose, on the basis of common sense and some psychological or sociological theory, we expect achievement to be caused by both beliefs (X) and knowledge from related courses (Z). This predicted causal relation can be represented as a model with arrows corresponding to the direction of the causal links:

I.

Model I states that X causes Y, Z causes Y, but X and Z are not causally related.

A rival model of the causal relationship might assert that beliefs (X) caused

---

[5]One variable Z may not be enough; two or more may be needed. However, for simplicity only one extra variable is considered here.

both achievement (Y) and grades in related courses (Z). This model can be written as

II.

$$X \nearrow Y \\ \searrow Z.$$

Still another plausible model asserts that the causal relationship between beliefs (X) and achievement (Y) is mediated by grades in related courses (Z). In this case, beliefs have an indirect effect on achievement through grades in other courses:

III.
$$X \rightarrow Z \rightarrow Y.$$

Finally, a fourth model might account for the observed relation between beliefs (X) and achievement (Y) as due to the fact that knowledge from related courses (Z) caused both X and Y:

IV.

$$Z \nearrow X \\ \searrow Y.$$

In order to determine whether model I provides an accurate representation of the causal relation between beliefs and achievement, the data from the correlational study can be fitted with model I and each of the three competing models to see if the data fit the proposed model better than the rival models.[6] If not, doubt is cast on the proposed model and further conceptual and empirical work is needed to clarify the causal relation between X and Y.

In examining causal relations in correlational studies, then, both theory and data are combined. On the basis of theory, certain rival hypotheses can be eliminated (e.g., temporal order) and causal relations within a proposed model can be justified. Then, data from the study can be used to test whether the proposed model or some alternative provides the most accurate representation of the causal relationship (for details, see Kerlinger & Pedhazur, 1973; for more advanced treatments, see Blalock, 1964, 1971; Duncan, 1975).

♦   ♦   ♦   ♦   ♦

Summary   This chapter presents procedures for calculating and interpreting the *correlation coefficient*, a measure of the strength of association between two variables. Two types of correlation coefficients are presented: the *Pearson product-moment correlation coefficient*, used when X and Y are linearly related and the *Spearman*

[6]For example, Model I accounts for a greater proportion of the variance in Y than does Model IV.

rank-order correlation coefficient, a special case of the Pearson coefficient, used when X or Y is measured on an ordinal scale or when X and Y are monotonically related. Then, several *sources of misleading correlation coefficients* are discussed. Finally, the relation between correlation and causality is discussed.

♦ ♦ ♦ ♦ ♦

Key Words

causal model	monotonically decreasing function
common (shared) variance	monotonically increasing function
correlation coefficient	negative relationship
covariance	Pearson product-moment correlation coefficient
cross-product	
curvilinear relationship	percentage of variance accounted for
deviation-score formula	positive relationship
extreme groups	raw-score formula
linear relationship	restriction of range
monotonic relationship	Spearman rank correlation coefficient

♦ ♦ ♦ ♦ ♦

Exercises

1–3 Three joint distributions are shown in Table 7-8. Examine each distribution and determine whether it is appropriate to calculate r_{XY} as a measure of the strength of association of the variables. Explain your answer. If r_{XY} is inappropriate, suggest the appropriate correlation coefficient.

Table 7-8

Exercise 1		Exercise 2		Exercise 3	
Anxiety *(X)*	Performance on cognitive task *(Y)*	Abstract reasoning *(X)*	Performance on mathematical puzzle *(Y)*	Ranking of leadership ability *(X)*	Ranking of extroversion *(Y)*
2	5	10	2	5	4
3	7	10	2	7	3
3	10	11	3	8	10
4	15	11	4	2	6
5	20	12	4	1	9
5	19	12	3	4	8
6	19	12	4	3	5
6	20	13	6	6	7
7	16	13	5	10	2
8	9	13	5	9	1
8	6	14	6		
9	3	14	7		

Table 7-9

Student	Creative performance	Creative thinking	Intelligence
1	1	1	101
2	1	2	100
3	2	2	108
4	2	3	98
5	3	4	105
6	3	3	106
7	4	2	99
8	4	4	107
9	5	3	102
10	5	4	100

4–12 Researchers studying the relationship between different aspects of creativity and intelligence administered the following three measures to a sample of high school students: (1) a self-report questionnaire measuring creative performance, which asked about talented nonacademic accomplishments during high school; (2) a paper-and-pencil test of creative thinking; and (3) a group intelligence test. The data in Table 7-9 were obtained.

4. Calculate the correlation between creative performance and creative thinking, using the *deviation-score formula*.

5. What can you conclude about the relationship between these two aspects of creativity?

6. What percentage of the variance in creative thinking is accounted for by creative performance?

7. Calculate the correlation between intelligence and creative thinking, using the *raw-score formula*.

8. How much of the variance in creative thinking is accounted for by intelligence?

9. A major issue in research on creativity is whether or not tests of creative thinking measure the same or different competences than tests of general intelligence. Based on these data, what would you conclude?

10. Calculate the correlation between creative performance and intelligence, using either the deviation-score or the raw-score formula.

11. How much of the variance in creative performance is accounted for by intelligence?

12. Compare the relationship between creative thinking and intelligence with the relationship between creative performance and intelligence. What can you conclude?

13. Another group of researchers studying the relationship between creative thinking and intelligence administered different measures of creative thinking and intelligence to a sample of high school students. They obtained an r_{XY} of .80 and concluded that high intelligence results in high scores on creative thinking. Is this conclusion warranted from the data? Explain.

14–19. The following study investigated the relationship between viewing violence

Table 7-10

Hours per week of violent television	Fantasy aggression	Reality aggression
8	2	35
10	2	5
13	3	25
14	3	20
16	5	20
17	4	15
18	7	25
19	7	35
20	10	40
22	9	40

on television and aggressive behavior in children. Three measures were collected from a sample of children aged 9 to 12: (1) hours per week viewing violent television shows; (2) score on a measure of fantasy aggression; and (3) score based on observations of child's aggressive behavior at home (reality aggression). The data in Table 7-10 were obtained.

14. Calculate the Spearman rank correlation coefficient (r_S) for fantasy aggression and time viewing violent television.

15. What can you conclude?

16. Calculate r_S for violent television time and reality aggression.

17. What can you conclude?

18. Suppose the researchers had not included a measure of reality aggression in their study, on the assumption that aggressive tendencies are expressed similarly in reality and in fantasy. How would their conclusions have changed?

19. Several popular women's magazines reported this study and recommended that mothers should discourage their children from watching violent television shows so that their children would not become hostile and aggressive. Does this conclusion follow from these data? Explain.

20–22 Estimate r_{XY} for each scatterplot below.

20.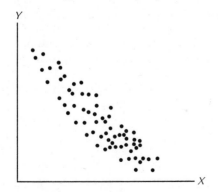

21.

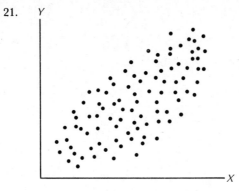

22.

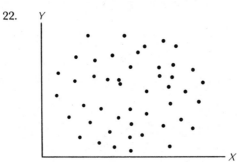

23–26 Indicate which of the following factors is most likely to produce a misleading correlation coefficient in the measurement described:

    I. restriction of range
   II. use of extreme groups
  III. combining groups
   IV. outliers
    V. curvilinearity

23. The correlation between income and feelings of alienation computed on a sample of New York City residents where one member of the sample was a member of the Rockefeller family.

24. The correlation between need for affiliation and interpersonal openness computed on subjects scoring extremely high or extremely low on a need-for-affiliation scale.

25. The correlation between LSAT score and grade-point average in the first year of law school computed on a sample of law students enrolled at ten major universities in the United States.

26. The correlation between measures of daily stress and job satisfaction computed on a sample of inner-city and suburban blue-collar workers.

8 ♦

Linear Regression

Establishing a Systematic Relationship between Variables

Prediction of Y from X: Intuitive Approach

Prediction Using Linear Regression

♦ Development of the Equation for Linear Regression ♦

♦ Interpretation of the Components of the Linear Regression Equation ♦

♦ Application of the Regression Equation ♦

Errors in Prediction

♦ Standard Error of Estimate ♦

♦ Interpretation of the Standard Error of Estimate ♦

Linear Regression Equation for Predicting X from Y

♦ Comparison of Regression of Y on X and X on Y ♦

♦ Standard Error for Estimating X from Y ♦

Percentage of Variance

Summary

♦ Key Words ♦

♦ Exercises ♦

O~NE GOAL~ of science is **prediction**. Theories are built to predict one variable from other variables. For example, the force on an object can be predicted perfectly by knowing its mass and acceleration. In many cases, of course, prediction is less than perfect. For example, weather conditions such as rainfall can be predicted from barometric pressure and other indicators, but sometimes not very reliably. Prediction is as important a goal in the behavioral sciences as in other sciences. For example, job performance as a typist can be predicted from scores on a typing test, but of course not perfectly. College grade-point averages can be predicted from scores on the Scholastic Aptitude Test, but again not perfectly. Such a functional relationship does not imply that one variable causes the other. It only says that values of one variable can be predicted by knowing values of the other. For example, a functional relationship can be specified between college GPA and scores on the SAT so that a student's GPA can be predicted from knowledge of her SAT score. This relationship does not suggest, however, that a high GPA, say, is caused by a high SAT score.

Much of the research and theory building in the behavioral sciences, then, is aimed at not only providing an index of the relationship between two variables as the correlation coefficient does, but at improving predictions by specifying a functional relationship between two variables. This functional relationship is based on data collected from the same subjects on the "predictor" variable—the variable with which predictions are to be made (e.g., SAT scores) and on the "outcome" variable—the variable to be predicted (e.g., GPAs). Once the functional relationship between the two variables is specified, scores on the predictor variable can be used to predict scores on the outcome variable for similar individuals. The purpose of this chapter, in broad terms, is to present a technique for specifying the functional relationship which statistically predicts one variable (e.g., GPAs) from another variable (e.g., SAT scores) and to provide the skills necessary to compute and interpret the descriptive statistics involved in prediction.

ESTABLISHING A SYSTEMATIC RELATIONSHIP BETWEEN VARIABLES

In order to predict one variable from another, there must be some **systematic relationship** between the two variables. And, as you know from Chapters 6 and 7, both the joint distribution and the correlation coefficient provide information about the relationship between two variables. If there is a systematic relationship between X and Y, the points in a scatterplot will form a pattern and the correlation coefficient will not be zero. In this case, one variable (Y) is some function of the other variable (X) and the functional relation between X and Y can be found. This functional relationship tells us how many score points Y is expected to change if scores on X change by a certain number of points. For example, the relationship between SAT scores and GPAs, shown in Figure 8-1, is systematic. This strong, positive, linear relationship is reflected by the correlation between the scores on the two variables: $r_{XY} = 0.89$. As SAT scores increase, GPAs tend to increase. This suggests that if a person's SAT score were known, his or her GPA could be predicted because of the systematic relationship between SAT scores and GPA. Further, this systematic relationship between scores on the SAT and GPA can be translated into a functional relationship which goes something like this: for every 100-point increase in SAT scores, there is an increase of .3 points in GPA.

In Majasan's study (see Chapter 2 for a review), achievement in introductory psychology was systematically related to students' beliefs about psychology (humanistic versus behavioristic). In classroom 3, the relationship between beliefs and achievement was linear and positive (Figure 8-2a); the points fall along a straight line rising from lower left to upper right. The correlation coefficient is 0.98. By knowing a person's score on the belief scale, his or her final exam score can be predicted almost exactly. This systematic relationship can be translated into the following functional relationship: for every increase of 1.39 points on the belief scale, final-exam scores are expected to increase by one point.

In another classroom, the relationship between beliefs and achievement was curvilinear (Figure 8-2b); the points fall along a curved line. Since there is a systematic relationship between X (beliefs) and Y (achievement), final-exam

Figure 8-1 ◆ Scatterplot of scores on the Scholastic Aptitude Test (SAT) and Grade-Point Averages (GPA)

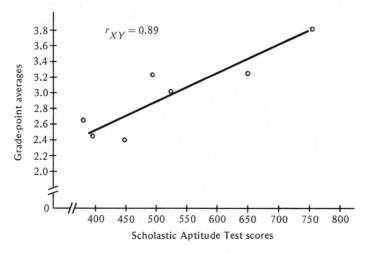

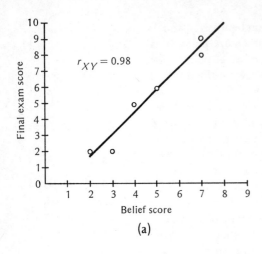

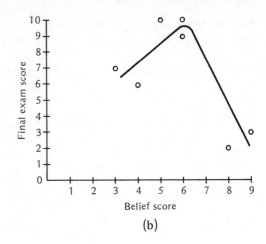

Figure 8-2 ◆ Scatterplot of scores on the Belief Scale and final exam in two classrooms of the Majasan study

scores can still be predicted from scores on the belief scale. The prediction would go something like this: for scores below $X = 5.5$, achievement-test scores are predicted to increase; for scores above $X = 5.5$, achievement-test scores are predicted to decrease. In this more complicated case a functional relationship can be specified mathematically, but the techniques are beyond the scope of this book.

The purpose of this chapter is to formalize these notions about prediction. In particular, this chapter translates the statement "final-exam scores can be predicted from scores on the belief scale" into an equation which predicts a score on the final exam from a score on the belief scale. In so doing, only the *linear* (straight-line) case is considered;[1] the process of fitting such a straight line is called **linear regression**.

PREDICTION OF *Y* FROM *X*: INTUITIVE APPROACH

In developing a rule for predicting a person's score on some variable *Y* from his score on some variable *X*, the obvious place to start is with the scatterplot of *X* and *Y*. The scatterplot contains the information needed to develop the prediction rule. But, of course, the scatterplot is something like an inkblot; what is seen depends on who is doing the looking. One way to reduce this potential ambiguity is to simplify matters by looking at scatterplots with a few points, all of which fall on a straight line. Three such scatterplots are presented in Figure 8-3. In (a), all points lie on a horizontal line; in (b), all points lie on a line

[1]Other textbooks such as Draper & Smith (1968) provide treatments of the case of prediction with curvilinear relationships.

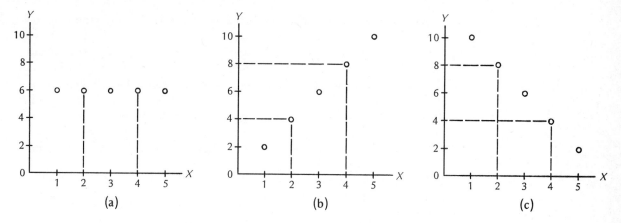

Figure 8-3 ♦ Scatterplots of hypothetical errorless data representing zero (a), positive (b) and negative (c) slopes

rising from left to right; and in (c), all points lie on a line descending from left to right.

A second way to reduce the ambiguity in looking at a scatterplot in order to develop a rule for predicting Y from X is to recall those factors which influence the sign and magnitude of a correlation coefficient in a scatterplot. Two factors are important (see Chapter 7, "Characteristics of Correlation Coefficients"): (1) the slope of the scatterplot and (2) the degree to which the points in the scatterplot cluster about a line representing the slope.

Armed with the scatterplots in Figure 8-3 and the critical features of a scatterplot which give rise to a systematic relationship between X and Y, we can develop a rule which specifies the **functional relation** between X and Y which in turn will enable us to predict Y from X. To begin, consider what is known about scatterplot (a). First, all points lie on a straight line. Second, as the values of X increase, Y stays the same. Third, since the line is flat, it has zero elevation or slope. In this case, perfect prediction is possible (even without knowing X) and a prediction rule can be stated: Regardless of a person's score on X, predict a Y score of 6—the mean, $\bar{Y}$, of Y—for each person. While this seems like too simple a case to be useful, it is quite important in developing a general prediction rule. First, it points out two critical factors which must be included in the prediction rule: (1) the mean of the Y variable, $\bar{Y}$, and (2) the slope of the imaginary line in the scatterplot. Second, it points out that if the slope is zero, the rule should predict $\bar{Y}$ for each value of X. In short, Figure 8-3a shows that any rule for predicting Y from X must include a piece of information pertaining to the mean of Y and another, separate, piece of information pertaining to the slope of the line in the scatterplot.

Next, consider the case presented in Figure 8-3b. There is a perfect, positive relationship between X and Y. Furthermore, there is a clear pattern in the relationship between X and Y: if $X = 1$, $Y = 2$; if $X = 2$, $Y = 4, \ldots$; if $X = 5$, $Y = 10$. This pattern in the relationship between X and Y, reflected in Figure 8-3b as a positive slope (rising from left to right), can be summarized as follows: As X increases 1 point, Y increases 2 points. This suggests that the **slope** of the scatterplot indicates how much of a change in Y is associated with a unit change in X. Or, put a slightly different way, the slope tells us how many points Y changes if X changes by 1 point. In developing a rule for predicting Y from X, then, information is needed about the magnitude and direction of the slope of the imaginary line.

In order to determine the magnitude and direction of the slope—how rapidly Y changes with a unit change in X—the change in Y can be divided by the change in X:

$$\text{Slope} = \frac{\text{change in } Y}{\text{change in } X}. \qquad [\mathbf{8\text{-}1}]$$

And in order to determine the change in Y and the change in X, the values for two score pairs falling on the imaginary straight line in scatterplot (b) can be used. Let's denote a pair of scores, X and Y, as (X, Y). If (X_1, Y_1) represents one point on the scatterplot and (X_2, Y_2) represents the second point, then the equation for the slope of the data points is

$$\text{Slope} = \frac{Y_2 - Y_1}{X_2 - X_1}. \qquad [\mathbf{8\text{-}2}]$$

For example, let (X_1, Y_1) be the lowest point in the scatterplot, so that $X_1 = 1$ and $Y_1 = 2$, and let (X_2, Y_2) be the next lowest point, so that $X_2 = 2$ and $Y_2 = 4$. Then as X changes one unit (as X goes from 1 to 2), Y changes 2 units (Y goes from 2 to 4):

$$\text{Slope} = \frac{Y_2 - Y_1}{X_2 - X_1} = \frac{4 - 2}{2 - 1} = \frac{2}{1} = 2.$$

No matter which pair of points is selected from the points on the imaginary straight line, the ratio of their changes will be the same and will equal the slope. Thus, if (X_1, Y_1) is the lowest point in Figure 8-3(b) and (X_2, Y_2) is the highest point, then inserting these values in Formula 8-2 should produce a slope equal to 2:

$$\text{Slope} = \frac{Y_2 - Y_1}{X_2 - X_1} = \frac{10 - 2}{5 - 1} = \frac{8}{4} = 2.$$

A rule for predicting Y from X, then, should include information about the mean of Y, information about the slope of the imaginary line describing the scatterplot, and, of course, information about a person's relative standing on X. This rule would then add to or subtract from the mean of Y a value which depends on the slope of the imaginary straight line and how far above or below $\overline{X}$ the person's score, X, stands. The rule can be stated in the following forms:

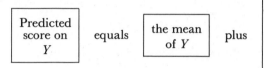

| Predicted score on Y | equals | the mean of Y | plus | an increment or decrement based on the slope and the person's standing on X relative to the mean of X |

or

$$\underset{\substack{\text{predicted} \\ \text{score on } Y}}{\hat{Y}} \;=\; \underset{\text{mean of } Y}{\overline{Y}} \;+\; \underset{\text{slope}}{\frac{Y_2 - Y_1}{X_2 - X_1}} \; \underset{\substack{\text{relative} \\ \text{standing on } X}}{(X - \overline{X})} . \qquad [\textbf{8-3}]$$

(Notice that a carat (ˆ) has been placed above Y to denote a predicted score of Y.)

Now, let's apply this formula to the data in the scatterplots in Figure 8-3. The rule for predicting Y from X in scatterplot (a) was to predict $\overline{Y}$ regardless of X. If Formula 8-3 is correct, it should make the same prediction. From scatterplot (a), $\overline{Y}$ is known to be 6 and $\overline{X}$ is known to be 3. In order to calculate the slope, let's use the lowest and highest points in the scatterplot: (1, 6) and (5, 6). (Remember, we reasoned the slope should be zero because the points fell on a horizontal line.) Finally, let's determine the predicted Y score for X scores of 2 and 4:

$$\hat{Y}_{\text{for } X=2} = 6 + \frac{6-6}{5-1}(2-3) = 6 + 0(-1) = 6 + 0 = 6;$$

$$\hat{Y}_{\text{for } X=4} = 6 + \frac{6-6}{5-1}(4-3) = 6 + 0(+1) = 6 + 0 = 6.$$

So far so good. Now let's apply the formula to the data in scatterplot (b). In looking at these data we developed a rule for predicting Y from X which said: For every increase of one point in X, increase Y by 2 points. Thus, if one point on the scatterplot is $X = 1$ and $Y = 2$, then if $X = 2$ for a second point, $\hat{Y}$ will equal $2 + 2$, or 4. Equation 8-3 should make the same prediction. In using this equation, note that $\bar{X} = 3$ and $\bar{Y} = 6$. Again, in calculating the slope, let's use the lowest and highest points in the scatterplot:

$$\hat{Y}_{X=2} = 6 + \frac{10 - 2}{5 - 1}(2 - 3)$$

$$= 6 + 2(-1)$$

$$= 6 + (-2)$$

$$= 4;$$

$$\hat{Y}_{X=3} = 6 + \frac{10 - 2}{5 - 1}(3 - 3)$$

$$= 6 + 2(0)$$

$$= 6.$$

Again, Formula 8-3 predicts accurately. As a final test, let's use this equation to predict the Y scores in scatterplot (c) from the X scores. Note that the slope of the points in this figure is negative, so that the slope calculated in Formula 8-3 should also be negative:

$$\hat{Y}_{X=2} = 6 + \frac{2 - 10}{5 - 1}(2 - 3)$$

$$= 6 + (-2)(-1)$$

$$= 8;$$

$$\hat{Y}_{X=4} = 6 + \frac{2 - 10}{5 - 1}(4 - 3)$$

$$= 6 + (-2)(+1)$$

$$= 4.$$

The data in Figure 8-3 have led to the development of a prediction rule which fits a straight line to the scatterplot. This straight line passes through each of the points in the scatterplot. This can be verified by drawing a straight line through any two values of predicted Y scores and determining whether this line passes through the other three points in the scatterplot. For example, data from Figure 8-3c led to a predicted Y of 8 for $X = 2$ and a predicted Y of 4 for $X = 4$. This means that if this line were graphed, it would pass from upper left to lower right on the graph and it would include the following points (pairs of scores): (1, 10); (2, 8); (3, 6); (4, 4); (5, 2). This corresponds precisely to the scatterplot in Figure 8-3c. The prediction rule, then, states that when there is a linear relation between X and Y: (1) a straight line can be fitted to the data in the scatterplot, (2) the functional relation between the predicted Y score and the predictor variable X specifies the nature of the straight line and takes the form $\hat{Y}_X = \bar{Y} + b(X - \bar{X})$, where b is the slope, and (3) for each value of X, the predicted Y score lies on the straight line fitted to the scatterplot.

In the ideal case for the joint distribution of two variables shown in Figure 8-3, **PREDICTION USING** all pairs of scores (points) fell on a straight line. While these data were used to **LINEAR REGRESSION** develop an equation for a straight line intuitively, the relationship between X and Y could have been described directly by the general mathematical equation for a straight line:

$$Y = a + bX, \qquad [\mathbf{8\text{-}4}]$$

where $\quad a$ is the Y intercept, and
$\qquad b$ is the slope of the line.

The **Y-intercept** a is the score value of Y when X equals zero. The slope b of the line has the same definition as given above. It specifies the amount of change in Y for a unit change in X:

$$\text{slope} = b = \frac{Y_2 - Y_1}{X_2 - X_1}, \qquad [\mathbf{8\text{-}2}]$$

where (X_1, Y_1) and (X_2, Y_2) are any two points on the straight line.

Formula 8-4 can be applied to the data in Figure 8-3b to predict Y from X. In scatterplot (b), the intercept—the value of Y when X equals zero—is zero. (Just extend the line below the lowest data point.) The slope has already been calculated, $b = 2$. The predicted value of Y for $X = 3$ is

$$\hat{Y}_{X=3} = 0 + 2(3) = 6.$$

In scatterplot (a), the intercept is 6. The slope has already been calculated: $b = 0$. The predicted value of Y for $X = 3$ is:

$$\hat{Y}_{X=3} = 6 + 0(3) = 6.$$

Finally, in scatterplot (c), the intercept is 12 ($a = 12$), the slope is -2 ($b = -2$), and the predicted value of Y for $X = 3$ is:

$$\hat{Y}_{X=3} = 12 + (-2)(3) = 12 - 6 = 6.$$

◆　　◆　　◆　　◆　　◆

In the special case in which all of the points in a joint distribution fall along a **Development of the** straight line, Formula 8-4 can be used to predict Y from X. The line developed **Equation for Linear** by this equation gives the predicted values of Y for each value of X. Both a and **Regression**

b in the equation can be determined from the data available in the joint distribution. However, data in a joint distribution almost never fall on a straight line; rather, the points often tend to cluster along a straight line. Some of the points may fall on the line, others will not. This more usual case is shown in Figure 8-4a. If the intercept of Y (i.e., a) is defined as the value of Y when X equals zero, which value of Y should be chosen when X equals zero? If the slope is the rate of change in Y divided by the rate of change in X, which pair of points should be chosen in order to use Formula 8-2 to calculate the slope?

The problem, in short, is that when all the points in a joint distribution do *not* fall on a straight line, it is not clear how to determine the value of a and b in Formula 8-4:

$$Y = a + bX.$$

The solution to this problem is to specify that some criterion should be met in estimating a and b and then determine the values of a and b that meet the criterion. The criterion used to estimate a and b in prediction studies is called the criterion of **least squares**. This criterion states that a and b should be determined so as to minimize the variability of points about the line fitted to the joint distribution. Thus, in fitting a straight line to the data in Figure 8-4a, the line in Figure 8-4b is placed in the swarm of points so that the mean squared distance of the points from the line is as small as possible. (In Figure 8-4b, note that the distance from a point to the regression line is measured by drawing a perpendicular line to the abscissa and not to the slope.) This is called the criterion of least squares because the regression line is fitted to the swarm of

Figure 8-4 ◆ Scatterplot of X and Y (a) and illustration of least squares criterion in fitting regression line to scatterplot (b)

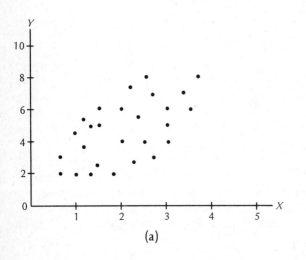

(a)

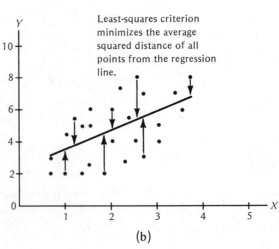

Least-squares criterion minimizes the average squared distance of all points from the regression line.

(b)

points in the scatterplot so that the sum of the squared deviations between the points and the regression line [i.e., $\Sigma(Y - \hat{Y})^2$] is minimized.

When the criterion of least squares is applied to the general equation for a straight line, the following estimates of a and b are found (for details on this estimation, see Draper & Smith, 1968):

$$a = \bar{Y} - b_{Y \cdot X} \bar{X}, \qquad [\mathbf{8\text{-}5}]$$

$$b_{Y \cdot X} = \frac{\text{Cov}_{XY}}{s_X^2}, \qquad [\mathbf{8\text{-}6}]$$

where $a = Y$ intercept,

   $b_{Y \cdot X} =$ slope of line predicting Y from X (read "Y dot X").

If, in the general equation for a straight line ($Y = a + bX$), a is replaced by its definition, the result is

$$\hat{Y} = \bar{Y} - b_{Y \cdot X} \bar{X} + b_{Y \cdot X} X. \qquad [\mathbf{8\text{-}7a}]$$

If the terms on the right side of 8-7a are rearranged, the result is

$$\hat{Y} = \bar{Y} + b_{Y \cdot X} X - b_{Y \cdot X} \bar{X}. \qquad [\mathbf{8\text{-}7b}]$$

Finally, notice that both X and $\bar{X}$ are multiplied by b. So b can be factored out to arrive at a general equation for predicting Y from X:

$$\hat{Y} = \bar{Y} + b_{Y \cdot X}(X - \bar{X}). \qquad [\mathbf{8\text{-}7}]$$

This equation is called a **linear regression equation.** It is used to predict the values of one variable (Y) from the values of another variable (X). It is similar to Formula 8-3, which was developed intuitively:

$$\hat{Y} = \bar{Y} + \frac{Y_2 - Y_1}{X_2 - X_1}(X - \bar{X}).$$

The one exception is that $b_{Y \cdot X}$, in Equation 8-7, is estimated by $(\text{Cov}_{XY})/s_X^2$.

However, if all of the points in a joint distribution fall on a straight line, the two estimates of the slope of the regression line are the same:

$$\frac{Y_2 - Y_1}{X_2 - X_1} = \frac{\text{Cov}_{XY}}{s_X^2}.$$

♦   ♦   ♦   ♦   ♦

Interpretation of the Components of the Linear Regression Equation

The purpose of the equation for linear regression is to specify a functional relation between X and Y so that Y can be predicted from X (or vice versa; see discussion preceding Formula 8-12 below). The regression equation accomplishes this by fitting a straight line or **regression line** to the points in a joint distribution, using the criterion of least squares. The prediction is accomplished in that *for each value of X, the regression line gives the predicted value of Y.*

There are two components in the linear regression equation which accomplish the task of fitting a straight line to a scatterplot: (1) $\overline{Y}$ and (2) $b_{Y \cdot X}(X - \overline{X})$. The first component, $\overline{Y}$, provides the information needed to adjust the regression line to the *height* or *elevation* of the swarm of points in the joint distribution. The second component, $b_{Y \cdot X}(X - \overline{X})$, provides the information needed to adjust the slope of the regression line. The second component also provides information on how much to increase or decrease $\overline{Y}$ in order to obtain a predicted value of Y from a particular value of X.

The criterion of least squares leads to a definition of the slope, $b_{Y \cdot X}$, which looks somewhat different from the one given in the intuitive approach. So some additional discussion is needed. The slope using the criterion of least squares is

$$b_{Y \cdot X} = \frac{\text{Cov}_{XY}}{s_X^2}. \qquad [\textbf{8-6}]$$

The numerator is the covariance of X and Y. It provides information on the degree to which changes in Y are associated with changes in X, i.e., how much X and Y covary. The denominator, s_X^2, is the variance of X. This ratio adjusts the rate-of-change information, Cov_{XY}, so that it corresponds to a unit increase in X. Thus, the slope has the same interpretation using the least-squares formula as it does using the change formulas given earlier in Formulas 8-1 and 8-2. That is, the *slope* provides information on *how many units Y increases for every one-unit increase in X.*

An alternative way of defining the regression slope $b_{Y \cdot X}$ is in terms of the correlation coefficient. Since the correlation coefficient is defined as

$$r_{XY} = \frac{\text{Cov}_{XY}}{s_X s_Y}, \qquad [\textbf{7-2}]$$

this equation can be solved for the covariance of X and Y as follows:

$$\text{Cov}_{XY} = (r_{XY})(s_X)(s_Y).$$

By substituting $(r_{XY})(s_X)(s_Y)$ into the equation for the regression slope, we get

$$b_{Y \cdot X} = \frac{(r_{XY})(s_X)(s_Y)}{s_X^2}$$

$$= r_{XY} \frac{s_Y}{s_X}. \qquad [8\text{-}6a]$$

This new formula states that the slope adjusts the correlation—a measure of how X and Y go together—according to how large an increase in Y results from a unit increase on the X scale (s_Y/s_X). Again, it tells us how many units to increase Y for every increase in X of one unit.

♦ ♦ ♦ ♦ ♦

Enough talk about the regression equation for a while; how is it applied? The steps in applying the regression equation will be described with the help of the data from classroom 3 in the Majasan study.

Application of the Regression Equation

In using linear regression, we assume that X and Y are approximately linearly related. This assumption can be checked by examining the scatterplot of X and Y to insure that a straight line provides an appropriate description of the data.[2] (See Figure 8-2a.) If the scatterplot shows a linear relation between X and Y, Formula 8-7 can be used to fit a regression line to the data:

$$\hat{Y} = \overline{Y} + b_{Y \cdot X}(X - \overline{X}).$$

The next steps involve the calculation of the statistics used in this equation. In Table 8-1, the mean and standard deviation of X and Y have been calculated along with the covariance and correlation of X and Y. The only value needed in the equation but not provided in Table 8-1 is the slope, $b_{Y \cdot X}$. This can be calculated using either Formula 8-6 or 8-6a:

$$b_{Y \cdot X} = \frac{\text{Cov}_{XY}}{s_X^2} \qquad [8\text{-}6]$$

$$= \frac{7.17}{(2.27)^2}$$

$$= 1.39$$

[2]There are statistical tests which can be used in deciding whether or not a straight line provides a good fit of the points in a scatterplot. If a straight line is not an appropriate fit, consult advanced texts on regression analysis to determine the appropriate model for fitting a curvilinear regression line to the data.

Table 8-1 ♦ Descriptive statistics for data from classroom 3 in the Majasan study

Belief score				Final-exam Scores				
X	$\bar{X}$	x	x^2	Y	$\bar{Y}$	y	y^2	xy
8	5.14	2.86	8.18	10	6	4	16	11.44
7	5.14	1.86	3.46	8	6	2	4	3.72
3	5.14	−2.14	4.58	2	6	−4	16	8.56
5	5.14	−0.14	0.02	6	6	0	0	0.00
7	5.14	1.86	3.46	9	6	3	9	5.58
2	5.14	−3.14	9.86	2	6	−4	16	12.56
4	5.14	−1.14	1.30	5	6	−1	1	1.14
Σ 36	36	0	30.86	42	42	0	62	43.00

$$s_X = \sqrt{\frac{30.86}{6}}$$
$$= 2.27$$

$$s_Y = \sqrt{\frac{62}{6}}$$
$$= 3.21$$

$$\text{Cov}_{XY} = \frac{\Sigma xy}{N-1}$$
$$= \frac{43}{6}$$
$$= 7.17$$
$$r_{XY} = \frac{\text{Cov}_{XY}}{s_X s_Y}$$
$$= \frac{7.17}{2.27 \times 3.21}$$
$$= 0.98$$

or

$$b_{Y \cdot X} = r_{XY} \frac{s_Y}{s_X} \qquad [\textbf{8-6a}]$$

$$= (.98) \frac{3.21}{2.27}$$

$$= 1.39.$$

Procedure 8-1 summarizes the steps in computing $b_{Y \cdot X}$ with Formula 8-6a—the most commonly used form of this equation.

The slope of the regression line, $b_{Y \cdot X}$, can also be calculated directly from raw scores using the following equation:

$$b_{Y \cdot X} = \frac{N(\Sigma XY) - (\Sigma X)(\Sigma Y)}{N \Sigma X^2 - (\Sigma X)^2} . \qquad [\textbf{8-8}]$$

Operation	Example
1 Look up Formula 8-6a: $$b_{Y \cdot X} = r_{XY} \frac{s_Y}{s_X}$$	
2 Compute r_{XY}, s_Y, and s_X. *See Procedures 7-1 or 7-2 and 4-7 or 4-8, respectively, to review procedures for these calculations.*	$r_{XY} = 0.98$, $s_Y = 3.21$, $s_X = 2.27$.
3 Insert appropriate values into Formula 8-6a and solve.	$b_{Y \cdot X} = 0.98 \left(\dfrac{3.21}{2.27} \right)$ $= 1.39$

Steps in computing $b_{Y \cdot X}$ using the correlation coefficient (data taken from Table 8-1) ♦ Procedure 8-1

Calculation of $b_{Y \cdot X}$ using raw scores (data taken from Table 8-1) ♦ Procedure 8-2

Operation	Example			
1 Look up Formula 8-8: $$b_{Y \cdot X} = \frac{N(\Sigma XY) - (\Sigma X)(\Sigma Y)}{N \Sigma X^2 - (\Sigma X)^2}.$$				
2 Set up a table with the following four columns: X, Y, X^2, XY.	X	Y	X^2	XY
3 List scores on X and Y in their respective columns.	X	Y	X^2	XY
4 Square each X score and enter in column labeled X^2.	8	10	64	80
	7	8	49	56
	3	2	9	6
5 Multiply each X by the corresponding Y and enter in column labeled XY.	5	6	25	30
	7	9	49	63
6 Sum scores in each column to obtain ΣX, ΣY, ΣX^2, ΣXY.	2	2	4	4
	4	5	16	20
	ΣX $= 36$	ΣY $= 42$	ΣX^2 $= 216$	ΣXY $= 259$
7 Square ΣX to obtain $(\Sigma X)^2$.	$36^2 = 1296$.			

(continued on p. 238)

8 Enter appropriate values into general equation to obtain $b_{Y \cdot X}$:

$$b_{Y \cdot X} = \frac{N(\Sigma XY) - (\Sigma X)(\Sigma Y)}{N\Sigma X^2 - (\Sigma X)^2}.$$

Remember that N refers to the number of subjects or pairs or scores.

$$\frac{7(259) - (36)(42)}{7(216) - 1296} = 1.39.$$

This procedure may be more convenient when r_{XY} or the standard deviation of X or Y is not readily available. For reference, the steps in using this formula are shown in Procedure 8-2.

Now that $b_{Y \cdot X}$ has been calculated, the symbols in the regression equation can be replaced by their respective values for predicting achievement from belief:

$$\hat{Y} = 6 + 1.39(X - 5.14).$$

In order to draw a straight line, two points on the line must be determined. Any two values of X, then, can be used for drawing the regression line onto the scatterplot. For $X = 2$ and $X = 8$, the predicted Y scores are

$$\hat{Y}_{X=2} = 6 + 1.39(2 - 5.14) = 6 + (-4.36) = 1.64,$$

$$\hat{Y}_{X=8} = 6 + 1.39(8 - 5.14) = 6 + 3.98 = 9.98.$$

Figure 8-5 ◆ Scatterplot (a), regression line (b) and scatterplot with regression line (c) for data from Classroom 3 in the Majasan study

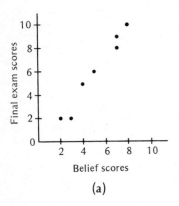

(a)

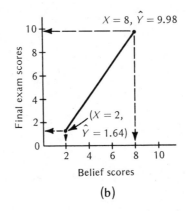

(b)

(c)

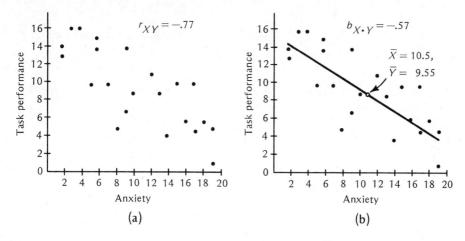

Figure 8-6 ◆ Scatterplot (a) with regression line (b) of scores earned on a measure of anxiety and on a measure of performance on a complex cognitive task

These two points—($X = 2$, $\hat{Y} = 1.64$) and ($X = 8$, $\hat{Y} = 9.98$)—are used to draw the regression line in Figure 8-5. Notice that the points in the scatterplot cluster tightly about the regression line, as expected from a correlation of 0.98 between X and Y.

The data in Figure 8-6 are taken from a hypothetical study of the relation between anxiety and task performance. One theory of anxiety predicts a negative relationship between anxiety (X) and performance on a complex cognitive task (Y). Data in this figure support the prediction: $r_{XY} = -.77$, $b_{Y \cdot X} = -.57$. In order to draw the regression line in Figure 8-6b, the predicted Y scores need to be determined for two values of X:

$$\hat{Y}_{X=2} = 9.55 + (-.57)(2 - 10.5) = 14.4,$$

$$\hat{Y}_{X=19} = 9.55 + (-.57)(19 - 10.5) = 4.7.$$

These two sets of points—($X = 2$, $\hat{Y} = 14.4$) and ($X = 19$, $\hat{Y} = 4.7$)—are used to draw the regression line.

When a regression line is drawn on a scatterplot, it can be used to predict Y from any value of X. For example, for an anxiety score of 10.5 (the mean of X), the predicted performance score is 9.55 (the mean of Y). Thus, *in order to determine the predicted score $\hat{Y}$ from any value of X, the regression equation can be used to provide the value, or $\hat{Y}$ can be read directly from a scatterplot in which the regression line has been drawn.* The steps for calculating the regression line are summarized in Procedure 8-3.

EXAMPLE PROBLEM 1   The data reported in Table 8-2 were obtained in a study of predictors of job success.

a. Compute $b_{Y \cdot X}$.
b. Calculate the linear regression equation for predicting job performance from the simulation test.
c. Compute values of $\hat{Y}$ for $X = 1$ and $X = 6$.
d. Using the two points computed in c, plot the regression line for Y on X.

Procedure 8-3 ◆ Steps for computing the regression line (data from Table 8-1)

Operation	Example
1 Verify that assumptions have been met by examining: (a) sampling procedures, (b) measurement scale of X and Y, and	(a) Subjects were randomly selected. (b) Belief scores and final exam scores represent continuous variables.
(c) scatterplot of X and Y. *See Procedure 6-1 to review procedure for constructing a scatterplot.* *(a) Each pair of scores is independent of every other pair (i.e., subjects were randomly selected);* *(b) X and Y are continuous variables (i.e., scores can theoretically assume an infinite number of values;* *(c) The relationship between X and Y is linear.*	(c)

Students' scores on the psychological belief scale (X)

2 Look up Formula 8-7:

$$\hat{Y} = \bar{Y} + b_{Y \cdot X}(X - \bar{X}).$$

3 Compute $\bar{Y}$ and $\bar{X}$. $\bar{Y} = 6,$

See Procedure 4-5 to review procedures for calculating a mean.

$\bar{X} = 5.14$.

4 Compute $b_{Y \cdot X}$ using Formula 8-6a.

$b_{Y \cdot X} = 1.39$.

$$b_{Y \cdot X} = r_{XY} \frac{s_Y}{s_X},$$

or Formula 8-8:

$$b_{Y \cdot X} = \frac{N(\Sigma XY) - (\Sigma X)(\Sigma Y)}{N \Sigma X^2 - (\Sigma X)^2}$$

See Procedures 8-1 and 8-2 for computing these formulas.

5 Insert appropriate values into Formula 8-7 and solve.

Usually values of $\hat{Y}$ for two values of X are computed so that the regression line can be plotted.

For $X = 2$:

$$\hat{Y} = 6 + 1.39(2 - 5.14)$$

$$= 6 + (-4.36)$$

$$= 1.64.$$

The predicted final-exam score for a belief score of 2 is 1.64.

For $X = 8$:

$$\hat{X} = 6 + 1.39(8 - 5.14)$$

$$= 6 + 3.98$$

$$= 9.98.$$

The predicted final-exam score for a belief score of 8 is 9.98.

6 Plot the regression line.

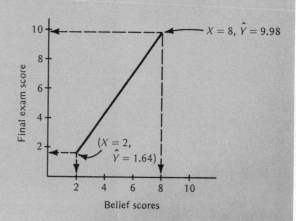

Table 8-2 ◆ Hypothetical scores on simulated and actual job performances

Performance on job simulation test, X	Actual performance on the job, Y
2	5
3	4
3	6
4	9
5	7

$\bar{X} = 3.4$	$r_{XY} = .64$	$\bar{Y} = 6.2$
$s_X = 1.14$		$s_Y = 1.92$

ERRORS IN PREDICTION

It does not take Sherlock Holmes to realize that not all of the points in Figure 8-5c and 8-6b fall on the regression line. In fact, most of the points do not fall exactly on the line, even in Figure 8-5c where $r_{XY} = 0.98$. Since the regression line represents the predicted value of Y for each value of X and the points in the joint distribution represent the actual values of Y for each value of X, *the discrepancy between the points and the regression line constitutes* **error in prediction** *of Y from X.*

◆　◆　◆　◆　◆

Standard Error of Estimate

Figure 8-7 reproduces Figure 8-5c and highlights the discrepancy between the predicted values of Y on the regression line and the actual values of Y represented by the points in the figure. The numerical value of the discrepancy is obtained by subtracting the predicted value of Y from the actual value of Y for a given value of X: Discrepancy $= Y - \hat{Y}$. This discrepancy shows the magnitude of the error of estimating Y from a particular value of X. For example, the predicted Y score for an X score of 3 is 3.03. The actual value of Y is 2. The prediction is in error by $2 - 3.03 = -1.03$ points; the minus sign indicates that the actual value fell below the predicted value.

One possible measure of the amount of error involved in estimating Y from X would be to add up the discrepancy scores and divide this sum in order to get an "average discrepancy score" as an index of error. However, as might be expected, the algebraic sum of the positive and negative discrepancy scores is zero.

The solution to this problem is analogous to the solution for the standard deviation. The discrepancy scores can be squared and summed, and then divided by N. (Actually $N - 2$ is used when estimating the parameter.) Finally,

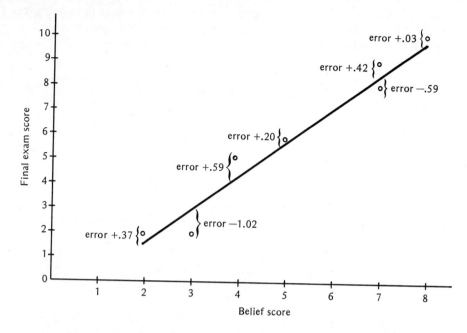

Figure 8-7 ◆ Errors in predicting final exam scores from belief scores from Classroom 3 in the Majasan study

the square root can be taken to return this average value to the original scale of measurement. This measure of the error in predicting Y from X is called the **standard error of estimate**; it is an index of the magnitude of error made in estimating Y from X. The formula can be written as

$$s_{Y \cdot X} = \sqrt{\frac{\Sigma(Y - \hat{Y})^2}{N - 2}} \qquad [8\text{-}9]$$

where $s_{Y \cdot X}$ = standard error of estimate,[3]
Y = actual value(s) of Y for a given value of X,
$\hat{Y}$ = predicted value of Y for a given value of X,
$N - 2$ = number of observations minus 2.[4]

---

[3]The similarity of the symbols used for the standard error of estimate ($s_{Y \cdot X}$) and the standard deviation (s_X or s_Y) is intentional. Both are essentially measures of variability, as will become clearer in the next section.

[4]Note that $N - 2$ rather than N is used to calculate the "average" of the squared discrepancy scores. While the standard error is defined as the mean of the squared deviations of the points from the regression line, the formula given here provides a statistic that is used as an estimator (see

In order to determine the standard error of estimate for the data in Figure 8-7, the discrepancy scores in the figure are squared, and these squares are then summed. This sum of the squared discrepancy scores is divided by $N - 2$ and then the square root of this value is taken:

$$s_{Y \cdot X} = \sqrt{\frac{(.37)^2 + (-1.02)^2 + (.59)^2 + (.20)^2 + (.42)^2 + (-.59)^2 + (.03)^2}{5}}$$

$$= \sqrt{\frac{2.0908}{5}}$$

$$= \sqrt{.42}$$

$$= .65.$$

An alternative formula, computationally much easier than Formula 8-9, is:

$$\boxed{s_{Y \cdot X} = s_Y \sqrt{1 - r_{YX}^2}. \qquad [\textbf{8-10}]}$$

Since r_{XY}^2 equals the proportion of variance in Y predictable from X, $1 - r_{XY}^2$ represents the proportion of variance in Y that is not predictable from X, i.e., the error in prediction. Multiplying $\sqrt{1 - r_{XY}^2}$ by s_Y adjusts the error to the scale of measurement of the variable being predicted. From Table 8-1, we know that $r_{XY} = .98$ and that $s_Y = 3.21$. Since r_{XY} equals r_{YX}, we can insert these values into Formula 8-10, obtaining

$$s_{Y \cdot X} = 3.21 \sqrt{1 - .98^2}$$

$$= 3.21 \sqrt{1 - .9604}$$

$$= 3.21 \sqrt{.0396}$$

$$= .64.$$

The difference between .65 and .64 is minor and due to the fact that in Formula 8-9 we divided by $N - 2$, whereas in Formula 8-10 there is an implicit division by $N - 1$. The steps in computing $s_{Y \cdot X}$ using Formula 8-10 are summarized in Procedure 8-4.

The standard error of estimate can also be calculated directly from raw

---

Chapter 1, "Relation between Descriptive and Inferential Statistics"). Hence, the denominator reflects an adjustment for degrees of freedom (see footnote 6 in Chapter 4, or see Chapter 14 on degrees of freedom).

Operation	Example
1 Look up Formula 8-10:	
$$s_{Y \cdot X} = s_Y \sqrt{1 - r_{YX}^2} \ .$$	
2 Compute s_Y and r_{YX}. *See Procedures 4-8 and 7-1 or 7-2 for making these calculations.*	$s_Y = 3.21,$ $r_{YX} = .98.$
3 Insert the appropriate values into Formula 8-10 and solve.	$s_{Y \cdot X} = 3.21 \sqrt{1 - .98^2}$ $= 3.21 \sqrt{1 - .9604}$ $= 3.21 \sqrt{.0396}$ $= .64.$

Steps in calculating $s_{Y \cdot X}$ using the correlation coefficient (data taken from Table 8-1) ◆ Procedure 8-4

scores using the following formula:

$$s_{Y \cdot X} = \sqrt{\left[\frac{1}{N(N-2)} \right] \left[N \Sigma Y^2 - (\Sigma Y)^2 - \frac{[N \Sigma XY - (\Sigma X)(\Sigma Y)]^2}{N \Sigma X^2 - (\Sigma X)^2} \right]} \qquad [8\text{-}11]$$

This procedure may be preferred if r_{XY} or s_Y is unavailable. For reference, the steps in using this formula are shown in Procedure 8-5.

Steps in calculating $s_{Y \cdot X}$ using raw scores (data taken from Table 8-1) ◆ Procedure 8-5

Operation	Example
1 Look up Formula 8-11:	
$$s_{Y \cdot X} = \sqrt{\frac{1}{N(N-2)} \left[N \Sigma Y^2 - (\Sigma Y)^2 - \frac{[N \Sigma XY - (\Sigma X)(\Sigma Y)]^2}{N \Sigma X^2 - (\Sigma X)^2} \right]}$$	
	(continued on p. 246)

SECTION III ◆ JOINT DISTRIBUTIONS

2 Set up a table with the following five columns: X, X^2, Y, Y^2, XY.

3 List scores on X and Y in their respective columns.

4 Square each X and enter in column labeled X^2.

5 Square each Y and enter in column labeled Y^2.

6 Multiply each X by the corresponding Y and enter in column labeled XY.

7 Sum scores in each column to obtain: $\Sigma X, \Sigma X^2, \Sigma Y, \Sigma Y^2, \Sigma XY$.

X	X^2	Y	Y^2	XY
8	64	10	100	80
7	49	8	64	56
3	9	2	4	6
5	25	6	36	30
7	49	9	81	63
2	4	2	4	4
4	16	5	25	20
ΣX $= 36$	ΣX^2 $= 216$	ΣY $= 42$	ΣY^2 $= 314$	ΣXY $= 259$

8 Square ΣX to obtain $(\Sigma X)^2$. $\qquad 36^2 = 1296.$

9 Square ΣY to obtain $(\Sigma Y)^2$. $\qquad 42^2 = 1764.$

10 Enter appropriate terms into the general equation to obtain $s_{Y \cdot X}$:

$$s_{Y \cdot X} = \sqrt{\frac{1}{N(N-2)}\left[N \Sigma Y^2 - (\Sigma Y)^2 - \frac{[N \Sigma XY - (\Sigma X)(\Sigma Y)]^2}{N \Sigma X^2 - (\Sigma X)^2}\right]}$$

Remember that N refers to the number of subjects or pairs of scores.

$$s_{Y \cdot X} = \sqrt{\frac{1}{7(7-2)}\left[7(314) - 1764 - \frac{[7(259) - (36)(42)]^2}{7(216) - 1296}\right]}$$

$$= 0.64.$$

EXAMPLE PROBLEM 2

Calculate the standard error of estimate for predicting actual job performance from performance on a job simulation test. (See Table 8-2 for data.)

◆ ◆ ◆ ◆ ◆

Interpretation of the Standard Error of Estimate

The standard error of estimate for a joint distribution is analogous to the standard deviation for a univariate distribution. Just as the standard deviation provides a measure of the dispersion of scores about the mean of a univariate distribution, the standard error of estimate provides a measure of the dispersion of points about the regression line.

The analogy can be carried even further. The regression line can be thought of as a *moving mean*. At each value of X, theoretically there can be an

246

indefinitely large number of Y values. The mean of these Y values, $\overline{Y}$ for a given X, falls on the regression line. The standard error of estimate, then, is the standard deviation of actual Y scores about the mean of Y for a given value of X. Thus, for the standard error of estimate, we write $s_{Y \cdot X}$, which can be read as the standard deviation of Y for a given value of X.

This reasoning is reflected in Figure 8-8. The predicted Y score is the mean of the Y scores at a particular value of X. Thus, the regression line, representing the predicted Y scores, can be thought of as a line of means. If the standard deviation of Y scores about $\hat{Y}$ at each level of X were calculated and averaged, this average standard deviation of Y at each value of X would be the standard error of estimate.

If the Y values are normally distributed about their mean—$\hat{Y}$ in the joint distribution—the standard error of estimate can be used to mark off the areas in the normal distribution. From Table B at the back of the book, we know that about 68 percent of the scores in the normal distribution fall between 1 standard deviation below the mean and 1 standard deviation above the mean. Thus, 68 percent of the Y scores at a particular $\hat{Y}$ will fall within ± 1 standard error of estimate. The relation of the standard error of estimate to the normal distribution and the joint distribution is shown in Figure 8-9.

The standard error of estimate was 0.65 for the data from Majasan's study of the relation between beliefs in psychology and achievement in introductory psychology. It is reasonable to assume that in the population the achievement test scores are normally distributed so if the hypothetical data from Majasan's study were not based on seven hypothetical observations (used for pedagogical purposes), but were based on 1000 cases, then approximately 68 percent of the

Figure 8-8 ◆ Interpretation of the standard error of estimate as the average standard deviation of Y scores about their predicted Y scores

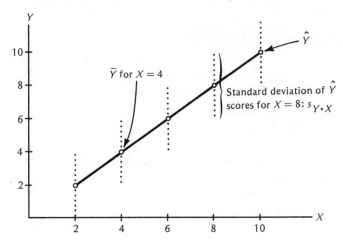

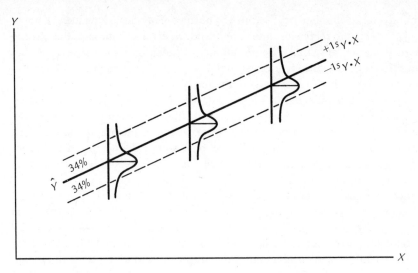

Figure 8-9 ◆ Relationship of the standard error of estimate to the normal distribution

raw scores in this large sample would fall within $\pm s_{Y \cdot X}$ or $\pm.65$ points of the predicted Y score.

Table B also shows that 95 percent of the cases in the normal distribution fall between 1.96 standard deviation units below the mean and 1.96 standard deviation units above the mean. (Note that this amounts to virtually 2 standard deviations above and below the mean. This corresponds to our earlier discussion in Chapter 5, in which we stated that approximately 95 percent of the cases fall within ± 2 standard deviations.) Thus, assuming normality, 95 percent of the observed Y scores would fall within $\pm 1.96 s_{Y \cdot X}$ or $1.96 \times .65 = 1.27$ points of the predicted value of Y.

LINEAR REGRESSION EQUATION FOR PREDICTING X FROM Y

Earlier discussions in this chapter have shown that linear regression establishes a functional relationship between X and Y. In establishing this relationship, X may be written as a function of Y or Y may be written as a function of X:

$$X = f(Y),$$

$$Y = f(X).$$

Since linear regression is most often used in *prediction studies* in the behavioral sciences and since X is typically used to label the predictor variable which is measured prior to the outcome variable, the functional relation of interest is usually the one defining Y as a function of X.

The equation for predicting Y from X, then, can be used to predict college grade-point averages from Scholastic Aptitude Test scores. Since SAT scores are measured prior to college GPA, SAT scores are labeled X and GPAs are labeled Y. In prediction research, then, we are interested primarily in the functional relation predicting Y from X and therefore tend to ignore the functional relation predicting X from Y.

In some research, however, the focus is not on prediction of one variable (Y) from another variable (X). Rather, the focus is on identifying the functional relation between two variables. In this case, predicting X from Y is just as important as predicting Y from X. The researcher, then, is interested in both of the functional relations written above. In this case, scores on either variable might be labeled X; neither variable occurs prior to the other.

For example, a researcher might be interested in describing the functional relation between scores on the Stanford-Binet intelligence test and scores on the Wechsler intelligence test. In this case, scores on either measure might be labeled X; neither variable occurs prior to the other. And the researcher is probably just as interested in the relation of X to Y as she is in the relation of Y to X. Likewise, a researcher may want to describe the functional relation between scores on measures of trait and state anxiety. Again, either measure could be labeled X, since neither occurs prior to the other and the researcher is probably just as interested in relating state anxiety to trait anxiety as she is in relating trait anxiety to state anxiety.

An equation for predicting X from Y could be developed in exactly the same way that the equation for predicting Y from X was developed. The only change would be that, in the formula for predicting X from Y with a straight line ($X = a + bY$), the least-squares estimates of a and b would be found by minimizing the mean squared distance between subjects' actual scores on X and their predicted scores on X (i.e., $X - \hat{X}$). If this is done, the linear regression equation for predicting X from Y is

$$\hat{X}_Y = \bar{X} + b_{X \cdot Y}(Y - \bar{Y}). \qquad [\textbf{8-12}]$$

The predicted value of X depends on the mean of X and the number of units that X increases for each unit increase in Y, $b_{X \cdot Y}$. Only one term in Formula 8-12 remains undefined: $b_{X \cdot Y}$. The least-squares estimate of $b_{X \cdot Y}$ is

$$b_{X \cdot Y} = r_{XY}\frac{s_X}{s_Y}. \qquad [\textbf{8-13}]$$

By using the standard deviation of Y in the denominator, the X scores are adjusted for one unit increase in Y. Procedure 8-1 shows procedures for calculating $b_{Y \cdot X}$ using the correlation coefficient. Note that the same procedure can be followed for calculating $b_{X \cdot Y}$ except that s_X is divided by s_Y in step 1. Raw scores can also be used for calculating $b_{X \cdot Y}$ in the following formula:

$$b_{X \cdot Y} = \frac{N(\Sigma XY) - (\Sigma X)(\Sigma Y)}{N \Sigma Y^2 - (\Sigma Y)^2}. \qquad [8\text{-}14]$$

Procedure 8-2 gives an explanation of how to set up this raw-score calculation for $b_{Y \cdot X}$. The same procedure can be followed for calculating $b_{X \cdot Y}$ from raw scores except that the appropriate Y terms must be inserted in step 1.

Table 8-3 presents scores and descriptive statistics for measures of trait and

Table 8-3 ♦ Descriptive statistics for data from a hypothetical study of the relationship between trait and state anxiety

Trait anxiety				State anxiety				
X	$\bar{X}$	x	x^2	Y	$\bar{Y}$	y	y^2	xy
4	6.6	−2.6	6.76	5	7.3	−2.3	5.29	5.98
5	6.6	−1.6	2.56	4	7.3	−3.3	10.89	5.28
9	6.6	2.4	5.76	10	7.3	2.7	7.29	6.48
3	6.6	−3.6	12.96	6	7.3	−1.3	1.69	4.68
6	6.6	−0.6	0.36	6	7.3	−1.3	1.69	.78
5	6.6	−1.6	2.56	8	7.3	0.7	0.49	−1.12
10	6.6	3.4	11.56	9	7.3	1.7	2.89	5.78
7	6.6	0.4	0.16	7	7.3	−0.3	0.09	−0.12
8	6.6	1.4	1.96	8	7.3	0.7	0.49	0.98
9	6.6	2.4	5.76	10	7.3	2.7	7.29	6.48
Σ 66	66	0	50.40	73	73	0	38.10	35.20

$$s_X = \sqrt{\frac{50.40}{9}} \qquad s_Y = \sqrt{\frac{38.10}{9}} \qquad \text{Cov}_{XY} = \frac{35.20}{9}$$

$$= 2.37 \qquad\qquad = 2.07 \qquad\qquad = 3.91$$

$$r_{XY} = \frac{3.91}{(2.37)(2.07)}$$

$$= .80$$

state anxiety for a random sample of 10 subjects in a hypothetical study. The data in this table can be used in Equation 8-12 to predict X from Y.

$$\hat{X}_Y = 6.60 + \frac{3.91}{2.07^2}(Y - 7.30)$$

$$= 6.60 + (0.91)(Y - 7.30).$$

For a score of 4 on the measure of state anxiety (Y), the predicted score on the measure of trait anxiety (X) is

$$\hat{X}_4 = 6.60 + 0.91(4 - 7.30)$$

$$= 6.60 + 0.91(-3.3)$$

$$= 6.60 - 3.00$$

$$= 3.60.$$

◆ ◆ ◆ ◆ ◆

Comparison of Regression of Y on X and X on Y

As noted in Chapter 7, the correlation or strength of association between two variables X and Y is the same regardless of whether scores on X are correlated with scores on Y or scores on Y are correlated with scores on X. This equality can be seen in the formula for a correlation coefficient:

$$r_{XY} = \frac{\text{Cov}_{XY}}{s_X s_Y}, \qquad r_{YX} = \frac{\text{Cov}_{YX}}{s_Y s_X}. \qquad [7\text{-}2]$$

First, the denominators are clearly equivalent, since the same value is obtained by multiplying s_Y by s_X as by multiplying s_X by s_Y, due to the commutative property of multiplication. So what remains to be shown is what may be intuitively obvious: $\text{Cov}_{XY} = \text{Cov}_{YX}$. By definition,

$$\text{Cov}_{XY} = \frac{1}{N-1}\Sigma xy \quad \text{and} \quad \text{Cov}_{YX} = \frac{1}{N-1}\Sigma yx.$$

Again, since multiplication is commutative, we have $xy = yx$ and $\Sigma xy = \Sigma yx$, and thus Cov_{XY} equals Cov_{YX}.

Our intuition may lead us to conclude further that the equation for predicting X from Y should be the same as the equation for predicting Y from X. In this case, intuition leads us somewhat astray. While the general form of the equation remains the same, the exact functional relationship for predicting X from Y is *not* the same as that for predicting Y from X.

In order to see this difference, compare the two regression equations. Recall that the equation for predicting Y from X is

$$\hat{Y}_X = \bar{Y} + b_{Y \cdot X}(X - \bar{X}). \qquad [8\text{-}7]$$

This equation states that the predicted value of $Y(\hat{Y}_X)$ depends upon the mean of Y ($\bar{Y}$) which is increased or decreased by the value $b_{Y \cdot X}(X - \bar{X})$. This amount depends on (1) the rate of change in Y that corresponds to a one-unit change in X—that is, the slope $b_{Y \cdot X}$, and (2) how far X is from $\overline{X}$—that is, $X - \overline{X}$.

Now examine the equation for predicting X from Y:

$$\hat{X}_Y = \overline{X} + b_{X \cdot Y}(Y - \overline{Y}). \qquad [8\text{-}12]$$

This equation states that the predicted score, $\hat{X}_Y$, depends on the mean of X $(\overline{X})$ which is increased or decreased by an amount which depends on (1) the rate of change in X corresponding to a one-unit change in Y $(b_{X \cdot Y})$ and (2) the distance of Y from $\overline{Y}$ $(Y - \overline{Y})$.

There are three major differences between the equation for predicting Y from X and the equation for predicting X from Y: (1) the mean used as the starting point of the regression equation $(\overline{X}$ or $\overline{Y})$, (2) the distance of the score on the predictor from the mean on the predictor $[(X - \overline{X})$ or $(Y - \overline{Y})]$, and (3) the slope $(b_{Y \cdot X}$ or $b_{X \cdot Y})$. The first two differences are obvious. The mean of X (or Y) tells us about the scale on which X (or Y) is measured, and adjusts the predicted value to that scale. The deviation of Y from $\overline{Y}$ or X from $\overline{X}$ tells us about an individual's standing (relative position) on the variable used to make the prediction.

The third difference, the slope $b_{Y \cdot X}$ and $b_{X \cdot Y}$, requires some further explanation. First, recall that the slope is a measure of how much the predicted variable changes as a consequence of a one-unit change in the predictor variable. For example, $b_{Y \cdot X}$ tells how much Y changes for each one-unit increase in X. Similarly, $b_{X \cdot Y}$ tells how much X changes for each unit increase in Y. Suppose Y changes drastically for each unit change in X. In this case, the slope for predicting Y from X $(b_{Y \cdot X})$ will be relatively large. Conversely, if X were predicted from Y, then X would show a very small change for each unit increase in Y. Thus, $b_{X \cdot Y}$ would be relatively small. The reason for this difference in size is also illustrated by the following formulas:

$$b_{Y \cdot X} = \frac{\text{Cov}_{XY}}{s_X^2}, \qquad [8\text{-}6]$$

$$\boxed{b_{X \cdot Y} = \frac{\text{Cov}_{XY}}{s_Y^2} \qquad [8\text{-}13a]}$$

where $b_{Y \cdot X}$ = slope for predicting Y from X,
$\quad\quad\quad b_{X \cdot Y}$ = slope for predicting X from Y.

Note that we have already shown that the numerators of the two equations are identical $(\text{Cov}_{XY} = \text{Cov}_{YX})$. As shown in the last chapter, the covariance between X and Y provides a measure of how closely X and Y are related. Note also that the denominator of each equation contains the variance of the variable used to make the prediction. Thus, the equation for $b_{Y \cdot X}$ contains the variance of X (s_X^2) in the denominator, while the equation for $b_{X \cdot Y}$ contains the variance of Y (s_Y^2) in the denominator. The process of dividing Cov_{XY} by the variance of the variable used to make the prediction adjusts the increase in the predicted variable to a one-unit increase in the predictor variable. Suppose, again, that the variance of X is much smaller than the variance of Y. It follows, then, that $b_{Y \cdot X}$ will be relatively large, since Cov_{XY} is divided by a relatively small number (s_X^2). This means that for each increase of one unit in X, Y will increase drastically. Conversely, $b_{X \cdot Y}$ will be relatively small, since Cov_{XY} is divided by a relatively large number (s_Y^2). That is, for an increase of one unit in Y, X will increase only slightly. If $s_X = s_Y$, then $b_{Y \cdot X} = b_{X \cdot Y}$ and the slopes will be the same.

In order to see this relationship between the two slopes pictorially, Figure 8-10 presents the regression line for predicting Y from X ($b_{Y \cdot X}$) and the regression line for predicting X from Y ($b_{X \cdot Y}$) for two variables, where $r_{XY} = 0.60$, $\text{Cov}_{XY} = 9.6$, $\overline{X} = 4$, $\overline{Y} = 6$, $s_X = 2.00$, and $s_Y = 8.00$. Before examining this figure closely, let's make some predictions about the slopes from these descriptive statistics. First, notice that s_Y is four times greater than s_X. This means that for a small change in X, there will be a large change in Y. Therefore, we predict that $b_{Y \cdot X}$ will be large compared to $b_{X \cdot Y}$. Put another way, if $r_{XY} = 1$, a unit change in X would lead to a four-unit change in Y. However, since r_{XY} is considerably less than 1 in this example, the change will not be 1 to 4; it will be less.

In order to check this reasoning, the two regression slopes can be calculated:

$$b_{Y \cdot X} = \frac{\text{Cov}_{XY}}{s_X^2} = \frac{9.6}{2^2} = 2.40;$$

$$b_{X \cdot Y} = \frac{\text{Cov}_{XY}}{s_Y^2} = \frac{9.6}{8^2} = .15.$$

When predicting Y from X, $b_{Y \cdot X}$ tells us that for an increase of 1 point on X, Y increases by 2.40 points. When predicting X from Y, $b_{X \cdot Y}$ tells us that for an increase of 1 point on Y, X increases by .15 point.

These calculations verify our reasoning. The slope coefficient for predicting Y from X ($b_{Y \cdot X}$) is considerably larger than the one for predicting X from Y ($b_{X \cdot Y}$). Since $b_{Y \cdot X}$ is greater than $b_{X \cdot Y}$, the regression line for predicting Y from X is steeper than that for predicting X from Y. (See Figure 8-10.)

In summary, the difference in the regression lines for Y on X and X on Y arises from three differences in the two regression equations: (1) the mean of the variables to be predicted ($\overline{Y}$ for Y on X, or $\overline{X}$ for X on Y); (2) the

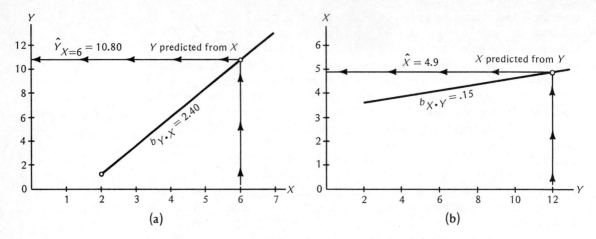

Figure 8-10 ♦ Regression lines for predicting Y from X (a) and X from Y (b)

individual's relative standing on the variable used to make the prediction ($X - \bar{X}$ for Y on X, or $Y - \bar{Y}$ for X on Y); and (3) the slope of the line ($b_{Y \cdot X}$ or $b_{X \cdot Y}$).

EXAMPLE PROBLEM 3 Using the data in Table 8-2:

a. Compute $b_{X \cdot Y}$.
b. Calculate the general linear regression equation for X on Y.
c. Compute X for $Y = 8$ and $Y = 3$.
d. Plot the regression line for X on Y on the same scatterplot you constructed in Example Problem 1d.

♦ ♦ ♦ ♦ ♦

Standard Error for Estimating X from Y Just as errors are made in predicting Y from X, errors are made in predicting X from Y. In order to determine the magnitude of this error in prediction, Formula 8-15 can be used:

$$s_{X \cdot Y} = s_X \sqrt{1 - r_{XY}^2} \, . \qquad [8\text{-}15]$$

This notation, $s_{X \cdot Y}$, indicates that this is the formula for finding the error involved in estimating X from Y. The major difference between this formula and the formula for the error in estimating Y from X ($s_{Y \cdot X} = s_Y \sqrt{1 - r_{YX}^2}$) is the replacement of s_Y by s_X. This adjusts the estimation errors to the variability in the X scale. In our example of anxiety measures, the error in predicting X from Y is

$$s_{X \cdot Y} = 2.37 \sqrt{1 - .80^2}$$

$$= 2.37 \sqrt{1 - .64}$$

$$= 2.37 \sqrt{.36}$$

$$= (2.37)(.6)$$

$$= 1.42.$$

Procedure 8-4 shows the steps for calculating $s_{Y \cdot X}$ using the correlation coefficient. Note that the procedure for calculating $s_{X \cdot Y}$ using the correlation coefficient is the same except that s_X should be used in the formula and not s_Y (see step 1).

The standard error of estimate can also be calculated directly from the raw scores using the following formula:

$$s_{X \cdot Y} = \sqrt{\frac{1}{N(N-2)} \left[N\Sigma X^2 - (\Sigma X)^2 - \frac{[N\Sigma XY - (\Sigma X)(\Sigma Y)]^2}{N\Sigma Y^2 - (\Sigma Y)^2} \right]}. \qquad [8\text{-}16]$$

Procedure 8-5 shows the calculation of $s_{Y \cdot X}$ from raw scores. The procedure for calculating $s_{X \cdot Y}$ from raw scores is the same except that X terms are substituted for Y terms and vice versa.

The standard error for estimating X from Y has the same interpretation as the standard error for estimating Y from X. If, for each value of Y, the X scores are normally distributed, then approximately 68 percent of the observed X values will fall within $\pm 1 s_{X \cdot Y}$ of the predicted value of X. Thus, assuming normality, about 68 percent of the X scores are expected to fall within ± 1.42 points of the predicted X value. For $\hat{X} = 5.48$—the predicted value of X when Y is 4—approximately 68 percent of the actual X values will fall between $X = 4.06$ and $X = 6.90$.

Using the data in Table 8-2, calculate $s_{X \cdot Y}$.   EXAMPLE PROBLEM 4

In Chapter 7 the proportion of variability in one variable that could be accounted for by knowing the variability in the second variable was found by   PERCENTAGE OF VARIANCE squaring the correlation coefficient. For example, in the study of the relationship between trait and state anxiety, we found that r_{XY} was .80. Therefore, the proportion of variability in state anxiety that is accounted for by knowing trait anxiety is found by squaring r_{XY}:

Proportion of variance in Y accounted for by X

$$= r_{XY}^2 = (.80)^2 = .64.$$

The proportion of variance in state anxiety accounted for by trait anxiety is .64. To obtain the **percentage of variance** accounted for in Y by knowing X, simply multiply the proportion found above by 100:

Percentage of variance in Y accounted for by X

$$= r_{XY}^2 \times 100 = (.80)^2 \times 100 = 64\%. \qquad [7\text{-}4]$$

Thus, 64 percent of the variance in state anxiety is accounted for by trait anxiety.

In Chapter 7 the predictable variability—the variability that could be accounted for—was represented by the slope of an imaginary straight line fitted to a scatterplot. This imaginary straight line is now known to you as a regression line. Since the regression line provides information about the predictable variability, there should be some relation between the slope and the proportion of variance in one variable that can be accounted for by knowing variability in the second variable. This is the case:

$$\text{Proportion of variance} = r_{XY}^2 = (b_{X \cdot Y})(b_{Y \cdot X}), \qquad [8\text{-}17]$$

$$\text{Percentage of variance} = 100 r_{XY}^2 = 100(b_{X \cdot Y})(b_{Y \cdot X}). \qquad [8\text{-}17a]$$

The data from the study of anxiety can be used to demonstrate the equivalence implied in Formulas 8-17 and 8-17a:

$$\text{Proportion of variance} = .80^2 = .91 \times .70 = .64,$$

$$\text{Percentage of variance} = 100(.64) = 64\%.$$

Thus, 64 percent of the variance in trait anxiety can be accounted for by state anxiety.

EXAMPLE PROBLEM 5

What percentage of variance in job performance is accounted for by knowing performance on the job simulation test (see Table 8-2)?

♦   ♦   ♦   ♦   ♦

Summary

This chapter presents statistical techniques for specifying the *functional relationship* between two variables so that scores on one variable can be predicted from scores on the other. Procedures for computing a *linear regression equation* for predicting Y from X, and for calculating the *standard error of estimate* to measure the error in predicting Y from X are discussed. Similar procedures are also presented for predicting X from Y. Finally, procedures for identifying the *proportion* or *percentage of variance* in one variable accounted for by the other are described.

♦   ♦   ♦   ♦   ♦

Key Words

error in prediction	prediction
functional relation	proportion of variance
intercept	regression line
least-squares criterion	slope
linear regression	standard error of estimate
linear regression equation	systematic relationship
percentage of variance	

♦   ♦   ♦   ♦   ♦

Exercises

1–14 The following data were obtained in a study examining the relationship between creativity as measured by a drawing completion test and openness to experience as measured by a perceptual awareness scale:

Person	Drawing Completion Test (X)	Perceptual Awareness Scale (Y)
1	4	6
2	5	9
3	1	4
4	2	5
5	3	4
	$\bar{X} = 3$	$\bar{Y} = 5.6$
	$s_X = 1.58$	$s_Y = 2.07$
	$r_{XY} = .84$	

1. Calculate $b_{Y \cdot X}$.

2–3 What score on the Perceptual Awareness Scale would you predict for persons with the following scores on the Drawing Completion Test?

2. 6

3. 3

4. What is the standard error of estimate when predicting Y from X?

5. Suppose that $\hat{Y} = 5.6$. Assuming normality, between what two scores will 68 percent of the actual Y scores fall?

6. Again, suppose $\hat{Y} = 5.6$. Assuming normality, between what two scores will 95 percent of the actual Y scores fall?

7. Calculate $b_{X \cdot Y}$.

8–9 What score on the Drawing Completion Test would you predict for persons with the following scores on the Perceptual Awareness Scale?

8. 7

9. 3

10. Calculate $s_{X \cdot Y}$.

11. Suppose that $\hat{X} = 3.90$. Assuming normality, between what two scores will 68 percent of the actual X scores fall?

12. Suppose that $\hat{X} = 1.34$. Assuming normality, between what two scores will 95 percent of the actual X scores fall?

13. What percentage of variance in openness to experience is explained by knowing creativity?

14–17 A parole board wants to predict potential parolees who will successfully readjust to life outside prison. A study was instituted in order to examine the relationship between several variables and readjustment. One variable examined was number of prior arrests. Readjustment outside prison was measured by the parole officer's rating on a scale of 1 to 10 of the parolee's readjustment after six months on the outside. These data are shown below:

Parolee	Number of prior arrests (X)	Readjustment outside prison (Y)
1	0	8
2	1	8
3	4	2
4	2	5
5	1	6
6	3	5
7	2	7
8	0	9
	$\bar{X} = 1.63$	$\bar{Y} = 6.25$

14. What is the general linear regression equation for predicting readjustment from number of prior arrests? (*Note*: Use the raw-score formula to calculate $b_{Y \cdot X}$)

15–16 What is the parole board's best estimate of a parolee's readjustment if he has:

15. 2 prior arrests?

16. 5 prior arrests?

17. Calculate the standard error of estimate of this prediction using the raw-score formula.

18. Explain the least-squares criterion in your own words. How is this principle used in fitting a regression line to a set of data?

19. What information does the slope of a regression line provide?

20. How does a line with a slope of 3 differ from a line with a slope of -3?

21. Compare the standard error of estimate in predicting Y from X ($s_{Y \cdot X}$) with the standard deviation of Y (s_Y). In what ways are they similar? In what ways are they different?

22. In which of the following units is $s_{Y \cdot X}$ expressed?

    a. units of X

    b. units of Y

    c. not directly interpretable in units of X or Y.

23. Given the data below, what Y score would you predict for a person who received an X score of 16?

Variable X	Variable Y
$\bar{X} = 12.00$	$\bar{Y} = 21$
$s_X = 3.42$	$s_Y = 5.92$
$r_{XY} = 0.00$	

SECTION IV

Reasoning
Behind
Statistical Inference

THE first three sections have focused on designing research and summarizing and describing what happened to subjects in that research. However, research seldom stops at the point where a lot is known about the particular subjects in the study. Rather, it attempts to generalize from the behavior of the subjects in the study to what is probably true of the behavior of similar people in general.

Psychologists and sociologists build theories by generalizing from the results of a particular study or series of studies to what might be true of human behavior in general. Educators, making recommendations on how to improve education, generalize from the results of a particular study or series of studies to what is probably true for all students like the ones observed in the studies. And politicians base their policies on generalization from the results of a particular study to what might be true for an entire population of people.

So research must be designed with the need for generalization in view. In order to be able to generalize from a particular group of subjects in a study, called a *sample*, to a larger group of subjects of interest, called a *population*, a sample of subjects is selected randomly from the larger population. If the sampling is random, the behavior of the people in the population may be inferred from that of the people in the sample. In other words, random sampling will produce samples which, *in the long run*, are representative of the population. The phrase "in the long run" means that even though any one random sample may not be representative of the population, most will be. The great value of random sampling is that we can determine the nature of the representativeness to be expected over repeated sampling from a population.

In this scheme, descriptive statistics play an important role. Not only do they describe what happened to the subjects in a particular study; they can be used to estimate what probably would happen if the entire population participated in the study. When descriptive statistics are used to estimate population *parameters* (descriptive measures for populations), they are called, as you might expect, "estimators" (cf. Chapter 1). An *estimator*, then, is a statistic defined by some formula for combining scores in a sample (e.g., $\overline{X} = \Sigma X \div N$). Accordingly, the sample mean, for example, may be used as an estimator of the mean of the population from which the sample was drawn. In using sample statistics to estimate population parameters, behavioral scientists are able to draw inferences from the sample to the population.

Research, then, ideally operates by randomly selecting samples from a population and observing the behavior of subjects in the sample. Based on the observed behavior (e.g., described as a mean or variance), an inference is drawn to what is probably true in the population. This is the basis of **statistical inference**.

Without observing the behavior of every person in the population, however, we can never be absolutely certain that the inference from sample to population is correct. The best that can be done is to indicate the possibility that the inference is in error. More formally, it is possible to state the probability that an inference from sample to population may be wrong.

Finally, research design, descriptive statistics and probability can be brought together in drawing inferences from one or more samples to what is probably true in the population. In this section of the text, the beginning and underpinnings of a large variety of statistical tests are presented.

9.

Statistical Inference: By Intuition

Statistical Inference and Past Experience

Statistical Inference from the Researcher's Perspective

A Model of Statistical Inference

Statistical Inference in Behavioral Research

Hypothesis Testing and Statistical Inference

♦ Case I—Does the Sample Belong to a Hypothesized Population? ♦

♦ Case II—Are Two Groups Drawn from Populations with Equal Means? ♦

Errors in Statistical Inference

Summary

♦ Key Words ♦

♦ Exercises ♦

In BEHAVIORAL research, inferences (generalizations) are drawn from the behavior of a small group of people to the behavior of people in the larger group of interest. This larger set of people is called a *population*, while the smaller subset is called a *sample*. In order to infer from sample to population, researchers follow a standard set of procedures underlying statistical inference. A random sample of subjects is drawn from a population. In drawing a *random sample*, each person in the population has an equal chance of being included in the sample. Over many such samples, then, the behavior of the subjects in the typical sample is representative of the behavior of the people in the population.

Descriptive statistics play an important role in this sampling scheme. Recall from Chapter 4 that statistics (e.g., the mean) are measures describing a sample. Analogously, *parameters* are measures describing a population. So, in addition to describing a sample, statistics can be used to estimate parameters. An *estimator*, then, is a statistic that is used to estimate a population parameter. Thus, a sample mean is used to estimate the mean of a population. By using statistics as estimators of parameters, behavioral scientists draw inferences from sample data to the population of interest. Unfortunately, the value of a sample estimate of a parameter may not exactly equal the value of the parameter. After all, the sample estimate is based only on a small subset of subjects from the population. So errors may arise in inferring characteristics of the population (i.e., values of parameters) from sample statistics. A major contribution of statistical theory is to enable researchers to indicate the probability that their inferences are in error.

In this chapter, the basic concepts underlying statistical inference are presented. The chapter is conceptual in nature, and it is intended to give you an overview of how statistical inference operates. Subsequent chapters will provide the skills for drawing inferences from sample data.

STATISTICAL INFERENCE AND PAST EXPERIENCE

One way to get an idea of what statistical inference is all about is to draw on past experience. For example, have you ever met a person that you liked immediately? Based on a limited sample of information—looks, dress, initial behavior—you draw the inference that Charlie's a nice guy. Or perhaps you've met someone you didn't like right off. Again, you're drawing an inference about that person in general from a limited set of observations.

Consider another example. Jujyfruits are chewy candies that come in a package with several different flavors mixed together. Some of the candies are red (cherry), some yellow (lemon), some black (licorice), some orange (orange), some purple (grape), and some green (lime). Suppose the red (cherry) Jujyfruits are my favorites. But the company that makes the candy skimps on the number of cherry candies in the box. I drew this generalization, of course, by inference after having eaten the candy from numerous boxes. (While this is an example of an inference, I make no claim that it is a *valid* inference. Valid inferences are the focus of the remaining sections of this chapter.)

One last example should bring the concept of inference home: the weather report. Weather forecasters sample wind conditions, temperature, and barometric pressure and infer from these and other observations what the weather will be. From my sample of weather reports, I infer that the forecasts are often incorrect. (Again, I make no claim that this is a valid inference, although most people would agree with it.)

The common element in each of these examples is that people draw generalizations or inferences about themselves, other people, and the world in general from a limited sample of information (observations, data). Sometimes these inferences are valid and sometimes they are not (Shavelson, Cadwell, & Izu, 1977; Tversky & Kahneman, 1974). Statistical inference refers to a particular procedure for making inferences or generalizations from a limited sample of data.

The procedures of statistical inference differ from the intuitive procedures used in everyday life in that they involve random sampling. The great value of random sampling is that we can determine the sort of representativeness of a sample to be expected in the long run (see Section IV). So the validity of statistical inference can be readily evaluated, while the validity of everyday, intuitive inferences cannot be.

In research, a group of "subjects" is observed, and the researcher attempts to draw valid generalizations or inferences from this sample to a population of people like the subjects observed in the research. For example, a researcher might collect achievement-test scores from 50 third-grade students and attempt to generalize what she finds for this small group to all third-graders like those observed in the study. In other words, research works from the particular to the general. We almost always deal with a limited number of data and attempt to make valid generalizations by inference from these data. This is done because there is not time enough, energy enough, or money enough to make all possible observations of interest. And even if there were, all possible observations probably could not be made, because they are not available at one point in time. So a limited number of observations must be used to make inferences about the larger group of observations of interest. If the observed data are representative of this larger group, then conclusions drawn from our data will generalize to the larger group; that is, they will be valid. If the sample data are not representative of the larger group to which the researcher wants to generalize, conclusions drawn about this larger group may not be valid.

STATISTICAL
INFERENCE FROM
THE RESEARCHER'S
PERSPECTIVE

To make these abstract ideas more concrete, reconsider some of the studies described in Chapter 2. In Rosenthal and Jacobson's study of teacher expectancy, a sample of elementary-school students was randomly assigned to either the experimental (expectancy) group or the control group. Data were collected on these students before and after teachers were provided information about the expected intellectual performance of their students. By inference from these sample data, Rosenthal and Jacobson made the following generalization: "The evidence presented . . . suggests rather strongly that children who are expected by their teachers to gain intellectually in fact do show greater intellectual gains after one year than do children of whom gains are not expected." Thus, from a sample of 320 students—65 in the expectancy group and 255 in the control group—in grades 1–6, Rosenthal and Jacobson made an inference which applied to *all children*. While this is an example of an unusually broad generalization, it points out one purpose of research noted earlier: to reach important generalizations by making inferences from a limited number of observations (i.e., sample data).

In a study of the development of moral judgment from childhood to adulthood, Weiner and Peter drew a sample of children and adults ranging in age from 4 to 18 years. All subjects read stories in which the *intent* of the actor and the *outcome* of the actor's behavior were varied. After each story, the subjects judged whether the actor should be rewarded or punished for his or her acts. Based on sample data from 300 subjects drawn from five different age levels, Weiner and Peter reached the following generalization: " . . . a progressive decline [was found] in use of objective outcome information and an increment [was found] in the use of subjective intent information, given both positive and negative outcomes and intents, until the age of 18." Note that at this point, Weiner and Peter no longer have in mind just the 300 subjects they observed in their study; rather, they infer from these subjects to a whole population of people, aged 4 to 18 years. This points out, once again, that one intent of research is to reach important generalizations by making inferences from sample data.

In Majasan's study of the relation between achievement in an introductory psychology course and the congruence between teacher and student beliefs about the study of psychology, a sample of twelve classrooms was drawn. Teachers' and students' beliefs were measured prior to the course. At the end of the course, student examination scores were collected. In eleven of the twelve classes, the closer the correspondence between the teacher's and student's beliefs, the higher was the student's achievement. Note that the intent of this study was not only to describe the relation between belief and achievement in twelve classes but also to generalize the findings from the twelve classes to psychology courses in general like those observed.

Finally, in Hewett and Goldman's study, over 13,000 students were sampled from four campuses of the University of California to determine relationships between student sex, college major, grade-point average, and aptitude level. From these sample data, Hewett and Goldman reached the following generalization: "It seems very clear that men and women tend to major in different college fields. This difference in major field is sufficient to account for much, if not most, of the apparent 'overachievement' of college women." Again, note the generalization—from a sample of students at four campuses of the University of California to *all college men and women*.

From these four studies, the intent of behavioral research becomes quite clear: to go beyond data describing a particular sample and reach important generalizations which apply to a larger group of people, the population. In order to reach these generalizations, each of the studies followed a set procedure for drawing statistical inferences from sample data. These procedures are set forth in the remainder of this chapter and in Chapters 10 through 13.

In a way, people operate like intuitive statisticians. They draw inferences about themselves, other people, and the world in general from sample data. While they act as if their sample data were representative of a class of data to which they wish to make inferences, in real-life situations these data may or may not be representative or valid (see, for example, Shavelson & Atwood, 1977; Tversky & Kahneman, 1974). In behavioral research an attempt is made to obtain representative, unbiased data in order to make valid generalizations from a small sample to a larger class of data. To do this, the researcher follows steps prescribed by a statistical model of inference.

A MODEL OF STATISTICAL INFERENCE

One model of statistical inference takes the following form. We assume an indefinitely large—perhaps infinite—set of observations we would like to know about (e.g., achievement-test scores for all third-graders in the U.S. or reaction times for all college sophomores in a memory experiment). This *set of observations* is called a **population**.[1] As noted in Chapter 1, the population is so large that all possible observations cannot be made, so a subset of all possible observations must be drawn. This subset of observations on a more limited number of people is called a **sample**. A sample, then, is a *subset or part of a population*. Inferences about the population are drawn from information found in the sample.

In drawing inferences from the sample to the population, the statistical model requires that the sample be random.[2] A **random sample** is a sample

---

[1]In some cases, the populations may be finite and small. The statistical methods presented in this textbook do not apply to that case. For an outstanding treatment of "finite statistics," see Cochran (1966). As Glass and Stanley (1970, p. 241) point out, "for the purposes of statistical inference it is generally not necessary to worry about the distinction between finite and infinite populations whenever the size of the population is more than 100 times greater than the sample taken from the population."

[2]Various techniques other than simple random sampling are available for drawing samples and making inferences from these samples to populations. See, for example, Cochran (1966).

drawn so that each member of the population has an equal and independent chance of being included in the sample. Throughout this textbook, we assume that samples are random. This assumption of random selection of subjects from the population represents an ideal situation. When it is satisfied, sample findings can be generalized to a known population. For example, political opinion surveys and the Neilson ratings of television programs may approximate this ideal, since it is not too difficult to phone or mail questionnaires to people throughout the country. However, researchers often are not able to randomly select subjects, due to logistical, financial, and time constraints. In this case, samples may be selected for convenience or availability (e.g., volunteers, college sophomores). For example, Rosenthal and Jacobson used subjects at one elementary school in their study of teacher expectancy because they were readily available. (Jacobson was associated with the school district in which the study was conducted.) Likewise, Weiner and Peter used subjects from local schools in their study of moral judgments. As Cornfield and Tukey (1956) pointed out, when available samples are used, inferences from the sample should be made to the accessible population, i.e., the population of subjects like those observed in the study. (The validity of these inferences can be tested by replicating the study with a new sample.) Notice that the accessible population may differ from the population to which the researcher wishes to generalize. In reporting the results of a study, researchers should be careful to point out the limits of their generalizations.

In drawing inferences about a population, we are interested in describing the characteristics of the population—such as its central tendency or variability—using the characteristics of the sample. Descriptive measures of the characteristics of the population—such as the mean or variance—are called **parameters**. Descriptive measures of the characteristics of the sample are called **statistics**. Parameters, then, describe populations, while statistics describe samples. The importance of this distinction, if not already apparent, will become apparent in the remainder of this chapter. As a convention for maintaining this distinction, parameters are denoted by Greek letters, while statistics are denoted by Latin letters. For example, the population mean (a parameter) is denoted by the Greek letter μ (mu) while the sample mean (a statistic) is denoted by the Latin letter $\overline{X}$ (with a bar). The population variance is denoted by σ^2 (sigma squared), while the sample variance is denoted by s^2.

When a statistic is used to **estimate** a parameter, it is called an "estimator." For example, the sample mean is often used as an estimator of the population mean. An **estimator**, then, is a statistic defined by some formula for combining scores from sample data. The sample mean, $\overline{X} = \Sigma X \div N$, is a statistic which is used as an estimator of the population mean μ. The value of a particular sample mean is taken as our "best estimate" of the value of μ. Likewise, the sample variance s^2—defined by the formula $s^2 = \Sigma x^2 \div (N-1)$—is used to estimate the population variance σ^2. The value of a particular sample variance is taken as our best estimate of σ^2.

Since a sample provides only a small subset of data from a population, it is highly unlikely for, say, a particular sample mean to equal exactly the population mean. Indeed, $\overline{X}$ and μ probably will not be the same, since all sorts of factors of which the researcher is unaware may make the particular sample mean a poor representation of the population mean. Such factors are lumped together and called chance or random effects. Just as chance factors give rise to differences between a sample mean and the population mean it is intended to estimate, they also give rise to differences between means of samples, all of which were drawn from the same population. So, although sample statistics such as $\overline{X}$ are used as our best guess of a population parameter such as μ, this estimate may be in error due to random effects. This being the case, it is important to know something about the characteristics of estimators such as $\overline{X}$ and σ^2.

Three important characteristics of estimators are: (1) unbiasedness, (2) consistency, and (3) relative efficiency. Each is discussed briefly here. It should be noted at the outset that few statistics possess all of these desirable characteristics. Nevertheless, each characteristic is important for an estimator to possess, if possible.

An estimator is said to be *unbiased* in estimating a parameter if, for an indefinitely large number of random samples, the mean of the estimator equals the value of the parameter being estimated. For example, the sample mean is an unbiased estimator of the population mean μ. That is, if many samples are randomly selected from a population, and a sample mean $\overline{X}$ calculated for each sample, the mean of the sample means will equal μ. Likewise, the sample variance $s^2 = \Sigma x^2 \div (N - 1)$ is an unbiased estimator of σ^2, because the mean of the sample variances, calculated for an extremely large number of samples from a population, equals σ^2. If, instead, the formula $\Sigma x^2 \div N$ for a sample variance is used, the sample variance will be a *biased* estimator of σ^2. This happens because the average value of this sample variance, calculated over an indefinitely large number of random samples, is *less than* or equal to the population variance. (See Glass & Stanley, 1970, p. 253, for a table showing the biasedness of various estimators of various population parameters.)

A *consistent* estimator tends to get closer and closer to the parameter it estimates as sample size increases. The sample mean is a consistent estimator of the population mean; if the sample included the entire population, the sample mean would equal the population mean. The sample mean, then, is both an unbiased and consistent estimator of the population mean. The sample standard deviation s is also a consistent estimator of the population standard deviation σ, but it is biased. The larger the sample, the more closely s estimates σ, but it never equals σ.

The *efficiency* of an estimator is the degree to which the estimate of a population parameter varies from sample to sample. Put another way, the efficiency of an estimator is the precision with which it estimates a parameter. The *relative efficiency* of an estimator is the ratio of the variance of that estimator to the variance of another estimator of the same population parameter. For example, suppose we are interested in estimating the mean of a normal population. If a large number of random samples were drawn from this population and the mean and median for each sample were calculated, both would provide unbiased estimates of μ. But the variance of sample means would be less than the variance of sample medians. Hence, relative to the median, the sample mean is a more efficient estimator of μ.

From this discussion, it should be clear that in the long run (i.e., over many samples), sample statistics tell us what we want to know about the parameters they estimate. And some statistics are "better" estimators than others. It should also be abundantly clear that, on the basis of limited evidence from a single sample, our estimate of a parameter may be in error. This is a central problem addressed by inferential statistics—given sample data, what should we conclude is true of the population? In describing how inferential statistics addresses this problem, a hypothesis-testing approach is taken in this chapter. This approach, instead of one using estimation and confidence intervals, is taken for pedagogical reasons. It may be easier for students to conceptualize statistical inference initially from a hypothesis-testing approach than from an estimation approach. In subsequent chapters, both approaches are presented.

STATISTICAL INFERENCE IN BEHAVIORAL RESEARCH

In behavioral research, statistical inference can be used to help answer two somewhat similar, commonly posed questions about a population:

Case I. Does a particular sample of observations belong to a hypothesized population of observations?

Case II. Do observations taken on two groups of subjects differ from one another? That is, do the two sets of observations represent samples from identical populations or from different populations?

In the first case (Case I research), sample data are drawn to determine whether the data came from some hypothesized population. For example, the average score on an intelligence test is 100 in the general population. A school administrator might wonder whether the mean IQ of students in his school district is 100. So a random sample of students from the school is given an intelligence test, and the mean of the sample is calculated and used to estimate the population parameter. If the sample mean is close to 100, the administrator might conclude that the students in the district belong to the population of students with mean IQ of 100. If, however, the sample mean deviates from 100 drastically, he might conclude that the students differ from the general population. In Case I research, then, a particular population is hypothesized (e.g., the general population with an average IQ of 100). This hypothesis about the population is usually based on previous research findings or the researcher's best hunch about the nature of the population. A sample of subjects is drawn randomly. Based on data from the sample, an inference is made as to whether the students were drawn from the hypothesized population *or* from some alternative population (e.g., from the general population with an average IQ of 100 or another population with an average IQ of, say, 110).

Case II research addresses the question: Do observations on two groups of subjects differ from one another? In this case, two sets of observations are made. The problem, then, is to infer whether the two groups represent samples from populations with a common mean or from populations with different means. If the samples were drawn from populations with a common mean, then the researcher should conclude from his sample data that the population means do not differ from one another. If the samples were drawn from populations with different means, then the researcher should conclude from his sample data that the population means differ from one another. For example, suppose that subjects are randomly assigned either to an experimental group which received programmed text material in a logical sequence or to a control group which received the material in a scrambled sequence. After reading the programmed text, subjects in both groups are given an achievement test. The researcher is interested in whether there was an effect due to the sequence of programmed material. To answer this question, the sample data for both groups are compared. Prior to reading the material, the two samples represented populations with the same mean. If, after reading the material, the mean scores of the two groups are similar, the inference is that both groups still represent populations with the same mean. Thus the researcher concludes that the treatment did not have an effect. If the means differ greatly, the inference is that the groups represent samples from populations with different means. In this case, the researcher concludes that there was a treatment effect.

These two types of research questions, Case I and Case II, are extremely common in research in the behavioral sciences. The two examples given below illustrate in further detail the types of research questions associated with Case I and Case II studies. In addition, steps are provided for answering the research questions posed—a procedure known as hypothesis testing.

Suppose, for example, that a state board of education wanted to estimate the mean reading level of its high-school seniors, i.e., the entire population (see Figure 9-1a). Since it is difficult and costly to test all of the high-school seniors in the state at one time, a random sample of seniors is tested in the spring of 1975. From this sample of test scores, the mean and standard deviation of the sample distribution are calculated (see Figure 9-1b). These sample data are used to estimate the mean and standard deviation of the entire population of scores for high-school seniors in the state (see Figure 9-1c).

The next question the state board might ask about the mean reading level of its high-school seniors is whether it differs from that of high-school seniors in

HYPOTHESIS TESTING AND STATISTICAL INFERENCE

Case I—Does the Sample Belong to a Hypothesized Population?

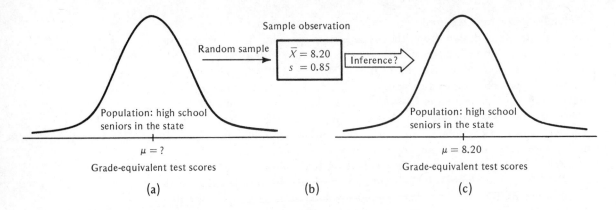

Figure 9-1 ♦ Schematic representation of the steps involved in statistical inference from sample data to the population

the entire United States. Suppose that from national test norms, the mean reading level of high school seniors is known to be 7.89 on a grade-equivalent scale. The question of interest, then, is: *How likely are we to observe a sample mean of 8.20 or greater when, in fact, the sample was drawn from a population with a mean of 7.89?*

The answer to this question will help in deciding whether the high-school seniors in this particular state are similar in reading level to high school seniors across the United States. Clearly, if a sample mean of 8.20 or greater is likely to occur when random samples are drawn from a population with $\mu = 7.89$, the conclusion that the seniors are similar to those in the country as a whole seems to be warranted. However, if a sample mean of 8.20 or greater is quite unlikely to occur when the population mean is 7.89, the conclusion that high school seniors in this state differ in reading level from seniors in other states seems reasonable. In short, should we infer that the sample data were drawn from a population with $\mu = 7.89$, or should we conclude that they were drawn from a different population with $\mu > 7.89$ (μ greater than 7.89)? This problem of inference is shown in Figure 9-2c (a and b are the same as in Figure 9-1).

In reaching a decision on whether a sample mean differs from some known or expected population mean, the following strategy is used. The hypothesis to be tested is set forth. This hypothesis is called the **null hypothesis** (denoted H_0). For the reading study, the null hypothesis would be H_0: $\mu = 7.89$. An **alternative hypothesis** (denoted H_1) is also stated. It may take one of three forms: (1) The population mean is not equal to some specified value (H_1: $\mu \neq 7.89$). This is often called a "nondirectional" alternative hypothesis. (2) The population mean is less than some specific value (H_1: $\mu < 7.89$), or (3) the population mean is greater than some specific value (H_1: $\mu > 7.89$). These last two forms are often called "directional" alternative hypotheses. The choice of an alternative hypothesis is not arbitrary. If theory, prior research, or (preferably) both suggest that μ may be less than or greater than the value specified in the null

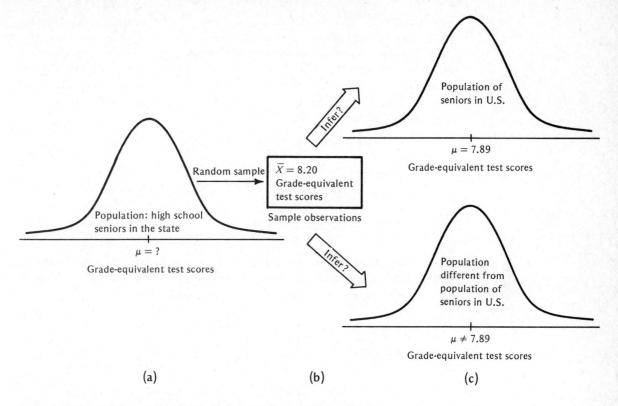

Figure 9-2 ◆ Schematic representation of the steps involved in inference—
Case I ($\overline{X}$ represents the sample mean; μ represents the population mean.)

hypothesis, a directional alternative hypothesis should be used. In the absence
of such evidence, the nondirectional alternative hypothesis should be used. On
the basis of sample data (e.g., $\overline{X} = 8.20$), the researcher decides whether or not
to reject the null hypothesis. A decision not to reject the null hypothesis lends
no support to the alternative hypothesis. However, a decision to reject the null
hypothesis indirectly confirms the alternative hypothesis. The following enumerates the steps in hypothesis testing:

1. Assume that the sample was drawn from the known or expected population. This is equivalent to saying that the seniors in this particular state have
the same reading level as seniors in the United States. This assumption which is
to be tested is known as the *null hypothesis*, H_0. The null hypothesis is denoted as

$$H_0: \mu = \text{some specific value,}$$

where H denotes "hypothesis,"
        0 denotes "null" or "naught,"
        μ denotes the population mean.

273

In our example, H_0: $\mu = 7.89$, or, in words, the average reading level of seniors in the state is 7.89—the average reading level of seniors in the country.

2. Test the assumption of the null hypothesis against an *alternative hypothesis* H_1. The alternative hypothesis asserts that the sample differs from the population specified in the null hypothesis. That is, it asserts that the sample is drawn from a *different* population than the one specified in the null hypothesis. The alternative hypothesis is denoted as:

$$H_1: \mu \neq \text{ some specified value } (\neq \text{ denotes ``not equal''}),$$

or

$$H_1: \mu > \text{ some specified value } (> \text{ denotes ``greater than''}),$$

or

$$H_1: \mu < \text{ some specified value } (< \text{ denotes ``less than''}).$$

In our example (research on reading level), this would be H_1: $\mu \neq 7.89$, or, in words, the average reading level of seniors in the state is different from 7.89—the average reading level of seniors in the country.

Table 9-1 ◆ Summary of the steps involved in hypothesis testing for Case I Research: does a particular sample of observations belong to a hypothesized population of observations?

---

1.   Specify hypotheses:

        H_0: $\mu =$ some specific value   (H_0 is the hypothesis that is tested. It represents the best information about the population available prior to the study.)

        H_1 : $\mu \neq$ some specific value   (H_1 is the hypothesis which remains
                or   tenable if the null hypothesis is
        $\mu >$ some specific value   rejected. It represents the revised
                or   information about the population.)
        $\mu <$ some specific value

2. Procedures:
    Draw random sample from population of interest.
    Observe average (mean) score in sample.

3. Decision rules:
    If the difference between the sample mean and the hypothesized population mean is *likely to arise by chance, do not reject H_0*.
    If the difference between the sample mean and the hypothesized population mean is quite *unlikely to arise by chance, reject H_0 and conclude H_1*.

---

3. In order to test the null hypothesis, draw a random sample of subjects from the population of interest (high school seniors in the state).

4. Based on the sample data, decide whether or not to reject the null hypothesis that the reading level of the population of seniors in the state is the same as in the country.[3] If you decide not to reject the null hypothesis, you decide that the difference between the sample mean and the hypothesized population mean was likely to be due to chance. If you decide to reject the null hypothesis, you decide that a difference as large as or larger than that between the sample mean and the hypothesized population mean was unlikely to have arisen by chance. In this case you accept the alternative hypothesis that the average reading level of high-school seniors in the state differed from the average reading level of seniors in the United States.

These steps in making statistical inferences are summarized in Table 9-1.

♦   ♦   ♦   ♦   ♦

In a study to determine the effect of organization or structure on remembering and recalling a list of words, a random sample of 100 college sophomores was drawn from a population of sophomores (Figure 9-3a and b). Half of these sophomores were randomly assigned to the experimental group ($n_E = 50$) and half to the control group ($n_C = 50$; see Figure 9-3c). Note that at this point in the study, no "treatment" had been given. Thus, the two samples should look very similar and each should provide a picture of what the entire population of sophomores looks like. In this way, sophomores in the experimental group and the control group began the experiment on equal footing.

Case II—Are Two Groups Drawn from Populations with Equal Means?

Next, both groups of sophomores were presented a list of related words to learn. The list was arranged in its proper hierarchical form for the experimental group and in a scrambled order for the control group. After studying the words, the sophomores were asked to recall as many of the words as possible. Figure 9-3d indicates that the mean number of words recalled in the experimental group was greater than in the control group. From these sample data, we must decide between one of two alternatives:

1. The two groups represent populations with a common mean—i.e., in the population there was no difference between the groups in mean recall. In this case, the conclusion drawn from the experiment is that organization did not affect recall.

2. The two samples represent populations with different means—i.e., there were differences between the groups in recall. In this case, the conclusion is that organization did affect recall.

[3]Specific procedures for making this decision will be discussed at length in Chapters 11 and 12. Our concern here is with the nature of the inferences that are drawn from research. Note that the decision is "not to reject" rather than to "accept" H_0. The reason for this distinction is explained at length in Chapter 11.

If the difference between the sample distributions of the experimental and control groups was likely to occur by chance, we should decide that there was no treatment effect and conclude that both samples (groups) belong to the same population. If the difference was not likely to occur by chance, we should decide that there was a treatment effect and conclude that the samples (groups) represent different populations. This decision is made by inferring from the sample data to the population or populations (see Figure 9-3e).

The problem of deciding whether the two samples—experimental and control groups—belong to populations with a common mean or different means is the fundamental problem addressed by statistical inference. The problem is to decide whether the observed differences between sample data may have arisen by *chance* or whether the observed differences arose because, after the experimental treatment, the two samples represent two different populations.

Figure 9-3 ♦ Schematic representation of the steps involved in statistical inference from a true experiment. ($\bar{X}$ represents the sample mean; μ represents the population mean. E represents the experimental group and C represents the control group.)

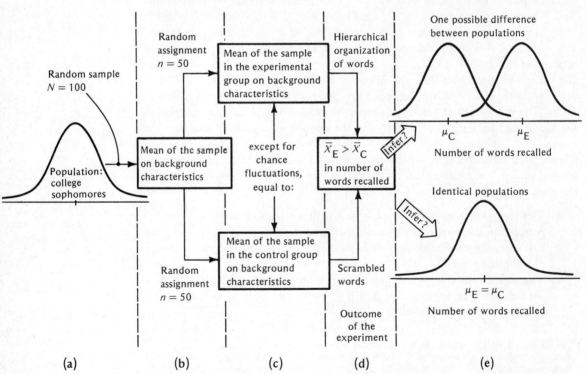

This element of chance introduced into the sample observations suggests that we can never be absolutely sure of the true state of affairs in the population. The best we can do is state *how likely* we are to observe sample differences as large or larger than the ones we have observed if the samples were drawn from the same population. If the observed sample differences are *likely* to arise by sampling from the same population, we infer the sample data represent the same population—i.e., there was no treatment effect. However, if the observed sample differences are quite *unlikely* to arise by sampling from the same population, we infer that the sample data represent different populations—i.e., there was a treatment effect.

The steps in reaching a decision about whether sample differences represent differences in populations are similar to Case I. There are differences, however, in the hypotheses and procedures, since a different research question is being asked. These steps in **hypothesis testing** are summarized below and outlined in Table 9-2.

1. Assume that the samples represent the *same* population. This is equivalent to the assumption that there is no treatment effect. This assumption is called the *null hypothesis*, H_0. In this case, H_0 predicts *no difference* between the populations from which the two sets of observations were taken. That is, it assumes that the two samples of observations came from two populations with a common mean. (Recall that, in Case I, H_0 also predicted *no difference*; however, it predicted no difference between the population from which one set of sample observations was drawn and a hypothesized population.) The null hypothesis is denoted as

$$H_0: \mu_E = \mu_C$$

where H denotes the "hypothesis,"
        0 denotes "null" or "naught,"
        μ denotes the population mean from which the sample was drawn,
        E and C denote experimental and control groups, respectively.

Or, in words, the mean of the experimental population equals the mean of the control population.

2. Test the assumption of the null hypothesis against an *alternative hypothesis*, H_1. H_1 asserts that the null hypothesis is incorrect; in the example, it asserts that the two samples represent different populations. The alternative hypothesis is denoted as

$$H_1: \mu_E \neq \mu_C$$

(the mean of the experimental group is not equal to the mean of the control group), or

$$H_1: \mu_E > \mu_C$$

Table 9-2 ◆ Summary of the steps involved in hypothesis testing for Case II Research: do two samples represent the same or different populations?

---

1. Hypotheses

   H_0: $\mu_E = \mu_C$ (The mean of the experimental group equals the mean of the control group; that is, there is *no difference* between the means of the populations from which the two samples were drawn.)[a]

   H_1: $\mu_E \neq \mu_C$ (The mean of the experimental group does not equal the mean of the control group; that is, the samples represent *different* populations.)

   or

   H_1: $\mu_E > \mu_C$ (The mean of the experimental group is greater than the mean of the control group.)

   or

   H_1: $\mu_E < \mu_C$ (The mean of the experimental group is less than the mean of the control group.)

2. Procedures

   Take a random sample from the population of interest.

   Randomly assign subjects in sample to either the experimental or control group.

   Present the treatment.

   Observe the average (mean) score in each group ($\bar{X}_E$ and $\bar{X}_C$).

3. Decision Rules

   If the observed difference between $\bar{X}_E$ and $\bar{X}_C$ is *likely to arise by chance, do not reject H_0.*

   If the observed difference between $\bar{X}_E$ and $\bar{X}_C$ is *quite unlikely to arise by chance, reject H_0 and conclude H_1.*

---

[a]In some cases, the null hypothesis might be written so that the difference between the control and experimental groups equals some value and not zero: H_0: $\mu_E - \mu_C = $ a specified value. Thus, a null hypothesis does not always imply "no difference."

(the mean of the experimental group is greater than the mean of the control group), or

$$H_1: \mu_E < \mu_C$$

(the mean of the experimental group is less than the mean of the control group). Thus, H_1 specifies a difference between the means of the populations from which the two samples were drawn.

3. In order to test these hypotheses, draw a random sample of subjects from

278

some known population. Then randomly assign the subjects in this sample to either the experimental or the control group.[4]

4. Perform the experiment—i.e., introduce the independent variable or "treatment"—and observe the outcome or dependent variable in each group.

5. Based on the sample data, decide whether or not to reject the null hypothesis. If you decide *not* to reject the null hypothesis, you decide that the observed differences between the experimental and control group were *likely to have arisen by chance*. If you decide to reject the null hypothesis, you decide that the observed differences between the experimental and control group after the treatment were *quite unlikely to have arisen by chance*. In this case, you accept the alternative hypothesis that there was a "treatment effect."

In making inferences about what is true of the population or populations, we can never be certain that our decision to reject or not reject the null hypothesis will be correct. The possibility of making the wrong decision (that is, making an error) is always there. An error can be made in two ways:

ERRORS IN
STATISTICAL INFERENCE

1. Decide to *reject* the null hypothesis when it is *true*. In this case, we infer that the two groups represent different populations when in fact they represent identical populations.
2. Decide *not to reject* the null hypothesis when it is *false*. In this case, we infer that the two groups represent identical populations when, in fact, they represent different populations.

This decision problem is represented in Table 9-3. The *true state of affairs* in the population—the state of affairs that we attempt to find out about through our sample data—is that the *populations are either the same* (null hypothesis) *or different* (alternative hypothesis). From the sample data, we can decide that the observed differences between the two groups represent identical populations (not reject H_0) or that the observed differences between the two groups represent characteristics of different populations (reject H_0). The cells in this 2×2 decision matrix indicate the conditions under which a correct decision is made and the conditions under which an incorrect decision is made.

As we have seen in our discussion of the concepts involved in statistical inference, the decision about whether or not to reject the null hypothesis has depended on *how likely the observed differences in sample data were to arise by chance*. The notion of chance was not explained in this chapter. Furthermore, no

---

[4]Case II procedures are also used to compare two groups of subjects who differ on some personal characteristic such as sex or high or low anxiety prior to the study. In this case, subjects are not randomly assigned to levels of the treatment; the treatment has been performed by nature. The question answered by these hypothesis-testing procedures is whether or not the observations (e.g., reaction times in a memory study) drawn from these groups represent populations with the same or different means. This point will be discussed at length in later chapters.

Table 9-3 ♦ Decision matrix: to reject or not to reject the null hypothesis—that is the question

		True state of affairs in the population	
		Identical populations	Different populations
Decision	Identical populations (not reject H_0)	Correct decision	Error
	Different populations (reject H_0)	Error	Correct decision

criterion was given for deciding how large a difference between the two sets of sample data is necessary in order to conclude that the differences between sample data were unlikely to arise by chance. In a sense, the remainder of this book deals with the definition of chance and the decision about whether sample data arose by chance or from true differences. Specifically, the next three chapters develop the concept of chance and provide methods for determining whether sample data arose by chance. Chapter 13 presents methods for estimating the magnitude of errors in our decisions.

♦　　♦　　♦　　♦　　♦

Summary
This chapter introduces basic concepts underlying *statistical inference* such as *random sampling*, *sample*, *population*, *statistic*, *parameter*, and *estimator*. With these concepts, researchers can make valid inferences or generalizations about a population from a limited sample of data. Two types of questions about populations are presented which are commonly posed in behavioral research: Case I: (Does a particular sample of observations belong to a hypothesized population of observations?) and Case II (Do observations taken on two groups of subjects differ from one another?). Procedures, called *hypothesis testing*, for answering these questions are presented. Finally, possible *errors* that can be made in statistical inference are presented.

♦　　♦　　♦　　♦　　♦

Key Words

alternative hypothesis	population
estimator	random sample
hypothesis testing	sample
null hypothesis	statistical inference
parameters	statistic

♦   ♦   ♦   ♦   ♦

1. What is the difference between a *population* and a *sample*?
2. Why are researchers concerned with *statistical inference*?

3–7 The manager of one branch of a large industrial firm claimed that employee morale was significantly higher due to increased employee participation in management decisions than at the other branch, where no such administrative changes had occurred. To test this hypothesis, 100 employees were randomly selected from each plant and asked to complete a questionnaire measuring job satisfaction. The mean score was 10 for employees from the first branch and 8 for those from the second branch.

3. What research questions does the study intend to answer?
4. Specify H_0 (null hypothesis) and H_1 (alternative hypothesis) for this study.

5–7 Suppose the difference in employee morale was shown to be unlikely to have arisen by chance.

5. What decision would you make regarding the null and alternative hypotheses?
6. What inference would you draw?
7. a. What error might result from this inference?
   b. What is the major threat to the internal validity of this study?

8–12 Scores on a measure of leadership ability were collected on *all* Army recruits since the draft was abolished. The mean of the distribution was found to be 35, and the standard deviation was 10. Recently a new advertising campaign was instituted stressing responsible career opportunities in the military. Recruitment officers were interested in whether individuals recruited under the new advertising program were any different in leadership ability than other individuals recruited since the end of the draft.

8. What research question does the study intend to answer?
9. Specify H_0 and H_1 for this study.

10–12 Suppose the difference in leadership ability between recruits since the end of the draft and recruits under the new advertising program was shown to be likely to have arisen by chance.

10. What decision would you make regarding the null and alternative hypotheses?
11. What inference would you draw?
12. What error might result from this inference?

13–18 A professional golf association was interested in evaluating the effect of two golf clinics on the scores of participating golfers. Based on personal observation, the association felt that clinic B was more effective than clinic A due to better organization and instruction. Twenty golfers participating in each clinic were randomly selected, and their scores in the tournament were collected immediately following completion of the clinic. The average score of golfers participating in clinic A was 2 below par, and for those in clinic B was 4 below par. (Remember that a low golf score is better than a high one.)

13. What research question does this study intend to answer?
14. Specify H_0 and H_1.

15–18 Suppose the differences in golf scores were shown to be likely to have arisen by chance.

15. What decision would you make regarding the null and alternative hypotheses?
16. What inference would you draw?
17. What error might result from this inference?
18. What is the major threat to the internal validity of this study?

19. Supt. Forbes hired a consultant to see if his fifth graders were performing below grade level in history. He said that if the mean achievement for a sample of students was below grade level, he would initiate a new remedial program. Which of the following will he most likely choose as null and alternative hypotheses?

a. H_0: $\mu > 5$ b. H_0: $\mu \leqslant 5$
    H_1: $\mu = 5$ H_1: $\mu > 5$
c. H_0: $\mu \geqslant 5$ d. H_0: $\mu \neq 5$
    H_1: $\mu < 5$ H_1: $\mu = 5$

20. What is the difference between a parameter and a statistic?

21–25 Identify the following as Case I or Case II research questions:

21. How likely are we to observe a sample mean of 9.8, when the sample was drawn from a population with a mean of 12.0?
22. Do the reading scores from two sixth-grade classes differ from one another, or do they represent samples from the same population?
23. Does a group of randomly sampled college sophomores represent the population of college sophomores in terms of political party preference?
24. How likely are we to find a difference between an experimental and control group on posttest scores?
25. Does a particular sample belong to a hypothesized population?

10 ♦

Probability Theory
and
Mathematical Distributions

As POINTED out in Chapter 9, behavioral research, ideally, operates by randomly selecting samples from a population and observing the behavior of subjects in the sample. Based on the observed behavior (described by a sample statistic such as a mean or a variance), an inference is drawn to what is probably true in the population. Without observing the behavior of every person in the population, however, researchers can never be absolutely certain that the inference from sample to population is correct. The best that can be done is to indicate the chance that the inference is incorrect. Or, put another way, the best researchers can do is to indicate the probability that their inferences are correct.

The purposes of this chapter are to introduce, formally, the concept of probability and to provide you with skills in finding probabilities by a counting procedure or from probability distributions. In order to keep the technical discussions at a minimum, just the bare bones of **probability theory** are presented.[1] Throughout some of the more technical parts of the presentation here, keep in mind that the goal of this chapter is to provide you with something more than an intuitive understanding of the question underlying statistical inference: "How likely are we to get the sample results assuming that the null hypothesis is true?"

AN INTUITIVE APPROACH TO PROBABILITY

Most people are pretty good intuitive statisticians. They have a reasonably clear concept of probability without any formal education on the topic. When you ask people what the probability of rain is, they can answer the question—perhaps almost as well as the weather forecaster. The purpose of this section is to extend your knowledge about probability by adding some concepts in probability theory.

What is the probability of tossing a fair coin—one for which a head or a tail is equally likely to occur—and getting heads? Most people will probably answer that there is a "50-50 chance." This is usually expressed as a proportion in probability theory: ".50." This response is the same one you would get if you used probability theory to answer the question. Probability theory would reason as follows (assuming equally likely outcomes):

1. What are the possible outcomes in flipping a coin? Heads or tails.
2. Of all possible outcomes, how many ways can I toss a head? One.

[1]For a more complete presentation of probability theory, see Hays, 1971.

284

3. The probability of heads, then, is given by the number of ways the favored outcomes occur (i.e., one way—heads) divided by the total number of possible outcomes (two ways—heads or tails): $1/2 = 0.50$.

Steps 1 through 3 are summarized in Table 10-1. Note that at step 2, a frequency distribution can be constructed (column 4 of Table 10-1). Along the abscissa are the possible outcomes: "not heads" or "heads." Along the ordinate are the number of ways an outcome can occur. At step 3, the probability of getting a head (and the probability of not getting a head) is given. Notice that a *relative frequency distribution* can also be constructed at this step. The frequencies from the frequency distribution are divided by N, the total number of outcomes possible. These relative frequencies can be read as probabilities. Thus, the relative frequency distribution can be used as a *probability distribution*.

Let's try estimating another probability, one that may hit closer to home. What is the probability of guessing on a true-false test and getting the right answer? To get you into a guessing frame of mind (if you aren't already there), try answering this question:

T   F   Johnny Bench hit two home runs in the fifth game of the 1975 World Series.

Most of you probably guessed at the answer to the question. For those of you who know Johnny Bench, you know that he is quite capable of hitting home runs so you might take an "educated guess" and say true. But many of you could just as easily have flipped a coin: heads I say true, tails I say false. In this case, you're guessing at random. You are as likely to guess heads as tails. Finally, some baseball buffs will know the correct answer: false. (It was Tony Perez who hit two home runs in the fifth game.)

Now, the question again: What is the probability of guessing (*randomly*) on a true-false test and getting the right answer? Most students will readily say "50-50" or, expressed as a proportion, ".50." Or, since guessing randomly is the same as flipping a coin—heads you're right and tails you're wrong—you can get the answer. Probability theory would use the same three steps as described before: (1) list the possible, equally likely outcomes of guessing on the test (right or wrong); (2) determine how many of those outcomes will give a right answer (one); and (3) calculate the probability of a right answer as the number of ways the favored outcome occurs (i.e., the right answer) divided by the total number of outcomes ($1/2 = 0.50$). This reasoning is also summarized in Table 10-1.

Now let's try a last example with a potentially bigger payoff. What is the probability of getting a 2 by rolling a die? Good gamblers—and many not-so-good gamblers—will quickly answer "one out of six" or "$\frac{1}{6}$" or ".17." By using the three steps in probability theory, the same conclusion is found: (1) what are the possible, equally likely outcomes of rolling a die? (there are six: 1, 2, 3, 4, 5, and 6); (2) of all possible outcomes, how many will give a 2? (one: a 2 occurs only once in the list of possible outcomes); thus (3) the probability of

Table 10-1 ◆ Theoretical distributions of outcomes of three experiments

Experiment	Number of equally likely possible outcomes	Number of favored outcomes	Theoretical frequency distribution	Probability (p) = $\dfrac{\text{\# of favored outcomes}}{\text{\# of possible outcomes}}$	Theoretical relative frequency distribution (probability distribution)
a. Flipping a fair coin	2 ⟨ heads, tails	tossing heads: 1		$p(\text{heads}) = 1/2 = .50$	
b. Guessing on true-false	2 ⟨ right, wrong	guessing correctly: 1		$p(\text{right}) = 1/2 = .50$	
c. Rolling a die	1 2 3 4 5 6	rolling a 2: 1		$p(2) = 1/6 = .17$	

getting a 2 by rolling a die is given by the number of ways the favored outcome occurs (i.e., 1) divided by the total number of outcomes (i.e., 6): $1/6 = 0.17$. This reasoning is summarized in Table 10-1. Notice that on the abscissa of the frequency distribution and on the relative-frequency distribution (*probability distribution*), the possible values of rolling a die are either "2" or "not 2." There is one way to get a 2; there are five ways to get "not 2."

What is the probability of guessing right (*randomly*) on a four-alternative multiple-choice question? (If necessary, refer to Table 10-1 for help.)

EXAMPLE PROBLEM 1

At this point, our intuition can be summarized formally in probability theory. Flipping a coin, guessing on a true-false question, rolling a die, and guessing on a multiple-choice question are all examples of trials that produce an **outcome**: heads or tails; right or wrong; and 1, 2, . . . , 6. All possible individual outcomes of a trial are collectively called the **outcome space** (*OS*) of the experiment. The outcome space for the coin experiment is $OS = \{H, T\}$; the outcome space for the true-false item experiment is $OS = \{R, W\}$; and the outcome space for the die experiment is $OS = \{1, 2, 3, 4, 5, 6\}$. In short, the outcome space corresponds to the set of all possible outcomes.

A MORE FORMAL APPROACH TO PROBABILITY

An event (E) is any specific combination of possible, individual outcomes. Put another way, an **event** is a subset of the outcome space. In the coin experiment, we were interested in the event "heads." In the true-false experiment, we were interested in the event "correct." In the die experiment, we were interested in the event "2." In short, events correspond to what we were calling the favored outcome(s).

Note that the unfavored outcome is also an event, but not the one of interest. For example, for the event "2" in the die experiment, there is another event, "not 2." The event "not 2" includes the following outcomes: 1, 3, 4, 5, and 6. In notation form,

$$OS = \{1, 2, 3, 4, 5, 6\},$$

$$E(2) = \{2\},$$

$$E(\text{not } 2) = \{1, 3, 4, 5, 6\}.$$

Similarly, some other event can be selected in the die experiment. For example, what outcomes would be included in the event, "even numbers" on the roll of a die?

$$OS = \{1, 2, 3, 4, 5, 6\},$$

$$E(\text{even numbers}) = \{2, 4, 6\}.$$

At this point, probability can be defined in a formal way. Under the assumption of a finite or countably infinite outcome space with equally likely outcomes, the **probability** p of an event is defined as the number of outcomes in the event divided by the number of outcomes in the outcome space:

$$p(E) = \frac{\#E}{\#OS},$$ [10-1]

where $\#E$ = number of outcomes in the event,
  $\#OS$ = number of outcomes in the outcome space.

The steps in computing the probability of an event are summarized in Procedure 10-1 using the die experiment as an example.

EXAMPLE PROBLEM 2

What is the probability of getting an even number on a roll of a die? [*Hint:* Remember that in order to calculate probability, you assume equally likely outcomes and identify: (1) the number of all possible individual outcomes in the experiment and (2) the number of outcomes falling within the event "even numbers."]

If you feel that you need more practice in calculating probabilities, solve the following additional problems.

Procedure 10-1 ◆ Steps in computing the probability of an event

Operation	Example
1 Look up Formula 10-1: $$p(E) = \frac{\#E}{\#OS}$$ where $\#E$ = number of outcomes of the event, and $\#OS$ = number of outcomes in the outcome space.	Die experiment: What is the probability of rolling a 2 in one throw?
2 Identify the number of outcomes in the event ($\#E$).	$\#E = 1$. (There is only one way to roll a 2.)
3 Identify the number of outcomes in the outcome space ($\#OS$).	$\#OS = 6$. (There are six possible outcomes from rolling a die.)
4 Divide $\#E$ by $\#OS$.	$\frac{1}{6} = 0.17$.

The probability of rolling a 2 in one throw is 0.17. |

What is the probability of getting either a 1 or 6 on a roll of a die?	EXAMPLE PROBLEM 3

What is the probability of drawing a king from a deck of 52 cards?	EXAMPLE PROBLEM 4

What is the probability of drawing a heart from a deck of 52 cards?	EXAMPLE PROBLEM 5

In each of the examples, it was easy to count the outcomes in the outcome space and in an event. However, when four or five true-false questions are considered in an experiment or when two or three dice are rolled, the counting gets quite tedious. In general, as the number of repetitions increases, the amount of counting needed to specify the outcome space increases dramatically.

I'M TOO BUSY TO DO ALL THAT COUNTING

As a first example, consider a fairly small outcome space such as that produced by guessing on a two-item true-false test. By "guessing" we mean that outcomes (right, wrong) on each item are equally likely and that a guess on one item has no effect whatsoever on the response to the second item (i.e., guesses on the items are mutually independent). The outcome space, then, contains four equally likely outcomes (see Table 10-2). Further, there are three possible score values on a two-item true-false test: 0, 1, 2 (see Table 10-2). These score values can be considered events. There is only one way to obtain a score value of zero—both answers must be wrong. Thus, there is one outcome in the event, zero correct: $E(0 \text{ correct}) = \{WW\}$. A score value of 1 can be obtained by answering either the first or second item correctly. Thus, there are two

Table 10-2 ♦ Representation of guessing on the two-item true-false test in probability terms

Outcomes on first item	Outcomes on second item	Total number of items correct (score value)
R	R	2 (RR)
	W	1 (RW)
W	R	1 (WR)
	W	0 (WW)
	#(Outcome space) = 4	

outcomes in the event "1 correct": $E(1 \text{ correct}) = \{RW, WR\}$. Finally, there is only one way to obtain a score value of 2—both answers must be correct. So there is one outcome in the event "2 correct": $E(2 \text{ correct}) = \{RR\}$.

From this information, the probability of getting each event or score value can be found:

$$p(E = 0) = \frac{\#E}{\#OS} = \frac{1}{4} = 0.25,$$

$$p(E = 1) = \frac{\#E}{\#OS} = \frac{2}{4} = 0.50,$$

$$p(E = 2) = \frac{\#E}{\#OS} = \frac{1}{4} = 0.25.$$

This counting is summarized in Figure 10-1 a and b. Figure 10-1a shows the three possible events or score values—0, 1, and 2—on the abscissa and the number of outcomes or frequency with which each score value can occur on the ordinate.

Figure 10-1 ◆ Frequency distributions and probability distributions based on two items (a, b) and three items (c, d)

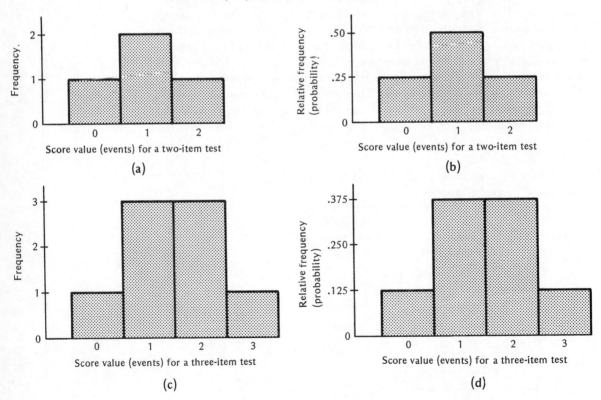

Like any frequency distribution, Figure 10-1a can be converted into a *relative frequency distribution* by dividing each frequency value (number of outcomes in an event) by N, the total number of outcomes in the outcome space (see Figure 10-1b). In symbol form,

$$\text{relative frequency} = \frac{\text{number of outcomes on ordinate}}{\text{number of outcomes in } OS} = \frac{\# E}{\# OS} \qquad [10\text{-}1a]$$

At this point, the value of a relative frequency distribution should be clear. By converting a frequency distribution into a relative frequency distribution, a **probability distribution** is formed:

$$p(E) = \text{relative frequency of } E = \frac{\# E}{\# OS} \qquad [10\text{-}1b]$$

Now, let's derive the probability distribution for scores on a three-item test. First, the outcome space needs to be enumerated. As shown in Table 10-3, there are eight possible, equally likely outcomes: RRR, RRW, RWR, RWW, WRR, WRW, WWR, WWW.

Table 10-3 ◆ Representation of guessing on the three-item true-false test in probability terms

One item	Outcomes on Two items	Three items	Number of items correct (score value)
R	R	R	3 (RRR)
		W	2 (RRW)
	W	R	2 (RWR)
		W	1 (RWW)
W	R	R	2 (WRR)
		W	1 (WRW)
	W	R	1 (WWR)
		W	0 (WWW)
#OS = 2	#OS = 4	#OS = 8	

Four events (four score values) can be observed with a three-item test: E(score value $= 0$), E(score value $= 1$), E(score value $= 2$), E(score value $= 3$). In short, a person can get a score ranging from 0 to 3 on a three-item true-false test. There is one outcome associated with a score of 0: $E(0) = \{WWW\}$. There are three outcomes associated with (ways to get) a score of 1: $E(1) = \{RWW, WRW, WWR\}$. Likewise, there are three outcomes associated with a score of 2: $E(2) = \{RRW, RWR, WRR\}$. Finally, there is only one way to guess correctly on all the items: $E(3) = \{RRR\}$. These frequencies, or numbers of outcomes, associated with the events (score values) are the same as those shown in Figure 10-1c, as expected.

In order to convert the frequency distribution in Figure 10-1c into the probability distribution in Figure 10-1d, the probability of each event needs to be calculated:

$$p(E = 0) = \frac{\# E}{\# OS} = \frac{1}{8} = 0.125,$$

$$p(E = 1) = \frac{\# E}{\# OS} = \frac{3}{8} = 0.375,$$

$$p(E = 2) = \frac{\# E}{\# OS} = \frac{3}{8} = 0.375,$$

$$p(E = 3) = \frac{\# E}{\# OS} = \frac{1}{8} = 0.125.$$

These probabilities are placed on the ordinate of a graph and the score values are placed on the abscissa to form Figure 10-1d.

A lot of time and tedious counting could have been saved if we already had the probability distribution for guessing randomly on the three-item true-false test. Figure 10-1d can be used to find the answer to the following question: "What is the probability of getting a score of 1 correct by guessing on a three-item true-false test?" From this figure, the probability of a score of 1 is 0.375. Likewise, the probabilities of the scores 0, 2, and 3 can be found (0.125, 0.375, and 0.125, respectively). Moreover, the probability of getting a score of two *or more* can be found by adding up the probabilities for a score of two and a score of three: $.375 + .125 = .500$.

MATHEMATICAL DISTRIBUTIONS

At this point, three conclusions can be made about probability distributions. First, as the number of items on a true-false test increases, the amount of counting needed to determine the size of the outcome space and the event of interest increases greatly. A ten-item true-false test has an outcome space of 1024 outcomes. This also holds as the number of dice rolled increases, as the number of coins flipped increases, as the number of multiple-choice questions increases, and in general as the number of trials increases.

Second, the number of outcomes increases in an orderly, lawlike manner as the number of trials (coins, true-false items, etc.) increases. For example, a toss of one coin produces an outcome space of 2, a toss of two coins produces an outcome space of 4, a toss of three coins produces an outcome space of 8, and a toss of four coins produces an outcome space of 16 outcomes. This means that the counting process we have just gone through can be modelled mathematically (i.e., described by a mathematical formula) and the probability of each event of interest can be calculated directly without counting.

Third, reading probabilities from a probability distribution is a lot easier and less time consuming than calculating probabilities by counting. Mathematical models that produce probabilities instead of our doing a lot of counting, then, are worthy of consideration.

When a distribution is derived from a mathematical model, it is referred to as a **mathematical distribution**. A very common mathematical model is the **binomial expansion**. It models experiments in which each trial is independent of every other trial, two outcomes are possible on each trial, and the probability of "success" is the same from one trial to the next. Some examples of such experiments are tossing coins (each coin is a trial), guessing on a true-false or multiple-choice test (each item is a trial), or rolling dice (each die is a trial). The mathematical distribution produced by the binomial expansion is called the binomial distribution; it can be used as a probability distribution for tossing coins or guessing on tests.

The purpose of developing the binomial distribution here is threefold: (1) to give you a sense of what a probability distribution is, (2) to show you that mathematical distributions can be used as probability distributions, and (3) to show you that these distributions provide information about the probability of an event. To begin, the binomial expansion is probably most familiar to you as presented in your elementary algebra course. There you were taught to expand an expression such as $(a + b)^2$ as follows:

$$(a + b)^2 = a^2 + 2ab + b^2.$$

If, in this expression, a is replaced by the probability of success (p), b by the probability of "not success" (q; remember, there are only two possible outcomes on each trial), and the power (2 in this case) by the number of trials (N), then the binomial expansion can be written as

$$(p + q)^N. \qquad [\textbf{10-2}]$$

To see how the binomial expansion can be used to produce a binomial distribution, consider a two-item true-false test in which the examinee guessed the answer to each item. The probability of guessing correctly on an item is one-half, while the probability of guessing incorrectly is also one-half. Moreover, there are two items on the test, so there are two trials ($N = 2$). In this case, the binomial expansion can be written as

$$\left(\tfrac{1}{2} + \tfrac{1}{2}\right)^2.$$

Notice that on a two-item test, the examinee can receive one of three scores: 0, 1, 2. The binomial expression, then, should produce a probability for each of the three possible score values. This is exactly what happens:

$$\left(\tfrac{1}{2} + \tfrac{1}{2}\right)^2 = \left(\tfrac{1}{2}\right)^2 + 2\left(\tfrac{1}{2}\right)\left(\tfrac{1}{2}\right) + \left(\tfrac{1}{2}\right)^2$$

$$= \tfrac{1}{4} + \tfrac{1}{2} + \tfrac{1}{4}.$$

Score: 0   1   2.

If the results of this binomial expansion are cast into a relative frequency distribution with score values (0, 1, 2) on the abscissa and relative frequencies ($\tfrac{1}{4}, \tfrac{1}{2}, \tfrac{1}{4}$) on the ordinate, the result is a **binomial distribution** (shown in Figure 10-1b).

In general, the binomial distribution can be found for any number of trials (N) and for any different values of p and q. (Note that $p + q = 1.00$.) For example, consider a three-item multiple-choice test with four alternatives on each item. Assuming guessing, $p = \tfrac{1}{4}$, $q = \tfrac{3}{4}$, $N = 3$:

Binomial expression	Binomial expansion	Probability	Score value
$(\tfrac{1}{4} + \tfrac{3}{4})^3 =$	$(\tfrac{1}{4})^3$	.02	3
	$+ 3(\tfrac{1}{4})^2(\tfrac{3}{4})$	.14	2
	$+ 3(\tfrac{1}{4})(\tfrac{3}{4})^2$	.42	1
	$+ (\tfrac{3}{4})^3$	.42	0

Actually, the binomial distribution is not one distribution but rather a whole family of distributions which depend on two parameters: (1) N, the number of trials in an experiment and (2) p, the probability of success on any one trial. To see this, just compare the true-false example with the multiple-choice example. Figure 10-2 presents three binomial distributions in which $p(\text{success}) = \tfrac{1}{2}$ and $N = 3$, 10, and infinity. Notice that as the number of trials increases, the binomial distribution becomes increasingly "bell shaped." It can be shown that, when $N =$ infinity (e.g., an infinite number of coin tosses) and $p = \tfrac{1}{2}$, the binomial distribution becomes a *normal distribution*[2] (Figure 10-2c).

---

[2]Probabilities in the binomial distribution for an infinity of trials are given by the proportion of area under the normal curve (cf. Chapter 5). This concept is presented in detail in Chapters 11 and 12.

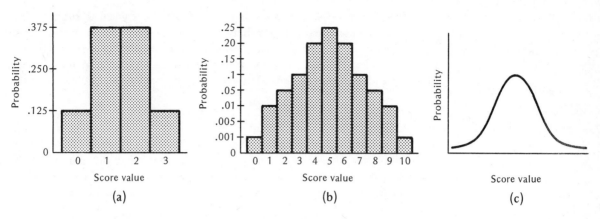

Figure 10-2 ◆ Binomial distributions with probability = .50 for (a) 3, (b) 10, and (c) infinite trials

Like the binomial distribution, the **normal distribution** is a family of mathematical distributions. It is particularly important because this theoretical distribution can be used to model many kinds of data collected in the behavioral sciences. Applications of the normal distribution are discussed extensively in the next two chapters.

The purpose in mentioning normal distributions here is that they too, like the binomial distribution, could be derived mathematically or by counting—given enough time. We do not intend to take the time. However, by developing the binomial distribution, you should get a sense of what a probability distribution is, and recognize that mathematical distributions can be used as probability distributions by representing them as relative frequency distributions and that these distributions provide information about the probability of an event.

TO ANSWER THE QUESTION "HOW LIKELY?"

By now, you may be having some difficulty remembering why we got into so much probability theory. If you think way back to the last chapter, you will remember that in answering research questions with empirical data, the researcher can never be absolutely certain his answer is correct. Rather, the best that can be done is to collect data and state how likely those data are to arise if the null hypothesis is true. In order to make statements about how likely sample results are to occur under the null hypothesis, it was necessary to develop some probability theory. Having developed the theory, it can be applied in answering the question. In fact, the remainder of this book deals just with this problem: "How likely are we to get the sample results under the null hypothesis?"

In order to show how the probability theory developed in this chapter can be used to answer the question "How likely?" consider an example using a true-false test. Suppose that a ten-item true-false test is given to subjects after some experimental treatment. Perhaps the first question the researcher would like to answer is whether or not the subjects were guessing on the test. His null hypothesis, then, is that the subjects were guessing, that is, that their performance was due to chance alone. His alternative hypothesis is that they were not guessing.[3]

Under the null hypothesis—that the subject's performance is due to chance or random guessing—we can think of each subject's score as being drawn from a binomial distribution in which the number of trials (N) is equal to 10 and the probability of success on each trial (p) is $\frac{1}{2}$. The theoretical distribution for the number of correct responses under the null hypothesis is shown in Figure 10-2b. The null hypothesis is that subjects are guessing and should get about half of the true-false items correct ($10 \div 2 = 5$):

$$H_0: \mu = 5.$$

The alternative hypothesis is that subjects' performance is not due to chance; that is, they are not randomly guessing. Thus the research hypothesis can be formally stated as follows:

$$H_1: \mu \neq 5$$

(see footnote 3).

In order to test this hypothesis, a subject is drawn at random from the population proposed under the null hypothesis (the population of persons guessing at random), given the experimental treatment, and then tested. The question of interest is: How likely is it that this subject could have obtained her score if she were actually guessing? Suppose the person earned a score of 10 on the test. Under the null hypothesis that this person was guessing, how likely is she to obtain a score of 10 correct out of 10 possible? Intuition says that this is *quite unlikely*. However, we can do better. Using the probability distribution under the null hypothesis (Figure 10-2b), we see that if the person were guessing, the probability of his or her earning a score of 10 would be 0.001. Quite unlikely! Based on this sample data, we should decide to reject the null hypothesis that the person was guessing. We therefore accept the research hypothesis that the person was not guessing at random.

While there are many variations on this theme, this example can serve as a basis for all statistical inference. Assuming the null hypothesis is true, a probability distribution can be identified. Sample data are collected. Then the question is asked: How likely would we be to get these sample data if they were

---

[3]As indicated in Chapter 9, alternative hypotheses can take one of three forms. The alternative hypothesis here is nondirectional, since no predictions about the effects of the treatment have been made. If theory or past evidence suggested that the experimental treatment would facilitate performance, the following research hypothesis might have been specified: $H_1: \mu > 5$. Similarly, if the treatment was expected to interfere with performance, we might have specified $H_1: \mu < 5$.

drawn from the probability distribution identified under the null hypothesis? If they are likely to arise from the hypothesized distribution, the null hypothesis is not rejected. If they are quite unlikely to arise under the null hypothesis (i.e., the probability is quite low), the null hypothesis should be rejected with the conclusion that the research hypothesis is correct. The chance of being incorrect in this case is quite small, depending on the criterion used to decide whether or not to reject the null hypothesis.

◆   ◆   ◆   ◆   ◆

Summary

This chapter presents basic concepts and skills in *probability theory* that are necessary to understand how that theory is used in making statistical inferences. Procedures for calculating *probabilities* are presented, and the use of *probability distributions* such as the *binomial* and *normal distributions* is discussed. Finally, the use of probability theory in statistical inference is illustrated.

◆   ◆   ◆   ◆   ◆

Key Words

binomial distribution	outcome
binomial expansion	outcome space
event	probability
mathematical distribution	probability distribution
normal distribution	probability theory

◆   ◆   ◆   ◆   ◆

Exercises

1–4 A particular game of chance in Las Vegas shows numbers from 1 to 100. The even numbers are red and the odd numbers are black. Assuming that the game is fair, what is the probability of obtaining the specified result?

1. A red number.
2. An odd number.
3. A 10.
4. Either 1 or 100.

5–8 A card game called canasta uses two decks of playing cards at once. Assuming that you have a canasta deck, what is the probability of randomly choosing the following?

5. A queen.
6. A spade or club.
7. An ace of spades.
8. A jack, queen, or king of hearts.

9–12 Sixty restaurants are advertised in the Yellow Pages for a city. Of these, 10 serve Chinese food, 17 Mexican, 5 French, 8 Italian, and 20 American. What is the probability of randomly choosing a restaurant that serves the following?

9. American food.
10. Mexican or French food.

11. Chinese or American food.
12. Mexican, French, Italian or Chinese food.

13–16 A particular school has four sixth-grade classes. They contain the following number of boys and girls:

	Class 1	Class 2	Class 3	Class 4
Boys	15	14	8	13
Girls	15	16	14	10

When the names of all sixth-graders are combined, what is the probability of randomly selecting the following?

13. A boy.
14. A girl from Class 2.
15. A girl from Class 1 or Class 4.
16. A boy or girl from Class 3.

17. How is probability theory related to statistical inference?

18–20 Suppose a student takes a three-item multiple-choice test. If each item has three alternatives and the student performs at the chance level (i.e., guessing), what is the probability that he will get the following scores? (Hint: see Formula 10-2.)

18. All three items correct.
19. Two items correct.
20. None of the items correct.

21–25 Consider a four-alternative multiple-choice test with four items. What is the probability of getting the following scores by guessing? (Hint: see Formula 10-2.)

21. No items correct.
22. One item correct.
23. Two items correct.
24. Three items correct.
25. Four items correct.

Inferences about a Population Mean
from
Sample Means

Basic Concepts Underlying Hypothesis Testing
◆ Sampling Distribution of Means ◆
◆ Characteristics of the Sampling Distribution of Means ◆

Statistical Test Underlying Inference from a Sample Mean
◆ Finding Probabilities in the Sampling Distribution of Means ◆
◆ The Alternative Hypothesis and the Tail You Seek ◆

Applications of Hypothesis Testing: Inferences about a
Population Mean Based on Sample Means

Confidence Intervals
◆ Interval Estimates for a Population Mean ◆
◆ Relationship between Confidence Intervals and Hypothesis Testing ◆

Summary
◆ Key Words ◆
◆ Exercises ◆

IN THIS chapter, statistical procedures are developed to test hypotheses arising from Case I research questions: "Does a particular sample belong to a specified population?" A statistical test used to help answer Case I research questions, the $z_{\bar{X}}$ test, is presented along with some important concepts underlying the use of this test. The $z_{\bar{X}}$ test is used in deciding whether or not the difference between a sample mean and a hypothesized population mean may have been due to chance.

Two fundamental ideas underlie this and many other statistical tests. The first idea is that the null hypothesis is *assumed* to be true until it is shown to be false. In other words, the difference between the sample mean and the hypothesized population mean is *assumed* to be due to chance. The greater the difference between the sample mean and the hypothesized population mean, the lower the probability that the difference is due to chance (all other things being equal, of course). If the difference is extremely large, we should conclude that the difference is not due to chance (i.e., reject the null hypothesis). Rather, the difference is probably due to the fact that the sample was drawn from a different population than the one with the hypothesized mean.

The problem of determining the probability of the difference is solved by the second idea. Namely, a piece of research uses just one sample out of an indefinitely large number of samples that could have been taken from the population specified by the null hypothesis. Furthermore, if a large number of samples were drawn from this population, each sample mean would not be exactly the same value as most of the others. Rather, sample means would differ from one another and from the true mean of the population. In order to determine whether the particular sample mean obtained in a research study actually was drawn from the population specified in the null hypothesis, we need to know something about the nature of the distribution of means sampled from that population. A distribution with values of the sample mean on the abscissa and relative frequencies on the ordinate is called a *sampling distribution of means*. The sample mean, then, can be located within this sampling distribution of means to determine whether it falls in the center of the distribution or at the extreme ends of the sampling distribution. The further the sample mean lies from the center of the sampling distribution—the further it lies from the hypothetical population value—the greater the chances are that the discrepancy is not due to chance but represents a systematic difference.

This chapter is divided into four sections. The first section presents three fundamental concepts in hypothesis testing: (1) the *sampling distribution*; (2) the characteristics of the sampling distribution, including its approximate shape, its central tendency, and its variability; and (3) the sampling distribution as a probability distribution which provides an answer to the question of "how likely?"

The second section presents: (1) a statistical test, the "$z_{\bar{X}}$ test," which is used to determine the probability that a sample mean was drawn from a specified population; (2) the concept of the *level of significance* of a statistical test which provides a basis for deciding whether a sample mean is likely or unlikely to have arisen from a particular population; and (3) the concept of one-tailed (directional) and two-tailed (nondirectional) statistical tests. The third section presents *applications* of these statistical tests, and the final section discusses procedures for constructing *confidence-interval* estimates of the population mean.

Recall from the discussion of statistical inference in Chapter 9 that research sets out to reject the null hypothesis and gain support for the alternative hypothesis. A decision about H_0, based on sample data, bears on what the population of students, subjects, observations, and so on looks like. In order to make a decision, we need to know what to expect in a study if the null hypothesis actually is true. In making inferences about the mean of a population from a sample mean, *a model is needed to indicate just how much variability to expect in sample means drawn randomly from the population under the null hypothesis.* From this model of chance sample means, we can decide whether or not our sample mean was within the expected range. If it is expected, the null hypothesis cannot be rejected. (We speak of not rejecting the null hypothesis rather than accepting the null hypothesis because, even though we cannot reject the null hypothesis on the basis of sample data, we do not know that its value is exactly that of the true population mean. After all, we could be off a few tenths of a point, or even more.) If it is unexpected—unlikely to arise by chance under the null hypothesis—we might decide to reject the null hypothesis and conclude that our alternative hypothesis is true. Here a model is presented of the variability of sample means drawn from a population specified by the null hypothesis: the sampling distribution of means.

In theory, an indefinitely large number of samples could be drawn from the population specified by the null hypothesis. Furthermore, in theory, a mean could be calculated for each sample. For example, suppose the null hypothesis is that the mean IQ score in a population is 100 (Figure 11-1a). As shown in Figure 11-1b, means of samples drawn from this population will differ from one another; however, they also will cluster about the central value: $\mu = 100$.

In order to get a picture of the variability in sample means that could be expected from sampling under the null hypothesis, the sample means could be plotted as a frequency polygon with the abscissa representing the values of the sample means and the ordinate representing the frequency or relative frequency with which each value is observed. Such a theoretical distribution is

BASIC CONCEPTS UNDERLYING HYPOTHESIS TESTING

Sampling Distribution of Means

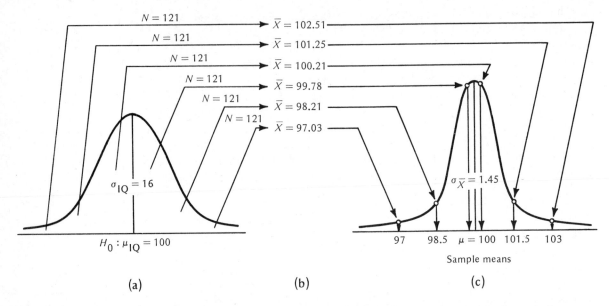

Figure 11-1 ♦ The concept of a sampling distribution of means: (a) theoretical population of IQ scores with mean IQ (μ_{IQ}) equal to 100 and standard deviation (σ_{IQ}) of 16 IQ points; (b) six means which were drawn randomly from the population with $\mu_{IQ} = 100$ and $\sigma_{IQ} = 16$. Each mean is based on a sample of 121 subjects (scores from the population; (c) sampling distribution of means based on samples of size 121.

called a **sampling distribution of means**. The theoretical sampling distribution of means for samples of 121 subjects, each drawn from the population specified by the null hypothesis, is shown in Figure 11-1c. Notice that the mean of the sampling distribution of means is equal to the population mean and that the variability of the sample means (Figure 11-1c) is much less than the variability of the IQ scores themselves (Figure 11-1a). This happens because (1) there are more scores in the middle of a score distribution than at the ends of the distribution, so that (2) the sample mean is more likely to be based on these middle scores than on the extreme scores. (We will return to this point shortly.) *The sampling distribution, then, provides a model of the variability of sample means* based on samples of 121 subjects from the population specified by the null hypothesis.

To illustrate how the sampling distribution of means is used in research, consider a hypothetical study. A group of researchers want to know whether the population of subjects from which they plan to randomly sample has a mean IQ of 100 or whether the subjects represent a population with a mean IQ different than 100. They begin by stating the null and alternative hypotheses: $H_0: \overline{X}_{IQ} = 100$; $H_1: \overline{X}_{IQ} \neq 100$. Then a sample of 121 subjects is drawn randomly and the mean IQ calculated. Under the assumption that the null hypothesis is true, the sampling distribution shown in Figure 11-1c suggests that the sample mean is most likely to fall within the range of 97 to 103 and that it should be close to 100, the center of the distribution. Suppose the sample mean was found to be 95.45. Is a mean of 95.45 or less a likely outcome under the null hypothesis? What is the basis for your decision?[1]

The importance of the sampling distribution of means is that it provides a model of what is likely to occur if the null hypothesis is true. Conceptually, this model is formed by assuming that repeated, random samples of size N can be drawn from a population specified under the null hypothesis. The sample for a study, then, is just one of many that might have been drawn. If a mean is calculated for each sample, these sample means will differ from one another just by chance. These differences give rise to errors in inferring from the sample to the population. By taking repeated samples, we can specify just how much variability to expect among sample means. Using this variability as a yardstick, we can determine how likely it is that an observed sample mean in a research study arose under the null hypothesis. If, according to the yardstick, the mean falls close to the hypothesized population mean, the null hypothesis should not be rejected. If the mean does not fall close to the hypothesized population mean, a decision to reject H_0 should be made.

◆ ◆ ◆ ◆ ◆

From mathematical statistics, we know that if repeated random samples of size N are drawn from a normally distributed population, the distribution of sample means:

Characteristics of the Sampling Distribution of Means

1. will be normally distributed;
2. will have a mean equal to the population mean;
3. will have a standard deviation—called the standard error of the mean— equal to the population standard deviation divided by the square root of the sample size.

Furthermore, if N is large, the central limit theorem states that the sampling distribution of means will be approximately normal, even though the population is not normally distributed. Furthermore, the mean of the sampling distribution will equal μ, and the standard error will equal the population standard deviation (σ) divided by the square root of the sample size ($\sqrt{N}$), regardless of the shape of the population distribution. Each of these points is covered in detail below.

Shape of the sampling distribution   For samples of 30 subjects or more, the sampling distribution of means will be approximately normal for a wide variety

---

[1]This is an unlikely outcome, since this sample mean falls (approximately) two standard deviations below the hypothesized population mean (assuming Figure 11-1c is drawn to scale—which it is, of course).

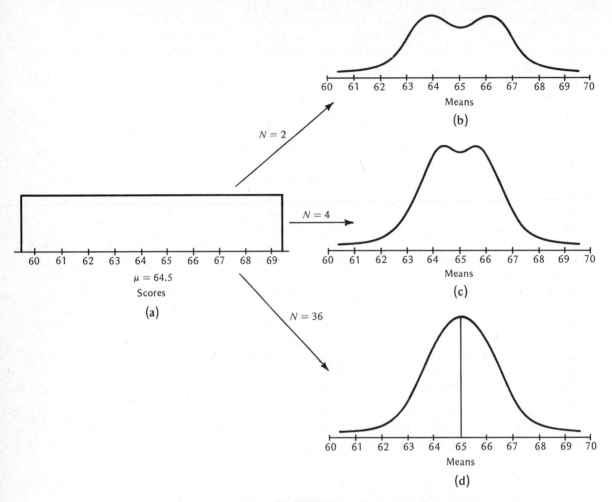

Figure 11-2 ◆ Relationship between sample size and shape of the sampling distribution of means (after Clarke et al., 1965): (a) frequency distribution of scores in the population; (b) sampling distribution based on samples of size 2; (c) sampling distribution based on samples of size 4; (d) sampling distribution based on samples of size 36

of differently shaped population distributions.[2] The relation between sample size and shape of the sampling distribution of means is shown in Figure 11-2. Figure 11-2a shows the distribution of scores in the population. A population distribution which is flat or "rectangular" rather than normal was intentionally

[2]If the distribution of scores in the population is normal, so will be the sampling distribution of means, regardless of N. However, if there is no available information about the shape of the distribution of scores in the population, the **central limit theorem** states that as the sample size increases, the shape of the sampling distribution of means becomes increasingly like the normal

chosen to show that even in this case, with samples of size 30 or more, the sampling distribution of means approaches normality. Figure 11-2b shows the sampling distribution of means based on a sample size of 2. Notice that the distribution has a slight peak in the center. Figure 11-2c shows the sampling distribution based on samples of size 4. The distribution is becoming increasingly symmetric about the population mean. Finally, Figure 11-2d shows the sampling distribution based on samples of size 36. This sampling distribution of means can be described as normal in form.

Mean of the sampling distribution   The mean of the sampling distribution of means is the population mean. This arises from the fact that the sample mean is an unbiased estimator of the population mean (cf. Chapter 9). That is, for random sampling from any population, the long-run average of the sample means will equal the population mean.

Standard error of the mean   The standard deviation of sample means in a sampling distribution of means is called the **standard error of the mean**. It provides an index of how much the sample means vary about the population mean (the mean of the sampling distribution). Thus it provides information about the amount of error likely to be made by inferring the value of the population mean from a sample mean. The greater the variability among sample means, the greater the chance that the inference about the population mean from a single sample mean will be in error.

The standard error of the mean ($\sigma_{\bar{X}}$) is a function of the population standard deviation (σ_X) and the sample size (N):

$$\sigma_{\bar{X}} = \frac{\sigma_X}{\sqrt{N}} \, . \qquad [11\text{-}1]$$

Formula 11-1 indicates that as N increases, $\sigma_{\bar{X}}$ decreases, since σ is the same regardless of sample size. This relationship between sample size and the standard error makes intuitive sense if we take note of two things: (1) the mean is greatly influenced by extreme scores, and (2) there are usually more scores near the center of a distribution than at the extremes. In a small sample (e.g., $N = 4$), most of the scores would fall around the population mean, but one extreme score would greatly influence the value of a sample mean. Thus, from sample to sample (of $N = 4$), considerable variability between means should be expected. However, in a large sample (e.g., $N = 121$), the existence of a few extreme scores might be balanced by scores at either extreme of the distribution

---

one. For a sample size of 30, the normal distribution provides a reasonably good approximation of the sampling distribution of means. So $N = 30$ is used, as a rule, for inferring the shape of the sampling distribution.

and greatly outweighed by the large number of scores close to the population mean. In this case, the differences between sample means should be small.

In order to illustrate the importance of this relationship between sample size and standard error, consider the sampling distributions shown in Figure 11-3. Figure 11-3a shows the distribution of scores in some hypothetical population with a mean equal to 50 and a standard deviation of 10 points. Figure 11-3b shows the distribution of means based on a sample size of 1. Notice that this sampling distribution of means is the same as the population distribution, since there is no difference between a mean based on one score and the score itself. Figure 11-3c shows a sampling distribution based on samples of size 2. The variability of this sampling distribution is less than that of the population distribution. Figure 11-3d shows a sampling distribution based on samples of size 16. The variability of this distribution is considerably smaller than that of

Figure 11-3 ◆ Relationship between sample size and the standard error of the mean (samples drawn from a population with scores normally distributed): (a) distribution of scores in a hypothetical population with $\mu = 50$, $\sigma = 10$; (b) sampling distribution of means based on sample sizes of $N = 1$: $\sigma_{\bar{x}} = 10/\sqrt{1} = 10$; (c) sampling distribution of means based on sample sizes of $N = 2$: $\sigma_{\bar{x}} = 10/\sqrt{2} = 7.07$; (d) sampling distribution of means based on sample sizes of $N = 16$: $\sigma_{\bar{x}} = 10/\sqrt{16} = 2.50$; (e) sampling distribution of means based on sample sizes of $N = 36$: $\sigma_{\bar{x}} = 10/\sqrt{36}$ 1.67

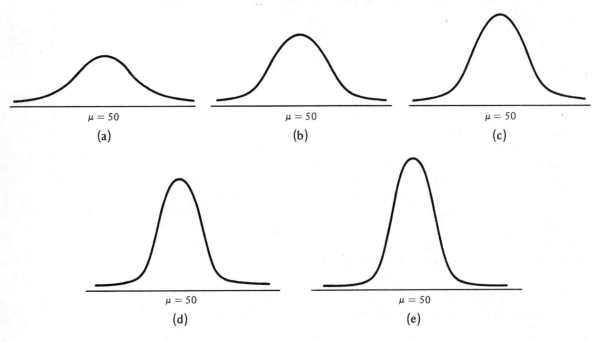

$\mu = 50$

(a)

$\mu = 50$

(b)

$\mu = 50$

(c)

$\mu = 50$

(d)

$\mu = 50$

(e)

the preceding sampling distributions. The variability of the sampling distribution based on samples of size 36 is the smallest of all. Finally, if a sample of "size infinity" were drawn, the standard error would equal zero. *As sample size increases, the standard error of the mean decreases.* The larger the sample on the average, the smaller the error made in inferring the population mean from a sample mean.

The results of a statewide testing program of high-school seniors in California showed a mean of 50 and standard deviation of 14 on a measure of mechanical ability. Suppose a large number of samples of 49 seniors were drawn at random and a mean calculated for each sample.

EXAMPLE PROBLEM 1

a. What *shape* will this sampling distribution of means take?
b. What is the *mean* of this sampling distribution of means?
c. What is the standard error of the mean (i.e., the standard deviation of the sampling distribution of means)?

Sampling distribution as a probability distribution   The sampling distribution of means can be used as a probability distribution to answer questions about how likely a particular sample mean is to arise under the null hypothesis. Recall that in the last chapter probability was defined as the relative frequency of an event. Thus, a frequency distribution of scores can be converted into a probability distribution by converting it to a relative frequency distribution. Since the sampling distribution is a frequency distribution for means, means are sampled and not scores. An event is defined as a mean equal to or less than a particular value. Thus, the probability of an event—a sample mean—is

$$p(\text{Event}) = p(\overline{X} \leqslant \text{particular value})$$
$$\approx \frac{\text{frequency of (sample means} \leqslant \text{particular value)}}{\text{total number of means sampled}}$$
$$= \text{cumulative relative frequency.} \qquad [11\text{-}2]$$

Suppose 200 sample means were drawn and 10 of them were less than or equaled 55. The probability of observing a sample mean ⩽ 55, then, is given by Formula 11-2:

$$p(\overline{X} \leqslant 55) = \frac{\text{frequency of (sample means} \leqslant 55)}{\text{total number of means sampled}}$$
$$= \frac{10}{200} = .05.$$

The probability of observing a sample mean $\leqslant 55$ is the cumulative relative frequency of that event, i.e., $10/200 = .05$. Thus, by converting the sampling distribution of means to a cumulative relative frequency distribution, this distribution can be used as a probability distribution. Since the sampling distribution is a normal distribution with a mean equal to μ under the null hypothesis and a standard deviation (standard error) equal to $\sigma_{\overline{X}}$, this distribution can be used to find probabilities and answer the question "How likely was this sample mean to arise assuming the null hypothesis is true?"

STATISTICAL TEST
UNDERLYING
INFERENCE FROM A
SAMPLE MEAN

**Finding Probabilities
in the Sampling
Distribution of Means**

The sampling distribution of means is approximately normal for sample sizes of 30 or more. With this rule of thumb, we usually need not worry about the shape of the distribution of scores in the population. When the area under the normal curve is considered as relative area (cumulative relative frequency), it may be interpreted as probability (see Figure 11-4a). And when the area is divided into blocks of one standard deviation each as in Figure 11-4b, the probabilities in various parts of the distribution are known. For example, the relative area beyond two standard errors (standard deviations) above the mean is 0.0228; the probability of observing a sample mean two standard errors or more above the population mean specified in the null hypothesis is 0.0228 (Figure 11-4b).

In order to use Table B near the end of the book to find the probabilities under the normal curve, the means on the abscissa of the sampling distribution of means can be converted to z scores in a manner analogous to converting raw scores to $z_{\overline{X}}$ scores (see Chapter 5):

Raw scores:
$$z = \frac{X - \overline{X}}{s},$$
[5-1]

Sample means:
$$z_{\overline{X}} = \frac{\overline{X} - \mu}{\sigma_{\overline{X}}}.$$
[11-3]

Notice that the z scores corresponding to means in the sampling distribution are denoted by $z_{\overline{X}}$; this reminds us that we are dealing with a sampling distribution of means and not raw scores. Further, note that $\sigma_{\overline{X}}$ indicates how many standard errors (standard deviations in a sampling distribution) a sample mean falls below or above the mean of the distribution, μ. Hence the statistical test based on the normal distribution is called the $z_{\overline{X}}$ **test**.

In order to become familiar with using the sampling distribution of means as a probability distribution, an example is helpful. Consider a sampling distribution with $\mu = 50$ and $\sigma_{\overline{X}} = 5$ (Figure 11-5a). What is the probability of

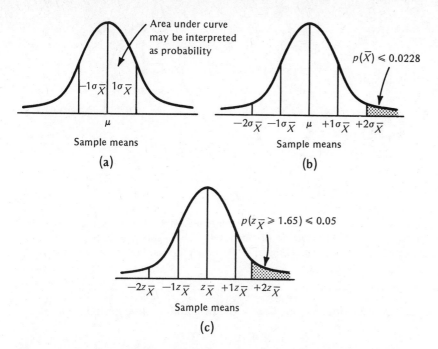

Figure 11-4 ◆ The sampling distribution of means as a probability distribution: (a) the sampling distribution of means as a probability distribution with mean μ and standard error (standard deviation) $\sigma_{\bar{X}}$; (b) probabilities may be found by dividing the normal sampling distribution into standard error (standard deviation) units

observing a sample mean of 55 or above? The conceptual problem is shown in Figure 11-5b. First, convert the sample mean of 55 to $z_{\bar{X}=55}$:

$$z_{\bar{X}} = \frac{55 - 50}{5}$$

$$= \frac{5}{5}$$

$$= 1.$$

Note that we are dealing with the upper tail of the sampling distribution and that we need to know the relative area in the small portion of the normal distribution. Using Table B, locate a score of 1 in the left column and find the relative area under the smaller portion of the curve—in this case 0.1587. Finally, since relative area can be interpreted as probability, the probability of observing a sample mean of 55 or more is 0.1587. Procedure 11-1 summarizes these steps.

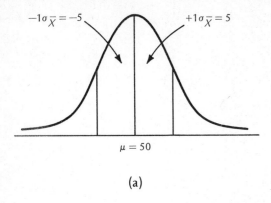

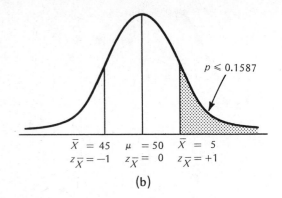

Figure 11-5 ♦ Finding probabilities using the normal sampling distribution of means: (a) sampling distribution of means with $\mu = 50$ and $\sigma_{\bar{X}} = 5$; (b) probability of observing a sample mean $\geqslant 55$ shown in shaded area

EXAMPLE PROBLEM 2

Suppose $\mu = 20$ and $\sigma_{\bar{X}} = 2$. What is the probability of observing a sample mean of:

a. 26 or greater?
b. 16 or less?
c. 16 or less or 24 or more?

Procedure 11-1 ♦ Steps in identifying the probability of observing a sample mean at or above (below) some value

Operation	Example
1 Convert $\bar{X}$ to $z_{\bar{X}}$ using Formula 11-3: $$z_{\bar{X}} = \frac{\bar{X} - \mu}{\sigma_{\bar{X}}}$$	Example 1: What is the probability of observing a sample mean of 55 or more if $\mu = 50$ and $\sigma_{\bar{X}} = 5$? $$z_{\bar{X}} = \frac{55 - 50}{5} = 1.$$ Example 2: What is the probability of observing a sample mean of 38.40 if $\mu = 50$ and $\sigma_{\bar{X}} = 5$? $$z_{\bar{X}} = \frac{38.40 - 50}{5} = \frac{-11.60}{5} = -2.32.$$ Example 3: What is the probability of observing a sample mean of 60 or more or 40 or less?

310

$$z_{\bar{X}=60} = \frac{60-50}{5} = 2.00,$$

$$z_{\bar{X}=40} = \frac{40-50}{5} = -2.00.$$

2 Specify the tail of the sampling distribution to be identified.

Example 1:

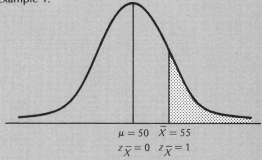

$\mu = 50$ $\bar{X} = 55$
$z_{\bar{X}} = 0$ $z_{\bar{X}} = 1$

Example 2:

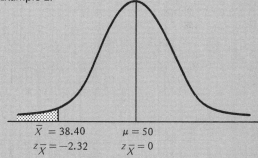

$\bar{X} = 38.40$ $\mu = 50$
$z_{\bar{X}} = -2.32$ $z_{\bar{X}} = 0$

Example 3:

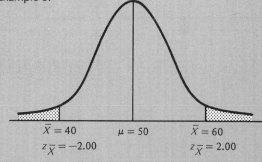

$\bar{X} = 40$ $\mu = 50$ $\bar{X} = 60$
$z_{\bar{X}} = -2.00$ $z_{\bar{X}} = 2.00$

3 Using Table B, locate the probability of $z_{\bar{X}}$. (*See Procedure 5-3 for a review.*)

Example 1: Since the area to be identified constitutes the smaller portion of the curve, locate a z score of 1 in the first column of Table B and read across to column 4: $p = 0.1587$. The probability of (continued on p. 312) observing a sample mean of 55 or more under H_0: $\mu = 50$ is .16.

Example 2: This area also constitutes the smaller tail of the curve. Since the normal distribution is symmetric, the area above a score of 2.32 is the same as that below a score of -2.32. From column 4 of Table B, $p = .0102$. The probability of observing a sample mean of 38.40 or less under H_0: $\mu = 50$ is 0.01. Quite improbable!

Example 3: First, locate the area above a $z_{\bar{x}}$ score of 2.00 (small tail of curve) by locating a $z_{\bar{x}}$ of 2.00 in column 1 of Table B and reading across to column 4. This probability is $p = .0228$. Since the normal curve is symmetric, the area below a $z_{\bar{x}}$ score of -2.00 is equal to the area above a $z_{\bar{x}}$ score of 2.00. Thus, this probability is also .0228. To find the total probability, simply sum these values:

$$p = .0228 + .0228$$
$$= .0456.$$

The probability of observing a sample mean of 60 or more or 40 or less is about .05.

Significance level α: what do you mean, "unlikely"?   Since the sampling distribution of means can be modeled by a normal probability distribution, this distribution can be used to answer the question "Assuming the null hypothesis is true, what is the probability of obtaining a sample mean as large or larger than the one observed?" If sample means of this size or greater are quite *unlikely* to be observed (i.e., quite improbable), a decision to reject the null hypothesis should be made. However, if sample means are likely to arise under the null hypothesis, a decision not to reject the null hypothesis should be made.

The problem, then, is to define operationally what is meant by unlikely. By convention, an unlikely sample result—e.g., a sample mean at or above (below) some extreme value—is defined as one whose probability of occurrence is less than or equal to a fixed small quantity: 0.05 or 0.01. This convention grew out of experimental settings in which the error of rejecting a true H_0 was very serious. For example, in medical research, the null hypothesis might be that a particular drug produces undesirable effects. Deciding that the medicine is safe (i.e., rejecting H_0) can have serious consequences. Hence, conservatism is desired. Often in behavioral research, however, the consequences are not so dire. For example, suppose an instructor is to select one of two texts of approximately equal cost. The instructor might conduct a study to determine which book leads to greater achievement, satisfaction, or both. In this case, the instructor might be willing to reject the null hypothesis on the basis of a probability less than or equal to .25. If, in fact, there is no true difference between the texts, the "error" of selecting one over the other is not particularly serious. If the decision is correct, teacher and students alike benefit. Some wisdom, then, should be exercised in setting the level of significance (see "Tradeoff between Level of Significance and Power" in Chapter 13).

This definition of an unlikely sample result in probability terms is called the **level of significance** of the statistical test. The level of significance is often denoted by the Greek letter α (alpha): $\alpha = 0.05$ or $\alpha = 0.01$. It leads to the following decision rule. *Reject the null hypothesis if the probability of obtaining a sample mean at or beyond a certain value is less than or equal to* 0.05 (*or* 0.01); *otherwise do not reject the null hypothesis*:

$$\text{Reject } H_0 \text{ if } p \leqslant 0.05 \ (\text{or } 0.01);$$
$$\text{Do not reject } H_0 \text{ if } p > 0.05 \ (\text{or } 0.01).$$

This decision rule, then, defines an unlikely event in a research study as one that occurs 5 times in 100 or less (0.05) or 1 time in 100 or less (0.01) when the null hypothesis is true. Thus, the rule implies that we are willing to make an error 5 times in 100 (or 1 time in 100) and reject the null hypothesis when it is actually true. The probability of making this error—rejecting a true null hypothesis—is denoted by the level of significance, α. When $\alpha = 0.05$, this means that we are willing to make an error by rejecting a true null hypothesis in 5 studies out of 100. This margin of error seems reasonable since it is much more probable that extreme sample means are drawn from an alternative population with a different mean. Note also that by setting $\alpha = 0.05$, a correct decision *not to reject the null hypothesis* will be made 95 times in 100 ($1 - .05 = .95$).

Significance level and the sampling distribution of means   The significance level defines unlikely sample means as those that would occur in no more than (say) 5 samples in 100 if the null hypothesis were true. Since the sampling distribution of means for $N = 30$ can be modeled by a normal probability distribution, the level of significance can be marked off in the sampling distribution. This is done by identifying that part of the sampling distribution beyond which the probability of observing a sample mean is less than 0.05. In order to find this part of the sampling distribution, identify the critical value of $z_{\bar{x}}$ beyond which 5 percent of the sample means fall (i.e., $p < .05$); this critical value of $z_{\bar{x}}$ is often called $z_{\bar{x}}$(critical). From Table B, $z_{\bar{x}}$(critical) equals 1.65 for $\alpha = .05$. Figure 11.6a shows a sampling distribution with $\mu = 50$ and $\sigma_{\bar{x}} = 5$ in which $\alpha = 0.05$ is denoted by the shaded area. A sample mean falling in the shaded area would lead to a decision to reject the null hypothesis, H_0: $\mu = 50$. Likewise, Figure

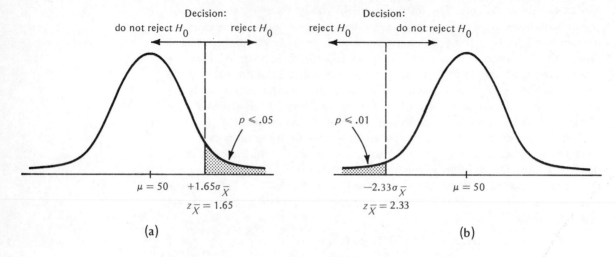

Figure 11-6 ♦ Critical regions for rejecting the null hypothesis: (a) level of significance: $\alpha = 0.05$ in upper tail; (b) level of significance: $\alpha = 0.01$ in lower tail

11-6b shows the level of significance at $\alpha = 0.01$ in the lower tail of the sampling distribution; $z_{\bar{X}}$(critical) equals -2.33. A sample mean falling in this shaded area would lead to a decision to reject the null hypothesis, $\mu = 50$. Notice that as the level of significance becomes more stringent, the area under the distribution leading to a rejection of the null hypothesis becomes smaller.

The only problem now is to decide which tail of the normal distribution to use as the critical region for rejecting the null hypothesis. As will be seen in the next section, this decision is not as arbitrary as Figure 11-6 suggests.

EXAMPLE PROBLEM 3

Suppose a study was conducted with $\alpha = 0.05$ so that $z_{\bar{X}}$(critical) $= 1.65$. What decision would you make about H_0 if the observed (calculated) value of $z_{\bar{X}}$ equaled:

a. 1.90?

b. 1.50?

♦   ♦   ♦   ♦   ♦

The Alternative Hypothesis and the Tail You Seek   The tipoff as to which tail to seek in the sampling distribution is given by the alternative hypothesis. Recall from Chapter 9 that there are three possible alternative hypotheses that can be posed as a rival to the null hypothesis:

$$H_1: \mu > 50,$$

314

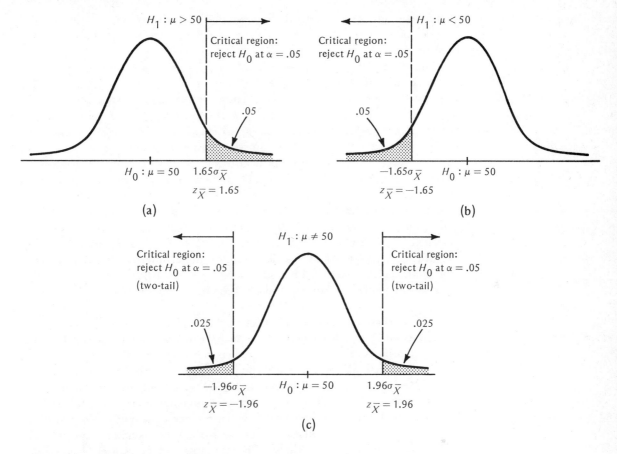

Figure 11-7 ◆ Critical regions of the sampling distribution of means for rejecting H_0 under directional (one-tail) and nondirectional (two-tail) research hypothesis when $\alpha = .05$; (a) directional H_1 (one-tail test); (b) directional H_1 (one-tail test); (c) nondirectional H_1 (two-tail test)

$$H_1: \mu < 50,$$

$$H_1: \mu \neq 50.$$

The first two hypotheses are **directional**; they indicate the direction of the difference between the mean of the population under the null hypothesis and the mean of the population under the alternative hypothesis. *If the alternative hypothesis predicts the true population mean to be above the mean in the null hypothesis, the critical region for rejecting the null hypothesis lies in the upper tail of the sampling distribution* (Figure 11-7a). *If the alternative hypothesis predicts the true population mean to be below the mean in the null hypothesis, the critical region for rejecting the null hypothesis lies in the lower tail of the sampling distribution* (Figure 11-7b). Directional hypotheses are sometimes called **one-tailed hypotheses** because the critical region for rejecting the null hypothesis is in only one tail of the probability distribution.

The third alternative hypothesis, H_1: $\mu \neq 50$, is **nondirectional**. It predicts that the true mean does not equal the mean in the null hypothesis, but it does not say whether it is below or above. Thus, we must consider the critical region to be either tail of the distribution. *If the alternative hypothesis is nondirectional, the critical region for rejecting the null hypothesis lies in both tails of the sampling distribution.*

In order to test the null hypothesis against a nondirectional alternative hypothesis at $\alpha = .05$, mark off critical regions in both tails of the distribution as $\alpha/2 = .05/2 = .025$. (See Figure 11-7c.) This is necessary because we want to mark off no more than a total of 5 percent of the normal sampling distribution as a critical region for testing the null hypothesis: $.025 + .025 = .05$. Note that if we marked off both tails at $\alpha = .05$, we would have actually marked off 10 percent of the distribution: $.05 + .05 = .10$. By using $\alpha/2$, the significance level is set at $\alpha = .05$. Nondirectional alternative hypotheses are sometimes called **two-tailed hypotheses** because the critical region for rejecting the null hypothesis lies in both tails of the probability distribution.

Basis for choosing a one-tailed or two-tailed test   The choice of a directional or nondirectional hypothesis depends upon how much is known about the phenomena being studied. If a *theory* predicts the direction of the outcome of a study, a directional alternative hypothesis may be used. If there is strong *empirical evidence* (i.e., prior research studies) suggesting the direction of the outcome of a study, a directional alternative hypothesis may also be used. Of course, if both theory and empirical evidence suggest the outcome of a study, a directional research hypothesis should be used. But whenever there is doubt about the outcome of a study either because prior research has yielded conflicting outcomes or because theory inadequately predicts the outcome, a nondirectional alternative hypothesis should be used. When in doubt as to whether to use a directional or nondirectional hypothesis, use a nondirectional hypothesis. Null hypotheses rejected on the basis of the two-tailed hypothesis will also be rejected with a one-tailed hypothesis. In making decisions about whether or not to reject the null hypothesis, conservatism is usually preferred (but see the beginning of the section on "Significance Level α").

The question often arises, "What if you test a one-tailed hypothesis and the sample mean turns out to be significantly far from H_0 in the *opposite* direction?" The answer to this question can be seen from a precise statement of the null hypothesis for a directional statistical test:[3]

---

[3]In testing the null hypothesis of, say, H_0: $\mu \leqslant 50$, we actually test the exact hypothesis, H_0 : $\mu = 50$. If H_0 can be rejected using the largest value of μ (50), it will also be rejected for all values of the population mean less than 50.

$$H_0: \mu \leqslant \text{some value,}$$

$$H_1: \mu > \text{some value}$$

or

$$H_0: \mu \geqslant \text{some value,}$$

$$H_1: \mu < \text{some value.}$$

Once the null hypothesis is stated in its fullest form, we see that a sample mean falling in an extreme but opposite direction falls within the domain of the null hypothesis and so the null hypothesis should not be rejected. Furthermore, if this happens, it raises serious doubts as to the basis for originally specifying the directional hypothesis. A two-tailed test should have been used from the start.

---

a. Suppose that $H_0: \mu = 10$, $H_1: \mu \neq 10$, and $\alpha = .05$. What is $z_{\bar{X}}$ (critical)?

b. Suppose that $H_0: \mu = 15$, $H_1: \mu < 15$, and $\alpha = .05$. What is $z_{\bar{X}}$ (critical)?

EXAMPLE PROBLEM 4

At this point, the concepts in the preceding section can be put together in order to test hypotheses with data from a study. Recall that the hypothesis and significance level are established *before* the study is conducted. The logic of hypothesis testing demands this. (Obviously, it is not fair to look at your data first and then decide H_0, H_1, and α.) Then, suppose a random sample of 30 or more subjects is drawn from a population and a sample mean calculated. Finally, for our statistical model, the act of drawing a random sample of 30 or more subjects and calculating a sample mean implies that the sampling distribution of means will be approximately normal with mean equal to μ and standard error equal to $\sigma_{\bar{X}}$. Furthermore, the sampling distribution can be considered a normal probability distribution and can be used to determine the probability of a sample mean at or beyond a certain value given the null hypothesis.

APPLICATIONS OF HYPOTHESIS TESTING: INFERENCES ABOUT A POPULATION MEAN BASED ON SAMPLE MEANS

Based on the sample data, a decision is made to reject or not reject the null hypothesis. Statistically, the decision is made by comparing the $z_{\bar{X}}$ value for the observed sample mean with the $z_{\bar{X}}$ (critical) value. If $z_{\bar{X}}$ (observed) $\geqslant z_{\bar{X}}$ (critical), reject the null hypothesis. The steps in this reasoning are given in Table 11-1.

Case I research addresses the question: "Is this sample of subjects drawn from a population with μ equal to some specific value or was the sample drawn from some alternative population?" An example of a Case I study is the study of reading achievement conducted by a state school board. Recall that the board wanted to know whether the reading level of high-school seniors in the state differed from the national reading level of high-school seniors. From

Table 11-1 ◆ Correspondence between the steps in hypothesis testing and the features of the statistical model

Steps in hypothesis testing	Features of the statistical model
1. Assume the null hypothesis is true: $H_0: \mu = $ specific value.	1. Identifies the population from which sample assumed to be drawn: 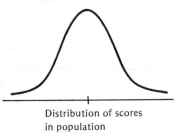 Distribution of scores in population
2. State a research hypothesis which, if the null hypothesis is rejected, will be accepted: $H_1: \mu \neq$ specific value, or $H_1: \mu <$ specific value, or $H_1: \mu >$ specific value.	2. Identifies alternate population from which sample may be drawn. It also provides information needed for establishing a rule for deciding whether or not to reject H_0. 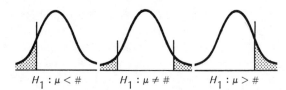 $H_1 : \mu < \#$ $H_1 : \mu \neq \#$ $H_1 : \mu > \#$ Sampling distribution of means
3. State decision rule: Reject H_0 if probability is ≤ 0.05; otherwise, do not reject H_0.	3. Identifies critical value of $z_{\bar{x}}$ in sampling distribution which corresponds to a probability of 0.05.
4. Draw a random sample of $N > 30$ from the population and calculate a sample mean.	4. Identifies the nature of the sampling distribution of means: a. normal distribution, b. mean equal to μ, c. standard error equal to $\sigma/\sqrt{N}$.
5. Based on sample data, decide whether or not to reject the null hypothesis.	5. Is $\|z_{\bar{x}}$ (observed)$\|$—[= $\|(\bar{X} - \mu)/\sigma_{\bar{x}}\|$]—equal to or greater than $z_{\bar{x}}$ (critical)? If so, reject H_0; otherwise do not reject H_0.

national test norms, the mean reading level of seniors in the population was known to be 7.87 ($\mu = 7.87$) on a grade-equivalent scale with a standard deviation of 1.10 ($\sigma = 1.10$) grade-equivalent points.

In this study, the null hypothesis was that the mean reading level of seniors in the state was 7.87 on a grade-equivalent scale:

$$H_0: \mu = 7.87.$$

In order to show the application of a one-tailed test, assume the board had good reason for believing that the mean reading level of seniors in the state was greater than 7.87 on a grade-equivalent scale. The alternative hypothesis is

$$H_1: \mu > 7.87.$$

In testing the null hypothesis, a significance level of $\alpha = .05$ was chosen.

Since the alternative hypothesis is directional, one tail—the upper tail—of the sampling distribution corresponds to the critical region. The critical value of $z_{\bar{x}}$ which identifies the small portion in the upper tail is 1.65 (see Figure 11-8a). If $z_{\bar{x}}$ (observed) is greater than or equal to $z_{\bar{x}}$ (critical) $= 1.65$, the decision to reject the null hypothesis should be made.

In order to test the null hypothesis, a random sample of 100 seniors was drawn from the state. The mean reading score was found to be 8.20. In order to decide whether or not to reject the null hypothesis on the basis of this sample mean, we need to transform the observed sample mean into a $z_{\bar{x}}$ score as follows:

Figure 11-8 ♦ Critical regions for rejecting the null hypothesis in the state reading study: (a) critical region for rejecting H_1: (one-tailed test); (b) critical region for rejecting H_1: (two-tailed test)

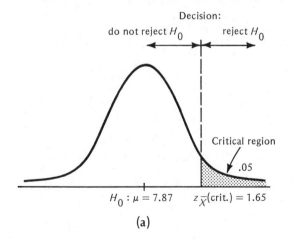 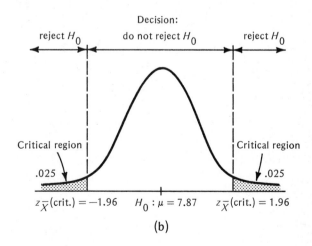

Decision:

do not reject H_0 reject H_0

Critical region

.05

$H_0: \mu = 7.87$ $z_{\bar{x}}$(crit.) = 1.65

(a)

Decision:

reject H_0 do not reject H_0 reject H_0

Critical region   Critical region

.025   .025

$z_{\bar{x}}$(crit.) = -1.96 $H_0: \mu = 7.87$ $z_{\bar{x}}$(crit.) = 1.96

(b)

$$z_{\bar{X}}(\text{observed}) = \frac{\bar{X} - \mu}{\sigma_{\bar{X}}} = \frac{8.20 - 7.87}{1.10/\sqrt{100}} = \frac{.33}{.11} = 3.00. \qquad [\textbf{11-3}]$$

Since $z_{\bar{X}}$(observed) exceeds $z_{\bar{X}}$(critical), the decision is made to reject the null hypothesis, accept the alternative hypothesis, and conclude that the mean reading score of the seniors in the state is greater than that of seniors in the nation. The steps in the hypothesis testing are summarized in Procedure 11-2.

In deciding whether or not to reject the null hypothesis in the reading study,

Procedure 11-2 ♦ Steps in hypothesis testing (one-tailed test with $\alpha = .05$)

Operation	Example
1 Specify null and alternative hypotheses: $H_0: \mu = $ particular value; **a** $H_1: \mu > $ particular value, or **b** $H_1: \mu < $ particular value. *Since the direction of difference between the population mean and a particular value is specified, the alternative hypothesis is "directional" or "one-tailed."*	$H_0: \mu = 7.87,$ $H_1: \mu > 7.87.$
2 Specify decision rule with one-tailed test at $\alpha = .05$. **a** Reject H_0 if $\|z_{\bar{X}}(\text{obs.})\| > z_{\bar{X}}(\text{crit.}) = 1.65.$ **b** Do not reject H_0 if $\|z_{\bar{X}}(\text{obs.})\| < z_{\bar{X}}(\text{crit.}) = 1.65.$	**a** Reject H_0 if $z_{\bar{X}}$ (obs.) $\geqslant 1.65.$ **b** Do not reject H_0 if $z_{\bar{X}}$ (obs.) $< 1.65.$
3 Compute $z_{\bar{X}}$ (observed) using Formula 11-3: $$z_{\bar{X}} = \frac{\bar{X} - \mu}{\sigma_{\bar{X}}}$$ where $\sigma_{\bar{X}} = \dfrac{\sigma}{\sqrt{N}}$ [11-1].	$\sigma_{\bar{X}} = \dfrac{1.10}{\sqrt{100}} = \dfrac{1.10}{10} = .11,$ $z_{\bar{X}}$ (observed) $= \dfrac{8.20 - 7.87}{.11} = \dfrac{.33}{.11}$ $= 3.00.$
4 Make decision (see step 2) and reach conclusion.	For a one-tailed test with $\alpha = .05$, $z_{\bar{X}}$ (crit.) $= 1.65$. Since $z_{\bar{X}}$ (obs.) $> z_{\bar{X}}$ (crit.), reject H_0. Conclude that the mean grade-equivalent reading level of seniors in the state is greater than that of seniors nationwide.

we have not been critical of the State Board's decision to use a one-tailed alternative hypothesis. However, there is insufficient evidence to warrant a directional research hypothesis. Theory is not cited and empirical evidence is not mentioned, although the state may have such evidence from past years. To play things conservatively, our decision to reject H_0: $\mu = 7.87$ should be based on a two-tailed test. In this case, the hypothesis-testing procedures are given in Procedure 11-3. One change is that the alternative hypothesis is stated in its nondirectional form:

$$H_1: \mu \neq 7.87.$$

A second change is the specification of the critical region for rejecting the null hypothesis. Since we are not sure whether the state's seniors will score

Steps in hypothesis testing (two-tailed test at $\alpha = .05$) ◆ Procedure 11-3

Operation	Example
1 Specify null and alternative hypotheses:	
H_0: μ = particular value,	H_0: μ = 7.87,
H_1: $\mu \neq$ particular value.	H_1: $\mu \neq$ 7.87.
Since the direction of difference between the population mean and a particular value is not specified, the alternative hypothesis is "nondirectional" or "two-tailed."	
2 Specify decision rules with $\alpha = .05$ (two-tailed): **a** Reject H_0 if	**a** Same as Operation 2a.
$\qquad \|z_{\bar{x}}(\text{obs.})\| \geqslant \|z_{\bar{x}}(\text{crit.})\| = 1.96.$	
b Do not reject H_0 if	**b** Same as Operation 2b.
$\qquad \|z_{\bar{x}}(\text{obs.})\| < \|z_{\bar{x}}(\text{crit.})\| = 1.96.$	
3 Compute $z_{\bar{x}}(\text{obs.})$ using Formula 11-3:	$\sigma_{\bar{x}} = \dfrac{1.10}{\sqrt{100}} = \dfrac{1.10}{10} = .11,$
$\boxed{z_{\bar{x}} = \dfrac{\bar{X} - \mu}{\sigma_{\bar{x}}}}$	$z_{\bar{x}}(\text{obs.}) = \dfrac{8.20 - 7.87}{.11} = \dfrac{.33}{.11}$
where $\sigma_{\bar{x}} = \sigma/\sqrt{N}$ [11-1].	$= 3.00.$
4 Make decision (see step 2) and reach conclusions.	Two-tailed test at $\alpha = .05$: $z_{\bar{x}}(\text{crit.}) = 1.96$. Since $\|z_{\bar{x}}(\text{obs.})\| > z_{\bar{x}}(\text{crit.})$, reject H_0. Conclude that the mean grade-equivalent reading level of seniors in the state differs from the nationwide mean.

above or below the national mean, we need to identify both tails of the normal sampling distribution as critical regions, as shown in Figure 11-8b. Furthermore, since we want to keep α at .05, each tail is marked off at

$$\frac{\alpha}{2} = \frac{.05}{2} = .025.$$

The $z_{\bar{X}}$(critical) corresponding to 0.025 is 1.96 (Table B). Our decision rule for rejecting the null hypothesis is:

Reject H_0 if $z_{\bar{X}}$ (observed) is greater than or equal to 1.96 or less than or equal to -1.96; that is, reject H_0 if $|z_{\bar{X}}$ (observed)$|$ is greater than or equal to 1.96. Otherwise, do not reject H_0.

Since $z_{\bar{X}}$ (observed) = 3.00, $z_{\bar{X}}$ (observed) is greater than $z_{\bar{X}}$ (critical). Therefore, the decision is to reject the null hypothesis. In accepting the alternative hypothesis, we conclude that the mean reading level of seniors in the state is greater than the nationwide mean. (In this case, H_0 was rejected using both a one- and two-tailed test. This will not always happen, as mentioned above and discussed further in Example Problem 5.)

EXAMPLE PROBLEM 5

The mean score of a sample of 49 seniors enrolled in a particular vocational education program was 53.4 on a measure of mechanical ability. The principal of the program wants to test the hypothesis that seniors from her school are superior in mechanical ability to seniors in general throughout the state. State norms show that mean mechanical ability is 50 with a standard deviation of 14.

a. Test the principal's hypothesis at $\alpha = .05$ using the format for a one-tailed test shown in Procedure 11-2, noting hypotheses, decision rules, computation, decision, and conclusion.
b. Suppose the principal did not have sufficient evidence to warrant a directional hypothesis. Perform a two-tailed test with $\alpha = .05$ using the format shown in Procedure 11-3.
c. Compare conclusions based on the one-tailed and the two-tailed test. Are they the same or different? Why?

CONFIDENCE INTERVALS

Suppose a friend offered you the following choice in making a bet for a pitcher of beer: (1) you say that Mt. Everest is 29,000 feet high or (2) you say that Mt. Everest is between 29,000 and 31,000 feet high. Which bet would you prefer making? Probably you would choose the latter bet since it allows you a fair margin for error; there is a good chance that the true height falls within the interval. Suppose this character offers you another pair of bets: that, in the 1969 NCAA basketball championships, UCLA beat Purdue by (1) 20 points or (2) between 15 and 25 points. You would probably prefer the latter bet, since there is a greater probability that the true difference falls within the interval than that you will hit the true difference by making a **point estimate** of 20 points. In sum, you could be more certain of winning the bet by choosing an interval which included the point estimate of the true value than by choosing the bet with only the point estimate and no margin for error.

◆   ◆   ◆   ◆   ◆

These betting situations are somewhat analogous to point estimation and interval estimation (confidence intervals). The reasoning goes something like this for Case I situations. A sample is drawn randomly from a population and the sample mean is calculated. This is equivalent to drawing a sample mean from a sampling distribution of means. This sample mean is interpreted as an estimate of the true population mean. However, since the estimate is based on

Interval Estimates for a Population Mean

Figure 11-9 ◆ Confidence intervals for μ: (a) sampling distribution of means; (b) confidence interval about $\bar{X} = 50.7$; (c) confidence interval about $\bar{X} = 55$; (d) confidence intervals for each of four randomly sampled means

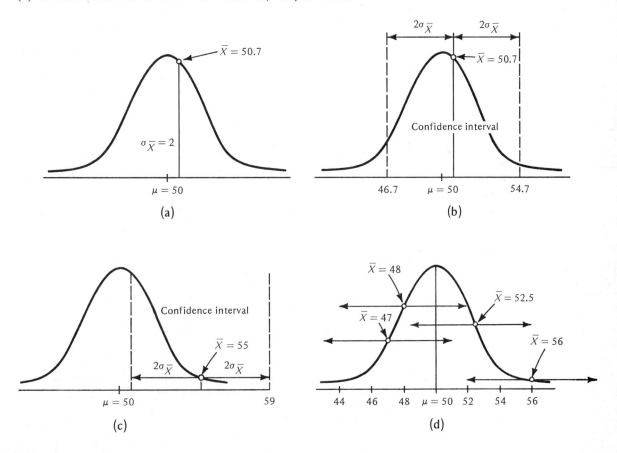

sample data, this estimate may be in error. The magnitude of the error in estimating μ from $\overline{X}$ depends on how much sample means differ from one another on repeated sampling from the population—in short, on the standard error of the mean, $\sigma_{\overline{X}}$. The smaller the standard error, the smaller the error likely to arise in estimating μ from $\overline{X}$.

The sample mean is the best *point estimate* of the population mean, but just like the bet about the height of Mt. Everest, a single point estimate can easily be in error. In estimating the true value of the population mean, just as in estimating the true height of Mt. Everest, it would be convenient to hedge our bets by constructing an interval in which the population mean is likely to fall. In this way, we could increase our confidence by supposing that our **interval estimate** contained the population mean.

In order to understand the rationale underlying the **confidence interval**, let's assume, for the moment, that we are omniscient and know that the mean of a certain population on an English proficiency test is 50, with a standard deviation of 20. For samples of size 100, Figure 11-9a shows the corresponding sampling distribution of means. (Notice that $\sigma_{\overline{X}} = 20/\sqrt{100} = 2$.) Now suppose we took a particular random sample of 100 subjects and found the mean proficiency score to be 50.7. This amounts to selecting randomly a mean from the sampling distribution. As ordinary mortals—we are no longer omniscient—our best estimate of the mean proficiency score in the population, μ, is 50.7. But just to be sure we have not made a mistake about the value of μ, we decide to hedge our bet by saying that μ falls within 2 standard errors on either side of this sample mean:

$$\mu \text{ falls within the interval:} \quad \overline{X} \pm 2\sigma_{\overline{X}}.$$

This is a reasonably conservative proclamation—two standard deviations account for a large part of the area under a normal distribution. The result of constructing the confidence interval about the sample mean is

$$\mu \text{ falls within the interval:} \quad 50.7 \pm (2)(2),$$

or

$$46.7 \leqslant \mu \leqslant 54.7.$$

In words, this says that we are reasonably certain that the mean proficiency score in the population falls within an interval such as 46.7 and 54.7. Figure 11-9 shows the sampling distribution of means and provides a visual representation of the confidence interval constructed about the sample mean of 50.7. Notice that in this case the interval actually includes $\mu = 50$.

Suppose we draw another mean randomly from the sampling distribution in Figure 11-9a. This time the sample mean is 55. Again, our single best estimate of μ is the sample mean, but to be on the safe side, we construct a confidence interval two standard errors above and below the sample mean:

$$55 \pm 2(2),$$

$$51 \leqslant \mu \leqslant 59.$$

In this case, the interval says that we are confident that the population mean falls within an interval such as 51 and 59. If we become omniscient for the moment, we are bound to have an all-knowing grin on our faces because we know that drawing a sample mean of 55—two and a half $\sigma_{\bar{x}}$'s beyond μ—was quite unlikely and that even the wide confidence bands do not include μ in this case.

Figure 11-9 b and c exemplify an important point about the use and interpretation of confidence intervals. A confidence interval constructed about a single, randomly sampled mean either does or does not include the population mean μ. Since we are not actually omniscient, we can never be absolutely sure that a particular confidence interval includes μ. Therefore, we must resort to a statement about the probability that a confidence interval includes μ. The reasoning goes something like this. Suppose we select a large number of means randomly from Figure 11-9a and construct confidence intervals for each mean. Since most of the randomly sampled means will fall within plus or minus two standard errors of μ, most of the confidence intervals constructed within plus or minus two standard errors of the sample mean will include the population mean μ. This situation is shown in Figure 11-9d for a few randomly sampled means. Notice that almost all of the confidence intervals in the figure include μ.

The probability statement, then, is about randomly sampled means and the intervals constructed about them. Since 95 percent of the sample means fall roughly within two standard errors of the population mean ($1.96\sigma_{\bar{x}}$, to be exact), approximately 95 out of 100 sample confidence intervals will include μ. Or, put another way, *over all possible randomly sampled means, the probability is .95 that*

$$\bar{X} - 1.96\sigma_{\bar{x}} \leqslant \mu \leqslant \bar{X} + 1.96\sigma_{\bar{x}}. \qquad [\textbf{11-4a}]$$

This confidence interval is called the *95-percent confidence interval* (CI$_{.95}$). Its two boundaries, $\bar{X} - 1.96\sigma_{\bar{x}}$ and $\bar{X} + 1.96\sigma_{\bar{x}}$, are called the *95-percent confidence limits*. The steps in constructing the 95-percent confidence interval are summarized in Procedure 11-4, using the sample of scores for the 100 subjects on the English proficiency test (see above).[4]

---

[4]Once actual values—confidence limits—are obtained, the probability statement no longer refers to the particular values, since the interval either does or does not include μ. Rather, we can say that the probability is, for example, approximately .95 that the true value of μ is covered by an interval *such as* that between the particular confidence limits in our data.

Operation	Example
1 Identify the values of $\bar{X}$ and σ.	From a sample of scores for 100 subjects on an English proficiency test, $\bar{X} = 50.7$, $\sigma = 20$.
2 Compute $\sigma_{\bar{X}}$ using Formula 11-1: $$\sigma_{\bar{X}} = \frac{\sigma_X}{\sqrt{N}}$$	$$\sigma_{\bar{X}} = \frac{20}{\sqrt{100}}$$ $$= \frac{20}{10}$$ $$= 2.0.$$
3 Compute the 95% confidence interval by inserting the appropriate values into Formula 11-4a and solving: $$\bar{X} - 1.96\sigma_{\bar{X}} \leqslant \mu \leqslant \bar{X} + 1.96\sigma_{\bar{X}}.$$	$$50.7 + (1.96)(2.0) \leqslant \mu \leqslant 50.7 + (1.96)(2.0),$$ $$50.7 - 3.92 \leqslant \mu \leqslant 50.7 + 3.92,$$ $$46.78 \leqslant \mu \leqslant 54.62.$$ Over all possible samples, the probability that a randomly sampled confidence interval like this one includes the true population mean μ is .95. The confidence limits are 46.78 and 52.86.

Procedure 11-4 ◆ Steps in constructing the 95-percent confidence interval

The *99-percent confidence interval* (CI$_{.99}$) is given by

$$\bar{X} - 2.58\sigma_{\bar{X}} \leqslant \mu \leqslant \bar{X} + 2.58\sigma_{\bar{X}} \qquad [\text{11-4b}]$$

The value of 2.58 corresponds to the upper and lower area of .005 (i.e., .01/2) in the normal distribution (Table B). The procedures for constructing the 99-percent confidence interval are identical to those for constructing the 95-percent confidence interval except that $\sigma_{\bar{X}}$ is multiplied by 2.58 rather than 1.96 (see Formula 11-4a). If the 99-percent confidence interval is constructed for the sample data from the English study, we have

$$\text{CI}_{.99}: \quad 50.7 - 2.58(2.0) \leqslant \mu \leqslant 50.7 + 2.58(2.0),$$

$$50.7 - 5.16 \leqslant \mu \leqslant 50.7 + 5.16,$$

$$45.54 \leqslant \mu \leqslant 55.86.$$

Over all possible samples, the probability that a randomly sampled confidence interval, such as the one above, includes the true population mean μ is .99.

By comparing the limits for $CI_{.99}$ with the confidence limits for $CI_{.95}$ (Procedure 11-4), we see that increasing our confidence from .95 to .99 increases the width of the interval. The price of greater confidence, then, is a wider confidence interval. If we want to be perfectly confident, a 100-percent confidence interval could be constructed:

$$\overline{X} - \infty \sigma_{\overline{X}} \leqslant \mu \leqslant \overline{X} + \infty \sigma_{\overline{X}}.$$

However, this interval is, perhaps, a bit large for our needs. You never get something for nothing—or hardly ever, anyway.

Construct the 95-percent and 99-percent confidence intervals for μ given the following information:

$$\overline{X} = 30, \qquad \sigma_{\overline{X}} = 4.$$

EXAMPLE PROBLEM 6

♦   ♦   ♦   ♦   ♦

Two-tailed tests   In hypothesis testing, the focus is on whether a sample mean was obtained from a population specified by the null hypothesis or whether the sample mean was drawn from some alternative population. Put another way, hypothesis testing focuses on how likely we are to observe the sample mean—a point estimate of the population mean—under the null hypothesis. For a two-tailed test, by convention, a sample mean was likely if it lies no less than two standard errors above or below the population mean. (Actually, we use 1.96 standard errors.) A sample mean is deemed unlikely if it lies at or beyond two (or 1.96) standard errors of the mean of the population designated by the null hypothesis. Figure 11-10a provides a pictorial representation of the hypothesis-testing strategy for this two-tailed alternative hypothesis with $\alpha = .05$. As this figure shows, the area for rejecting the null hypothesis lies in both tails of the sampling distribution of means.

Relationship between Confidence Intervals and Hypothesis Testing

In constructing a confidence interval, the focus is on the range of values that have a high probability of including the population mean. Thus, the 95-percent confidence interval will include the population mean for all randomly sampled means falling within two (1.96) standard errors of the true population mean. This focus is represented pictorially in Figure 11-10b. Notice that all but one of the intervals include μ. In the long run, 95 out of 100 randomly sampled means will fall within two (1.96) standard errors of either side of μ. In hypothesis testing, then, 95 out of 100 times we will reach the correct decision not to reject the null hypothesis.

From Figure 11-10c, it is clear that any confidence interval centered more than $1.96\sigma_{\overline{X}}$ away from μ will *not* include the value of $\mu = 7.87$. In general,

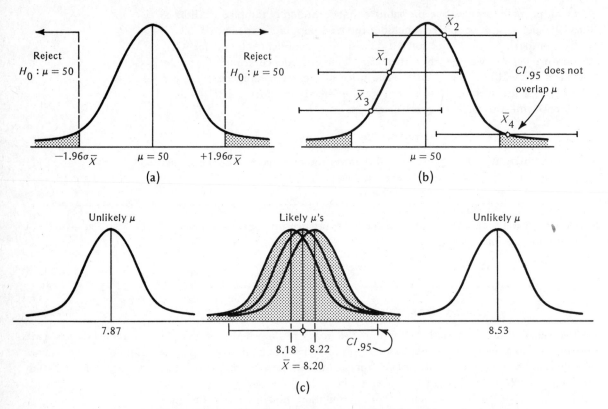

Figure 11-10 ♦ Pictorial representations of the focus of hypothesis testing and confidence intervals: (a) focus of hypothesis testing: assumes H_0 is true until shown to be false; (b) relation between hypothesis testing and confidence intervals; (c) some likely and unlikely estimates of sampling distribution from which $\bar{X} = 8.20$ was sampled ($\sigma_{\bar{x}} = .10$ in all cases)

then, if a sample mean falls in the $\alpha = .05$ (two-tailed) region for rejecting the null hypothesis in the hypothesis-testing framework, then the 95-percent confidence interval constructed about this sample mean will not contain the hypothesized population mean. Likewise, if a mean falls in the $\alpha = .01$ (two-tailed) rejection region, the 99-percent confidence interval constructed about this sample mean will not contain the hypothesized population mean. In short, if the $(1 - \alpha)$-percent confidence interval constructed about a sample mean does not include μ under the null hypothesis, then the hypothesis test at $\alpha/2$ will lead to a decision to reject the null hypothesis.

Perhaps a concrete example will bring this point home. In the study of reading achievement (see "Application of the Significance Test for a Single Mean" above), the null hypothesis was that $\mu = 7.87$. The population standard deviation was 1.10. From a random sample of 100 seniors, $\bar{X} = 8.20$. With $N = 100$, $\sigma_{\bar{x}} = .11$,

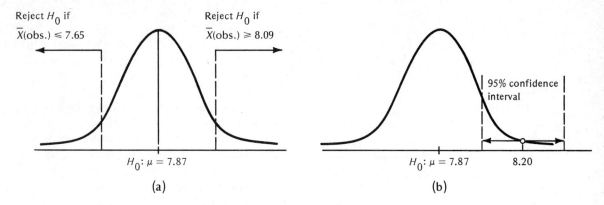

Figure 11-11 ◆ Pictorial representation of hypothesis testing and confidence intervals for the hypothetical study of reading achievement: (a) hypothesis testing ($\alpha = .05$, $\sigma_{\bar{X}} = .11$); (b) 95-percent confidence interval

$$z_{\bar{X}}(\text{observed}) = \frac{8.20 - 7.87}{.11} \qquad [\textbf{11-3a}]$$

$$= 3.00.$$

Since $z_{\bar{X}}$ (observed) is greater than 1.96, it exceeds $z_{\bar{X}}$ (critical, $\alpha = .05$, two tail) and we should decide to reject the null hypothesis. This situation is represented pictorially in Figure 11-11a.

The $1 - \alpha$ $(1 - .05)$ or 95-percent confidence interval can be constructed using Formula 11-4 (see Procedure 11-4 for the computational steps):

$$\text{CI}_{.95}: \quad 8.20 - 1.96(.11) \leqslant \mu \leqslant 8.20 + 1.96(.11),$$

$$7.984 \leqslant \mu \leqslant 8.416.$$

This situation is shown in Figure 11-11b. As can be seen from the figure or from the lower confidence limit, the 95-percent confidence interval does not include the hypothesized population mean of 7.87. Thus we should decide to reject the null hypothesis. For the two-tailed case, then, either the method of hypothesis testing or a confidence interval estimation can be used to test the null hypothesis.

Using the data in Example Problem 5:

a. Construct 95-percent confidence limits for the sample mean.
b. What decision would you make about H_0 based on these results?
c. Compare this decision with the decision in Example Problem 5b based on hypothesis-testing procedures.

EXAMPLE PROBLEM 7

One-tailed tests   One-tailed tests, by their nature, do not have an analog with symmetric confidence intervals. That is, if there is good reason to perform a one-tailed test, the confidence interval, too, should take advantage of this information. Hence, the confidence interval should be unidirectional, too.

◆   ◆   ◆   ◆   ◆

Summary   This chapter presents hypothesis testing procedures for answering the following Case I research question: "Does a particular sample mean belong to a specified population?" The discussion began with two basic ideas in hypothesis testing. First, the null hypothesis is assumed to be true until it is shown to be false. Second, since just one sample out of an indefinitely large number of samples is taken from the population, sample means will differ from the population mean by chance alone (i.e., sampling error).

In the first section of the chapter, three fundamental concepts following from these ideas were presented. First, the *sampling distribution of means* was introduced as a model of the variability in sample means expected under H_0. Second, the characteristics of the sampling distribution—the shape (cf. central limit theorem), central tendency, and variability of the sampling distribution—were introduced. Third, procedures for interpreting the sampling distribution as a *probability distribution* were presented.

In the second section of the chapter, the $z_{\bar{X}}$ test—a statistical test for determining the probability that a sample mean arose from a specified population—was described. Then the concept of *level of significance* was presented as a basis for deciding whether or not to reject a null hypothesis. Finally, *one-tailed* (directional) and *two-tailed* (nondirectional) statistical tests were described.

The third section discussed applications of the $z_{\bar{X}}$ test, and the final section presented procedures for constructing and interpreting *confidence intervals*.

◆   ◆   ◆   ◆   ◆

Key Words

central limit theorem	point estimate
confidence interval	population mean
directional alternative hypothesis	probability distribution
hypothesis testing	sample mean
interval estimate	sampling distribution of means
level of significance	standard error of the mean
nondirectional alternative hypothesis	two-tailed hypothesis
null hypothesis	$z_{\bar{X}}$ test
one-tailed hypothesis	

◆   ◆   ◆   ◆   ◆

Exercises   1–7 Scores on a reading readiness test are available for all students completing kindergarten in a large metropolitan school district. Consider this group of scores as a *population* of measures with a mean of 75 and a standard deviation of 10. Assume that an infinite number of samples of 36 scores were selected at random from the population.

1. Would you expect the means of these samples to be the same? Explain.
2. Suppose a frequency distribution of these sample means is constructed. What is this frequency distribution called?
3. What would be plotted on the ordinate and abscissa of this graph?
4. What is the mean of this distribution?
5. What is the standard deviation of this distribution called? Calculate.
6. Describe the shape of the distribution.
7. Suppose that each of the samples were based on 121 scores. How would the variability of the distribution change?

8. How does a sampling distribution of means differ from frequency distributions discussed previously?
9. Define the following measures of variability: σ, $\sigma_{\bar{X}}$.

10–13 Specify the mean and standard deviation (standard error) of the sampling distribution of the mean given the following data:

10. $\mu = 5$, $\sigma_X = 2$, $N = 36$.
11. $\mu = 25$, $\sigma_X = 5$, $N = 121$.
12. $\mu = 50$, $\sigma_X = 8$, $N = 144$.
13. $\mu = 63$, $\sigma_X = 11$, $N = 64$.

14. What is the probability of observing the following sample means when $\mu = 90$, $\sigma_X = 8$, and $N = 64$?
   a. 93.0 or greater,
   b. 91.5 or greater,
   c. 89.0 or less,
   d. 87.5 or less.

15–18 Draw a sampling distribution which indicates $z_{\bar{X}}$(critical) and the critical region for rejecting H_0 when H_0: $\mu = 10$ and H_1 is as follows.

15. H_1: $\mu \neq 10$, $\alpha = .05$.
16. H_1: $\mu > 10$, $\alpha = .05$.
17. H_1: $\mu \neq 10$, $\alpha = .01$.
18. H_1: $\mu < 10$, $\alpha = .01$.

19. Name two conditions in which a directional research hypothesis is warranted.

For exercises 20, 24, 25, 26, include the following information:
   (1) Null and alternative hypotheses
   (2) Decision rule
   (3) Statistical test
   (4) Decision
   (5) Conclusions

20–23 After a survey of all employees, a large company reported that mean job satisfaction was 18 with a standard deviation of 6 on a scale of job satisfaction. The Western regional manager noticed that the mean based on the 121 employees in his area was 19.5.

20. Conduct a test at $\alpha = .05$ (two-tail).
21. Construct a 95-percent confidence interval around the sample mean.

22. What decision would you make about H_0 based on this confidence interval?

23. Compare your decisions in 20 and 22. Are they the same? Why?

24. A community mental-health center routinely administered a measure of self-esteem to each of its clients. The following results were obtained: $\mu = 20$, $\sigma = 4$. Based on past research, a psychologist at the center hypothesized that clients completing a special program designed to build self-confidence would show significantly higher self-esteem than clients in general. The mean self-esteem of a random sample of 49 clients completing the special program was 21. Test the psychologist's hypothesis at $\alpha = .01$ (one-tail).

25. A survey of all markets in a large city showed that the average price of selected high-quality meats such as top sirloin and filet mignon was $2.41 per pound with a standard deviation equal to .20. A random sample of 36 markets in a particular chain which advertised significantly lower prices for high-quality meats showed a mean of $2.39 per pound. Test this advertising claim at $\alpha = .05$ (one-tail).

26–27 Results of a statewide survey showed that the mean score on a driver safety test for all students who had completed driver training was 80 with $\sigma = 12$. School administrators were interested in whether there was a significant difference in driver safety since a new driving simulator was incorporated into the program. A random sample of 81 students completing the new program showed a mean of 84.

26. Conduct a test at $\alpha = .01$ (two-tail).

27. Construct a 99-percent confidence interval.

12 ◆

Inferences
about
Differences between Means

SOMETIMES IN behavioral research, a random sample of N subjects is drawn from a population and n_1 subjects in this sample are randomly assigned to an experimental group while the other n_2 subjects are randomly assigned to a control group.[1] After the experimental group has received the treatment, the control group has received the "placebo," and the effects have been measured, the following question of statistical inference arises: "Might the observed difference between the sample means of the experimental and control group be due to chance, or does the difference represent a systematic treatment effect?"

For example, in the hypothetical study of teacher expectancy (Chapter 2), a random sample of 60 elementary-school children was drawn from a population of elementary-school children. Half of the subjects were randomly assigned to the treatment group (and labeled "bloomers") and half to the control group ($n_1 = n_2 = 30$; see Figure 12-1c). Teachers were told that half of their students (experimental group) were expected to show exceptional intellectual progress over the school year. At the end of the year, the subjects in both groups received a test of intellectual ability. The dependent variable, then, was IQ score. Means and standard deviations on the intelligence test are presented in Figure 12-1d. From these sample data, we must decide whether the two groups represent populations with a common mean (i.e., H_0: There was no effect on intellectual ability due to teacher expectancy) or whether the two samples now represent different populations with different means (i.e., H_1: Teacher expectancy improves intellectual ability) (Figure 12-1e).

In order to decide whether or not the observed difference in sample means arose by chance, the first step is to specify a sampling distribution for differences in sample means. A *sampling distribution of differences between means* is a theoretical distribution with values of differences between sample means ($\overline{X}_1 - \overline{X}_2$) on the abscissa and probabilities on the ordinate. Once the sampling distribution is specified, it can be used as a probability distribution in deciding whether or not the difference between sample means was likely to occur under the null hypothesis. These topics are the subject of the next section. More specifically, the next section illustrates how the sampling distribution of differences between means is used for testing hypotheses. The final section discusses procedures for constructing confidence intervals or interval estimates of the difference between population means.

---

[1]This is Campbell and Stanley's "control-group, posttest-only" design (see Chapter 1). We will continue to refer to this type of experiment as a Case II study. Case II studies also encompass other designs such as the criterion-group design.

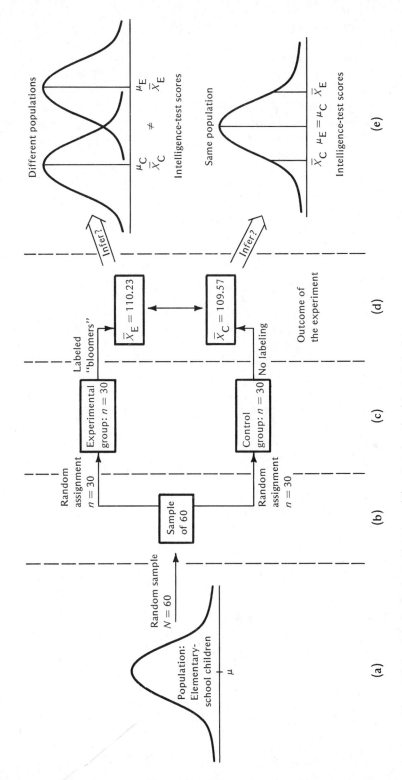

Figure 12-1 ◆ Schematic representation of the steps involved in statistical inference from a true experiment. ($\bar{X}$ represents the sample mean; μ represents the population mean. E represents the experimental group and C represents the control group.)

SAMPLING
DISTRIBUTION OF
DIFFERENCES
BETWEEN MEANS

At this point, let's conceptualize what is going on in a Case II study, assuming the null hypothesis is true (Figure 12-2a). From a population, two random samples of size n (number of subjects in each of the two groups) are drawn, a mean score for each group is calculated, and the **difference between the means** is found by subtracting one sample mean from the other: $\overline{X}_1 - \overline{X}_2$. Theoretically, at least, this study could be replicated over and over again by drawing pairs of random samples from the population and finding the difference $(\overline{X}_1 - \overline{X}_2)$ between the sample means of the two groups. If this were done, the difference between pairs of sample means would be expected to vary from one replication of the study to the next. In order to get a picture of the variability between differences in sample means, the differences between means could be graphed in the form of a frequency polygon with the values of $\overline{X}_1 - \overline{X}_2$ on the abscissa and the frequency with which each value of $\overline{X}_1 - \overline{X}_2$ is observed on the ordinate (Figure 12-2b).

This frequency distribution shows a sampling distribution of the differences between means. It shows the variability that is expected to arise from randomly sampling differences between pairs of means from the population under the null hypothesis. Since it is a frequency distribution, it can be converted into a relative frequency distribution and treated as a probability distribution. Formally, a **sampling distribution of differences between means** is a theoretical probability distribution with differences between sample means $(\overline{X}_1 - \overline{X}_2)$ on the abscissa and probabilities on the ordinate. By treating the sampling distribution of differences between means as a probability distribution, we can answer such questions as: "What is the probability of observing a difference between sample means $(\overline{X}_1 - \overline{X}_2)$ as large or larger than the observed sample difference, assuming that the null hypothesis is true?"

In the study of teacher expectancy, the difference between the means of the experimental and control groups, $\overline{X}_1 - \overline{X}_2$, represents a random sample from a

Figure 12-2 ◆ Making inferences about differences between means: (a) finding the difference between two sample means, assuming the null hypothesis is true; (b) differences between sample means $(\overline{X}_1 - \overline{X}_2)$

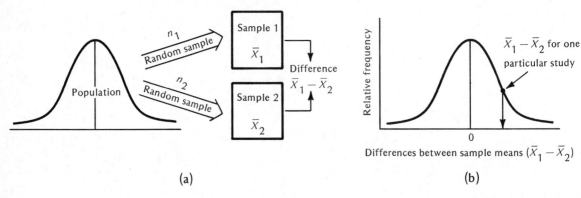

sampling distribution of differences between means. Such a sampling distribution can be used to answer the question: "If the null hypothesis is true, what is the probability of observing a difference between sample means equal to $\overline{X}_1 - \overline{X}_2$ or greater?" If the probability is greater than 0.05, the null hypothesis (in this case, "no treatment effect") cannot be rejected. If the probability is 0.05 or less, the null hypothesis can be rejected and the conclusion is that teacher expectancy improves intellectual ability.

◆ ◆ ◆ ◆ ◆

In order to use the sampling distribution of differences between means as a probability distribution, first we need to assume that the null hypothesis is true, and second we need to know something about the nature of this sampling distribution. According to mathematical statistics, if repeated random samples of size n are drawn from a normally distributed population, the sampling distribution of the difference between means:

Characteristics of the Sampling Distribution of Differences between Means

1. is normally distributed;
2. has a mean equal to zero (i.e., since the samples are taken from the same population, $\mu_1 = \mu_2$ and $\mu_1 - \mu_2 = 0$); and
3. has a standard deviation called the **standard error of the difference between means**. (The formula for this quantity, $\sigma_{\overline{X}_1 - \overline{X}_2} = \sqrt{\sigma_{\overline{X}_1}^2 + \sigma_{\overline{X}_2}^2}$, will be discussed shortly.)

For samples of size approximately 30 or more ($n \geqslant 30$), the *central limit theorem* states that, for a wide variety of different population distributions, the sampling distribution of the differences between means will be approximately normal. Further, the mean of the sampling distribution will equal zero and the variability of sample means will equal the standard error of the difference between means.

Shape of the sampling distribution As sample size increases, the sampling distribution of differences between means becomes increasingly close to the normal distribution. If the difference between sample means, $\overline{X}_1 - \overline{X}_2$, is thought of as a single mean representing this difference, $\overline{X}_d$, then Figure 11-2 in Chapter 11 shows this effect of increasing sample size on the shape of the sampling distribution of differences between means.

Mean of the sampling distribution In most behavioral research, the null hypothesis is that of no difference between population means: $\mu_1 - \mu_2 = 0$. Assuming the null hypothesis is true, the mean of the sampling distribution of differences between means will be equal to $\mu_1 - \mu_2 = 0$. In order to see this intuitively, suppose we take an indefinitely large number of pairs of sample means and calculate the difference between each pair. Some of the differences will be positive (i.e., $\overline{X}_1 > \overline{X}_2$, so that $\overline{X}_1 - \overline{X}_2 > 0$), some will be zero ($\overline{X}_1 = \overline{X}_2$, so that $\overline{X}_1 - \overline{X}_2 = 0$), and some will be negative ($\overline{X}_1 < \overline{X}_2$, so that $\overline{X}_1 - \overline{X}_2 < 0$).

Since the sample pairs are drawn from what amounts to the same population, the same number of positive differences as negative differences would be expected in the long run. Thus, in calculating the mean of the sampling distribution of differences between means, the positive and negative sample differences should cancel each other out and the mean of the distribution should be zero.

Standard error of the difference between means Subtracting pairs of sample means can be conceived of as subtracting sample means drawn from two identical sampling distributions, each with a standard error (standard deviation of sampling distribution of sample means) equal to $\sigma_{\bar{X}}$. The error involved in calculating differences between sample means, then, will depend on the standard error of the mean in one sampling distribution ($\sigma_{\bar{X}_1}$) as well as that in the other sampling distribution ($\sigma_{\bar{X}_2}$). So the error which arises in estimating the difference in population means ($\sigma_{\bar{X}_1 - \bar{X}_2}$) is an additive combination of these two individual errors in estimating the means: The *standard error of the difference between means* is defined as

$$\sigma_{\left(\text{difference between } \bar{X}_1 \text{ and } \bar{X}_2\right)} = \sigma_{\bar{X}_1 - \bar{X}_2} = \sqrt{\sigma_{\bar{X}_1}^2 + \sigma_{\bar{X}_2}^2} \ . \qquad [\,12\text{-}1\,].$$

As mentioned earlier, this is the error involved in estimating the difference between population means from sample means. Put another way, it is the standard deviation of the difference between means. These conclusions are represented graphically in Figure 12-3a.

For the study on the effects of teacher expectancy, the sampling distribution of the difference between means is approximately normally distributed, since

Figure 12-3 ◆ Characteristics of the sampling distribution of the difference between means: normally distributed with mean ($\mu_1 - \mu_2$) = 0 and standard error of the difference, $\sigma_{\bar{X}_1 - \bar{X}_2}$

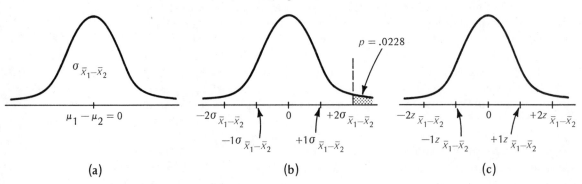

(a)   (b)   (c)

$n_E = n_C = 30$ and $N = 60$. Under the null hypothesis, the mean of this sampling distribution is zero. Suppose that $\sigma_E = \sigma_C = 10$.[2] Then the standard error of the difference between means is found using Formula 12-1 as follows:

$$\sigma_{\bar{X}_E - \bar{X}_C} = \sqrt{\sigma_{\bar{X}_E}^2 + \sigma_{\bar{X}_C}^2} \ .$$

The first step is to find $\sigma_{\bar{X}_E}$ and $\sigma_{\bar{X}_C}$:

$$\sigma_{\bar{X}_E} = \frac{\sigma_E}{\sqrt{n_E}} = \frac{10}{\sqrt{30}} = \frac{10}{5.48} = 1.82,$$

and

$$\sigma_{\bar{X}_C} = \frac{\sigma_C}{\sqrt{n_C}} = \frac{10}{\sqrt{30}} = \frac{10}{5.48} = 1.82.$$

So

$$\sigma_{\bar{X}_E - \bar{X}_C} = \sqrt{(1.82)^2 + (1.82)^2}$$

$$= \sqrt{3.31 + 3.31}$$

$$= \sqrt{6.62}$$

$$= 2.57.$$

What is the standard error of differences between means ($\sigma_{\bar{X}_E - \bar{X}_C}$) if $\sigma_E = 8$, $\sigma_C = 8$, $n_E = 64$, and $n_C = 64$?

EXAMPLE PROBLEM 1

♦   ♦   ♦   ♦   ♦

We know from the central limit theorem that for sample sizes $n_1, n_2 \geqslant 30$, the sampling distribution of the difference between means is approximately normal (Figure 12-3a). When the frequency polygon is converted to a relative frequency polygon, the areas under the curve in this normal distribution may be interpreted as probabilities. And when the area is divided into blocks of one standard deviation each, as in Figure 12-3b, the probabilities corresponding to the various parts of the normal distribution can be seen. For example, the relative area beyond two standard deviations (standard errors of the difference between means) above the mean is 0.0228; the probability of observing a difference between sample means of two or more standard errors (deviations) above the mean is 0.0228 (Figure 12-3b).

The Sampling Distribution of the Difference between Means as a Probability Distribution

---

[2]Under the null hypothesis, sample 1 and sample 2 are drawn randomly from the same population with a standard deviation of σ. Thus, if the population standard deviation for sample 1 is σ_1 and for sample 2 is σ_2, then $\sigma_1 = \sigma_2 = \sigma$.

In order to use Table B to find probabilities under the normal curve, the differences between means on the abscissa of the sampling distribution must be converted to z scores in a manner analogous to converting raw scores to z scores (Chapter 5): for raw scores,

$$z = \frac{X - \bar{X}}{s},$$ [5-1]

whereas for the sample difference between means,

$$z_{\bar{X}_1 - \bar{X}_2} = \frac{\overbrace{(\bar{X}_1 - \bar{X}_2)}^{\substack{\text{Difference} \\ \text{in sample} \\ \text{means } (\bar{X}_D)}} - \overbrace{(\mu_1 - \mu_2)}^{\substack{\text{Difference} \\ \text{in population} \\ \text{means}(\mu_D)}}}{\sigma_{\bar{X}_1 - \bar{X}_2}}.$$ [12-2]

Notice that the z score corresponding to the difference between means in the sampling distribution is denoted by $z_{\bar{X}_1 - \bar{X}_2}$, or $z_{\bar{X}_E - \bar{X}_C}$ for experimental and control groups. This reminds us that we are dealing with a sampling distribution of the differences between means and not raw scores. Further, note that $z_{\bar{X}_1 - \bar{X}_2}$ tells us how many standard errors (standard deviations in a sampling distribution) the difference between sample means falls above or below the mean of the sampling distribution of the difference between means. Figure 12-3c shows this sampling distribution marked off in units of $z_{\bar{X}_1 - \bar{X}_2}$.

In order to get used to using the sampling distribution of the difference between means as a probability distribution, a few examples may be helpful. In the study of teacher expectancy, under the null hypothesis the sampling distribution of the difference between means is approximately normal ($n_E = n_C = 30$ and $N = 60$) with a mean equal to zero and a standard error of the difference between means, $\sigma_{\bar{X}_E - \bar{X}_C}$, equal to 2.57 (see preceding section). What is the probability of observing a difference between sample means of 3.00 points or more (i.e., $\bar{X}_E - \bar{X}_C \geqslant 3.00$)? Should the null hypothesis be rejected? This problem is shown conceptually in Figure 12-4a. In answering this question, the first step is to set forth the null and alternative hypotheses along with the level of significance: $H_0: \mu_E - \mu_C = 0$; $H_1: \mu_E - \mu_C > 0$; $\alpha = .05$. Next, convert the difference between means ($\bar{X}_E - \bar{X}_C$) to a $z_{\bar{X}_E - \bar{X}_C}$ score using Formula 12-2:

$$z_{\bar{X}_E - \bar{X}_C} = \frac{(\bar{X}_E - \bar{X}_C) - (\mu_E - \mu_C)}{\sigma_{\bar{X}_E - \bar{X}_C}}$$

$$= \frac{3.00 - 0}{2.57}$$

$$= 1.17.$$

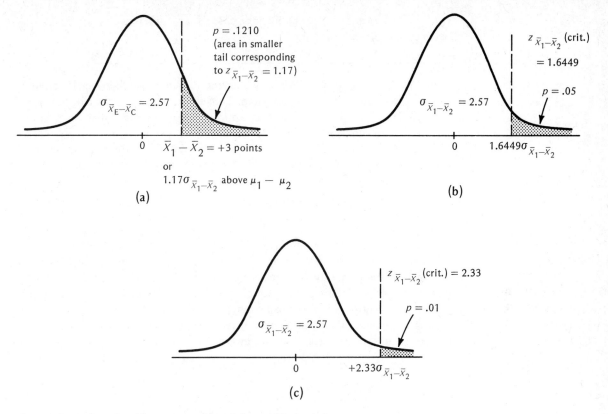

Figure 12-4 ◆ Conceptual representation of the problem of determining probability with the sampling distribution of differences between means

Then use Table B to find the relative area under the normal curve corresponding to the smaller portion of the upper tail of the curve. For a z of 1.17, this area is 0.1210. The probability of observing a difference of 3 points or greater between sample means is 0.1210, or .12. Since .12 is greater than α, the null hypothesis should not be rejected.

In hypothesis testing, the z(critical) value corresponding to α is commonly found from Table B, and z(observed) is compared with it in order to decide whether or not to reject the null hypothesis. For example, suppose we wished to identify the critical value of $z_{\bar{X}_E - \bar{X}_C}$ beyond which the probability is 0.05 or less of observing a difference between sample means *above* the difference between population means—i.e., above zero. This question can be interpreted as follows: "What is the $z_{\bar{X}_E - \bar{X}_C}$ at or above which 5 percent of the differences between sample means fall?" This problem is presented conceptually in Figure 12-4b. Referring to Table B, we see that the $z_{\bar{X}_E - \bar{X}_C}$ value corresponding to .05 of the area in the upper tail of the curve is 1.65. Hence, the critical value of

$z_{\overline{X}_E - \overline{X}_C}$ is 1.65, and the probability of observing a difference of $z_{\overline{X}_E - \overline{X}_C} \geqslant 1.65$ between sample means is .05.

EXAMPLE PROBLEM 2

a. What is the probability of observing a difference between sample means equal to or greater than 2.50, if the sampling distribution of differences between means is approximately normal, with a mean equal to zero and $\sigma_{\overline{X}_1 - \overline{X}_2} = 1.20$?

b. What is the critical value of $z_{\overline{X}_1 - \overline{X}_2}$ beyond which the probability is 0.01 or less of observing a difference in sample means above the difference between population means (i.e., above zero)?

APPLICATIONS OF HYPOTHESIS TESTING: INFERENCES ABOUT DIFFERENCES BETWEEN POPULATION MEANS BASED ON DIFFERENCES BETWEEN TWO INDEPENDENT SAMPLE MEANS

With the nature of the sampling distribution of the differences between means specified, this sampling distribution can be used as a probability distribution for testing hypotheses about differences between group means. At this point, the steps in hypothesis testing are analogous with Case I research. As an example, consider the study on teacher expectancy. In this case, the null hypothesis was that there would be no difference between mean intelligence scores of the control group and the experimental group:

$$H_0: (\mu_E - \mu_C) = 0,$$

or, more generally,

$$H_0: (\mu_1 - \mu_2) = 0.$$

The alternative hypothesis, based on symbolic interactionist theory and prior research, was that the mean intelligence of the experimental group is greater than that of the control group:

$$H_1: (\mu_E - \mu_C) > 0,$$

or,

$$H_1: (\mu_1 - \mu_2) > 0.$$

In testing the null hypothesis, let's use $\alpha = 0.01$ as the level of significance.

Since the research hypothesis is directional, one tail of the sampling distribution of the difference between means—the upper tail—is identified as a critical region in Figure 12-4c. The critical value of $z_{\overline{X}_E - \overline{X}_C}$ which identifies the small portion of the upper tail is 2.33 (see Table B).[3] Note that we now speak of $z_{\overline{X}_E - \overline{X}_C}$ or $z_{\overline{X}_1 - \overline{X}_2}$ and not $z_{\overline{X}}$, since we are dealing with the sampling distribu-

---

[3]The same critical values of z are used for both Case I and Case II research, since the alternative hypothesis in both types of research designs refers to the same parts of the normal distribution.

342

tion of the *difference between two means*. If $z_{\bar{X}_E - \bar{X}_C}$(observed) is greater than $z_{\bar{X}_E - \bar{X}_C}$(critical), the null hypothesis should be rejected.

The observed sample means are 110.23 for the experimental group and 109.57 for the control group; the standard error of the means is 2.57. In order to decide whether or not to reject the null hypothesis, convert these sample data to a z score as follows:

$$z_{\bar{X}_E - \bar{X}_C}(\text{observed}) = \frac{(\bar{X}_E - \bar{X}_C) - (\mu_E - \mu_C)}{\sigma_{\bar{X}_E - \bar{X}_C}} \qquad [12\text{-}2]$$

Since $\mu_E - \mu_C = \mu_D = 0$ under the null hypothesis, Formula 12-2 can be rewritten as

$$z_{\bar{X}_E - \bar{X}_C}(\text{observed}) = \frac{\bar{X}_E - \bar{X}_C}{\sigma_{\bar{X}_E - \bar{X}_C}} \qquad [12\text{-}2a]$$

$$= \frac{110.23 - 109.57}{2.57}$$

$$= \frac{0.66}{2.57}$$

$$= 0.26.$$

Steps in hypothesis testing—Case II (example data from hypothetical study of teacher ♦ Procedure 12-1 expectancy)

Operation	Example
1 Specify null and alternative hypotheses: $\qquad H_0\!: \mu_1 - \mu_2 = 0.$ For a two-tailed test: $\qquad H_1\!: \mu_1 - \mu_2 \neq 0;$ For a one-tailed test: $\qquad H_1\!: \mu_1 - \mu_2 > 0$ or $\qquad H_1\!: \mu_1 - \mu_2 < 0.$ E *and* C *(for experimental* and *control* groups) may be substituted as subscripts if the mnemonic helps.	In the teacher-expectancy study, a one-tailed test was conducted as follows: $\qquad H_0\!: \mu_E - \mu_C = 0,$ $\qquad H_1\!: \mu_E - \mu_C > 0,$ $\qquad \alpha = .01.$ (continued on p. 344)

2 Specify decision rule at α:

a For a one-tailed test at $\alpha = .01$:

Reject H_0 if

$$|z_{\bar{x}_1 - \bar{x}_2}(\text{obs.})| \geq z_{\bar{x}_1 - \bar{x}_2}(\text{crit.}) = 2.33.$$

Do not reject H_0 if

$$|z_{\bar{x}_1 - \bar{x}_2}(\text{obs.})| < z_{\bar{x}_1 - \bar{x}_2}(\text{crit.}) = 2.33. \; .$$

b For a two-tailed test at $\alpha = .01.$:

Reject H_0 if

$$|z_{\bar{x}_1 - \bar{x}_2}(\text{obs.})| \geq z_{\bar{x}_1 - \bar{x}_2}(\text{crit.}) = 2.58.$$

Do not reject H_0 if

$$|z_{\bar{x}_1 - \bar{x}_2}(\text{obs.})| < z_{\bar{x}_1 - \bar{x}_2}(\text{crit.}) = 2.58.$$

Reject H_0 if

$$|z_{\bar{x}_E - \bar{x}_C}(\text{obs.})| \geq 2.33.$$

Do not reject H_0 if

$$|z_{\bar{x}_E - \bar{x}_C}(\text{obs.})| < 2.33.$$

3 Draw a random sample of N subjects from the population of interest. Randomly assign each subject to one of the two groups. Conduct the study and collect data.

Sixty elementary school children are selected and randomly assigned to the experimental or control groups. Experimental subjects are labeled as "bloomers," while control subjects are not. Intelligence-test scores are collected at the end of the school year, and the following data are obtained:

$$\bar{X}_E = 110.23,$$

$$\bar{X}_C = 109.57.$$

Assume that it is known that

$$\sigma_E = \sigma_C = 10$$

(See the example in the section on "Standard error of the difference between means").

4 Compute $\sigma_{\bar{x}_1 - \bar{x}_2}$ using Formula 12-1:

$$\sigma_{\bar{x}_1 - \bar{x}_2} = \sqrt{\sigma_{\bar{x}_1}^2 + \sigma_{\bar{x}_2}^2}.$$

$$\sigma_{\bar{x}_E} = \frac{\sigma_E}{\sqrt{n_E}} = \frac{10}{\sqrt{30}} = \frac{10}{5.48} = 1.82,$$

$$\sigma_{\bar{x}_C} = \frac{\sigma_C}{\sqrt{n_C}} = \frac{10}{\sqrt{30}} = \frac{10}{5.48} = 1.82,$$

$$\sigma_{\bar{x}_E - \bar{x}_C} = \sqrt{(1.82)^2 + (1.82)^2}$$

$$= \sqrt{3.31 + 3.31}$$

$$= \sqrt{6.62}$$

$$= 2.57.$$

5 Compute $z_{\bar{x}_1 - \bar{x}_2}$(observed) using Formula 12-2a:

$$z_{\bar{x}_1 - \bar{x}_2}(\text{observed}) = \frac{\bar{X}_1 - \bar{X}_2}{\sigma_{\bar{x}_1 - \bar{x}_2}}.$$

$$z_{\bar{x}_E - \bar{x}_C}(\text{obs.}) = \frac{110.23 - 109.57}{2.57}$$

$$= \frac{0.66}{2.57}$$

$$= 0.26.$$

| **6** Make decision about whether or not to reject H_0 (see step 2), and draw conclusion about the outcome of the experiment. | Since $|z_{\bar{X}_E - \bar{X}_C}(\text{obs.})| < z_{\bar{X}_E - \bar{X}_C}(\text{crit.})\ (0.26 < 2.33)$, do not reject H_0. Conclude that there is insufficient evidence in the sample data to reject the null hypothesis. This does not mean the null hypothesis is true—the sample difference was 0.66 and not 0—but the evidence is not strong enough to allow us to reject H_0. It is just too likely that a sample difference of 0.66 arose when the true difference is zero. |

Since $z_{\bar{X}_E - \bar{X}_C}(\text{observed})$ does not exceed $z_{\bar{X}_E - \bar{X}_C}(\text{critical})$, the decision is made *not* to reject the null hypothesis. The steps for conducting tests of one- and two-tailed hypotheses are summarized in Procedure 12-1. Example data are taken from the hypothetical study of teacher expectancy.

In a study of the effects of special class placement on the achievement of educably mentally retarded (EMR) children, 36 EMR children were randomly assigned to special education classes and 36 were randomly assigned to regular classes. The following results were obtained:

$$\bar{X}_{SC} = 50, \qquad \bar{X}_{RC} = 48;$$

assume: $\qquad \sigma_{SC} = 5, \qquad \sigma_{RC} = 5,$

where SC = special class and RC = regular class.

Using the format in Procedure 12-1, test the null hypothesis at $\alpha = .01$ (two-tailed).

EXAMPLE PROBLEM 3

The logic behind and the procedures for constructing a confidence interval for differences between population means is the same as that for a single population mean (Chapter 11). As a reminder of this logic and these procedures, suppose we randomly sample a difference between means from the sampling distribution of differences in Figure 12-5a. (The sample, then, is drawn from a distribution with $\mu_1 - \mu_2 = 0$ and $\sigma_{\bar{X}_1 - \bar{X}_2} = 2$.) For this sample, the difference between means is $+.70$ points. This difference is our single best estimate of $\mu_1 - \mu_2$. However, recognizing that the sample difference might be in error, a confidence interval can be constructed to hedge our bet (see Figure 12-5b):

CONFIDENCE INTERVALS FOR A DIFFERENCE BETWEEN MEANS

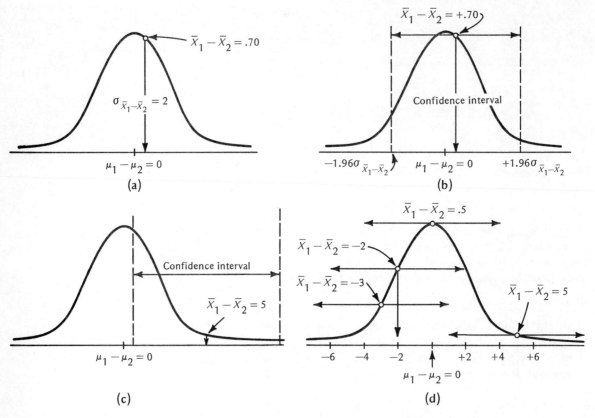

Figure 12-5 ♦ Confidence intervals for $\mu_1 - \mu_2$: (a) sampling distribution of differences between means; (b) confidence interval about $\bar{X}_1 - \bar{X}_2 = .70$; (c) confidence interval about $\bar{X}_1 - \bar{X}_2 = 5$; (d) confidence intervals for each of four randomly sampled differences between means

$$\text{CI}_{.95} = (\text{mean difference}) \pm 1.96 \times (\text{standard error}) \qquad [\,12\text{-}3\,]$$

$$= .7 \pm (1.96)(2).$$

Thus

$$-3.22 \leqslant \mu_1 - \mu_2 \leqslant 4.62.$$

The probability, then, is approximately .95 that the difference between population means lies within an interval *such as* −3.22 to +4.62.

Notice that this statement does *not* mean that the *particular interval* contains $\mu_1 - \mu_2$. For a specific confidence interval, the probability is 0 or 1 that it contains $\mu_1 - \mu_2$, since the particular interval either does or does not contain the difference. This point is illustrated in Figure 12-5c. Here a difference of 5 points was randomly sampled from the sampling distribution with $\mu_1 - \mu_2 = 0$; this difference is an unlikely occurrence. The 95-percent confidence interval $(CI_{.95})$ is

$$5 \pm (1.96)(2),$$

or

$$1.08 \leqslant \mu_1 - \mu_2 \leqslant 8.92.$$

While the probability is approximately .95 that an interval *such as* 1.08 to 8.92 contains $\mu_1 - \mu_2$, this particular interval does not contain the true value, 0.

Since 95 out of 100 randomly sampled differences between means will fall within plus or minus 1.96 standard errors of $\mu_1 - \mu_2$, most confidence intervals will include the true value of $\mu_1 - \mu_2$. However, we never know exactly which ones do and which ones do not. This situation is shown in Figure 12-5d for a few randomly sampled differences between means.

◆   ◆   ◆   ◆   ◆

The 95-percent confidence interval $(CI_{.95})$ for $\mu_1 - \mu_2$ is defined by

The 95-Percent Confidence Interval

$$\left(\overline{X}_1 - \overline{X}_2\right) \pm 1.96\sigma_{\overline{X}_1 - \overline{X}_2}. \qquad [12\text{-}3a]$$

$CI_{.95}$ can also be written as

$$\left(\overline{X}_1 - \overline{X}_2\right) - 1.96\sigma_{\overline{X}_1 - \overline{X}_2} \leqslant \mu_1 - \mu_2 \leqslant \left(\overline{X}_1 - \overline{X}_2\right) + 1.96\sigma_{\overline{X}_1 - \overline{X}_2}. \qquad [12\text{-}3b]$$

In the hypothetical study of the teacher-expectancy effect, the difference between the expectancy group's mean and the control group's mean was $110.23 - 109.57 = 0.66$. The standard error of the difference between means, $\sigma_{\overline{X}_1 - \overline{X}_2}$, was 2.57 (see Procedure 12-1). The 95-percent confidence interval is constructed by inserting the appropriate values into Formula 12-3b:

$$CI_{.95}: \quad .66 - 1.96(2.57) \leqslant \mu_1 - \mu_2 \leqslant .66 + 1.96(2.57),$$

$$.66 - 5.04 \leqslant \mu_1 - \mu_2 \leqslant .66 + 5.04,$$

$$-4.38 \leqslant \mu_1 - \mu_2 \leqslant 5.70.$$

The probability is .95 that a randomly selected confidence interval such as this one includes the true difference between population means.

♦   ♦   ♦   ♦   ♦

The 99-Percent Confidence Interval

The 99-percent confidence interval ($CI_{.99}$) for $\mu_1 - \mu_2$ is defined by

$$\left(\overline{X}_1 - \overline{X}_2\right) \pm 2.58\sigma_{\overline{X}_1 - \overline{X}_2}. \qquad [12\text{-}4]$$

$CI_{.99}$ can also be written as

$$\left(\overline{X}_1 - \overline{X}_2\right) - 2.58\sigma_{\overline{X}_1 - \overline{X}_2} \leqslant \mu_1 - \mu_2 \leqslant \left(\overline{X}_1 - \overline{X}_2\right) + 2.58\sigma_{\overline{X}_1 - \overline{X}_2}. \qquad [12\text{-}4a]$$

The 99-percent confidence interval for the data from the hypothetical study on teacher expectancy is

$$CI_{.99}: .66 - 2.58(2.57) \leqslant \mu_1 - \mu_2 \leqslant .66 + 2.58(2.57),$$

$$.66 - 6.63 \leqslant \mu_1 - \mu_2 \leqslant .66 + 6.63,$$

$$-5.97 \leqslant \mu_1 - \mu_2 \leqslant 7.29.$$

EXAMPLE PROBLEM 4

Suppose $\overline{X}_E = 56$, $\overline{X}_C = 53$ and $\sigma_{\overline{X}_E - \overline{X}_C} = 1.50$. Construct a 95-percent confidence interval and a 99-percent confidence interval around the observed difference between sample means.

♦   ♦   ♦   ♦   ♦

Summary

This chapter presents procedures for answering the Case II research question: "Might the observed difference between the sample means of the experimental and control groups be due to chance or to a systematic treatment effect?" The *sampling distribution of differences between means* is introduced and used for significance testing. Finally, procedures are discussed for constructing *confidence intervals* for the *difference between means*.

♦   ♦   ♦   ♦   ♦

Key Words

central limit theorem	interval estimate
confidence intervals	sampling distribution of differences
difference between means	between means
hypothesis testing	standard error of the difference
independent sample means	between means

♦   ♦   ♦   ♦   ♦

1–7 Scores on a Spanish proficiency test measuring reading and writing skills are   **Exercises**
available on two populations of students: those receiving an inductive and those
receiving a deductive method of instruction. Suppose that repeated samples of 144
students are randomly selected from these populations and the differences between pairs
of sample means are calculated.

1. Assuming that there is no difference between the two populations, would you
expect the differences between all pairs of sample means to be the same? Explain.

2. Suppose a frequency distribution of the differences between these sample means is
constructed. What is this frequency distribution called?

3. What would be plotted on the abscissa and ordinate of this graph?

4. Under H_0, what would you expect the mean of this distribution to be?

5. What is the standard deviation of this distribution called?

6. Describe the shape of the distribution.

7. How does this distribution differ from the sampling distribution discussed in
Chapter 11?

8–11 Calculate the standard error of the differences between means.

8. $\sigma_1 = 3$, $n_1 = 36$, $\sigma_2 = 2$, $n_2 = 36$.
9. $\sigma_1 = 5$, $n_1 = 81$, $\sigma_2 = 10$, $n_2 = 81$.
10. $\sigma_1 = 7$, $n_1 = 49$, $\sigma_2 = 8$, $n_2 = 64$.
11. $\sigma_1 = 6$, $n_1 = 121$, $\sigma_2 = 6$, $n_2 = 144$.

12–15 Assuming that there are no differences between populations, what is the
probability of observing the following differences between sample means when $\sigma_{(\bar{X}_1 - \bar{X}_2)} =$
1.50?

12. $\bar{X}_1 - \bar{X}_2 \geqslant 3.00$.
13. $\bar{X}_E - \bar{X}_C \geqslant 5.00$.
14. $\bar{X}_E - \bar{X}_C \leqslant -4.50$.
15. $\bar{X}_1 - \bar{X}_2 \leqslant -2.75$.

16, 19, 22 Include the following information:

(1) Null and alternative hypotheses
(2) Decision rule
(3) Statistical test
(4) Decision
(5) Conclusion.

16–18 In a study of the effects of verbal and imaginal strategies on learning lists of
words, 36 children were randomly assigned to a verbal strategy (constructing a story
using the words from the list) and 36 to an imaginal strategy (constructing an image
involving words from the list). The following data were obtained on a recall test:

$$\bar{X}_i = 20, \qquad \bar{X}_v = 18.$$

16. Test the hypothesis that the groups are significantly different at $\alpha = .05$ (two-
tailed). The population standard deviations were known to be $\sigma_i = \sigma_v = 4$.

17. Construct a 95-percent confidence interval for the differences between means.
18. What conclusion would you reach about H_0 from Exercise 17? Why?

19–21 In a study of the effectiveness of counseling techniques, 49 counselees at a student counseling center at a major university were randomly assigned to a program teaching problem-solving skills, and 49 were randomly assigned to a client-centered program stressing personal growth and self-actualization. The following results were obtained on a measure of personal adjustment:

$$\bar{X}_{PS} = 15, \qquad \bar{X}_{CC} = 13.$$

19. Test whether the two groups are significantly different at $\alpha = .01$ (two-tailed). The population standard deviations were known to be $\sigma_{PS} = \sigma_{CC} = 3$.
20. Construct a 99-percent confidence interval around this difference between means.
21. What decision would you make about H_0 at $\alpha = .01$ based on the confidence interval constructed in Exercise 20? Why?

22. Some psychological research suggests that children who are given material rewards (candy, tokens, etc.) for performing an intrinsically satisfying task will be less likely to persist at the task on a subsequent occasion than children who are not given such material rewards. In a study designed to replicate these findings, 72 preschoolers were presented with several types of paper in different sizes and shapes and a variety of brightly colored marking pens. A random half of the subjects were given candy for engaging in the task (Group 1), while the other half were not (Group 2). One week later, all subjects were given an opportunity to engage in the task again. The number of minutes which they persisted on the task was measured. The following results were obtained:

$$\bar{X}_1 = 8, \qquad \bar{X}_2 = 13.$$

Test the hypothesis that the time on task in Group 1 is significantly less than in Group 2 ($\alpha = .05$); $\sigma_1 = \sigma_2 = 4$.

13 •

Decisions, Error,
and
Power

I$_N$ MAKING statistical inferences, the researcher is cast in the role of a decision-maker: "To reject or not to reject the null hypothesis? That is the decision." In order to be *absolutely* certain about making a correct decision, the researcher would have to observe the entire population. But since, in the behavioral sciences, populations are often infinite or at least indefinitely large, this is impossible.

Thus, the decision-maker usually operates under conditions of *uncertainty*. In order to make decisions about what is true in the population, she must draw a random sample from the population and, based on this random sample, *infer* what is true of the population. Based on this inference, the researcher decides whether or not to reject the null hypothesis.

One example used in Chapter 9 to illustrate this problem in decision making was the problem of determining whether or not students in a particular school district differed from the general population in intelligence. The researcher suspected that these students, on the average, would score higher than persons in the general population. In order to test this supposition, a random sample of students ($N = 64$) was drawn from the school district and given an intelligence test. The average score for these students was 105, and the population standard deviation was equal to 16 points. Since the mean IQ in the population was known to be 100, should the researcher decide that the population of students in the school district would score higher than students in general?

In order to answer this question, first recognize that since the entire student population was not observed, the sample mean of 105 might not be the true value for this population. Thus, there is some degree of uncertainty about whether the value of the sample mean accurately estimates the population mean. This makes the researcher's decision less than absolutely certain. This uncertainty leads to a second question, "What is the probability of observing a sample mean of 105 when, in fact, the true mean of the population is 100?" Chapters 10 and 11 provided the information needed to answer questions like this one. If the probability were less than .05 of observing a sample mean of 105 or greater when the true population mean was 100, we decided to conclude that the population mean for these students was above 100. If the probability was greater than .05, we decided that there was insufficient evidence to conclude that the population mean for the students differed from 100.

The major purpose of this chapter is to formalize this decision-making process further. The chapter is divided into three sections. The first section describes the types of errors in inference that can arise from hypothesis-testing procedures. The second section defines the *power* of a statistical test, the probability of rejecting a false null hypothesis. It also presents procedures for calculating power with one-sample (Case I) and two-sample (Case II) research, and describes factors that influence the power of a statistical test. The final section describes methods for estimating sample size.

In the example above, the researcher was interested in determining whether the average IQ score in a population of students in a particular school district is greater than the mean IQ of 100 in the general population. If he were omniscient, he would know the answer: either the students' average IQ was 100 or it was greater than 100. These two alternative answers to the researcher's question are shown in Figure 13-1. Thus, there are two possible states of affairs in the population: either the mean IQ in the student population is 100 ($\mu = 100$), or it is greater than 100 ($\mu > 100$). DECISIONS IN
STATISTICAL
INFERENCE

However, the researcher does not in fact know the true state of affairs in the population. Hence he must make an inference from sample data to decide whether or not 100 is the true value.

This decision problem has two features. First, there is a true state of affairs which the researcher would like to know about—in this case, the true situation in the population of students. Second, he must infer the true state of affairs from sample data with some chance of error.

◆   ◆   ◆   ◆   ◆

This decision problem can be cast into the familiar hypothesis-testing frame-work. For our example, we have **Probabilities of Type I and II Errors**

$$H_0: \mu = 100,$$
$$H_1: \mu > 100.$$

Figure 13-1 ◆ Alternative inferences in hypothetical IQ study

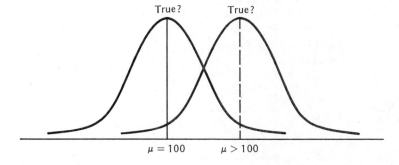

In the population, the null hypothesis is either true or false. The sample data may lead the researcher to decide to reject or not reject the null hypothesis, and he may be correct or incorrect. Table 13-1 shows this decision problem. The researcher makes a correct decision when he decides to:

1. not reject a true null hypothesis,
2. reject a false null hypothesis.

This table also shows that the researcher can make *two types of* **errors**:

Type I: Reject a true null hypothesis
Type II: Not reject a false null hypothesis.

In Chapters 11 and 12, attention was focused on the first column of Table 13-1; the null hypothesis was assumed to be *true*. In particular, we were quite concerned with the error of rejecting a true null hypothesis. In order to avoid making this Type I error, we quite conservatively set the level of statistical significance, α—the probability of rejecting a true null hypothesis—at .05 or .01. The probability of making a correct decision—not to reject the null hypothesis when it is true—is then $1 - \alpha$. If $\alpha = .05$, the probability of a correct decision when the null hypothesis is true is $1 - .05 = .95$.

However, Table 13-1 points out that, in the population, *the null hypothesis can be false*, and this leads to a different set of considerations. In order to give this situation some reality, let's step back for a moment and consider what research is all about. A study is conducted because there is good reason to believe that the null hypothesis is false—otherwise, why do the study? Thus, Rosenthal and Jacobson conducted their study of teacher expectancy because theory and research suggested an expectancy effect. Majasan conducted his study because he believed that the congruence between teachers' and students' beliefs in-

Table 13-1 ♦ The decision problem in making inferences from sample data within the hypothesis-testing framework

		True situation in the population	
		H_0 is true	H_0 is false
Decision alternatives based on inferences from sample data	Do not reject H_0	Correct $(1 - \alpha)$	Type II error (β)
	Reject H_0	Type I error (α)	Correct Power $(1 - \beta)$

fluenced the students' achievement. In all cases, researchers set up the null hypothesis and attempt to *knock it down* (reject it). If they succeed in rejecting the null hypothesis, they indirectly receive support for their alternative hypothesis. It is the alternative hypothesis that led to the study in the first place. This short sermon should have convinced you that the second column in Table 13-1 has great relevance to research.

When the null hypothesis is false, the researcher—the decision-maker—commits an error by not rejecting the null hypothesis. The probability of making this **Type II error** is labeled β (beta):

$$p(\text{not rejecting a false } H_0) = p(\text{Type II error}) = \beta.$$

When the null hypothesis is false and the researcher decides to reject it—something she set out to do—the researcher makes a correct decision. Appropriately, *the probability of correctly rejecting a false null hypothesis is called the* **power** *of the statistical test.*

The power of a statistical test tells you the probability that your experiment will detect the difference, if the difference truly exists. For example, the power of a statistical test gives the probability of detecting a true difference between IQs of students in a particular school district from the general population or the probability of detecting true differences between two treatments, if the difference truly exists. This being the case, researchers should take a power trip. They should strive to design the most powerful experiments possible. There seems little reason to spend time and money on an experiment which has little chance of detecting a difference when the difference is actually there.

Since the probabilities in either column of Table 13-1 sum to 1, and since the probability of a Type II error—not rejecting a false null hypothesis—is β, then the *power*—the probability of rejecting a false null hypothesis—is $1 - \beta$:

$$\text{power} = p(\text{rejecting a false } H_0) = 1 - \beta.$$

A method for calculating the power of a statistical test will be presented. From this method, it is possible to estimate the power of a statistical test either before or after conducting the experiment.

In designing a piece of research, then, the researcher should strive to maximize the power of the statistical test (i.e., minimize the probability of a Type II error) and minimize the probability of a Type I error (α). While this is an admirable goal, like most admirable goals, it is easier said than done.

TRADEOFF BETWEEN LEVEL OF SIGNIFICANCE AND POWER OF THE STATISTICAL TEST

In trying to decrease α (the probability of rejecting a true null hypothesis—Type I error) and at the same time to decrease β (the probability of not rejecting a false null hypothesis—Type II error), a problem arises. As one type of error (e.g., α) decreases, the other (e.g., β) tends to increase. Or, put another way, as α decreases (becomes more conservative), the power of the statistical test $(1 - \beta)$ also tends to decrease, since β tends to increase. In short, α and β are *inversely* related. (This inverse relationship is not a simple one, as will be shown later on in the chapter.)

In order to deal with this tradeoff, some conventions have been established for setting the level of significance, α. Since α refers to a decision error when the null hypothesis is true, it corresponds to the null hypothesis—the hypothesis which is stated exactly. Thus, α, or the probability of a Type I error, is directly under the researcher's control. This being the case, by convention α is set at .05 or .01 (prior to collecting data, of course). This convention is a conservative one; researchers tend to consider rejecting a true null hypothesis a serious error. By committing such an error, for example, the researcher could be led up a blind alley and not realize it until several additional studies had been conducted. Or the substance of the research might involve potential harm to people such that the probability of a Type I error should be minimized (see Chapter 11). For example, medical studies seek to determine safe drug dosages. If the null hypothesis is that the drug is harmful at a certain level, the researcher does not want to reject this hypothesis until he is virtually certain that no harm will come to the potential patient. Thus, in this case, α might be set extremely conservatively (at, say, .0001).

However, there are situations in which the risk of a Type II error is of greater concern than the risk of a Type I error. In many educational studies, for example, two or more instructional methods may cost about the same and have no adverse effects on students. In this case, a Type I error—concluding that one treatment is better than the others when, in fact, it is not—seems not to be too costly in dollars or risks to students. However, a Type II error—concluding that there is no difference between treatments when, in fact, there is a true difference—seems costly in the sense that students may be denied an instructional treatment which would truly help them learn.

In summary, since there is an inverse relationship between α and β, the researcher must trade off one type of error against the other in decision making. To help make this tradeoff, a convention has been established which sets α at either .05 or .01 (or sometimes even lower). However, the decision about the appropriate level of significance (α) should not be made on the basis of statistical convention alone; common sense should also be used in considering the risk involved in making a Type I or a Type II error.

POWER OF A
STATISTICAL TEST

**Single-Sample
(Case I) Research**

In developing the skills to estimate the power of statistical tests, it is easiest to begin with the single-sample or Case I research. Recall that this research is designed to answer the question: "Does a particular sample belong to a hypothesized population?" (See Chapters 9 and 11 for detailed discussions.) Also recall that a statistical test may be one- or two-tailed. We will start with a discussion of the power of one-tailed tests, since it is conceptually easier.

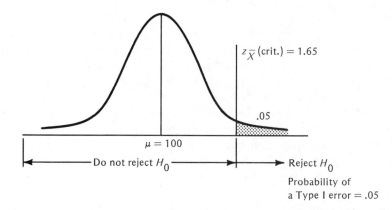

Figure 13-2 ◆ Distribution of scores under H_0 in the hypothetical IQ study

One-tailed tests In discussing power, a review of the hypothesis-testing framework is helpful. In doing this, the example of the IQ study will be used. The hypothesis-testing perspective works with the first column in Table 13-1—the case where H_0 is true. The following steps are taken in hypothesis testing:

1. An exact hypothesis about the population parameter μ is stated:

$$H_0: \mu = 100.$$

2. An inexact, alternative hypothesis is stated:

$$H_1: \mu > 100.$$

Note that this is a *directional* alternative hypothesis: μ is *greater than* 100. It is tested indirectly by testing H_0 directly. This alternative hypothesis is *inexact*, since it is not stated as one value. We should be equally ready to reject H_0 if, in fact, $\mu = 100.10$, 101.00, or 150.10.

3. The level of significance (α) is set at .05 by convention.
4. Students are randomly sampled from the school district in question. The sample mean $\overline{X}$ is used as an estimate of μ.
5. Given the sample data, a decision is made on whether or not to reject the null hypothesis. For a one-tailed test, the decision rule is:

a. If $z_{\overline{X}}$ (observed) equals or exceeds 1.65, reject the null hypothesis.
b. If $z_{\overline{X}}$ (observed) is less than 1.65, do not reject the null hypothesis, where

$$z_{\overline{X}}(\text{observed}) = \frac{\overline{X} - \mu}{\sigma_{\overline{X}}}.$$

(See Figure 13-2.)

Several features of this hypothesis-testing framework are important for understanding power. First, the distribution shown in Figure 13-2 is a sampling distribution of means. It is also a probability distribution. It indicates that, assuming H_0 is true, an extremely high sample mean will be drawn from that population 5 times in 100. That is, the probability of Type I error is .05. Second, by using this distribution for testing the null hypothesis, we have *assumed that the null hypothesis is true*. Remember, the null hypothesis is always assumed to be true until shown to be unlikely. Thus, Figure 13-2 shows the sampling distribution under the null hypothesis with a mean of 100. Third, the hypothesis-testing framework focuses on the first column of Table 13-3: the probability of a correct or incorrect decision when the null hypothesis is true.

Now, let's move slowly into the power trip. In order to do so, Table 13-3 suggests that we must consider the case in which the null hypothesis is, in fact, false. If the null hypothesis is false, Figure 13-2 is not the sampling distribution from which the researcher sampled. Rather, some alternative sampling distribution would provide the correct picture. Using the value of $z_{\bar{X}}$ (critical) = 1.65, which is always determined with the assumption that H_0 is true, what would we decide to do about our sample mean, which in fact was sampled from a different sampling distribution? If we decide to reject the null hypothesis, the decision is a correct one. But if we decide not to reject the null hypothesis when we should have, we have committed a Type II error.

Since the case of a false null hypothesis corresponds to the alternative hypothesis, the problem is as follows. The alternative hypothesis is not an exact hypothesis. All it says is that the true population mean is greater than 100. There are an infinite number of means greater than 100. Which one is true? At first glance, it may seem that an impossible problem has been identified. However, there is a heuristic solution.[1] The solution is to select one of the infinity of alternative means and assume that it is the "true" mean. *We can determine the power by assuming that a specific value of μ is correct*—a value different from *μ* under the null hypothesis—*and then determine whether we would have correctly rejected the null hypothesis*.

One way to make this selection is to decide how much of a deviation from a mean IQ of 100 would be important to know about from the school district's point of view. Suppose the district administrators are interested only in a difference of 3 IQ points or more. They would not mind making a Type II error on the basis of less than 3 IQ points. That is, they would not be concerned if we falsely concluded that the school district's mean is 100 when, in fact, it is 101 or 102. In this case, let's choose a mean of 103 as the true value of *μ* for students in the district. In so doing, we have an *exact* alternative hypothesis to work with.

---

[1]There is also a statistical solution, of course. For an intuitive description of it, see Guilford and Fruchter (1973, pp. 179–184).

At this point, we know that H_0 is false and that the true population mean is 103. The question remains whether our statistical test would be powerful enough to detect this 3-point difference.

This reasoning is presented pictorially in Figure 13-3. The critical region for rejecting the null hypothesis is shown in Figure 13-3a, the theoretical sampling distribution under H_0. The critical region is established in the usual way and does not depend on the particular value of μ chosen for the exact alternative hypothesis. If the critical region is projected into the true alternative sampling distribution (Figure 13-3b), less than half of the alternative sampling distribution falls above the rejection region. This means that if repeated samples were drawn from the sampling distribution under the true alternative hypothesis, over 50 percent of the sample means would not lead us to reject the null hypothesis. In other words, the probability of not rejecting a false null hypothesis—the probability (β) of a Type II error—is greater than .50. The power of this statistical test for detecting a difference of 3 IQ points from the mean under the null hypothesis is less than .50, since the power is $1 - \beta$.

Figure 13-3 ◆ Sampling distributions under H_0: $\mu = 100$ (a) and H_1: $\mu = 103$ (b) (one-tail test) in the hypothetical IQ study

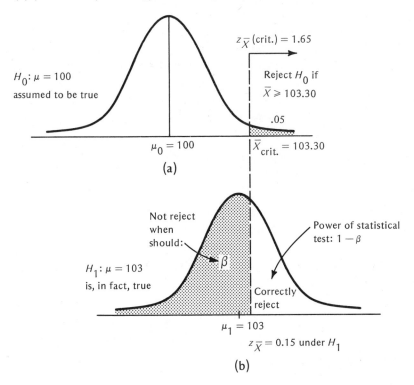

$z_{\overline{X}}$ (crit.) $= 1.65$

H_0: $\mu = 100$
assumed to be true

Reject H_0 if
$\overline{X} \geqslant 103.30$

.05

$\mu_0 = 100$

$\overline{X}_{crit.} = 103.30$

(a)

Not reject
when
should:

Power of statistical
test: $1 - \beta$

H_1: $\mu = 103$
is, in fact, true

β

Correctly
reject

$\mu_1 = 103$

$z_{\overline{X}} = 0.15$ under H_1

(b)

In order to calculate the power of a statistical test exactly, we need to determine the area in the sampling distribution under the alternative hypothesis in which we will correctly reject H_0—the unshaded area in Figure 13-3b labeled "correctly reject." This poses a problem, because a z score is needed to find an area in a normal distribution. In this case (Figure 13-3b), we need the $z_{\overline{X}}$ score corresponding to the point where the shaded and unshaded portions meet:

$$z_{\overline{X}(H_1)} = \frac{\overline{X}_{meet} - \mu_1}{\sigma_{\overline{X}}}. \qquad [13\text{-}1]$$

So, in order to find $z_{\overline{X}(H_1)}$, we need the value of $\overline{X}_{meet}$; the values of μ_1 (μ under H_1) and $\sigma_{\overline{X}}$ are already known. While $\overline{X}_{meet}$ cannot be determined directly from Figure 13-3b, we know that it corresponds to the sample mean falling 1.65 standard errors above $\mu_0 = 100$ ($\mu_0 =$ value of μ under H_0), as shown by the projection of the critical region from Figure 13-3a to b. So the problem can be solved by finding the value of the sample mean corresponding to the critical region in the sampling distribution under H_0 (Figure 13-3a) and noting that $\overline{X}_{critical}$ under H_0 equals $\overline{X}_{meet}$ under H_1.

The first step in calculating the power, then, is to determine the value of the sample mean ($\overline{X}_{critical}$) at or beyond which H_0 will be rejected. From Figure 13-3a, we see that $\overline{X}_{critical}$ lies 1.65 standard errors above μ_0, so in general,

$$\overline{X}_{critical} = \mu_0 + z_{\overline{X}(critical)}\sigma_{\overline{X}}. \qquad [13\text{-}2]$$

In the example problem, $\mu_0 = 100$, $z_{\overline{X}}(critical) = 1.65$, and $\sigma_{\overline{X}} = 2$:

$$\overline{X}_{critical} = 100 + (1.65 \times 2)$$

$$= 103.30.$$

The critical value of $\overline{X}$ at or beyond which the null hypothesis will be rejected is 103.30.

The second step is to recognize that $\overline{X}_{critical}$ under H_0 (Figure 13-3a) equals $\overline{X}_{meet}$ under H_1, so

$$\overline{X}_{meet} = \overline{X}_{critical} = 103.30.$$

The third step is to find the value of $z_{\overline{X}(H_1)}$, so that Table B at the end of the book can be used to find the area in the unshaded portion of Figure 13-3b—the area corresponding to the power of the statistical test:

$$z_{\bar{X}(H_1)} = \frac{\bar{X}_{\text{meet}} - \mu_1}{\sigma_{\bar{X}}}$$

[**13-1**]

$$= \frac{103.30 - 103}{2}$$

$$= \frac{.3}{2}$$

$$= .15.$$

The last step is straightforward. The area at or above a $z_{\bar{X}(H_1)}$ score of .15 can be found by identifying the area in the smaller tail of the curve. Using Table B, we find that the probability of observing a sample mean at or above $z_{\bar{x}} = .15$ is .44. The power of this statistical test—the probability of detecting a mean difference of 3 IQ points—is .44. This power of .44 means that, given a true mean of 103, our statistical test will lead us to reject the null hypothesis in only about four out of ten replications of the study.

The probability of a Type II error can also be determined with the aid of Figure 13-3. The shaded area of the sampling distribution for the alternative hypothesis represents the values of sample means that would *not* lead to a correct decision, to reject the null hypothesis. These sample means do not fall in the rejection region under the null hypothesis. Thus, the shaded area represents the probability of not rejecting the null hypothesis—the probability of a Type II error, β. So in order to determine β, we need to find the area in the larger part of the curve below $z_{\bar{x}} = .15$. From Table B, column 3, this area is 0.56. The probability of a Type II error, β, is .56.

As you have probably already noticed, it is unnecessary to calculate the power *and* β. Once you know one, you know the other, since the power plus β equals unity:

$$\text{power} = 1 - \beta = 1 - .56 = .44.$$

These steps in calculating the power of a statistical test are summarized in Procedure 13-1. Ignore, for the moment, two-tailed tests. This topic is covered next.

The concept of power is a difficult one to learn. Perhaps another example will help. Suppose, in another school district, the administration believes its students are below the mean on IQ. The administrators are interested in detecting a difference of 4 IQ points or more; anything less does not matter to them. They plan to randomly sample 144 students and the standard deviation of the scores, σ, is known to be 16 IQ points ($\sigma_{\bar{x}} = 16/\sqrt{144} = 1.33$). What is the power of this statistical test?

First, set up the null and alternative hypotheses. Remember that the administrators are only interested in an IQ difference of 4 points or more and

Procedure 13-1 ♦ Steps in calculating power: one-sample (Case I) research, one-tailed and two-tailed tests

Operation	Example
1 Set up exact null and alternative hypotheses. *The exact alternative hypothesis is based on the difference between means that the researcher wishes to detect.*	*One-tailed tests* The data in this example are taken from the hypothetical study of IQ (see beginning of this chapter). From this information, H_0, H_1, and α are listed below. Note also that $\sigma_{\bar{x}} = 2$ for the example data.[a]

$H_0: \mu = 100,$

$H_1: \mu = 103,$

$\alpha = .05$ (one-tailed).

Two-tailed tests

The data in this example are taken from a hypothetical study of IQ in which H_0, H_1, and α are as specified below. The researcher, then, wants to detect a 4.3-point difference in IQ. Further, $\sigma_{\bar{x}}$ was known to be 1.33 IQ points.

$H_0: \mu = 100,$

$H_1: \mu = 104.3,$

$\alpha = .05$ (two-tailed).

2 Draw a figure of the sampling distributions specified in H_0 and H_1.
In drawing this figure to scale, it is helpful to calculate $\sigma_{\bar{x}}$ first. Then the two distributions can be scaled—placed in relation to one another —accurately.

Note that the location of these distributions relative to each other is determined by the means specified under H_0 and H_1 and $\sigma_{\bar{x}}$.

One-tailed Tests

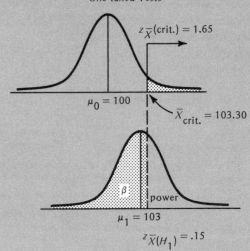

$z_{\bar{X}}(\text{crit.}) = 1.65$

$\mu_0 = 100$

$\bar{X}_{\text{crit.}} = 103.30$

β power

$\mu_1 = 103$

$z_{\bar{X}(H_1)} = .15$

Note: $\sigma_{\bar{X}} = 2$

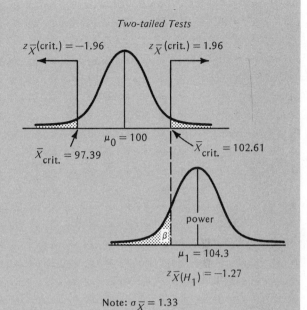

Two-tailed Tests

$z_{\bar{X}}(\text{crit.}) = -1.96$ $z_{\bar{X}}(\text{crit.}) = 1.96$

$\mu_0 = 100$

$\bar{X}_{\text{crit.}} = 97.39$ $\bar{X}_{\text{crit.}} = 102.61$

power

β

$\mu_1 = 104.3$

$z_{\bar{X}}(H_1) = -1.27$

Note: $\sigma_{\bar{X}} = 1.33$

3 a Identify values of $z_{\bar{X}}(\text{crit.})$ in the distribution under H_0.

  b For the two-tailed test, identify tail(s) of distribution under H_0 beyond $z_{\bar{X}}(\text{crit.})$ that intersect(s) the distribution specified by H_1. *Note: In some cases, both tails in the distribution under H_0 will intersect the distribution specified by H_1 (see Figure 13-8).*

4 Calculate $\bar{X}_{\text{crit.}}$ corresponding to $z_{\bar{X}}(\text{crit.})$ in the distribution under H_0, using Formula 13-2:

$$\bar{X}_{\text{crit.}} = \mu + z_{\bar{X}}(\text{crit.})\sigma_{\bar{X}}.$$

See footnote a for calculation of $\sigma_{\bar{X}}$.

(continued on p. 364)

One-tailed tests
Let $\alpha = .05$, so $z_{\bar{X}}(\text{crit.})$ under $H_0 = 1.65$.

Two-tailed tests
Let $\alpha = .05$, so $z_{\bar{X}}(\text{crit.})$ under $H_0 = -1.96$ and 1.96. In this example, the tail beyond $z_{\bar{X}}(\text{crit.}) = 1.96$ (right tail) intersects the distribution under H_1.

One-tailed tests

$$\bar{X}_{\text{crit.}} = 100 + 2(1.65)$$
$$= 103.30.$$

Two-tailed tests

$$\bar{X}_{\text{crit.}}(\text{right tail}) = 100 + (1.96 \times 1.33)$$
$$= 102.61,$$

where $\sigma_{\bar{X}} = 16/\sqrt{144} = 1.33$.

---

[a] $\sigma_{\bar{X}}$ is calculated from the data at the beginning of this chapter: $\sigma = 16$ and $N = 64$, so

$$\sigma_{\bar{X}} = \frac{\sigma}{\sqrt{N}} = \frac{16}{\sqrt{64}} = \frac{16}{8} = 2.$$

5 Calculate the value of $z_{\bar{X}}$ in the distribution under H_1, noting that $\bar{X}_{crit.} = \bar{X}_{meet}$ in Eq. 13-1:

$$z_{\bar{X}(H_1)} = \frac{\bar{X}_{meet} - \mu_1}{\sigma_{\bar{X}}}.$$

One-tailed tests

$$z_{\bar{X}(H_1)} = \frac{103.30 - 103}{2} = .15.$$

Two-tailed tests

$$z_{\bar{X}(H_1)} = \frac{102.61 - 104.3}{1.33} = -1.27.$$

6 Using Table B, identify the area under the curve corresponding to the power (i.e., the area in the distribution under H_1 in which you will correctly reject H_0).

One-tailed tests

From Table B, the area above $z_{\bar{X}(H_1)} = .15$ is .44. Thus,

$$\text{power} = .44.$$

Two-tailed tests

From Table B, the area above $z_{\bar{X}(H_1)} = 1.27$ is .90. Thus,

$$\text{power} = .90.$$

7 β, the probability of not rejecting a false H_0, is easily calculated:

$$\beta = 1 - \text{power}.$$

One-tailed tests

$$\beta = 1 - .44$$
$$= .56.$$

Two-tailed tests

$$\beta = 1 - .90$$
$$= .10.$$

that they have good reason to suspect that their students are below the national average (100) on IQ. Thus,

$$H_0: \mu = 100;$$
$$H_1: \mu < 100.$$

However, for the purposes of calculating the power, we need an exact alternative hypothesis. Since the school officials are only interested in a difference of 4 IQ points, assume that the true population mean is 96 ($= 100 - 4$). Thus, we can state an exact alternative hypothesis:

$$H_1: \mu = 96.$$

The next step is to draw a picture of the situation (see Figure 13-4). The sampling distribution for $H_1: \mu = 96$ can be located accurately by noting that

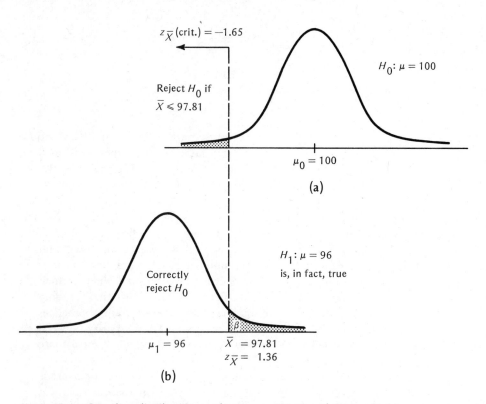

Figure 13-4 ◆ Sampling distributions under H_0: $\mu = 100$ (a) and H_1: $\mu = 96$ (b) (one-tailed test) in the hypothetical IQ study

$\mu = 96$ falls 4 points *below* $\mu = 100$ and that $\sigma_{\bar{X}} = 1.33$. Thus, $\mu = 96$ falls 3 standard errors ($4 \div 1.33$) below $\mu = 100$. In drawing the critical region on the sampling distribution under H_0 and projecting it onto the distribution under H_1, note that a one-tail test, H_1: $\mu < 100$, was specified, and so the critical region lies in the *lower* tail of Figure 13-4a ($\alpha = .05$).

Next, determine the value of the sample mean ($\bar{X}_{\text{critical}}$) which corresponds to $z_{\bar{X}}(\text{critical}) = -1.65$ in the sampling distribution under H_0:

$$\bar{X}_{\text{critical}} = \mu_- + z_{\bar{X}}(\text{critical})\sigma_{\bar{X}} \qquad [\mathbf{13\text{-}2}]$$

$$= 100 + (-1.65 \times 1.33)$$

$$= 97.81.$$

Since $\bar{X}_{\text{critical}}$ equals $\bar{X}_{\text{meet}}$, the point where the shaded and unshaded areas of Figure 13-4b meet, we have all of the information needed to find the unshaded area in 13-4b:

$$z_{\bar{X}(H_1)} = \frac{\bar{X}_{\text{meet}} - \mu_1}{\sigma_{\bar{X}}} \qquad [\,13\text{-}1\,]$$

$$= \frac{97.81 - 96}{1.33}$$

$$= 1.36.$$

The power, then, will correspond to the larger part of the normal distribution for $z_{\bar{X}} = 1.36$. The probability of rejecting a false null hypothesis with a true alternative hypothesis of $\mu = 96$ is .91 from Table B. Since the power is .91, the shaded portion of the alternative distribution, β, is .09.

EXAMPLE PROBLEM 1

In the study of men's and women's achievement in college described in Chapter 2, information about students' college major, aptitude, and achievement was collected for a large number of undergraduates at four University of California campuses in order to determine whether men and women choose different major fields of study, whether grading practices differ from one field to another, and whether grading practices account for the differences in achievement. (See "The Disparity between College Grades Earned by Men and Women" in Chapter 2 for a more complete description.)

An initial question of the researchers was whether or not the average SAT score of the University of California students in their sample was significantly higher than the national average SAT score (1000), as they had reason to believe. Suppose that: (1) the researchers are interested in detecting a 100-point difference or more, (2) the sample consisted of 40 students, and (3) the standard deviation in the population is known to be 200.

What is the power of this statistical test at $\alpha = .05$? What is the value of β?

(Hint: Set up (a) an exact H_0 and H_1; (b) a graph of the sampling distribution under H_0 with $\bar{X}_{\text{critical}}$ specified; (c) a graph of the sampling distribution under H_1 with $\bar{X}_{\text{meet}}$ corresponding to $\bar{X}_{\text{critical}}$ under H_0 specified.)

Two-tailed tests The problem of determining the power of a statistical test under a nondirectional (two-tailed) alternative hypothesis is quite similar to that of a one-tailed test. As an example, suppose that an administrator in a school district does not have good reason to believe students to be above or below a mean IQ of 100. In this case, a two-tailed statistical test would be set

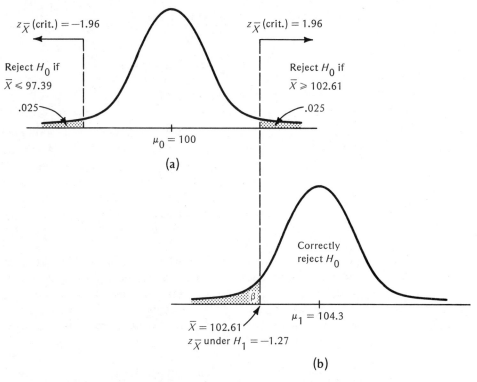

$z_{\bar{X}}$(crit.) = −1.96

Reject H_0 if
$\bar{X} \leqslant 97.39$

.025

$z_{\bar{X}}$(crit.) = 1.96

Reject H_0 if
$\bar{X} \geqslant 102.61$

.025

$\mu_0 = 100$

(a)

Correctly
reject H_0

β

$\bar{X} = 102.61$
$z_{\bar{X}}$ under $H_1 = -1.27$

$\mu_1 = 104.3$

(b)

Figure 13-5 ◆ Sampling distributions under (a) H_0: $\mu = 100$ and (b) H_1: $\mu = 104.3$ (two-tailed test) in the hypothetical IQ study. (Note: $\sigma_{\bar{x}} = 1.33$.)

up under the null hypothesis ($\alpha = .05$; $\alpha/2 = .025$ in one tail and .025 in the other). Thus, the critical values of $z_{\bar{x}}$ for rejecting H_0 are -1.96 and 1.96. This situation is represented in Figure 13-5a.

Suppose further that the true population mean is 104.3. The sampling distribution for this true alternative hypothesis is shown in Figure 13-5b. In order to determine the power of this statistical test, first $\bar{X}_{\text{critical}}$ must be calculated (let $\sigma_{\bar{x}} = 1.33$ as in the last example). Since μ under H_1 is way above μ under H_0, the tail in the lower distribution can be ignored. In this case,

$$\bar{X}_{\text{critical}} = \mu + \sigma_{\bar{x}}(z_{\text{critical}})$$
$$= 100 + 1.33(1.96)$$
$$= 102.61.$$

Next, note that $\bar{X}_{\text{critical}}$ under H_0 equals $\bar{X}_{\text{meet}}$ under H_1, so a $z_{\bar{X}(H_1)}$ score can be calculated to find the unshaded area in the alternative distribution, the power of the statistical test:

$$z_{\overline{X}(H_1)} = \frac{102.61 - 104.3}{1.33}$$

$$= \frac{-1.69}{1.33}$$

$$= -1.27.$$

From Table B, the area in the greater (unshaded) portion of the curve marked off by $z_{\overline{X}} = -1.27$ is .90. Thus, the power of the statistical test is .90, and β equals .10. These steps in calculating power are summarized in Procedure 13-1.

In this example, the operations involved in calculating power were almost identical to those under the one-tailed case. The one exception was identifying two tails in the sampling distribution under the null hypothesis; this resulted in a more restrictive rejection region than would have occurred with a one-tailed test.

However, this is not the only situation which may arise. Consider the situation in which the true population mean is 99. Figure 13-6 provides a picture of this situation.[2] Notice that the sampling distribution under H_1 (Figure 13-6b) is intersected by the region of rejection under the null hypothesis in both of its tails. This occurs because the true population mean is quite close to the mean under the null hypothesis. From this figure, we see that a correct decision to reject the null hypothesis can be made in two ways: (1) if a sample mean is greater than or equal to 102.61, or (2) if a sample mean is less than or equal to 97.39. However, most of the sample means drawn from this true alternative distribution will fall between 97.39 and 102.61. In this case, an incorrect decision not to reject the null hypothesis will be made.

In order to determine the power of this statistical test, we need to determine the area in each of the tails where the sample means lead to a correct decision.[3] To do so, the first step is to determine $z_{\overline{X}(H_1)}$ for 97.39 and $z_{\overline{X}(H_1)}$ for 102.61 in the alternative distribution:

$$z_{\overline{X}(H_1)} = \frac{97.39 - 99}{1.33} = \frac{-1.61}{1.33} = -1.21;$$

$$z_{\overline{X}(H_1)} = \frac{102.61 - 99}{1.33} = \frac{3.61}{1.33} = 2.71.$$

Next, we find the area in the smaller tail marked off by the $z_{\overline{X}}$ scores. From Table B, this area will be .1131 for a $z_{\overline{X}}$ score of -1.21, and .0034 for a $z_{\overline{X}}$ score

---

[2] Since $\overline{X}_{\text{critical}} = \mu + z_{\overline{X}}$ (critical)$\sigma_{\overline{X}}$ (Formula 13-2), we have $\overline{X}_{\text{critical}}$(right tail) $= 100 + (1.96) \times$ (1.33) $= 102.61$ and $\overline{X}_{\text{critical}}$(left tail) $= 100 - (1.96) \times (1.33) = 97.39$.

[3] Curiously, a correct decision to reject a false null hypothesis can be made for the wrong reason. In this example, for instance, a sample mean way above 100 (the opposite direction from the true $\mu_1 = 99$) can lead to a correct decision. This has been called, by some, a Type III error.

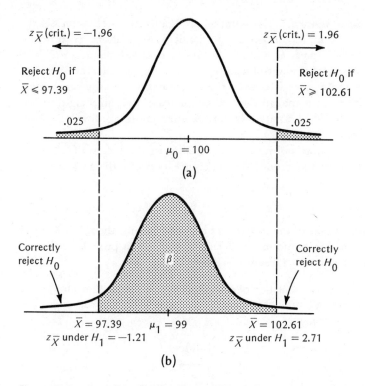

$z_{\bar{X}}(\text{crit.}) = -1.96$

$z_{\bar{X}}(\text{crit.}) = 1.96$

Reject H_0 if
$\bar{X} \leqslant 97.39$

Reject H_0 if
$\bar{X} \geqslant 102.61$

.025

.025

$\mu_0 = 100$

(a)

Correctly
reject H_0

β

Correctly
reject H_0

$\bar{X} = 97.39$
$z_{\bar{X}}$ under $H_1 = -1.21$

$\mu_1 = 99$

$\bar{X} = 102.61$
$z_{\bar{X}}$ under $H_1 = 2.71$

(b)

Figure 13-6 ◆ Sampling distributions under (a) H_0: $\mu = 100$ and (b) H_1: $\mu = 99$ (two-tailed test) in the hypothetical IQ study

of 2.71. Finally, by adding these two areas together, we have the area of the normal sampling distribution under the true alternative hypothesis which leads to the correct decision to reject the false null hypothesis:

$$.1131 + .0034 = .1165.$$

Thus, the probability of rejecting a false null hypothesis—the power of the statistical test—is .1165. The probability of not rejecting a false null hypothesis—the probability of a Type II error, β—is $1 - .1165 = .8835$.

Suppose that the researchers in the study of female "overachievement" referred to in Example Problem 1 had no reason to believe that the SAT scores of University of California students were above the national average. What is the power of a two-tail statistical test at $\alpha = .05$? What is β? (Hint: Set up steps a–c as in Example Problem 1.)

EXAMPLE PROBLEM 2

Two-sample (Case II) research   Two-sample, or Case II, research addresses the question: "Are two samples drawn from identical populations or different populations?" (See Chapters 9 and 12 for more detailed discussions.) The rationale for estimating the power of a statistical test for the difference between two means (two-sample case) is exactly the same as that for the one-sample case. The only difference is that in the two-sample case, the sampling distributions under the null and alternative hypotheses are sampling distributions of differences between means.

Under the null hypothesis of no difference between the means of a control group and an experimental group, the difference between the means in the population is zero:

$$H_0: \mu_1 - \mu_2 = 0.$$

The sampling distribution of the differences between means, then, has a mean of zero and is assumed to be normal in form. (Figure 13-7a provides a picture of this situation for a one-tailed test at $\alpha = .05$.)

Figure 13-7 ♦ Conceptual representation of power for the two-sample case ($\sigma_{\bar{X}_1 - \bar{X}_2} = 2.50$): (a) sampling distribution under $H_0: \mu_1 - \mu_2 = 0$; (b) sampling distribution under $H_1: \mu_1 - \mu_2 = 5$

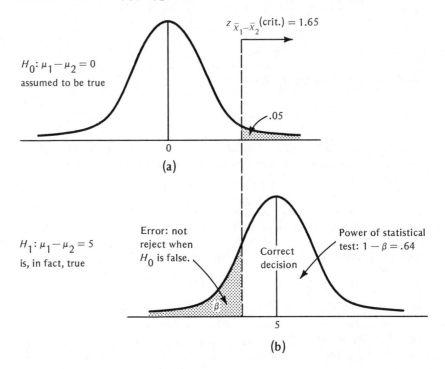

Under the alternative hypothesis, a difference between the mean performance of the control and experimental groups is expected. The difference may be nondirectional (two-tailed) or, as shown in Figure 13-7, directional (one-tailed). In any case, the sampling distribution of the differences between means is normal in form and has a mean different from zero. Figure 13-7 shows the sampling distribution of differences between means for a specific alternative hypothesis:

$$H_1: \mu_1 - \mu_2 = 5.$$

A specific alternative hypothesis is used, since the power of a statistical test is always determined with respect to the magnitude of the difference between means that the researcher wishes to detect. In Figure 13-7, the researcher wants to detect a difference of 5 points between the means of the control and experimental groups.

Once the problem of estimating power has been cast in the form of sampling distributions of differences between means under the null and alternative hypotheses, the solution to the problem is exactly the same as that for the one-sample case described in detail above. The next step is to identify the critical difference between means, $(\overline{X}_1 - \overline{X}_2)_{\text{critical}}$ (cf. $\overline{X}_{\text{critical}}$), that must be observed in order to reject H_0. In Figure 13-7a, this is the value of the difference between means falling 1.65 standard errors above zero. In general,

$$
\boxed{
\begin{aligned}
\left(\overline{X}_1 - \overline{X}_2\right)_{\text{critical}} &= 0 + z_{\overline{X}_1 - \overline{X}_2(\text{critical})} \cdot \sigma_{\overline{X}_1 - \overline{X}_2} \\
&= z_{\overline{X}_1 - \overline{X}_2(\text{critical})} \cdot \sigma_{\overline{X}_1 - \overline{X}_2}.
\end{aligned}
\qquad [\textbf{13-3}]
}
$$

If $\sigma_{\overline{X}_1 - \overline{X}_2}$ equals 2.50, then $(\overline{X}_1 - \overline{X}_2)_{\text{critical}}$ in Figure 13-7a is

$$\left(\overline{X}_1 - \overline{X}_2\right)_{\text{critical}} = 1.65(2.50)$$
$$= 4.13.$$

Thus, under the null hypothesis and $\alpha = .05$ (one-tailed), any difference between sample means $\geqslant 4.13$ will lead to a correct decision to reject the null hypothesis (the unshaded portion of Figure 13-7a). However, a difference of less than 4.13 will lead to an incorrect decision not to reject the false null hypothesis. The shaded area of Figure 13-7b represents the probability of making this Type II error.

The power of the statistical test can be found by determining the area in the unshaded portion of Figure 13-7b. This can be done by first noting that

$(\overline{X}_1 - \overline{X}_2)_{\text{critical}}$ falls at the point in Figure 13-7b where the shaded and unshaded areas meet, say $(\overline{X}_1 - \overline{X}_2)_{\text{meet}}$ (cf. $\overline{X}_{\text{meet}}$). Then, the z score corresponding to this point, $z_{(\overline{X}_1 - \overline{X}_2)(H_1)}$, can be found so that the area in the unshaded portion of Figure 13-7b can be determined:

$$
z_{(\overline{X}_1 - \overline{X}_2)(H_1)} = \frac{\left(\overline{X}_1 - \overline{X}_2\right)_{\text{meet}} - (\mu_1 - \mu_2)_{H_1}}{\sigma_{\overline{X}_1 - \overline{X}_2}} \qquad [\mathbf{13\text{-}4}]
$$

$$
= \frac{4.13 - 5}{2.50}
$$

$$
= -.35.
$$

Finally, the area to the right of a $z_{(\overline{X}_1 - \overline{X}_2)(H_1)}$ score of $-.35$ can be found. This is the area corresponding to the power of the statistical test (Figure 13-7b). Table B shows that this area is .64. Thus, the power of the statistical test is .64, and β—the probability of a Type II error—is .36. These steps in calculating power are summarized in Procedure 13-2.

As another example of calculating power for the two-sample case, consider

Procedure 13-2 ♦ Steps in calculating power: two-sample (Case II) research, one-tailed and two-tailed tests

Operation	Example
1 Set up exact null and alternative hypotheses. *The exact alternative hypothesis is based on the difference between means that the researcher wishes to detect.*	*One-tailed tests* Data for this example are taken from Figure 13-9. $H_0: \mu_1 - \mu_2 = 0$ $H_1: \mu_1 - \mu_2 = 5$ $\alpha = .05$ (one-tailed) *Two-tailed tests* Data are taken from the hypothetical study of teacher expectancy (see Figure 13-8). $H_0: \mu_1 - \mu_2 = 0$ $H_1: \mu_1 - \mu_2 = .66$ $\alpha = .05$ (two-tailed)

2 Draw a graph of the sampling distributions specified in H_0 and H_1.

In drawing this graph to scale, it is helpful to calculate $\sigma_{\bar{x}_1 - \bar{x}_2}$ first. Then the two distributions can be scaled—placed in relation to one another—accurately.

Note that the location of these distributions relative to each other is determined by the means specified under H_0 and H_1 and by $\sigma_{\bar{x}_1 - \bar{x}_2}$.

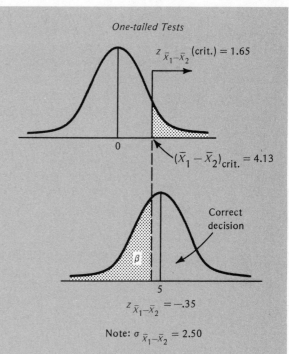

One-tailed Tests

$z_{\bar{X}_1 - \bar{X}_2}$ (crit.) = 1.65

$(\bar{X}_1 - \bar{X}_2)_{\text{crit.}} = 4.13$

0

Correct decision

β

5

$z_{\bar{X}_1 - \bar{X}_2} = -.35$

Note: $\sigma_{\bar{X}_1 - \bar{X}_2} = 2.50$

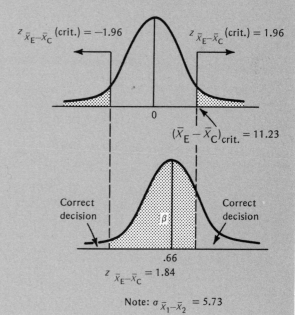

Two-tailed Tests

$z_{\bar{X}_E - \bar{X}_C}$ (crit.) = −1.96

$z_{\bar{X}_E - \bar{X}_C}$ (crit.) = 1.96

0

$(\bar{X}_E - \bar{X}_C)_{\text{crit.}} = 11.23$

Correct decision

β

Correct decision

.66

$z_{\bar{X}_E - \bar{X}_C} = 1.84$

Note: $\sigma_{\bar{X}_1 - \bar{X}_2} = 5.73$

(continued on p. 374)

3 a Identify value(s) of $z_{\bar{X}_1 - \bar{X}_2}(\text{crit.})$ in the distribution under H_0.

One-tailed tests

Let $\alpha = .05$, so $z_{\bar{X}_1 - \bar{X}_2}(\text{crit.}) = 1.65$

b For the two-tailed test, identify tail(s) of the distribution under H_0 beyond $z_{\bar{X}_E - \bar{X}_C}(\text{crit.})$ that intersect(s) the distribution specified under H_1.

Two-tailed tests

Let $\alpha = .05$, so $z_{\bar{X}_E - \bar{X}_C}(\text{crit.}) = 1.96$ and -1.96.

In this example, both critical regions (-1.96 and 1.96) intersect the distribution under H_1.

4 Calculate $(\bar{X}_1 - \bar{X}_2)_{\text{crit.}}$ corresponding to $z_{\bar{X}_1 - \bar{X}_2}(\text{crit.})$ in the distribution under H_0 by using Formula 13-3:

$$\boxed{\left(\bar{X}_1 - \bar{X}_2\right)_{\text{crit.}} = z_{\bar{X}_1 - \bar{X}_2}\sigma_{\bar{X}_1 - \bar{X}_2}}$$

and Formula 12-1b:

$$\sigma_{\bar{X}_1 - \bar{X}_2} = \sqrt{\frac{\sigma_1^2}{n_1} + \frac{\sigma_2^2}{n_2}}$$

One-tailed tests

$$\left(\bar{X}_E - \bar{X}_C\right)_{\text{crit.}} = (2.50)(1.65)$$

$$= 4.13.$$

(Note: $\sigma_{\bar{X}_1 - \bar{X}_2}$ is 2.50; see text.)

Two-tailed tests

For the upper region,

$$\left(\bar{X}_E - \bar{X}_C\right)_{\text{crit.}} = (1.96)(5.73)$$

$$= 11.53.$$

For the lower region,

$$\left(\bar{X}_E - \bar{X}_C\right)_{\text{crit.}} = (-1.96)(5.73)$$

$$= -11.53,$$

(Note: $\sigma_{\bar{X}_E - \bar{X}_C} = 5.73$; see text.)

5 Calculate the value of $z_{(\bar{X}_1 - \bar{X}_2)(H_1)}$ in distribution under H_1 noting that

$$\left(\bar{X}_1 - \bar{X}_2\right)_{\text{crit.}} = \left(\bar{X}_1 - \bar{X}_2\right)_{\text{meet,}}$$

and using Formula 13-4:

$$\boxed{z_{(\bar{X}_1 - \bar{X}_2)(H_1)} = \frac{\left(\bar{X}_1 - \bar{X}_2\right) - \left(\mu_1 - \mu_2\right)_{H_1}}{\sigma_{\bar{X}_1 - \bar{X}_2}}}$$

One-tailed tests

$$z_{(\bar{X}_1 - \bar{X}_2)(H_1)} = \frac{4.13 - 5}{2.50}$$

$$= -.35.$$

Two-tailed tests

For the upper region

$$z_{(\bar{X}_E - \bar{X}_C)(H_1)} = \frac{11.23 - .66}{5.73}$$

$$= 1.84.$$

For the lower region,

$$z_{(\bar{X}_E - \bar{X}_C)(H_1)} = \frac{-11.23 - .66}{5.73}$$

$$= 2.08.$$

6 Using Table B, identify the area under the curve corresponding to the power (i.e., the area in the distribution under H_1 in which you will correctly reject H_0).

One-tailed tests

From Table B, the area to the right of a $z_{(\bar{X}_1 - \bar{X}_2)(H_1)}$ score of $-.35$ is .64. Thus,

$$\text{power} = .64.$$

Two-tailed tests

From Table B, the area to the right of a $z_{(\bar{X}_E - \bar{X}_C)(H_1)}$ score of 1.84 is .0329 while the area below -2.08 is .0188. Thus,

$$\text{power} = .0329 + .0188$$
$$= .0517.$$

7 β, the probability of not rejecting a false H_0, is easily calculated:

$$\beta = 1 - \text{power}.$$

One-tailed tests

$$\beta = 1 - .64$$
$$= .44.$$

Two-tailed tests

$$\beta = 1 - .0517$$
$$= .9483.$$

the data from the hypothetical study of teacher expectancy described in Chapter 2. In this study, students, randomly assigned to the experimental condition, were expected by their teachers to "spurt" intellectually, while the teachers did not hold this expectation for students randomly assigned to the control condition. At the end of the study, the mean IQ score for the experimental group was 109.57 with a standard deviation of 9.16 points, while the mean IQ score for the control group was 110.23 with a standard deviation of 9.38 points. Thus, the observed difference between the means of the two groups is 0.66; the standard error of the difference between means is known to be

$$\sigma_{\bar{X}_1 - \bar{X}_2} = 5.73.$$

Let's assume that the researchers were interested in finding the power of the statistical test they had already conducted with $\alpha = .05$ (two-tailed). In this case, then, the researchers are interested in determining the power of their statistical test for detecting a true difference between means equal to the observed difference of 0.66. With this information, the problem of determining the power of their statistical test can be represented graphically as in Figure 13-8. Notice that, since a two-tailed hypothesis is used, the critical region in the tail of the distribution is $.05/2 = .025$. Also, since the difference (.66) is so small, we have to consider both tails in calculating the power.

The first step is to determine the values of $\bar{X}_E - \bar{X}_C$ which correspond to the upper and lower regions of significance under the null hypothesis (the cutoffs for the shaded area in Figure 13-8a). For the upper tail,

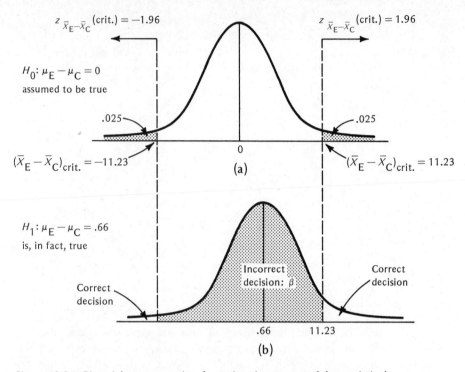

Figure 13-8 ♦ Pictorial representation for estimating power of the statistical test for the hypothetical Pygmalion study: (a) sampling distribution under H_0; (b) sampling distribution under H_1

$$\left(\bar{X}_E - \bar{X}_C\right)_{\text{critical}} = z_{\bar{X}_E - \bar{X}_C}(\text{critical}) \cdot \sigma_{\bar{X}_E - \bar{X}_C} \qquad [13\text{-}3]$$

$$= (1.96)(5.73)$$

$$= 11.23.$$

For the lower tail,

$$\left(\bar{X}_E - \bar{X}_C\right)_{\text{critical}} = (-1.96)(5.73)$$

$$= -11.23.$$

Thus, any difference between the means of the control and experimental groups of ± 11.23 points or more would lead to the correct decision to reject the null hypothesis. However, any difference between means of less than 11.23 points would lead to the erroneous decision not to reject the false null hypothesis.

From Figure 13-8, it is clear that the power of the statistical test for detecting a difference of less than 1 IQ point between groups (in particular, 0.66 IQ point) is quite low. In order to determine the power precisely, the area in the upper and lower unshaded areas of Figure 13-8b needs to be determined. This is done by finding the $z_{(\bar{X}_E - \bar{X}_C)(H_1)}$ score in the alternative distribution corresponding to this area and consulting Table B. For the upper portion,

$$z_{(\bar{X}_E - \bar{X}_C)(H_1)} = \frac{(\bar{X}_E - \bar{X}_C)_{\text{meet}} - (\mu_E - \mu_C)_{H_1}}{\sigma_{\bar{X}_E - \bar{X}_C}} \qquad [13\text{-}4]$$

$$= \frac{11.23 - .66}{5.73}$$

$$= 1.84.$$

For the lower portion,

$$z_{(\bar{X}_E - \bar{X}_C)(H_1)} = \frac{-11.23 - .66}{5.73}$$

$$= -2.08.$$

From Table B, the area in the smaller tail of the curve corresponding to $z_{(\bar{X}_E - \bar{X}_C)(H_1)}$ scores of 1.84 and -2.08 are .0329 and .0188, respectively. The power of the statistical test for detecting a difference of .66 IQ points between the control group and the experimental group is $.0329 + .0188 = .0517$. (See Procedure 13-2 for a summary of these calculations.) The probability β of a Type II error is .9483.

It was hardly worth the effort to run a study such as this in which a small difference between groups might reasonably be expected, unless something could be done to increase the power of the statistical test. This is just the topic of the next section— factors affecting the power of a statistical test.

A researcher, interested in strategies for learning from prose, plans to randomly assign 15 subjects to each of two groups, tested respectively under (1) a *subject-generated* (SG) underlining condition in which subjects were instructed to underline the most important sentence in each paragraph, and (2) an *experimenter-provided* (EP) condition in which subjects were provided with materials in which the most important sentence in each paragraph was already underlined. All subjects will be given a comprehension test after reading the passage.

EXAMPLE PROBLEM 3

Suppose that: (a) the experimenter is interested in detecting a two-point difference between the groups; (b) he has a theory and pilot data to suggest that the SG group would show significantly greater comprehension than the EP group; and (c) $\sigma_{SG} = \sigma_{EP} = 2.5$.

What is the power of this statistical test at $\alpha = .05$ (one-tailed)? What is the value of β? (Hint: Set up steps a–c as in Example Problem 1.)

♦   ♦   ♦   ♦   ♦

Factors Influencing the Power of a Statistical Test At this point, you know how to determine the power of a statistical test, but that does not necessarily help unless you can do something to improve the power if your statistics suggest that you should. The purpose here is to identify a number of factors which influence the power of a statistical test and to identify those which are under your control. By systematically manipulating such factors as sample size, you can manipulate the power of your statistical test.

There are four factors which influence the power of statistical tests, and three of them are under your control.

Level of significance One factor under your control is the level of significance, α. *The power of a statistical test increases as α increases.* Thus, if all other factors influencing power are held constant, as α increases from .01 to .05 to .10, and so on, power increases. This relationship between power and α is shown in Figure 13-9. As you can see, as α increases, so does the power of the

Figure 13-9 ♦ Illustration of the relationship between α and power: (a) sampling distributions under H_0; (b) sampling distributions under H_1 (assume true $\mu = 52$; $\sigma_{\bar{X}} = 2$)

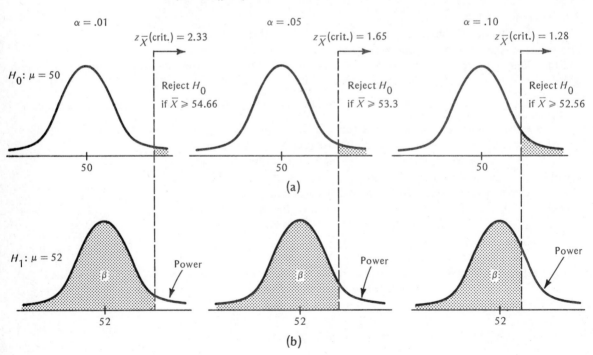

statistical test (unshaded area under the sampling distribution for the alternative, "true" hypothesis).

Magnitude of the treatment effect   The **magnitude of the treatment effect** is a second factor affecting the power of a statistical test. *The greater the treatment effect is, the greater the power* (all other things being equal). This relation between power and treatment effect works as follows. If the treatment effect is small, the sampling distributions under H_0 and H_1 will overlap greatly, reducing the probability of detecting a true difference. If the effect is large, the sampling distributions under H_0 and H_1 will scarcely overlap one another. In this case, the difference will be easy to detect and power will be high.

While the magnitude of the treatment effect is not directly under the researcher's control, it behooves the researcher to carefully develop a treatment by pilot-testing and revising it. In this way, noise or error in estimating the difference between population means from sample data can be reduced.

Variability in the population   A third factor affecting the power of a statistical test is the variability in the population. All other factors being equal (α constant, sample size constant, and treatment effect constant), *the smaller the standard deviation of the population, the more powerful the statistical test*. The reason is the following. First, as the overlap between the sampling distribution under the null and specific alternative hypotheses decreases, power increases, since all sample means from the "true" alternative distribution fall in the rejection region. Second, the spread of these sampling distributions (and hence, potential overlap) depends, in part, on the population standard deviation σ. Recall from Chapter 11 that the standard deviation in a sampling distribution of means—called the standard error of the mean—is

$$\sigma_{\bar{X}} = \frac{\sigma}{\sqrt{N}}. \qquad [11\text{-}1]$$

Thus, if N is held constant, as we assumed above, the spread or potential overlap of the sampling distribution under the null and specific alternative hypotheses increases as σ increases. This relationship is shown in Figure 13-10.

The population variance, σ, can be controlled by the researcher, at least to some extent. This control can be achieved in a number of ways. One way to control σ is to sample subjects from a homogeneous population. Instead of sampling subjects from all ranges of socioeconomic status, for example, the researcher might sample from a population of middle-class subjects. A second way to control σ is to make sure that the dependent variable is reliable, since an unreliable dependent variable will increase σ by introducing unnecessary error. A third way to control σ is to use statistical techniques such as the analysis of covariance or a randomized-block design (see, for example, Hays, 1973; Winer, 1971).

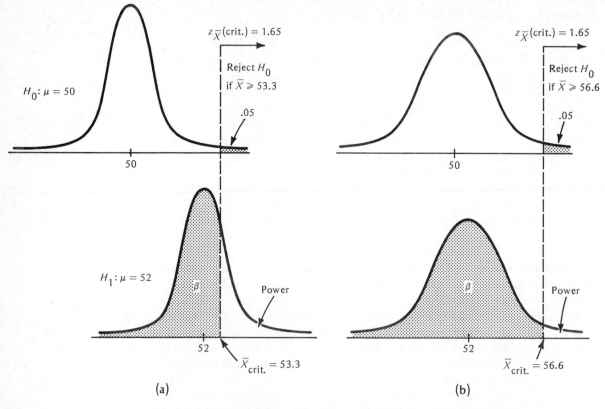

Figure 13-10 ◆ Illustration of the relationship between power and variability ($N = 64$): (a) sampling distributions under H_0 and H_1 with $\sigma = 16$ so $\sigma_{\bar{x}} = 2$; (b) sampling distribution under H_0 and H_1 with $\sigma = 32$ so $\sigma_{\bar{x}} = 4$

Sample size As shown above, the sample size influences the power of a statistical test by influencing the spread of the sampling distributions under H_0 and H_1. By increasing the sample size and holding all other factors constant (α, treatment effect, and σ), one decreases the variability of the sampling distribution. One thereby also decreases the overlap between the distribution under the null hypothesis and the distribution under the alternative hypothesis. Thus more and more of the sample means drawn from the distribution under the "true" alternative hypothesis fall in the rejection region of the null hypothesis. Hence, the power of the statistical test is increased. The effect of sample size on power is shown in Figure 13-11.

Some wisdom As you might guess, sample size influences the power of statistical tests indirectly by affecting the variability of the sampling distribution(s). However, sample size is one of the most important factors underlying

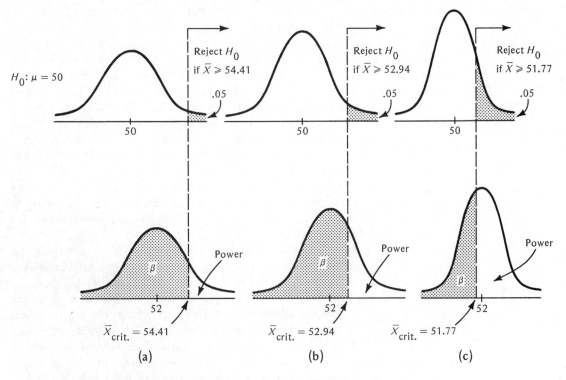

$H_0: \mu = 50$

Reject H_0 if $\bar{X} \geqslant 54.41$

.05

Reject H_0 if $\bar{X} \geqslant 52.94$

.05

Reject H_0 if $\bar{X} \geqslant 51.77$

.05

50

50

50

Power

Power

Power

β

β

β

52

52

52

$\bar{X}_{crit.} = 54.41$

$\bar{X}_{crit.} = 52.94$

$\bar{X}_{crit.} = 51.77$

(a)

(b)

(c)

Figure 13-11 ◆ Illustration of relationship between power and sample size ($\sigma = 16$): (a) sampling distribution under H_0 and H_1 with $N = 36$ so $\sigma_{\bar{x}} = 2.67$; (b) sampling distributions under H_0 and H_1 with $N = 81$ so $\sigma_{\bar{x}} = 2.94$; (c) sampling distribution under H_0 and H_1 with $N = 225$ so $\sigma_{\bar{x}} = 1.07$

power. It is possible to design an experiment which is extremely powerful just by increasing sample size, which in turn decreases the variability of the sampling distribution(s) and decreases the overlap between distributions specified by H_0 and H_1 if differences exist. Thus, differences are more easily detected. This means that trivial differences from a practical standpoint may be statistically significant. It also means that even poor experimental treatments may be found to differ significantly from control treatments. Wisdom comes into play when the researcher balances the factors influencing the power of statistical tests by designing a study with: (1) the best treatments possible, so that the treatment effect is as strong as possible; (2) α set at a conservative level (e.g., .05 or .01), so that the probability of a Type I error is minimized; and (3) sample sizes large enough so that theoretically and/or practically significant differences are detected. Since the sample size is such an important factor influencing the power of a statistical test, some methods for estimating the needed sample size for an experiment are given below.

METHODS FOR
ESTIMATING THE
SAMPLE SIZE

**When the Standard
Deviation Is Known**

In estimating the size of a sample needed for a study, there are a number of factors to be taken into consideration: the probability of a Type I error (α), the probability of a Type II error (β, or alternatively power which is $1 - \beta$), the size of the difference between means to be detected in the study, and the population variance (σ). Prior to a study, a researcher should be able to state desired levels of the first three factors influencing the sample size. For example, α might be set at .05 by convention, and β might be set at .10, giving a power of $1 - \beta = .90$. While the conventions for setting β are not as well established as those for setting α, often β is set at .20 or lower (power $\geqslant .80$). With $\beta \leqslant .20$, the researcher assures a reasonable probability of detecting a difference if the difference exists. Notice also that, as is almost always the case, α is more conservative than β. This reflects most researchers' greater concern for a Type I than a Type II error. However, as pointed out earlier, there may be situations in which a Type II error is more costly than a Type I error and you may want to make corresponding adjustments in α and β.

The researcher should also have some notion of how big a difference the study must detect. This can be approached in several ways. In applied research, a statistically significant difference should also be significant for practice, i.e., application. For example, in one of the IQ studies of students in a particular school district, the district administration was interested in detecting a mean IQ of 3 points or more above the national norm of 100; this difference had practical value for the administration. In a curriculum evaluation study in which a decision is to be made about which of two reading curricula to adopt, the difference might have to be reasonably large to have practical value, especially when differential costs of implementing the curricula are considered. In basic research, theory might indicate how large a difference an experimental treatment should make in comparison with the control treatment. Or it may be important to detect very small differences if such differences are important in testing the theory. Regardless of the magnitude of the difference expected, the researcher should be able to state how much of a difference he or she would like the study to detect.

There are some cases, however, in which the researcher has some notion of the magnitude of difference to be detected but cannot translate the size of the difference into a number because he is not sure of the measurement scale: should the difference be 1 point? 5 points? In this case, the desired magnitude of difference will depend on the variability of scores on the dependent variable. The researcher might state that he would like to detect a difference of, say, a half a standard deviation between the experimental and control groups (see below, "When the Standard Deviation Is Unknown").

Sample size for single-sample (Case I) research: one-tailed tests   At this point, the problem of determining sample size can be presented conceptually. We will begin with single-sample (Case I) research designed to determine whether a sample belongs to a population with a certain hypothesized mean. One-tailed tests are used first, not because the conclusion or formula used for calculating sample size will differ in important ways for two-tailed tests, but because the one-tailed test is easier to understand.

In developing ideas about determining sample size, one of the IQ studies will be used as an example. Recall that in one of the hypothetical studies, a researcher set out to determine the mean IQ of students in a school district, and α was set at .05. Let's assume that for this study the desired power of the statistical test was .90, so β was set at .10. Finally, the difference between the national norm mean of 100 and the district mean had to be +3 IQ points or more to be of practical value. So the researcher set the difference D at +3. With these three pieces of information, we can set up two sampling distributions: one representing the null hypothesis, H_0: $\mu = 100$, and one representing the specific alternative hypothesis, H_1: $\mu = 103$. In drawing these two sampling distributions, the figures must be scaled to represent the situation in which $\beta = .10$, i.e., 10 percent of the distribution under the alternative hypothesis falls in the nonrejection region of the distribution under the null hypothesis. This is the 10 percent of the sample means that would lead the researcher to fail to

Figure 13-12 ◆ Hypothetical sampling distributions when $\alpha = .05$, $\beta = .10$ and $D = 3$ (one-tailed test): (a) sampling distribution under H_0; (b) sampling distribution under H_1

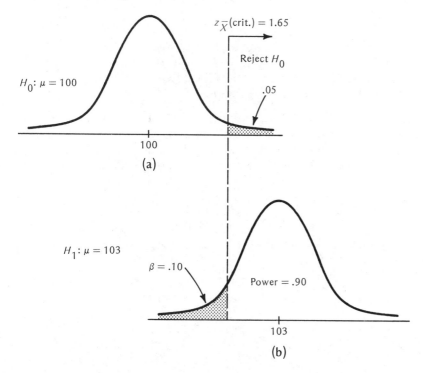

$z_{\bar{X}}(\text{crit.}) = 1.65$

Reject H_0

H_0: $\mu = 100$

.05

100

(a)

H_1: $\mu = 103$

$\beta = .10$

Power = .90

103

(b)

reject a false null hypothesis, i.e., to commit a Type II error. Figure 13-12 provides a picture of this situation.

The key point to notice is that in drawing the figures to the appropriate scale, there is only one value of the standard error of the mean—the index of the spread or variability of each sampling distribution—which allows the two distributions to overlap exactly so that $\beta = .10$. As mentioned earlier, the variability of the sampling distribution—i.e., the standard error, $\sigma_{\bar{X}}$—depends on the standard deviation in the population and the sample size. As $\sigma_{\bar{X}}$ decreases, the likelihood of detecting true differences between the sample and the population—power—increases, since the overlap between the distributions under H_0 and H_1 is decreased. The figure can be drawn to scale by finding the exact value of N, the sample size, which adjusts the standard error so that the overlap of the two distributions produces $\beta = .10$. The formula for determining the sample size needed to adjust the two distributions so that $\beta = .10$ when $\alpha = .05$ and $D = 3$ is

$$N = \frac{\sigma^2(z_\beta - z_\alpha)^2}{D^2}, \qquad [\mathbf{13\text{-}5}]$$

where $\sigma^2 =$ population standard deviation squared, i.e., the population variance;

$z_\beta = z$ score corresponding to the area in the smaller portion of the sampling distribution under H_1, i.e., β;

$z_\alpha = z$ score corresponding to the area in the smaller portion of the sampling distribution under H_0, i.e., α;

$D =$ scale distance between μ_0 and μ_1.

In order to use this formula, values are needed for each of its terms. The population standard deviation for IQ is 16; thus $\sigma^2 = 16^2 = 256$. Now z_β is the standard score *below* which the probability of observing a sample mean is .10 under H_1. The value of z_β corresponding to .10 in the smaller tail can be found in Table B. This value is -1.28. It is negative because, in this example, we are interested in the area of the lower tail on the distribution under H_1. On the other hand, z_α is the standard score *above* which the probability of observing a sample mean is .05 under H_0. From Table B, this value is $+1.65$. Finally, $D = +3$. Substituting this information into Formula 13-5, we have

$$N = \frac{256(-1.28 - 1.65)^2}{3^2}$$

$$= \frac{256(-2.93)^2}{9}$$

$$= 244.19.$$

Since .19 of a subject cannot be observed in the study, round off to $N = 244$. Thus, this procedure tells us that 244 subjects are needed to detect a difference of 3 IQ points when $\alpha = .05$ and $\beta = .10$.

In calculating the sample size, the factor $(z_\beta - z_\alpha)^2$ will always result in adding the two absolute values inside the parentheses and squaring their sum, assuming $\beta \leqslant .50$. (This assumption is quite reasonable, since in determining N we are usually interested in a statistical test with power $\geqslant .80$.) Thus, $(-1.28 - 1.65)^2$ amounted to taking the sum of two negative numbers, $(-1.28) + (-1.65)$, and squaring the sum, $(-2.93)^2$. Since the sum is squared, we need not worry about the sign of the two numbers. Thus, the values of z_β and z_α can be expressed as absolute values in which the sign is ignored: $(|z_\beta| + |z_\alpha|)^2$. This makes the formula for determining the sample size much easier to work with. Assuming $\beta \leqslant .50$, Formula 13-5 can be rewritten as:

$$N = \frac{\sigma^2(|z_\beta| + |z_\alpha|)^2}{D^2}. \qquad [\,13\text{-}5a\,]$$

The steps for calculating the sample size are summarized in Procedure 13-3.

Suppose that the researchers in the study of female "overachievement" decided to replicate their study with another sample of University of California students. They decided that they wanted to detect a 100-point difference or more above the national average of 1000 on the GRE, and that they wished to set $\alpha = .05$ (one-tailed) and $\beta = .10$. Assuming that $\sigma = 200$, what sample size should they use?

EXAMPLE PROBLEM 4

Sample size for single-sample (Case I) research: two-tailed tests   The formula for calculating the sample size for a one-tailed test can be modified slightly for use with two-tailed tests. This modification involves using the critical value for a two-tailed test, $z_{\alpha/2}$, instead of the critical value for a one-tailed test, z_α:

$$N = \frac{\sigma^2(z_\beta - z_{\alpha/2})^2}{D^2}, \qquad [\,13\text{-}5b\,]$$

where $z_{\alpha/2} = z$ score corresponding to the area in the smaller portion of the sampling distribution under H_0; this area corresponds to $\frac{1}{2}\alpha$, or $\alpha/2$, so that, if $\alpha = .05$, $\alpha/2 = .05/2 = .025$.

Procedure 13-3 ♦ Steps in calculating sample size when σ is known: one sample (Case I) research, one-tailed and two-tailed tests

Operation	Example
1 Set up exact H_0 and H_1.	*One-tailed test*
	$$H_0: \mu = 100,$$
	$$H_1: \mu = 103.$$
	Two-tailed test
	$$H_0: \mu = 100,$$
	$$H_1: \mu = 103.$$
2 Define α, β, and D (the difference between values of μ specified in H_0 and H_1).	*One-tailed test*
	$$\alpha = .05,$$
	$$\beta = .10,$$
	$$D = 103 - 100 = 3.$$
	Two-tailed test
	$$\alpha = .05,$$
	$$\beta = .10,$$
	$$D = 103 - 100 = 3.$$

3 Use the appropriate formula to compute sample size:

One-tailed tests

$$N = \frac{\sigma^2(|z_\beta| + |z_\alpha|)^2}{D^2}, \quad \text{[13-5a]}$$

where
σ^2 = population standard deviation
z_β = z score corresponding to the area in the smaller portion of the sampling distribution under H_1 (i.e., $\beta \leqslant .50$),
z_α = z score corresponding to the area in the smaller portion of the sampling distribution under H_0,
D = scale distance between μ_0 and μ_1.

Two-tailed test

$$N = \frac{\sigma^2(|z_\beta| + |z_{\alpha/2}|)^2}{D^2}, \quad \text{[13-5c]}$$

where $z_{\alpha/2}$ = z score corresponding to the area in the smaller portion of the sampling distribution under H_0.

One-tailed test

$$N = \frac{16^2(|-1.28| + |1.65|)^2}{3^2}$$
$$= 244.19 \approx 244 \text{ subjects.}$$

Two-tailed test

$$N = \frac{16^2(|-1.28| + |1.96|)^2}{3^2}$$
$$= 298.60 \approx 299 \text{ subjects.}$$

If $\beta \leqslant .50$, Formula 13-5b can be rewritten as

$$N = \frac{\sigma^2(|z_\beta| + |z_{\alpha/2}|)^2}{D^2} . \qquad [13\text{-}5c]$$

As an example of the use of this formula, suppose a researcher is not sure whether the mean IQ of students in a particular district falls above or below 100. So a two-tailed test is to be used at $\alpha = .05$. (Note that the criterion for rejecting H_0 cuts off $\alpha/2$, or .025, in either tail.) Suppose further that she wanted to detect a difference from 100 of 3 points or more, $\sigma = 16$, and $\beta = .10$. Formula 13-5c, then, can be used to determine sample size for this two-tailed case:

$$N = \frac{16^2(|-1.28| + |1.96|)^2}{3^2}$$

$$= \frac{256(3.24)^2}{9}$$

$$= 298.60.$$

Since the value of N is not a whole number, this value is rounded to 299. These calculations indicate that the sample size needed to detect a difference of 3 IQ points when $\alpha = .05$ (two-tailed: $\alpha/2 = .025$) and $\beta = .10$ is 299 subjects. These steps in calculating sample size are summarized in Procedure 13-3.

Suppose that the researchers in Example Problem 4 wished to conduct a two-tailed test. What sample size should they use?

EXAMPLE PROBLEM 5

Sample size for two-sample (Case II) research: one-tailed tests   The formula for calculating the size of the sample needed for *each* of the two groups (control and experimental) in the two-sample case is the same as that for the single-sample case, with one exception. Assuming σ is known, the formula must adjust for the fact that *two* samples are involved in determining the differences between means. Hence, the formula for sample size takes this into account:

$$n = \frac{2\sigma^2(z_\beta - z_\alpha)^2}{D^2} . \qquad [13\text{-}6]$$

Assuming $\beta \leqslant .50$, Formula 13-6 can be rewritten as

$$n = \frac{2\sigma^2(|z_\beta| + |z_\alpha|)^2}{D^2}. \qquad [13\text{-}6a]$$

As an example of how to use this formula, consider the data from the hypothetical study of teacher expectancy. In that study, the desired difference between the means of the control and experimental groups was .66 IQ points. While this difference certainly has little practical importance, it may be theoretically important, since expectancy theory predicts a difference but does not indicate the magnitude. Suppose that the data showing the difference of .66 points were taken from a pilot study. The researchers then wished to determine the sample size needed to detect this difference in their major study, in which a one-tailed test is planned at $\alpha = .05$ and the power of that test is to be .90 ($\beta = .10$). The values of z_β (-1.28) and z_α (1.65) can be determined from Table B, and $D = .66$. The population variance, σ^2, is known to be $16^2 = 256$. The sample size may be found from Formula 13-6 or 13-6a:

$$n = \frac{2(16^2)(-1.28 - 1.65)^2}{.66^2} = \frac{2(16^2)(|-1.28| + |1.65|)^2}{.66^2}$$

$$= \frac{2(256)(8.56)}{.4356}$$

$$= \frac{4392.96}{.4356}$$

$$= 10084.85.$$

Procedure 13-4 ◆ Steps in calculating the sample size when σ is known: two-sample (Case II) research, one-tailed and two-tailed tests

Operation	Example
1 Set up exact H_0 and H_1.	*One-tailed test*
	$H_0: \mu_E - \mu_C = 0,$
	$H_1: \mu_E - \mu_C = .66.$
	Two-tailed test
	$H_0: \mu_E - \mu_C = 0,$
	$H_1: \mu_E - \mu_C = .66.$

2 Define α, β, and D (the size of the difference between values of μ specified in H_0 and H_1).

One-tailed test

$$\alpha = .05,$$
$$\beta = .10,$$
$$D = .66.$$

Two-tailed test

$$\alpha = .05,$$
$$\beta = .10,$$
$$D = .66.$$

3 Use the appropriate formula for sample size:

One-tailed test

$$n = \frac{2\sigma^2(|z_\beta| + |z_\alpha|)^2}{D^2} \quad [\text{13-6a}]$$

($\sigma = 16$ for IQ scores). z_β, z_α, and D are defined in Procedure 13-3.

Two-tailed test

$$n = \frac{2\sigma^2(|z_\beta| + |z_{\alpha/2}|)^2}{D^2} \quad [\text{13-6c}]$$

($\sigma = 16$ for IQ scores). $z_{\alpha/2}$ is defined in Procedure 13-3.

One-tailed test

$$n = \frac{2(16^2)(|-1.28| + |1.65|)^2}{.66^2}$$
$$= 10{,}084.85$$
$$\approx 10{,}085 \text{ subjects in } each \text{ group.}$$

Two-tailed test

$$n = \frac{2(16^2)(|-1.28| + |1.96|)^2}{.66^2}$$
$$= 12{,}338.75$$
$$\approx 12{,}339 \text{ subjects in } each \text{ group.}$$

The results of the computation of sample size indicate that a sample of 10,085 subjects is needed in *each* of the two groups, or a total of 20,170 subjects are needed for the study. These steps are summarized in Procedure 13-4.

Suppose that the researchers in the prose learning study in Example Problem 3 wish to determine the sample size needed to detect a 2-point difference between the groups when $\alpha = .01$ (one-tail) and $\beta = .05$. Assuming that $\sigma = 2.5$, what sample size is necessary?

EXAMPLE PROBLEM 6

Sample size for two-sample (Case II) research: two-tailed tests   For a two-tailed statistical test, the only change that needs to be made involves z_α. The z value corresponding to $\alpha/2$ is used in place of z_α. Thus, the general formula for the two-sample case is:

$$n = \frac{2\sigma^2(z_\beta - z_{\alpha/2})^2}{D^2}. \qquad [\mathbf{13\text{-}6b}]$$

If $\beta \leqslant .50$, Formula 13-6b can be rewritten as

$$n = \frac{2\sigma^2(|z_\beta| + |z_{\alpha/2}|)^2}{D^2}, \qquad [\mathbf{13\text{-}6c}]$$

$$n = \frac{2(16^2)(|-1.28| + |1.96|)^2}{.66^2}$$

$$= 12,338.75.$$

In order to conduct a two-tailed test at $\alpha = .05$ with the power equal to .90, 12,339 subjects are needed in each of the two cells of the design, or a total of 24,678 subjects are needed for the study. These steps are summarized in Procedure 13-4.

EXAMPLE PROBLEM 7   Suppose that the researchers in Example Problem 6 want to conduct a two-tailed test at $\alpha = .01$. What sample size is necessary?

♦   ♦   ♦   ♦   ♦

When the Standard Deviation is Unknown   **Sample size for single-sample (Case I) research**   In many cases, the population variance σ is not known. Nevertheless, the sample size still can be estimated (Dixon & Massey, 1969; Hays, 1973; Levin, 1975). The first step is to express D, in the formulas above, as a *difference in standard deviation units* (Δ). Using population parameters, Δ is defined as

$$\Delta = \frac{|\mu_1 - \mu_0|}{\sigma}, \qquad [\mathbf{13\text{-}7}]$$

where $\mu_1 =$ population mean specified under H_1,
        $\mu_0 =$ population mean specified under H_0.

In words, Δ tells how large a difference we are interested in—not in terms of actual scores, but in terms of a z score. If Δ were .33, this would mean that the researcher wanted to detect a difference of $\frac{1}{3}$ of a standard deviation between μ_1 and μ_0. As a rule of thumb, Cohen (1969, pp. 22–25) defines a "small effect" as $\Delta = .20$; the researcher wants to detect a difference of $\frac{1}{5}$ of a standard deviation between μ_1 and μ_0. A "medium effect" is defined as $\Delta = .50$, and a "large effect" is defined as $\Delta = .80$. As you become more comfortable with Δ, you will be able to express the difference of theoretical or practical importance in your own research without reference to this rule of thumb.

With Δ defined, an approximate formula (Dixon & Massey, 1969) can be written for determining the sample size for a single sample when σ is unknown:

$$N = \frac{(z_\beta - z_\alpha)^2}{\Delta^2}. \qquad [\textbf{13-8}]$$

Assuming $\beta \leqslant .50$, Formula 13-8 can be rewritten as

$$N = \frac{(|z_\beta| + |z_\alpha|)^2}{\Delta^2}. \qquad [\textbf{13-8a}]$$

As an example of how to use this formula, data from the hypothetical IQ study can be used. The null hypothesis was that the mean IQ in the district equaled the mean IQ of 100 in the general population: $\mu_0 = 100$. Now, suppose the researcher does not know σ and is interested in detecting a "small effect," so that $\Delta = .20$. In this case, then, the researcher wants to detect a difference of about $\frac{1}{5}$ of a standard deviation. Furthermore, she sets α at .05 (one-tailed) and wants the power of the statistical test to be .90, so that $\beta = .10$. Thus, the terms in Formula 13-8 or 13-8a can be replaced by the corresponding values of Δ, z_α, and z_β, and N can be determined:

$$N = \frac{(|z_\beta| + |z_\alpha|)^2}{\Delta^2} \qquad [\textbf{13-8a}]$$

$$= \frac{(1.28 + 1.65)^2}{.20^2}$$

$$= 214.5.$$

The sample for this study, then, should include 215 subjects. These steps are summarized in Procedure 13-5.

Suppose instead that the researcher intended to conduct a two-tailed statisti-

Operation	Example
1 Define α, β.	*One-tailed test*

$\alpha = .05,$

$\beta = .10.$

Two-tailed test

$\alpha = .05,$

$\beta = .10.$

2 Use the appropriate formula for calculating sample size when σ is unknown.

One-tailed tests

$$N = \frac{(|z_\beta| + |z_\alpha|)^2}{\Delta^2}, \quad [13\text{-}8a]$$

One-tailed tests

To detect a small effect,

$$N = \frac{(|-1.28| + |1.65|)^2}{.20^2}$$

$$= 214.5 \approx 215 \text{ subjects.}$$

Two-tailed tests

$$N = \frac{(|z_\beta| + |z_{\alpha/2}|)^2}{\Delta^2}, \quad [13\text{-}9a]$$

where $\Delta =$ size of the difference between the sample and the population that is of interest in terms of z scores.

Two-tailed tests

To detect a small effect,

$$N = \frac{(|-1.28| + |1.96|)^2}{.20^2}$$

$$= 262.20 \approx 263 \text{ subjects.}$$

Rule of thumb (Cohen, 1969):

small effect: $\quad \Delta = .20,$

medium effect: $\quad \Delta = .50,$

large effect: $\quad \Delta = .80.$

z_β, z_α, and $z_{\alpha/2}$ are defined in Procedure 13-3.

Procedure 13-5 ♦ Steps in calculating the sample size when σ is unknown: single-sample (Case I) research, one-tailed and two-tailed tests

cal test at $\alpha = .05$. In this case, too, Formula 13-8 can be modified:

$$N = \frac{(z_\alpha - z_{\alpha/2})^2}{\Delta^2} . \qquad [13\text{-}9]$$

Assuming $\beta \leqslant .50$, Formula 13-9 can be rewritten as

$$N = \frac{(|z_\beta| + |z_{\alpha/2}|)^2}{\Delta^2} \qquad [\text{13-9a}]$$

$$= \frac{((|-1.28| + |1.96|)^2}{.20^2}$$

$$= 262.44.$$

The sample size for this study, then, should be 263 subjects. These steps are also summarized in Procedure 13-5.

If these values for N are compared with the corresponding values for one- and two-tail tests using Formula 13-5, the sample sizes using the approximate formula when σ is unknown are found to be less than when σ is known. What can account for these differences, given that α and β were the same throughout the calculations? Note that there is a difference between the formulas even when the values of α and β are the same. Formula 13-5 uses σ and D (where $D = |\mu_1 - \mu_0|$), while Formula 13-8 uses Δ. However, Δ can be calculated from the information in Formula 13-5, since σ is known to be 16 and D is known to be 3:

$$\Delta = \frac{|\mu_1 - \mu_0|}{\sigma} \qquad [\text{13.7}]$$

$$= \frac{3}{16}$$

$$= 0.1875.$$

Thus, for a direct comparison of the two formulas, Δ should be set at 0.1875. If this is done, the result using Formulas 13-9 and 13-8a is:

One tail	Two tails
$N = \dfrac{(|1.28| + |1.65|)^2}{.1875^2}$	$N = \dfrac{(|1.28| + |1.96|)^2}{.1875^2}$
$= \dfrac{8.58}{.035}$	$= \dfrac{10.50}{.035}$
$= 245.14$	$= 298.67$

Thus, when Δ is equated in the calculations using the two formulas, there is agreement on the sample size: $N(\text{one tailed}) = 245$ and $N(\text{two-tailed}) = 299$.

EXAMPLE PROBLEM 8   Suppose that the researchers in the study of college GPAs discussed in Example Problem 1 did not know σ and were interested in detecting a "medium effect." What sample size is required if $\alpha = .01$ (one-tailed) and $\beta = .05$?

Sample size for two-sample (Case II) research   Sample size also can be determined for two-sample tests when σ is unknown. The formula differs from that of the one-sample case only in that the numerator is multiplied by a factor of two:

$$
\text{One-tail:} \qquad n = \frac{2(z_\beta - z_\alpha)^2}{\Delta^2}, \qquad [13\text{-}10]
$$

$$
\text{Two-tail:} \qquad n = \frac{2(z_\beta - z_{\alpha/2})^2}{\Delta^2}. \qquad [13\text{-}11]
$$

Assuming that $\beta \leqslant .50$, Formulas 13-10 and 13-11 can be rewritten as

$$
\text{One-tail:} \qquad n = \frac{2(|z_\beta| + |z_\alpha|)^2}{\Delta^2}, \qquad [13\text{-}10a]
$$

$$
\text{Two-tail:} \qquad n = \frac{2(|z_\beta| + |z_{\alpha/2}|)^2}{\Delta^2}. \qquad [13\text{-}11a]
$$

The data from the hypothetical study of teacher expectancy can be used to illustrate how this formula can be used to estimate the sample size. For the one-tailed case, recall that $\alpha = .05$, $\beta = .20$, $D = .66$, and $\sigma = 16$. First, let's use information about D (which is $|\mu_1 - \mu_0|$) and σ to determine Δ (we could have decided on Δ independently of this information, but then we could not compare the results of Formulas 13-6a and 13-10a):

$$
\Delta = \frac{|\mu_1 - \mu_0|}{\sigma} \qquad [13\text{-}7]
$$

$$
= \frac{.66}{16}
$$

$$
= .0413.
$$

Thus, using the results of the pilot study, the researchers determined the sample size needed to detect a difference between the means of the control and experimental groups of $\frac{4}{100}$ of a standard deviation.

The next step is to replace the terms in Formula 13-10a with the appropriate values of Δ (.04), z_β (-0.84), and z_α (1.65), and calculate n:

$$n = \frac{2(|-0.84| + |1.65|)^2}{.0413^2} \qquad [\text{13-10a}]$$

$$= \frac{2(6.20)}{.0017}$$

$$= 7294.12.$$

Steps in calculating sample size when σ is unknown: two-sample (Case II) research, ♦ Procedure 13-6 one-tailed and two-tailed tests

Operation	Example
1 Define α, β.	*One-tailed test*
	$\alpha = .05,$
	$\beta = .20.$
	Two-tailed test
	$\alpha = .05,$
	$\beta = .20.$
2 Use the appropriate formula for calculating sample size when σ is unknown.	
One-tailed tests	*One-tailed test*
$$n = \frac{2(|z_\beta| + |z_\alpha|)^2}{\Delta^2}, \quad [\text{13-10a}]$$	For a "*very* small effect",
	$$n = \frac{2(|-0.84| + |1.65|)^2}{.0413^2}$$
	$$= 7294.12$$
	$$\approx 7294 \text{ subjects in each group.}$$
Two-tailed tests	*Two-tailed test*
$$n = \frac{2(|z_\beta| + |z_{\alpha/2}|)^2}{\Delta^2} \quad [\text{13-11a}]$$	For a "*very* small effect",
	$$n = \frac{2(|-0.84| + |1.96|)^2}{.0413^2}$$
where z_β, z_α, and $z_{\alpha/2}$ are defined in Procedure 13-3, and Δ is defined in Formula 13-7.	$$= 9223.53$$
	$$\approx 9224 \text{ subjects in each group.}$$

A sample of 7294 subjects is needed in each of the two groups in order to have a statistical test with power equal to .80. These steps are summarized in Procedure 13-6.

In order to determine sample size for a two-tailed test, the only change to be made is in z_α. In the two-tailed case, the z value corresponding to $\alpha/2$ is used. For $\alpha/2 = .05/2$, we have $z_\alpha = 1.96$ and

$$n = \frac{2(|-0.84| + |1.96|)^2}{.0413^2} \qquad [13\text{-}11a]$$

$$= \frac{2(7.84)}{.0017}$$

$$= 9223.53.$$

A sample size of 9,224 subjects in each of the two cells, then, is needed to conduct the two-tailed test at $\alpha = .05$ with a power of .80. These steps are also summarized in Procedure 13-6.

EXAMPLE PROBLEM 9   Suppose that the researchers in the prose learning study of underlining strategies described in Example Problem 3 did not know σ and were interested in detecting a "large effect." What sample size would be required if $\alpha = .05$ (two-tailed) and $\beta = .10$?

♦ ♦ ♦ ♦ ♦

Summary   This chapter discusses *errors* associated with making statistical inferences. *Type I errors* and *Type II errors* are defined and their relationship discussed. *Power* of a statistical test is defined, procedures for calculating it with one-sample (Case I) and two-sample (Case II) research are presented, and factors influencing the power of a statistical test are described. Finally, methods for estimating *sample size* are discussed.

♦ ♦ ♦ ♦ ♦

Key Words

alpha (α)	magnitude of treatment effect
beta (β)	power
decisions	sample size
errors	statistical inference
hypothesis testing	Type I error
level of significance	Type II error

♦ ♦ ♦ ♦ ♦

Exercises   1. A researcher conducting a study of the effects of premature birth on later development was interested in determining whether the average motor development of infants born prematurely was below that of the general population of infants on a particular measure of infant motor development ($\mu = 70$). In making an inference from the sample data, what are the two situations in which the research will make an inference that is:

  a. correct?
  b. incorrect?

2–5 Name the following probabilities:

2. p(rejecting a false H_0).
3. p(rejecting a true H_0).
4. p(not rejecting a false H_0).
5. p(not rejecting a true H_0).

6–7 What is the relationship between the following?

6. Power and β.
7. β and α.

8–12 In a study of the effects of creativity training, 36 randomly selected college freshmen participated in a creativity program for one semester. Based on past empirical data, the researchers had reason to believe that the mean score on a divergent-thinking test (a measure of creativity) of students participating in the program would be significantly higher than the average score based on national norms ($\mu = 15$). Suppose that: (a) the experimenters are interested in detecting a 4-point difference, and (b) σ is 5.

8. What is the power of this statistical test at $\alpha = .01$?
9. What sample size would be required to replicate this study with $\alpha = .01$ and $\beta = .10$?
10. Suppose that the experimenters did not have reason to believe that divergent thinking in the creativity-training sample was significantly higher than the national mean. What is the power of their statistical test at $\alpha = .01$?
11. What sample size would be required to replicate the study in Exercise 10 with $\alpha = .01$ and $\beta = .10$?
12. Suppose σ is not known and the experimenters are interested in detecting a "medium effect." What sample size is required if $\alpha = .01$ (two-tailed) and $\beta = .10$?

13–17 A chemistry instructor was interested in whether students learn more from being provided with notes and listening to a lecture or from taking notes during lecture. He randomly assigned his students ($N = 72$) into two sections: a note-having group (NH) and a note-taking group (NT). All students took the same final examination at the end of the quarter. Suppose that: (a) the instructor is interested in detecting a 5-point difference between the groups; (b) he has theoretical and empirical evidence suggesting that the NH group will show significantly lower performance than the NT group; and (c) $\sigma_{NH} = \sigma_{NT} = 6$.

13. What is the power of this statistical test at $\alpha = .05$?
14. What sample size would be required to replicate this study with $\alpha = .05$ and $\beta = .15$?

15. Suppose the instructor did not have evidence to suggest that either group would perform significantly better on the final examination. What is the power of his statistical test at $\alpha = .05$?

16. What sample size would be required to replicate the study in Exercise 15 with $\alpha = .05$ and $\beta = .15$?

17. Suppose σ is not known and the instructor is interested in detecting a "large effect." What sample size is required if $\alpha = .05$ (two-tailed) and $\beta = .15$?

18. Suppose a researcher wants to examine the effects of achievement motivation training on academic performance. He sets α at .01 and then calculates the power of his statistical test. He finds, much to his dismay, that power $= .45$. What alternatives are available to increase the power of his test?

19–22 An educational psychologist plans to compare two modes of instruction: student-centered instruction (S) and teacher-centered instruction (T). What type of error will he make in testing his hypothesis if he concludes the following?

19. S is better than T, but there is in fact no difference in the population.
20. S is no different than T, and there is in fact no difference in the population.
21. S is no different than T, and there is in fact a real difference in the population.
22. S is better than T, and there is in fact a real difference in the population.

23. A remedial reading laboratory was set up in Jackson School, and elementary-school children with remedial problems were assigned at random either to the experimental laboratory group (E) or to a traditional instructional control group (C). After a semester of instruction, an achievement test was administered and a statistical test was made on the mean achievement scores for the groups. It was concluded that the mean achievement was higher for the experimental than the control group, $\alpha = .05$. Does this mean that the probability of
a. not rejecting a true null hypothesis was .05?
b. rejecting a true null hypothesis was .05?
c. rejecting a false null hypothesis was .05?
d. accepting a false null hypothesis was .05?

SECTION V

Statistical Tests
for
Between-Subjects Designs

Iɴ behavioral research, subjects may be randomly sampled from some population—often sophomores enrolled in introductory courses in psychology, sociology, or statistics—and then randomly assigned to one of two or more groups constituting control and experimental groups. A comparison of the groups tells something about the effect of the treatments. Or subjects may be randomly sampled from each of two or more populations—"normals" and "schizophrenics," or low, middle, and high socioeconomic status—and differences between these samples examined. In either type of study, each group of subjects receives or has received a different treatment. And in either study, a comparison which reveals something about the differences between groups involves a comparison between different groups of subjects.

Research designs from which inferences are drawn about treatment effects on several populations of subjects are called **between-subjects designs**. Between-subjects designs may qualify as true experiments, or they may represent ex post facto designs. The prototype of the true experimental between-subjects design is the posttest-only, control-group design. Subjects are randomly sampled from some population and then randomly assigned to a control or experimental group. This true experiment can be extended to include more than one experimental group and more than one control group, so that subjects are randomly assigned to one and only one control or experimental group. Kirk (1968) calls such designs completely randomized designs. The true experiment can also be extended to factorial experiments in which two or more independent variables are examined simultaneously. Subjects are randomly assigned to one and only one cell of the design representing a unique combination of two or more variables. Kirk (1968) calls such designs completely randomized factorial designs. As with all true experimental designs, statements can be made about the cause-and-effect relationship between the independent variable or variables and the dependent variable.

Criterion-group designs—a type of ex post facto design—are also between-subjects designs. The prototype of the criterion-group design is the comparison of randomly sampled groups of subjects from a "normal" population and a "deviant" population. The study comparing normals and schizophrenics is a criterion-group design. The criterion-group design can be extended to include more than two groups, and not necessarily a comparison of normals and deviates. The study comparing samples of subjects from the three levels of socioeconomic status is a case in point. Finally, two or more individual difference variables can be combined in factorial fashion for a factorial criterion-group design. For the sake of an example, consider the comparison of normals and schizophrenics drawn from three socioeconomic levels. As with all ex post facto designs, statements *cannot* be made about the cause-and-effect relationship between the independent variable or variables and the dependent variable.

A third type of between-subjects design is a factorial design which combines a true experimental design with a criterion-group design. For example, an experimenter might randomly assign subjects who are either high or low on some variable (such as anxiety) to a control group or an experimental group. This produces a 2×2 factorial design with two levels of anxiety (low, high) and two levels of treatment (control, experimental). The design contains four cells corresponding to the combinations of the two independent variables (1) low anxiety—control, (2) low anxiety—experimental, (3) high anxiety—control, and (4) high anxiety—experimental. A comparison of the mean performance of the low- and high-anxiety groups constitutes a criterion-group design. Causal interpretations of the effect of anxiety on the dependent variable are not warranted. However, the comparison of the difference between the means of the control and experimental groups represents a true experimental design, and so a causal interpretation of this difference is warranted. Finally, a comparison of the four means corresponding to each cell of the design provides information about the interaction of anxiety and treatment (cf. Chapter 1). If the means of the control and experimental groups are compared at each of the two levels of the anxiety variable, causal interpretations of the differences are warranted.

A number of well-known statistical tests are available for examining the data from between-subjects designs. In this section, three such tests are covered: (1) the *t* test, (2) the analysis of variance, and (3) chi square. The *t test* is used to compare means from single-sample (Case I) and two-sample (Case II) research designs. It is used instead of the *z* test (see Chapters 11 and 12) because it does not require that the population variance be known. Chapters 14 and 15 in this section and Chapter 19 in the next section describe the *t* test.

The *analysis of variance* is used to compare the means of two or more groups. Furthermore, it can be used to compare means from a factorial design. So, it can test the effects of each of two (or more) independent variables *and* their unique combinations. Chapters 16 and 17 discuss the analysis of variance.

The *chi-square test* is used with frequency data. It enables the researcher to compare the numbers of subjects falling into two or more groups (e.g., the number of Democrats, Republicans, and "others"). It can also be used with frequency data from factorial designs (e.g., the numbers of male and female voters in the three political-party categories). Chapter 18 describes the chi-square test.

14 .

t Test
for
Single-Sample Research

C_{ASE} I research problems were characterized by the question, "Does a particular sample belong to a hypothesized population?" In order to answer this question, a single sample of subjects is drawn randomly from some population. A sample statistic such as a mean is calculated. Then a null hypothesis of no difference between the sample mean and the hypothesized population mean is tested. For example, "Does the *mean* reading score of a sample of high-school seniors from a certain school district suggest that seniors in that district belong to the general population of seniors in the state with mean equal to μ?"

Chapter 11 presented a method for deciding whether a sample with a particular *mean* was drawn from the hypothesized population (specified by the null hypothesis) or some other population (specified by the alternative hypothesis). The decision of whether or not to reject the null hypothesis rested on the *probability* of observing the sample mean under the assumption that the null hypothesis is true. The normal distribution was used as the model for determining this probability on the basis that the population value of the standard error of the mean ($\sigma_{\bar{X}}$) is known, and, for samples of size 30 or more, the sampling distribution of means is approximately normal (a consequence of the central limit theorem).

The purpose of this chapter is to provide a statistical test for handling data on Case I research problems. Specifically, this chapter provides a technique for comparing a sample mean with a hypothesized population mean when, as is the usual case, the population value for the standard error of the mean is unknown and has to be estimated from sample data. This statistical test is called the *t* test.

PURPOSE AND UNDERLYING LOGIC

The purpose of the *t* test for a mean, like that of the $z_{\bar{X}}$ test, is to help decide whether the sample mean was drawn from a hypothesized population with a specified mean μ, or whether it was drawn from some other population. The *t* test—unlike the $z_{\bar{X}}$ test—can be used when the standard error of the mean, $\sigma_{\bar{X}}$, is unknown and has to be estimated from sample data. In practice, then, the *t* test is used much more frequently than the $z_{\bar{X}}$ test, since we seldom know $\sigma_{\bar{X}}$.

The logic behind the *t* test is quite similar to that underlying the $z_{\bar{X}}$ test described in Chapter 11, even though the technical development is a bit more complicated for the *t* test. To briefly review the hypothesis-testing framework, the purpose of the *t* test is to help decide whether or not to reject the null hypothesis. Since this decision is never made with complete certainty, the decision is a probabilistic one. The problem, then, is to determine the probability of observing a sample mean at or beyond some value assuming that the null hypothesis is true.

In solving this problem, several steps must be taken. The first step is to provide a sample estimate for the standard error of the mean:

$$\sigma_{\bar{X}} = \frac{\sigma}{\sqrt{N}} . \qquad [11\text{-}1]$$

This can be accomplished by using the sample standard deviation as an estimate of the population standard deviation. Then an estimate of $\sigma_{\bar{X}}$ is

$$s_{\bar{X}} = \frac{s}{\sqrt{N}} . \qquad [14\text{-}1]$$

The next step is to find the distance between a sample mean and the population mean in terms of $s_{\bar{X}}$, and not in terms of $\sigma_{\bar{X}}$ as is done to get $z_{\bar{X}}$:

$$z_{\bar{X}\text{observed}} = \frac{\bar{X} - \mu}{\sigma_{\bar{X}}} . \qquad [11\text{-}2]$$

This can be achieved by replacing $\sigma_{\bar{X}}$ in Formula 11-2 with its estimator, $s_{\bar{X}}$. When this is done, t is defined:

$$t_{\text{observed}} = \frac{\bar{X} - \mu}{s_{\bar{X}}} . \qquad [14\text{-}2]$$

Thus t is a measure of the distance between $\bar{X}$ and μ in standard-error units ($s_{\bar{X}}$), estimated from the sample data.

To specify the sampling distribution of t, it must be recognized that there is a very important difference between $z_{\bar{X}}$ and t. In the expression for $z_{\bar{X}}$, $\sigma_{\bar{X}}$ is constant over all samples of size N. So only the numerator varies from sample to sample due to random fluctuations in $\bar{X}$ (since μ is constant). However, in the expression for t, $s_{\bar{X}}$ varies from sample to sample along with $\bar{X}$. This is because $s_{\bar{X}}$ depends on the sample standard deviation s, which varies like any other sample estimate of a population parameter. If several random samples, then, produced exactly the same mean (e.g., $\bar{X} = 10$), the value of $z_{\bar{X}}$ would be exactly the same over the samples (since μ and $\sigma_{\bar{X}}$ are constants) while t_{observed} would probably vary, since $s_{\bar{X}}$ is not constant from one sample to the next. So for repeated samples, t will vary due to random fluctuations in $\bar{X}$ and s. If the value of $t = (\bar{X} - \mu)/s_{\bar{X}}$ is calculated for each of a very large number of samples from a normal population, a frequency distribution for t can be graphed with the values of *t* on the abscissa and the frequencies on the ordinate. The resulting frequency polygon can be modeled by a theoretical (mathematical) distribution of *t*. When this is done, the theoretical model is called the *sampling distribution of t*, or **t distribution**. It can be used as a probability distribution under the null hypothesis for determining the probability of observing a sample mean at or beyond some value when $\sigma_{\bar{X}}$ is unknown.

Like the normal distribution, the sampling distribution of *t* is symmetric in shape (Figure 14-1). Also like the normal distribution, the *t* distribution can be interpreted as a probability distribution and therefore can be used to determine the probability of observing a sample mean at or beyond some value, assuming that the null hypothesis is true.

There are, however, several important differences between the *t* and the normal distributions. One difference is that there is a different *t* distribution for

Figure 14-1 ♦ The normal sampling distribution and members of the family of the sampling distribution of *t* (critical regions with $\alpha = .05$, two-tailed): (a) normal sampling distribution (b) sampling distribution of *t* ($df = 2$) (c) sampling distribution of *t* ($df = 9$) (d) sampling distribution of *t* ($df = 30$)

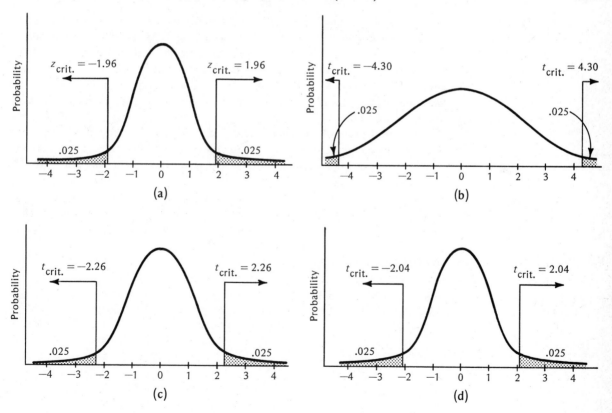

each possible sample size from 2 to infinity, whereas there is only one standard normal distribution regardless of sample size. Thus, the sampling distribution of t is actually a family of distributions with a different member for each sample size.

Another difference is that the tails of the t distribution are higher than those of the normal distribution, i.e., there is a greater area under the tails of the t distributions (compare Figure 14-1a and b). This arises because t is influenced by the variability of $\overline{X}$ and s from samples, while $z_{\overline{X}}$ is influenced only by the variability of $\overline{X}$, since $\sigma_{\overline{X}}$ is constant. One implication of this is that the critical values of t for rejecting a null hypothesis are higher than the critical values of z, since you have to go farther out in the higher tails of the t distribution to mark off the 5-percent or one-percent region (see Figure 14-1).

Finally, as sample size increases, the t distributions become increasingly normal in form. With sample sizes of 30 or more, there is a close fit between the t distribution and the normal distribution (compare Figure 14-1a and d). With an infinite sample size, the t distribution and the normal distribution are identical. Intuitively, this is because as the sample size increases the sample estimate of $\sigma_{\overline{X}}$ becomes more and more like the parameter itself.

DEGREES OF
FREEDOM

Rather than describing the family of t distributions with respect to sample size, this family is more accurately described according to each of the possible *degrees of freedom* (*df*) from 1 to infinity. This is because the t distribution is based on degrees of freedom rather than on sample sizes (although there is a close connection between *df* and N, especially for the single-sample case). As a consequence, this seems an appropriate place for a discussion of the concept of degrees of freedom.

The term **degrees of freedom** refers to the independent pieces of information on which a sample statistic is based. For brevity, it is often used for the *number* of such pieces of information. For example, a mean based on a sample of 30 scores is determined from all 30 scores. That is, each score provides an independent piece of information in the calculation of the mean. Or, put another way, until the mean of the 30 scores is known, we know nothing about the values of each of the scores. However, once the mean of the 30 scores is known, we know something about the 30 scores. To see how this works, a numerical example is helpful. Suppose a random sample of four scores which range from 0 to 20 is drawn from a population and three of the scores are 5, 8, and 11. Can you determine the value for the last score without any further information? No, unless you make a lucky guess. Each score provides an independent piece of information for calculating the mean; the mean is based on N degrees of freedom. Suppose now you are told that the mean of the scores is 7. Can you determine the value of the fourth score? The answer is yes. Since the sum of the deviation scores, $\Sigma(X - \overline{X})$, is zero, the fourth score will be that score which makes the sum of the four scores in deviation form equal zero:

$(5 - 7) = - 2$, $(8 - 7) = 1$, and $(11 - 7) = 4$. The algebraic sum of these three deviation scores is 3. Thus, the fourth score must be, in deviation form, -3. In raw-score form, it is the score value 3 points below the mean: $7 - 3 = 4$. Thus, given a random sample of N scores *and* the mean, there are $N - 1$ independent pieces of information or $N - 1$ degrees of freedom.

Any sample statistic that uses the sample mean in its calculation must be based on no more than $N - 1$ degrees of freedom. For example, a sample variance is calculated by subtracting the mean from each score in the sample. In calculating the variance, then, how many independent pieces of information are used to estimate the statistic? Since there are only $N - 1$ independent pieces of information in a set of deviation scores, the variance is estimated with $N - 1$ degrees of freedom.

Furthermore, different sample statistics are based on different numbers of degrees of freedom. As noted above, the mean is based on N degrees of freedom and the sample variance and standard deviation are based on $N - 1$ degrees of freedom. Recall that the correlation coefficient uses the mean of X and the mean of Y in its calculation. Thus, the correlation coefficient is based on $N - 2$ degrees of freedom. In general, the number of degrees of freedom on which a sample statistic is based depends on the sample size (N) and on the number of sample statistics used in its calculation.

The reason that the t distribution is based on degrees of freedom and not sample size is easy to explain now. In estimating the standard error of the t distribution (a sample statistic), the standard deviation s is used:

$$s_{\bar{X}} = \frac{s}{\sqrt{N}}. \qquad [14\text{-}1]$$

So, for the single-sample case, the t distribution is based on $N - 1$ degrees of freedom rather than on the sample size N.

From here on out, you can coast. When the t test is carried out on a single mean, the procedures are the same as the procedures for a single-sample $z_{\bar{X}}$ test (see Chapter 11). The only exception is that the sampling distribution of t is used instead of the normal distribution. The procedures for carrying out the t test are outlined below.

SIGNIFICANCE TEST FOR SINGLE-SAMPLE RESEARCH

◆ ◆ ◆ ◆ ◆

The hypotheses tested with the t distribution are the same as those tested with the normal sampling distribution. In the case of a two-tailed alternative hypothesis, the null and alternative hypotheses are

Hypotheses

$$H_0\colon \mu = \text{specified value,}$$

$$H_1\colon \mu \neq \text{specified value.}$$

In the case of directional (i.e., one-tailed) alternative hypotheses, the null and alternative hypotheses are

$$H_0: \mu = \text{specified value},$$

$$H_1: \mu > \text{specified value}$$

or

$$H_0: \mu = \text{specified value},$$

$$H_1: \mu < \text{specified value}.$$

♦   ♦   ♦   ♦   ♦

Assumptions   In using the sampling distribution of t to test hypotheses about means, the following assumptions are made:

1. The scores are randomly sampled from some population, and
2. The scores in the population are normally distributed.

These assumptions should be examined before the t test is performed. Assumption 1 is examined logically. Did the sampling procedures meet the criteria for sampling at random? In order to examine assumption 2, a frequency distribution of scores in the sample should be inspected visually. Look for a symmetric, bell-shaped distribution of scores. Any radical departure of these scores from the expected distribution—such as a couple of very extreme scores—suggests that the assumption of normality does not hold.

This procedure for examining the assumption of normality, however, immediately suggests a paradox. One important feature of the t test is its ability to handle small samples—as small as $N = 2$. But frequency distributions based on small samples seldom tell you much about the distribution of scores in the population; there are just too few scores to get a good idea of the shape of the distribution. How, then, can this assumption be examined? The answer is that for very small samples, the assumption of a normal population cannot be examined. Nevertheless, prior information from larger, similar samples can be used to check this assumption. For example, a sample of four SAT scores will probably not tell you anything about this distribution of scores in the general population of students applying to college. But other data sources with quite large sample sizes show the distribution of SAT scores to be approximately normal. For samples of $N \geqslant 15$, a frequency distribution of sample data can be used to examine this assumption.

The assumption of a normal distribution of scores in the population, however, does not pose a problem for the t test if N is large (above 30). The t test can be used even if the distribution of scores in the parent population is somewhat nonnormal.[1] However, if N is small, nonnormality may give rise to errors. In this case, tests described by Siegel (1956) can be used.

---

[1] There is obviously something of a logical contradiction in our stating that a normal distribution is an assumption underlying the t test, and then later saying that violation of this assumption usually

◆   ◆   ◆   ◆   ◆

The formula for the *t* test has already been given as:

$$t_{observed} = \frac{\bar{X} - \mu}{s_{\bar{X}}} . \qquad [\textbf{14-2}]$$

As an example of the use of the *t* test, suppose that a random sample of 9 subjects was drawn from a population of freshmen in a university. The mean score of the sample on the verbal section of the Scholastic Aptitude Test (SAT-V) was 625 with a standard deviation of 90 points. Since the SAT-V was developed so that the mean equals 500 in the general population of high-school graduates applying to college, the question arises whether freshmen in this university have, on the average, higher SAT-V scores than the population of high-school students who apply to college.

The *t* test can be used in order to decide whether the freshmen in this sample are drawn from a population with a mean of 500 or are drawn from some alternative population. First, the null and alternative hypotheses need to be stated along with the level of significance:

$$H_0: \mu = 500,$$

$$H_1: \mu > 500,$$

$$\alpha = .05.$$

Next, the value of $t_{observed}$ is calculated:

$$t_{observed} = \frac{X - \mu}{s_{\bar{X}}} = \frac{\bar{X} - \mu}{s/\sqrt{N}} \qquad [\textbf{14-2}]$$

$$= \frac{625 - 500}{90/\sqrt{9}}$$

$$= 4.17.$$

The observed value of *t* is 4.17. The next step is to decide whether or not to reject the null hypothesis on the basis of $t_{observed}$.

◆   ◆   ◆   ◆   ◆

In order to decide whether or not to reject the null hypothesis, the critical value of *t* must be determined. This is the value at or beyond which less than 5 (or 1) percent of the sample *t*'s lie in the sampling distribution of *t*. Since the critical

---

is not problematic. In *deriving* any statistical test, certain assumptions are made, such as normality. The assumptions are formal requirements, and it is best not to violate them. However, in practice, statisticians have found that certain violations of these assumptions do not appreciably affect the outcome of the statistical test. This is one such case.

value of t depends on the sample size (degrees of freedom), the first step is to determine the number of degrees of freedom for the statistical test. There are $N - 1$ degrees of freedom for the single-sample t test. For our example, there are $9 - 1 = 8$ df.

The next step is to find the critical value of t at $\alpha = .05$. Table C at the end of the book provides these values. The numbers of degrees of freedom are listed in the left-hand column of the table. The body of the table lists the critical values of t. For one-tailed tests, use the upper set of column headings with the appropriate level of significance α, and for two-tailed tests, use the lower set of column headings with the appropriate level of significance. For the example with $\alpha = .05$, one-tailed, and 8 df, first locate .05 under the heading for the one-tailed test—the second column of the table—and read down that column to the value which corresponds to 8 df. The value of $t_{\text{critical}(.05, 8)}$ is 1.860. Since t_{observed} (4.17) exceeds t_{critical} (1.860), the null hypothesis should be rejected. The mean score of freshmen at the university is greater than the mean score for the population of high-school graduates taking the SAT-V.

More generally, the following set of criteria can be established for deciding whether or not to reject the null hypothesis:

1. For a two-tailed test,
   a. reject H_0 if $|t_{\text{observed}}| \geqslant t_{\text{critical}(\alpha/2, df)}$
   b. do not reject H_0 if $|t_{\text{observed}}| < t_{\text{critical}(\alpha/2, df)}$
2. For a one-tailed test,
   a. reject H_0 if $|t_{\text{observed}}| \geqslant t_{\text{critical}(\alpha, df)}$
   b. do not reject H_0 if $|t_{\text{observed}}| < t_{\text{critical}(\alpha, df)}$

The notation $t_{\text{critical}(\alpha/2, df)}$ can be read as the critical value of t at $\alpha/2$ for a specified number of degrees of freedom.

The data from the example can be used to illustrate how these criteria for deciding about the null hypothesis are applied. To begin, t_{observed} equals 4.17. For a nondirectional test at $\alpha = .05$, $\alpha/2 = .05/2 = .025$. With $df = 8$, Table C provides $t_{\text{critical}(.05/2, 8)} = 2.306$. Since $|t_{\text{observed}}| > t_{\text{critical}}$, the null hypothesis should be rejected. For a nondirectional test at $\alpha = .01$, $\alpha/2 = .01/2 = .005$. Again, with $df = 8$, Table C provides $t_{\text{critical}(.01/2, 8)} = 3.355$. The null hypothesis should be rejected. Finally, for a one-tailed test at $\alpha = .01$, $t_{\text{critical}(.01, 8)} = 2.896$; again, the null hypothesis should be rejected.

♦   ♦   ♦   ♦   ♦

Numerical Example   In the hypothetical study of men's and women's college achievement described in Chapter 2, SAT scores were collected on a sample of students from four campuses of the University of California. Table 14-1 presents hypothetical data on the SAT total scores (verbal plus quantitative) for a sample of students at one of these campuses, UCLA. Based on these sample data, are UCLA students representative of the entire population taking the SAT, or do these students represent, as expected, a group of students who score above the mean?

Table 14-1 ♦ Hypothetical
SAT data on a random
sample of ten students
from UCLA

Student ID	Score
1	1050
2	1200
3	1100
4	1130
5	1160
6	1075
7	1100
8	1025
9	1000
10	1000

$$\bar{X} = 1084$$
$$s = 67.24$$

Steps in conducting a *t* test for single-sample designs (example data from Table 14-1) ♦ Procedure 14-1

Operation	Example
1 Specify the null and alternative hypotheses and level of significance. *Level of significance is generally set at .05 or .01.*	H_0: $\mu = 1000$, H_1: $\mu > 1000$, $\alpha = .01$,
2 Compute $t_{obs.}$ using Formula 14-2: $$t_{obs.} = \frac{\bar{X} - \mu}{s_{\bar{X}}}$$	$t_{obs.} = \dfrac{1084 - 1000}{67.24/\sqrt{10}}$ $= \dfrac{84}{21.26}$ $= 3.95.$
where $$s_{\bar{X}} = \frac{s}{\sqrt{N}} \quad . \textbf{[14-1]}$$	

(continued on p. 412)

3 Locate $t_{crit.}$ at the specified level of significance with $N - 1$ df using Table C.

$t_{crit.(.01, 9)} = 2.821$

4 Decide whether or not to reject the null hypothesis:
Reject H_0 if $|t_{obs.}| \geqslant t_{crit.}$.
Do not reject H_0 if $|t_{obs.}| < t_{crit.}$.

Since $|t_{obs.}| > t_{crit.}$ (3.95 > 2.821), reject H_0. Conclude that students at UCLA have a higher mean SAT score than the general population of students taking the test.

In order to answer this question, we need to know the mean score on the SAT for all students taking the examination. Since both the SAT verbal and quantitative subscales are constructed to have means of 500, the mean score on the total test is 1000. With this information in hand, a t test can be conducted. Procedure 14-1 summarizes the steps for conducting this test, using data from Table 14-1.

The results of the t test indicate that the null hypothesis should be rejected. Students at UCLA—from which the sample was randomly selected—have a higher mean SAT score than do high-school graduates who take the SAT.

CONFIDENCE
INTERVALS FOR
THE MEAN USING
THE t DISTRIBUTION

Confidence intervals can also be established using the t distribution with $N - 1$ degrees of freedom. In general, the 95-percent confidence interval is constructed when $\alpha = .05$ and the 99-percent confidence interval is constructed when $\alpha = .01$. These intervals, then, will be referred to as the $100 \times (1 - \alpha)$-percent confidence intervals. The general form of the confidence interval can be expressed as

$$\overline{X} \pm t_{critical(\alpha/2, \, df)}(s_{\overline{X}}) \qquad [\textbf{14-3}]$$

$$or$$

$$\overline{X} - \left(t_{critical(\alpha/2, \, df)}(s_{\overline{X}}) \leqslant \mu \leqslant \overline{X} + t_{critical(\alpha/2, \, df)}(s_{\overline{X}})\right).$$

The major differences between this confidence interval and the one developed in Chapter 11 are that (1) the t distribution $t_{critical(\alpha/2, \, df)}$ is used instead of the normal distribution $z_{\overline{X} \, (critical, \, \alpha/2)}$, and $s_{\overline{X}}$ is used instead of $\sigma_{\overline{X}}$.

The 95-percent confidence interval for the data in the example study of SAT-V scores (see discussion following Formula 14-2 above) can be written as follows:

$CI_{.95}$: $\overline{X} - t_{\text{critical}(.05/2,\,8)}(s_{\overline{X}}) \leqslant \mu \leqslant \overline{X} + t_{\text{critical}(.05/2,\,8)}(s_{\overline{X}})$

$$625 - (1.86)(30) \leqslant \mu \leqslant 625 + (1.86)(30),$$

$$625 - 69.18 \leqslant \mu \leqslant 625 + 69.18,$$

$$555.82 \leqslant \mu \leqslant 694.18.$$

The probability is .95 that an interval formed in this manner will include the population mean μ.[2]

The 99-percent confidence interval can be written as

$CI_{.99}$: $\overline{X} - t_{\text{critical}(.01/2,\,8)}(s_{\overline{X}}) \leqslant \mu \leqslant \overline{X} + t_{\text{critical}(.01/2,\,8)}(s_{\overline{X}}),$

$$625 - (2.896)(30) \leqslant \mu \leqslant 625 + (2.896)(30),$$

$$625 - 100.65 \leqslant \mu \leqslant 625 + 100.65,$$

$$524.35 \leqslant \mu \leqslant 725.65.$$

The results of our hypothesis-testing procedures indicated that freshmen in this particular university have, on the average, higher SAT-V scores than the population of high-school graduates applying to college. However, notice that the confidence intervals are quite large. These confidence intervals make it abundantly clear that the value of the true population mean for freshmen at the university is in some doubt.

Hypothetical SAT total scores for a sample of students at the University of California at San Diego (UCSD) are shown below. Based on these sample data, test whether UCSD students are representative of the general population of students taking the SAT or whether they represent an alternative population of students. Include in your answer:

EXAMPLE PROBLEM 1

a. Null and alternative hypotheses
b. t_{observed}
c. t_{critical} at $\alpha = .01$ (two-tailed)
d. Conclusions
e. 99-percent confidence interval
f. Based on the *t* test, would you expect the 99-percent confidence interval to include μ under H_0? Why or why not?

[2]Note that the probability statement is about confidence intervals formed in this manner and not the particular interval constructed. Once the sample values are placed in the formula, the probability statement does not hold for that particular instance. (See Chapter 11 for details.)

Hypothetical SAT data on a random sample of ten students at UCSD	
Student ID number	SAT total score
31	1150
32	1185
33	1200
34	1160
35	1200
36	1150
37	1100
38	1120
39	1080
40	1150

$$\overline{X} = 1149.5$$
$$s = 40.31$$

◆   ◆   ◆   ◆   ◆

Summary   This chapter presents a statistical test for *single-sample designs*. These designs address the Case I research question: "Does a particular sample of observations belong to a hypothesized population of observations?" The *t test* is used to determine whether a sample mean based on sample sizes of 2 or more is drawn from a hypothesized population with a specified mean. The *t distribution* is also used to construct 95- or 99-percent *confidence intervals* around a sample mean. Confidence intervals provide an interval estimate of the population mean. In the long run 95 (or 99) percent of the confidence intervals constructed in this manner will contain the true population mean.

◆   ◆   ◆   ◆   ◆

Key Words

between-subjects design	population mean
confidence intervals	random sampling
degrees of freedom	sample mean
directional test	single-sample design
nondirectional test	*t* distribution
normality	*t* test
one-tailed test	two-tailed test

◆   ◆   ◆   ◆   ◆

Exercises   1–7 An electronics company is interested in whether the mechanical aptitude of recently hired college graduates was representative of those hired in the past. A

414

standardized mechanical aptitude test with a mean of 100 and a standard deviation of 50 was given to a random sample of the new employees, with the following results:

Employee number	Mechanical-aptitude score
1	110
2	95
3	82
4	120
5	135
6	78
7	140
8	138

$$\bar{X} = 112.25,$$
$$s = 25.07.$$

Using these sample data, determine whether the mean score of the college graduates is representative of the mean score of those hired in the past.

1. Formulate null and alternative hypotheses.
2. Provide a test of each assumption or an explanation for not conducting the test.
3. Find $t_{observed}$.
4. Find $t_{critical}$ at $\alpha = .05$ (two-tailed).
5. State your conclusions.
6. Determine the 95-percent confidence interval.
7. Based on the t test, would you expect the 95-percent confidence interval to include μ under H_0? Why or why not?

8–12. Research on human memory indicates that, on the average, people can remember 5 pieces of new information (such as unrelated words read from a long list). A random sample of 16 subjects trained in mnemonics for remembering information were read a list of 20 words to remember, then asked to count backwards from 1000 for a minute, and then asked to recall as many of the words as possible. Their mean recall was 8 words with a standard deviation of 2 words. Using this information, determine whether subjects in this sample were representative of the general population in average recall.

8. Formulate null and alternative hypotheses (one-tailed).
9. Discuss each assumption.
10. Find $t_{observed}$.
11. Find $t_{critical}$ at $\alpha = .01$.
12. State your conclusions.

13–19. In a random sample of $N = 25$ observations, $\bar{X} = 30$ and $s = 10$. From national norm data, μ is known to be 36.

13. Formulate null and alternative hypotheses (two-tailed).
14. Discuss each assumption.
15. Find $t_{observed}$.

16. Find $t_{critical}$ at $\alpha = .10$.
17. State your conclusions.
18. Determine the 90-percent confidence interval.
19. Based on the t test, would you expect the 90-percent confidence interval to include μ under H_0? Explain.

Statistical Tests
for
Two Independent Groups

THIS CHAPTER presents statistical tests for examining data from two basic between-subjects designs. The first type of design is a true experimental design in which subjects are randomly assigned either to a control group or to an experimental group (see Chapter 1; see also Campbell & Stanley, 1966). The researcher may make causal interpretations of the results. That is, the researcher is able to conclude that the independent variable caused the observed differences between the control group and the experimental group on the dependent variable.

The second type of design is a criterion-group design. Subjects are selected because they represent one or another population of interest. For example, one group of subjects might be drawn randomly from a population of "neurotics," the other from a population of "normals." Notice that the experimenter does *not* randomly assign subjects to the two groups. The treatment—whatever it was—has been provided by nature (see Chapter 1 and Campbell & Stanley, 1966, on ex post facto designs). In general the criterion-group design sorts subjects into two discrete groups on some individual difference variable (e.g., sex, personality, ability, interest) and compares these two groups on some measure (dependent variable) thought to be related to group membership. The criterion-group design, then, is a correlational design, and the results of such a study *cannot* support an interpretation that the independent variable (e.g., type of subject population) caused the differences between the two groups. Rather, a significant difference between the two groups can only be interpreted as demonstrating a relationship between the independent and dependent variables. Thus, the mean difference in reading-test scores for girls and boys indicates a relationship between sex and reading ability. However, it does not imply that being a girl, for example, causes higher reading ability. Many variables may underlie the relationship between sex and reading ability, such as social reinforcement for practicing reading or exposure to appropriate models (e.g., primarily female teachers of reading in elementary schools).

Both types of designs attempt to provide answers to Case II research questions (see Chapter 9): "Are the two groups drawn from the same population or different populations?" Notice that in the formulation of the Case II research problem, the focus is on the differences between distributions, not necessarily on the differences between distribution means. In this chapter, then, statistical tests are provided for examining differences between means *and* distributions of populations.

The purpose of the t test for two independent means is to help the researcher decide whether the observed difference between two sample means arose by chance, or represents a true difference between populations. In the language of hypothesis testing, the purpose of the t test is to help decide whether or not to reject the null hypothesis of no difference between the means of the two groups.

Since this decision cannot be made with complete certainty, it is a probabilistic one. The problem, then, is to determine the probability of observing the difference between the sample means of the two groups under the assumption that the null hypothesis is true (i.e., there is no difference between the two groups).

In solving this problem, several steps must be taken. The first step is to provide an estimate of the unknown standard error of the differences between means:

$$\sigma_{\bar{X}_1 - \bar{X}_2} = \sqrt{\sigma_{\bar{X}_1}^2 + \sigma_{\bar{X}_2}^2} \qquad [12\text{-}1]$$

$$= \sqrt{\frac{\sigma^2}{n_1} + \frac{\sigma^2}{n_2}} \ .$$

This can be achieved by using the standard deviation from each sample as an estimate of σ. For samples of equal size ($n_1 = n_2 \geqslant 2$), the estimate of the standard error of the difference between means is

$$s_{\bar{X}_1 - \bar{X}_2} = \sqrt{s_{\bar{X}_1}^2 + s_{\bar{X}_2}^2} \qquad [15\text{-}1]$$

$$= \sqrt{\frac{s^2}{n_1} + \frac{s^2}{n_2}} \ .$$

Figure 15-1 ♦ Sampling distribution of t for differences between means ($df = (n_1 - 1) + (n_2 - 1) = 9 + 9 = 18$)

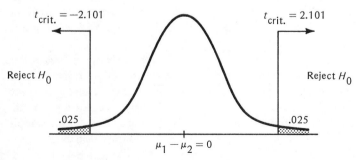

THE t TEST FOR DIFFERENCES BETWEEN TWO INDEPENDENT MEANS

Purpose and Underlying Logic

The next step is to provide a measure of the distance between the difference of the sample means $(\overline{X}_1 - \overline{X}_2)$ and the difference of their corresponding population means $(\mu_1 - \mu_2)$. If the standard error of the differences between means $(\sigma_{\overline{X}_1 - \overline{X}_2})$ were known, then $z_{\overline{X}_1 - \overline{X}_2}$ could be used as the measure:

$$z_{\overline{X}_1 - \overline{X}_2} = \frac{(\overline{X}_1 - \overline{X}_2) - (\mu_1 - \mu_2)}{\sigma_{\overline{X}_1 - \overline{X}_2}}. \qquad [12\text{-}2]$$

In fact, $\sigma_{\overline{X}_1 - \overline{X}_2}$ is not known. But this parameter can be estimated by $s_{\overline{X}_1 - \overline{X}_2}$. By making this substitution, t for differences between means is defined:

$$t_{\overline{X}_1 - \overline{X}_2\text{observed}} = \frac{(\overline{X}_1 - \overline{X}_2) - (\mu_1 - \mu_2)}{s_{\overline{X}_1 - \overline{X}_2}}. \qquad [15\text{-}2]$$

In this case, t is a measure of the distance between the difference of the sample means $(\overline{X}_1 - \overline{X}_2)$ and the difference of their corresponding population means $(\mu_1 - \mu_2)$. Notice that since we sample from populations with identical means in setting up the sampling distribution under H_0, $\mu_1 = \mu_2$ and so $\mu_1 - \mu_2 = 0$. Thus, t can be simplified as follows:

$$t_{\overline{X}_1 - \overline{X}_2}(\text{observed}) = \frac{\overline{X}_1 - \overline{X}_2}{s_{\overline{X}_1 - \overline{X}_2}}. \qquad [15\text{-}2a]$$

The final step in specifying the sampling distribution of t is to recognize that the value of t will vary from one sample to the next due to random fluctuation in both $\overline{X}$ and s. If the value of t [which is $(\overline{X}_1 - \overline{X}_2)/s_{\overline{X}_1 - \overline{X}_2}$] is calculated for each of a very large number of samples from a normal population, a frequency distribution for t can be graphed with the values of t on the abscissa and the frequencies on the ordinate. This frequency distribution can be modeled by the theoretical (mathematical) distribution of t. When this is done, the theoretical model is called the *sampling distribution of t for differences between means*. It can be used as a probability distribution for deciding whether or not to reject the null hypothesis when $\sigma_{\overline{X}_1 - \overline{X}_2}$ is unknown.

Actually, the sampling distribution of t for differences between means is a family of distributions. Each particular member of the family of t distributions depends on degrees of freedom. (For a discussion of the t distribution and degrees of freedom, see Chapter 14). Specifically, the t distribution for differences depends on the number of degrees of freedom in the first sample $(n_1 - 1)$ and in the second sample $(n_2 - 1)$ of the pair. So the t distribution used to model the sampling procedure described above is based on $(n_1 - 1) + (n_2 - 1)$ degrees of freedom or on $N - 2$ degrees of freedom, where $N = n_1 + n_2$. In the example with $n_1 = n_2 = 10$, a t distribution with 18 df would be used to model the sampling distribution $[(10 - 1) + (10 - 1) = 9 + 9 = 18$; see Figure 15-1].

The t distribution of differences has the following characteristics. (See Chapter 14 for a more detailed discussion.) First, its mean is equal to zero $(\mu_1 - \mu_2 = 0)$. This happens because some differences between sample means are positive $(\overline{X}_1 - \overline{X}_2 > 0)$, some are zero $(\overline{X}_1 - \overline{X}_2 = 0)$, and some are negative $(\overline{X}_1 - \overline{X}_2 < 0)$. Over all differences between pairs, the positive differences cancel the negative differences, so that the average difference is zero. Second, the distribution is symmetric in shape and looks like a bell-shaped curve. However, the mathematical rule specifying the t distribution is not the same as the rule for the normal distribution, so the t and the normal distributions are not the same. Nevertheless, as the sample size increases, the t distribution becomes increasingly normal in shape. With an infinite sample size, the t distribution and the normal distribution are identical.

◆   ◆   ◆   ◆   ◆

Hypotheses

The hypotheses about differences between population means using the sampling distribution of t are the same as those tested with the normal sampling distribution described in Chapter 12. In the case of a two-tailed alternative hypothesis, the null and alternative hypotheses are:

$$\left\{ \begin{array}{l} H_0: \mu_1 - \mu_2 = 0 \\ H_1: \mu_1 - \mu_2 \neq 0 \end{array} \right\}, \quad \text{i.e.,} \quad \left\{ \begin{array}{l} H_0: \mu_1 = \mu_2 \\ H_1: \mu_1 \neq \mu_2 \end{array} \right\}.$$

In the case of a directional alternative hypothesis, the null and alternative hypotheses are either

$$\left\{ \begin{array}{l} H_0: \mu_1 - \mu_2 = 0 \\ H_1: \mu_1 - \mu_2 > 0 \end{array} \right\}, \quad \text{i.e.,} \quad \left\{ \begin{array}{l} H_0: \mu_1 = \mu_2 \\ H_1: \mu_1 > \mu_2 \end{array} \right\},$$

or

$$\left\{ \begin{array}{l} H_0: \mu_1 - \mu_2 = 0 \\ H_1: \mu_1 - \mu_2 < 0 \end{array} \right\} \quad \text{i.e.,} \quad \left\{ \begin{array}{l} H_0: \mu_1 = \mu_2 \\ H_1: \mu_1 < \mu_2 \end{array} \right\}.$$

◆   ◆   ◆   ◆   ◆

Design Requirements for the Use of the t Test

The use of the t test imposes a number of requirements on the collection of data:

1. There is one independent variable with two levels (i.e., groups).
2. A subject appears in one and only one of the two groups.
3. The levels of the independent variable may differ from one another either qualitatively or quantitatively. Qualitative differences are, for example, that between individualized and traditional reading curricula, or that of sex (male versus female). Quantitative variables are, for example, the amount of time studying or the number of reinforcements.

♦ ♦ ♦ ♦ ♦

Assumptions   In using the sampling distribution of t to test for differences between independent means, the following assumptions are made:

1. The scores in the two groups are randomly sampled from their respective populations and are independent of one another.
2. The scores in the respective populations are normally distributed.
3. The variances of scores in the two populations are equal (i.e., $\sigma_1^2 = \sigma_2^2$). This assumption is often called the assumption of **homogeneity of variance**.

The assumption of independence deserves some discussion. It actually has two parts. First, the scores of subjects in one group must be unrelated to the scores of subjects in the other group. This is called **independence of groups**. Second, scores must be independent of the basis for the administration of the treatments: the application of the treatment to one subject in a group must not influence the way in which the treatment is applied to any other subject in the group. This is called **independence of treatments**.

In order to clarify these two parts of the independence assumption, some examples may help. The assumption of independence of groups will be violated if (1) Harry and Charlie are both assigned to group 1 because Charlie refused to participate in the study unless he could be with Harry, or if (2) both Harry and Charlie were given their choice of group and chose group 1. Some examples of a violation of the assumption of independence of treatments are the following: (1) Subjects are assigned to small groups to learn some material. What each subject learns depends, in part, upon what each of them contributes in the group discussion. (2) A group of subjects are listening to a lecture when a gardener distracts them at a critical part by mowing the lawn nearby. Since many subjects were distracted at the same point in time, what one subject did not learn is related to what some other subject did not learn. (3) During the course of a four-day study, subjects in one group describe what they are learning to subjects in another group. In effect, all of the subjects receive bits and pieces of all the treatments.

The assumption of independence is tested logically. Close inspection of the sampling procedures should reveal, in a true experiment, that subjects were assigned to one or the other group randomly and received their treatments independently. In a criterion-group study, subjects in each group should be randomly sampled from their respective populations.

The assumption of normality can be examined empirically if the sizes of the two groups are about 15 or more. For each group, the scores should be arranged in a frequency distribution. The shape of this distribution can be examined visually to see if the distribution of scores is *roughly* normal. If sample sizes are too small to inspect the distributions visually, prior information about the distribution of scores from similar subjects can be used. In general, the t test is not seriously affected by a violation of the normality assumption. However, this is no excuse for not inspecting the frequency distribution. If one or both of these distributions (e.g., distributions for scores in the control and experimental groups) are extremely skewed, a nonparametric statistical test such as the Mann-Whitney U, described in a subsequent section of this chapter, should be considered.

Assumption 3, homogeneity of variance, can be tested empirically with a number of different statistical tests (e.g., see Winer, 1971). The effect of violating this assumption on the probabilities of Type I and Type II errors depends on n_1 and n_2. If the number of subjects in both groups is the same ($n_1 = n_2$), the t test is not affected seriously by a violation of this assumption. This should be motivation in itself to design studies with equal sample sizes if possible. If, however, the sample sizes are quite different (e.g., 3 to 1), a nonparametric test (see the section on the Mann-Whitney U test below) may provide a preferable alternative. Notice, though, that this difference between the variances of the two groups may have substantive meaning and may deserve interpretation in its own right.

♦   ♦   ♦   ♦   ♦

The formula for the t test when the sample sizes are equal ($n_1 = n_2$) is

Formulas for the *t* Test

$$t_{\bar{X}_1 - \bar{X}_2}(\text{observed}) = \frac{\bar{X}_1 - \bar{X}_2}{s_{\bar{X}_1 - \bar{X}_2}}. \qquad [\,15\text{-}2a\,]$$

However, in order to use the t test for the more general case where sample sizes may be either equal or unequal, $s_{\bar{X}_1 - \bar{X}_2}$ must be defined more generally than it was in Formula 15-1. The goal in defining $s_{\bar{X}_1 - \bar{X}_2}$, then, is to find the best estimate of the population variance using sample variances. This can be done as follows. Under the assumption of equal population variances ($\sigma_1^2 = \sigma_2^2 = \sigma^2$), s_1^2 and s_2^2 each estimate σ^2. The best estimate of the value of σ^2, then, is the average of s_1^2 and s_2^2. This average is called a **pooled estimate**.[1] So the formula for the t test can be written to reflect this pooling:

$$t_{\bar{X}_1 - \bar{X}_2}(\text{observed}) = \frac{\bar{X}_1 - \bar{X}_2}{\sqrt{\dfrac{s_{\text{pooled}}^2}{n_1} + \dfrac{s_{\text{pooled}}^2}{n_2}}} \qquad [\,15\text{-}2b\,]$$

$$= \frac{\bar{X}_1 - \bar{X}_2}{\sqrt{s_{\text{pooled}}^2 \left(\dfrac{1}{n_1} + \dfrac{1}{n_2} \right)}}.$$

---

[1] The pooled variance is the best estimate in that the standard error of the pooled estimate will be less than the standard error of the pooled estimate of either of the sample statistics taken singly.

Table 15-1 ♦ Descriptive statistics for the hypothetical posttest data from the teacher-expectancy study: first-graders

	Control group				Experimental group		
X	$\bar{X}$	$X - \bar{X}$	x^2	X	$\bar{X}$	$X - \bar{X}$	x^2
90	105.2	-15.2	231.04	107	116.4	-9.4	88.36
99	105.2	-6.2	38.44	111	116.4	-5.4	29.16
102	105.2	-3.2	10.24	117	116.4	0.6	0.36
114	105.2	8.8	77.44	125	116.4	8.6	73.96
121	105.2	15.8	249.64	122	116.4	5.6	31.36
Σ 526	526	0	606.80	Σ 582	582	0	223.20

$$s^2 = \frac{606.80}{5-1} = 151.70 \qquad\qquad s^2 = \frac{223.20}{5-1} = 55.8$$

$$s = \sqrt{151.70} = 12.32 \qquad\qquad s = \sqrt{55.8} = 7.47$$

The pooled variance estimate s^2_{pooled} is found by computing a weighted average of s_1^2 and s_2^2:

$$s^2_{\text{pooled}} = \frac{(n_1 - 1)s_1^2 + (n_2 - 1)s_2^2}{(n_1 - 1) + (n_2 - 1)}$$

$$= \frac{(n_1 - 1)s_1^2 + (n_2 - 1)s_2^2}{n_1 + n_2 - 2}.$$

Incorporating the pooled estimate of the population variance into Formula 15-2b, we have

$$t_{\bar{X}_1 - \bar{X}_2}(\text{observed}) = \frac{\bar{X}_1 - \bar{X}_2}{\sqrt{\left[\dfrac{(n_1 - 1)s_1^2 + (n_2 - 1)s_2^2}{n_1 + n_2 - 2}\right]\left(\dfrac{1}{n_1} + \dfrac{1}{n_2}\right)}}. \qquad [\textbf{15-2c}]$$

This formula can be used for samples of equal or different sizes. If the sample sizes are equal ($n_1 = n_2 = n$), the cumbersome denominator in Formula 15-2c reduces to $\sqrt{(s_1^2 + s_2^2)/n}$ and the t test can be written as

$$t_{\bar{X}_1 - \bar{X}_2}(\text{observed}) = \frac{\bar{X}_1 - \bar{X}_2}{\sqrt{\dfrac{s_1^2 + s_2^2}{n}}}. \qquad [\textbf{15-2d}]$$

As an example of how to apply Formulas 15-2c and 15-2d, consider the hypothetical posttest scores for first-graders in the teacher-expectancy study. (See Table 15-1 for the data and Chapter 2 for a complete description of the study.) In this study, the experimental group (students designated at random to be intellectual "spurters") was expected to score higher than the control group (students not designated as spurters) on a measure of intellectual ability which was given at the end of the school year. To test whether there was a significant difference between the two groups, t can be calculated by inserting the appropriate values from Table 15-1 into Formula 15-2c as shown below:

$$t_{\bar{X}_1 - \bar{X}_2}(\text{observed}) = \frac{\bar{X}_1 - \bar{X}_2}{\sqrt{\left[\dfrac{(n_1 - 1)s_1^2 + (n_2 - 1)s_2^2}{n_1 + n_2 - 2}\right]\left(\dfrac{1}{n_1} + \dfrac{1}{n_2}\right)}} \qquad [\textbf{15-2c}]$$

$$= \frac{105.2 - 116.4}{\sqrt{\left[\dfrac{(5 - 1)151.70 + (5 - 1)55.8}{5 + 5 - 2}\right]\left(\dfrac{1}{5} + \dfrac{1}{5}\right)}}$$

$$= \frac{-11.20}{\sqrt{\left(\dfrac{606.8 + 223.2}{8}\right)\left(\dfrac{2}{5}\right)}}$$

$$= \frac{-11.20}{\sqrt{(103.75)(.4)}}$$

$$= \frac{-11.20}{\sqrt{41.5}} = \frac{-11.20}{6.44}$$

$$= -1.74.$$

Since the sample sizes are equal, Formula 15-2d can also be used to obtain t. These computations are shown in Procedure 15-1.

◆   ◆   ◆   ◆   ◆

In order to decide whether or not to reject the null hypothesis, the observed value of t (-1.74 in the example) must be compared with a critical value of t. The symbol t_{critical} designates the points in the t distribution beyond which

Decision Rules for Rejecting the Null Hypothesis

Procedure 15-1 ♦ Steps in conducting a t test for two independent groups (example data from the hypothetical study of teacher expectancy shown in Table 15-1)

Operation	Example
1 Specify the null and alternative hypotheses and the level of significance.	H_0: $\mu_C - \mu_E = 0$, H_1: $\mu_C - \mu_E < 0$, where C represents the control group, and E represents the experimental group. $\alpha = .01$.
2 Examine the assumptions of the t test: **a** independent and random sampling	**a** A description of the sampling procedures for the study given in Chapter 2 suggests that subjects were independently sampled from each age group. (It is unlikely that subjects were actually randomly selected from their respective populations. They were selected from a convenient sample representing each population.)
b Normality within each population	**b** The assumption of normality within each population cannot be tested directly here by constructing a frequency distribution, since the number of scores in each group is so small. However, since the t test is not sensitive to violations of this assumption, we can proceed.
c Homogeneity of variances (equal variances in two populations)	**c** When cell sizes are equal, the t test is not sensitive to violations of this assumption. Since cell sizes are equal here ($n_1 = n_2 = 5$), we need not be concerned with testing this assumption.
3 Compute $t_{\bar{X}_1 - \bar{X}_2}$ (observed) by inserting appropriate values into Formula 15-2c or 15-2d (if $n_1 = n_2$) and solving:	From Table 15-1 we have

$$\bar{X}_C = 105.2, \qquad \bar{X}_E = 116.4,$$
$$s_C^2 = 151.70, \qquad s_E^2 = 55.8,$$
$$n_C = 5, \qquad n_E = 5.$$

$t_{\bar{X}_1 - \bar{X}_2}(\text{observed})$

$$= \frac{\bar{X}_1 - \bar{X}_2}{\sqrt{\left[\dfrac{(n_1 - 1)s_1^2 + (n_2 - 1)s_2^2}{n_1 + n_2 - 2}\right]\left(\dfrac{1}{n_1} + \dfrac{1}{n_2}\right)}}, \quad \textbf{[15-2c]}$$

or, if $n_1 = n_2$:

$$t_{\bar{X}_1 - \bar{X}_2}(\text{observed}) = \frac{\bar{X}_1 - \bar{X}_2}{\sqrt{\dfrac{s_1^2 + s_2^2}{n}}}. \quad \textbf{[15-2d]}$$

Since cell sizes are equal, Formula 15-2d can be used:

$$t_{\bar{X}_1 - \bar{X}_2}(\text{observed}) = \frac{105.2 - 116.4}{\sqrt{\dfrac{151.70 + 55.80}{5}}} = \frac{-11.2}{\sqrt{\dfrac{207.5}{5}}}$$

$$= \frac{-11.2}{\sqrt{41.5}} = \frac{-11.2}{6.44} = -1.74.$$

4 Identify $t_{crit.}$ with $n_E + n_C - 2$ degrees of freedom using Table C.

$df = 5 + 5 - 2 = 8,$

$t_{crit.(.01, 8)} = 2.896.$

5 Decide whether or not to reject the null hypothesis:

  a Reject H_0 if $|t_{obs.}| \geqslant t_{crit.}$.

  b Do not reject H_0 if $|t_{obs.}| < t_{crit.}$.

Since $|t_{obs.}| < t_{crit.}$ ($|-1.74| < 2.896$), do not reject H_0. Conclude that, while the difference between means was in the expected direction, there is insufficient evidence to lead us to believe that this difference represents anything but a chance occurrence.

differences between sample means are unlikely to arise under the null hypothesis. Since there is a different critical value of t for each degree of freedom, the first step is to determine the number of degrees of freedom. For the example data from the teacher-expectancy study, there were 5 subjects in the control group (n_1) and 5 subjects in the experimental group (n_2). The degrees of freedom, then, for the critical value of t are:

$$df = (5 - 1) + (5 - 1)$$
$$= 4 + 4$$
$$= 8.$$

The next step is to find the critical value of t for 8 degrees of freedom at a specified level of significance α. In the example study, assume that a one-tailed test at $\alpha = .01$ was planned before the study was conducted. From Table C,

$$t_{critical(.01, 8)} = 2.896.$$

Since the *absolute value* of $t_{observed}$ (1.74) does not exceed the critical value of t (2.896), the null hypothesis should not be rejected. While the difference between the means was in the expected direction, the evidence leads us to the conclusion that this difference probably represents a chance occurrence.

In general, the following set of criteria can be established for deciding whether or not to reject the null hypothesis:

	Reject H_0 if:	Do not reject H_0 if:
Nondirectional (two-tailed)	$|t_{obs.}| \geqslant t_{crit.(\alpha/2, df)}$	$|t_{obs.}| < t_{crit.(\alpha/2, df)}$
Directional (one-tailed)	$|t_{obs.}| \geqslant t_{crit.(\alpha, df)}$	$|t_{obs.}| < t_{crit.(\alpha, df)}$

(For an application of these criteria, see Chapter 14, "Decision Rules for Rejecting the Null Hypothesis.")

The steps in conducting the t test for two independent groups are summarized in Procedure 15-1 using data from Table 15-1.

◆   ◆   ◆   ◆   ◆

Confidence Intervals The $100(1 - \alpha)$-percent confidence interval can be established around the observed differences between means using the t distribution. This procedure is similar to that described in Chapter 12 for constructing confidence intervals using the normal distribution. The major difference is that, since the standard error is estimated from sample data, t_{critical} with $df = n_1 + n_2 - 2$ is used rather than z_{critical} in constructing the interval. The general form of the confidence interval is

$$\left(\bar{X}_1 - \bar{X}_2\right) - t_{\text{critical}(\alpha/2,\, df)} s_{\bar{X}_1 - \bar{X}_2} \leqslant \mu_1 - \mu_2$$
$$\leqslant \left(\bar{X}_1 - \bar{X}_2\right) + t_{\text{critical}(\alpha/2,\, df)} s_{\bar{X}_1 - \bar{X}_2}. \qquad [\textbf{15-3}]$$

As an example of constructing confidence intervals, let's set up the 95-percent confidence interval $[95 = 100(1 - .05)]$ for the data from the example study. Three pieces of information are needed: (1) $\bar{X}_1 - \bar{X}_2$, (2) $s_{\bar{X}_1 - \bar{X}_2}$, and (3) t_{critical}. All three pieces of information are already available. From Procedure 15-1,

$$\bar{X}_1 - \bar{X}_2 = -11.2,$$

$$s_{\bar{X}_1 - \bar{X}_2} = 6.44.$$

The value of t_{critical} for $\alpha/2 = .05/2$ and 8 degrees of freedom can be found in Table C: 2.306.

The 95-percent confidence interval is found as follows (pay attention to negative numbers):

$$CI_{.95}: \quad -11.2 - (2.306)(6.44) \leqslant \mu_1 - \mu_2 \leqslant -11.2 + (2.306)(6.44),$$

$$-11.2 - 14.85 \leqslant \mu_1 - \mu_2 \leqslant -11.2 + 14.85,$$

$$-26.05 \leqslant \mu_1 - \mu_2 \leqslant 3.65.$$

The interval tells us that over all random samples of differences between means, the true value of $\mu_1 - \mu_2$ lies within the rather large interval such as that bounded by -26.05 to $+3.65$ IQ points, with a probability of .95.

The 99-percent confidence interval can be constructed in a similar way. Only one piece of information is missing: t_{critical} at $.01/2$. With 8 degrees of freedom, the value of t_{critical} can be found from Table C:

$$t_{\text{critical}(.01/2,\, 8)} = 3.355.$$

With this information, the 99-percent confidence interval can be written

$CI_{.99}$: $-11.2 - (3.355)(6.44) \leqslant \mu_1 - \mu_2 \leqslant -11.2 + (3.355)(6.44),$

$$-11.2 - 21.61 \leqslant \mu_1 - \mu_2 \leqslant -11.2 + 21.61,$$

$$-32.81 \leqslant \mu_1 - \mu_2 \leqslant 10.41.$$

The 99-percent confidence interval tells us that over all possible samples, one must allow an enormous range of values (e.g., -32.81 to $+10.41$) in order to include the true difference between means with probability equal to .99.

Table 15-2 presents moral judgments, along with descriptive statistics, for subjects in age group 1 (4–6 years old) and in age group 5 (16–18 years old) for an event in which the *outcome* was positive while the *intent* was negative. In this situation, Piaget's theory predicts that young children will give positive ratings (since the outcome was positive) and adults will give negative ratings (since the intent was negative). Test this hypothesis at $\alpha = .05$. Include the following in your answer:

EXAMPLE PROBLEM 1

a. Null and alternative hypotheses
b. Test of each assumption or explanation for not conducting the test
c. $t_{observed}$
d. $t_{critical}$
e. Conclusions
f. 95-percent confidence interval

Table 15-2 ♦ Hypothetical moral judgments and descriptive statistics from the moral-judgment study: judgments about a moral act in which the outcome was positive but the actor's intent was negative

Subject	Young children (group 1)	Young adults (group 5)
1	1	-5
2	-1	-2
3	-1	-2
4	1	-2
5	2	-3
Σ	2	-14
$\bar{X}$	0.40	-2.80
s^2	1.80	1.70
s	1.34	1.30

MANN-WHITNEY
U TEST FOR TWO
INDEPENDENT GROUPS

**Parametric and
Nonparametric Tests**

Classical statistical methods such as the *t* test and the analysis of variance (described briefly in Section V and presented in detail in Chapters 16 and 17) are called *parametric tests* because they test hypotheses about parameters such as $H_0 : \mu_1 - \mu_2 = 0$. They are developed on the assumptions that scores are measured at least on an interval scale and are normally distributed in the populations and that the variances of the populations are all equal.

In contrast, **nonparametric tests** do not (necessarily) test hypotheses about specific population parameters. Rather, they test hypotheses about, for example, the shapes of distributions or their central tendencies. Moreover, they do not assume interval measurement and normal populations with equal variances. Rather, nonparametric tests rest on weaker assumptions about the measurement scale (e.g., they can be used with an ordinal scale and a discrete sampling distribution) and the nature of the parent populations (which may be similar in shape in some cases and symmetric in others).

While the less stringent assumptions make nonparametric tests attractive to the behavioral scientist, a word of caution is appropriate. Nonparametric tests have been "sold" as a panacea. "In some miraculous way, using such a technique is supposed to solve all the problems raised by unknown measurement level, objectionable assumptions, and so on (including, some apparently believe, sloppy data). If this is true, this is the only known example of something for nothing in statistics or anywhere else" (Hays, 1971, p. 763).

In choosing between a parametric and a nonparametric test, then, the potential costs and benefits of each must be weighed. In situations in which certain of the assumptions of parametric tests are not met, the consequences of violating the assumptions should be taken into consideration. In many cases, the parametric tests are not seriously affected by the violation of their assumptions (see the discussion of the assumption of normality and homogeneity of variance above) and may be more powerful than their nonparametric counterparts. In many other cases, however, parametric tests are not as powerful as their nonparametric counterparts when certain of their assumptions (e.g., homogeneity) have been violated. And in some cases (e.g., unequal sample sizes and variances), assumptions of parametric tests are untenable and so the accuracy of the statistical results is problematic. Furthermore, with small sample size ($n < 10$), assumptions underlying parametric tests tend to be untenable and the nonparametric counterpart may be more appropriate. Finally, for computational ease, the nonparametric methods carry the day.

In summary, there's more than one way to skin a rabbit—or analyze a set of data. The choice between parametric and nonparametric tests is not always an easy one. While the emphasis of this text is clearly on the parametric methods, one or more nonparametric methods may be presented along with their parametric counterparts. The **Mann-Whitney *U* test**, a counterpart of the *t* test, is such an example and is presented below. An understanding of both techniques will help you make an appropriate choice of tests. And, since parametric and nonparametric methods view and array the same data somewhat differently, you will acquire some skill in looking at data from different perspectives. Such a flexible outlook often reveals information about the effects of an experiment that otherwise might be overlooked.

♦   ♦   ♦   ♦   ♦

The purpose of the Mann-Whitney U test is to help the researcher decide whether or not the distributions of scores in two independent groups were drawn from two identical population distributions. If the shapes of the population distributions are similar, the U test can be used to examine the null hypothesis that the two populations are identical with respect to their *central tendency*. In this case, the U test is a nonparametric analog to the t test for two independent groups. It may be used as an alternative to the t test or when the t test's assumptions of normality and equal variances are untenable.

Purpose and Underlying Logic

The decision whether or not to reject the null hypothesis cannot be made with certainty; it is a probabilistic one. The problem, then, is to determine the probability of observing differences between the distributions of scores in two independent groups assuming the null hypothesis is true.

The first step in coming up with a probability statement is to define a statistic which reflects differences between the two distributions of scores. This statistic is called the U statistic. It is based not on the raw scores, but on the rank order of scores from lowest to highest, since these ranks adequately reflect differences between two distributions. In order to see this, consider the data in Table 15-3 from the teacher-expectancy study. (For details in computing U, see "Formula for the U Statistic" below.) Notice that most of the high scores are associated with the experimental group. So the ranks associated with the experimental group (4, 5, 7, 9, 10) are generally higher than those associated with the control group (1, 2, 3, 6, 8). The difference between the two distributions of scores, then, can be seen in the rank ordering of subjects' scores in the two groups: CCCEECECEE. The U statistic is simply the number of E scores preceding each C score. In counting the number of E scores preceding each C score, some E scores will be counted more than once. In the example, no E

Table 15-3 ♦ Using data from the study of teacher expectancy (see Table 15-1)

Group	C	C	C	E	E	C	E	C	E	E
Raw score	90	99	102	107	111	114	117	121	122	125
Rank	1	2	3	4	5	6	7	8	9	10

Sum of ranks:
    Control group, $1 + 2 + 3 + 6 + 8 = 20$
    Experimental group, $4 + 5 + 7 + 9 + 10 = 35$

score precedes the first three C scores, 2 E scores precede the fourth C score, and a total of 3 E scores (counting the first two E scores for a second time) precede the fifth C score. So $U = 0 + 0 + 0 + 2 + 3 = 5$.

The next step is to determine the probability of observing U at or beyond some value, assuming the null hypothesis is true. With the U test, as with many nonparametric tests, this problem is solved by capitalizing on two pieces of information. First, all possible orderings of subjects' scores (e.g., all possible orderings of Es and Cs) can be determined by knowing only the number of subjects in each of the two groups. Second, all possible random orderings, under the null hypothesis, are equally likely. From this information, the probability of a particular event (e.g., $U \leqslant$ some value) can be determined by the ratio of the number of ways subjects' scores can be rank ordered in that event to the total possible orderings of subjects' scores.

♦　　♦　　♦　　♦　　♦

Hypotheses　　The hypotheses tested with the U statistic are somewhat different than the hypotheses presented so far. The null hypothesis is that the distributions of scores in the two populations from which the groups were drawn are identical. The alternative hypothesis is that the distributions of scores in the two populations from which the groups were drawn are different in some way. If the U statistic is used to test for differences between means, an additional restrictive assumption must be made: the population distributions are identical in all other respects. In this case, the null and alternative hypotheses can be written as in Table 15-4.

♦　　♦　　♦　　♦　　♦

Design Requirements for　　The use of the U test implies that certain design requirements have been met.
the Use of the U Test　　They are the same as for the t test:

1. There is one independent variable with two levels (i.e., groups).
2. A subject appears in one and only one group.
3. The levels of the independent variable may differ from one another either qualitatively or quantitatively.

♦　　♦　　♦　　♦　　♦

Assumptions　　In using the Mann-Whitney U test, the assumption of independence of scores is made. If the U test is used to test hypotheses about central tendency, an additional assumption is made that the distributions of scores in the two populations are similar except for central tendency.

♦　　♦　　♦　　♦　　♦

Formula for the　　While it is possible to use the counting method described above to calculate U,
U Statistic　　this method is tedious for fairly large samples. An alternative method which gives identical results is the following. First, the scores from both groups are pooled together so that there are $n_1 + n_2 = N$ scores considered together.

Table 15-4 ♦ Hypotheses for the U test

	Nondirectional hypotheses	Directional hypotheses
H_0:	The distributions of scores in the two populations from which the groups were drawn are identical.	The distributions of scores in the two populations from which the groups were drawn are identical.
H_1:	The distributions of scores in the two populations from which the groups were drawn differ in their means: $\mu_1 \neq \mu_2$.	The distributions of scores in the two populations from which the groups were drawn differ in their means: $\mu_1 > \mu_2$ or $\mu_1 < \mu_2$.

Second, these N scores are arranged in order of their magnitude regardless of group. Each score, however, is labeled with the group from which it came. For example, the scores from the teacher-expectancy study (Table 15-1) were pooled so that there are $5 + 5 = 10$ scores. These scores are arranged in order of their magnitude—lowest to highest—in the second row of Table 15-3. The group from which each score came—experimental (E) or control (C)—is identified in the first row.

Third, a rank is assigned to each score according to its magnitude. A rank of 1 is assigned to the lowest score, a rank of 2 is assigned to next highest score, and so on, until a rank of N is assigned to the highest score. In Table 15-3, the lowest score is 90 and a rank of 1 has been assigned to it. The highest score is 125 and a rank of 10 (because $N = 10$) has been assigned to it. In some cases, two or more scores may be tied for a particular rank. For example, suppose that in Table 15-3, the score of 102 was actually a score of 99. Now there would be two scores of 99 tied for ranks of 2 and 3. In this case, the average of the two ranks is assigned to both scores. For example, the two scores of 99 would each be assigned a rank of 2.5.[2]

Fourth, find the sum of the ranks for each of the two groups and then take the larger sum. In the example, the sum of the ranks for the experimental group would be taken, because it is larger than the sum of the ranks for the control group ($35 > 20$; see Table 15-3). This sum is called T_L:

$$T_L = \text{larger sum of the ranks}$$
$$= 4 + 5 + 7 + 9 + 10$$
$$= 35.$$

[2]The Mann-Whitney test assumes no two scores are exactly the same. In other words, there are no "ties" in theory. However, in practice, ties occur. If the ties occur between two observations *in the same group*, U is unaffected. If the ties occur between observations *in different groups*, U is affected. Usually this effect is negligible. For large samples ($n_L \geqslant 20$), a correction exists (see Hays, 1973; Siegel, 1956).

The fifth step is to calculate the Mann-Whitney U statistic as follows:

$$U_1 = n_L n_S + \frac{n_L(n_L + 1)}{2} - T_L,$$

$$U_2 = n_L n_S - U_1 \qquad \textbf{[15-4]}$$

where $\quad n_L$ = number of subjects in the group with the larger sum of ranks,
$\qquad n_S$ = number of subjects in the other group.

Mann-Whitney U equals the smaller of U_1 and U_2.

Using the information from the example, we have

$$U = (5)(5) + \frac{5(5 + 1)}{2} - 35$$

$$= 5$$

$$U_2 = (5)(5) - 5 = 20$$

The value of U_1, calculated with Formula 15-4, is the smaller of the two and is exactly the same as that obtained with the counting method, as expected.

♦ ♦ ♦ ♦ ♦

Decision Rules for Rejecting the Null Hypothesis In order to decide whether or not to reject the null hypothesis, the probability of observing a value of less than or equal to U (5 in the example) is needed. This decision is made one of three ways, depending on the size of the two groups. If $n \leqslant 8$, Table J at the end of the book can be used to determine the probability of U directly. If $9 \leqslant n \leqslant 20$, U must be compared with the critical value of U in Table K. These critical values of U designate the regions beyond which differences between the means of the two groups are unlikely to arise. Finally, if $n > 20$, the normal distribution (Table B) can be used to determine the critical value.

$\textbf{\textit{n}} \leqslant \textbf{8}$ If the larger of the two samples is less than or equal to 8, Table J can be used to find the probability of U. The following steps are taken in using this table to identify the critical values:

1. Locate the table corresponding to the larger of the two sample sizes (labeled N_2 in the table).
2. Locate the column of the table corresponding to the smaller of the two sample sizes (labeled N_1 in the table).
3. Locate the row of the table corresponding to U.
4. Read the probability from the table which corresponds to the row and column appropriate to your data. This is the one-tailed probability of observing the difference between means given the null hypothesis. The two-tailed probability is obtained by doubling this value.

5. If a *directional* (one-tailed) *alternative hypothesis* has been specified, reject the null hypothesis if the probability value in the table is less than or equal to α.

6. If a *nondirectional* (two-tailed) *alternative hypothesis* has been specified, double the probability value in the table. Reject the null hypothesis if this value is less than or equal to α.

In the example, $n_1 = n_2 = 5$. So first locate the table for $n_L = 5$ in Table J. Next find the column which indicates the value of N_1, which is 5. Finally, locate the row corresponding to $U = 5$. Now, read the probability value corresponding to the row value of 5 and the column value of 5. This value is .075. Since this is the one-tailed probability of U, the null hypothesis cannot be rejected at $\alpha = .05$ for either a one-tailed test ($p = .075$) or a two-tailed test ($p = 2 \times .075 = .15$).

$9 \leqslant n \leqslant 20$ If the larger of the two sample sizes falls in between 9 and 20, the critical values for U can be found in Table K. In order to use Table K, the following steps should be taken:

1. Locate the table corresponding to the level of significance (α)—one- or two-tailed—which you have planned to use.
2. Locate the smaller sample size (N_1) along the rows of the table, and the larger (N_2) along the columns.
3. Read the critical value of U which corresponds to the appropriate row (N_1) and column (N_2).
4. Reject the null hypothesis if U is *less than or equal to* the critical value.

For example, suppose that a researcher set $\alpha = .05$ (two-tailed) and conducted a study in which $n_1 = 8$, $n_2 = 15$, and $U = 12$. On the basis of $U = 12$, should the null hypothesis be rejected? In order to answer this question, $U_{critical}$ must be found from Table K. First, locate the table corresponding to $\alpha = .05$, two-tailed. Next, locate $N_1 = 8$ among the rows of the table and $N_2 = 15$ among the columns. Then, read the critical value of U corresponding to the intersection of the row and column:

$$U_{critical} = 29.$$

Since $U = 12$ is less than $U_{critical} = 29$, the null hypothesis of identical population distributions should be rejected in favor of the alternative hypothesis of a difference in the central tendency of the two populations.

$n > 20$ If the larger sample is greater than 20, the sampling distribution of U is approximately normal.[3] By converting U into a z score, z_U, Table B can be

---

[3]The effect of sample size on the sampling distribution of the U statistic is analogous to that described for the sampling distribution of means in Chapter 12. As a consequence of the central limit theorem, the shape of the sampling distribution approaches normality as sample size increases. Note, however, that this does not imply that the distributions of scores on which the U statistic is computed are necessarily normal.

used to decide whether or not to reject the null hypothesis. First, z_U is defined as

$$z_U = \frac{U - \dfrac{n_1 n_2}{2}}{s_U} \qquad [\mathbf{15\text{-}5}]$$

$$= \frac{U - \dfrac{n_1 n_2}{2}}{\sqrt{\dfrac{n_1 n_2 (n_1 + n_2 + 1)}{12}}} . \qquad [\mathbf{15\text{-}5a}]$$

As an example of how to use and interpret the results of Formula 15-5a, suppose that random samples of 30 "normals" and 30 "neurotics" were drawn from their respective populations in order to test the following hypotheses at $\alpha = .05$:

H_0: The distributions of self-concept scores in the two populations from which the samples were drawn are identical;

H_1: The distributions of self-concept scores in the two populations from which the samples were drawn differ only in their means, with $\mu_{\text{normals}} > \mu_{\text{neurotics}}$.

The original self-concept scores in the sample were converted to ranks and U was found to be 580.[4] With this information, z_U can be found from Formula 15-5a:

$$z_U = \frac{580 - \dfrac{(30)(30)}{2}}{\sqrt{\dfrac{(30)(30)(30 + 30 + 1)}{12}}}$$

---

[4]In detail,

$$U = n_L n_S + \frac{n_L(n_L + 1)}{2} - T_L \qquad [\mathbf{15\text{-}4}]$$

$$= (30)(30) + \frac{30(30 + 1)}{2} - 785$$

$$= 900 + \frac{930}{2} - 785$$

$$= 900 + 465 - 785$$

$$= 580.$$

$$= \frac{580 - 450}{\sqrt{54900/12}}$$

$$= 1.92$$

From Table B, the probability of observing $z_U \geq 1.92$ is .027. Since this value is less than .05 (one-tailed), the null hypothesis can be rejected. The mean self-concept score for "normals" is greater than for "neurotics."

Procedure 15-2 summarizes the steps in conducting the U test with sample sizes of less than 9, between 9 and 20, and greater than 20.

Steps in conducting the Mann-Whitney U test (using hypothetical data) ♦ Procedure 15-2

Operation	Example
1 Specify null and alternative hypotheses and level of significance.	H_0: The distributions of scores in the populations from which the experimental and control groups were drawn are identical.
	H_1: The distributions of scores from which the experimental and control groups were drawn differ in their means, with $\mu_E > \mu_C$.
2 Test assumptions of the U test: **a** Independent and random sampling **b** Distributions of similar shape	For the purposes of this computational example, we will assume that all assumptions have been met. The data are:

	C	E
	10	14
	12	17
	15	17
		20
		24
		25

Operation	Example
3 Arrange scores in order of magnitude, regardless of group. Identify group above each judgment.	C C E C E E E E E 10 12 14 15 17 17 20 24 25
4 Assign a rank of 1 to the lowest score and a rank of N to the highest score. If scores are tied, assign the average rank to each.	Group: C C E C E E E E 1 2 3 4 5.5 5.5 7 8 9
5 Calculate T_L, the larger sum of the ranks.	The sum of ranks in the experimental group is the larger. $$T_L = 3 + 5.5 + 5.5 + 7 + 8 + 9$$ $$= 38$$

(continued on p. 438)

6 Compute U by inserting appropriate values into Formula 15-4 and solving:

$$U = n_L n_S + \frac{n_L(n_L + 1)}{2} - T_L.$$

$$U = (6)(3) + \frac{6(6 + 1)}{2} - 38$$

$$= 1.$$

7 Determine whether or not to reject H_0 by using one of the following procedures, depending on size of n:

a If $n \leqslant 8$, determine probability of U using Table J (see text).

b If $8 < n < 20$, determine the critical value of U using Table K (see text).

c If $n > 20$, convert U to z_U using Formula 15-5:

$$z_U = \frac{U - (n_1 n_2/2)}{s_U}$$

and determine $z_{critical}$ using Table B.

If ties occur within the same group (as in the example data), U is unaffected. If ties occur between groups, U is affected, but for small samples (n < 20), a correction does not exist. For large samples (n ≥ 20), see Hays (1973) or Siegel (1956).

Since $n < 8$, Table J can be used to determine the probability of U. First, locate the table for $n_L = 6$. Then, find the column of the table for $n_S = 3$. Next, identify the row of the table corresponding to $U = 1$. Finally, read the probability value associated with $n_S = 3$ and $U = 1$: .024.

EXAMPLE PROBLEM 2

Using the data presented in Example Problem 1, test whether there are differences between the moral judgments of adults and children when given a short story in which the outcome is positive and the actor's intent is negative, using the Mann-Whitney U Test ($\alpha = .05$, two-tailed). Include the following in your answer:

a. Null and alternative hypotheses
b. Test of assumptions or explanation if not conducting test
c. Table showing conversion of scores to ranks
d. U
e. The probability of U given that H_0 is true.

♦   ♦   ♦   ♦   ♦

Summary This chapter presents statistical tests for comparing differences between two independent groups with respect to their *central tendency*. Procedures for conducting a *t test* to compare differences between the means of two independent groups are presented, and procedures for constructing *confidence intervals* around this difference are discussed. Procedures for conducting the *Mann-Whitney U test*, a nonparametric analog to the *t* test, are also presented.

♦   ♦   ♦   ♦   ♦

central tendency	Mann-Whitney *U* test
confidence intervals	nonparametric test
criterion-group design	normality
homogeneity of variance	pooled estimate
independence of groups	random sampling
independence of treatments	*t* test

♦   ♦   ♦   ♦   ♦

Exercises

1–9 A psychologist was interested in the voluntary production of alpha waves. (Alpha is a brain wave pattern recorded by the EEG, with a frequency of 8–13 cps. It has been associated with the conscious experience of relaxation.) Twelve volunteers were randomly assigned to two groups. The experimental group received training in voluntary alpha production for 15 minutes. A tone was presented to the subject each time his EEG recording showed the alpha pattern. The subject was instructed to focus on the conscious state he experienced at the tone onset. The control group was randomly presented with a tone during the 15-minute session. Then all subjects were asked to produce alpha waves during a 5-minute period. The following hypothetical data were obtained from this study:

	Duration (in minutes) of alpha produced	
Subject	Control group	Experimental group
1	1.0	4.0
2	2.4	2.0
3	2.0	3.4
4	1.5	4.2
5	2.9	3.0
6	.9	2.5
$\overline{X}$	1.78	3.18
s	.79	.85

Using these data, test the difference between means for the two groups using a *t* test.

1. Formulate null and alternative hypotheses (two-tailed).
2. Find $t_{observed}$.
3. Find $t_{critical}$ at .05.
4. State your conclusions.
5. Find the 95-percent confidence interval.
6. Give the design requirements for the *t* test as they relate to this study.

7. Under what conditions would you decide to use the Mann-Whitney U test instead of the t test for two independent groups?

8. Suppose you had reason to believe that the scores were drawn from nonnormal populations. For these data, is the U test appropriate?

9. Explain your answer to Exercise 8.

10–15 Suppose the subjects in Exercises 1–9 were also asked to rate the depth of relaxation they were able to achieve on a scale from 1 to 10 (1 = not relaxed; 10 = very relaxed). The following hypothetical scores were obtained from these ratings:

Subject	Control group	Experimental group
1	1	9
2	3	7
3	2	4
4	5	8
5	3	6
6	1	6

Using these data, test the difference between means for the two groups using a t test.

10. Formulate null and alternative hypotheses (two-tailed).
11. Find the means and standard deviations for the two groups.
12. Find $t_{observed}$.
13. Find $t_{critical}$ at $\alpha = .05$.
14. State your conclusions.
15. Find the 95-percent confidence interval.

16–20 Using the Mann-Whitney U test, test whether there is a difference between groups in the rating of the level of relaxation ($\alpha = .05$).

16. Formulate null and alternative hypotheses (two-tailed).
17. Draw up a table showing conversion of scores to ranks.
18. Find $U_{observed}$.
19. Find $U_{critical}$ for $\alpha = .05$.
20. State your conclusions.
21. Given $n_1 = n_2 = 25$, $U_{observed} = 15$; find z_U.

16 ♦

One-Way Analysis of Variance

THIS CHAPTER presents a statistical method for analyzing data from *two or more* independent samples of subjects. This method is the one-way ANalysis Of VAariance (ANOVA). It is used to test hypotheses about differences between two or more population means. Sample data for the ANOVA may be obtained from true experiments or from criterion-group designs.

As an example of a true experiment with more than two groups, suppose a researcher examined the effectiveness of different counseling practices for helping clients reduce their fear of heights (acrophobia). She might compare the effectiveness of behavior modification and client-centered (Rogerian) therapy with each other and with a control group in which subjects talked informally to a therapist. In this study, then, subjects would be randomly assigned to one of three groups: (1) behavior modification, (2) client-centered therapy, or (3) control. They would receive their treatments and then be flown to Pisa, Italy. There they would be placed at the top of the Leaning Tower and asked to walk to the edge. The dependent variable would be the distance between the subject and the edge after the subject fell to all fours. The differences between the mean distances for each group can be compared using a one-way analysis of variance.

As an example of the application of the one-way ANOVA to data collected using a criterion-group design, suppose a researcher was interested in determining the relationship between socioeconomic status (SES) and achievement. In this study, children ten years of age would be randomly sampled from each of three groups—low, middle, and high SES—and given an achievement test. Differences in the mean achievement of subjects in the three groups could be examined using a one-way ANOVA.

DESCRIPTION OF
THE ANOVA

**Purpose and
Underlying Logic**

Purpose The purpose of the one-way ANOVA is to compare the means of two or more groups[1] in order to decide whether the observed differences between them represent a chance occurrence or a treatment effect. The test is called a **one-way** ANOVA because it compares groups which differ on *one* independent variable with two or more levels. For example, in the study of acrophobia, one variable was systematically manipulated—type of counseling technique. This variable had three levels: behavior modification, client-centered therapy, and a control treatment.

---

[1]In comparing the means of *two* independent groups, either the *t* test described in Chapter 15 or the one-way analysis of variance presented here may be used.

Table 16-1 ♦ Subjects' scores and descriptive statistics from the hypothetical study of counseling methods (Scores represent distances from the edge of the tower.)

	Control	Behavior Modification	Rogerian
	5	1	3
	6	2	3
	8	3	4
$\overline{X}$	6.33	2.00	3.33
s	1.53	1.00	0.57
s^2	2.34	1.00	0.33

In order to get an intuitive idea of how the ANOVA works, this example may be helpful. Based on the hypothetical data for the counseling study shown in Table 16-1, would you conclude that there is a treatment effect? Or did the difference between the three means (6.33, 2.00, 3.33) arise by chance?

In providing an answer to this question, the ANOVA compares the variability of scores within a group—variability due to sampling error alone—with the variability between the group means—variability due to sampling error and possible treatment effects. If the variability between groups is considerably greater than the variability within groups, this is evidence of a treatment effect.

Now consider this approach in more detail. Since all subjects within a group receive the same treatment, the variability of scores within a group is considered error; it represents unsystematic variation. For example, all subjects in the behavior-modification group received this type of therapy. The variation of the subjects' scores about the mean ($\overline{X} = 6.33$) represents error variation. Unsystematic error variation may be due to measurement error, random events which occur during the conduct of the study, or both.[2] Within-group variability, then, introduces "noise" in obtaining an estimate of the population mean (μ) for each group.

The variability, or differences between the group means, is viewed as a combination of error variability *and* variability due to treatment effects. Treatment effects represent systematic variations in the scores which can be attri-

---

[2]Variability between scores within a group also may be due to systematic differences between subjects. For example, subjects may differ in ability. The ANOVA, however, assumes that variability within a group is unsystematic, or not worth accounting for, or both. If there is important, systematic variation within a group, the ANOVA directs us to remove it by adding a second variable—ability in this example—to the design. This would create a two-way design, ability × treatment. In this way, the effect of ability on the scores can be estimated.

buted to the independent variable. These effects represent the "signal" that the researcher is attempting to isolate from the "noise" or error in the data. For example, the differences between the means of the behavior-modification, Rogerian, and control groups—2.00, 3.33, and 6.33, respectively—reflect error variation and possibly treatment effects as well.

These two sources of variability, within-group and between-group variability, can be written symbolically as

$$s^2_{within} = \text{error variability,}$$

$$s^2_{between} = \text{error variability} + \text{treatment effects.}$$

If the variability between group means is much greater than the variability within groups, the ANOVA will lead to a decision to reject the null hypothesis of no difference between population means. That is, there is a treatment effect. If, however, the difference between the sources of variability—within groups and between groups—falls within the range expected from sampling error, the ANOVA will lead to a decision not to reject the null hypothesis. In this case, conclude that there was not a treatment effect and that differences between group means were due to chance.

The decision of whether or not to reject the null hypothesis is never made with certainty; it is a probabilistic decision. As with the statistical tests discussed previously, the basic problem is to determine the probability of observing chance differences between two or more sample means when the null hypothesis is true. In order to do this, a sampling distribution is needed. This theoretical distribution should provide a model of what happens when repeated samples of two or more means are drawn from the same population and compared with one another.

Underlying logic: the F distribution The *F* **distribution**, a mathematical distribution, provides a model of what happens when repeated random samples of two or more means are drawn from the same population and compared with one another. Intuitively, it works like this. Suppose a researcher draws a random sample of three groups, each of size 10, from the same population. This is equivalent to sampling under the null hypothesis of no difference between population means. For each sample, a mean and a variance are calculated. The sample means will probably differ from one another due only to sampling error. (Recall that the standard error of the mean is $\sigma/\sqrt{N}$.) Likewise, the scores within each group will probably differ from each other according to the variation of scores in the population, σ. In this case, then, the variation within groups provides one estimate of **error variability**. And since the sample means are drawn from the same population, so that there is no difference in the population means, the variation between groups provides a second, independent estimate of error variability:

$$s^2_{within} \approx \text{error variability,}$$

$$s^2_{between} \approx \text{error variability} + \left[\text{treatment effect} = 0 \text{ under } H_0\right].$$

Since s^2_{within} and $s^2_{between}$ are independent sample estimates of the sampling error, they will not be exactly the same. The degree to which they fluctuate can be measured by dividing one by the other:

$$F_{observed} = \frac{s^2_{between}}{s^2_{within}}. \qquad [\textbf{16-1}]$$

Now, suppose this sampling procedure under the null hypothesis was carried out many times and each time the ratio of $s^2_{between}$ and s^2_{within} was formed. For each sample, different values of $F_{observed}$ would be obtained. If a frequency distribution were formed by placing values of $F_{observed}$ on the abscissa and the relative frequency on the ordinate, the result would be the sampling distribution of F shown in Figure 16-1. It enables us to state the probability of obtaining $F_{observed}$ at or beyond some value, assuming that the null hypothesis is true. If $F_{observed}$ is quite improbable, the null hypothesis should be rejected, the conclusion being that the population means differ—indicating a treatment effect.

The sampling distribution of F has several important characteristics. First, the mean of the distribution approaches 1 as the sample size increases. Second, the F distribution is unimodal. Third, since the F distribution has a lower limit of zero, the sampling distribution is positively skewed. Extremely high values of $F_{observed}$ are more likely to occur than are extremely low values. Or, put another way, $s^2_{between}$ tends to take on more extreme values than does s^2_{within}. Fourth, the F distribution, like the t distribution, is actually a family of distributions, each member of the family differing from the others according to its degrees of freedom. Unlike the t distribution, the shape of the F distribution depends on *two* different numbers of degrees of freedom. One set of degrees of freedom depends on the number of sample means (groups) being compared, while the

Figure 16-1 ◆ Sampling distribution of $F(df = 2, 27)$

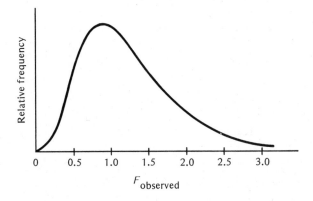

other set depends on the number of subjects in each group. Each is now discussed in turn:

Degrees of freedom between groups (df_B)   In the sampling example, there were three groups. The degrees of freedom for the between-group comparison ($s^2_{between}$) is equal to the number of groups (k) minus 1:

$$df_B = \text{number of groups} - 1$$

$$= k - 1.$$

In the sampling example with three groups, then, $df_B = 3 - 1 = 2$.

Degrees of freedom within groups (df_W)   The second type of degrees of freedom is *within* each group of the design. Again, consider the sampling example with three groups and ten subjects in each group. Once the mean of a group is known along with nine of the scores in the group, the last score is also known. Thus, with n subjects in a group, there are $n - 1$ degrees of freedom within a group. For example, if $n = 10$, $df = 10 - 1 = 9$. The total number of degrees of freedom, within all groups, then, is equal to the sum of the numbers of degrees of freedom within each group across all groups:

$$df_W = df \text{ within group 1} + df \text{ within group 2}$$

$$+ \cdots + df \text{ within group } k.$$

In the example experiment, with three groups and ten subjects in each group, we have $df_W = 9 + 9 + 9 = 27$.

The fifth characteristic of the F distribution is its relation to the t distribution. Since both the F test and the t test can be used to compare two means (i.e., 1 df between two groups), there must be some relation between the F distribution and the t distribution. As expected, for a two-tailed t test, the relationship is

$$F_{(1, df_W)} = t^2_{(df_W)}.$$

This means that the one-way ANOVA and the two-tailed t test can be used interchangeably in comparing the difference between two means.

◆   ◆   ◆   ◆   ◆

Overview of the ANOVA   The ANOVA partitions the total variation in scores into variation within groups (s^2_{within}) and variation between groups ($s^2_{between}$). For example, it partitions the variability of all the scores in Table 16-1 (5, 6, . . . , 4) into variability within groups (e.g., variability within the control group: 3, 3, 4) and variability between groups (6.33, 3.33, 2.00). Then it divides $s^2_{between}$ by s^2_{within} to obtain $F_{observed}$. Finally, $F_{observed}$ can be located in the sampling distribution of F in order to decide whether or not to reject the null hypothesis.

In presenting the results of the ANOVA, typically an ANOVA source table is used (see Table 16-2). In its simplest form, it represents: (1) the two sources of

Table 16-2 ◆ ANOVA source table (data from Table 16-1)

Source of variation	df^a	Mean square (variance)	$F_{observed}$
Between groups	$k - 1 = 2$	14.78	$\dfrac{s^2_{between}}{s^2_{within}} = \dfrac{14.78}{1.22} = 12.11^b$
Within groups (error)	$N - k = 6$	1.22	

[a] k = the number of levels of the independent variable, i.e., the number of groups; N = the total number of subjects in the study.
[b] Significant at $\alpha = .05$; $p < .05$ in this case.

variation in the dependent variable—between groups and within groups; (2) the degrees of freedom for estimating variability from each of the two sources of variation; (3) the numerical values representing the variability due to the between-group and within-group sources of variation;[3] and (4) the value of $F_{observed}$. Table 16-2 presents an ANOVA source table for the data from Table 16-1. Notice that the $F_{observed}$ is 12.11. This means that $s^2_{between}$ is twelve times greater than s^2_{within}.

Finally, the value of $F_{observed}$ can be compared with the value of $F_{critical}$ in order to decide whether or not to reject the null hypothesis of no treatment effects. The $F_{critical}$ value depends on the degrees of freedom for each source of variation and on the level of significance (α). If $F_{observed}$ exceeds $F_{critical}$, conclude that the difference between $s^2_{between}$ and s^2_{within} did not arise from sampling error. Rather, the population means differ due to a treatment effect. Of course, we could be wrong, as indicated by the probability of a Type I error, α. In the counseling study with $\alpha = .05$, $F_{critical}$ with 2 and 6 degrees of freedom can be found in Table E at the end of the book: $F_{critical(.05, 2, 6)} = 5.14$. Since $F_{observed}$ exceeds $F_{critical}$, the null hypothesis of no treatment effects should be rejected. Conclude that the counseling method (or absence of it) influenced how closely subjects would approach the edge of the Leaning Tower of Pisa.[4]

Why not multiple t tests? A frequently asked question is, "What is wrong with doing a series of t tests to compare pairs of means?" In the counseling study, for example, a t test might be used to test the following differences: control (C) versus behavior modification (B), C versus Rogerian (R), and B versus R.

The major problem with this procedure is that the three statistical tests are

[3] Procedures for making these calculations will be presented in later parts of this chapter.

[4] On the basis of this test, we can only conclude that there was a treatment effect. We cannot conclude that the behavior modification alleviated subjects' fears more effectively than the procedures used in the other two groups. In order to define the exact nature of this overall effect, comparisons between means (discussed in later sections of this chapter) must be conducted.

not independent of one another; if B is significantly more effective than R, and R more effective than C, we already know that B is more effective than C.

The problem of the lack of independence with multiple t tests is reflected in the probability of a Type I error. If three *independent* t tests are conducted, each at $\alpha = .05$, the probability of obtaining a significant result from any one of the three statistical tests is *not* .05. The probability is given by

$$p(\text{Type I error}) = 1 - (1 - \alpha)^c, \qquad [16\text{-}2]$$

where c is the number of independent t tests. For the example of three independent t tests,

$$p(\text{Type I error}) = 1 - (1 - .05)^3$$
$$= 1 - (.95)^3$$
$$= 1 - .86$$
$$= .14.$$

When t tests are not independent, a complicated pattern of dependence emerges, and it is extremely difficult to specify the probability of a Type I error.

The moral of the story, then, is that the ANOVA should be used to compare the means of three or more independent groups. For two independent groups, only one t test is needed, so either the t test *or* the ANOVA can be used. Both tests will yield equivalent results, since for a two-tailed t test the following relation holds:

$$F_{(1, df_{\text{w}})} = t^2_{(df_{\text{w}})}.$$

◆ ◆ ◆ ◆ ◆

Hypotheses The analysis of variance is used to test hypotheses about population means. The null and alternative hypotheses are similar to those tested by the t test, with the exception that additional notation is needed to represent population means for two or more groups. The null hypothesis is

$$H_0: \mu_1 = \mu_2 = \cdots = \mu_i = \cdots = \mu_k.$$

In the null hypothesis, μ_i represents the mean of the population for the ith group, and μ_k represents the mean of the population for the kth, or last, group. The null hypothesis in the counseling study, for example, could be written:

$$H_0: \mu_1 = \mu_2 = \mu_3$$

or

$$H_0: \mu_\text{C} = \mu_\text{B} = \mu_\text{R}.$$

The alternative hypothesis is that at least some pair of population means differ from one another. In symbols, we can write that some pair of means, μ_i and $\mu_{i'}$, differ from one another:

$$H_1: \mu_i \neq \mu_{i'} \qquad \text{for some } i \text{ and } i'.$$

The alternative hypothesis, then, states that, of the k means, two or more in the population differ from one another. The alternative hypothesis in the counseling study would be written in the same way:

$$H_1: \mu_i \neq \mu_{i'} \qquad \text{for some } i \text{ and } i'.$$

Directional hypotheses are not tested with the analysis of variance. As noted above, the alternative hypothesis states merely that two or more means differ from one another. To see why the alternative hypothesis in the ANOVA is nondirectional, suppose, for example, you expected the following alternative hypothesis:

$$H_1: \mu_1 < \mu_2 > \mu_3 < \mu_4.$$

What tail are you talking about now?

The results of the analysis of variance, then, enables us to decide whether there was a significant treatment effect. That is, the ANOVA indicates whether any combination of the treatment group means is significantly different from any other combination. However, it does not indicate which particular treatment means are significantly different from each other. If the analysis of variance suggests a significant treatment effect, comparisons between means, discussed in a later section of this chapter, must be conducted in order to determine which means are significantly different from each other.

♦   ♦   ♦   ♦   ♦

In using the sampling distribution of F to test hypotheses about two or more means, three familiar assumptions are made.   **Assumptions**

Independence This assumption states that the score for any particular subject is independent of the scores of all other subjects; that is, it provides a unique piece of information about the treatment effect.

Normality The assumption of normality states that the scores within each treatment population are normally distributed. Put another way, the scores in a particular treatment group are assumed to be sampled from a population of scores which is normal in form.

Homogeneity of variances This last assumption states that the variances of scores in each treatment population are equal (i.e., $\sigma_1^2 = \sigma_2^2 = \cdots = \sigma_i^2 = \cdots = \sigma_k^2$).

These assumptions are the same as those underlying the t test for two independent means. They are discussed in some detail in Chapter 15, as are methods for examining them. The ANOVA is not sensitive to violations of the assumption of normality for an independent variable with a fixed number of levels.

When cell sizes are equal, the ANOVA also is not sensitive to violations of the assumption of homogeneity of variances. In the example study of counseling methods, we need not be concerned with testing either of these assumptions, since the cell sizes were equal in all groups (see Table 16-1). For unequal cell sizes, Winer (1971) presents some methods for statistically testing the assumption of homogeneity of variances. As long as the assumption of normality is tenable, the use of tests for the homogeneity assumption is reasonable.

◆　　◆　　◆　　◆　　◆

Computation of the ANOVA As noted earlier, the ANOVA focuses on a comparison of the variability within groups (variability due to error) and the variability between groups (variability due to error plus treatment effects, if they exist). In arriving at estimates of these two sources of variation in scores, the ANOVA divides the total variability between scores (regardless of group) into variability within groups and variability between groups:

> Total variability
> = Within-group variability + Between-group variability.　　$\left[\textbf{16-3}\right]$

The total variance over all scores, regardless of group, is defined as the square of the deviation of each individual's (p) score from the mean of all the scores, called the **grand mean** ($\overline{X}_G$), divided by $N - 1$:[5]

$$ s^2_{\text{total}} = \frac{\sum\limits_i \sum\limits_p \left(X_{pi} - \overline{X}_G\right)^2}{N - 1}. \qquad \left[\textbf{16-4}\right] $$

(For an explanation of Σ, see the Review of Summation Notation at the end of the book.) In calculating variances such as the total variance, it is cumbersome

---

[5] The total variance over all subjects and groups is analogous to the variance for a single set of scores presented in Chapter 4:

$$ s^2 = \frac{\Sigma(X - \overline{X})^2}{n - 1}. $$

The variance for a single set of scores is defined as the sum of squared deviations of scores from the mean of the group divided by the appropriate degrees of freedom. Notice that the total variance is defined as the sum over persons and groups (hence the double summation signs) of the squared deviations of scores from the grand mean—the mean over all persons and groups—divided by the appropriate degrees of freedom.

to worry about dividing by $N - 1$ until all other calculations are carried out. So, in order to get rid of the $N - 1$ for the time being, we multiply it into both sides of the equation to obtain

$$(N - 1)s_{total}^2 = \sum_i \sum_p \left(X_{pi} - \bar{X}_G \right)^2. \qquad [16\text{-}4a]$$

Formula 16-4a is the formula for the sum of squared deviations of scores from the grand mean. It is most often called the **sum of squares total**:

$$\text{Sum of squares total} = SS_T = \sum_i \sum_p \left(X_{pi} - \bar{X}_G \right)^2. \qquad [16\text{-}4b]$$

(This formula is not generally used in computation; an equivalent computational formula is given in Procedure 16-1.) Likewise, the **sum of squares within groups** (SS_W) can be calculated by squaring the difference between each score in a group and the group mean, and then summing these squared differences over groups:

$$\text{Sum of squares within} = SS_W = \sum_i \sum_p \left(X_{pi} - \bar{X}_i \right)^2. \qquad [16\text{-}5]$$

The **sum of squares between groups** (SS_B) can be found by squaring the difference between each group mean and the grand mean and then summing these squared differences:

$$\text{Sum of squares between} = SS_B = \sum_i n_i \left(\bar{X}_i - \bar{X}_G \right)^2. \qquad [16\text{-}6]$$

In this last formula, n_i appears because we are, in effect, counting the between-group variability once for every subject in a group. Since these are deviation-score formulas for the sums of squares and raw-score formulas are commonly used in calculating the sums of squares, numerical examples are not given.

All sums of squares, then, are variances that have not yet been divided by their respective degrees of freedom. In calculating the ANOVA, we work with sums of squares, and after the major work in calculation is completed, the sums of squares are divided by their appropriate degrees of freedom to get estimates of the within- and between-group variability. These estimates are called **mean**

squares. Note that in Table 16-2 the sums of squares were omitted. But the degrees of freedom and the mean squares (variances) were included.

The formulas for computing the sums of squares are given in Procedure 16-1 and summarized in Table 16-3. They are raw-score formulas. They are

Procedure 16-1 ◆ Steps in calculating sums of squares for the one-way ANOVA[a]

Operation	Example
1 Set up data summary table.	

	Treatment level		
	Control T_1	Behavior modification T_2	Rogerian T_3
	5	1	3
	6	2	3
	8	3	4
$\sum_{p=1}^{n} X_{pi} =$	19	6	10

2 Make the following *preliminary computations*:

a Sum the scores in each group

$$\left[\sum_{p=1}^{n} X_{pi} \right].$$

See table above.

b Square the sum of the scores in each group (step 2a) and divide each sum by the number of subjects (n) in the group

$$\left[\frac{\left(\sum_{p=1}^{n} X_{pi} \right)^2}{n_i} \right].$$

$$\frac{\left(\sum_{p=1}^{n} X_{p1} \right)^2}{n_1} = \frac{19^2}{3} = 120.33,$$

$$\frac{\left(\sum_{p=1}^{n} X_{p2} \right)^2}{n_2} = \frac{6^2}{3} = 12,$$

$$\frac{\left(\sum_{p=1}^{n} X_{p3} \right)^2}{n_3} = \frac{10^2}{3} = 33.33.$$

c Sum all scores in the summary table, regardless of group, to obtain a total sum

$$\left[\sum_{1}^{N} X_p \right].$$

$$\sum_{1}^{N} X_p = 5 + 6 + 8 + 1 + 2 + 3 + 3 + 3 + 4$$

$$= 35.$$

3 Compute the following *intermediate quantities*. Note that these are labeled with symbols in braces, { }, to simplify matters later on.

a Sum the values computed in step 2b to obtain

$$\{1\} = \left[\dfrac{\displaystyle\sum_{i=1}^{k} \left(\displaystyle\sum_{p=1}^{n} X_{pi} \right)^2}{n_i} \right].$$

$$\{1\} = \sum_{i=1}^{k} \dfrac{\left(\displaystyle\sum_{p=1}^{n} X_{pi} \right)^2}{n_i} = 120.33 + 12 + 33.33$$

$$= 165.66.$$

b Square the total sum (step 2c) and divide by N to obtain

$$\{2\} = \dfrac{\left(\displaystyle\sum_{p=1}^{N} X_p \right)^2}{N}.$$

$$\{2\} = \dfrac{\left(\displaystyle\sum_{p=1}^{N} X_p \right)^2}{N} = \dfrac{35^2}{9}$$

$$= 136.11.$$

c Square each score in the summary table and sum these squared scores to obtain

$$\{3\} = \sum_{p=1}^{N} X_p^2.$$

$$\{3\} = \sum_{p=1}^{N} X_p^2 = (5)^2 + (6)^2 + \cdots + (4)^2$$

$$= 173.$$

4 Compute the sums of squares using the following computational formulas:

a Sum of squares total,

$$SS_T = \sum_{p=1}^{N} X_p^2 - \dfrac{\left(\displaystyle\sum_{p=1}^{N} X_p \right)^2}{N} \quad \text{[16-7]}$$

$$= \{3\} - \{2\}.$$

$$SS_T = \{3\} - \{2\}$$
$$= 173 - 136.11$$
$$= 36.89.$$

b Sum of squares between groups,

$$SS_B = \sum_{i=1}^{k} \dfrac{\left(\displaystyle\sum_{p=1}^{n} X_{pi} \right)^2}{n_i} - \dfrac{\left(\displaystyle\sum_{p=1}^{N} X_p \right)^2}{N} \quad \text{[16-8]}$$

$$= \{1\} - \{2\}.$$

$$SS_B = \{1\} - \{2\}$$
$$= 165.66 - 136.11$$
$$= 29.55.$$

c Sum of squares within groups,

$$SS_W = \sum_{p=1}^{N} X_p^2 - \sum_{i=1}^{k} \dfrac{\left(\displaystyle\sum_{p=1}^{n} X_{pi} \right)^2}{n_i} \quad \text{[16-9]}$$

$$= \{3\} - \{1\}.$$

$$SS_W = \{3\} - \{1\}$$
$$= 173 - 165.66$$
$$= 7.34.$$

---

[a]N = the total number of subjects; n_i = the number of subjects in group i; $\sum_1^N X_p$ = the sum of scores over all persons in the study = $\sum_i \sum_p X_{pi}$. All other notation is standard; see the Review of Summation Notation at the end of the book.

equivalent to the deviation-score formulas, but are easier to use in computations.[6] As a way of presenting the computations in the ANOVA, the data from the counseling study will be used. These data are reproduced in Procedure 16-1, along with instructions on how to display the data and to calculate the sums of squares total, between, and within. In order to simplify these calculations, certain preliminary computations and intermediate quantities are used in computing the sums of squares.

Once the sums of squares have been calculated, they are entered in the summary table in which the final set of computations is carried out to obtain $F_{observed}$. Table 16-4 is an ANOVA summary table for the analysis of the data from the counseling study (see Procedure 16-1). Two sources of variation in scores are shown in the first column—between groups and within groups. The third row, labeled "Total," serves here as a computational check, since $SS_T = SS_B + SS_W$ (see Formula 16-3).

The second column of Table 16-4 gives the values of the sums of squares. These values are taken from the computations shown in Procedure 16-1. [Notice that the value of the total sum of squares (36.89) equals the sum of SS_B and SS_W (29.55 + 7.34).]

The third column of Table 16-4 gives the values of between-group and within-group degrees of freedom using formulas from Table 16-3. The degrees

---

[6]As an example of the equivalence of the deviation-score and raw-score formulas, consider the equivalence of these formulas for the total sum of squares. The deviation-score formula is

$$SS_T = \sum_i \sum_p (X_{pi} - \bar{X}_G)^2 \qquad \text{[16-4b]}$$

$$= \sum_i \sum_p (X_{pi}^2 - 2X_{pi}\bar{X}_G + \bar{X}_G^2) \qquad \text{Squaring}$$

$$= \sum_i \sum_p X_{pi}^2 - 2\bar{X}_G \sum_i \sum_p X_{pi} + \sum_i \sum_p \bar{X}_G^2 \qquad \begin{array}{l}\text{Distributing summation}\\\text{and rule for summation}\\\text{of a constant}\end{array}$$

$$= \sum_i \sum_p X_{pi}^2 - 2\bar{X}_G(N\bar{X}_G) + N\bar{X}_G^2 \qquad \bar{X} = \frac{\sum X}{N}\,;\ \sum X = N\bar{X}$$

$$= \sum_i \sum_p X_{pi}^2 - 2N\bar{X}_G^2 + N\bar{X}_G^2 \qquad \text{Combining terms}$$

$$= \sum_i \sum_p X_{pi}^2 - N\bar{X}_G^2 \qquad \text{Combining terms}$$

$$= \sum_i \sum_p X_{pi}^2 - N\frac{\left(\sum_i \sum_p X_{pi}\right)^2}{N^2} \qquad N\bar{X}_G = \sum_i \sum_p X_{pi}\,;\ \text{thus,}$$

$$= \sum_i \sum_p X_{pi}^2 \frac{-\left(\sum_i \sum_p X_{pi}\right)^2}{N}\,. \qquad \bar{X}_G = \frac{\sum_i \sum_p X_{pi}}{N}\,.$$

Thus we have Formula 16-7 (in Procedure 16-1), which is the raw-score formula. The raw-score formulas corresponding to the deviation-score formulas for SS_B and SS_W (Formulas 16-5 and 16-6) are given in Table 16-3 and Procedure 16-1.

Table 16-3 ◆ Computational formulas for the one-way ANOVA[a]

Source of variation	Sum-of-squares formula	df formula	Mean-square formula	F
Between groups	$SS_B = \sum\limits_{i=1}^{k} \dfrac{\left(\sum\limits_{p=1}^{n} X_{pi} \right)^2}{n_i} - \dfrac{\left(\sum\limits_{p=1}^{N} X_p \right)^2}{N}$ [16-8]	$df_B = k - 1$	$\dfrac{SS_B}{df_B}$	$\dfrac{MS_B}{MS_W}$
Within groups	$SS_W = \sum\limits_{p=1}^{N} (X_p)^2 - \sum\limits_{i=1}^{k} \dfrac{\left(\sum\limits_{p=1}^{n} X_{pi} \right)^2}{n_i}$ [16-9]	$df_W = N - k$	$\dfrac{SS_W}{df_W}$	
Total	$SS_T = \sum\limits_{p=1}^{N} (X_p)^2 - \dfrac{\left(\sum\limits_{p=1}^{N} X_p \right)^2}{N}$ [16-7]	$df_T = N - 1$		

[a]See Procedure 16-1.

of freedom for estimating the between-group variance is the number of groups (k) minus 1: $df_B = 3 - 1 = 2$. These $k - 1$ degrees of freedom reflect the fact that the variability between groups is estimated from the variability of the k group means about the grand mean. (One degree of freedom is lost by calculating and thus knowing $\bar{X}_G$.)

The within-group degrees of freedom are simply $N - k$: $df_W = 9 - 3 = 6$. The formula for df_W follows from this reasoning: The within-group variance is simply the average of the variances within each group. Since the variances within each group are assumed to be equal (this is the assumption of homogeneity of variance), this average represents a pooled estimate of the common population variance. Each estimate of the population variance is based on $n - 1$ degrees of freedom. If there are k groups, there are k estimates of the common population variance, each based on $n - 1$ degrees of freedom. So $df_W = (n_1 - 1) + (n_2 - 1) + \cdots + (n_k - 1) = N - k$.

The fourth column in Table 16-4, labeled "Mean square," gives the result of dividing each sum of squares by its respective degrees of freedom. The mean squares provide measures of the variability between and within groups. Under the null hypothesis of no difference between means, MS_B and MS_W provide two independent estimates of error variance. Under the alternative hypothesis of a difference between means,

$$MS_B = \frac{\text{variability}}{\text{due to error}} + \frac{\text{variability}}{\text{due to treatment effects}}$$

(Note: Mean squares are not additive, so there is no entry in the Total row of the table.)

Table 16-4 ♦ Analysis of variance summary table (data from Table 16-1)

Source of variation	Sum of squares[a] SS	df	Mean square MS	F
Between groups	29.55	$3 - 1 = 2$	$29.55/2 =$ 14.78	$14.78/1.22 =$ 12.11[b]
Within groups	7.34	$9 - 3 = 6$	$7.34/6 =$ 1.22	
Total	36.89	$9 - 1 = 8$		

[a]From Procedure 16-1.
[b]$p < .05$.

Finally, the last column of Table 16-3 gives the formula for $F_{observed}$:

$$F_{observed} = \frac{MS_B}{MS_W}. \qquad [16\text{-}10]$$

From Table 16-4, this value is 12.11 for the data from the counseling study.

♦   ♦   ♦   ♦   ♦

Decision Rules for Rejecting the Null Hypothesis   In order to determine whether to reject the null hypothesis and conclude that there is a significant treatment effect, $F_{observed}$ must be compared with $F_{critical}$ using df_B, df_W, and α. For $\alpha = .05$, $F_{critical}$ can be found in Table E:

$$F_{critical(.05, 2, 6)} = 5.14.$$

Table 16-5 ♦ Hypothetical data from the study on study time and learning

Person	Study time (minutes)			
	10	20	45	75
1	7	9	20	10
2	10	14	18	11
3	6	12	19	13
4	7	11	16	12
5	8	13	18	11
$\bar{X}$	7.6	11.8	18.2	11.4
s	1.52	1.92	1.48	1.14
s^2	2.30	3.70	2.20	1.30

Since $F_{observed}$ exceeds $F_{critical}$, the null hypothesis should be rejected. This decision is noted in Table 16-4 (footnote b). We can conclude that the counseling method produced a significant treatment effect. The observed differences between the three means are not likely to have arisen by chance.

In a study of the relationship between study time and learning, high-school students were randomly assigned to one of four study time conditions: 10, 20, 45, 75 minutes. Students were given written material on international relations to study and were given an achievement test at the end of the study session. Based on the data shown in Table 16-5, test whether there was a significant treatment effect at $\alpha = .05$. Include in your answer:

EXAMPLE PROBLEM 1

a. Null and alternative hypotheses
b. Tests of assumptions or explanation for not doing so
c. Computation of sums of squares (see Procedure 16-1 for format)
d. ANOVA summary table (see Table 16-3 for format)
e. $F_{critical}$
f. Conclusions

The overall F test with the one-way ANOVA indicates whether or not the observed differences between treatment means were likely to arise by chance. However, the F test does not give information about the *strength* of the treatment effect. One measure of the strength of the treatment effect is the proportion of the total variability in a set of scores that can be accounted for by the levels of the independent variable. This proportion of variance is analogous to the proportion of variance discussed in the chapter on correlation (Chapter 7). Recall that r_{XY}^2 could be interpreted as the proportion of variance in Y that can be accounted for by knowing X. In the case of the ANOVA, the measure of the strength of a treatment effect indicates how much variance in scores can be accounted for by knowing about differences in treatment groups. This statistic is called **omega square** (ω^2).[7]

STRENGTH OF
ASSOCIATION

Omega square can be used with data from the study of counseling methods to obtain a measure of the **strength of association** between counseling method (the independent variable) and distance from the edge of the Tower of Pisa (the dependent variable). The formula for omega square is

$$\omega^2 = \frac{SS_B - (k-1)\, MS_W}{SS_T + MS_W}. \qquad [\textbf{16-11}]$$

[7]This statistic has a number of limitations. See Glass and Hakstian (1969).

Operation	Example
1 Use Formula 16-11: $$\omega^2 = \frac{SS_B - (k-1)MS_W}{SS_T + MS_W}.$$	$SS_B = 29.55,$ $MS_W = 1.22,$ $SS_T = 36.89.$
2 Insert appropriate values from ANOVA source table into Formula 16-11 and solve.	$\omega^2 = \dfrac{29.55 - (3-1)(1.22)}{36.89 + 1.22}$ $= \dfrac{27.11}{38.11}$ $= 0.71.$ 71% of the variance in the dependent variable is accounted for by the differences in counseling treatments.

Procedure 16-2 ◆ Steps in computing omega square (data from Table 16-4)

The steps in calculating ω^2 are summarized in Procedure 16-2 using the counseling study as an example. Note that $\omega^2 = .71$. This suggests that variations in the independent variable (counseling method) account for a large portion—71 percent—of the variability of the distance measure. In other words, there is a strong relationship between counseling method and reduction of fear of heights as measured by the distance from the edge of the tower.

EXAMPLE PROBLEM 2

Compute the strength of association for the study-time experiment described in Example Problem 1. Include in your answer:

a. Computation
b. Interpretation.

METHODS FOR COMPARING MEANS IN THE ANALYSIS OF VARIANCE

To summarize briefly, the overall F test in the analysis of variance indicates whether or not there are significant differences between means. Omega square (ω^2) indicates the strength of the treatment effect. However, when the study includes *more than two groups*, neither statistic indicates which means differ statistically from the others. For example, in the counseling study, the overall F indicated a significant effect for the method. Several questions still remain. For example, is the mean of the behavior modification (B) group significantly less than the mean of the Rogerian (R) group? Or is the mean of the Rogerian group significantly less than the mean of the control (C) group? Does the mean

458

of the B group differ from the average of the other two means (R and C)? In order to determine just where the differences between means lie, additional statistical tests are needed.

In conducting tests for differences between means, a number of options are available. The first decision is made prior to conducting the study. If there is prior theory or empirical evidence to suggest hypotheses about differences between means, **planned (a priori) comparisons** may be conducted. In this case, the ANOVA and planned comparisons between means are used for theory testing. If the study is exploratory in nature, all possible differences between means can be examined after the study has been conducted using **post hoc comparisons**. In this case, the ANOVA and post hoc comparisons between means are used to analyze data for the purpose of theory building. As might be expected, planned comparisons are more powerful than the data-snooping permitted by post hoc comparisons. There is always a price for examining all possible combinations of means after the study has been conducted.

◆　　◆　　◆　　◆　　◆

In making planned comparisons, hypotheses about differences between means must be set forth before the study is conducted. In doing so, the researcher should have strong theoretical reasons, strong empirical evidence, or preferably both. Once the hypotheses have been set forth, comparisons between means for each hypothesis can be identified. These comparisons are written as a set of weighted means with the sum of the weights equal to zero (see below). Finally, for the statistical test presented here, each comparison must be independent of every other comparison. These comparisons are often referred to as "orthogonal contrasts" because they contain independent or nonoverlapping pieces of information. Each of these points is discussed in detail below.

Planned Comparisons

Comparisons planned prior to the conduct of the study　Comparisons between the k treatment means must be planned prior to the conduct of the study. There should be a strong theoretical basis, empirical basis, or both, underlying the comparisons. As an example, consider the counseling study. Contrary to popular belief, the results of prior research suggest that psychotherapy is more effective than control treatments (Smith & Glass, 1977). However, the results of research are equivocal with respect to whether behavior modification or Rogerian therapy is more effective with phobias like acrophobia. (Some evidence suggests the former is more effective, but the research has methodological problems.) Thus, on the basis of theory and prior research, it seems safe to hypothesize that subjects in the control group will not come as close to the edge of the Pisa tower as will subjects in the two counseling groups. The mean of the control group, then, will be greater than the average of the means for the two therapy groups:

$$H_1: \mu_C > \frac{\mu_B + \mu_R}{2}.$$

Since the research is equivocal with respect to whether the behavior modification or Rogerian technique will decrease fear more, a second alternative hypothesis might specify that a difference is expected between the two groups but the direction cannot be specified:

$$H_2: \mu_B \neq \mu_R.$$

(See step 1 of Procedure 16-3.)

The sum of weighted means in the comparison equals zero A planned comparison between means may be written as a set of weighted means where the sum of the weights is equal to zero. A comparison, then, is defined formally as the weighted sum of k population means. If w_i represents the weight (a number) assigned to the mean of treatment i, a comparison can be defined formally as

$$C = w_1\mu_1 + w_2\mu_2 + \cdots + w_k\mu_k$$
$$= \sum_1^k w_i\mu_i. \qquad [16\text{-}12]$$

A **sample comparison** is defined in exactly the same way as the population comparison, except that sample means are used:

$$\hat{C} = w_1\overline{X}_1 + w_2\overline{X}_2 + \cdots + w_k\overline{X}_k$$
$$= \sum_1^k w_i\overline{X}_i. \qquad [16\text{-}12a]$$

Since this sample comparison is used to estimate the population comparison of interest, a caret (^) is placed over the C.

The weights assigned to each mean may consist of any set of real numbers not all equal to zero. They are determined by the comparison the researcher wishes to make. For example, two alternative hypotheses were identified for the counseling study:

$$H_1: \mu_C > \frac{\mu_B + \mu_R}{2}$$

and

$$H_2: \mu_B \neq \mu_R.$$

These hypotheses can be translated into comparisons. H_2 specifies a comparison between the means of the behavior modification and the Rogerian groups. A set of k weights, then, should be constructed to compare $\overline{X}_B$ with $\overline{X}_R$ and to ignore $\overline{X}_C$ for the purposes of this comparison. This can be accomplished by assigning the following set of weights to $\bar{X}_C$, $\bar{X}_B$, and $\bar{X}_R$ respectively: 0, $+1$, and -1. More formally, this comparison can be defined as the weighted sum of $k = 3$ means:

$$\hat{C}_2 = (0)\bar{X}_C + (1)\bar{X}_B + (-1)\bar{X}_R$$

$$= \bar{X}_B - \bar{X}_R.$$

Notice that by using zero, the control group can be ignored for this comparison. Finally, there is nothing magic about this set of weights. A different set of weights could have been assigned (e.g., 0, $+2$, -2; or 0, -2, $+2$; or 0, $+\frac{1}{2}$, $-\frac{1}{2}$; or 0, $-\frac{1}{2}$, $+\frac{1}{2}$).

The procedure for assigning a set of weights to the first alternative hypothesis is somewhat more complex:

$$H_1\colon \mu_C > \frac{\mu_B + \mu_R}{2}.$$

The trick is to recognize that this hypothesis identifies a comparison between the mean for the control group against the average of the means for the B and R groups. This can be accomplished by the following sets of weights: $+1$, $-\frac{1}{2}$, $-\frac{1}{2}$, or $+2$, -1, -1:

$$\hat{C}_1 = (1)\bar{X}_C + \left(-\tfrac{1}{2}\right)\bar{X}_B + \left(-\tfrac{1}{2}\right)\bar{X}_R = \bar{X}_C - \frac{\bar{X}_B + \bar{X}_R}{2};$$

or

$$\hat{C}_1 = (2)\bar{X}_C + (-1)\bar{X}_B + (-1)\bar{X}_R = 2\bar{X}_C - \left(\bar{X}_B + \bar{X}_R\right).$$

In writing weights for planned comparison, then, any set of real numbers, not all equal to zero, can be used. *The only restriction is that the sum of the weights equals zero.* More formally, the requirement is

$$\boxed{\begin{array}{c} w_1 + w_2 + \cdots + w_k = 0; \\[1mm] \sum\limits_{1}^{k} w_i = 0. \qquad [\,16\text{-}13\,] \end{array}}$$

In order to check this requirement, the algebraic sum of the weights can be obtained. For the weights representing the comparison suggested by H_1, the algebraic sum of the weights is:

$$+1 - \tfrac{1}{2} - \tfrac{1}{2} = 0$$

or

$$2 - 1 - 1 = 0.$$

This set of weights satisfies the requirement of summing to zero, as do all sets of weights given in this section. (See step 2 in Procedure 16-3.)

Independence of pairs of comparisons   The third requirement is that each comparison is independent of every other comparison.[8] The independence of a set of comparisons depends only on the set of weights assigned to each mean and in no way depends on the values of the means observed. Assuming equal cell sizes, *two comparisons are independent if the sum of the cross-products of their corresponding weights is zero.*[9] If w_{1i} represents the weight assigned to the mean from treatment i in the first comparison and w_{2i} the weight assigned to the mean from treatment i in the second comparison, the requirement for independence can be written formally as

$$w_{11}w_{21} + w_{12}w_{22} + \cdots + w_{1k}w_{2k} = 0;$$
$$\sum_1^k w_{1i}w_{2i} = 0. \qquad [\textbf{16-14}]$$

(See step 5 of Procedure 16-3 for verifying the independence of comparisons.)

For k treatment groups, $k - 1$ independent comparisons can be defined. Thus, in any study, one set of $k - 1$ planned orthogonal comparisons may be conducted. However, for k means, it is possible to write more than one set of $k - 1$ comparisons.

In the counseling study with $k = 3$ groups, $3 - 1 = 2$ independent comparisons can be defined. Once the two comparisons have been identified, a third comparison cannot be specified which will be independent—that is, it will not satisfy the requirement that the sum of the cross-products of the weights equals

---

[8]Planned comparisons need not be independent. However, the dependent case is not presented in this text. For a discussion of it, see Kirk (1968, pp. 79–81).

[9]The assumption of equal sample sizes is not a requirement for planned comparisons. But by making this assumption, the identification of independent comparisons is simplified. If sample sizes are unequal, the requirement in Formula 16-14,

$$\sum_1^k w_{1i}w_{2i} = 0,$$

can be modified as follows:

$$\sum_1^k \frac{w_{1i}w_{2i}}{n_i} = 0. \qquad [16\text{-}14a]$$

Here the cross-product of the comparison weights for each sample is weighed inversely by n_i before the sum is taken. If this weighed sum of weights equals zero, the comparisons may be regarded as independent.

zero. For example, suppose that prior empirical evidence suggested a third comparison—the control group versus the Rogerian group:

$$\hat{C}_3 = (1)\overline{X}_C + (0)\overline{X}_B + (-1)\overline{X}_R.$$

This comparison will not be independent of $\hat{C}_1$ or $\hat{C}_2$ (see step 6 of Procedure 16-3). Further, no set of weights can be identified such that $\hat{C}_3$ will be independent of both $\hat{C}_1$ and $\hat{C}_2$.

Steps in specifying weights for planned comparisons (data from Table 16-1) ♦ Procedure 16-3

Operation	Example
1 Identify hypotheses based on prior theory, research, or both. *Strong evidence must exist for these predictions.*	$H_1: \mu_C > \dfrac{\mu_B + \mu_R}{2},$ $H_2: \mu_B \neq \mu_R.$

2 Assign weights to means so that the comparisons identified by the hypotheses in step 1 are specified. *The sum of the weights for each comparison must equal zero:*

$$\boxed{\sum_{1}^{k} w_i = 0. \quad [16\text{-}13]}$$

	$\overline{X}_C = 6.33$	$\overline{X}_B = 2.00$	$\overline{X}_R = 3.33$
$\hat{C}_1 \, [\overline{X}_C \text{ vs. } (\overline{X}_B + \overline{X}_R)/2]$	1	$-\frac{1}{2}$	$-\frac{1}{2}$
$\hat{C}_2 \, [\overline{X}_B \text{ vs. } \overline{X}_R]$	0	$+1$	-1

3 Add the weights for each comparison in order to verify the accuracy of step 2.

$$\hat{C}_1: (+1) + \left(-\tfrac{1}{2}\right) + \left(-\tfrac{1}{2}\right) = 0,$$
$$\hat{C}_2: 0 + (+1) + (-1) = 0.$$

4 Write the comparisons in the form of a weighted sum of means:

$$\boxed{\hat{C} = \sum_{1}^{k} w_i \overline{X}_i. \quad [16\text{-}12]}$$

$$\hat{C}_1 = (+1)\overline{X}_C + \left(-\tfrac{1}{2}\right)\overline{X}_B + \left(-\tfrac{1}{2}\right)\overline{X}_R,$$
$$\hat{C}_2 = (0)\overline{X}_C + (+1)\overline{X}_B + (-1)\overline{X}_R.$$

5 For each pair of comparisons, cross-multiply the weights corresponding to each mean, using Formula 16-14:

$$\boxed{\sum_{1}^{k} w_{1i} w_{2i} = 0.}$$

For each pair of comparisons, the sum of the cross-products of corresponding weights must equal zero.

$\hat{C}_1$ vs. $\hat{C}_2$:
$$(+1)(0) + (-\tfrac{1}{2})(+1) + (-\tfrac{1}{2})(-1) = 0.$$

(continued on p. 464)

6 Only $k - 1$ independent comparisons may be defined.

Since $k = 3$, only 2 independent comparisons can be specified. Suppose a third hypothesis was specified:

$$H_3: \bar{X}_C \neq \bar{X}_R.$$

Then

$$\hat{C}_3 = (1)\bar{X}_C + (0)\bar{X}_B + (-1)\bar{X}_R.$$

$\hat{C}_3$ is not independent of $\hat{C}_1$ or $\hat{C}_2$:

$\hat{C}_1$ vs. $\hat{C}_3$:
$$(1)(1) + \left(-\tfrac{1}{2}\right)(0) + \left(-\tfrac{1}{2}\right)(-1) \neq 0,$$

$\hat{C}_2$ vs. $\hat{C}_3$:
$$(0)(1) + (+1)(0) + (-1)(-1) \neq 0.$$

Computation of the value of a comparison   Once the comparison between means has been written, the value of the comparison ($\hat{C}$) can be found by simply inserting the appropriate values and carrying out the arithmetic operations. For example,

$$\hat{C}_1 = (1)\bar{X}_C + \left(-\tfrac{1}{2}\right)\bar{X}_B + \left(-\tfrac{1}{2}\right)\bar{X}_R.$$

Procedure 16-4 ◆ Steps in computing a comparison ($\hat{C}$) between means (data from Table 16-1)

Operation	Example
1 Begin with a comparison written in the form of a weighted sum of means: $$\hat{C} = \sum_{1}^{k} w_i \bar{X}_i \qquad \text{[16-12a]}$$ (See step 4 of Procedure 16-3.)	$\hat{C}_1 = (+1)\bar{X}_C + \left(-\tfrac{1}{2}\right)\bar{X}_B + \left(-\tfrac{1}{2}\right)\bar{X}_R$ $\hat{C}_2 = (0)\bar{X}_C + (+1)\bar{X}_B + (-1)\bar{X}_R$
2 Insert appropriate values for each mean and solve.	$\hat{C}_1 = (+1)(6.33) + \left(-\tfrac{1}{2}\right)(2) + \left(-\tfrac{1}{2}\right)(3.33)$ $\quad = 6.33 - 1 - 1.67$ $\quad = 3.66,$ $\hat{C}_2 = (0)(6.33) + (+1)(2) + (-1)(3.33)$ $\quad = 0 + 2 - 3.33$ $\quad = -1.33.$

The values of $\bar{X}_C$, $\bar{X}_B$, and $\bar{X}_R$ can be obtained from Table 16-1 and inserted into the comparisons (see Procedure 16-4):

$$\hat{C}_1 = (1)(6.33) + \left(-\tfrac{1}{2}\right)(2) + \left(-\tfrac{1}{2}\right)(3.33)$$
$$= 6.33 - 1 - 1.67$$
$$= 3.66.$$

The difference between the mean of the control group and the average of the means of the other two groups is 3.66.

Notice that the value of the contrast will depend on the particular set of weights chosen. For example, suppose the following weights were used for contrast 1: 2, -1, -1. Then

$$\hat{C}_1 = (2)\bar{X}_C + (-1)\bar{X}_B + (-1)\bar{X}_R$$
$$= (2)6.33 + (-1)(2) + (-1)(3.33)$$
$$= 12.66 - 2 - 3.33$$
$$= 7.33.$$

In this case, the value 7.33 represents the difference between two times the mean of the control group and the sum of the two means for the counseling groups. While differences in weights influence the magnitude of $\hat{C}$, they are taken into account in conducting a statistical test. This is the topic of the next section.

Statistical test for planned comparisons   For each planned orthogonal comparison, the t distribution can be used to determine whether or not the differences between two means or between combinations of means arose by chance. For each comparison, the null and alternative hypotheses are: H_0: $C = 0$ and H_1: $C \neq 0$ for a nondirectional alternative hypothesis; or H_1: $C > 0$ or H_1: $C < 0$ for directional alternative hypotheses.

In addition, α is also set before the data are collected. Typically, each t test is performed at $\alpha = .05$ or $\alpha = .01$.

In order to test each comparison statistically, the following general formula for a t test is used to obtain the *observed value* of t:

$$t_{observed} = \frac{\hat{C}}{\sqrt{MS_W\left(\dfrac{w_1^2}{n_1} + \dfrac{w_2^2}{n_2} + \cdots + \dfrac{w_k^2}{n_k}\right)}}, \qquad [\mathbf{16\text{-}15}]$$

where $\hat{C}$ = value of the contrast,
$\quad MS_W$ = mean square within groups (error) from the ANOVA table,
$\quad k$ = number of groups.

If the number of subjects in each of the groups is the same (i.e., $n_1 = n_2 = \cdots = n_k$), then Formula 16-15 can be simplified as follows:

$$t_{observed} = \frac{\hat{C}}{\sqrt{\dfrac{MS_W}{n}(w_1^2 + w_2^2 + \cdots + w_k^2)}}. \qquad [16\text{-}15a]$$

Finally, if the comparison is between only two of the k means with equal cell size, the formula can be simplified even further:

$$t_{observed} = \frac{\hat{C}}{\sqrt{\dfrac{2\,MS_W}{n}}}. \qquad [16\text{-}15b]$$

This is equivalent to the formula given for the t test in Chapter 15 when $n_1 = n_2$. Notice that $\hat{C}$ amounts to $\overline{X}_1 - \overline{X}_2$ and the denominator involves the pooled sample variance divided by n:

$$\sqrt{\frac{2s_{pooled}^2}{n}} = \sqrt{\frac{s_1^2 + s_2^2}{n}}.$$

The critical value of t can be found in Table C. The number of degrees of

Procedure 16-5 ♦ Steps in conducting a statistical test of a planned comparison (data from hypothetical counseling study)

Operation	Example
1 Specify null and alternative hypotheses for each contrast.	For contrast 1: H_0: $C_1 = 0$, H_1: $C_1 > 0$. For contrast 2: H_0: $C_2 = 0$, H_2: $C_2 \neq 0$.
2 Set α level for each comparison.	$\alpha = .05$.

3 Compute $t_{obs.}$ by inserting the appropriate values into one of the following formulas and solving:

a If the number of subjects in each group is unequal, use Formula 16-15:

$$t_{obs} = \frac{\hat{C}}{\sqrt{MS_W\left(\dfrac{w_1^2}{n_1} + \dfrac{w_2^2}{n_2} + \cdots + \dfrac{w_k^2}{n_k}\right)}},$$

where $\hat{C}$ = value of the contrast;
MS_W = mean square within-groups (error) from the ANOVA table;
k = number of groups.

b If the number of subjects in each group is equal, and the comparison is between two or more means, use Formula 16-15a:

$$t_{obs} = \frac{\hat{C}}{\sqrt{\dfrac{MS_W}{n}\left(w_1^2 + w_2^2 + \cdots + w_k^2\right)}}.$$

c If the number of subjects in each group is the same and the comparison is between two means, use Formula 16-15b:

$$t_{obs.} = \frac{\hat{C}}{\sqrt{\dfrac{2MS_W}{n}}}.$$

(continued on p. 468)

(See Procedure 16-4 for contrasts.)

With 3 subjects in each group, Formula 16-15a can be used to test contrast 1 ($\hat{C}_1$):

$$t_{obs.} = \frac{3.66}{\sqrt{\dfrac{1.22}{3}\left[(+1)^2 + \left(-\frac{1}{2}\right)^2 + \left(-\frac{1}{2}\right)^2\right]}}$$

$$= \frac{3.66}{\sqrt{.404\left(1 + \frac{1}{4} + \frac{1}{4}\right)}}$$

$$= \frac{3.66}{\sqrt{.606}}$$

$$= \frac{3.66}{.778}$$

$$= 4.70.$$

Since there were 3 subjects in each group and since $\hat{C}_2$ tests the difference between two means, Formula 16-15b can be used to test contrast 2 ($\hat{C}_2$):

$$t_{obs.} = \frac{-1.33}{\sqrt{\dfrac{2(1.22)}{3}}}$$

$$= \frac{-1.33}{\sqrt{\dfrac{2.44}{3}}}$$

$$= \frac{-1.33}{\sqrt{.81}}$$

$$= \frac{-1.33}{.9}$$

$$= -1.478.$$

4 Locate critical value of t in Table C. Degrees of freedom equals $N - k$ or the df_W from the ANOVA table. Recall that the critical value of t will also depend on whether the alternative hypothesis is nondirectional (two-tailed) or directional (one-tailed).

Contrast 1:
  $\alpha_1 = .05$ (see step 2),
  $df_W = 6$,
  test one-tailed (see step 1),
  $t_{crit.} = 1.943$.

Contrast 2:
  $\alpha_2 = .05$ (see step 2),
  $df_W = 6$,
  test two-tailed (see step 1),
  $t_{crit.} = 2.447$.

5 If $|t_{obs.}| \geq t_{crit.}$, reject H_0.
  If $|t_{obs.}| < t_{crit.}$, do not reject H_0.

Contrast 1:
Since $|t_{obs.}| > t_{crit.}$ ($|4.70| > 1.943$), reject H_0. Conclude that μ_C is significantly higher than the average of μ_B and μ_R.

Contrast 2:
Since $|t_{obs.}| < t_{crit.}$ ($|-1.478| < 2.447$), do not reject H_0. Conclude that μ_B and μ_R are not significantly different from each other.

freedom for the critical value equals $N - k$ or the df_W from the ANOVA table. If $|t_{observed}|$ is greater than or equal to $t_{critical}$, reject H_0. If $|t_{observed}|$ is less than $t_{critical}$, do not reject H_0. The steps in conducting a statistical test for planned comparisons are summarized in Procedure 16-5.

Planned (a priori) comparisons represent the most powerful method for statistically testing for differences between three or more means. With planned comparisons, the ANOVA is used to calculate the mean square within groups (error); *the F value need not be computed.* Thus, planned comparisons are more powerful than the overall ANOVA.

However, as history tells us, one always pays a price for power. Planned comparisons are no exception. In order to conduct these comparisons, two requirements must be met:

1. Comparisons must be planned and justified prior to conducting the study, and
2. The comparisons must be independent of one another, so that $k - 1$ comparisons can be conducted at most.

EXAMPLE PROBLEM 3

The following results were obtained in a replication of the experiment on study time (described in Example Problem 1) with 20 subjects in each group:

	Study time (minutes)			
	10	20	45	75
$\overline{X}$	6	10	18	11

The summary table for the one-way ANOVA for these data is shown below:

Source of variation	SS	df	MS	F
Between groups	345	3	115.00	10.66
Within group	820	76	10.79	
Total	1165			

Prior to the study, the researchers predicted that:

1. $\mu_{45\text{ min}}$ is greater then $\mu_{75\text{ min}}$, and
2. $\mu_{10\text{ min}}$ is less than the average for the other 3 groups.

Test both comparisons between means at $\alpha = .05$. Include in your answer:

a. Table showing weights for each contrast with verification that $\Sigma w_i = 0$ and that the contrasts are independent (see Procedure 16-3)
b. Null and alternative hypotheses for C_1
c. Computation of $\hat{C}_1$
d. The t test for contrast 1
e. t_{critical} for contrast 1
f. Conclusion
g. Steps 2–6 for contrast 2.
h. Maximum number of independent comparisons that could be conducted.

◆   ◆   ◆   ◆   ◆

Post Hoc Comparisons

If the research is exploratory, so that none or only some of the $k - 1$ independent planned comparisons can be set forth prior the study, pairs of means or more complex combinations of means still can be examined by a variety of statistical techniques called *post hoc* comparisons. **Post hoc comparisons**, then, refer to comparisons of means which have not been planned but which look interesting to the researcher on the basis of the sample data. They allow the researcher to snoop through the data to find out where the differences occurred which gave rise to the significant, overall F. Put another way, if the overall F is significant, at least one out of all possible comparisons between pairs of means or complex combinations of means will be significant. Post hoc comparisons are methods for discovering where the difference or differences lie.

The only requirement for using post hoc comparisons as a statistical test of differences between means is that the *overall F in the* ANOVA *must be significant*. If the overall F is significant, post hoc comparisons permit you to make a large number of statistical tests, all of them at a preset level of significance. For example, in the counseling study with three groups (means), six comparisons can be examined: B versus R, B versus C, R versus C, BR versus C, BC versus R, and RC versus B. Using Scheffé's method of post hoc comparison, for example, all six statistical tests can be so conducted that the level of significance (α) for all six tests taken together does not exceed a preset value of α such as .05 or .01.

If the overall F is *not* significant, post hoc comparisons can still be conducted, but *the statement about the probability of a Type I error (α) is not necessarily true*. In this case, the comparisons simply flag differences between means which might be interesting to explore in future studies.

There is a method of post hoc comparison for almost any occasion. For example, Scheffé's method can be used for comparing pairs of means or for comparing complex combinations of means. Tukey's honestly-significant-difference test is designed solely for the purpose of comparing pairs of means, as is the Newman-Keuls test. And Dunnett's test has been developed specifically for comparing the mean of each experimental group against the mean of the control group. Since the smorgasbord of post hoc comparisons is so full, only the most frequently used tests are presented here: Scheffé's test and Tukey's test. Texts such as Kirk (1968) and Winer (1971) contain most of the smorgasbord if you still have an appetite for post hoc comparisons after this presentation.

Scheffé's test The most widely applicable of all the methods of post hoc comparison is **Scheffé's test**. It permits comparisons of pairs of means and of complex combinations of means. Furthermore, it is the most widely accepted test for making post hoc comparisons.

Scheffé's test is carried out in exactly the same way as planned comparisons except that *the comparisons need not be planned a priori and they need not be independent of one another*. Thus, Scheffé's test uses the t test given in Formulas 16-15 a, b.

This seems too good to be true; there must be a catch. Well, there is. The catch comes in when the value of t_{critical} is calculated. The value of t_{critical} for Scheffé's test, labeled t'_{critical} to distinguish it from planned comparisons, is

$$t'_{\text{critical}} = \sqrt{(k-1)F_{\text{critical}(\alpha,\,k-1,\,df_{\text{w}})}} \, , \qquad \left[\,16\text{-}16\,\right]$$

where $k =$ number of groups, and
$F_{\text{critical}} =$ critical value of the F distribution with $k-1$ degrees of freedom in the numerator and df_{w} in the denominator.

The steps in conducting post hoc comparisons using Scheffé's test are summarized in Procedure 16-6. When the value of $t'_{critical}$ (3.21 in our example) is compared with the value of $t_{critical}(\alpha = .05, 6\ df)$ which would be used in a planned comparison (3.143), the price for making all possible comparisons becomes apparent. In order to control for the probability of a Type I error, the Scheffé method increases the critical value for determining significance.

Steps in conducting Scheffé's test for making post hoc comparisons between means ♦ Procedure 16-6 (data from Tables 16-1 and 16-4)

Operation	Example
1 Identify hypotheses between means to be tested. *These may be based on the researcher's "hunches" about the results, snooping through the data, or both. Alternative hypotheses are nondirectional, since the direction of differences between means is not specified prior to the conduct of the study.*	Suppose the researcher wished to test $\bar{X}_C$ vs. $\bar{X}_R$, $H_1: \mu_C \neq \mu_R.$
2 Assign weights to means so that the comparisons identified by the hypotheses in step 1 are specified. *Comparisons need not be independent, but the sum of the weights must equal zero (16-13):* $$\sum_i^k w_i = 0.$$	$\begin{array}{ccc} \bar{X}_C = 6.33 & \bar{X}_B = 2.00 & \bar{X}_R = 3.33 \\ \hline +1 & 0 & -1 \end{array}$
3 Write the comparison(s) in the form of a weighted sum of means (16-12a): $$\hat{C} = \sum_1^k w_i \bar{X}_i.$$	$\hat{C} = (+1)(\bar{X}_C) + (0)(\bar{X}_B) + (-1)(\bar{X}_R).$
4 Insert appropriate values for each mean and solve.	$\hat{C} = (+1)(6.33) + (0)(2.00) + (-1)(3.33)$ $= 6.33 + 0 - 3.33$ $= 3.00.$
5 To conduct Scheffé's test: **a** Specify null and alternative hypotheses for each contrast. *Alternative hypotheses are always nondirectional (see step 1).*	$H_0: C = 0,$ $H_1: C \neq 0.$ (continued on p. 472)

b Compute $t_{obs.}$ using Formula 16-15, 16-15a, or 16-15b. (See step 3 of Procedure 16-5.)

Using Formula 16-15b,

$$t_{obs} = \frac{3.00}{\sqrt{\dfrac{2(1.22)}{3}}}$$

$$= \frac{3.00}{\sqrt{\dfrac{2.44}{3}}}$$

$$= \frac{3.00}{\sqrt{.81}}$$

$$= \frac{3.00}{.9}$$

$$= 3.33.$$

c Compute $t'_{crit.}$ by inserting the appropriate values into Formula 16-16 and solving:

$$t'_{crit.} = \sqrt{(k-1)F_{crit.(\alpha,\, k-1,\, df\, W)}}$$

where $k =$ number of groups, and
$F_{crit.} =$ the F distribution at specified α level with $k-1$ degrees of freedom in the numerator and df_W in the denominator.

Let $\alpha = .05$. Since there were 3 groups, $k = 3$. F_{crit} with $k - 1 = 2$ df in the numerator and 6 df in the denominator (see df in Table 16-2) equals 5.14 (see Table E). Thus,

$$t'_{crit} = \sqrt{2(5.14)}$$

$$= \sqrt{10.28}$$

$$= 3.21.$$

d If $|t_{obs.}| \geq t'_{crit.}$, reject H_0.
If $|t_{obs.}| < t'_{crit.}$, do not reject H_0.

Since $|3.33| > 3.21$, reject H_0. Conclude that μ_C is significantly higher than μ_R.

EXAMPLE PROBLEM 4

Using the data from the study described in Example Problem 3, make the following post hoc comparison using Scheffé's method ($\alpha = .05$):

$$\mu_{20\ min} \text{ versus } \mu_{45\ min}.$$

Include in your answer:

a. Null and alternative hypotheses
b. Set of weights for the comparison
c. Computation of $\hat{C}$
d. t test
e. $t'_{critical}$
f. Conclusions.

Tukey's HSD test Tukey's HSD (honestly-significant-difference) test is designed for making all possible pairwise comparisons between means at an overall level of significance α. This test is more powerful than Scheffé's all-purpose test for comparing *pairs* of means; it should not be used for testing complex comparisons (i.e., a comparison involving more than two means).

Tukey's HSD test is conducted by comparing the difference between each pair of means with the value of *HSD*. The value of *HSD* is given by

$$HSD = q_{(\alpha,\, df_{\mathrm{w}},\, k)} \sqrt{\frac{MS_{\mathrm{w}}}{n}}\ , \qquad [\,16\text{-}17\,]$$

where q = value of studentized range statistic from Table F,
α = probability of a Type I error,
df_{W} = degrees of freedom for MS_{w},
k = number of groups,
n = number of subjects within a group. (If n differs greatly from group to group, see Kirk, 1968, p. 90.)

The value of *HSD* is based on a sampling distribution called the *studentized range statistic*. The sampling distribution of q builds on the fact that, for random samples from the same population (i.e., groups with no systematic differences), the range of sample differences tends to increase as the sample size increases (cf. Kirk, 1968, p. 88). This distribution is given in Table F.

Three pieces of information are needed to locate the value of q in Table F in the appendix: α, df_{W}, and k. The value of q is found by locating the number of

Steps in conducting Tukey's *HSD* test: post hoc comparisons between all pairs of ♦ Procedure 16-7
means (example from hypothetical counseling study)

Operation	Example
1 Specify null and alternative hypotheses: $\qquad H_0\colon C = 0,$ $\qquad H_1\colon C \neq 0,$ and $\qquad C = \mu_i - \mu_{i'}.$ *Hypotheses are specified for all pairs of means, since Tukey's HSD test is designed for making all pairwise comparisons among means. The alternative hypothesis is nondirectional, since the direction of differences between means is not specified prior to the study.*	$H_0\colon C = 0,$ $H_1\colon C \neq 0,$ where $C = \mu_i - \mu_{i'}$ for all pairs. (continued on p. 474)

2 a Set up a table with the mean of each group listed along the rows and columns of the table. Means are listed in *order of size* from smallest to largest.
The table should have k rows and k columns where k is the number of groups.

	$\bar{X}_B = 2.00$	$\bar{X}_R = 3.33$	$\bar{X}_C = 6.33$
$\bar{X}_B = 2.00$	—	1.33	4.33
$\bar{X}_R = 3.33$		—	3.00
$\bar{X}_C = 6.33$			—

b Compute the difference between each pair of means by subtracting the mean listed in each row from the mean listed in each column. Enter this value into the appropriate cell of the table. *Only the differences above the diagonal must be calculated, since the values below the diagonal will be the same except for sign.*

3 Compute *HSD* using Formula 16-17:

$$HSD = q_{(\alpha,\, df_w,\, k)} \sqrt{\frac{MS_w}{n}},$$

where q = value of studentized range statistic from Table F,
α = probability of Type I error,
df_w = degrees of freedom for MS_w,
k = number of groups,
n = number of subjects within groups.

Let

$$\alpha = .05,$$
$$df_w = 6,$$
$$k = 3,$$

$$HSD = q_{(.05,\, 6,\, 3)} \sqrt{\frac{1.22}{3}}$$

$$= 4.34 \sqrt{\frac{1.22}{3}}$$

$$= 4.34(0.64)$$

$$= 2.78.$$

4 Compare differences between means listed in the table (step 2) with the value of *HSD*. If any difference is greater than the value of *HSD*, reject H_0. For differences which are greater than *HSD*, conclude that the means are significantly different at the specified α level.

	$\bar{X}_B = 2.00$	$\bar{X}_R = 3.33$	$\bar{X}_C = 6.33$
$\bar{X}_B = 2.00$	—	1.33	4.33[a]
$\bar{X}_R = 3.33$		—	3.00[a]
$\bar{X}_C = 6.33$			—

[a] $p < .05$.

Reject H_0. Conclude that, in the population:
a means of the behavior-modification and control groups are significantly different and
b means of the Rogerian and control groups are significantly different.

degrees of freedom for MS_w (df_w) and the specified α level in the rows of the table and the number of groups in the columns of the table. The intersection of this row and column gives the value of q.

The differences between all pairs of means are then compared with the value of *HSD*. If the difference between a pair of means is greater than or equal to *HSD*, the two means are (honestly) significantly different at the specified level of α.

The steps in conducting all pairwise comparisons between means using

474

Tukey's HSD test are summarized in Procedure 16-7, using an example from the hypothetical counseling study. Notice that Tukey's test indicates that the mean of the control group is significantly different from the mean of both the counseling groups. These results suggest that the counseling groups produced greater effects than did the control group.

Using the data from the experiment on study time in Example Problem 3, compare all pairs of means using Tukey's HSD test. (Let $\alpha = .05$.) Include in your answer:

a. Null and alternative hypotheses
b. Table of differences between means
c. Computation of *HSD*
d. Conclusions.

EXAMPLE PROBLEM 5

♦   ♦   ♦   ♦   ♦

Summary

This chapter presents the *one-way analysis of variance* (ANOVA), a statistical method for determining whether observed differences between the means of two or more independent samples of subjects are likely to have arisen by chance. The purposes, underlying logic, and procedures for computing and interpreting the ANOVA are discussed. *Omega square* (ω^2), a measure of strength of association or the strength of the treatment effect, is also presented. Finally, methods for making *comparisons between means* to determine which means differ statistically from the others are discussed. *Planned*, or *a priori*, *comparisons* are used when comparisons have been planned before the study is conducted and strong theoretical and/or empirical bases exist for specifying these comparisons. *Post hoc comparisons* are used when the overall F in the ANOVA is significant and comparisons have not been planned prior to the study but look interesting on the basis of the sample data. The most widely applicable methods for making post hoc comparisons, *Scheffé's test* and *Tukey's HSD test*, are presented here.

♦   ♦   ♦   ♦   ♦

Key Words

analysis of variance (ANOVA)	mean square within groups
ANOVA source table	normality
a priori comparisons	omega square
between-group variability	one-way analysis of variance
error variability	planned comparisons
F distribution	post hoc comparisons
grand mean	random error
homogeneity of variance	sample comparisons
independence	Scheffé's test
mean square between groups	strength of association

sum of squares between groups

sum of squares total

sum of squares within groups

total variability

treatment effects

Tukey's HSD test

within-group variability

♦　　♦　　♦　　♦　　♦

Exercises

1. In a study of the effects of three levels of drug dosage on the number of trials rats needed to run a maze without error, $F = 4.15$, $df = 2, 10$. What conclusions can be drawn from the results of the ANOVA?

2. Why is the ANOVA preferable to multiple t tests?

3. When are a priori comparisons of means appropriate?

4. Do you need to calculate the F value in order to use planned comparisons? Why or why not?

5. When are post hoc comparisons appropriate?

6. Do you need to calculate the F value in order to use post hoc comparisons? Why or why not?

7–11 Define the following terms:

7. Error variability.

8. Omega square.

9. Homogeneity of variance.

10. Mean squares.

11. $s^2_{between}$.

12–27 A zoo was having problems with the monkeys throwing garbage at the human onlookers. An animal psychologist was brought in to try and remedy the situation. He decided to try to find which type of reinforcement could be used to reduce the monkeys' negative behavior. He randomly assigned twelve monkeys, four each to three special cages. A large garbage can was placed in each cage during the training sessions. Each time a monkey in cage 1 placed his garbage in the can, he received a small piece of his favorite food. The monkeys in cage 2 received a new toy, and the monkeys in cage 3 did not receive any reward for putting the garbage in the can. After 5 days of training for a half hour each day, all monkeys were observed for a half-hour period. The number of times each monkey threw garbage into the can was counted. The following hypothetical data were obtained from this study:

	Number of times garbage thrown into can		
	Cage 1: Food reward	Cage 2: Toy reward	Cage 3: No reward
	5	7	3
	10	8	1
	6	10	0
	4	5	2
Sum	25	30	6
$\overline{X}$	6.25	7.50	1.50

12–19 Based on the data given above, test whether there was a significant treatment effect at $\alpha = .05$.

12. Formulate null and alternative hypotheses.
13. Make tests of assumptions or give explanations for not doing so.
14. Compute sums of squares.
15. Construct ANOVA summary table.
16. Find $F_{critical}$.
17. Find $F_{observed}$.
18. Calculate omega square.
19. State your conclusions.

20–25 Make a post hoc comparison of cages 1 and 2 with cage 3 using Scheffé's method ($\alpha = .05$).

20. Formulate null and alternative hypotheses.
21. Choose a set of weights for the comparison.
22. Compute $\hat{C}$.
23. Perform a t test.
24. Find $t'_{critical}$.
25. State your conclusions.

26. Make all possible post hoc comparisons between pairs of means using Tukey's HSD, following the procedures given in Procedure 16-7 ($\alpha = .05$).

27. Suppose that the psychologist had strong evidence from past research to suggest that some type of reinforcement was better than no reinforcement. Test the following comparison:

$$\hat{C}: \quad \bar{X}_3 < \frac{\bar{X}_1 + \bar{X}_2}{2}, \qquad \alpha = .05.$$

17 •

Factorial Analysis
of
Variance

Two-Way Analysis of Variance
♦ Purpose and Rationale ♦
♦ Design Requirements ♦
♦ Hypotheses ♦
♦ Assumptions ♦
♦ Computation of the Two-Way ANOVA ♦
♦ Decision Rules for Rejecting the Null Hypothesis ♦
♦ Interpretation of the Results of the Two-Way ANOVA ♦
Strength of Association
Methods for Comparing Means in the Two-Way ANOVA
♦ Planned Comparisons ♦
♦ Post Hoc Comparisons ♦
Summary
♦ Key Words ♦
♦ Exercises ♦

THE **factorial analysis of variance** is a statistical method for examining data from factorial designs (see Chapter 1). It is used to test several hypotheses about differences between means in the factorial design. In this chapter, the conceptual underpinnings and the techniques for using the factorial analysis of variance are presented along with two general methods for interpreting the results. One method is to measure the strength of association between each independent variable (and combination of independent variables) and the dependent variable. This measure of the strength of association is *omega square*, introduced in Chapter 16. The second method for interpreting the results of the factorial ANOVA is *post hoc comparisons*. These comparisons test for differences between specific pairs or combinations of means. *Scheffé's* and *Tukey's* methods of post hoc comparison, presented in Chapter 16, are extended to test differences between means in factorial designs. Finally, the method of *planned comparisons*, an alternative approach to the overall ANOVA, is extended from Chapter 16 to test differences between means in factorial designs.

Sample data for the factorial ANOVA may be obtained in true experiments, from factorial criterion-group designs, or from combinations of the two (see Section V). For example, the ANOVA may be used to examine data from four of the five studies described in Chapter 2. The study of teacher expectancy is a true experiment employing a 2×6 factorial design with two levels of a treatment variable ("bloomers" or experimental group, and control group) and six levels of a grade-level factor (grades 1 through 6). The study of moral judgments is also a true experiment, using a $2 \times 2 \times 5$ factorial design with two levels of outcome (positive and negative), two levels of intent (positive and negative), and five levels of age (4 through 18 years).[1] The study of men's and women's achievement in college is a $2 \times 4 \times 4$ factorial criterion-group design with two levels of sex (male and female), four levels of subject-matter major (physical sciences, biological sciences, social sciences, and humanities) and four levels of campus (UCLA, UCSD, UCI, and UCD). Finally, the study of the determinants of emotion is a true experiment employing a 2×4 factorial design with two levels of a situation variable (euphoria and anger) and four levels of a treatment variable (drug + accurate explanation, drug + inaccurate explanation, drug + no explanation, and placebo).

---

[1]These ages were divided into five levels of 3 years each (4–6 years, 7–9 years, etc.). In most of our examples, two age levels—young children (4–6 years) and young adults (16–18 years)—were used to simplify matters.

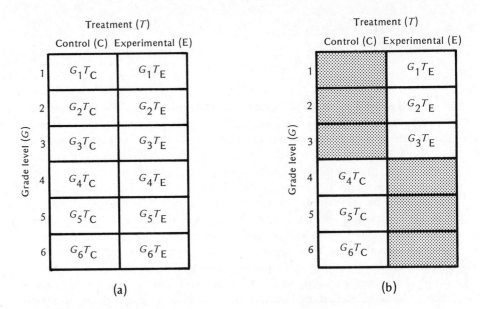

Figure 17-1 ♦ Examples of crossed and not crossed factorial designs: (a) 2×6 crossed, factorial design; (b) 2×6 factorial design which is not crossed

While factorial designs with many factors can be (and have been) conceptualized and conducted, this text is restricted to factorial designs with two independent variables. The analysis of variance applied to factorial designs with two factors is often called the two-way ANOVA. Restricting the focus to the two-way ANOVA is not a major limitation, since the material presented in this chapter can be extended directly to factorial designs with any number of factors. A second restriction is that the presentation will be limited to designs with equal numbers of subjects in each cell. This simplifies the presentation and the interpretation of the results of the factorial ANOVA. (For a presentation of the ANOVA with unequal cell sizes, see Applebaum and Cramer, 1974; Kirk, 1968; and Winer, 1971.) Finally, the presentation will be limited to **completely crossed designs**, that is, designs in which each level of one factor occurs with (i.e., is "crossed" with) each level of the other factor. In the study of teacher expectancy, treatment is crossed with grade level, so that both levels of the treatment factor (control and experimental) are observed with each level of the grade factor (see Figure 17-1a). That is, subjects were randomly selected from each grade level and randomly assigned to one of the two treatment groups (i.e., cells of the design). If all levels of one factor do not occur with all levels of the other factor, the design is not crossed. For example, suppose that in the hypothetical study of teacher expectancy, "bloomers" were randomly selected from grades 1 through 3 and control-group subjects were randomly selected from grades 4 through 6. In this case, some cells of the design are empty. Every level of one variable (grade level) does not occur with every level of the other variable (treatment group) (see Figure 17-b). The material presented in this chapter does not bear directly on such designs (see Dayton, 1970; Kirk, 1968; and Winer, 1971).

Purpose The purpose of the two-way ANOVA is to compare the mean scores from four or more groups[2] in a factorial design in order to decide whether the differences between means may be due to chance or to the effect of the first factor (called the **main effect** for factor A), the second factor (main effect for factor B), or a combination of certain levels of the first factor with certain levels of the second factor (called the **interaction effect**). As a concrete example of the possible effects in a two-way design, consider the data from the expectancy study shown in Table 17-1. Information about the effect of the expectancy treatment on IQ scores can be obtained by comparing the mean scores of the control group and experimental group at the bottom of Table 17-1. These mean scores are calculated by ignoring the grade-level factor; they are based on 6 (grade levels) $\times$ 5 (subjects within a cell) = 30 scores. Notice that the means can be compared without bias because both are based on scores from the same number of subjects in each of the six grades, who were randomly assigned to the experimental or control group. Finally, the difference between the two means is quite small—.66 points. A t test or one-way ANOVA probably would not show the difference to be statistically significant.[3]

Information about the effect of grade level on the IQ scores can be obtained by comparing the means for each grade level in the right-hand column of Table 17-1. These means are calculated by ignoring the treatment factor; they are based on 2 (treatment groups) $\times$ 5 (subjects within a cell) = 10 scores. Again, they can be compared without bias because in each case the same number of scores from both the experimental and control groups enters into the calculation. Finally, the differences between the means are reasonably small (range = 4.9 IQ points). A one-way ANOVA could be run to test the differences between these six means statistically.

Finally, the main body of the table contains information about the effects of combinations of grade level and treatment. Notice that the high mean IQ scores occur in only three of the twelve cells of the design. The greatest expectancy advantage occurs with first- and second-graders, while the reverse

TWO-WAY ANALYSIS OF VARIANCE

Purpose and Rationale

---

[2]In a crossed factorial design, the smallest number of groups, 4, arises from a 2×2 design ($2 \times 2 = 4$ groups).

[3]The main effect in a two-way ANOVA is not the same as the between-group effect in a one-way ANOVA, ignoring the other independent variable. The within-group error term for the one-way ANOVA will include variation due to the main effect of the ignored second variable and the interaction effect of the two independent variables. One of the values of the two-way ANOVA is that the systematic variation of scores between subjects due to a second independent variable can be isolated and so removed from the error term.

Table 17-1 ◆ Mean posttest scores from the study of teacher expectancy ($n = 5$; raw data in Table 2-1)

		Treatment		Mean scores representing the effect for grade level
		Control	Experimental	
	1	105.20	116.40	110.80
	2	105.80	117.20	111.50
Grade	3	109.00	106.60	107.80
level	4	109.40	106.20	107.80
	5	116.20	109.20	112.70
	6	111.80	105.80	108.80
Mean scores representing the effect for treatment		109.57	110.23	

occurs with fifth-graders in the control group. The data in the cells of the design, then, suggest that the expectancy effect may occur at certain grade levels (1 and 2), does not occur at other grade levels (3 and 4), and reverses itself at other grade levels (5 and 6).

Often the question is asked, "Why not run two separate one-way research studies testing each factor separately instead of using a factorial design?" There are three good reasons. The first reason is economy of time and resources. The second, more important reason is that more information is gained from the factorial design than from the combination of two one-way designs. For example, if the expectancy study had been conducted as two separate one-way designs, information about the effects of treatment and grade level would be obtained, but information would not have been obtained about certain combinations where the largest differences between means arose. A major benefit of the factorial design over several one-way designs, then, is that factorial designs test three hypotheses—one for each of the two independent variables and one for the combination of the two independent variables—while separate one-way designs only test hypotheses about the main effect of each independent variable. The third, equally important reason is that the error variance will be more precisely estimated in a factorial design than in a one-way design. For example, systematic variation of subjects' scores within a cell of a one-way design might be due to (say) differences in subjects' knowledge, in addition to other, unidentified sources of variations. By treating "level of knowledge" as a second factor in a factorial design, this systematic variation can be removed from the variation within groups. In this way, a more precise estimate of unsystematic variation—error—can be obtained in the factorial design (cf. footnote 3).

In summary, the two-way ANOVA tests three hypotheses statistically. One hypothesis refers to the main effect for the first variable, another to the main effect for the second variable, and the third to the unique effect of certain levels of one variable paired with certain levels of the other variable.

This last hypothesis is called an interaction hypothesis. It is viewed as a *unique* effect because it cannot be predicted from knowledge of the main effect for factor 1 or for factor 2. Perhaps an analogy will help explain this concept. Knowing the properties of hydrogen and oxygen allows us to predict that they will combine (can be "crossed" in factorial fashion), but it does not permit us to predict all of the properties that, when they are combined, we will get with water. Knowing the properties of sodium and chlorine allows us to predict that they will combine, but it does not allow us to predict all of the properties that, when they are combined, we will get with salt. Finally, knowing that there is no effect due to treatment in the study of teacher expectancy and, at best, there is a weak effect due to grade level, does not allow us to predict that the expectancy effect will operate as hypothesized at certain grade levels (1 and 2) and not at others (5 and 6).

Often, in order to examine the interaction hypothesis, the data from a study are presented in a graph. The mean values on the dependent variable are identified on the ordinate of the graph, and one of the two independent variables is identified on the abscissa. If one of the two independent variables is an individual-difference variable, it is identified on the abscissa. If both are

Figure 17-2 ◆ Interaction between treatment and grade level in the study on teacher expectancy (data from Table 17-1)

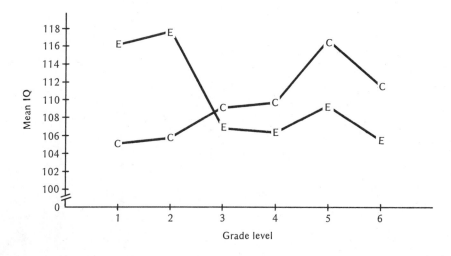

individual-difference variables, either may be placed on the abscissa. Finally, the remaining independent variable is represented as two or more lines on the graph (depending on the number of levels of that variable).

Figure 17-2 presents a graph of the data from the expectancy study. The means from the main body (cells) of Table 17-1 are plotted, with one line representing the control group and the other line representing the experimental group. From this figure, it is clear that there is an interaction effect: (1) a large difference between means in favor of the experimental group occurs at grades 1 and 2; (2) a very small difference occurs at grades 3 and 4; and (3) a moderate difference in favor of the control group occurs at grades 5 and 6.

In general, interactions can take on several visual representations when graphed. Some examples are shown in Figure 17-3. A **disordinal interaction** occurs when the lines in a graph cross (see Figures 17-2 and 17-3a). A

Figure 17-3 ◆ Some examples of graphs displaying disordinal, ordinal, and no interactions: (a) disordinal interaction; (b) ordinal interaction; (c) ordinal interaction; (d) no interaction

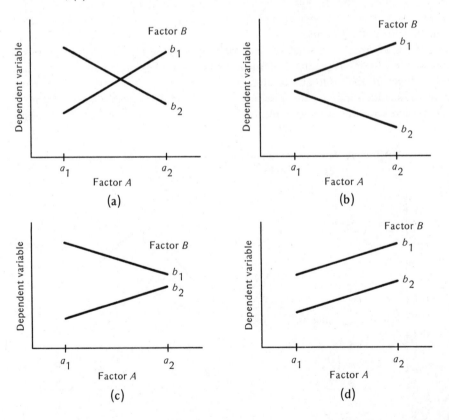

disordinal interaction indicates that the effects of the levels of one factor (e.g., factor B) reverse themselves as the levels of the other factor (e.g., factor A) change. For example, at level a_1 in Figure 17-3a, the mean of the group receiving level b_2 is considerably higher than the mean of the group receiving level b_1. However, this pattern is reversed at level a_2. At a_2 the mean of the group receiving level b_1 is higher than the mean of the group receiving level b_2.

An **ordinal interaction** occurs when the lines on the graph are not parallel and they do not cross (Figure 17-3b and c). This pattern suggests a greater difference between groups at one level of a factor than at the other level of the same factor. For example, in Figure 17-3b, the difference between means at level a_1 (group a_1b_1 versus a_1b_2) is quite small. However, at level a_2, the difference between the means (group a_2b_1 versus a_2b_2) is quite large.

Finally, parallel lines on such a graph (Figure 17-3d) indicate the absence of an interaction. This pattern suggests a similar pattern of means on one factor at each level of the other factor. For example, in Figure 17-3d, the means for levels b_1 and b_2 show a similar pattern at a_1 and a_2. In both cases, the means of groups receiving level b_1 are higher than the means of groups receiving b_2.

Rationale The statistical rationale underlying the two-way ANOVA is similar to that of the one-way ANOVA (see Chapter 16 for a full discussion). The two main-effect hypotheses and the interaction hypothesis in a two-way design are independent of one another, and so a separate F test is conducted for each of them. Thus, in the study of teacher expectancy, one hypothesis refers to the effect of the treatment (i.e., experimental versus control) and an F test would be conducted as follows:

$$F = \frac{MS_{\text{treatment}}}{MS_{\text{within}}}.$$

Just as with the one-way ANOVA, $MS_{\text{treatment}}$ is estimated from the differences between the means of the control and the experimental groups and MS_{within} is the average within-cell variance over all of the cells in the design.

The hypothesis related to the effect of grade level is evaluated with a second F test:

$$F = \frac{MS_{\text{grade level}}}{MS_{\text{within}}}.$$

The $MS_{\text{grade level}}$ is estimated from the differences between the six row means in Table 17-1, while MS_{within} is the same as defined above.

Finally, the interaction hypothesis is tested with a third F test:

$$F = \frac{MS_{\text{interaction}}}{MS_{\text{within}}}.$$

The $MS_{\text{interaction}}$ is estimated from the pattern of the differences between the twelve means in the main body of Table 17-1, while MS_{within} is the same as defined above.

Each of the three F tests test the null hypothesis that there are no effects. For example, under the null hypothesis of no expectancy effect, the difference between the means of the experimental and control groups is hypothesized to arise by chance. In this case, the variance due to treatment ($MS_{\text{treatment}}$) is assumed to represent an independent sample of error variability.

In presenting the results of the two-way ANOVA, an ANOVA source table is used (see Table 17-2). As with the one-way ANOVA, the sources of variation in the dependent variable are identified. However, in the case of the two-way ANOVA, there are three sources of between-group variation, and not just one source as in the one-way ANOVA. These three sources correspond to each of the three independent hypotheses tested: main effect for A, main effect for B, and interaction of A and B. Finally, the fourth source of variability is within-group (error) variability.

For each of the four sources of variation, the corresponding sums of squares, degrees of freedom, and mean squares are presented. And a separate F test is conducted for each of the three independent hypotheses.

Finally, the value of F_{observed} for each hypothesis can be compared with its corresponding value of F_{critical} in order to decide whether or not to reject the null hypothesis. The value of F_{critical} depends on the degrees of freedom for each source of variation in the F test and the level of significance (α). If F_{observed} exceeds F_{critical}, we conclude that the difference between means did not arise from sampling error, but rather from a treatment effect. Of course, we could be wrong, as indicated by the probability of a Type I error, α. In Table 17-2, three hypotheses are tested, one with 1 and 48 df and two with 5 and 48 df. The value of F_{critical} for 1 and 48 df is (approximately) 4.04, while for 5 and 48 df it is (approximately) 2.41. By comparing F_{observed} with F_{critical}, we conclude that

Table 17-2 ◆ Source table for the two-way ANOVA (data taken from the study of teacher expectancy)

Source of variation	Sum of squares	df	MS	F_{observed}
Treatment (A)	6.67	1	6.67	0.082
Grade level (B)	212.40	5	42.48	0.525
Treatment × grade level (A × B)	884.32	5	176.86	2.185
Within-group variability (Error)	3885.97	48	80.96	

there is no main effect due to treatment or grade level and no effect due to the interaction of treatment and grade level. However, the results in Table 17-2 suggest the possibility of an interaction, which might be examined in future research with a larger sample of subjects.

♦ ♦ ♦ ♦ ♦

The use of the two-way ANOVA presupposes that the data have been collected as follows: **Design Requirements**

1. There are two independent variables, each with two or more levels. In this chapter, the two variables are assumed to be completely crossed.
2. The levels of the independent variables may differ either qualitatively or quantitatively. The distinction between "bloomers" and controls in the teacher-expectancy study is an example of a qualitative difference. The distinction between grade levels is an example of a quantitative difference.
3. A subject may appear in one and only one cell of the design.

♦ ♦ ♦ ♦ ♦

The two-way ANOVA is used to test three hypotheses. Two of these hypotheses refer to the main effects of factor A and factor B, while the third refers to the interaction effect of factors A and B. For factor A with q levels, the null hypothesis is **Hypotheses**

$$H_0: \mu_1 = \mu_2 = \cdots = \mu_i = \cdots = \mu_q.$$

The null hypothesis states that in the population, the means for all of the levels of factor A are equal. The notation μ_i refers to the mean at any unidentified level of factor A. The alternative hypothesis is

$$H_1: \mu_i \neq \mu_{i'} \text{ for some } i \text{ and } i'.$$

This hypothesis states that at least some distinct pair of means (μ_i and $\mu_{i'}$) differ from one another in the population.

A similar interpretation can be given to the null and alternative hypotheses for factor B with r levels:

$$H_0: \mu_1 = \mu_2 = \cdots = \mu_j = \cdots = \mu_r,$$

$$H_1: \mu_j \neq \mu_{j'} \text{ for some } j \text{ and } j'.$$

In this case, j refers to any unidentified level of the B factor, and μ_j and $\mu_{j'}$ represent a distinct pair of means.

Intuitively, it would seem as if the null and alternative hypotheses for the interaction should be written in a manner similar to the main effects using the cell means. However, this is not the case, because the cell means reflect not only the interaction effect but also the effects of factors A and B if one or both exist. Since the interaction provides information about the unique effect of the combination of the levels of factor A with the levels of factor B, the main effects of A and B have to be removed from the cell means. In order to avoid the cumbersome notation showing the effects of A and B removed from the cell means, the interaction hypotheses will be written as

$$H_0: \text{interaction effect} = 0,$$

$$H_1: \text{interaction effect} \neq 0.$$

By testing each of these hypotheses, a decision about the null hypothesis can be made for each effect. That is, the two-way ANOVA indicates whether there is an effect due to factor A, factor B, and the interaction of A and B. However, if there are, for example, more than two levels of factor A, it will not indicate which treatment means are significantly different from each other. Likewise, if there is a significant interaction effect, the overall F test of the interaction will not indicate where it lies. In order to determine specific differences, comparisons between means using procedures such as Scheffé's or Tukey's methods must be conducted, just as was done with the one-way ANOVA.

◆　　◆　　◆　　◆　　◆

Assumptions　　Three assumptions are made in using the sampling distribution of F to test each of the three hypotheses in the two-way ANOVA.

1. *Independence.* The score for any particular subject is independent of the scores of all other subjects; i.e., it provides a unique piece of information about the effect.
2. *Normality.* The scores within each cell of the design are drawn from a population in which scores are normally distributed. Put another way, the scores in a particular cell of the design are assumed to be sampled from a population of scores which is normal in form.
3. *Homogeneity of variances.* The variances of scores in the populations underlying all the cells of the design are equal.

These assumptions are the same as those underlying the t test with two independent groups. Methods for examining these assumptions are given in Chapter 15.

The two-way ANOVA is not sensitive to the violation of the assumption of normality. When cell sizes are equal, the ANOVA is also not sensitive to violations of the assumption of homogeneity of variances.

◆　　◆　　◆　　◆　　◆

Computation of the　In the one-way ANOVA, the total variability between scores was partitioned into
Two-Way ANOVA　two independent sources of variability, within-group variability and between-group variability:

$$\text{Total variability} = \text{Variability between groups}$$

$$+ \text{Variability within groups (error)}. \qquad [\textbf{16-3}]$$

In a similar manner, the total variability between scores in the two-way ANOVA is partitioned into four sources of variability—the effects of factor A, of factor B, of the interaction of A and B, and of variability within groups, or error:

$$
\begin{aligned}
\text{Total variability} = &\text{ variability due to factor } A \\
&+ \text{variability due to factor } B \\
&+ \text{variability due to interaction } (A \times B) \\
&+ \text{variability within groups (error)}. \qquad [\textbf{17-1}]
\end{aligned}
$$

As with the one-way ANOVA, in the two-way ANOVA we work with sums of squares instead of variances (mean squares) when the computations are carried out (see Chapter 16, "Computation of the ANOVA"). Then, once the computations are completed, the sums of squares are divided by their respective degrees of freedom in order to get mean squares or variances. Finally, $F_{observed}$ is calculated for each of the three effects by dividing the variability for each effect by the within-group variance.

Procedure 17-1 gives the raw-score formulas and steps for calculating the sums of squares in the two-way ANOVA. In presenting those formulas, the data shown in Table 17-3 will be used. Let's suppose that the data are from a study of the effects of certain instructional treatments on the reading comprehension of subjects classified as low or high in verbal ability. Specifically, the experimenter provided three different versions of text material to the subjects. In one version, factual questions were inserted after every four paragraphs and subjects

Table 17-3 ♦ Results of the hypothetical study of reading comprehension

		Type of question (B)			
		b_1	b_2	b_3	
		None	Factual	Comprehension	Row mean
Verbal ability (A)	a_1 Low	1 2 $\bar{X}=1.5$	1 2 $\bar{X}=1.5$	7 8 $\bar{X}=7.5$	3.50
	a_2 High	8 9 $\bar{X}=8.5$	3 4 $\bar{X}=3.5$	3 4 $\bar{X}=3.5$	5.17
Column mean		5.00	2.50	5.50	

were asked to answer the questions as they read. A second version of the text contained questions after every four paragraphs which tested comprehension of the material. The third version did not contain questions (control group). Twelve college sophomores were divided into groups of low and high verbal ability and then randomly assigned to one of the three text groups so that there were two subjects per cell. This, then, is a 2×3 (verbal ability $\times$ type of question) design. After reading the text material, subjects took an achievement test. (See Table 17-3 for the results of this test.)

Just by "eyeballing" the data in Table 17-3 we can get some idea of what happened in the study. First, as expected, subjects high in verbal ability scored higher than subjects low in verbal ability, on the average (5.17 versus 3.50, respectively). Second, subjects in the control group and comprehension group tended to earn higher scores, on the average, than did subjects in the factual group (5.00 and 5.50 versus 2.50). Third, low-ability subjects profited most from the comprehension questions, while high-ability subjects profited most from the text without questions. Finally, the variability of scores within each cell is the same, and this variability is quite small.

The pattern of results in the two-way ANOVA should reflect these descriptive data. In order to verify this, the sums of squares calculated in Procedure 17-1 can be entered into an ANOVA summary table and the three F ratios calculated using the formulas in Table 17-4. The first column of the source table enumerates the sources of variation in the achievement-test sources. The second

Procedure 17-1 ♦ Steps in calculating sums of squares for the two-way ANOVA[a]

Operation	Example
1 Set up a data summary table as shown. A score in this table is denoted as X_{pij}, where p refers to the person, i refers to any unidentified level of factor A, and j refers to any unidentified level of factor B.	Data summary table

Data summary table

		Factor B (treatment)		
		b_1 (Control)	b_2 (Factual)	b_3 (Comprehensive)
Factor A (verbal ability)	a_1	1	1	7
		2	2	8
	a_2	8	3	3
		9	4	4

[a]N is the total number of subjects. n is the number of subjects in a cell of the design. q is the number of levels of factor A. r is the number of levels of factor B.

2 Make the following preliminary computations:

a Sum the scores in each of the cells of the design, and place these sums in a table of cell sums as shown.

Table of cell sums

	b_1	b_2	b_3
a_1	3	3	15
a_2	17	7	7

b Sum the cell sums in the table of cell sums in order to get total sums for each row and each column, and place these values in the table as shown.

Table of cell sums

	b_1	b_2	b_3	Total sum for rows
a_1	3	3	15	21
a_2	17	7	7	31
Total sum for columns	20	10	22	

c Square the values in the table of cell sums and divide this new value by n, the number of scores that entered the sum.

$$\frac{3^2}{2}, \frac{3^2}{2}, \frac{15^2}{2}, \frac{17^2}{2}, \frac{7^2}{2}, \frac{7^2}{2}$$

$$= \frac{9}{2}, \frac{9}{2}, \frac{225}{2}, \frac{289}{2}, \frac{49}{2}, \frac{49}{2}$$

$$= 4.5, 4.5, 112.5, 144.5, 24.5, 24.5.$$

d Square each row sum and then divide the new value by nr, the number of scores that entered the sum.

$$\frac{21^2}{2 \times 3}, \frac{31^2}{2 \times 3}$$

$$= \frac{441}{6}, \frac{961}{6}$$

$$= 73.5, 160.17.$$

e Square each column sum and then divide the new value by nq, the number of scores that entered the sum.

$$\frac{20^2}{2 \times 2}, \frac{10^2}{2 \times 2}, \frac{22^2}{2 \times 2}$$

$$= \frac{400}{4}, \frac{100}{4}, \frac{484}{4}$$

$$= 100, 25, 121.$$

f Sum all of the scores in the data summary table regardless of cells, to get the total sum ($\sum_1^N X_p$).

$$\sum_1^N X_p = 1 + 2 + 1 + 2 + 7 + 8$$

$$+ 8 + 9 + 3 + 4 + 3 + 4$$

$$= 52.$$

3 Compute the following intermediate quantities. Note that these quantities are labeled with symbols in braces, {}, to simplify matters later on.

(continued on p. 492)

a Square the total sum calculated in step 2f and divide this new value by nqr, the number of scores that entered the sum:

$$\{1\} = \frac{\left(\sum\limits_{p=1}^{N} X_p\right)^2}{nqr}.$$

b Sum the values in step 2d to obtain

$$\{2\} = \sum_{i=1}^{q} \frac{\left(\sum\limits_{j=1}^{r}\sum\limits_{p=1}^{n} X_{pij}\right)^2}{nr}.$$

c Sum the values in step 2e to obtain

$$\{3\} = \sum_{j=1}^{r} \frac{\left(\sum\limits_{i=1}^{q}\sum\limits_{p=1}^{n} X_{pij}\right)^2}{nq}.$$

d Sum the values in step 2c to obtain

$$\{4\} = \sum_{i=1}^{q}\sum_{j=1}^{r} \frac{\left(\sum\limits_{p=1}^{n} X_{pij}\right)^2}{n}.$$

e Square each score in the data summary table (step 1), and sum all of the squared scores regardless of cell:

$$\{5\} = \sum_{p=1}^{N} X_p^2.$$

4 Compute the sums of squares using the following computational formulas:

a

$$SS_T = \sum_{p=1}^{N} X_p - \frac{\left(\sum\limits_{p=1}^{N} X_p\right)^2}{nqr} \quad [17\text{-}2]$$

b

$$SS_A = \sum_{i=1}^{q} \frac{\left(\sum\limits_{j=1}^{r}\sum\limits_{p=1}^{n} X_{pij}\right)^2}{nr} - \frac{\left(\sum\limits_{p=1}^{N} X_p\right)^2}{nqr} \quad [17\text{-}3]$$

$$\{1\} = \frac{\left(\sum\limits_{p=1}^{12} X_p\right)^2}{2\cdot 2\cdot 3} = \frac{52^2}{12} = \frac{2704}{12}$$
$$= 225.33.$$

$$\{2\} = \sum_{i=1}^{2} \frac{\left(\sum\limits_{j=1}^{3}\sum\limits_{p=1}^{2} X_{pij}\right)^2}{2\cdot 3} = 73.5 + 160.17$$
$$= 233.67.$$

$$\{3\} = \sum_{j=1}^{3} \frac{\left(\sum\limits_{i=1}^{2}\sum\limits_{p=1}^{2} X_{pij}\right)^2}{2\cdot 2} = 100 + 25 + 121$$
$$= 246.$$

$$\{4\} = \sum_{i=1}^{2}\sum_{j=1}^{3} \frac{\left(\sum\limits_{p=1}^{2} X_{pij}\right)^2}{2}$$
$$= 4.5 + 4.5 + 112.5 + 144.5 + 24.5 + 24.5$$
$$= 315.$$

$$\{5\} = \sum_{1}^{12} X_p^2 = 1^2 + 2^2 + \cdots + 3^2 + 4^2$$
$$= 1 + 4 + \cdots + 9 + 16$$
$$= 318.$$

$$SS_T = \{5\} - \{1\}$$
$$= 318 - 225.33$$
$$= 92.67.$$

$$SS_A = \{2\} - \{1\}$$
$$= 233.67 - 225.33$$
$$= 8.34.$$

c

$$SS_B = \sum_{j=1}^{r} \frac{\left(\sum_{i=1}^{q}\sum_{p=1}^{n} X_{pij}\right)^2}{nq} - \frac{\left(\sum_{p=1}^{N} X_p\right)^2}{nqr} \quad [17\text{-}4]$$

$SS_B = \{3\} - \{1\}$

$= 246 - 225.33$

$= 20.67.$

d

$$SS_{AB} = \sum_{i=1}^{q}\sum_{j=1}^{r} \frac{\left(\sum_{p=1}^{n} X_{pij}\right)^2}{n} - \sum_{i=1}^{q} \frac{\left(\sum_{j=1}^{r}\sum_{p=1}^{n} X_{pij}\right)^2}{nr}$$

$$- \sum_{j=1}^{r} \frac{\left(\sum_{i=1}^{q}\sum_{p=1}^{n} X_{pij}\right)^2}{nq} + \frac{\left(\sum_{p=1}^{N} X_p\right)^2}{nqr} \quad [17\text{-}5]$$

$SS_{AB} = \{4\} - \{2\} - \{3\} + \{1\}$

$= 315 - 233.67 - 246 + 225.33$

$= 60.66$

e

$$SS_W = \sum_{p=1}^{N} X_p^2 - \sum_{i=1}^{q}\sum_{j=1}^{r} \frac{\left(\sum_{p=1}^{n} X_{pij}\right)^2}{n} \quad [17\text{-}6]$$

$SS_W = \{5\} - \{4\}$

$= 318 - 315$

$= 3.$

column contains the sums of squares from Procedure 17-1. Note that the sums of squares total (SS_T) can be used as a computational check, since

$$SS_T = SS_A + SS_B + SS_{AB} + SS_W. \quad [17\text{-}7]$$

The third column of the table gives the formulas for finding the degrees of freedom associated with each source of variation. Note that, like the sums of squares, the degrees of freedom for each source of variation are additive, so df_T can be used as a computational check:

$$df_T = df_A + df_B + df_{AB} + df_W. \quad [17\text{-}8]$$

The fourth column gives the formulas for calculating mean squares, and the fifth column gives the formulas for calculating $F_{observed}$.

Table 17-4 ◆ Formulas used in completing the source table for the two-way ANOVA

Source of variation	Sums of squares[a]	df[b]	Mean square	$F_{observed}$
Factor A	$SS_A =$ [17-3]	$df_A = q - 1$	$\dfrac{SS_A}{df_A}$	$F_A = \dfrac{MS_A}{MS_W}$
Factor B	$SS_B =$ [17-4]	$df_B = r - 1$	$\dfrac{SS_B}{df_B}$	$F_B = \dfrac{MS_B}{MS_W}$
Interaction of factors A and B	$SS_{AB} =$ [17-5]	$df_{AB} = (q - 1)(r - 1)$	$\dfrac{SS_{AB}}{df_{AB}}$	$F_{AB} = \dfrac{MS_{AB}}{MS_W}$
Within-group variability (Error)	$SS_W =$ [17-6]	$df_W = qr(n - 1)$	$\dfrac{SS_W}{df_W}$	
Total	$SS_T =$ [17-2]	$df_T = qrn - 1$		

[a]Formulas (numbers in brackets) are in Procedure 17-1.
[b]n is the number of subjects in a cell. q is the number of levels of factor A. r is the number of levels of factor B.

The results of the two-way ANOVA of the data from the comprehension study are presented in Table 17-5. These results are consistent with our "eyeball" analysis of the descriptive data.

◆   ◆   ◆   ◆   ◆

Decision Rules for Rejecting the Null Hypothesis
In order to determine whether or not to reject the null hypothesis for each of the three hypotheses tested by the two-way ANOVA, $F_{observed}$ must be compared with $F_{critical}$. Furthermore, since $F_{critical}$ depends on the degrees of freedom associated with each effect and the error term, there will be different values of $F_{critical}$ for different pairs of degrees of freedom. In order to find the value of $F_{critical}$ in Table E, three pieces of information need to be known: α, df_{effect}, and df_{error}. For the data from the hypothetical study of comprehension from prose material (Table 17-5), two critical values of F are needed, since there are two different pairs of degrees of freedom: 1 and 6, and 2 and 6. If α is .05, the values of $F_{critical}$ are

$$F_{critical(.05, 1, 6)} = 5.99,$$

$$F_{critical(.05, 2, 6)} = 5.14.$$

Since $F_{observed}$ in each case exceeds its corresponding value of $F_{critical}$, the null hypothesis for factors A and B and the interaction should be rejected. There is a significant effect due to A, B, and AB.

Table 17-5 ◆ ANOVA summary table: results of the study of comprehension from prose material

Source of variation	Sum of squares	df	Mean squares	$F_{observed}$ [a]
Verbal ability (A)	8.34	1	8.34	16.68
Instructional treatment (B)	20.67	2	10.34	20.67
A × B	60.66	2	30.33	60.66
Within-group (error)	3.00	6	0.50	
Total	92.67	11		

[a] $F_{crit.(\alpha = .05, df = 1, 6)} = 5.99$, $F_{crit.(\alpha = .05, df = 2, 6)} = 5.14$; $p < .05$.

◆　　◆　　◆　　◆　　◆

In interpreting the results of the two-way ANOVA, start with the interaction effect and work upward. The rationale for doing this is as follows. An interaction effect implies that certain combinations of the levels of factors A and B have different effects than do other combinations. This means that the effect of factor A may depend on the level of factor B with which it is combined. Similarly, the effect of factor B may depend on the level of factor A with which it is combined. For example, the data from the reading study show that there is *no best* treatment (b_1 versus b_2 versus b_3). Rather, the effects of treatments depend on the verbal ability of the subject. Thus the effect of factor B (treatment) depends on the level of factor A (ability) with which it is combined. In short, the existence of a significant interaction in the data means the main effects of factors A and B must be qualified. One level of factor A does not always produce the "best" results, nor does one particular level of factor B. The effects of factors A and B depend on each other.

In interpreting a significant interaction such as the one shown in Tables 17-3 and 17-5, the first step is to plot the interaction. The steps in plotting an interaction are given in Procedure 17-2, using data from the comprehension study. The completed graph of this interaction is shown in step 4. This graph shows that subjects low in verbal ability benefited most from the comprehension treatment and least from either the factual or the control treatment. Subjects high in verbal ability benefited most from the control treatment and least from either the factual or the comprehension treatment. Clearly, the graph shows that both the main effects for factor A (ability) and factor B (treatment) must be qualified. Subjects high in verbal ability do not always have the highest performance. And one treatment does not always produce the highest performance. The effect of ability depends on what treatment the person received, and the effect of treatment depends on the verbal ability of the subject.

In order to be sure that this interpretation of the effects of the interaction in terms of differences between all means is accurate (and does not depend on

Interpretation of the Results of the Two-Way ANOVA

Procedure 17-2 ♦ Steps in plotting an interaction (example from hypothetical study of reading comprehension; data from Table 17-5)

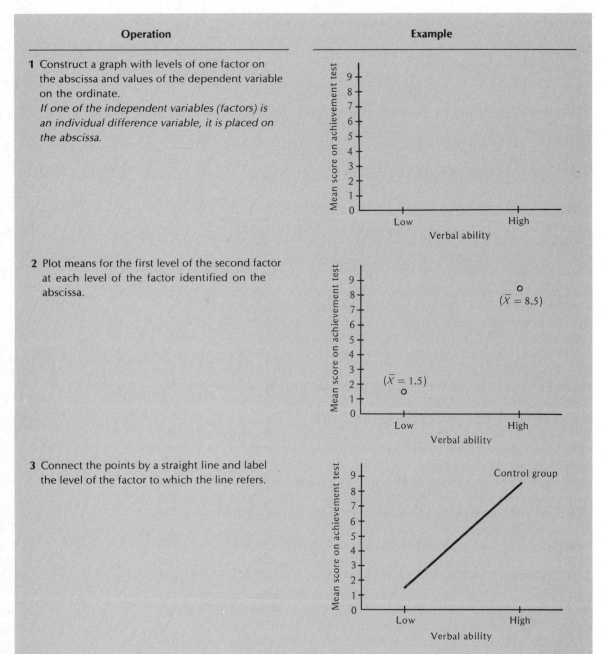

Operation	Example
1 Construct a graph with levels of one factor on the abscissa and values of the dependent variable on the ordinate. *If one of the independent variables (factors) is an individual difference variable, it is placed on the abscissa.*	
2 Plot means for the first level of the second factor at each level of the factor identified on the abscissa.	$(\bar{X} = 8.5)$ $(\bar{X} = 1.5)$
3 Connect the points by a straight line and label the level of the factor to which the line refers.	Control group

4 Repeat steps 2–3 for the remaining levels of the
factor.
*Different types of lines (dotted, dashed, etc.) are
often used to identify different levels of the factor.*

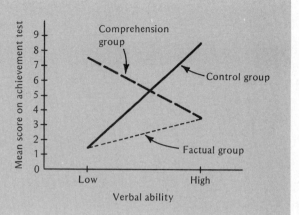

chance), post hoc comparisons of means should be conducted. The methods for
conducting these tests are described in a later section of this chapter.

If, however, there is no interaction effect, then it is appropriate to interpret
the main effects. Suppose a study was conducted to determine the effects of
motivation level and treatment on performance. The results showed no interaction effect. In this case, statements such as the following can be made: "The
experimental treatment produced a significantly greater effect than the control
treatment (factor A), regardless of the motivation level of the subjects (factor
B)." Or, "Subjects randomly assigned to the high-motivation treatment (B)
performed significantly better than did subjects assigned to the low-motivation
treatment, regardless of whether they were in the experimental or control
groups (A)."

In interpreting the main effects of factors with only two levels, a significant
overall F for those factors indicates that the difference between the two means
corresponding to the two levels is significant. In this case, a post hoc comparison is unnecessary. In interpreting the main effects of factors with three or more
levels, a significant overall F indicates that there is at least one significant
difference between the means corresponding to the levels of the factor. In this
case, additional post hoc analyses must be conducted.

In the hypothetical study of the determinants of emotion (see Chapter 2),
two theories were compared. The physiological-state theory asserted that
emotion is the feeling accompanying a physiological state of arousal and
that different physiological states (e.g., heart rate, numbness) led to
different emotional states. The two-component theory asserted that emotion was produced by (1) general physiological arousal and (2) cognitive

EXAMPLE PROBLEM 1

Table 2-7 ♦ Hypothetical data for the study on the determinants of emotion[a]

Treatment	Situation	
	Euphoria	Anger
Drug + accurate explanation	5	2
	4	3
	6	2
	5	1
Drug + inaccurate explanation	6	1
	7	1
	5	0
	6	2
Drug + no explanation	6	2
	7	3
	5	2
	5	3
Placebo	4	4
	4	4
	4	3
	6	3

[a] Scores refer to subjects' ratings of their feelings on a scale from 0 (angry) to 8 (happy). (See "Determinants of Emotion" in Chapter 2.)

factors involved in identifying, labeling, and interpreting a stirred-up physiological state.

In order to examine these two theories, a hypothetical experiment was conducted using a 2 × 4 design. The factor with two levels is the situation in which subjects find themselves (euphoria versus anger). The physiological-state theory does not implicate this variable, while the two-component theory asserts that subjects will interpret (i.e., identify, label, and interpret) heightened physiological arousal with respect to the situation if no other explanation is readily available. The factor with four levels is a treatment factor with the following levels: (1) drug (arousal) + accurate explanation (for arousal), (2) drug + inaccurate explanation, (3) drug + no explanation, and (4) placebo. The physiological-state theory asserts that subjects will experience the same emotion in all three drug conditions and that subjects in the placebo condition will not experience emotion. In contrast, the two-component theory predicts differences in emotion in the three drug conditions. In the condition "drug + accurate explanation," the theory asserts that situational factors should play a minor role in determining emotion, while in the other two drug conditions, situational factors should play an important role. Hence, the two-component model posits an interaction between treatment and situation.

The data from this hypothetical study are given in Table 2-7 on page 498.

Using these data, test whether there were significant main effects for treatment and situation and whether there was a significant interaction effect at $\alpha = .05$. Include in your answer:

a. Null and alternative hypotheses for each effect
b. Tests of assumptions or explanation for not doing so
c. Computation of sums of squares (see Procedure 17-1)
d. ANOVA summary table (see Table 17-4)
e. F_{critical} for each effect
f. Conclusions for each effect
g. Graph of interaction (see Procedure 17-2)

The overall F test for each hypothesis in the two-way ANOVA indicates whether or not the observed differences between cell means, column means, and row means (see Tables 17-1, 17-3, and 17-5) were likely to arise by chance. However, the F test does not give information about the *strength* of each effect. As with the one-way ANOVA (Chapter 16), the statistic omega square (ω^2) can be used as an index of the strength of association between the levels of each effect (A, B, and AB) and the dependent variable. For each of the three effects, the numerator of the formula for omega square is slightly different:

STRENGTH OF ASSOCIATION

$$\omega_A^2 = \frac{SS_A - (df_A)MS_W}{SS_T + MS_W} ; \qquad [17\text{-}9]$$

$$\omega_B^2 = \frac{SS_B - (df_B)MS_W}{SS_T + MS_W} ; \qquad [17\text{-}10]$$

$$\omega_{AB}^2 = \frac{SS_{AB} - (df_{AB})MS_W}{SS_T + MS_W} . \qquad [17\text{-}11]$$

Procedure 16-2 provides the steps in calculating omega square. Typically, omega square is calculated only for significant effects in the two-way ANOVA. In the hypothetical study of reading comprehension, all three effects were significant and the omega-square statistic for each effect can be calculated using data from Table 17-5:

$$\omega_A^2 = \frac{8.34 - (1)(0.50)}{92.67 + 0.50} = \frac{7.84}{93.17} = .08,$$

$$\omega_B^2 = \frac{20.67 - (2)(0.50)}{92.67 + 0.50} = \frac{19.67}{93.17} = .21,$$

$$\omega_{AB}^2 = \frac{60.66 - (2)(0.50)}{92.67 + 0.50} = \frac{59.66}{93.17} = .64.$$

Clearly, the strongest effect in the data is due to the interaction. The unique interaction effect accounts for 64 percent of the variance in achievement-test scores. The treatment effect accounts for 21 percent, and the effect of verbal ability accounts for only 8 percent.

EXAMPLE PROBLEM 2

Using the data from Example Problem 1, compute the strength of association for the main effects of factor A and factor B and their interaction. Include in your answer:

a. Computation of ω^2 for each effect
b. Interpretation

METHODS FOR COMPARING MEANS IN THE TWO-WAY ANOVA

The overall F tests in the two-way ANOVA indicate whether or not there are significant differences between means, and omega square indicates the strength of each effect on the dependent variable. However, as pointed out before, if there are more than two levels of a variable, neither statistic indicates which means differ from each other. In this section, methods of planned and post hoc comparisons for the two-way ANOVA are presented. Since these methods are analogous to the methods for the one-way ANOVA, the details given in Chapter 16 should be reviewed if necessary.

◆　　◆　　◆　　◆　　◆

Planned Comparisons

In making planned comparisons, the researcher should have strong theory and empirical support for specifying the comparisons to be made. These comparisons must be formulated prior to the conduct of the study, and α set for each comparison. For the statistical test given here, they must be orthogonal, and the sum of the weights used to make the comparisons must equal zero. (See Chapter 16, "Planned Comparisons.") Once these requirements have been met, the researcher collects data and uses the two-way ANOVA to obtain the value of MS_W. There is no need to calculate $F_{observed}$ for each effect (A, B, and AB) since planned comparisons can be conducted in the absence of a significant overall F.

Planned comparisons with a two-way design are made in the same manner as with a one-way design (see Chapter 16). The key to the similarity is to recognize that a two-way design with $q \times r$ cells can be treated as a one-way design. Specifically, a $q \times r$, two-way ANOVA is treated as a one-way ANOVA with $q \times r = k$ levels. In this case, the two-way ANOVA is stretched into one long one-way ANOVA. Each cell in the two-way ANOVA is considered to be a separate level—one of the k levels of the treatment variable. In the hypothetical study of prose learning, for example, the 2×3 (ability × treatment) design would be stretched into a one-way design with $k = 2 \times 3 = 6$ levels (Table 17-6).

With k levels for a planned comparison, there are $k - 1$ degrees of freedom. A maximum, then, of $k - 1$ orthogonal comparisons can be made. Each comparison accounts for one degree of freedom. For the prose learning study, five orthogonal comparisons are possible ($k - 1 = 6 - 1 = 5$).

A comparison in a two-way design is defined in exactly the same way as for the one-way design with $q \times r = k$ levels:

$$\hat{C} = w_1 \overline{X}_1 + w_2 \overline{X}_2 + \cdots + w_k \overline{X}_k. \qquad [\textbf{16-12a}]$$

Table 17-7 presents three of five possible orthogonal comparisons for the hypothetical study of prose learning. The first comparison is between the low- and high-ability groups. The mean performance of the low-ability subjects is compared with the mean performance of the high-ability subjects. Notice that in order to compare the two ability groups, the means of the three treatment groups are combined. Since there are only two levels of the ability variable, the comparison is equivalent to testing the main effect of A. The second comparison is between the control group and the two treatment groups combined (fact + comprehension). And the third comparison is between the fact and comprehension treatments, using data from the low-ability subjects.

For a statistical test of each comparison, the null and alternative hypotheses

Table 17-6 ♦ Cell means from a two-way ($q \times r$) ANOVA arranged in a one-way design (see Table 17-3)

	Cells of the design					
Levels of A:	Low ability (a_1)			High ability (a_2)		
Levels of B:	Control (b_1)	Fact (b_2)	Comprehension (b_3)	Control (b_1)	Fact (b_2)	Comprehension (b_3)
	1.5	1.5	7.5	8.5	3.5	3.5

Table 17-7 ♦ Some planned comparisons for the hypothetical study of prose learning: a 2 × 3 design

Comparison	Levels of A:	Low ability (a_1)			High ability (a_2)		
	Levels of B:	Control (b_1)	Fact (b_2)	Compre. (b_3)	Control (b_1)	Fact (b_2)	Compre. (b_3)
	Mean:	1.5	1.5	7.5	8.5	3.5	3.5
1		−1	−1	−1	+1	+1	+1
2		−2	+1	+1	−2	+1	+1
3		0	−1	+1	0	0	0

for the two-way design are the same as for the one-way design:

$$H_0: C = 0;$$

$$H_1: C \neq 0 \quad \text{or}$$

$$C > 0 \quad \text{or}$$

$$C < 0.$$

Finally, the statistical test for planned comparisons in a two-way design is the same as in a one-way design. For equal cell sizes, the t test is

$$t_{observed} = \frac{\hat{C}}{\sqrt{\dfrac{MS_W}{n}(w_1^2 + w_2^2 + \cdots + w_k^2)}} \qquad [\textbf{16-15a}]$$

with $df = qr(n-1) = k(n-1) = N - k$.

The data from Table 17-7 can be used as a numerical example of how the planned comparison is carried out. In this example, comparison 1 (the main effect of A) is tested at $\alpha = .05$. On the basis of theory and prior research, the mean score of the high-ability group is expected to be higher than the mean score of the low-ability group. More specifically, the null and alternative hypotheses for this comparison are

$$H_0: C_1 = 0,$$

$$H_1: C_1 > 0.$$

The value of $\hat{C}_1$ is found with Formula 16-12a, and $t_{observed}$ with Formula 16-15a:

$$\hat{C}_A = (-1)(1.5) + (-1)(1.5) + (-1)(7.5) + (1)(8.5) + (1)(3.5) + (1)(3.5)$$

$$= -1.5 - 1.5 - 7.5 + 8.5 + 3.5 + 3.5$$

$$= 5,$$

$$t_{observed} = \frac{5}{\sqrt{\frac{.50}{2}\left[(-1)^2 + (-1)^2 + (-1)^2 + (1)^2 + (1)^2 + (1)^2\right]}}$$

$$= \frac{5}{\sqrt{\frac{.50}{2}(6)}}$$

$$= \frac{5}{\sqrt{1.50}}$$

$$= 4.08.$$

In order to decide whether or not to reject the null hypothesis, the critical value of t with $N - k = 12 - 6 = 6$ df is needed. From Table C, this value for a one-tailed test at $\alpha = .05$ is 1.943. Since $t_{observed}$ exceeds $t_{critical}$, the null hypothesis should be rejected. Subjects high in verbal ability scored, on the average, higher than subjects low in verbal ability.

The steps in testing each of the comparisons in a two-way design are identical to the test of the first comparison. And since they are identical to the steps in testing a comparison in a one-way design, Procedure 16-5 can be used in calculating planned comparisons in a two-way design.

---

a. Physiological state theory asserts that the three drug conditions should give rise to the same emotion regardless of the situation in which the subject finds himself. In contrast, the two-component theory predicts a difference due to situation. Using the data in Example Problem 1, write a comparison of the three means in the euphoria situation with the three means in the anger condition. Test the hypothesis at $\alpha = .05$, and include in your answer:

1. Table of weights for the contrast with verification that weights are properly specified
2. Null and alternative hypotheses
3. Computation of $\hat{C}$
4. t test
5. $t_{critical}$
6. Conclusion.

b. Both theories predict no difference between the means of the placebo condition in the euphoria and anger situations. Compare the means of the placebo group in the euphoria and anger situations ($\alpha = .05$). Include items 1–6 above in your answer as well as a check to see if this comparison is independent of the first one.

EXAMPLE PROBLEM 3

◆　◆　◆　◆　◆

Post Hoc Comparisons　If the research is exploratory, so that none or only some of the $k - 1$ independent planned comparisons can be set forth prior to conducting the study, pairs of means or more complex combinations of means can still be examined using post hoc comparisons. (For background on the use of post hoc comparisons, see Chapter 16, "Post Hoc Comparisons.") Two methods for post hoc comparisons are presented here: Scheffé's test and Tukey's test. More advanced texts contain a smorgasbord of tests, but they will not be treated here (see Kirk, 1968; Winer, 1971).

Scheffé's test　Scheffé's test for post hoc comparisons in the two-way ANOVA is somewhat analogous to its use in the one-way ANOVA (see Chapter 16). If a significant interaction is found in the data, Scheffé's method is used to examine patterns in cell means. (For an extensive discussion of comparisons for examining the interaction effect, see Betz & Gabriel, 1978; Games, 1973, 1978; Levin & Marascuilo, 1972, 1973; and Marascuilo & Levin, 1970, 1976.) These comparisons are guided by a graph of the interaction effect. The type of comparisons, pairwise or complex, would depend on the observed differences between the cell means as revealed by the graph. In the absence of a significant interaction, the significant main effects (with more than two levels) become the focus of post hoc comparisons. In this case, the row and column means are compared (cf. Tables 17-1 and 17-3). With Scheffé's method, as many comparisons as possible can be carried out, all at a specified level of significance (α).

Interaction effects　In conducting a post hoc examination of a significant interaction, a graph guides the comparison of means. The procedures for calculating t_{observed} for a particular comparison are exactly the same as those described above for planned comparisons and in Chapter 16 for Scheffé's method with a one-way ANOVA. The $q \times r$ cell means are treated as if they were k means in a one-way ANOVA. The null and alternative hypotheses are

$$H_0: C = 0,$$

$$H_1: C \neq 0.$$

A sample comparison is defined as

$$\hat{C} = w_1 \overline{X}_i + w_2 \overline{X}_2 + \cdots + w_k \overline{X}_k, \qquad [\,16\text{-}12a\,]$$

and t_{observed} is

$$t_{\text{observed}} = \frac{\hat{C}}{\sqrt{\dfrac{MS_{\text{W}}}{n}\left(w_1^2 + w_2^2 + \cdots + w_k^2\right)}}. \qquad [\,16\text{-}15\,]$$

In order to decide whether or not to reject the null hypothesis, a critical value is needed. Just as with the one-way ANOVA, the critical value for the

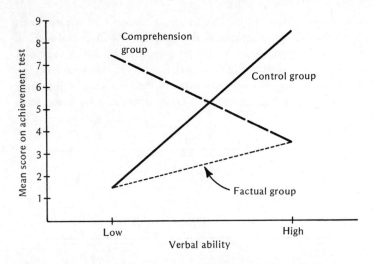

Figure 17-4 ♦ Interaction of verbal ability with treatment

Scheffé test takes into account the fact that all possible comparisons could be made at a particular level of significance (e.g., $\alpha = .05$). The critical value can be obtained from

$$t'_{\text{critical}} = \sqrt{(k-1)F_{\text{critical}(\alpha,\, k-1,\, df_{\text{w}})}} \ . \qquad [16\text{-}16]$$

Since the procedures for comparing cell means in a two-way ANOVA using Scheffé's method are virtually the same as the procedures for a one-way ANOVA, Procedure 16-5 can be used. As an example of how an interaction might be explored, consider the data from the prose-learning study (Tables 17-3 and 17-5). Since a significant interaction between verbal ability and treatment was found, post hoc comparisons are in order. Figure 17-4 provides a visual

Table 17-8 ♦ Some comparisons examining the interactions shown in Figure 17-4

Ability:	Low			High		
Treatment:	Control	Factual	Comprehension	Control	Factual	Comprehension
Means:	1.5	1.5	7.5	8.5	3.5	3.5
$\hat{C}_1$	-1	-1	2	0	0	0
$\hat{C}_2$	0	0	0	2	-1	-1
$\hat{C}_1 =$	$(-1)(1.5)$	$+(-1)(1.5)$	$+(2)(7.5)$	$+0$	$+0$	$+0 \qquad = 12$
$\hat{C}_2 =$	0	$+0$	$+0$	$+(2)(8.5)$	$+(-1)(3.5)$	$+(-1)(3.5) = 10$

representation of the interaction. From this figure, a number of comparisons can be identified to examine the interaction. For subjects low in verbal ability, the mean of the comprehension group should be compared with the means of the other two groups. For subjects high in verbal ability, the mean of the control group should be compared with the means of the two treatment groups (see Table 17-8). The value of $t_{observed}$ for each comparison can be found with Formula 16-7a:

$$\hat{C}_1: \quad t_{observed} = \frac{12}{\sqrt{\frac{.50}{5}\left[(-1)^2 + (-1)^2 + (2)^2 + (0)^2 + (0)^2 + (0)^2\right]}}$$

$$= 15.49,$$

$$\hat{C}_2: \quad t_{observed} = \frac{10}{\sqrt{\frac{.50}{5}\left[(0)^2 + (0)^2 + (0)^2 + (2)^2 + (-1)^2 + (-1)^2\right]}}$$

$$= 12.91.$$

In order to decide whether to reject the null hypothesis, $t'_{critical}$ has to be calculated with Formula 16-15:

$$t'_{critical} = \sqrt{(5)F_{critical(.05,\, 5,\, 6)}}$$

$$= \sqrt{(5)(4.39)}$$

$$= 4.69.$$

Since in both cases $t_{observed}$ exceeds $t'_{critical}$, the null hypothesis should be rejected, with the conclusion that the observed differences are reliable. Low-ability students perform best in the comprehension group, while high-ability students perform best in the control group.

One last comment. The comparisons made so far certainly are important in examining the interaction. However, other comparisons are also of interest, such as the comparison of means for subjects low and high in verbal ability for each of the treatment groups.

Main effects for A and B   In the absence of a significant interaction, comparisons between row means (main effect of A) and column means (main effect of B) become the focus of post hoc comparisons. For clarity, a row mean which reflects the effect of factor A will be denoted by $\bar{A}_i$, and a column mean which reflects the effect of factor B will be denoted by $\bar{B}_j$. The marginal means in Table 17-3 can be used to illustrate this new notation: $\bar{A}_1 = 3.50$, $\bar{A}_2 = 5.17$; $\bar{B}_1 = 5.00$, $\bar{B}_2 = 2.50$, $\bar{B}_3 = 5.50$.

For comparing the means representing the main effect of A, a comparison, $\hat{C}_A$, is defined as

$$\hat{C}_A = w_1\bar{A}_1 + w_2\bar{A}_2 + \cdots + w_q\bar{A}_q$$
$$= \sum_{i=1}^{q} w_i\bar{A}_i, \qquad [17\text{-}12]$$

and the formula for testing the usual hypotheses is

$$t_{\text{observed}(A)} = \frac{\hat{C}_A}{\sqrt{\dfrac{MS_W}{nr}\left(w_1^2 + w_2^2 + \cdots + w_q^2\right)}}. \qquad [17\text{-}13]$$

In order to decide whether or not to reject the null hypothesis, F_{observed} must be compared with F'_{critical} corresponding to the test of the A main effect:

$$t'_{\text{critical}(A)} = \sqrt{(df_A)F_{\text{critical}(\alpha,\, df_A,\, df_W)}} \qquad [17\text{-}14]$$

As an illustration of how the formula operates, the data from the prose-learning study will be used. However, in this example, normally the main effect of A would not be tested, for two reasons: (1) there are only two levels of A, so the overall significant F test indicates that they differ, and (2) there is an AB interaction, so that an examination of cell means is in order. With these caveats, the use of the formulas can be illustrated:

$$\hat{C}_A = (-1)(3.50) + (1)(5.17)$$
$$= 1.67,$$

$$t_{\text{observed}(A)} = \frac{1.67}{\sqrt{\dfrac{.5}{(2)(3)}\left[(-1)^2 + (1)^2\right]}}$$

$$= \frac{1.67}{.4}$$

$$= 4.18.$$

If the test is conducted at $\alpha = .05$, then $F_{\text{critical}(.05,\, 1,\, 6)}$ is equal to 5.99 and

$$t'_{\text{critical}(A)} = \sqrt{(1)(5.99)}$$
$$= 2.45.$$

Since $t_{observed(A)}$ exceeds $t'_{critical}$, the null hypothesis should be rejected and the conclusion drawn that subjects high in verbal ability scored, on the average, higher than subjects low in verbal ability on the achievement test.

For comparing the means representing the *main effect of B*, a comparison, $\hat{C}_B$, is defined as

$$\begin{aligned} \hat{C}_B &= w_1\bar{B}_1 + w_2\bar{B}_2 + \cdots + w_r\bar{B}_r \\ &= \sum_{j=1}^{r} w_j\bar{B}_j, \end{aligned} \qquad [17\text{-}15]$$

and the formula for testing the usual null and alternative hypotheses is

$$t_{observed(B_j)} = \frac{\hat{C}_{B_j}}{\sqrt{\dfrac{MS_W}{nq}\left(w_1^2 + w_2^2 + \cdots + w_r^2\right)}}. \qquad [17\text{-}16]$$

In order to decide whether or not to reject H_0: $C = 0$, $t_{observed}$ must be compared with $t'_{critical}$ corresponding to the test of the B main effect:

$$t'_{critical(B)} = \sqrt{(df_B)F_{critical(\alpha,\, df_B,\, df_W)}}. \qquad [17\text{-}17]$$

As an illustration of how this formula works, the data from the prose learning study will be used, with the caveat that since the interaction was significant, this main effect probably would not be of particular interest. For the purpose of this comparison, let's compare the two treatment groups ($\bar{B}_2 = 2.50$, $\bar{B}_3 = 5.50$) against the control group ($\bar{B}_1 = 5.00$):

$$\begin{aligned} \hat{C}_{B_j} &= (-2)(5.00) + (1)(2.50) + (1)(5.50) \\ &= -10 + 8 \\ &= -2, \end{aligned}$$

$$\begin{aligned} t_{observed(B)} &= \frac{(-2)}{\sqrt{\dfrac{.50}{(2)(2)}\left[(-2)^2 + (1)^2 + (1)^2\right]}} \\ &= \frac{-2}{.87} \\ &= -2.30. \end{aligned}$$

508

If the test is conducted at $\alpha = .05$, then $F_{critical(.05, 2, 6)}$ is equal to 5.14, and

$$t'_{critical(B)} = \sqrt{(2)(5.14)}$$
$$= 3.21.$$

Since $|t_{observed(B)}|$ does not exceed $t'_{critical(B)}$, the null hypothesis cannot be rejected. The steps in conducting Scheffé's test for examining the main effects of factors A and B are summarized in Procedure 17-3.

Steps in conducting Scheffé's test to examine main effects (data from the ♦ Procedure 17-3 reading-comprehension study)

Operation	Example
1 Specify null and alternative hypotheses for each contrast: $$H_0: C = 0,$$ $$H_1: C \neq 0.$$ *Note that H_1 is always nondirectional.*	$H_0: C = 0,$ $H_1: C \neq 0.$
2 *To examine the main effect of A:* **a** Assign weights to marginal row means so that comparison of interest is identified.	<table><tr><td>$\bar{A}_1$</td><td>$\bar{A}_2$</td></tr><tr><td>−1</td><td>1</td></tr></table>
b Compute $\hat{C}_A$ using Formula 17-12: $$\hat{C}_A = w_1\bar{A}_1 + w_2\bar{A}_2 + \cdots + w_q\bar{A}_q$$ $$= \sum_{i=1}^{q} w_i\bar{A}_i.$$	$\hat{C}_A = (-1)(3.50) + (1)(5.17)$ $= 1.67.$
c Compute $t_{obs.(A)}$ using Formula 17-13: $$t_{obs.(A)} = \frac{\hat{C}_A}{\sqrt{\frac{MS_W}{nr}(w_1^2 + w_2^2 + \cdots + w_q^2)}}$$ where n = number of subjects in a cell of the design, r = number of levels of factor B.	$t_{obs.(A)} = \dfrac{(1.67)}{\sqrt{\dfrac{.5}{(2)(3)}[(-1)^2 + (1)^2]}}$ $= 4.18.$
d Compute $t'_{crit.(A)}$ using Formula 17-14: $$t'_{crit.(A)} = \sqrt{(df_A)F'_{crit.(\alpha, df_A, df_W)}}$$ where q = number of levels of factor A	$df_A = 1,$ $\alpha = .05,$ $F_{crit.(.05, 1, 6)} = 5.99,$ $t'_{crit.(A)} = \sqrt{(1)(5.99)}$ $= 2.45.$

(continued on p. 510)

e If $|t_{obs.(A)}| \geq t'_{crit.(A)}$, reject H_0. If $|t_{obs.(A)}| < t'_{crit.(A)}$, do not reject H_0.

Since $|t_{obs.(A)}| > t'_{crit.(A)}$, reject H_0. Subjects of high verbal ability obtained a significantly higher mean achievement score than subjects of low verbal ability.

3 *To examine the main effect of B:*

a Assign weights to marginal column means so that comparison of interest is identified.

$\bar{B}_1$	$\bar{B}_2$	$\bar{B}_3$
-2	1	1

b Compute $\hat{C}_B$ using Formula 17-15:

$$\hat{C}_B = \sum_{j=1}^{r} w_j \bar{B}_j$$
$$= w_1 \bar{B}_1 + w_2 \bar{B}_2 + \cdots + w_r \bar{B}_r$$

$$\hat{C}_B = (-2)(5.00) + (1)(2.50) + (1)(5.50)$$
$$= -2.$$

c Compute $t_{obs.(B)}$ using Formula 17-16:

$$t_{obs.(B)} = \frac{\hat{C}_{B_j}}{\sqrt{\dfrac{MS_W}{nq}(w_1^2 + w_2^2 + \cdots + w_r^2)}}$$

$$t_{obs.(B)} = \frac{-2}{\sqrt{\dfrac{.50}{(2)(2)}\left[(-2)^2 + (1)^2 + (1)^2\right]}}$$
$$= -2.30.$$

where n = number of subjects in a cell of the design,

q = number of levels of factor A.

d Compute $t'_{crit.(B)}$ using Formula 17-17:

$$t'_{crit.(B)} = \sqrt{(df_B)F_{crit.(\alpha,\, df_B,\, df_W)}}$$

where r = number of levels of factor B.

$df_B = 2$
$\alpha = .05$
$F_{crit.(.05,\, 2,\, 6)} = 5.14$
$t'_{crit.(B)} = \sqrt{(2)(5.14)}$
$\quad\quad = 3.21.$

e If $|t_{obs.(B)}| \geq t'_{crit.(B)}$, reject H_0.
If $|t_{obs.(B)}| < t'_{crit.(B)}$, do not reject H_0.

Since $|t_{obs.(B)}| < t'_{crit.(B)}$, do not reject H_0. Conclude that mean achievement of subjects receiving factual and comprehension treatments did not differ significantly from the mean achievement of subjects in the control treatment.

EXAMPLE PROBLEM 4

a. The interaction effect in Example Problem 1 was significant. Using the data from this problem, compare the means of the three treatment groups against the placebo group in the euphoria situation using Scheffé's test. (Let $\alpha = .05$.) Include in your answer:

1. Null and alternative hypotheses
2. Set of weights for the comparison
3. Computation of $\hat{C}$

4. $t_{observed}$
5. $t'_{critical}$
6. Conclusions.

b. Examine the main effect of treatment by comparing the three means of the drug groups against the mean of the placebo group using Scheffé's test. (Let $\alpha = .05$.) Include steps 1–6 above in your answer.

Tukey's HSD test   In some cases, the researcher may be interested in examining differences between all possible pairs of means, given a significant main effect or interaction. This is data snooping at its best and serves to discover what happened in the present study and to formulate hypotheses for subsequent studies. For this purpose, Tukey's HSD (honestly significant difference) test can be used instead of Scheffé's method. For making pairwise comparisons, Tukey's test is more powerful than Scheffé's.

The use of Tukey's HSD test for comparing all possible pairs of cell means in a factorial design is analogous to its use in a one-way design. The only difference is that the factorial design must be arranged as a one-way design with $q \times r = k$ levels. In this case, each cell of the factorial design is considered a separate level of the treatment variable. In the hypothetical study of prose learning, a 2×3 (verbal learning × type of questioning treatment) factorial design was used. When it is treated as a one-way design, there are $2 \times 3 = 6$ levels of the treatment variable. Once the two-way factorial design is arranged as a one-way design, the procedure for conducting Tukey's HSD test is exactly the same as the one-way design. The procedure for using Tukey's test, then, is given in Procedure 16-7. Tukey's test can also be used with row and column means corresponding to the main effects for factors A and B, respectively. For factor A, divide MS_W by nr instead of n; and for factor B, divide MS_W by nq instead of n (see step 3 in Procedure 16-7).

Using the data from Example Problem 1, compare all pairs of means using Tukey's HSD test. (Let $\alpha = .05$.) Include in your answer:

EXAMPLE PROBLEM 5

a. Null and alternative hypotheses
b. Table of differences between means
c. Computation of HSD
d. Conclusions.

♦   ♦   ♦   ♦   ♦

This chapter presents the *factorial analysis of variance* (ANOVA), a statistical test used to test hypotheses about differences between means in true factorial

Summary

experiments or in factorial criterion-group designs. The discussion is restricted to the *two-way* ANOVA: the analysis of factorial designs with two factors having equal cell sizes. The purpose, underlying rationale, and procedures for computing and interpreting the two-way ANOVA are presented. Procedures for computing the strength of association (*omega square*) for main effects and the interaction effect are also discussed. Finally, methods for making *comparisons between means* in the two-way ANOVA are presented. Procedures for making *planned* (a priori) *comparisons* to test hypotheses about main effects or interactions formulated prior to the conduct of the study are described. Finally, methods are presented for making *post hoc comparisons* to test hypotheses formulated after data are collected, using *Scheffé's test* and *Tukey's test*.

◆　　◆　　◆　　◆　　◆

Key Words

a priori comparisons	normality
completely crossed design	omega square
degrees of freedom	ordinal interaction
disordinal interaction	planned comparisons
factorial analysis of variance	post hoc comparisons
factorial criterion-group design	Scheffé's test
factorial design	source of variation
homogeneity of variances	strength of association
independence	sum of squares
interaction effect	Tukey's test
main effect	two-way analysis of variance
mean squares	

◆　　◆　　◆　　◆　　◆

Exercises

1. What type of information can be obtained from a factorial ANOVA that cannot be obtained from separate one-way designs on each factor?

2–5 For each figure below, decide whether or not an interaction is suggested, and if so, name the type of interaction.

2.

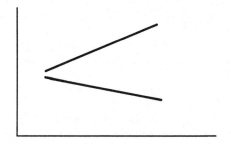

3.

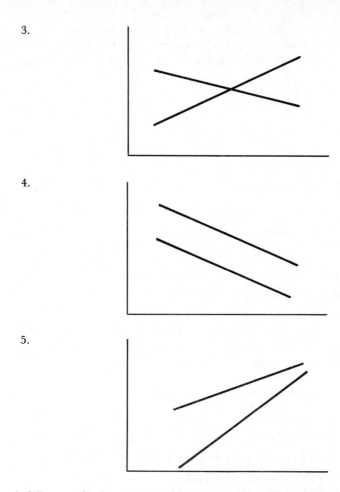

4.

5.

6. What are the three sources of between-group variation in the two-way ANOVA?

7. What are the sources of total variation in the two-way design?

8. Under what conditions is the ANOVA not sensitive to violations of the assumption of homogeneity of variances?

9. In interpreting the results of the two-way ANOVA, where do you start, and why?

10–22 A social psychologist was interested in the relation between self-concept and the ability to resist an authority figure. Six students scoring low on a measure of self-concept and six students with high scores on this measure were randomly assigned to two groups. Both groups were told that they would be participating in an experiment on the effects of punishment on learning a paired-associate word list. The subjects were asked to administer an electric shock to another student when that student made a mistake on the learning task. Actually, the other student was a confederate of the experimenter, who only pretended to receive a shock. The subjects administering the "shocks" could choose any level of shock, from 1 = low to 6 = high. Although the subject was not required to follow his directions, the experimenter in group 1 strongly suggested throughout the experiment that a high level of shock be given. In group 2, the experimenter merely observed the subjects. Subjects were scored on the total amount of shock given to the student. The following hypothetical data were collected from this study:

		Factor B (authority figure)	
		Group 1 (experimental)	Group 2 (control)
Factor A	High	2 3 3	1 2 3
(self-concept)	Low	6 14 10	4 5 4

Using the above data, test hypotheses for each effect at $\alpha = .05$.

10. Formulate null and alternative hypotheses for each effect.
11. Test assumptions or give an explanation for not doing so.
12. Compute sums of squares.
13. Construct the ANOVA summary table.
14. Find F_{critical} for each effect.
15. State your conclusions for each effect.
16. Draw a graph of the interaction.
17. Compute ω^2 for each effect.
18. State your conclusions on ω^2.

19–22 Compare all pairs of means using Tukey's HSD test ($\alpha = .05$).

19. Formulate null and alternative hypotheses.
20. Construct the table of differences between means.
21. Compute HSD.
22. State your conclusions.

23. A researcher had reason to conduct planned comparisons for an interaction effect. Given the following data, test the following planned comparisons for the interaction effect ($\alpha = .05$):

a. Levels of B at A_1 (expected $B_1 < B_2$)
b. Levels of B at A_2 (expected $B_1 > B_2$).

		Factor B	
		B_1	B_2
Factor A	A_1	$\bar{X} = 4.0$	$\bar{X} = 6.25$
	A_2	$\bar{X} = 12.0$	$\bar{X} = 2.8$
$(n = 3)$			

ANOVA summary table

Source	SS	df	Ms
Factor A	14.50	1	14.00
Factor B	18.50	1	18.50
$A \times B$	40.50	1	40.50
Error	15.20	8	1.90
Total	88.20	11	

24. In a study, a significant interaction was found ($F = 12.06$, $df = 1, 8$, $MS_W = 2.53$), so post hoc comparisons could be conducted at a specified level of significance. Given the data below, conduct Scheffé's test for post hoc comparisons for the interaction effects ($\alpha = .05$):

    a. Levels of B at A_1

    b. Levels of B at A_2.

		Factor B	
		B_1	B_2
Factor A	A_1	$\bar{X} = 4.25$	$\bar{X} = 2.10$
	A_2	$\bar{X} = 10.0$	$\bar{X} = 3.80$

18 ◆

Chi-Square Tests

The Uses of Chi-Square Tests

χ^2 for One-Way Designs: Goodness-of-Fit Test

◆ Purpose and Underlying Logic ◆

◆ Hypotheses ◆

◆ Assumptions and Requirements ◆

◆ Computational Procedures for the One-Way χ^2 Test ◆

◆ Decision Rules for Rejecting H_0 ◆

◆ Numerical Example ◆

◆ Correction for Continuity with One Degree of Freedom ◆

χ^2 for Two-Way Designs: Contingency-Table Analysis

◆ Purpose and Underlying Logic ◆

◆ Hypotheses ◆

◆ Assumptions and Requirements ◆

◆ Computational Procedures for the Two-Way χ^2 Test ◆

◆ Decision Rules for Rejecting H_0 ◆

◆ Numerical Example ◆

◆ Correction for Continuity for the 2×2 χ^2 ◆

◆ Collapsing Levels of a Variable in a χ^2 Test ◆

Summary

◆ Key Words ◆

◆ Exercises ◆

Cʜɪ-sQUARE TESTS are nonparametric statistical tests. They are used with frequency data which have been collected in either one-way or factorial designs. The chi-square test for one-way designs is called a *goodness-of-fit test* because it tests how closely observed frequencies from a sample fit theoretically expected frequencies based on a null hypothesis. The chi-square test for factorial designs tests the null hypothesis that two variables are independent of one another in the population. In this chapter the conceptual underpinnings of these tests, along with skills needed to apply them, are presented.

Chi-square tests are frequently used because behavioral researchers often are interested in counting the number of subjects falling into particular categories. The following example studies may give you some notion of how researchers come about counting frequencies.

USES OF
CHI-SQUARE TESTS

In a study of political opinions, researchers conducting a poll might be interested in whether the number of Democrats, Republicans, etc., in their sample is proportional to the number of voters in each party in the precincts from which the sample was taken. Or a researcher developing a measure of self-concept might want to know whether or not subjects' scores are normally distributed. In order to do this, the researcher would divide the theoretical, normal distribution into categories such as those shown in Figure 18-1a. He would then build a frequency polygon of the observed responses and divide it into the same categories (see Figure 18-1b). The observed number of responses falling in each area of the frequency distribution could be compared with the expected frequency based on the normal distribution to see if the responses were normally distributed.

Sometimes interval measurements are converted to categories[1] and the number of subjects falling into each category can be counted. For example, evaluators of remedial reading programs in California received reading achievement data based on four different published reading tests. (Different schools used different reading tests.) Since the tests could not be equated with one another, subjects' scores on the tests were converted to categories. For example, subjects with scores one-half a standard deviation above the mean of

---

[1]For example, subjects might be divided into groups of low and high anxiety depending upon whether their score on an anxiety scale was below or above the median of an appropriate norm group.

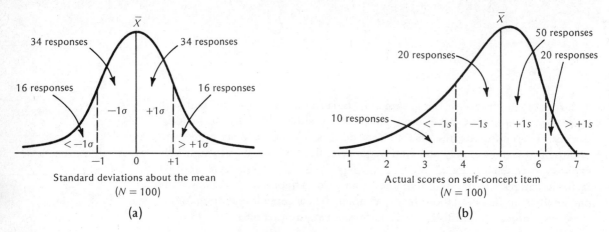

Figure 18-1 ♦ Theoretically expected and observed responses to a self-concept item: (a) theoretically expected frequency of scores if normally distributed; (b) observed responses

their norm group were labeled as "high" on reading achievement, subjects one-half a standard deviation below the norm were labeled "low," and subjects in the middle were labeled, of course, "middle." The number of subjects in each of two different remedial reading programs who fell in the "low," "middle," and "high" groups on reading achievement were counted and compared with the number in each category that would be expected if there was no relation between reading program and reading achievement.

Or a researcher might be interested in whether men with prior military experience have a different opinion about the development of the neutron bomb than men without military experience. Suppose that a random sample of 1000 men was drawn from the general population in the United States and asked two questions: (1) Have you served in the armed forces of the United States or any other country? (yes, no) and (2) Should the United States develop a neutron bomb? (yes, no, no opinion). Based on these responses, the sample could be divided into six groups (2×3) and the number of respondents falling in each cell could be counted. The pattern of frequencies in the six cells could then be compared with the frequencies that would be expected if there was no relationship between military experience and opinions about the neutron bomb.

In all of these examples, the **chi-square** statistic (χ^2) is used to test whether the observed frequencies differed significantly from the expected frequencies. Since all of these examples have a couple of features in common, they can be used to illustrate the circumstances under which the chi-square statistic can be used. First, χ^2 compares observed frequencies with **expected frequencies**. The expected frequencies might be based on prior information such as the number of Democrats and Republicans in a precinct. Or they might be based on a (null) hypothesis such as that the responses to self-concept items are normally distributed. Or they might be based on what would be expected if chance assigned subjects to categories, as in the study of opinions about the neutron bomb.

Second, χ^2 is used with data in the form of **counts** (in contrast, for example, to scores on a test). This means that χ^2 can be used with frequency data (f), proportion data ($f \div N$), probability data (number of outcomes in event $\div$ total number of outcomes), and percentages (proportion $\times 100$). In all of the example studies, observed frequencies were compared with expected frequencies. Nevertheless, if the data are in the form of proportions, the proportions can easily be converted to frequencies and the χ^2 statistic can be used to test whether the observed proportions differed from the expected proportions ($f = N \times$ proportion).

The third feature of the χ^2 test is the nature of the design in which the frequency data are collected. The independent variable or variables are in the form of **discrete categories**. For example, in the political-opinion poll, the categories were defined by voter registration. They are discrete, nonoverlapping categories. Likewise, subjects in the study of the relationship between military experience and opinion about the neutron bomb could be placed in nonoverlapping categories. Finally, in the example with reading achievement measures, subjects were placed in discrete categories: "low," "middle," and "high."

A fourth feature of the χ^2 test is that the data may be collected in a one-way design or in a two-way, factorial design.[2] In a one-way design, the independent variable may have two or more levels. For example, in the political-opinion poll, the independent variable—party affiliation—had many possible levels. Likewise, in a two-way design, each independent variable may have two or more levels. For example, in the study on opinions about the neutron bomb, the opinion variable had three levels and the military-experience variable had two levels.

Finally, a subject or a subject's response can fall in one and only one cell of the design. Thus, a voter could be classified as affiliated with one and only one political party. Problems can arise when more than one observation is available on a subject. The first observation (e.g., pretest score) might fall in category A while the second observation (e.g., posttest score) might fall in another category. This is not permitted in a χ^2 analysis.[3]

---

[2]More complicated factorial designs can be used; they are beyond the scope of this textbook.

[3]In this particular example, the problem can be overcome by reconceptualizing the pretest-posttest design. If the pretest is considered to be one independent variable with subjects categorized as low and high while the posttest is considered to be a second independent variable with two levels, a 2×2 (pretest $\times$ posttest) design is formed. In this case, subjects fall into one and only one cell of the design.

χ^2 FOR ONE-WAY
DESIGNS: GOODNESS-
OF-FIT TEST

In using the chi-square test for a one-way design, there must be one independent variable with two or more levels. A subject may be counted in one and only one cell of the design. And the dependent variable is a count in the form of frequencies, proportions, probabilities, or percentages.

◆　　◆　　◆　　◆　　◆

**Purpose and
Underlying Logic**

Purpose　The purpose of the χ^2 test for one-way designs is to determine whether the observed frequencies differ systematically from the theoretically expected frequencies, or whether the differences may be due to chance. Often the one-way χ^2 test is called a **goodness-of-fit test** because it examines how closely the observed frequencies fit the theoretically expected frequencies.

In order to use this statistical test, we must be able to specify, in advance, the theoretically expected frequencies. While this may seem like a monstrous task, actually it is straightforward. In some cases, researchers wish to compare an observed frequency distribution with some theoretical frequency distribution like the normal distribution. The normal distribution, then, can be divided into discrete categories such as standard-deviation units about the mean, and the theoretically expected frequency can be determined by multiplying the number of subjects in the sample by the proportion of cases expected in each area of the normal curve. For example, the proportion of cases falling between the mean and one standard deviation above it is approximately .34. So, in a sample of 100 subjects, approximately 34 ($100 \times .34$) should be found within one standard deviation above the mean if the sample data was drawn from a normal distribution (see Figure 18-1a).

In other cases, the theoretical frequencies can be specified by the researcher in much the same way the population mean μ was specified for Case I research studies (see Chapters 9, 11, and 14). Here, the researcher has some prior notion about frequencies in some population, and she wants to compare the observed frequencies with some set of hypothesized frequencies in the population. For example, in the political-opinion survey, the researcher wanted to compare the frequencies of Democrats, Republicans, etc. in the sample with the frequencies of registered voters in the precincts. The theoretical frequencies, then, can be determined by finding the proportion of Democrats, Republicans, etc. who are registered in the precincts. By multiplying the sample size by these proportions, the theoretically expected frequencies for the sample can be identified.

Or suppose a researcher wanted to determine whether the observed number of criminal homicides in a year differed from month to month. The expected frequencies can be determined by assuming that homicides are unrelated to time of year. Thus, in January with 31 days, the expected proportion of homicides would be $31/365 = .085$. In February (if it's not a leap year), the expected proportion would be $28/365 = .077$, and so on. The total number of criminal homicides in a year can be multiplied by these expected frequencies in order to determine the number of expected frequencies for each month. For example, if there were 100 homicides in a year, we should theoretically expect 8.5 homicides in January ($.085 \times 100$). In short, if the researcher specifies a null hypothesis such as "no relation between number of homicides and the month of the year," theoretical frequencies can be determined.

In developing the χ^2 statistic to measure how closely the observed frequencies (denoted by O) match the theoretically expected frequencies (denoted by E), it seems reasonable to subtract E from O in each category and then add up the differences over all of the k categories. But, alas, if this is done, the result will always be zero. This happens because the sum of the observed frequencies equals the total number of subjects in the sample (N), as does the sum of the expected frequencies:

$$\sum_{i=1}^{k}(O_i - E_i) = \sum_{i=1}^{k}O_i - \sum_{i=1}^{k}E_i$$

$$= N - N$$

$$= 0.$$

In order to avoid this problem—as before—the difference between O and E can be squared:

$$(O - E)^2.$$

The sum of the squared differences over all k categories will not be zero unless O equals E in every category. Thus, one possible statistic for comparing observed and expected frequencies is

$$\sum_{i=1}^{k}(O_i - E_i)^2.$$

However, one embellishment is needed to obtain the chi-square statistic. The chi-square statistic weights this squared difference (inversely) according to the expected frequency in each cell:

$$\chi^2_{observed} = \sum_{i=1}^{k}\frac{(O_i - E_i)^2}{E_i}. \qquad [\textbf{18-1}]$$

By weighting the squared difference within a cell inversely by the expected frequency (i.e., $1/E_i$), greater weight is given to those categories where we expect to find few subjects and *actually* find many. Intuitively, this seems appropriate, since we are more surprised to find many where few or none are expected than vice versa. This statistic, then, tells us how closely the observed and theoretical frequencies match each other. Notice that the closer the match between O and E, the smaller the value of the χ^2 statistic.

Underlying logic   The chi-square statistic provides a measure of how much the observed and expected frequencies differ from one another. But how much difference should be tolerated before concluding that the observed frequencies were not sampled from a distribution represented by the expected frequencies? In other words, how large should $\chi^2_{observed}$ be in order to reject the null hypothesis that the observed frequencies were sampled from a distribution represented by the expected frequencies?

Since this decision of whether or not to reject the null hypothesis cannot be made with certainty, it is a probabilistic one. The problem, then, is to determine the probability of finding $\chi^2_{observed}$ as large as or larger than some value, assuming the null hypothesis is true. In order to do so, a sampling distribution for the χ^2 is needed. To get an intuitive feel for this distribution, consider the following. Suppose a researcher takes a random sample of 100 subjects from a normal population and constructs a frequency polygon. Then he divides the observed frequency distribution into four categories according to standard-deviation units (see Figure 18-1). He then compares these observed frequencies with the theoretically expected frequencies based on the normal distribution. Since he is dealing with sample data, O will not agree with E in each category exactly. Rather, chance fluctuation should be expected. Thus, the value of χ^2 calculated with Formula 18-1 will not be zero for this sample. Suppose the researcher carries out this sampling procedure 2000 times. For each sample, χ^2 can be calculated; the 2000 χ^2 values will differ from one another. If the χ^2 values are placed in a frequency polygon with the value of χ^2 on the abscissa and the frequency with which each χ^2 value occurred on the ordinate, the frequency polygon will provide a *sampling distribution of chi-square* (see Figure 18-2). It tells us what to expect the chance fluctuations between O and E to be when, in fact, sampling was from a population specified by the theoretically expected frequencies. If the observed χ^2 value falls way out in the right-hand tail of the sampling distribution, its occurrence is quite improbable.

Figure 18-2 ◆ Sampling distribution of χ^2 when $df = 3$

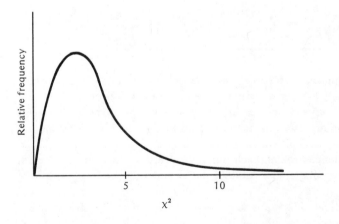

χ^2

In this case, the null hypothesis of no difference between the observed and expected frequencies should be rejected. If the observed value of χ^2 falls well within the sampling distribution of χ^2, the null hypothesis should not be rejected.

The chi-square distribution, like the t and F distributions, is a theoretical distribution—actually, a family of theoretical distributions. For one-way designs, the members of this family depend only on the number of distinct categories on which the statistic is based. Or, more accurately, there is a different member of the family for each number of degrees of freedom, since

$$df = \text{number of categories minus 1}$$
$$= k - 1.$$

Notice that the degrees of freedom for the χ^2 distribution depend on the number of categories (k) and *not* the number of subjects in the sample (N). This follows from the fact that the sum of the differences between O and E is zero (see above under "Purpose"). So, given $k - 1$ differences, the remaining difference is known.

Some important characteristics of the chi-square distribution can be seen in Figure 18-3, where several such distributions are shown, one for each of four numbers of degrees of freedom: 1, 6, 10, and 20. First, notice that as the number of categories (k) or degrees of freedom $(k - 1)$ increases, the value of χ^2_{observed} is expected to increase. This is because, for each category, we calculate

$$\frac{(O - E)^2}{E}.$$

Figure 18-3 ♦ Sampling distributions of χ^2 for differing degrees of freedom

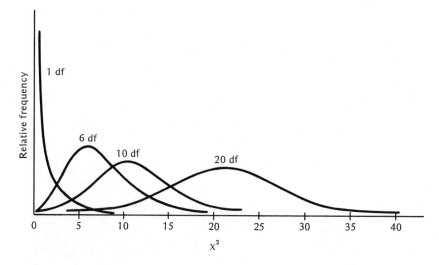

If there are two categories, $(O - E)^2/E$ will be summed twice. If there are 50 categories, . . . and so on.

Second, notice that the χ^2 distribution is unimodal. That is, it has one peak. And third, the χ^2 distribution is positively skewed. As the number of categories increases, however, the skewness decreases and, as the number of degrees of freedom grows infinitely large, the χ^2 distribution approaches the normal distribution.

In summary, the one-way χ^2 is used to test data in the form of frequency counts falling into one and only one category of a discrete, independent variable. The test is carried out by comparing the observed frequencies with the theoretically expected frequencies under the null hypothesis. Specifically, the χ^2 statistic is given by

$$\chi^2_{observed} = \sum_{i=1}^{k} \frac{(O_i - E_i)^2}{E_i}, \qquad [18\text{-}1]$$

with $k - 1$ degrees of freedom. The observed value of χ^2 can be compared with the critical value of χ^2 with $k - 1$ degrees of freedom in order to decide whether or not to reject the null hypothesis.

In order to get a feel for how the χ^2 test works, the data in Figure 18-1 can be used. The data in Figure 18-1b represent the observed frequency of subjects' responses on an item from a self-concept scale. The observed distribution appears to be negatively skewed, but this appearance may be due to chance. Instead, these data might have been sampled from a normal distribution (the null hypothesis) with expected frequencies shown in Figure 18-1a. For each category in the two graphs, the observed and expected frequencies can be compared and $\chi^2_{observed}$ can be computed:

$$\chi^2_{observed} = \frac{(10 - 16)^2}{16} + \frac{(20 - 34)^2}{34} + \frac{(50 - 34)^2}{34} + \frac{(20 - 16)^2}{16}$$

$$= \frac{(-6)^2}{16} + \frac{(-14)^2}{34} + \frac{(16)^2}{34} + \frac{(4)^2}{16}$$

$$= \frac{36}{16} + \frac{196}{34} + \frac{256}{34} + \frac{16}{16}$$

$$= 2.25 + 5.76 + 7.53 + 1,$$

$$= 16.54.$$

In order to determine whether or not to reject the null hypothesis, $\chi^2_{observed}$ is compared with $\chi^2_{critical}$ with $k - 1 = 4 - 1 = 3$ degrees of freedom.[4] From Table

---

[4]Actually, the chi-square test for normality has $k - 3$ degrees of freedom. One degree of freedom is associated with the chi-square test, one is associated with estimating the mean of the normal distribution (μ), and the last is associated with estimating the variance of the normal distribution (σ^2). This technicality need not concern us here. (For further details, see Hays, 1971, p. 727.)

D at the end of the book, $\chi^2_{critical(\alpha=.05,\ df=3)} = 7.815$. Since $\chi^2_{observed}$ exceeds $\chi^2_{critical}$, the null hypothesis should be rejected with the conclusion that the observed frequency distribution is nonnormal and negatively skewed.

At this point, we are ready to consider hypothesis testing with χ^2 more formally.

♦   ♦   ♦   ♦   ♦

Chi square is typically used for nondirectional (two-tailed) tests.[5] For such tests, **Hypotheses** the null and alternative hypotheses are:

H_0: The observed distribution of frequencies equals the expected (hypothetical) distribution of frequencies in each category.

H_1: The observed distribution of frequencies does not equal the expected (hypothetical) distribution of frequencies.

♦   ♦   ♦   ♦   ♦

For testing whether the observed frequencies in two or more categories come **Assumptions** from the hypothesized frequencies in these categories, five assumptions are **and Requirements** made:

1. Each observation must fall in one and only one category.
2. The observations in the sample are independent of one another.
3. The observations are measured as frequencies.
4. The *expected* frequency for each category is not less than 5 for $df \geqslant 2$ and not less than 10 for $df = 1$.
5. The observed values of χ^2 with one degree of freedom must be corrected for continuity in order to use the table of values of $\chi^2_{critical}$.

The first assumption can be checked by examining the categories to be used. The categories should be mutually exclusive so that each observation can belong to only one category. In the example of criminal homicides, the twelve months of the year served as categories. Each instance of criminal homicide could occur only in one particular month. A murder committed in May could not also occur in September. Assumption 2, independence, is discussed thoroughly in Chapter 15. Briefly, it can be examined by reviewing the sampling procedures.

Assumption 3 may be verified by examining the dependent variable to make sure that observations consist of frequencies or numbers of observations within

[5]The chi-square test is nondirectional (two-tailed). This follows because a negative deviation for $O - E$ is considered by the test just like a positive deviation. That is, the negative and positive deviations are squared and then combined. Thus, extremely negative values influence the value of χ^2 just like extremely positive values. A one-tailed test makes sense only when we are dealing with a simple outcome (two categories) that can go in one of two possible directions. In this case, see Cochran (1954).

each category. Observations in the form of proportions, probabilities, or percentages are also acceptable, since they are easily converted to frequencies.

Assumption 4 is required because the chi-square distribution is a theoretical distribution used to approximate the exact probability of the particular sampling distribution under assumptions 1 and 2 above. For large samples, probabilities from the χ^2 approximation are accurate. For small samples, they are not. Hence, assumption 4 provides a rule of thumb for identifying reasonably accurate probability values. This assumption can be checked by examining the *expected* frequencies for each category. If there are three or more categories, and if one or more of the categories has an expected frequency of less than 5, they may, in some cases, be combined in order to increase the expected frequency in a collapsed category. For example, in the homicide study, the incidence of criminal homicide could be examined for each three-month period by collapsing sets of three adjacent month categories into single categories. This procedure is only recommended when combinations of categories can be made meaningfully (see "Collapsing Levels of a Variable" below). Finally, assumption 5 is discussed under "Correction for Continuity" below.

◆　　◆　　◆　　◆　　◆

Computational Procedures for the One-Way χ^2 Test　The formula for testing whether an observed set of frequencies arose from an expected set of frequencies is given by Formula 18-1 above. The steps in calculating $\chi^2_{observed}$ are shown in Procedure 18-1 using the data from Figure 18-1. (Note that $N = 100$ in the example data.)

Procedure 18-1 ◆ Steps in computing χ^2 for a one-way design (example data from Figure 18-1; example shown below)

Operation	Example
1 Set up a computational table with 7 columns labeled as shown in the example.	See table on page 527.
2 List each cateogry in column 1.	
3 List the observed frequencies in column 2. *As a check for accuracy, the sum of the observed frequencies should equal N.*	
4 List the theoretically expected proportions for each category in column 3. (Note: The null hypothesis implies these proportions.) *As a computational check, the sum of the expected proportions should equal 1.*	

5 List the expected frequencies for each category in column 4. (E = expected proportion $\times$ N.) *As a computational check, the sum of the expected frequencies should equal N.*

6 a If $df = 1$ and all expected frequencies $\geqslant 10$, continue with the calculations. If an expected frequency is less than 10, the binomial test may be used (see Siegel, 1956).
 b If $df > 1$ and all expected frequencies exceed 5, continue with the calculations. If one or more expected frequency is less than 5, consider collapsing categories. Then proceed from step 2 again.

7 Compute the difference between O and E in column 5.
As a computational check, the sum of the differences between O and E should equal 0.

8 Square the differences in column 5 and enter these values in column 6.

9 Divide the value in column 6 by its corresponding value of E, and place these values in column 7.

10 Sum the values in column 7 to obtain χ^2_{observed}:

$$\chi^2_{\text{observed}} = \sum_{i=1}^{k} \frac{(O_i - E_i)^2}{E_i} \quad \textbf{[18-1]}$$

with $df = k - 1$.

			Example			
1	2	3	4	5	6	7
Category	Observed frequency (O)	Expected proportion	Expected frequency (E)	$O - E$	$(O - E)^2$	$\frac{(O - E)^2}{E}$
1	10	.16	16	−6	36	36/16 = 2.25
2	20	.34	34	−14	196	196/34 = 5.76
3	50	.34	34	16	256	256/34 = 7.53
4	20	.16	16	4	16	16/16 = 1.00
Σ	100	1.00	100	0		$\chi^2_{\text{obs.}} = 16.54$

◆   ◆   ◆   ◆   ◆

Decision Rules for Rejecting H_0

In order to decide whether or not to reject the null hypothesis, the critical value of χ^2 must be determined. Since there is a different χ^2 distribution for each possible number of degrees of freedom, the first step is to determine $k-1$, the number of degrees of freedom for the statistical test. In the example used in the computational model, $k = 4$, so there are $k - 1 = 3$ degrees of freedom for the statistical test (see footnote 4 above). Next, the critical value of χ^2 at a specified level of α can be found in Table D. In order to find χ^2_{critical} with 3 df, suppose the researcher set α at .05 prior to collecting the data. Then, enter the table by finding the degrees of freedom along the rows and the level of α along the columns. For $df = 3$ and $\alpha = .05$, $\chi^2_{\text{critical }(.05,\,3)} = 7.815$. Since χ^2_{observed} (16.54) in this example exceeds χ^2_{critical}, the null hypothesis should be rejected. Scores on the self-concept scale are not normally distributed. They are, in fact, negatively skewed; that is, people tended to rate themselves toward the high end of the scale. (This is a common, not so surprising, finding in research on self-concept; see Shavelson, Hubner, & Stanton, 1976.)

In general, the following rules can be used in deciding whether or not to reject the null hypothesis:

Reject H_0 if $\chi^2_{\text{observed}} \geqslant \chi^2_{\text{critical}(\alpha,\ df)}$,

Do not reject H_0 if: $\chi^2_{\text{observed}} < \chi^2_{\text{critical}(\alpha,\ df)}$.

Recall that the chi-square test is nondirectional. The tabulated values at α provide the critical values for the two-tailed test.

◆   ◆   ◆   ◆   ◆

Numerical Example

Suppose a researcher is interested in whether there are monthly differences in the number of homicides in a middle-sized city in the United States. Police records are examined for a particular year, and the researcher finds that 100 such crimes have been recorded during the year of interest. The researcher records the number of homicides committed during each month; these data are displayed in Table 18-1.

The question is, "Do these observed frequencies of homicides differ from what might be expected if the number of homicides was unrelated to the month of the year?" In order to answer this question, the χ^2 test can be used. For this statistical test, the null and alternative hypotheses are

Table 18-1 ◆ Number of homicides committed each month over a twelve-month period ($N = 100$)

Jan.	Feb.	Mar.	Apr.	May	Jun.	Jul.	Aug.	Sep.	Oct.	Nov.	Dec.
10	8	11	6	15	13	10	7	3	4	5	8

H_0: No difference in the population between observed and expected frequencies.

H_1: A difference in the population between observed and expected frequencies.

And let's set $\alpha = .01$.

Table 18-2 provides the necessary computations based on Procedure 18-1. The expected proportions were found as follows. If homicides are unrelated to the month of the year, then the number of such crimes in a month will depend only on the proportion of the 365 days in a year that occur in a particular month. For example, there are 31 days in January, so the proportion of days in a year occurring in January is $31 \div 365 = .085$. The expected frequencies are found by multiplying the expected proportion by the total number of homicides. So for January the expected frequency is $.085 \times 100 = 8.5$. Since all of the *expected* frequencies in Table 18-2 exceed 5, we can proceed with the χ^2 test for the one-way design.

The remaining entries in Table 18-3 are straightforward. Note that as a computational check, the column sums are calculated.

In order to decide whether or not to reject the null hypothesis at $\alpha = .01$,

Table 18-2 ♦ Computation of $\chi^2_{observed}$ for the data on homicides provided in Table 18-1

1 Category	2 Observed frequency (O)	3 Expected proportion	4 Expected frequency (E)	5 $O - E$	6 $(O - E)^2$	7 $\dfrac{(O - E)^2}{E}$
Jan.	10	.085	8.5	1.5	2.25	.26
Feb.	8	.077	7.7	0.3	0.09	.01
Mar.	11	.085	8.5	2.5	6.25	.74
Apr.	6	.082	8.2	−2.2	4.84	.59
May	15	.085	8.5	6.5	42.25	4.97
Jun.	13	.082	8.2	4.8	23.04	2.81
Jul.	10	.085	8.5	1.5	2.25	.26
Aug.	7	.085	8.5	−1.5	2.25	.26
Sept.	3	.082	8.2	−5.2	27.04	3.30
Oct.	4	.085	8.5	−4.5	20.25	2.38
Nov.	5	.082	8.2	−3.2	10.24	1.25
Dec.	8	.085	8.5	−0.5	0.25	.03
Sums	100	1.00	100	0		$\chi^2_{obs.} = 16.86$

χ^2_{critical} must be obtained from Table D. With $k - 1 = 12 - 1 = 11$ degrees of freedom,

$$\chi^2_{\text{critical}(.01, 11)} = 24.725.$$

Since χ^2_{observed} (16.86) does not exceed χ^2_{critical}, the null hypothesis should not be rejected. There is insufficient evidence to conclude that homicides occur more often in certain months than in others.

EXAMPLE PROBLEM 1

A weight-control clinic was interested in the types of foods that dieters found most difficult to avoid. Sixty clients were randomly selected and individually asked the following question: "Which of the following types of foods do you find *most* difficult to avoid when you are dieting?

a. Bread and rolls
b. Cookies and cakes
c. Ice cream and frozen desserts
d. Pastries and pies."

The following data were obtained:

Number of clients responding			
(a) Bread and rolls	(b) Cookies and cakes	(c) Ice cream and frozen desserts	(d) Pastries and pies
17	13	21	9

Conduct a χ^2 test at $\alpha = .01$ to determine if these observed frequencies differ from what would be expected if these foods were all equally difficult to avoid. Include in your answer:

a. Null and alternative hypotheses
b. Verification that assumptions and requirements have been met.
c. Computation of χ^2_{observed}
d. χ^2_{critical}
e. Conclusions.

♦ ♦ ♦ ♦ ♦

Correction for Continuity with One Degree of Freedom

The chi-square distribution, like the normal distribution, is a smooth, continuous curve. Observed frequencies, however, change discretely: from 1 to 2, from 2 to 3, etc. Thus, discrepancies may arise between the smooth curve of the values of the theoretical chi-square distribution and the bumpy distribution of observed values. This inconsistency between the theoretical and actual sampling distributions of chi square is only serious enough to affect the outcome of a test with one degree of freedom. In this case, a correction is applied to the observed frequencies in order to smooth them out.

The correction for the inconsistencies between the theoretical sampling distribution of χ^2 and the actual sampling distribution is called **Yates's correction for continuity**. It applies only when the number of degrees of freedom equals one. The following strategy is used in applying Yates's correction:

1. Subtract .5 from the observed frequency if the observed frequency is greater than the expected frequency; that is, if $O > E$, subtract .5 from O.
2. Add .5 to the observed frequency if the observed frequency is less than the expected frequency; that is, if $O < E$, add .5 to O.

The net effect of this correction is to smooth the data and to reduce, slightly, the observed value of χ^2.

As an example of how the correction is applied, consider the following study. A statistics class is required of all students in a graduate school of education in which two-thirds of the students are women and one-third are men. An instructor observes that in a class of 50 students, 30 are women and 20 are men. The instructor wonders whether there are more men in the class than would be expected from the distribution of men and women in the graduate school. In order to find out, the researcher conducts a χ^2 test at $\alpha = .05$. Since there are two groups, this a 1-df χ^2 test and a correction for continuity must be made. The actual correction is shown in Procedure 18-2 using these example data.

Steps in calculating χ^2 for a one-way design with 1 degree of freedom using Yates's ♦ Procedure 18-2 correction for continuity (example below)

Operation	Example
1 Set up a computation table with 8 columns labeled as shown in the example.	See table on p. 532.
2 List each category in column 1.	
3 List the observed frequencies in column 2. *As a check for accuracy, the sum of the observed frequencies should equal N.*	
4 List the theoretically expected proportions for each category in column 3. (Note: The null hypothesis implies these proportions.) *As a computational check, the sum of the expected proportions should equal 1.*	(continued on. p. 532)

5 List the expected frequencies for each category in column 4. (E = expected proportion $\times$ N.) *As a computational check, the sum of the expected frequencies should equal N.*

6 If all expected frequencies exceed 5, continue with the calculations. If not, do not use χ^2; use Fisher's exact test (see Siegel, 1956).

7 a If $O > E$, subtract .5 from O to obtain O^* which is corrected for continuity, and enter this value in column 5.

  b If $O < E$, add .5 to O to obtain O^* which is corrected for continuity, and enter this value in column 5.
As a computational check, the sum of the corrected observed frequencies should equal N.

8 Compute the difference between the corrected observed frequency and the expected frequency for each category ($O^* - E$) and enter in column 6.
As a computational check, the sum of the differences should equal zero.

9 Square the differences in column 6 and enter the squares in column 7.

10 Divide the values in column 7 by their corresponding expected frequencies and place the results in column 8.

11 Sum the values in column 8 to obtain $\chi^2_{observed}$, corrected for continuity.

Example

1	2	3	4	5	6	7	8
Category	Observed frequency (O)	Expected proportion	Expected frequency (E)	O corrected for continuity (O^*)	$O^* - E$	$(O^* - E^2)$	$\dfrac{(O^* - E)^2}{E}$
Male	20	.33	16.67	19.5	2.83	8.01	$\dfrac{8.01}{16.67} = .48$
Female	30	.67	33.33	30.5	-2.83	8.01	$\dfrac{8.01}{33.33} = .24$
Σ	50	1.00	50	50	0		$\chi^2_{obs.} = .72$

In order to decide whether or not to reject the null hypothesis, $\chi^2_{observed}$ must be compared with $\chi^2_{critical(.05, 1)}$ (see Table D):

$$\chi^2_{critical(.05, 1)} = 3.841.$$

Since $\chi^2_{observed}$ (0.72) does not exceed $\chi^2_{critical}$, the null hypothesis cannot be rejected. There is insufficient evidence to lead to the conclusion that more men than women enrolled in this statistics course than would be expected from the number of men and women in the graduate school.

EXAMPLE PROBLEM 2

A large industrial company recently instituted a new type of management training program. Records of previous training programs showed that about 75 percent of the participants in these programs were rated as "successful" managers by their superiors. Three months after completing the new management training program, participants were rated as "successful" or "unsuccessful" managers by their superiors. The number of participants in each category are shown below.

Number of participants rated	
"Successful"	"Unsuccessful"
37	3

Conduct a χ^2 test at $\alpha = .01$ to determine whether the number of participants rated as "successful" was greater than would be expected from previous experience. Include in your answer:

a. Computation of χ^2
b. $\chi^2_{critical}$
c. Conclusions.

χ^2 FOR TWO-WAY DESIGNS: CONTINGENCY-TABLE ANALYSIS

In using a chi-square test for a two-way design, there must be two independent variables, each with two or more levels, and a dependent variable in the form of a frequency count (viz., frequencies, proportions, probabilities, or percentages). As an example of a two-way design for which the χ^2 statistic is appropriate, recall the study of men's and women's achievement in college described in Chapter 2. Hewitt and Goldman (1975) found that the sex of the student and the student's choice of academic major were related; women tended to choose majors which gave higher grades. This explained the apparent difference in achievement between men and women; it was not necessary to invoke certain masculine and feminine characteristics as hypothesized in the

Table 18-3ᵃ ♦ Major-field choices of male and female undergraduates at UCLA

		Academic major				
		Physics	Engineering	English	Design	Total
Sex	Male	108	345	94	17	564
	Female	8	12	253	60	333
		116	357	347	77	897

ᵃFrom Table 2-6.

past. Table 18-3 presents data on choice of academic major for 897 male and female undergraduates at UCLA. The data are presented as a 2×4 (sex $\times$ major) design with frequencies entered in the cells of the design. Often such a table displaying a two-way design with frequencies in its cells is called a **contingency table**.

♦ ♦ ♦ ♦ ♦

Purpose and Underlying Logic

The purpose of the χ^2 test for the two-way design is to determine whether or not the two variables in the design are independent of one another. In the study of men's and women's achievement, for example, a two-way χ^2 would test whether or not sex and academic major are independent.

The formula for calculating the two-way χ^2 is the same as for the one-way χ^2; only the degrees of freedom change. The degrees of freedom for the two-way χ^2 depend on the number of rows (r) and the number of columns (c) in the design:

$$df = (r-1)(c-1).$$

The chi-square statistic with $(r-1)(c-1)$ degrees of freedom is used to compare the observed and expected frequencies in a two-way contingency table:

$$\chi^2_{observed} = \sum_{i=1}^{k} \frac{(O_i - E_i)^2}{E_i} \qquad [18\text{-}2]$$

with $df = (r-1)(c-1)$. The observed values of χ^2 can be referred to the theoretical sampling distribution of χ^2 described under "Purpose" near the beginning of this chapter. In so doing, a decision on whether or not to reject the null hypothesis can be made.

♦   ♦   ♦   ♦   ♦

The null and alternative hypotheses for the two-way chi-square test are:

Hypotheses

H_0: variables A and B are *independent* in the population;
H_1: variables A and B are *related* in the population.

For the data in Table 18-3, the null and alternative hypotheses are:

H_0: sex and choice of academic major are independent in the population;
H_1: sex and choice of academic major are related in the population.

♦   ♦   ♦   ♦   ♦

In using χ^2, the assumptions and requirements are:

Assumptions and Requirements

1. Each observation must fall in one and only one cell of the design.
2. Each observation is independent of every other observation.
3. The observations are measured as frequencies.
4. The expected frequency for any cell is not less than 5 for $df \geqslant 2$ and not less than 10 for $df = 1$.
5. The observed values of χ^2 with one degree of freedom (i.e., a 2×2 contingency table) must be corrected for continuity in order to use the table of values of $\chi^2_{critical}$.

Since these assumptions and requirements are discussed under that heading near the beginning of this chapter, there need not be further discussion here.

♦   ♦   ♦   ♦   ♦

Formula 18-2 is used for calculating the χ^2 statistic. The steps in calculating $\chi^2_{observed}$ for a two-way design are almost the same as for a one-way design. The major difference lies in the calculation of the expected frequencies.

Computational Procedures for the Two-Way χ^2 Test

In the two-way design, the expected frequencies represent the frequencies that would be expected if variables A and B were *independent*. Thus, regardless of the study, the expected frequencies for a two-way chi-square test are always calculated the same way:

$$E_{rc} = \frac{f_r f_c}{N}, \qquad [18\text{-}3]$$

where E_{rc} = expected frequency for a cell in row r and column c,
    f_r = number of observations (frequency) in the rth row,
    f_c = number of observations (frequency) in the cth column,
    N = total number of observations.

Procedure 18-3 ♦ Steps in calculating χ^2 for a two-way design with example data from Table 18-3 (example below)

Operation	Example
1 Set up a computational table with 6 columns labeled as shown in the example below.	See table on p. 537.

2 From the contingency table, list each of the k cells in column 1 by entering the row numbers in the left-hand subcolumn and the column numbers in the right-hand subcolumn.

3 List the observed frequencies in column 2. *As a check for accuracy, the sum of these observed frequencies should equal N.*

4 Calculate the expected frequencies using Formula 18-3:

$$E_{rc} = \frac{f_r fc}{N}$$

and enter these values in column 3. (See footnote in the example on p. 537 for computations.) *The sum of the expected frequencies should equal N.*

5 If $df > 1$ and any one expected frequency is less than 5, consider collapsing categories and then return to step 2; otherwise, continue. For $df = 1$, see section on "Correction for Continuity" below.

6 Calculate the difference between the observed and expected frequencies $(O - E)$, and enter these differences in column 4. *The sums of the differences should equal zero.*

7 Square the differences in column 4, and enter the squares in column 5.

8 Divide the values in column 5 by their corresponding expected frequencies, and place the results in column 6.

9 Sum the values in column 6 to obtain $\chi^2_{observed}$:

$$\chi^2_{observed} = \sum_{i=1}^{k} \frac{(O_i - E_i)^2}{E_i} \quad [\text{18-2}]$$

with $df = (r - 1)(c - 1)$.

	(1)		(2)	(3)	(4)	(5)	(6)
	Cell		Observed	Expected			
	row (sex)	column (major)	frequency (O)	frequency[a] (E)	O − E	(O − E)²	$\dfrac{(O-E)^2}{E}$
	1	1	108	72.94	35.06	1,229.20	16.85
	1	2	345	224.47	120.53	14,527.48	64.72
	1	3	94	218.18	−124.18	15,420.67	70.68
	1	4	17	48.42	−31.42	987.22	20.39
	2	1	8	43.06	−35.06	1,229.20	28.55
	2	2	12	132.53	−120.53	14,527.48	109.62
	2	3	253	128.81	124.19	15,423.16	119.74
	2	4	60	28.59	31.41	986.59	34.51
	Σ		897	897.00	0		$\chi^2_{obs.} = 465.06$

$$^a E_{11} = \frac{564 \times 116}{897} = 72.94, \quad E_{21} = \frac{333 \times 116}{897} = 43.06,$$

$$E_{12} = \frac{564 \times 357}{897} = 224.47, \quad E_{22} = \frac{333 \times 357}{897} = 132.53,$$

$$E_{13} = \frac{564 \times 347}{897} = 218.18, \quad E_{23} = \frac{333 \times 347}{897} = 128.82,$$

$$E_{14} = \frac{564 \times 77}{897} = 48.42, \quad E_{24} = \frac{333 \times 77}{897} = 28.59.$$

More specifically, then, the value of E_{rc} is what we would expect if the row and column variables are independent.[6]

For example, the expected frequency of the cell corresponding to the first row and the first column in Table 18-3 can be found by multiplying the number of observations in the first row (564 males) by the number of observations in the first column (116 physics majors) and dividing this value by N (897 undergraduates):

[6]Here E_{rc} is actually based on joint probability. In order to illustrate, E_{11} in Table 18-4—the expected number of males majoring in physics—will be used. In this case, E_{11} represents the probability of being male *and* being a physics major, assuming independence between sex and major. The probability of being male is the row total divided by N: 564 + 897 = .629. The probability of being a physics major is the column total divided by N: 116 + 897 = .129. The probability of being male *and* a physics major is $p(male) \times p(physics\ major) = .63 \times .13 = .08$. In order to convert the probability to a frequency, we multiply .08 by N: .0813 × 897 = 72.94.

$$E_{11} = \frac{564 \times 116}{897}$$

$$= \frac{65,424}{897}$$

$$= 72.94.$$

This procedure for calculating the expected frequencies is carried out for all cells of the design. With this one exception, the procedures for calculating the χ^2 for a contingency table are the same as for calculating the one-way χ^2 (see Procedure 18-3).

♦ ♦ ♦ ♦ ♦

Decision Rules for Rejecting H_0 In order to decide whether or not to reject H_0, $\chi^2_{observed}$ must be compared with $\chi^2_{critical\ (\alpha,\ df)}$. For a χ^2 contingency table, $df = (r-1)(c-1)$. With α and df known, Table D can be used to find $\chi^2_{critical}$. If $\chi^2_{observed}$ exceeds $\chi^2_{critical}$, reject the null hypothesis and conclude that variables A and B are related. If $\chi^2_{observed}$ does not exceed $\chi^2_{critical}$, conclude that there is insufficient evidence to say that variable A and B are not independent.

In the example problem with 2 rows and 4 columns (Table 18-3), $df = (2-1)(4-1) = 3$. If the test is conducted at $\alpha = .01$,

$$\chi^2_{critical(.01,\ 3)} = 11.345.$$

Since, in the example, $\chi^2_{observed}$ (465.06; see Procedure 18-3) exceeds $\chi^2_{critical}$, the null hypothesis should be rejected. Clearly, students' sex is related to choice of academic major. Specifically, women tend to choose majors in English and design, while men tend to choose majors in physics and engineering.

♦ ♦ ♦ ♦ ♦

Numerical Example A researcher wanted to determine whether there was any difference between boys' and girls' voting for president in a large school. The results of the election

Table 18-4 ♦ Votes cast by boys and girls for the three candidates running for class president

| | | Candidate | | | |
		A	B	C	Total
Sex	Boys	30	20	10	60
	Girls	15	10	15	40
	Total	45	30	25	100

are shown in Table 18-4 for a random sample of 100 voters. In order to determine whether or not there was a relationship between the sex of the voter and the choice of candidate, the following hypotheses were set forth to be tested at $\alpha = .05$:

H_0: sex and choice of candidate are independent in the population;

H_1: sex and choice of candidate are related in the population.

In order to decide whether or not to reject the null hypothesis, χ^2_{critical} with $df = (2 - 1)(3 - 1) = 2$ and $\alpha = .05$ is needed. From Table D,

$$\chi^2_{\text{critical}(.05, 2)} = 5.991.$$

If χ^2_{observed} equals or exceeds 5.991, the null hypothesis should be rejected.

Table 18-5 provides the necessary computations based on Procedure 18-3. Since $df \geqslant 2$ and all *expected* frequencies exceed 5, we can proceed with the χ^2 test: $\chi^2_{\text{observed}} = 5.55$. Since χ^2_{observed} does not exceed χ^2_{critical}, conclude that there is insufficient evidence to reject the null hypothesis of independence.

Table 18-5 ◆ Computation of χ^2_{observed} for data on the relation between sex and choice of candidate provided in Table 18-4

(1) Cell		(2)	(3)	(4)	(5)	(6)
Row (sex)	Column (candidate)	Observed frequency (O)	Expected frequency (E)	O − E	(O − E)²	$\dfrac{(O-E)^2}{E}$
1	1	30	$\dfrac{60 \times 45}{100} = 27$	3	9	$\dfrac{9}{27} = .333$
1	2	20	$\dfrac{60 \times 30}{100} = 18$	2	4	$\dfrac{4}{18} = .222$
1	3	10	$\dfrac{60 \times 25}{100} = 15$	−5	25	$\dfrac{25}{15} = 1.667$
2	1	15	$\dfrac{40 \times 45}{100} = 18$	−3	9	$\dfrac{9}{18} = .50$
2	2	10	$\dfrac{40 \times 30}{100} = 12$	−2	4	$\dfrac{4}{12} = .333$
2	3	15	$\dfrac{40 \times 25}{100} = 10$	5	25	$\dfrac{25}{10} = 2.50$
Sum:		100	100	0		$\chi^2_{\text{obs.}} = 5.55$

EXAMPLE PROBLEM 3

In a recent public-opinion survey, residents, sampled randomly in Los Angeles, were asked whether they supported the use of busing to desegregate city schools. The school board was interested in whether ethnic minority and nonminority residents felt differently about this issue. The data obtained are shown in the table below:

	"Yes"	"No"	"No opinion"	Totals
Minority	50	35	15	100
Nonminority	65	100	35	200
Totals	115	135	50	300

Conduct a χ^2 test at $\alpha = .05$ to test whether or not there is a relationship between minority-group membership and opinion on school busing. Include in your answer:

a. Null and alternative hypotheses
b. Verification that assumptions and requirements have been met
c. Computation of $\chi^2_{observed}$
d. $\chi^2_{critical}$
e. Conclusions.

◆   ◆   ◆   ◆   ◆

Correction for Continuity for the $2 \times 2\ \chi^2$

The 2×2 chi-square test is a statistical test with one degree of freedom: $(r - 1)(c - 1) = (2 - 1)(2 - 1) = 1$. Whenever the theoretical sampling distribution of chi square is used with 1 df, Yates's correction for continuity should be used (see page 20 of this chapter for the section on "Correction for Continuity" above for the rationale). This can be accomplished by subtracting .5 from the observed frequency whenever it exceeds the expected frequency, and adding .5 to the observed frequency whenever it is less than the expected frequency (see Procedure 18-2).

Since the 2×2 chi square is the only two-way design with one degree of freedom, a simple computational formula which incorporates Yates's correction is available. Consider the following 2×2 contingency table:

a	b	$a + b$
c	d	$c + d$
$a + c$	$b + d$	N

The lowercase letters represent frequencies in each of the four cells. From this table, the value of chi square can be found:

Table 18-6 ◆ Hypothetical survey of wine preferences of French and American businessmen

| Nationality | Do you prefer wine with lunch? | | |
	Yes	No	Total
French	$a = 54$	$b = 6$	$a + b = 60$
American	$c = 16$	$d = 24$	$c + d = 40$
Total	$a + c = 70$	$b + d = 30$	$N = 100$

$$\chi^2 = \frac{N\left(|ad - bc| - \dfrac{N}{2}\right)^2}{(a+b)(c+d)(a+c)(b+d)} \qquad [18\text{-}4]$$

with $df = 1$. The correction for continuity is made by the term $N/2$.

In order to see how Formula 18-4 works, consider some data taken from a hypothetical survey (Table 18-6) of French and American businessmen as to whether or not they preferred wine with lunch. In conducting the statistical test, the usual hypotheses are set forth and $\alpha = .05$. The critical value of chi square at $\alpha = .05$ with one degree of freedom, then, can be found in Table D:

$$\chi^2_{\text{critical}(.05,\, 1)} = 3.841.$$

If χ^2_{observed} is greater than or equal to 3.841, the null hypothesis should be rejected.

Before proceeding with the statistical test, the smallest expected frequency should be checked to see if it is at least 10 for this one-degree-of-freedom test. The smallest expected frequency is $(30 \times 40) \div 100 = 12$. Now all that need be done is to insert the appropriate values from Table 18-6 into Formula 18-4 and solve:

$$\chi^2 = \frac{100\left[|(54)(24) - (6)(16)| - \dfrac{100}{2}\right]^2}{(60)(40)(70)(30)}$$

$$= \frac{100(|1296 - 96| - 50)^2}{5,040,000}$$

$$= \frac{100(1150)^2}{5,040,000}$$

$$= \frac{132,250,000}{5,040,000}$$

$$= 26.24.$$

Since $\chi^2_{observed}$ exceeds $\chi^2_{critical}$, the null hypothesis should be rejected. Conclude that there is a relation between nationality and wine preference. French businessmen tend to prefer wine at lunch while American businessmen do not (see Table 18-6).

EXAMPLE PROBLEM 4

Half of the 44 students in poetry class were assigned to hear a lecture on techniques that can be used to capture the unique qualities of the sea. The other half viewed a series of slides showing well-known seascapes painted by well-acclaimed artists. Then all students were assigned to write a poem on the sea. In order to determine which teaching technique was most effective, poems were categorized as to their quality:

	Quality of poem		
Teaching technique	Low	High	Total
Lecture	14	8	22
Slides	10	12	22
Total	24	20	44

Conduct a χ^2 test at $\alpha = .01$ to determine whether teaching techniques and quality of poems are related. Include in your answer:

a. Computation of χ^2
b. $\chi^2_{critical}$
c. Conclusions.

♦   ♦   ♦   ♦   ♦

Collapsing Levels of a Variable in a χ^2 Test

Sometimes the *expected frequency* of one or more categories is less than 5 for χ^2 tests with $df \geq 2$ and less than 10 for a χ^2 test with $df = 1$. This is especially the case with small sample sizes. When this occurs, the next step depends on the size of the contingency table. For a 2×2 contingency table, **Fisher's exact test** may be used. This test does not rely on the χ^2 distribution; rather, exact probabilities are computed (see, for example, Hays, 1971; Siegel, 1956). For larger contingency tables, it may be possible to use the χ^2 test by collapsing levels of a variable. In this way, expected frequencies at different levels are combined, thus boosting the expected frequency. Collapsing can be achieved by combining the frequencies in adjacent cells in a one-way design or by combining the frequencies in adjacent rows, columns, or both in a contingency table. However, there is also a conceptual issue in collapsing cells and this is most important. Simply stated, it must make sense to collapse categories. For

Table 18-7 ◆ Data on the relation between the sex and age of respondents in the survey (N = 100)

	What is your sex?		
	Male	Female	Totals
How old **≤ 17**	35	15	50
were you on **18–23**	25	8	33
your last **24–29**	5	3	8
birthday? **≥ 30**	5	4	9
Total	70	30	100

example, in the absence of a good rationale, it might not make sense to collapse males with females, or physics majors with fine-arts majors.

As an example of the procedure of collapsing levels, consider the following survey. A random sample of 100 subjects answered, among many questions, the following two items:

1. What is your sex?
   a. Male
   b. Female
2. How old were you on your last birthday?
   a. 17 or younger
   b. 18–23
   c. 24–29
   d. 30 or older.

Hypothetical data from this study are presented in Table 18-7. In order to determine whether or not to collapse, the *smallest expected frequency* should be calculated. Since the expected frequency depends on the row and column frequencies,

$$E_{rc} = \frac{f_r f_c}{N}, \qquad [\textbf{18-3}]$$

the smallest expected frequency will be found by multiplying the smallest f_r by the smallest f_c. In Table 18-7, the smallest f_r is 8 and the smallest f_c is 30:

$$E_{rc(\text{smallest})} = \frac{8 \times 30}{100}$$

$$= \frac{240}{100}$$

$$= 2.4.$$

Table 18-8 ♦ Data from Table 18-7 with the two highest age categories collapsed

		What is your sex?		
		Male	Female	Totals
How old were you on your last birthday?	⩽ 17	35	15	50
	18–23	25	8	33
	⩾ 24	10	7	17
	Totals	70	30	100

Since this expected frequency is less than 5 with $df = 3$, we should consider collapsing adjacent ages. The two oldest age categories could be combined quite logically, and the combination of the two might solve the problem. This has been done in Table 18-8. Now the smallest expected frequency is

$$E_{rc(\text{smallest})} = \frac{17 \times 30}{100}$$

$$= \frac{510}{100}$$

$$= 5.10.$$

Since $df \geqslant 2$ and the smallest expected frequency exceeds 5, χ^2 for contingency tables can be calculated. We would then proceed with the calculations as shown in Procedure 18-3.

In summary, one requirement of the χ^2 test is that the *expected frequencies* are all 5 or greater for $df \geqslant 2$ and that the expected frequencies are 10 or greater for $df = 1$. This applies to one-way and two-way designs. Sometimes, especially with small sample sizes, one or more expected frequencies do not meet these criteria. In this case, it might be possible to collapse adjacent cells (one-way designs) or to collapse adjacent rows, columns, or both (two-way designs) in order to increase the expected frequency to its minimally required value. In collapsing, the combination of cells or rows (columns) must make conceptual sense.

EXAMPLE PROBLEM 5

Suppose that the following data were collected in a survey of the relationship between average number of hours spent studying per day and performance in advanced chemistry courses at a particular university.

Hours of study per day	Performance		Totals
	Pass	Fail	
⩽ 1	2	7	9
2	58	25	83
3	65	13	78
4	25	5	30
Totals	150	50	200

Determine whether categories should be collapsed in order to do a χ^2 test. If so, combine categories where appropriate. Include in your answer:

a. Smallest E_{rc} in noncollapsed data
b. Collapsed categories, if appropriate
c. Smallest E_{rc} of collapsed categories, if appropriate.

♦   ♦   ♦   ♦   ♦

Summary

This chapter presents statistical procedures for use in research designs in which data are collected in the form of counts (frequencies, proportions, probabilities, or percentages). In these designs, the independent variable takes the form of discrete categories and a subject's response may fall in only one of these categories. The *chi-square* (χ^2) test is used to determine whether the observed frequencies in these categories differ from the *expected frequencies*. Procedures for conducting the χ^2 test for *one-way* and *two-way* designs are presented. Procedures for applying *Yates's correction for continuity* when the χ^2 test has only one degree of freedom are also discussed for both types of designs. Finally, procedures are given for collapsing levels of a variable when the expected frequency of one or more categories is less than a certain criterion.

♦   ♦   ♦   ♦   ♦

Key Words

chi square	goodness-of-fit test
contingency table	observed frequency
counts	one-way design
degrees of freedom	percentage
discrete categories	probability
expected frequency	proportion
Fisher's exact test	two-way design
frequency	Yates's correction for continuity

♦   ♦   ♦   ♦   ♦

Exercises
1. List five important features of the χ^2 statistic.
2. Upon what is the critical value of χ^2 dependent?
3. How does the determination of the critical value of χ^2 differ from that of the critical value of t?
4. Why is the χ^2 for a one-way design called a goodness-of-fit test?
5. What is the relationship between the number of categories and the value of $\chi^2_{observed}$?
6. Why is a correction for continuity necessary for a χ^2 test with one degree of freedom?

7–14 Sixty randomly selected television viewers were asked to rate an idea for a television series as boring, exciting, or no opinion. The results are shown in the table below:

Boring	Exciting	No opinion
28	15	17

Conduct a χ^2 test at $\alpha = .01$ to find if these observed frequencies differ from what would be expected if there were no difference between the three categories.

7. Formulate null and alternative hypotheses.
8. Verify that assumptions and requirements have been met.
9. Compute $\chi^2_{observed}$.
10. Find $\chi^2_{critical}$.
11. State your conclusions.

12–14 Suppose that 40 television viewers were only given two rating categories: boring (28 responses) or exciting (12 responses). Again assume that no differences between response options were expected.

12. Compute $\chi^2_{observed}$.
13. Find $\chi^2_{critical}$ at $x = .01$.
14. State your conclusions.

15–19 A random sample of 40 patients from a metropolitan medical center were asked whether they were satisfied or dissatisfied with their doctors. A panel studying the quality of health care was interested in whether patients' opinions of their doctors were related to the severity of their illness. The data obtained are given below:

	Satisfied	Dissatisfied	Total
Severely ill	10	20	30
Not severely ill	40	10	50
Total	50	30	80

Conduct a χ^2 test at $\alpha = .05$.

15. Formulate null and alternative hypotheses.
16. Verify that assumptions and requirements have been met.

17. Compute $\chi^2_{observed}$.
18. Find $\chi^2_{critical}$.
19. State your conclusions.

20–24 An environmental protection agency was interested in whether there was a relationship between age and species for four kinds of cetacea off the coast of Baja California. A research team of marine biologists collected the following data:

		Sperm whale	Blue whale	Dolphin	Orca	
		Type of cetacea				
	1 mo–5 yr	2	5	9	10	26
Age	6–10 yr	2	7	7	8	24
	≥ 11 yr	12	14	15	20	61
	Total	16	26	31	38	111

Data from previous studies indicated that age was independent of the four types of cetacea. Conduct a χ^2 test at $\alpha = .05$ to see if these findings still hold.

20. Decide whether categories should be collapsed in order to do a χ^2. Explain.
21. Present the table for collapsed categories if necessary.
22. Compute χ^2 with $\alpha = .05$.
23. Find $\chi^2_{critical}$.
24. State your conclusions.

SECTION VI

Within-Subjects Designs
and
Mixed Designs

Iɴ ᴀ *between-subjects design*, a subject is observed in one and only one cell of the design. This is true of both one-way designs and factorial designs. Often it is desirable and sometimes it is possible to observe one subject in more than one treatment condition. Designs with repeated observations on the same subject are called **within-subjects designs**. An example may help clarify this distinction. Teachers' estimates of their students' academic performance depend on a number of factors such as the students' abilities, participation in class, work habits, and so on. In order to examine the influence of some of these factors on teachers' expectations, suppose a 3×3 design is constructed with three levels of ability (high, average, low) and three levels of participation (high, average, low). For each of the nine cells of the design, a description of a hypothetical student is written; e.g., one student is described as high in academic ability and participation, another is high in ability and average in participation, still another is low in ability and average in participation, and so on. A treatment, then, consists of having a subject (teacher) read the description of a particular hypothetical student. The dependent variable is the teacher's rating of how well that student would do in his or her class. Since it is possible to have all subjects (teachers) read and rate each of the nine descriptions (treatments), we have a *within-subjects design*. There are repeated observations on the same subjects, since each teacher reads about and rates each student description (treatment). A factorial ANOVA can be used to examine differences between mean ratings.

If, instead, *n* teachers are randomly assigned to each of the nine cells of the design, we have a *between-subjects design*; again, a two-way ANOVA can be used to examine differences between mean ratings. While the ANOVA can be used to examine data from between-subjects and within-subjects designs, the statistical procedures for the within-subjects design are somewhat different than for the between-subjects design.

Another example of a within-subjects design is the pretest-posttest preexperimental design (see Chapter 1). With this design, subjects are observed at pretest, then they receive a treatment, and finally they are observed at posttest. For each subject in the study, then, there are two observations. This design can be extended to include not only a pretest and a posttest but also a retention test one week after the treatment. In this case, three observations are made on each subject. If a delayed retention test (e.g., one month after treatment) is incorporated into the design, four observations are made on the same subjects. You can see why within-subjects designs are often called *repeated-measures designs*.

A final example will complete the description of the major types of within-subjects designs. Pairs of subjects, for example, could be *matched* on one (or more) individual-difference variables (IDV), such as academic ability, and then randomly assigned to one of two treatment groups. In this design, matched subjects are considered to be more similar to one another than to other subjects in the design. In fact, the idea behind this design is that subjects who are matched with one another are considered to be "images" of each other for the purpose of the study. They are treated as if the same subject were observed in each treatment. For example, 50 pairs of subjects ($N = 100$) might be matched on a measure of verbal ability and then randomly assigned to a control and an experimental group. They would receive an instructional treatment, and then the average performance of the two groups would be compared.

In constructing a within-subjects design using matching, two important requirements can be identified (among many). First, subjects should be matched on one or more individual-difference variables which are correlated with the dependent variable. In the example experiment, verbal ability was known to be correlated with the dependent variable (achievement) in the instructional setting ($r \approx 0.60$). Second, the number of subjects that have to be matched with one another depends on the number of cells in the design. If, as in the example study, there are two cells in the design, pairs of subjects are matched. One person in the pair is randomly assigned to the first cell, while the second person is assigned to the second cell. If there are six cells in a factorial design, six subjects have to be found who match on the IDV. In this way, *blocks* of six matched subjects are formed. Within each block, subjects are randomly assigned to one of the six cells of the design. You can see why within-subjects designs are sometimes called *randomized-block designs*.

In summary, *within-subjects designs* take three general forms: (1) the same subject is observed under all treatment conditions, (2) the same subject is observed before and after a treatment (e.g., pretest-posttest design), and (3) subjects are *matched* on an IDV and then randomly assigned to the treatments. All three forms of within-subjects designs are treated as if multiple observations had been made on the same subject.

In within-subjects designs, whatever is uniquely characteristic of a subject under one treatment will also be characteristic of him or her under the other treatments. For example, some subjects will be generally more responsive to treatments than others. This means that subjects' scores under different treatments will be related or dependent upon each other and that there will be (usually) a positive correlation between subjects' scores under the different treatment conditions. Statistical tests for data from within-subjects designs take this correlation into account.

The major advantage of the within-subjects design over the between-subjects design is that it provides a more powerful test of the null hypothesis. This happens because, by observing the same subjects under all treatment conditions, the measure of error variability ("error term") for the within-subjects design is smaller than for the between-subjects design. In the between-subjects design, variability within a group (error) may be due to experimental error *and* individual differences between subjects. In the within-subjects design, we can estimate the variability due to individual differences within a group from the repeated observations on the same subjects and remove this source of variability from the error term. Hence, in within-subjects designs, variability is due primarily to experimental error, so the error variability in this design is less than in the between-subjects design.

The major disadvantage of this design is that it does not always fit the research we wish to do. For example, it does not make sense to teach a group of subjects a social-studies lesson by method A and then teach them the same lesson by method B. Likewise, in a study of memory, it does not make sense to have the same subjects study and recall a list of words presented in a random order and then have them study and recall the same list of words in a conceptual order. In these and many other cases, we have *multiple-treatment interference*. In addition, studies with a large number of treatment conditions may fatigue or bore subjects participating in all conditions. While matching can be used to overcome fatigue or boredom, the greater the number of treatment conditions, the larger the blocks of matched subjects must be. It is extremely difficult to match two subjects adequately, let alone six or more.

The moral of the story is that whenever they are appropriate (and this is an important qualification), within-subjects designs get the job done with fewer subjects than between-subjects designs, if one holds *power* constant. If within-subjects designs cannot be implemented, between-subjects designs should be used. In some cases, it is possible and desirable to combine within-subjects and between-subjects designs. These designs are called, not surprisingly, *mixed designs*.

One familiar example of a mixed design is the pretest-posttest control-group design (see Chapter 1). Subjects are randomly assigned to a control or an experimental group; this is the between-subjects part of the design. They receive a pretest and then a posttest after the treatment; these repeated observations on all subjects constitute the within-subjects part of the design. This design is represented schematically in Table VI-1.

Perhaps an analogy will help make sense of a mixed design. Think of the control and experimental groups as two separate plots of land. This is the between-subjects part of the design. Each plot of land is split into sections (pretest and posttest in Table VI-1); this is the within-subjects part of the design. It turns out that this analogy has a history. The mixed design was developed for agricultural research; different fertilizers were applied within each of several plots of land. Hence, a mixed design is often called a *split-plot design*.

Another example of a mixed design may be helpful. Recall the study of the factors influencing teachers' estimates of how well students will perform academically. This was a 3×3 (ability $\times$ participation), within-subjects design. All N teachers provided ratings in all nine treatment conditions. Suppose,

Table VI-1 ♦ Schematic representation of a mixed design: pretest-posttest control-group design

		Between subjects	
		Control group	Experimental group
Within subjects	Pretest	$X_{1C\,pre}$ $X_{2C\,pre}$ $\vdots$ $X_{nC\,pre}$	$X_{1E\,pre}$ $X_{2E\,pre}$ $\vdots$ $X_{nE\,pre}$
	Posttest	$X_{1C\,post}$ $X_{2C\,post}$ $\vdots$ $X_{nC\,post}$	$X_{1E\,post}$ $X_{2E\,post}$ $\vdots$ $X_{nE\,post}$

before the study, teachers were divided into two groups on the basis of their beliefs about teaching: progressives (P) and traditionals (T). Since teachers can be assigned to one and only one of the two groups, P or T, this part of the design is a between-subjects design. Since all teachers, P and T alike, are observed under all nine treatment conditions, this part of the study is a within-subjects design. In all, we have a $2 \times 3 \times 3$ (belief $\times$ ability $\times$ participation), split-plot (mixed) design with beliefs as the between-subjects factor and information about student ability and participation as the within-subjects factors.

In this section, then, within-subjects and mixed designs have been discussed in order to introduce you to the range of possible designs. The analysis-of-variance techniques for analyzing data from these designs, however, are a bit more complicated than for between-subjects designs (see Chapters 16 and 17). So they are beyond the scope of this introductory textbook. (For presentations of the ANOVA for within-subjects and mixed designs, see intermediate texts by Dayton, 1970; Kirk, 1968; Myers, 1979; and Winer, 1971.) In the chapter that follows, the simplest statistical test for a within-subjects design is presented. This is the t test for dependent samples. It provides a statistical test of the difference between two means based on the same set of subjects.

19 ◆

The *t* Test
for
Dependent Samples

T_{HE} *t* **test for dependent samples** can be used to examine data from within-subjects designs when two observations are made on each subject or when one observation is made on each of the two members of a matched pair (see Section VI). In this chapter, the conceptual underpinnings are presented along with the techniques for using the *t* test for dependent samples.

As an example of a within-subjects design with two measures on the same subject or with matched pairs, consider a study of the effects of training on listening skills. In a study with repeated observations on the same group of subjects, subjects would be given a pretest on listening skills, a treatment to improve these skills, and then a posttest on listening skills. [(NB. This is a preexperimental design and is not recommended for drawing causal interpretations about the effect of listening training (see Chapter 1, "Designs for Behavioral Research").] In a study with matching, pairs of subjects would be matched on their scores from a pretest of listening skills. Then one member of each pair would be randomly assigned to (say) a control group, while the other member would be assigned to the group receiving the listening treatment. Afterwards, all subjects would be tested again for listening skills. More complicated, within-subjects designs can be conceived such as one-way designs with more than two observations (levels) or factorial designs. For them, the *randomized block* ANOVA is an appropriate statistical test. However, this ANOVA is beyond the scope of this text and will not be presented here (see Dayton, 1970; Kirk, 1968; Myers, 1979; Winer, 1971).

PURPOSE AND UNDERLYING LOGIC

The purpose of the *t* test for dependent samples is to help decide whether the difference between two sample means may be due to chance or to a true difference between population means. Even though the data come from the same sample or matched pairs of subjects, we speak of the difference between two sample means because the subjects received two different treatments. Nevertheless, since the scores in the two treatment or observation conditions are based on the same or matched subjects, they are correlated (see Section VI). The *t* test for dependent samples takes this correlation into account.

The sampling distribution of *t* can be used to determine the probability of observing a difference between means as large or larger than the difference in the sample data. The logic behind using the sampling distribution of *t* for examining differences between means with the dependent-sample *t* test is similar to that for the independent-sample *t* test (see Chapters 14 and 15). The major difference between the *t* test for independent samples (between-subjects design) and for dependent samples (within-subjects design) is in the standard error of the differences between means. The standard error is usually larger for independent samples than for dependent samples. This can be seen by comparing the two formulas for the standard errors. The standard error of the difference between means for the independent t test with equal cell sizes (Chapter 15) is

$$s_{\bar{X}_1 - \bar{X}_2} = \sqrt{s_{\bar{X}_1}^2 + s_{\bar{X}_2}^2} \; . \qquad\qquad [15\text{-}1]$$

For the correlated t test, the standard error of the difference between means, $s^*_{\bar{X}_1 - \bar{X}_2}$, is

$$s^*_{\bar{X}_1 - \bar{X}_2} = \sqrt{s_{\bar{X}_1}^2 + s_{\bar{X}_2}^2 - 2r_{12}s_{\bar{X}_1}s_{\bar{X}_2}} \; , \quad [19\text{-}1]$$

where   * indicates dependent samples,

$s_{\bar{X}}$ is the standard error of the mean $(s/\sqrt{N}\,)$, and

r_{12} is the correlation between subjects' scores in treatment 1 and treatment 2.

Equation 19-1 looks worse than it is. The standard error of the difference between means based on dependent samples depends on the standard error of the mean of sample 1 (squared), and the standard error (squared) for sample 2, just as in the formula for independent samples. Furthermore, $s^*_{\bar{X}_1 - \bar{X}_2}$ takes into account the fact that there is a correlation between subjects' scores in treatments 1 and 2, since the same subjects or matched pairs of subjects are observed in both treatments: $2r_{12}s_{\bar{X}_1}s_{\bar{X}_2}$. If subjects' scores are positively correlated—something we almost always expect—then some number will be subtracted from $s_{\bar{X}_1}^2 + s_{\bar{X}_2}^2$ in arriving at $s^*_{\bar{X}_1 - \bar{X}_2}$. This means that, usually, $s^*_{\bar{X}_1 - \bar{X}_2}$ will be smaller than $s_{\bar{X}_1 - \bar{X}_2}$.[1] This is because by subtracting out the correlation between subjects' scores in the two treatment conditions, we removed the variability within a group (error) due to individual differences between subjects. Hence, the error term for a within-subjects design is usually smaller than the error term for a between-subjects design (see Section VI).

While $s^*_{\bar{X}_1 - \bar{X}_2}$ and $s_{\bar{X}_1 - \bar{X}_2}$ refer to apparently different formulas, actually both come from the same general formula. In order to see why the apparent difference vanishes, think about an independent t test with subjects randomly assigned to one or the other group. What do you expect the correlation r between the scores of subjects in treatment 1 and treatment 2 to be? Well, since

---

[1]In rare cases, the correlation may be negative. In this case, $s^*_{\bar{X}_1 - \bar{X}_2}$ will be larger than $s_{\bar{X}_1 - \bar{X}_2}$. (However, the finding of a negative correlation may be substantively important—more so than the comparison of means.)

subjects were randomly assigned, the correlation should be zero. If $r = 0$ in Formula 19-1, then

$$s^*_{\bar{X}_1 - \bar{X}_2} = \sqrt{s^2_{\bar{X}_1} + s^2_{\bar{X}_2} - (2)(0)s_{\bar{X}_1}s_{\bar{X}_2}} \qquad [\mathbf{19\text{-}1}]$$

$$= \sqrt{s^2_{\bar{X}_1} + s^2_{\bar{X}_2}}$$

$$= s_{\bar{X}_1 - \bar{X}_2}. \qquad [\mathbf{15\text{-}1}]$$

So the formula for the standard error of the differences between means with independent samples has already taken into account the fact that r_{12} is expected to be zero.

The formula for the dependent t test is similar to the formula for the independent t test:

$$t^* = \frac{(\bar{X}_1 - \bar{X}_2) - (\mu_1 - \mu_2)}{\sqrt{s^2_{\bar{X}_1} + s^2_{\bar{X}_2} - 2r_{12}s_{\bar{X}_1}s_{\bar{X}_2}}}, \qquad [\mathbf{19\text{-}2}]$$

with $df = n - 1$,

where $t^* =$ a dependent-sample t test,

$n =$ is the number of subjects in *one* of the two cells.

(Notice that $n_1 = n_2 = n$, since the same subjects or matched pairs of subjects are observed in each of the two cells.)

One difference between the independent t test and the dependent test is that $s^*_{\bar{X}_1 - \bar{X}_2}$ is used for the standard error rather than $s_{\bar{X}_1 - \bar{X}_2}$. A second difference is that the t test for independent samples (t) is based on $n_1 + n_2 - 2$ degrees of freedom, while the dependent t test (t^*) is based on $n - 1$ degrees of freedom. We have fewer degrees of freedom for the dependent t test because the scores of subjects in treatment 1 are correlated with—not independent of—the scores in treatment 2. There are only n different subjects and so only n independent observations. Thus, there are $n - 1$ degrees of freedom for the dependent t test.

The hypotheses about differences between population means using the sampling distribution of t for dependent samples are exactly the same as the hypotheses for the independent t test. In the case of a two-tailed (nondirectional) alternative hypothesis, the null and alternative hypotheses are   HYPOTHESES

$$\left\{ \begin{array}{l} H_0: \mu_1 - \mu_2 = 0 \\ H_1: \mu_1 - \mu_2 \neq 0 \end{array} \right\}, \quad \text{i.e.,} \quad \left\{ \begin{array}{l} H_0: \mu_1 = \mu_2 \\ H_1: \mu_1 \neq \mu_2 \end{array} \right\}.$$

In the case of a directional alternative hypothesis, the null and alternative hypotheses are

$$\left\{ \begin{array}{l} H_0: \mu_1 - \mu_2 = 0 \\ H_1: \mu_1 - \mu_2 > 0 \end{array} \right\}, \quad \text{i.e.,} \quad \left\{ \begin{array}{l} H_0: \mu_1 = \mu_2 \\ H_1: \mu_1 > \mu_2 \end{array} \right\},$$

or

$$\left\{ \begin{array}{l} H_0: \mu_1 - \mu_2 = 0 \\ H_1: \mu_1 - \mu_2 < 0 \end{array} \right\}, \quad \text{i.e.,} \quad \left\{ \begin{array}{l} H_0: \mu_1 = \mu_2 \\ H_1: \mu_1 < \mu_2 \end{array} \right\}.$$

DESIGN REQUIREMENTS FOR THE USE OF THE t^* TEST

The use of the t^* test imposes a number of requirements on the collection of data:

1. There is one independent variable with two levels (i.e., two cells in the design).
2. The same group of subjects is observed under both treatment conditions, or matched pairs of subjects are observed so that one member of the pair is observed under treatment 1 and the other member of the pair is observed under treatment 2.
3. The levels of the independent variable may differ from one another either quantitatively or qualitatively. Qualitative differences are, for example, driving performance in cars with manual and automatic transmissions or strength before and after "pumping iron" (working with weights). Quantitative differences are, for example, a person's ability to recognize familiar objects at different distances, the amount of drug dosage given to rats, or the number of reinforcements.

ASSUMPTIONS

In using the sampling distribution of t to test for differences between dependent means, the following assumptions are made:

1. The scores of the n subjects are independently and randomly sampled from the two respective populations.
2. The scores in the respective populations are normally distributed.
3. The variance of scores in the respective populations are equal (homogeneity of variances: $\sigma_1^2 = \sigma_2^2$).

These assumptions and the (lack of) sensitivity of the t test to them have been discussed extensively in Chapter 15 (see "Assumptions" in Chapter 15), and will not be discussed again here.

CONCEPTUAL FORMULA

Since under the null hypothesis $\mu_1 - \mu_2 = 0$, the conceptual formula for the t^* test can be written as:

Table 19-1 ♦ Hypothetical pre- and posttest IQ scores for first-graders in the experimental group (see Table 2-1)

Subject	IQ scores	
	Pretest	Posttest
1	60	107
2	85	111
3	90	117
4	110	125
5	115	122
$\bar{X}$	92.00	116.40
s	21.97	7.47
r	0.946	

$$t^*_{observed} = \frac{\bar{X}_1 - \bar{X}_2}{\sqrt{s^2_{\bar{X}_1} + s^2_{\bar{X}_2} - 2r_{12}s_{\bar{X}_1}s_{\bar{X}_2}}} \qquad [19\text{-}2a]$$

with $df = n - 1$.

As an example of how this conceptual formula can be applied, some of the data from the hypothetical study of teacher expectancy will be used (see Chapter 2). Specifically, the pre- and posttest IQ scores of the first graders in the experimental group will be examined (see Table 19-1). Recall that these subjects were labeled "bloomers" and teachers expected them to "spurt" in intellectual development over the academic year.

The purpose of this analysis is to determine whether the mean difference of -24.4 IQ points between pre- and posttest scores ($92.00 - 116.40 = -24.40$) may have arisen by chance or represents a true difference between population means (i.e., the population before the treatment and the population after the treatment). Since the same subjects were observed at pretest and posttest, this is a within-subjects design with two groups, and so the t^* test is an appropriate statistic. One word of caution before proceeding: while we are testing differences between means before and after treatment, a significant difference does *not* imply that the treatment caused the change. Remember, this is a preexperimental design (see Chapter 1).

In order to conduct the statistical test, begin by stating the null and alternative hypotheses and the level of significance:

$$H_0: \mu_1 - \mu_2 = 0,$$

$$H_1: \mu_1 - \mu_2 \neq 0,$$

$$\alpha = .01.$$

Next, check the assumptions of independent random sampling, normality, and homogeneity of variance. Subjects were randomly sampled and IQ scores are known to be normally distributed; so much for the first two assumptions. However, the variances at pretest (21.97^2) and posttest (7.47^2) are not homogeneous. Nevertheless, the t test is not sensitive to a violation of this assumption, and so we can proceed.[2]

The next step is to insert the data from Table 19-1 into the formula for $t^*_{observed}$. Before doing so, two preliminary calculations have to be made:

$$s_{\bar{X}_{pre}} = \frac{s_{pre}}{\sqrt{n}} = \frac{21.97}{\sqrt{5}} = 9.83$$

and

$$s_{\bar{X}_{post}} = \frac{s_{post}}{\sqrt{n}} = \frac{7.47}{\sqrt{5}} = 3.34.$$

Now all values can be inserted into Formula 19-2, with the following result:

$$t^*_{observed} = \frac{92.00 - 116.40}{\sqrt{9.38^2 + 3.34^2 - 2(.946)(3.34)(9.83)}}$$

$$= \frac{-24.40}{\sqrt{96.629 + 11.156 - 62.119}}$$

$$= \frac{-24.40}{\sqrt{45.666}}$$

$$= \frac{-24.40}{6.758}$$

$$= -3.61.$$

DECISION RULES FOR REJECTING THE NULL HYPOTHESIS In order to decide whether or not to reject the null hypothesis, $t^*_{observed}$ (-3.61 in the example) must be compared with the critical value of t designating the regions of the t distribution beyond which differences between sample means are unlikely to arise under the null hypothesis. Since there is a different critical

---

[2]A difference between variances in a within-subjects design suggests that there may be an interaction between subjects and treatments. In this case, the t test represents a conservative test of the null hypothesis (see, for example, Kirk, 1968). This appears to have happened with this study.

value of t for each degree of freedom, the first step is to determine the number of degrees of freedom. With one group of subjects, there are $n - 1$ degrees of freedom:

$$df = n - 1.$$

For the example data from the teacher-expectancy study, there were five subjects, so the degrees of freedom for the critical value of t are

$$df = 5 - 1$$

$$= 4.$$

The next step is to find the critical value of t for 4 degrees of freedom at a specified level of significance (α). Table C at the end of the book provides these values. For $\alpha = .01$, two-tailed,

$$t_{\text{critical}(.01/2, 4)} = 4.604.$$

Since $|t^*_{\text{observed}}|$ does not exceed t_{critical}, the null hypothesis should not be rejected. There is insufficient evidence to conclude that the difference between the pre- and posttest means represented a true difference.

In the example study, suppose the mean score at posttest was expected to exceed the mean score at pretest. For this revision, then, the hypotheses would be

$$H_0: \mu_{\text{pre}} - \mu_{\text{post}} = 0,$$

$$H_1: \mu_{\text{pre}} - \mu_{\text{post}} < 0,$$

$$\alpha = .01.$$

For a one-tailed test at $\alpha = .01$ with 4 df, t_{critical} can be found in Table C:

$$t_{\text{critical}(.01, 4)} = 3.747.$$

Since the *absolute value* of t^*_{observed} (3.61) does not exceed the critical value of t (3.747), the null hypothesis should not be rejected. While the difference between means was in the expected direction, there is insufficient evidence to conclude that this difference represents anything but a chance occurrence.

In general, the following set of criteria can be established for deciding whether or not to reject the null hypothesis:

	Do not reject H_0 if	Reject H_0 if
Non-directional (two-tailed)	$|t^*_{\text{obs}}| < t_{\text{crit.}(\alpha/2, \, df)}$	$|t^*_{\text{obs}}| \geq t_{\text{crit.}(\alpha/2, \, df)}$
Directional (one-tailed)	$|t^*_{\text{obs}}| < t_{\text{crit.}(\alpha, \, df)}$	$|t^*_{\text{obs}}| \geq t_{\text{crit.}(\alpha, \, df)}$

While the conceptual formula for the dependent t test is reasonably straight-forward to use, the correlation between the observations under the two treatment conditions must be calculated. This calculation can be somewhat tedious for large samples, especially in the absence of a calculator or computer. Fortunately, there is a computationally easy formula for the t^* test which does not require calculation of the correlation or calculation of as many sample statistics as does the conceptual formula. The computational formula for the dependent t test is

$$t^*_{observed} = \frac{\bar{D} - \mu_D}{s_{\bar{D}}}$$

$$= \frac{\bar{D}}{s_{\bar{D}}}. \qquad [\mathbf{19\text{-}3}]$$

In this formula, $\bar{D}$ is the average of the difference between subjects' scores in one treatment condition (or at pretest) and their scores in the other treatment condition (or at posttest). More formally, if X_{p_1} represents subject p's score under treatment 1 (or pretest), and X_{p_2} represents this subject's score under treatment 2 (or posttest), then a difference score for this person is defined as

$$D_p = X_{p_1} - X_{p_2}. \qquad [\mathbf{19\text{-}4}]$$

The average difference score, $\bar{D}$, is simply $\bar{X}_1 - \bar{X}_2$:

$$\bar{D} = \frac{\sum_p D_p}{n}$$

$$= \frac{\sum_p (X_{p_1} - X_{p_2})}{n}$$

$$= \frac{\sum_p X_{p_1}}{n} - \frac{\sum_p X_{p_2}}{n}$$

$$= \bar{X}_1 - \bar{X}_2.$$

Further, μ_D is the mean difference in the population, assumed to be zero under the null hypothesis.

Finally, the standard error of the mean of differences is

$$s_{\bar{D}} = \frac{s_D}{\sqrt{n}}. \qquad [\textbf{19-5}]$$

And the standard deviation of the difference scores, s_D, is defined as

$$s_D = \sqrt{\frac{\sum\limits_{p}\left(D_p - \bar{D}\right)^2}{n-1}}. \qquad [\textbf{19-6}]$$

While, in presenting the computational formula, several new statistics had to be defined, they are easily and quickly calculated. Procedure 19-1 shows the application of the computational formula for the t^* test using as an example the data on first-graders in the hypothetical study on teacher expectancy (Table 19-1).

Procedure 19-1 Steps in testing the difference between means based on dependent samples (data from ♦ Table 19-1)

Operation	Example
1 Specify the null and alternative hypotheses for the statistical test. *If a directional alternative hypothesis is to be stated, it can be expressed as $H_1: \mu_D > 0$ or $H_1: \mu_D < 0$, depending on the direction of the alternative hypothesis.*	$H_0 : \mu_D = 0,$ $H_1 : \mu_D \neq 0.$
2 Specify the level of significance, α. *α is usually set at .05 or .01.*	$\alpha = .01.$
3 From Table C, determine t_{crit} for α using $n - 1$ degrees of freedom. $t_{crit(\alpha/2,\, n-1)}$ for two-tailed test; $t_{crit.(\alpha,\, n-1)}$ for one-tailed test.	$df = n - 1 = 5 - 1 = 4,$ $t_{crit.(01/2,\, 4)} = 4.604.$
4 Establish decision rules for rejecting the null hypothesis: **a** Do not reject H_0 if $|t^*_{obs}| < t_{crit}$. **b** Reject H_0 if $|t^*_{obs}| \geqslant t_{crit}$.	**a** If $|t^*_{obs}| < 4.604$, do not reject H_0. **b** If $|t^*_{obs}| \geqslant 4.604$, reject H_0.

(continued on p. 564)

5 Take a random sample of n subjects, conduct the study, and collect the data.

6 Set up a computational table with 7 columns:
 1. Subject ID number
 2. Score in treatment condition 1 (X_1)
 3. Score in treatment condition 2 (X_2)
 4. Difference score (D)
 5. The mean of the difference scores ($\overline{D}$)
 6. The deviation score ($D - \overline{D}$)
 7. The square of the deviation scores [$(D - \overline{D})^2$].

The descriptive data are presented in Table 19-1.

(1)	(2)	(3)	(4)	(5)	(6)	(7)
			$D=$			
Subject	X_1	X_2	$X_1 - X_2$	$\overline{D}$	$D - \overline{D}$	$(D - \overline{D})^2$
1	60	107	-47	-24.40	-22.60	510.76
2	85	111	-26	-24.40	-1.60	2.56
3	90	117	-27	-24.40	-2.60	6.76
4	110	125	-15	-24.40	9.40	88.36
5	115	122	-7	-24.40	17.40	302.76
Sum	460	582	(-122)	(-122)	0	911.20

7 Insert the subject's identification number in column 1.

8 Insert each subject's score under treatment 1 in column 2.

9 Insert each subject's score under treatment 2 in column 3.

10 Subtract each subject's score in column 3 from his or her score in column 2 to get the difference score D for each subject in column 4.

11 Sum the difference scores and divide the sum by n in order to get the mean of the difference scores to enter in column 5:

$$\overline{D} = \frac{\sum\limits_{p}(D_p)}{n}$$

$$\overline{D} = \frac{(-47) + (-26) + (-27) + (-15) + (-7)}{5}$$

$$= \frac{-122}{5}$$

$$= -24.40.$$

12 Subtract the mean of the difference scores ($\overline{D}$) from each subject's difference score (D) for column 6.
 (Note: in order to subtract a negative mean from a negative difference score, change the sign of the mean to + and take the sum. See example.)
 As a computational check, the sum of all $(D - \overline{D})$ should equal zero.

$(-47.00) - (-24.40) = -47.00 + 24.40 = -22.60$, etc., for each subject.

13 Square the values in column 6 and place the results in column 7.

$(-22.60)^2 = 510.76$, etc., for each subject.

14 Sum $(D - \overline{D})^2$ and enter the sum at the bottom of column 7.

$510.76 + 2.56 + 6.76 + 88.36 + 302.76 = 911.20$

15 Calculate the standard deviation of the difference scores by dividing the sum of column 7 (obtained in step 13) by $n - 1$, and then taking the square root:

$$s_D = \sqrt{\frac{\Sigma(D_p - \bar{D})^2}{n-1}} \quad \text{[19-6]}$$

$$s_D = \sqrt{\frac{911.20}{5-1}}$$

$$= \sqrt{227.8}$$

$$= 15.093.$$

16 Calculate the standard error of the mean differences by dividing the value in step 15 by the square root of *n*:

$$s_{\bar{D}} = \frac{s_D}{\sqrt{n}}. \quad \text{[19-5]}$$

$$s_{\bar{D}} = \frac{15.093}{\sqrt{5}}$$

$$= 6.750^a$$

17 Insert the values from steps 11 and 16 into formula 19-3 and calculate:

$$t^*_{obs.} = \frac{\bar{D}}{s_{\bar{D}}}. \quad \text{[19-3]}$$

$$t^*_{obs} = \frac{-24.40}{6.750} = -3.61.$$

18 Compare $|t^*_{obs}|$ (step 17) with t_{crit} (step 3) and decide whether or not to reject H_0.

Since $|t^*_{obs}| < t_{crit}$ (3.61 < 4.604), do not reject H_0. There is insufficient evidence to conclude that there is a significant difference between the two groups.

---

[a]You may have noticed a difference of .008 between $s_{\bar{D}}$ as it is calculated here and $s^*_{\bar{X}_1 - \bar{X}_2}$ as it appears in the denominator of the equation for $t^*_{observed}$ given in the "Conceptual Formula" section above. This difference is due to rounding error.

As an example of a within-subjects design with matching, consider a study on the effect of the organization of a list of words, all related to minerals, on subjects' recall of the words. In this study, subjects received a list of 50 words, either arranged in a conceptual hierarchy (experimental group) or arranged in a random order (control group). After studying the list for 4 minutes, all subjects worked on a filler task for 1 minute in order to prevent them from rehearsing the words in the list. Then all subjects recalled as many words from the list as possible.

Since there is a positive correlation between verbal ability and recall of conceptually related words, the researcher decided to match subjects on verbal ability in order to remove individual differences in verbal ability from the variability of scores within groups (error). From a random sample of 20

NUMERICAL EXAMPLE WITH MATCHED PAIRS

Table 19-2 ♦ Vocabulary scores for subjects in the study of the effects of organization on recall

Subject	Score	Pairing	Block	Subject	Score	Pairing	Block
1	30			11	19		
2	29	1, 2	A	12	19	11, 12	F
3	27			13	18		
4	25	3, 4	B	14	17	13, 14	G
5	24			15	15		
6	23	5, 6	C	16	14	15, 16	H
7	22			17	13		
8	22	7, 8	D	18	13	17, 18	I
9	20			19	9		
10	19	9, 10	E	20	5	19, 20	J

Table 19-3 ♦ Data from the study of the effects of organization on recall

Block	Experimental group (1)			Control group (2)		
	Subject ID	Vocabulary	Recall	Subject ID	Vocabulary	Recall
A	2	29	45	1	30	40
B	3	27	42	4	25	36
C	5	24	39	6	23	30
D	7	22	34	8	22	30
E	10	19	32	9	20	33
F	11	19	35	12	19	30
G	13	18	36	14	17	33
H	15	15	34	16	14	28
I	17	13	30	18	13	25
J	19	9	26	20	5	20
Mean		19.50	35.30		18.80	30.50
S.D.		6.22	5.60		7.02	5.58

$$r_{recall} = 0.894$$

subjects, 10 pairs of subjects were matched on the basis of their vocabulary test scores (blocks A–J; see Table 19-2). Then one member of the pair was randomly assigned to the experimental group, and the other member to the control group (see Table 19-3). Finally, the subjects participated in the experiment as described above. The results are summarized in Table 19-3. The mean number of words recalled in the experimental group was 35.30, while the mean number recalled in the control group was 30.50.

Before proceeding to an analysis of the data, consider more closely the data on matching in Table 19-2. Notice that only for subject pairs D, F, and I is the match on vocabulary scores perfect. Further, notice that the vocabulary score of subject 4 is closer to the vocabulary score of subject 5 than to the score of subject 3. Nevertheless, in order to find a match for subject 3, subject 4 had to be used. For block B, two points separate the subjects' scores. Finally, note that there is a four-point difference in block J. While matching is fine in theory, it is sometimes difficult to carry out in practice. The matching in Table 19-2 is reasonably good. Sometimes there are wide gaps between the scores of matched pairs. And if more than one variable is used for matching, matching may become quite difficult.

Table 19-4 ◆ Calculation of $t^*_{observed}$ using the data from the study of the effects of organization on recall

Block	Experimental X_1	Control X_2	$D = X_1 - X_2$	$\bar{D}$	$D - \bar{D}$	$(D - \bar{D})^2$
A	45	40	5	4.8	.20	.04
B	42	36	6	4.8	1.20	1.44
C	39	30	9	4.8	4.20	17.64
D	34	30	4	4.8	− .80	.64
E	32	33	−1	4.8	−5.80	33.64
F	35	30	5	4.8	.20	.04
G	36	33	3	4.8	−1.80	3.24
H	34	28	6	4.8	1.20	1.44
I	30	25	5	4.8	.20	.04
J	26	20	6	4.8	1.20	1.44
Σ	353	305	48	48	0	59.60

$$s_D = \sqrt{\frac{59.60}{10-1}} = 2.57, \quad s_{\bar{D}} = \frac{2.57}{\sqrt{10}} = 0.814,$$

$$t^*_{observed} = \frac{35.30 - 30.50}{.814} = \frac{4.8}{.814} = 5.90.$$

In order to conduct a statistical test, let's set forth the following hypotheses, level of significance, and decision rules:

$$H_0: \mu_D = 0,$$

$$H_1: \mu_D > 0,$$

$$\alpha = .05;$$

$$df = n - 1 = 10 - 1 = 9,$$

$$t_{critical(.05, 9)} = 1.883;$$

a. Do not reject H_0 if $|t^*_{observed}| < 1.883$.
b. Reject H_0 if $|t^*_{observed}| \geqslant 1.883$.

Table 19-4 shows the calculation of $t^*_{observed}$ using the computational formula (Procedure 19-1). Since $|t^*_{observed}|$ (5.90) is greater than $t_{critical}$ (1.883), the null hypothesis should be rejected. Conclude that organization caused the increase in recall.

EXAMPLE PROBLEM 1

A researcher wanted to determine whether army technicians' ability to track targets on a cathode-ray tube (CRT) differed under two conditions of visual display: white foreground on black background and yellow foreground on green background. In a pilot study, a random sample of eight technicians was selected; all eight were observed under both conditions. (In order to avoid practice effects, the order of presenting the two conditions was randomized so that half the subjects received the white-on-black condition first.) The number of targets accurately tracked (out of 5 possible) is shown below:

Technician	White on black	Yellow on green
1	0	2
2	1	1
3	0	3
4	1	2
5	0	0
6	1	4
7	2	3
8	3	4

Conduct a t^* test to determine whether there was a significant difference in the number of targets accurately tracked under the two CRT conditions. (Let $\alpha = .05$.) Include in your answer:

a. An explanation of why the dependent t test rather than the independent t test is appropriate,
b. Null and alternative hypotheses
c. $t_{critical}$
d. Decision rules
e. Computational table (see Procedure 19-1)
g. $t^*_{observed}$
h. Conclusions.

The $100(1 - \alpha)$-percent confidence interval can be constructed about the observed difference between means using the t distribution. The procedure and the interpretation of the confidence interval for correlated data are exactly the same as for independent data described in Chapter 15. However, where $s_{\bar{X}_1 - \bar{X}_2}$ was used for independent samples, $s^*_{\bar{X}_1 - \bar{X}_2}$ is used with dependent samples. And where $t_{critical}$ was based on $n_1 + n_2 - 2$ degrees of freedom with independent samples, $t_{critical}$ is based on $n - 1$ degrees of freedom with dependent samples. The general form of the confidence interval is:

CONFIDENCE INTERVALS

$$\left(\bar{X}_1 - \bar{X}_2\right) - t_{critical(\alpha/2, n-1)} s^*_{\bar{X}_1 - \bar{X}_2} \leqslant \mu_1 - \mu_2$$
$$\leqslant \left(\bar{X}_1 - \bar{X}_2\right) + t_{critical(\alpha/2, n-1)} s^*_{\bar{X}_1 - \bar{X}_2}. \qquad [\textbf{19-7}]$$

If the standard error has been calculated using difference scores, the general form of the confidence interval can be written as:

$$\left(\bar{X}_1 - \bar{X}_2\right) - t_{critical(\alpha/2, n-1)} s_{\bar{D}} \leqslant \mu_1 - \mu_2$$
$$\leqslant \left(\bar{X}_1 - \bar{X}_2\right) + t_{critical(\alpha/2, n-1)} s_{\bar{D}}. \qquad [\textbf{19-7a}]$$

As an example of constructing a confidence interval with correlated data, let's set up a 99-percent confidence interval for the data from the teacher-expectancy study (see Table 19-1 and Procedure 19-1). Three pieces of information are needed:

1. $\bar{X}_1 - \bar{X}_2 = \bar{D} = -24.40$,
2. $s^*_{\bar{X}_1 - \bar{X}_2} = s_{\bar{D}} = 6.758$, and
3. $t_{critical(.01/2, 4)} = 4.604$.

The 99-percent confidence interval can be found by inserting these values into Formula 19-7:

$$CI_{.99}: -24.40 - (4.604)(6.758) \leqslant \mu_1 - \mu_2 \leqslant -24.40 + (4.604)(6.758),$$
$$24.40 - 31.11 \leqslant \mu_1 - \mu_2 \leqslant -24.40 + 31.11,$$
$$-55.51 \leqslant \mu_1 - \mu_2 \leqslant 6.71.$$

Over all possible samples of $\bar{X}_1 - \bar{X}_2$, the probability is .99 that a confidence interval constructed like the one above will include the true difference between population means. (Notice that the probability statement is about all possible random samples of $\bar{X}_1 - \bar{X}_2$ or about intervals constructed like the one above, and not about the particular interval itself.)

♦   ♦   ♦   ♦   ♦

Summary   This chapter presents a statistical test—the *dependent-sample t test*—which is appropriate for *within-subjects designs* with two cells. These designs include cases where two observations are made on each subject or where one observation is made on each of the two members of a matched pair. Procedures for conducting the dependent t test and constructing confidence intervals around the difference between means are presented.

♦   ♦   ♦   ♦   ♦

Key Words

confidence intervals	normality
dependent samples	repeated observations
t test for dependent samples	standard error of the difference between means
homogeneity of variances	within-subjects designs
independent and random sampling	
matched pairs	

♦   ♦   ♦   ♦   ♦

Exercises   1–2 Under what two conditions is it appropriate to use the dependent t test instead of the independent t test?

3. Why are there fewer degrees of freedom for the dependent t test than for the independent t test?

4. Write the error terms for the independent t test and the dependent t test.

5. Explain the differences between them.

6–13 A clinical psychologist was interested in the effect of imagery on patients' emotional responses. He wanted to assess the differences in emotional responses to two types of exercises using imagery. In one exercise, subjects were asked to remember a room in their house as a child and to attempt to use imagery to picture the room in detail. The subject was instructed to "imagine that you are sitting in the middle of this room, and describe, as specifically as you can, all the sensory qualities of the room (i.e., what it looks like, sounds like, smells like, etc.)." In a second exercise, subjects were asked to picture a room in their house as a child, and to project this image on a blank wall in front of them. Subjects were then asked to describe the room in detail. The psychologist hypothesized that the more closely involved the subject was with the image, the greater would be the subject's emotional response. Thus, he hypothesized that exercise 1 would elicit a greater response than exercise 2. To test this hypothesis, he ran the following study. Twelve patients were selected and matched on their ability to form detailed images. Then one patient from each pair was randomly assigned to exercise 1, and the other was assigned to exercise 2. After performing the exercise, all subjects were asked to rate their emotional response on a scale from 1 (low) to 10 (high). The following hypothetical data were collected:

Subject pair	Rating of emotional response	
	Exercise 1	Exercise 2
1	4	2
2	6	3
3	7	1
4	9	5
5	2	2
6	9	6

Using these data, test whether there was a significant difference between the two groups ($\alpha = .05$).

6. Formulate null and alternative hypotheses.
7. Find $t_{critical}$.
8. Draw up the computational table.
9. Find $t_{observed}^{*}$.
10. State your conclusions.
11. Construct the 95-percent confidence interval for these data.
12. State your conclusion from this result.
13. From the hypothesis-testing results, should you expect this interval to include zero?

14–19 A psychologist is interested in determining the effect of two hours versus no food deprivation upon the amount of food intake of rats during a subsequent test period.

Subjects (matched)	Number of pellets eaten during test period	
	No food deprivation	Two hours deprivation
1	0.3	2.0
2	0.9	3.1
3	0.8	2.6
4	1.1	2.8
5	1.7	4.0
6	1.2	3.3
7	0.5	2.3
8	0.6	1.9
9	1.9	3.5
10	1.3	3.2

She uses a form of sampling where every animal in one condition has a litter mate in the other condition. The data for the experiment are given in the table above. Using these data, test whether there is a significant difference between the two groups ($\alpha = .01$).

14. Formulate null and alternative hypotheses (two-tailed).
15. Find $t_{critical}$.
16. State the decision rules.
17. Draw up the computational table.
18. Find $t^*_{observed}$.
19. State your conclusions.

⋅ Answers to Example Problems ⋅

CHAPTER 1
1. a, c, e are adequate hypotheses.
   b is not adequate, because it only concerns one variable and is not testable.
   d is vague, does not predict a relationship clearly.

2. **a.** Interval scale
   b. At least interval (ratio) scale
   c. Ordinal scale
   d. Interval scale
   e. Nominal scale

3. Study 1: Independent variables: type of legal argument and educational level
             Dependent variable: rating of defendant's guilt or innocence
   Study 2: Independent variable: length of breast-feeding
             Control variable: 3-year-old children
             Intervening variable: warmth, intimacy
             Dependent variable: rating of closeness of mother-child relationship

4. Study 1: Internal validity: history, maturation, testing
             External validity: selection of subjects, selection of treatments
   Study 2: Internal validity: none
             External validity: selection of subjects

5. **a.** One-group, pretest-posttest design
       Threats to internal validity: history, testing, instrumentation, selection
   b. One-shot case study
       Threats to internal validity: history, selection
   c. Intact-group comparison
       Threats to internal validity: selection

6. **a.** Posttest-only control-group design
   b. Factorial experimental design

7. **a.** Nonequivalent-control-group design
       Threats to internal validity: selection
   b. Time-series design
       Threats to internal validity: history

8. **a.** Correlational design
   b. Factorial criterion-group design

CHAPTER 3 **1.**

Persons	Treatment[a]	Grade	Posttest
31	2	1	90
32	2	1	99
33	2	1	102
34	2	1	114
35	2	1	121
36	2	2	99
37	2	2	95
38	2	2	104
39	2	2	108
40	2	2	123
41	2	3	102
42	2	3	106
43	2	3	107
44	2	3	111
45	2	3	119
46	2	4	102
47	2	4	102
48	2	4	107
49	2	4	116
50	2	4	120
51	2	5	112
52	2	5	110
53	2	5	115
54	2	5	119
55	2	5	125
56	2	6	96
57	2	6	120
58	2	6	117
59	2	6	110
60	2	6	116

[a]1 = experimental group, 2 = control group.

2. **a.**

Score value X	Tally	Frequency
125	/	1
124		0
123	/	1
122		0
121	/	1
120	//	2
119	//	2
118		0
117	/	1
116	//	2
115	/	1
114	/	1
113		0
112	/	1
111	/	1
110	//	2
109		0
108	/	1
107	//	2
106	/	1
105		0
104	/	1
103		0
102	////	4
101		0
100		0
99	//	2
98		0
97		0
96	/	1
95	/	1
94		0
93		0
92		0
91		0
90	/	1

b. Scores are about equally spread out in two groups; control-group scores are somewhat lower. Most frequently earned scores were 115 and 122 in experimental group and 102 in the control group.

3. a.

(1) Class Interval	(2) f	(3) Real limits	(4) Midpoint
123–125	2	122.5–125.5	124
120–122	3	119.5–122.5	121
117–119	3	116.5–119.5	118
114–116	4	113.5–116.5	115
111–113	2	110.5–113.5	112
108–110	3	107.5–110.5	109
105–107	3	104.5–107.5	106
102–104	5	101.5–104.5	103
99–101	2	98.5–101.5	100
96– 98	1	95.5– 98.5	97
93– 95	1	92.5– 95.5	94
90– 92	1	89.5– 92.5	91
	Sum = 30		

b. The pattern of frequencies in each class interval of the two groups is quite similar.

4. See column 3 of 3a above.

5. See column 4 of 3a above.

6.

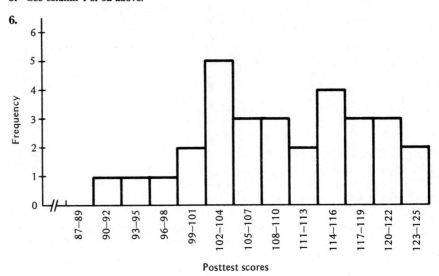

7.

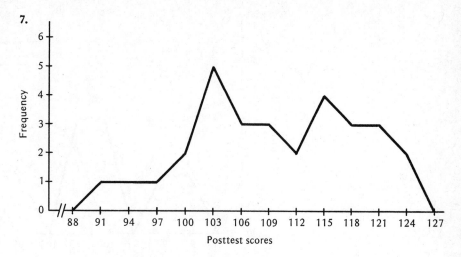

8. a.

Posttest scores	Grades 1–2		Grades 3–6	
	f	Rel. f	f	Rel. f
123–125	1	.10	1	.05
120–122	1	.10	2	.10
117–119	0	.00	3	.15
114–116	1	.10	3	.15
111–113	0	.00	2	.10
108–110	1	.10	2	.10
105–107	0	.00	3	.15
102–104	2	.20	3	.15
99–101	2	.20	0	.00
96– 98	0	.00	1	.05
93– 95	1	.10	0	.00
90– 92	1	.10	0	.00
Sum	10	1.00	20	1.00

b. Most "bloomers" (.90) in grades 1–2 tended to have relatively high posttest scores (i.e., above 111), while most "bloomers" in grades 3–6 (.75) tended to have somewhat lower scores (below 111). In the control group, the distributions for the two grade levels are similar. This pattern provides some evidence for our hunch. (This conclusion, however, is somewhat suspect, due to questions mentioned in Chapter 2 about the validity of the test for younger children.)

9.

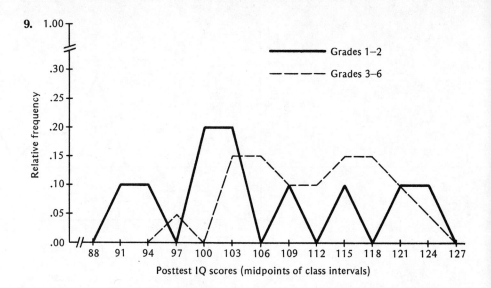

10.

(1) Class interval	(2) f	(3) Upper real limit	(4) Cum. f	(5) Cum. prop.	(6) Cum. %
123–125	2	125.5	30	1.00	100
120–122	3	122.5	28	.93	93
117–119	3	119.5	25	.83	83
114–116	4	116.5	22	.73	73
111–113	2	113.5	18	.60	60
108–110	3	110.5	16	.53	53
105–107	3	107.5	13	.43	43
102–104	5	104.5	10	.33	33
99–101	2	101.5	5	.17	17
96– 98	1	98.5	3	.10	10
93– 95	1	95.5	2	.07	7
90– 92	1	92.5	1	.03	3

11.

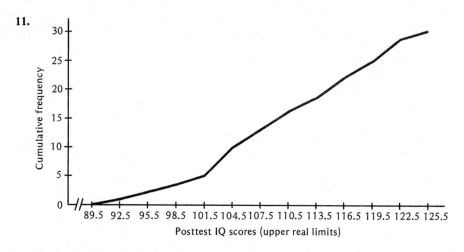

Cumulative frequency (y-axis); Posttest IQ scores (upper real limits) (x-axis)

12. See columns 5 and 6 of Example Problem 10 above.

13.

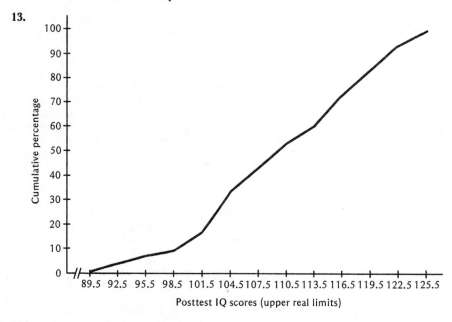

Cumulative percentage (y-axis); Posttest IQ scores (upper real limits) (x-axis)

14.

$$\text{Percentile} = \frac{cf_{ul} + \left(\dfrac{X - X_{ll}}{i}\right)fi}{N} \times 100$$

$$= \frac{10 + \left(\dfrac{106 - 104.5}{3}\right)3}{30} \times 100$$

$$= 38.33.$$

15.

$$\text{Score at given percentile} = X_{ll} + \frac{i(cf - cf_{ul})}{f_i}$$

First, compute

$$cf = \frac{\text{percentile rank} \times N}{100}$$

$$= \frac{70 \times 30}{100} = 21.$$

Enter appropriate values into Formula 3-2:

$$\text{Score at given percentile} = 113.5 + \frac{3(21 - 18)}{4}$$

$$= 115.75.$$

CHAPTER 4   **1. a.**

	Positive outcome (+O)	Positive intent (+I)	Negative outcome (−O)	Negative intent (−I)
Mode	+2.00	+2.50 −2.00	−2.50	−1.00

b. Young children seem to use outcome information, as Piaget predicts. They tended to reward when outcome was positive and punish when outcome was negative. They also seem to use intent, but to a much lesser degree. When intent was negative, subjects tended to punish. When intent was positive, the distribution is bimodal. This suggests that, regardless of the fact that the intent of the person in the story was positive, subjects tended to reward if the outcome was positive and punish if the outcome was negative.

2. a.

	+O	+I	−O	−I
Median	+2.00	+1.50	−2.00	−1.00

b. Conclusions are similar to Example Problem 1(b) except for the positive intent condition. Using the median as a measure of central tendency, subjects appear to be using positive intent information (i.e., they tended to reward in this condition).

3. a.

	+O	+I	−O	−I
Mean	+1.60	+.70	−2.00	−1.10

$\bar{X} = \Sigma X / N$ (Formula 4-2); the calculation for the positive outcome condition is

$$\bar{X} = \frac{(+4) + (+3) + (+3) + \cdots + (-1) + (-1)}{10} = 1.60.$$

b. Conclusions are similar to those above except that the use of positive intent appears somewhat less.

4.

$$\bar{X}_w = \frac{N_1 \bar{X}_1 + N_2 \bar{X}_2 + N_3 \bar{X}_3 + N_4 \bar{X}_4}{N_1 + N_2 + N_3 + N_4}$$

$$= \frac{(22)(71) + (30)(76) + (35)(79) + (28)(81)}{22 + 30 + 35 + 28}$$

$$= 77.2.$$

5. **a.**

	$+O$	$+I$	$-O$	$-I$
Range	5	7	5	6

Range $= X_{highest} - X_{lowest}$ (Formula 4-5); the calculation for positive outcome is

$$\text{Range} = +4 - (-1) = 5.$$

b. The ranges for the 4–6-year-olds are not similar to those of the 16–18-year-olds. In contrast to the 16–18-year-olds, the ranges of moral judgment for 4–6-year-olds were quite similar across the four conditions.

6. **a.**

	$+O$	$+I$	$-O$	$-I$
SIQR	1.00	2.25	0.875	1.75

SIQR $= (Q_3 - Q_1)/2$ (Formula 4-6); the calculation for positive outcome is

$$Q_3 = 2.5 + \frac{1(7.5 - 7)}{2} = 2.75,$$

$$Q_1 = 0.5 + \frac{1(2.5 - 2)}{2} = 0.75,$$

$$\text{SIQR} = \frac{2.75 - 0.75}{2} = 1.00.$$

b. No. $+I$ condition has the highest variability, $-I$ condition is slightly less variable, and $+O$ and $-O$ conditions have least variability.

7. **a.**

	$+O$	$-O$
Standard deviation	1.65	1.22

$s = \sqrt{\dfrac{\Sigma x^2}{N-1}}$ (Formula 4-7a); for positive outcome:

X	$\bar{X}$	x	x^2
4	1.6	2.4	5.76
3	1.6	1.4	1.96
3	1.6	1.4	1.96
2	1.6	0.4	.16
2	1.6	0.4	.16
2	1.6	0.4	.16
1	1.6	-0.6	.36
1	1.6	-0.6	.36
-1	1.6	-2.6	6.76
-1	1.6	-2.6	6.76
			$\Sigma x^2 = 24.4$

$$s = \sqrt{\frac{24.4}{9}} = \sqrt{2.71} = 1.65.$$

b. No. The standard deviations for the younger children are smaller than the standard deviations for the adults. This reflects Piaget's theory that children use outcome information and ignore intent information, while adults do just the opposite. See section on "The Range" for a discussion of this.

8. a.

	+I	−I
Standard deviations	2.50	1.97

$$s = \sqrt{\frac{\Sigma X^2 - \frac{(\Sigma X)^2}{N}}{N-1}}$$ (Formula 4-8). Calculation for positive intent:

$$s = \sqrt{\frac{61 - \frac{7^2}{10}}{10-1}} = 2.50.$$

b. No. The standard deviations are larger for 4–6-year-olds than for 16–18-year-olds in these conditions.

9.

	+O	+I	−O	−I
Variance	$(1.65)^2$	$(2.50)^2$	$(1.41)^2$	$(1.97)^2$
	= 2.72	= 6.25	= 1.99	= 3.88

CHAPTER 5 1. $z = \dfrac{2.65 - 2.93}{.33} = -.85.$

2. a. $z = \dfrac{2.25 - 2.93}{.33} = -2.06.$

b.

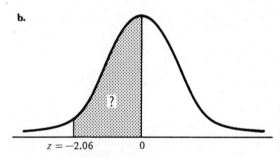

$$z = -2.06 \qquad 0$$

c. Area = .4803 (see column 2).

3. a. $z = \dfrac{2.75 - 2.93}{.33} = -.55.$

b.

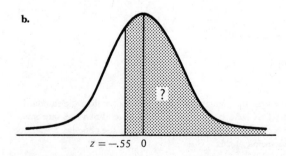

$$z = -.55 \quad 0$$

c. Area = .7088 (see column 3).

4. a. $z_{GPA} = 3.00 = \dfrac{3.00 - 2.93}{.33} = .21,$

$z_{GPA} = 3.35 = \dfrac{3.35 - 2.93}{.33} = 1.27.$

b.

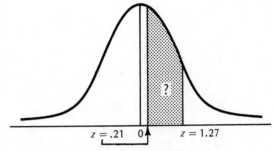

$z = .21 \quad 0 \qquad z = 1.27$

c. Area below $z = 1.27$ is .8980 (see column 3).
Area below $z = .21$ is .5832 (see column 3).
Difference in areas: $.8980 - .5832 = .3148.$

5. a.

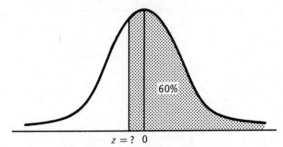

60%

$z = ? \quad 0$

b. Proportion of interest $= 60 + 100 = .60.$
c. Nearest proportion in column 3 $= .5987$, corresponding z score $= 0.25.$
d. Since z is below $\overline{X}$, z is negative: $z = -0.25.$
e. $X = .33(-0.25) + 2.93 = 2.85.$

1. $\overline{X} = 2.84,\ \overline{Y} = 1084,$

CHAPTER 7

$\mathrm{Cov}_{XY} = \dfrac{-39.6}{9} = -4.4,$

$r_{XY} = \dfrac{-4.4}{(.52)(67.24)} = -.13.$

2. $r_{XY} = \dfrac{N\Sigma XY - (\Sigma X)(\Sigma Y)}{\sqrt{[N\Sigma X^2 - (\Sigma X)^2][N\Sigma Y^2 - (\Sigma Y)^2]}}$

$= \dfrac{10(32856) - (29.2)(11270)}{\sqrt{[10(85.98) - (29.2)^2][10(12,714,100) - (11,270)^2]}}$

$= \dfrac{-524}{\sqrt{(7.16)(128,100)}}$

$= -.547.$

3. $r_{XY}^2 = (-.13)^2 = .02$, or 2%.

4.

Rank on X	$\bar{X}$	x	Rank on Y	$\bar{Y}$	y	xy
3	3.5	$-.5$	5	3.5	1.5	$-.75$
4	3.5	.5	2	3.5	-1.5	$-.75$
1	3.5	-2.5	1	3.5	-2.5	6.25
6	3.5	2.5	4	3.5	.5	1.25
5	3.5	1.5	3	3.5	$-.5$	$-.75$
2	3.5	-1.5	6	3.5	2.5	-3.75
						$\Sigma xy = 1.5$

$\text{Cov}_{XY} = \dfrac{1.5}{5} = .3,$

$s_X = \sqrt{\dfrac{17.5}{5}} = 1.87,$

$s_Y = \sqrt{\dfrac{17.5}{5}} = 1.87,$

$r_S = \dfrac{\text{Cov}_{XY}}{s_X s_Y},$

$= \dfrac{.3}{(1.87)(1.87)} = .0857.$

CHAPTER 8   **1.** **a.** $b_{Y \cdot X} = (r_{XY})\dfrac{s_Y}{s_X} = (.64)\dfrac{1.92}{1.14} = 1.08,$

or, using raw-score formula

$b_{Y \cdot X} = \dfrac{5(111) - (17)(31)}{5(63) - (17)^2} = 1.08.$

b. $\hat{Y} = \bar{Y} + b_{Y \cdot X}(X - \bar{X})$

$= 6.2 + 1.08(X - 3.4).$

c. $\hat{Y}_{X=1} = 6.2 + 1.08(1 - 3.4) = 3.61,$

$\hat{Y}_{X=6} = 6.2 + 1.08(6 - 3.4) = 9.01.$

d.

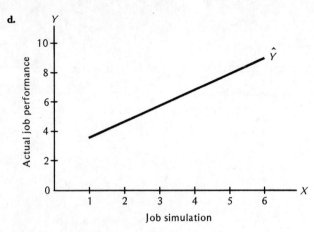

2. $s_{Y \cdot X} = s_Y \sqrt{1 - r_{YX}^2}$

$\quad = 1.92 \sqrt{1 - (.64)^2}$

$\quad = 1.48.$

3. a. $b_{X \cdot Y} = (r_{YX}) \dfrac{s_X}{s_Y}$

$\quad = (.64) \dfrac{1.14}{1.92} = .38.$

b. $\hat{X} = \bar{X} + b_{X \cdot Y}(Y - \bar{Y})$

$\quad = 3.4 + (.38)(Y - 6.2).$

c. $\hat{X}_{Y=8} = 3.4 + (.38)(8 - 6.2) = 4.08$

$\quad \hat{X}_{Y=3} = 3.4 + (.38)(3 - 6.2) = 2.18.$

d.

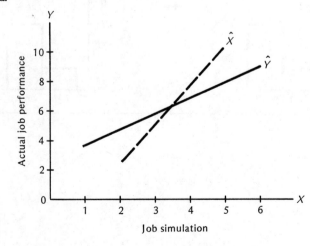

4. $s_{X \cdot Y} = s_X \sqrt{1 - r_{XY}^2}$

$= 1.14 \sqrt{1 - (.64)^2}$

$= .88.$

5. Percentage of variance in Y accounted for by X

$= (b_{X \cdot Y})(b_{Y \cdot X}) \times 100$

$= (.38)(1.08)(100)$

$= 41\%$

or

$= r_{XY}^2 \times 100$

$= (.64^2) \times 100$

$= 41\%.$

CHAPTER 10 **1.** Intuition says: 1/4 or .25. This is consistent with probability theory: (1) there are four possible equally likely outcomes in guessing; (2) of these possible outcomes, only one will give the correct answer; (3) the probability of guessing correctly is given by the number of ways the favored outcome occurs ("right") over the total number of outcomes—1/4 or .25. This is shown in the table below. Note also that the abscissa of the frequency distribution and probability distribution is labeled right and wrong (there are three ways to guess wrong).

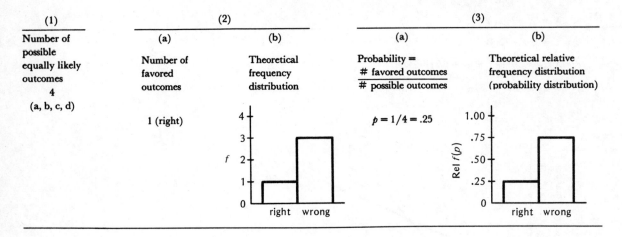

2. This question can be rephrased in probability-theory terms as: What is the probability of the event "even number" on a roll of a die? There are three steps in the calculation: (1) Identify all the possible equally likely outcomes in the experiment: $OS = \{1, 2, 3, 4, 5, 6\}$; $\# OS = 6$. (2) Identify the outcomes that fall within the event, even numbers: $E(\text{even numbers}) = \{2, 4, 6\}$; the number of outcomes in the event is $\# E = 3$. (3) The probability of guessing correctly, then is

$$p(E = \text{even numbers}) = \frac{\# E}{\# OS} = \frac{3}{6} = \frac{1}{2} = .50.$$

3. **a.** $OS = \{1, 2, 3, 4, 5, 6\}$, so $\# OS = 6$.
   b. $E_{(1 \text{ or } 6)} = \{1, 6\}$, so $\# E = 2$.
   c. $p_{(E=1, 6)} = \# E / \# OS = 2/6 = 1/3 = .33$.

4. **a.** $\# OS = 52$ cards.
   b. $\# E_{(\text{king})} = 4$.
   c. $p_{(E=\text{king})} = \# E / \# OS = 4/52 = 1/13 = .08$.

5. **a.** $\# OS = 52$ cards.
   b. $\# E_{(\text{heart})} = 13$.
   c. $p_{(E=\text{heart})} = \# E / \# OS = 13/52 = 1/4 = .25$.

1. **a.** Approximately normal.

CHAPTER 11

   b. The population mean (50).
   c.
$$\sigma_{\bar{X}} = \frac{\sigma}{\sqrt{N}} = \frac{14}{\sqrt{49}} = 2.00.$$

2. **a.**
$$z_{\bar{X}} = \frac{26 - 20}{2} = 3.00,$$

$$p(\bar{X} > 26) = .0013.$$

   b.
$$z_{\bar{X}} = \frac{16 - 20}{2} = -2.00,$$

$$p(\bar{X} < 16) = .0228.$$

   c.
$$z_{\bar{X}=16} = -2.00 \text{ (from Example Problem 2b)},$$

$$p(\bar{X} < 16) = .0228 \text{ (from Example Problem 2b)},$$

$$z_{X=24} = \frac{24 - 20}{2} = 2.00,$$

$$p(\bar{X} > 24) = .0228,$$

$$p(\bar{X} < 16 \text{ or } \bar{X} > 24) = .0228 + .0228 = .0456.$$

3. a. Reject H_0.
   b. Do not reject H_0.

4. a. $z_{\bar{X}}$ (critical) $= 1.96$ and -1.96.
   b. $z_{\bar{X}}$ (critical) $= -1.65$.

5. a. Step 1. Hypotheses:
      (a) H_0: $\mu = 50$,
      (b) H_1: $\mu > 50$.
  Step 2. Decision rule with $\alpha = .05$.
      (a) Reject H_0 if $z_{\bar{X}}$ (observed) > 1.65,
      (b) Do not reject H_0 if $z_{\bar{X}}$ (observed) < 1.65.
  Step 3. Computation of $z_{\bar{X}}$ (observed):

$$z_{\bar{X}} \text{ (observed)} = \frac{\bar{X} - \mu}{\sigma_{\bar{X}}}, \text{ where } \sigma_{\bar{X}} = \frac{\sigma}{\sqrt{N}};$$

$$z_{\bar{X}} \text{ (observed)} = \frac{53.4 - 50}{2} = 1.7, \text{ since } \sigma_{\bar{X}} = \frac{14}{\sqrt{49}} = 2.0.$$

  Step 4. Decision: $z_{\bar{X}}$ (critical) $= 1.65$. $z_{\bar{X}}$ (observed) $> z_{\bar{X}}$ (critical), so reject H_0.
  Step 5. Conclusion: The mean mechanical ability of seniors in the vocational program is greater than that of seniors statewide.

b. Step 1. Hypotheses:
      (a) H_0: $\mu = 50$,
      (b) H_1: $\mu \neq 50$.
  Step 2. Decision rule with $\alpha = .05$:
      (a) reject H_0 if $|z_{\bar{X}}(\text{observed})| > 1.96$,
      (b) do not reject H_0 if $|z_{\bar{X}}(\text{observed})| < 1.96$.
  Step 3. Computation of $z_{\bar{X}}(\text{observed})$: Same as for 5a. $z_{\bar{X}}(\text{observed}) = 1.7$
  Step 4. Decision: $|z_{\bar{X}}(\text{observed})| < z_{\bar{X}}(\text{critical})$, so do not reject H_0.
  Step 5. Conclusion: There is insufficient evidence to conclude that the mean mechanical ability of seniors in the vocational program is different from that of seniors statewide. The observed difference may have been due to chance.

c. Conclusions based on the two tests differ. This occurs because the value of $z_{\bar{X}}$ corresponding to the sample mean is greater than $z_{\bar{X}}$ (critical, one-tailed) but less than $z_{\bar{X}}$ (critical, two-tailed). Since the value of $z_{\bar{X}}$ (critical) marks off 5 percent of the area in *both* tails, the value of $z_{\bar{X}}$ (critical) at each tail marks off 2.5 percent of the distribution. This accounts for the larger value of $z_{\bar{X}}$ in the upper tail compared to the value of $z_{\bar{X}}(\text{critical})$ for a one-tailed test.

6. $CI_{.95}$: $\bar{X} - 1.96\sigma_{\bar{X}} < \mu < \bar{X} + 1.96\sigma_{\bar{X}}$,

$$30 - (1.96)(4) < \mu < 30 + (1.96)(4),$$
$$22.16 < \mu < 37.84;$$

$CI_{.99}$: $\bar{X} - 2.58\sigma_{\bar{X}} < \mu < \bar{X} + 2.58\sigma_{\bar{X}}$,

$$30 - (2.58)(4) < \mu < 30 + (2.58)(4),$$
$$19.68 < \mu < 40.32.$$

7. a. $CI_{.95}$: $\bar{X} - 1.96\sigma_{\bar{X}} < \mu < \bar{X} + 1.96\sigma_{\bar{X}}$,

$$53.4 - (1.96)(2) < \mu < 53.4 + (1.96)(2),$$
$$49.48 < \mu < 57.32.$$

b. Do not reject H_0, since the 95-percent confidence intervals such as this one includes μ.

c. Same decision about H_0, with two-tailed hypothesis test at $\alpha = .05$ and with 95-percent confidence interval.

1. $\sigma_{\bar{X}_E} = \dfrac{8}{\sqrt{64}} = 1.0, \ \sigma_{\bar{X}_C} = \dfrac{8}{\sqrt{64}} = 1.0,$

CHAPTER 12

$\sigma_{\bar{X}_E - \bar{X}_C} = \sqrt{(1.0)^2 + (1.0)^2} = \sqrt{1.00 + 1.00} = \sqrt{2.00} = 1.41.$

2. a.
$$z_{\bar{X}_1 - \bar{X}_2} = \frac{(\bar{X}_1 - \bar{X}_2) - (\mu_1 - \mu_2)}{\sigma_{\bar{X}_1 - \bar{X}_2}}$$

$$= \frac{2.50 - 0}{1.20}$$

$$= 2.08.$$

From Table B, $p(z_{\bar{X}_1 - \bar{X}_2} > 2.08) = .0188.$

b. From Table B, the value of $z_{(\text{critical})}$ corresponding to .01 of the area under the normal curve in the upper tail of the distribution is 2.33.

3. Step 1. Hypotheses:

$H_0: \mu_{SC} - \mu_{RC} = 0,$

$H_1: \mu_{SC} - \mu_{RC} \neq 0.$

Step 2. Decision rule with $\alpha = .01$ (two-tailed):

Reject H_0 if $|z_{\bar{X}_{SC} - \bar{X}_{RC}}(\text{observed})| > z_{\bar{X}_{SC} - \bar{X}_{RC}}(\text{critical}) = 2.58.$

Do not reject H_0 if $|z_{\bar{X}_{SC} - \bar{X}_{RC}}(\text{observed})| < z_{\bar{X}_{SC} - \bar{X}_{RC}}(\text{critical}) = 2.58.$

Step 3. Computation of $z_{\bar{X}_{SC} - \bar{X}_{RC}}(\text{observed})$:

$$z_{\bar{X}_{SC} - \bar{X}_{RC}}(\text{observed}) = \frac{(\bar{X}_{SC} - \bar{X}_{RC}) - (\mu_{SC} - \mu_{RC})}{\sigma_{\bar{X}_{SC} - \bar{X}_{RC}}}$$

$$= \frac{\bar{X}_{SC} - \bar{X}_{RC}}{\sigma_{\bar{X}_{SC} - \bar{X}_{RC}}},$$

$$\sigma_{\bar{X}_{SC} - \bar{X}_{RC}} = \sqrt{\sigma_{\bar{X}_{SC}}^2 + \sigma_{\bar{X}_{RC}}^2},$$

$$\sigma_{\bar{X}_{SC}} = \frac{\sigma_{SC}}{\sqrt{n_{SC}}} = \frac{5}{\sqrt{36}} = .83,$$

$$\sigma_{\bar{X}_{RC}} = \frac{\sigma_{RC}}{\sqrt{n_{RC}}} = \frac{5}{\sqrt{36}} = .83,$$

$$\sigma_{\bar{X}_{SC} - \bar{X}_{RC}} = \sqrt{(.83)^2 + (.83)^2} = \sqrt{.69 + .69} = 1.17,$$

$$z_{\bar{X}_{SC} - \bar{X}_{RC}} = \frac{50 - 48}{1.17} = 1.71.$$

Step 4. Decision: Since $|z_{\bar{X}_{SC} - \bar{X}_{RC}}(\text{observed})| < z_{\bar{X}_{SC} - \bar{X}_{RC}}(\text{critical})$, do not reject H_0.

Step 5. Conclusion: The achievement of EMR children in special classes does not differ significantly from that of EMR children in regular classes.

4. a. $CI_{.95}: \left(\bar{X}_E - \bar{X}_C\right) \pm 1.96\sigma_{\bar{X}_E - \bar{X}_C}$

$(56 - 53) \pm 1.96(1.50)$

$3 \pm 2.94.$

Thus,

$CI_{.95}: \quad .06 < \mu_E - \mu_C < 5.94$

b. $CI_{.99}: \left(\bar{X}_E - \bar{X}_C\right) \pm 2.58\sigma_{\bar{X}_E - \bar{X}_C}$

$(56 - 53) \pm 2.58(1.50)$

$3 \pm 3.87.$

Thus,

$CI_{.99}: \quad -0.87 < \mu_E - \mu_C < 6.87.$

CHAPTER 13   **1. a.** $H_0: \mu = 1000,$
$H_1: \mu = 1100.$

b.

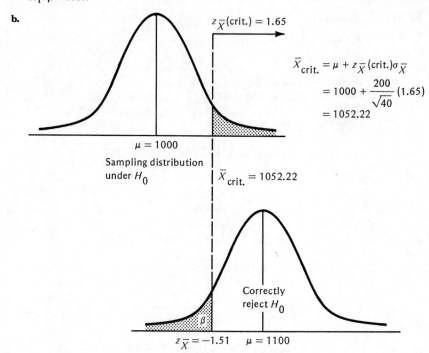

$z_{\bar{X}}(\text{crit.}) = 1.65$

$\bar{X}_{\text{crit.}} = \mu + z_{\bar{X}}(\text{crit.})\sigma_{\bar{X}}$

$= 1000 + \dfrac{200}{\sqrt{40}}(1.65)$

$= 1052.22$

$\mu = 1000$

Sampling distribution
under H_0

$\bar{X}_{\text{crit.}} = 1052.22$

Correctly
reject H_0

β

$z_{\bar{X}} = -1.51 \quad \mu = 1100$

Sampling distribution under H_1

c. Note: $\sigma_{\bar{X}} = 31.65$ so 1100 falls about 3 standard errors above 1000.

$$z_{\bar{X}(H_1)} = \frac{\bar{X}_{meet} - \mu_{H_1}}{\sigma_{\bar{X}}} = \frac{1052.22 - 1100}{31.65} = -1.51.$$

Thus, the power corresponds to the area under the greater part of the curve to the right of $z_{\bar{X}} = -1.51$. Since the normal distribution is symmetric, this area equals the area in the greater part of the curve to the left of $z_{\bar{X}} = 1.51$. From Table B,

power $= .93$.

Since β + power $= 1.00$,

$\beta = 1 -$ power $= .07$.

2. a. $H_0: \mu = 1000$,
   $H_1: \mu = 1100$.

b.

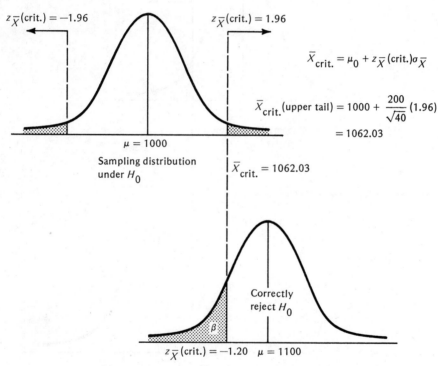

$$\bar{X}_{crit.} = \mu_0 + z_{\bar{X}}(crit.)\sigma_{\bar{X}}$$

$$\bar{X}_{crit.}(\text{upper tail}) = 1000 + \frac{200}{\sqrt{40}}(1.96)$$

$$= 1062.03$$

$z_{\bar{X}}(crit.) = -1.96$ $z_{\bar{X}}(crit.) = 1.96$

$\mu = 1000$

Sampling distribution under H_0

$\bar{X}_{crit.} = 1062.03$

Correctly reject H_0

β

$z_{\bar{X}}(crit.) = -1.20$ $\mu = 1100$

Sampling distribution under H_1

c. Note: $\sigma_{\bar{X}} = 31.65$,

$$z_{\bar{X}(H_1)} = \frac{1062.03 - 1100}{31.65} = -1.20.$$

Thus, the power corresponds to the greater portion of the curve to the right of -1.20. From Table B,

power $= .88$,

$\beta = 1 - \text{power} = .12$.

3. a. $H_0: \mu_{SG} - \mu_{EP} = 0$,
    $H_1: \mu_{SB} - \mu_{EP} = 2$.
    Note: $H_1: \mu_{EP} - \mu_{SG} = -2$ is equally correct; however, $H_1: \mu_{SG} - \mu_{EP} = 2$ is computationally easier, since the use of negative numbers is avoided.

b.

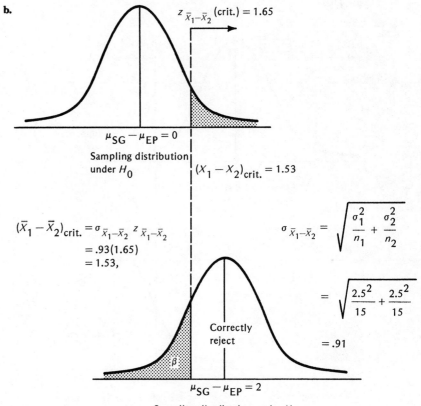

$z_{\bar{X}_1 - \bar{X}_2}$ (crit.) $= 1.65$

$\mu_{SG} - \mu_{EP} = 0$

Sampling distribution under H_0

$(X_1 - X_2)_{crit.} = 1.53$

$(\bar{X}_1 - \bar{X}_2)_{crit.} = \sigma_{\bar{X}_1 - \bar{X}_2} \ z_{\bar{X}_1 - \bar{X}_2}$
$= .93(1.65)$
$= 1.53$,

$\sigma_{\bar{X}_1 - \bar{X}_2} = \sqrt{\dfrac{\sigma_1^2}{n_1} + \dfrac{\sigma_2^2}{n_2}}$

$= \sqrt{\dfrac{2.5^2}{15} + \dfrac{2.5^2}{15}}$

$= .91$

Correctly reject

β

$\mu_{SG} - \mu_{EP} = 2$

Sampling distribution under H_1

c.

$$z_{(\bar{X}_1 - \bar{X}_2)(H_1)} = \frac{1.53 - 2}{.91} = -.52.$$

From Table B,

power $= .70,$

$\beta = .30.$

4.

$$N = \frac{\sigma^2(|z_\beta| + |z_\alpha|)^2}{D^2}$$

$$= \frac{200^2(1.28 + 1.65)^2}{100^2}$$

$$= \frac{40,000(8.58)}{10,000}$$

$$= 34.32 \approx 34.$$

5.

$$N = \frac{\sigma^2(|z_\beta| + |z_{\alpha/2}|)^2}{D^2}$$

$$= \frac{200^2(1.28 + 1.96)^2}{100^2}$$

$$= \frac{40,000(10.50)}{10,000}$$

$$= 42.$$

6.

$$n = \frac{2\sigma^2(|z_\beta| + |z_\alpha|)^2}{D^2}$$

$$= \frac{2(2.5)^2(|-1.65| + |2.33|)^2}{2^2}$$

$$= \frac{2(6.25)(15.84)}{4}$$

$$= 49.50 \approx 50 \text{ subjects in } \textit{each} \text{ group.}$$

7.

$$n = \frac{2\sigma^2(|z_\beta + z_\alpha|)^2}{D^2}$$

$$= \frac{2(2.5)^2(|-1.65| + |2.58|)^2}{2^2}$$

$$= \frac{2(6.25)(17.89)}{4}$$

$$= 55.91 \approx 56 \text{ per group.}$$

8. $N = \dfrac{(|z_\beta| + |z_\alpha|)^2}{\Delta^2}$

$= \dfrac{(|1.65| + |2.33|)^2}{.50^2}$

$= 63.36 \approx 63.$

9. $n = \dfrac{2(|z_\beta| + |z_{\alpha/2}|)^2}{\Delta^2}$

$= \dfrac{2(|1.28| + |1.96|)^2}{.80^2}$

$= 32.81 \approx 33$ per group.

CHAPTER 14

1. a. $H_0: \mu = 1000,$
   $H_1: \mu \neq 1000.$

b. $t_{observed} = \dfrac{1149.5 - 1000}{\left(40.31/\sqrt{10}\;\right)} = 11.72.$

c. $t_{critical(.01,\,9)} = 3.25.$

d. Since $t_{observed} > t_{critical}$, reject H_0. Conclude that students at UCSD belong to a population with a higher mean SAT total score than the general population of students taking the test.

e. $1149.5 - (3.25)(12.76) < \mu < 1149.5 + (3.25)(12.76),$
   $1108.03 < \mu < 1190.97$

f. No. The 99-percent confidence interval does not include μ under H_0, which is expected, since H_0 was rejected at $\alpha = .01$.

CHAPTER 15

1. a. $H_0: \mu_A - \mu_C = 0,$
   $H_1: \mu_A - \mu_C < 0,$
   where A represents adults and C represents children.

b. *Independent and random sampling*: Sampling procedures suggest independent sampling from each population.
   Normality: Unable to test with frequency distribution, due to small number of scores. However, t test is insensitive to violations of this assumption.
   Equal variances: Since cell sizes are equal, t test is not seriously affected by a violation of this assumption.

c. $t_{obs.} = \dfrac{\bar{X}_A - \bar{X}_C}{\sqrt{\dfrac{s_A^2 + s_C^2}{n}}}$ **[15-1d]**

$= \dfrac{-2.80 - 0.40}{\sqrt{\dfrac{1.70 + 1.80}{5}}} = -3.81.$

d. $t_{crit.(.05,\,8)} = 1.86.$

e. Since $|t_{obs.}| > t_{crit.}$, reject H_0. Conclude that children similar to those in our sample tend to use outcome information, while adults similar to those in our sample tend to use intent information in making moral judgments about short-story situations.

f. $CI_{.95}$: $-3.20 - 2.306(0.84) < \mu_1 - \mu_2 < -3.20 + 2.306(0.84)$,

$$-6.19 < \mu_1 - \mu_2 < -1.26.$$

2. **a.** H_0: The distributions of moral judgments in the populations of children and adults from which these groups were drawn are identical.

H_1: The moral judgments in the populations of children and adults from which these groups were drawn differ in their means:

$$\mu_C \neq \mu_A.$$

b. *Independent and random sampling*: Sampling procedures suggest that subjects were independently sampled from each population.

Distributions of similar shape. Unable to test with frequency distribution, given small number of scores.

c.

Group	A	A	A	A	A	C	C	C	C	C
Original moral judgment	-5	-3	-2	-2	-2	-1	-1	$+1$	$+1$	$+2$
Rank	1	2	4	4	4	6.5	6.5	8.5	8.5	10

d. $U = 25 + \dfrac{30}{2} - 40 = 0$.

e. .004.

f. Reject H_0. Conclude that there is a relationship between age and the basis on which a moral judgment is made.

CHAPTER 16

1. **a.** H_0: $\mu_1 = \mu_2 = \mu_3 = \mu_4$

H_1: $\mu_i \neq \mu_{i'}$ for some i and i'.

b. *Independence*: random assignment of subjects to groups and independent study of the material satisfy this assumption.

Normality: not tested, since ANOVA is not sensitive to violations of this assumption.

Homogeneity of variances: not tested, since ANOVA is not sensitive to violations of this assumption *when cell sizes are equal*.

c. *Step 1.*

Data summary table:

Person	Treatment level			
	T_1	T_2	T_3	T_4
p_1	7	9	20	10
p_2	10	14	18	11
p_3	6	12	19	13
p_4	7	11	16	12
p_5	8	13	18	11
$\sum_1^n X_{pi} =$	38	59	91	57

Step 2. **a.** See table above.

b.

$$\frac{\left(\sum\limits_{1}^{n} X_{p1}\right)^2}{n_1} = \frac{38^2}{5} = 288.8, \qquad \frac{\left(\sum\limits_{1}^{n} X_{p3}\right)^2}{n_3} = \frac{(91)^2}{5} = 1656.2,$$

$$\frac{\left(\sum\limits_{1}^{n} X_{p2}\right)^2}{n_2} = \frac{59^2}{5} = 696.2, \qquad \frac{\left(\sum\limits_{1}^{n} X_{p4}\right)^2}{n_4} = \frac{(57)^2}{5} = 649.8.$$

c.
$$\sum\limits_{1}^{N} X_p = 7 + 10 + 6 + 7 + 8 + 9 + 14 + 12 + 11 + 13 + 20 + 18 + 19$$
$$+ 16 + 18 + 10 + 11 + 13 + 12 + 11 = 245.$$

Step 3. **a.**

$$\{1\} = \frac{\sum\limits_{i=1}^{k}\left(\sum\limits_{p=1}^{n} X_{pi}\right)^2}{n_i} = 288.8 + 696.2 + 1656.2 + 649.8 = 3291.$$

b.

$$\{2\} = \frac{\left(\sum\limits_{p=1}^{N} X_p\right)^2}{N} = \frac{245^2}{20} = 3001.25.$$

c.
$$\{3\} = \sum\limits_{p=1}^{N} X_p^2 = (7)^2 + (10)^2 + (6)^2 + (7)^2 + (8)^2 + (9)^2 + (14)^2 + (12)^2 + (11)^2$$
$$+ (13)^2 + (20)^2 + (18)^2 + (19)^2 + (16)^2 + (18)^2 + (10)^2 + (11)^2$$
$$+ (13)^2 + (12)^2 + (11)^2 = 3329.$$

Step 4. **a.** $SS_T = \{3\} - \{2\} = 3329 - 3001.25 = 327.75.$

b. $SS_B = \{1\} - \{2\} = 3291 - 3001.25 = 289.75.$

c. $SS_W = \{3\} - \{1\} = 3329 - 3291 = 38.$

d. ANOVA summary table:

Source of variation	SS	df	MS	F
Between groups	289.75	3	96.58	40.58
Within groups	38.00	16	2.38	
Total	327.75			

e. $F_{\text{critical}(.05, 3, 16)} = 3.24.$

f. Since F_{observed} exceeds F_{critical}, reject H_0. Differences between means could not have arisen by chance.

2. a.
$$\omega^2 = \frac{SS_B - (k-1)MS_W}{SS_T + MS_W}$$

$$= \frac{289.75 - (4-1)2.38}{327.75 + 2.38}$$

$$= .86.$$

b. Study time accounted for 86 percent of the variance in achievement.

3. **a.** Set of weights:

Comparison	$\overline{X}_{10\text{ min}}$	$\overline{X}_{20\text{ min}}$	$\overline{X}_{45\text{ min}}$	$\overline{X}_{75\text{ min}}$	Sum of weights
$\hat{C}_1: \overline{X}_{45\text{ min}}$ vs. $\overline{X}_{75\text{ min}}$	0	0	1	-1	0
$\hat{C}_2: \overline{X}_{10\text{ min}}$ vs. $\dfrac{\overline{X}_{20} + \overline{X}_{45} + \overline{X}_{75}}{3}$	3	-1	-1	-1	0

Check on independence:

$$\hat{C}_1 \text{ vs. } \hat{C}_2 : \quad (0)(3) + (0)(-1) + (1)(-1) + (-1)(-1) = 0.$$

b. $H_0 : C_1 = 0,$
$H_1 : C_1 > 0.$

c. $\hat{C}_1 = \sum_1^k w_i \overline{X}_i = 1(18) + (-1)(11) = 7.$

d. $t = \dfrac{\hat{C}}{\sqrt{\dfrac{2\,MS_W}{n}}} = \dfrac{7}{\sqrt{\dfrac{2(10.79)}{20}}} = 6.74.$

e. Since α was set at .05, $t_{\text{critical}(.05,\,76)} = 1.671.$

f. Since $t_{\text{observed}} > t_{\text{critical}}$, reject H_0. Conclude that the mean of the study group given 45 minutes is significantly greater than the mean of the study group given 75 minutes.

g. Step 2. H_0: $C_2 = 0,$
    H_1: $C_2 < 0.$
Step 3. $\hat{C}_2 = (3)(6) + (-1)(10) + (-1)(18) + (-1)(11) = -21.$
Step 4. $\hat{C}_2$:

$$t = \dfrac{\hat{C}}{\sqrt{\dfrac{MS_W}{n}(w_1^2 + w_2^2 + \cdots + w_k^2)}}$$

$$= \dfrac{-21}{\sqrt{\dfrac{10.79}{20}\left[(3)^2 + (-1)^2 + (-1)^2 + (-1)^2\right]}}$$

$$= -8.25.$$

Step 5. $t_{\text{critical}(.05,\,76)} = 1.671.$
Step 6. Since $|t_{\text{observed}}| > t_{\text{critical}}$, reject H_0. Conclude that the mean of the study group given 10 minutes is significantly lower than the average of the other three groups.

h. $k - 1 = 4 - 1 = 3$ independent comparisons could be conducted.

4. **a.** H_0: $C = 0,$
H_1: $C \neq 0.$

b.

Comparison	Set of weights			
	$\overline{X}_{10\text{ min}} = 6$	$\overline{X}_{20\text{ min}} = 10$	$\overline{X}_{45\text{ min}} = 18$	$\overline{X}_{75\text{ min}} = 11$
$\overline{X}_{20\text{ min}}$ vs. $\overline{X}_{45\text{ min}}$	0	1	-1	0

    c. $\hat{C} = (0)(6) + (1)(10) + (-1)(18) + (0)(11) = -8.$

    d. $t = \dfrac{\hat{C}}{\sqrt{\dfrac{2MS_W}{n}}} = \dfrac{-8}{\sqrt{\dfrac{2(10.79)}{20}}} = -7.70.$

    e. $t'_{critical} = \sqrt{(k-1)F_{critical}} = \sqrt{(4-1)2.74} = 2.87.$

    f. Since $|t_{observed}| > t_{critical}$, reject H_0. Conclude that there is a significant difference between the means of the group given 20 minutes of study time and the group given 45 minutes of study time.

5. **a.** H_0: $C = 0$,
      H_1: $C \neq 0$
      for each pairwise comparison.

    b.

	$\bar{X}_{10\ min} = 6$	$\bar{X}_{20\ min} = 10$	$\bar{X}_{75\ min} = 11$	$\bar{X}_{45\ min} = 18$
$\bar{X}_{10\ min} = 6$	—	4*	5*	12*
$\bar{X}_{20\ min} = 10$		—	1	8*
$\bar{X}_{75\ min} = 11$			—	7*
$\bar{X}_{45\ min} = 18$				—

    * $p < .05.$

    c. $\text{HSD} = q_{(.05,\ 76,\ 4)}\sqrt{\dfrac{10.79}{20}}$

                 $= 3.74(0.73)$

                 $= 2.73.$

    d. Reject H_0. Differences between means marked * in the table shown in part b are significant at $\alpha = .05$. Note that the largest differences are found between the 45-minute group and the other three groups. This pattern of results suggests that 45 minutes is the optimal study time (i.e., produces the highest achievement).

CHAPTER 17   **1.** **a.** Main effect for factor A (situation):

          H_0: $\mu_E = \mu_A$;
          H_1: $\mu_E \neq \mu_A$.

          Main effect for factor B (treatment):

          H_0: $\mu_1 = \mu_2 = \mu_3 = \mu_4$;
          H_1: $\mu_i \neq \mu_{i'}$.

          Interaction effect (situation $\times$ treatment):

          H_0 : interaction effect $= 0$;
          H_1 : interaction effect $\neq 0$.

    b. *Independence*: random assignment of subjects to cells of the design and "treatment" given to individuals.
       Normality: not tested, since ANOVA is not seriously affected by violations of this assumption.
       Homogeneity of variances: not tested, since ANOVA is not seriously affected by violations of this assumption when cell sizes are equal.

c.   **Step 1.**   Data summary table is given in Example Problem 1.

    Step 2.   Table of cell sums:

a_1 = euphoria; a_2 = anger.

b_1 = drug + accurate explanation, b_2 = drug + inaccurate explanation,

b_3 = drug + no explanation; b_4 = placebo.

	b_1	b_2	b_3	b_4	Total sums for rows
a_1	20	24	23	18	85
a_2	8	4	10	14	36
Total sums for columns	28	28	33	32	

Step 3. $\dfrac{20^2}{4} = 100$, $\dfrac{24^2}{4} = 144$, $\dfrac{23^2}{4} = 132.25$, $\dfrac{18^2}{4} = 81$, $\dfrac{8^2}{4} = 16$, $\dfrac{4^2}{4} = 4$, $\dfrac{10^2}{4} = 25$,

$\dfrac{14^2}{4} = 49$.

Step 4. $\dfrac{85^2}{16} = 451.56$, $\dfrac{36^2}{16} = 81$.

Step 5. $\dfrac{28^2}{8} = 98$, $\dfrac{28^2}{8} = 98$, $\dfrac{33^2}{8} = 136.13$, $\dfrac{32^2}{8} = 128$.

Step 6. $\displaystyle\sum_{p=1}^{N} X_p = 5 + 4 + \cdots + 3 + 3 = 121$.

Step 7.   Intermediate quantities:

$$\{1\} = \frac{\left(\sum_{p=1}^{N} X_p\right)^2}{nqr} = \frac{121^2}{(4)(2)(4)} = 457.53,$$

$$\{2\} = \sum_{i=1}^{q} \frac{\left(\sum_{j=1}^{r} \sum_{p=1}^{n} X_{pij}\right)^2}{nr} = 451.56 + 81 = 532.56,$$

$$\{3\} = \sum_{j=1}^{r} \frac{\left(\sum_{i=1}^{q} \sum_{p=1}^{n} X_{pij}\right)^2}{nq} = 98 + 98 + 136.13 + 128 = 460.13,$$

$$\{4\} = \sum_{i=1}^{q} \sum_{j=1}^{r} \frac{\left(\sum_{p=1}^{n} X_{pij}\right)^2}{n} = 100 + 144 + 132.25 + 81 + 16 + 4 + 25 + 49$$

$$= 551.25,$$

$$\{5\} = \sum_{p=1}^{N} X_p^2 = 5^2 + 4^2 + \cdots + 3^2 + 3^2$$

$$= 567.$$

Step 8. Sums of squares:

$$SS_T = \{5\} - \{1\} = 567 - 457.53 = 109.47,$$

$$SS_A = \{2\} - \{1\} = 532.36 - 457.53 = 75.03,$$

$$SS_B = \{3\} \top \{1\} = 460.13 - 457.53 = 2.6,$$

$$SS_{AB} = \{4\} - \{2\} - \{3\} + \{1\} = 551.25 - 532.56 - 460.13 + 457.53$$

$$= 16.09,$$

$$SS_W = \{5\} - \{4\} = 567 - 551.25 = 15.75.$$

d. ANOVA summary table:

Source	Sum of squares	df	Mean square	$F_{obs.}$
Factor A	75.03	1	75.03	113.68
Factor B	2.60	3	0.87	1.32
A × B	16.09	3	5.36	8.12
Within groups	15.75	24	0.66	
Total	109.47	31		

e. $F_{critical(.05, 1, 24)} = 4.26$. This critical value applies to the test of A. $F_{critical(.05, 3, 24)} = 3.01$. This critical value applies to B and AB.

f. Main effect for A: Since $F_{observed} > F_{critical}$, reject H_0. There was a significant difference in the mean ratings of students in different situations. Main effect for B: Since $F_{observed} < F_{critical}$, do not reject H_0. There was not a significant difference in the mean ratings of subjects in the four treatment conditions. Interaction of A and B: Since $F_{observed} > F_{critical}$, reject H_0. There was a statistically significant interaction.

g. Graph of interaction.

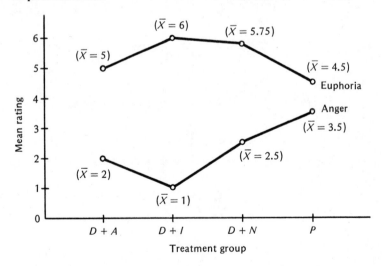

2. $\omega_A^2 = \dfrac{75.03 - (1)(.66)}{109.47 + .66} \approx .77;$

77 percent of the variance in ratings is accounted for by differences in situations.

$\omega_B^2 = \dfrac{2.60 - (3)(.66)}{109.47 + .66} \approx .01;$

1 percent of the variance in ratings is accounted for by differences in treatment group. (Since this effect was not statistically significant, ω^2 typically would not be calculated.)

$\omega_{AB}^2 = \dfrac{16.09 - (3)(.07)}{109.47 + .07} = .15;$

15 percent of the variance in ratings was due to the interaction of situation and treatment.

3. a. 1.

Euphoria (a_1)				Anger (a_2)			
b_1	b_2	b_3	b_4	b_1	b_2	b_3	b_4
1	1	1	0	-1	-1	-1	0

$[\sum w_i = 1 + 1 + 1 + 0 + (-1) + (-1) + 0 = 0.]$

2. $H_0 : C = 0,$
$H_1 : C \neq 0.$

3. $\hat{C} = (1)(5) + (1)(6) + (1)(5.75) + (0)(4.5) + (-1)(2) + (-1)(1) + (-1)(2.5)$
$\qquad + (0)(3.5) = 11.25.$

4.
$$t_{observed} = \dfrac{11.25}{\sqrt{\dfrac{.66}{4}\left[(1)^2 + (1)^2 + (1)^2 + (0)^2 + (-1)^2 + (-1)^2 + (-1)^2 + (0)^2\right]}}$$

$$= \dfrac{11.25}{\sqrt{.99}} = \dfrac{11.25}{.99} = 11.36.$$

5. $t_{critical(.05/2, 24)} = 2.064.$

6. Since $t_{observed} > t_{critical}$, reject H_0. Conclude that the mean ratings are higher in the euphoria condition than in the anger condition. This finding lends support to the two-component theory.

b. 1.

a_1				a_2			
b_1	b_2	b_3	b_4	b_1	b_2	b_3	b_4
0	0	0	1	0	0	0	-1

$[\sum w_i = 0 \text{ and } \sum w_{1i}w_{2i} = (1)(0) + (1)(0) + (1)(0) + (0)(1) + (-1)(0) + (-1)(0)$
$+ (-1)(0) + (0)(-1) = 0.]$

2. $H_0: C = 0,$
$H_1: C \neq 0.$

3. $\hat{C} = (1)(4.5) + (-1)(3.5) = 1.$

4. $t_{observed} = \dfrac{1}{\sqrt{\dfrac{2(.66)}{4}}}$ [16-15b]

$= \dfrac{1}{\sqrt{.33}} = \dfrac{1}{.57} = 1.74.$

5. $t_{critical(.05/2,\ 24)} = 2.064.$

6. Since $|t_{observed}| < t_{critical}$, do not reject H_0. Conclude that there is not a statistically significant difference between the means of the placebo groups in the euphoria and anger conditions.

4. a. 1. $H_0: C = 0,$
       $H_1: C \neq 0.$

2. For the euphoria situation (a_1),

	a_1				a_2			
	b_1	b_2	b_3	b_4	b_1	b_2	b_3	b_4
Means	5	6	5.75	4.5	2	1	2.5	3.5
$\hat{C}_1$	1	1	1	−3	0	0	0	0

3. $\hat{C}_1 = (1)(5) + (1)(6) + (1)(5.75) + (-3)(4.5) = 3.25.$

4. $t_{observed} = \dfrac{3.25}{\sqrt{\dfrac{.66}{4}\left[(1)^2 + (1)^2 + (1)^2 + (-3)^2\right]}}$

$= \dfrac{3.25}{\sqrt{1.98}} = \dfrac{3.25}{1.41} = 2.30.$

5. $t'_{critical} = \sqrt{(7)F_{critical(.05,\ 7,\ 24)}} = \sqrt{(7)(2.42)} = 4.12.$

6. Since $|t_{observed}| < t'_{critical}$, do not reject H_0. Conclude that the means of the drug groups in the euphoria situation do not differ significantly.

b. 1. $H_0: C = 0,$
      $H_1: C \neq 0.$

2.

	$\bar{B}_1$	$\bar{B}_2$	$\bar{B}_3$	$\bar{B}_4$
Column mean	3.50	3.50	4.13	4.00
$\hat{C}_B$	+1	+1	+1	−3

3. $\hat{C}_B = (1)(3.5) + (1)(3.5) + (1)(4.13) + (-3)(4) = .87.$

4. $t_{observed} = \dfrac{.87}{\sqrt{\dfrac{.66}{(4)(2)}\left[(1)^2 + (1)^2 + (1)^2 + (-3)^2\right]}}$

$= \dfrac{.87}{\sqrt{.99}} = \dfrac{.87}{.99} = .88.$

5. $t'_{critical(B)}$ = $\sqrt{(3)F_{critical(.05,\ 3,\ 24)}}$

= $\sqrt{(3)(3.01)}$ = $\sqrt{9.03}$

= 3.00.

6. Since $t_{observed}$ does not exceed $t'_{critical}$, do not reject H_0.

5. a. $H_0: \mu_1 = \mu_2 = \cdots = \mu_8$,

$H_1: \mu_i \neq \mu_{i'}$.

b.

	$\overline{X}_{22}$ = 1.00	$\overline{X}_{21}$ = 2.00	X_{23} = 2.50	$\overline{X}_{24}$ = 3.50	$\overline{X}_{14}$ = 4.50	$\overline{X}_{11}$ = 5.00	$\overline{X}_{13}$ = 5.75	$\overline{X}_{12}$ = 6.00
$\overline{X}_{22}$ = 1.00	—	1.00	1.50	2.50*	3.50*	4.00*	4.75*	5.00*
$\overline{X}_{21}$ = 2.00		—	.50	1.50	2.50*	3.00*	3.75*	4.00*
$\overline{X}_{23}$ = 2.50			—	1.00	2.00*	2.50*	3.25*	3.50*
$\overline{X}_{24}$ = 3.50				—	1.00	1.50	2.25*	2.50*
$\overline{X}_{14}$ = 4.50					—	.50	1.25	1.50
$\overline{X}_{11}$ = 5.00						—	.75	1.00
$\overline{X}_{13}$ = 5.75							—	.25
$\overline{X}_{12}$ = 6.00								—

c. $HSD = q(.05, 24, 8)\sqrt{\dfrac{.66}{4}}$

= (4.68)(.41) = 1.69.

d. For all starred entries in the table, reject the null hypothesis.

1. a. H_0: The observed distribution of frequencies equals the expected distribution of frequencies;

H_1: The observed distribution of frequencies does not equal the expected distribution of frequencies.

b. **1.** Mutually exclusive categories: Each subject could choose only one response.

2. Independence: Subjects were randomly selected and questioned individually.

3. Observations are measured as frequencies: The data consist of the *number* of subjects making each response.

4. Expected frequencies greater than 5 and $df > 2$: If all types of foods were equally difficult to avoid, the expected frequency for each of the four categories would be .25 × 60 = 15. Thus, no category has an expected frequency less than 5.

5. Correction for continuity: Does not apply, since df are greater than 1.

CHAPTER 18

c.

(1)	(2)	(3)	(4)	(5)	(6)	(7)
	Observed	Expected	Expected			
Category	frequency	proportion	frequency	$O - E$	$(O - E)^2$	$\dfrac{(O - E)^2}{E}$
	(O)		(E)			
a	17	.25	15	2	4	.27
b	13	.25	15	−2	4	.27
c	21	.25	15	6	36	2.40
d	9	.25	15	−6	36	2.40
Sum	60	1.00	60	0		$\chi^2_{obs.} = 5.34$

d. $\chi^2_{critical(.01,\,3)} = 11.345$.

e. Since $\chi^2_{observed} < \chi^2_{critical}$, do not reject H_0. There is insufficient evidence to conclude that certain types of foods are more difficult for dieters to avoid than others.

2. a.

(1)	(2)	(3)	(4)	(5)	(6)	(7)	(8)
	Observed	Expected	Expected	O Corrected			
Category	frequency	proportion	frequency	for contin-	$O* - E$	$(O* - E)^2$	$\dfrac{(O* - E)^2}{E}$
	(O)		(E)	uity $(O*)$			
"Successful"	37	.75	30	36.5	6.5	42.25	1.41
"Non-successful"	3	.25	10	3.5	−6.5	42.25	4.23
Sum	40	1.00	40	40	0		$\chi^2_{obs.} = 5.64$

b. $\chi^2_{critical(.01,\,1)} = 6.635$.

c. Since $\chi^2_{observed} < \chi^2_{critical}$, do not reject H_0. There is insufficient evidence to conclude that the number of "successful" managers is greater with the new training program than with previous programs.

3. a. H_0: Minority-group membership and opinion on school busing are independent in the population.

H_1: Minority-group membership and opinion on school busing are related in the population.

b. 1. Mutually exclusive categories: Each subject could choose only one response and belong to only one type of group.

2. Independence: Subjects were randomly selected and, presumably, polled individually.

3. Observations are measured as frequencies: The data consist of the *number* of subjects making each response.

4. Expected frequencies less than 5 with $df > 2$: The smallest expected frequency is $(50 \times 100)/300 = 16.67$. Thus, no cell has an expected frequency less than 5.

5. Correction for continuity: Does not apply since df are greater than 1.

c.

(1) Cell		(2) Observed	(3) Expected	(4)	(5)	(6)
Row (group)	Column (opinion)	frequency [a] (O)	frequency [a] (E)	$O - E$	$(O - E)^2$	$\dfrac{(O - E)^2}{E}$
1	1	50	38.33	11.67	136.19	3.55
1	2	35	45.00	-10.00	100.00	2.22
1	3	15	16.67	-1.67	2.79	0.17
2	1	65	76.67	-11.67	136.19	1.78
2	2	100	90.00	10.00	100.00	1.11
2	3	35	33.33	1.67	2.79	0.08
Sum		300	300	0		$\chi^2_{obs.} = 8.91$

$$^a E_{11} = 100 \times \frac{115}{300} = 38.33, \qquad E_{21} = 200 \times \frac{115}{300} = 76.67,$$

$$E_{12} = \frac{100 \times 135}{300} = 45.00, \qquad E_{22} = \frac{200 \times 135}{300} = 90.00,$$

$$E_{13(smallest)} = E_{13} = \frac{100 \times 50}{300} = 16.67, \quad E_{23} = \frac{200 \times 50}{300} = 33.33.$$

d. $\chi^2_{critical(.05, 2)} = 5.99.$

e. Since $\chi^2_{observed} > \chi^2_{critical}$, reject H_0. Conclude that minority-group membership and opinion on school busing are related.

4. a.

$$\chi^2 = \frac{N\left(|ad - bc| - \dfrac{N}{2}\right)^2}{(a + b)(c + d)(a + c)(b + d)} \quad [18\text{-}4]$$

$$= \frac{44\left[|(14)(12) - (8)(10)| - \dfrac{44}{2}\right]^2}{(22)(22)(24)(20)}$$

$$= \frac{44(|168 - 80| - 22)^2}{232,320} = \frac{44(66)^2}{232,320} = \frac{191,664}{232,320} = .83.$$

b. $\chi^2_{critical(.01, 1)} = 6.635.$

c. Since $\chi^2_{observed} < \chi^2_{critical}$, do not reject H_0. Conclude that teaching technique and quality of poems are independent.

5. a. $E_{rc} = \dfrac{9 \times 50}{200} = 2.25.$

b.

Hours of study per day	Performance		Total
	Pass	Fail	
$\leqslant 2$	60	32	92
3	65	13	78
4	25	5	30
Total	150	50	200

c. $E_{rc(smallest)} = \dfrac{(30)(50)}{200} = 7.5$ and $df = (3-1)(2-1) = 2.$

CHAPTER 19

1. a. Since the same group of subjects were observed on both occasions, this is a within-subject design. Subjects' scores at each occasion are *not* independent, and this correlation must be taken into account.

b. $H_0: \mu_D = 0,$
$H_1: \mu_D \neq 0.$

c. $t_{critical(.05, 7)} = 2.365.$

d. Do not reject H_0 if $|t^*_{observed}| < t_{critical}.$
Reject H_0 if $|t^*_{observed}| > t_{critical}.$

Subject	X_1	X_2	D	$\bar{D}$	$D - \bar{D}$	$(D - \bar{D})^2$
1	0	2	-2	-1.375	-0.625	0.39
2	1	1	0	-1.375	1.375	1.89
3	0	3	-3	-1.375	-1.625	2.64
4	1	2	-1	-1.375	0.375	0.14
5	0	0	0	-1.375	1.375	1.89
6	1	4	-3	-1.375	-1.625	2.64
7	2	3	-1	-1.375	0.375	0.14
8	3	4	-1	-1.375	0.375	0.14
Sum	8	19	-11	-11	0	9.87

f. $s_D = \sqrt{\dfrac{9.87}{7}} = \sqrt{1.41} = 1.19,$

$s_{\bar{D}} = \dfrac{1.19}{\sqrt{8}} = \dfrac{1.19}{2.83} = .042.$

g. $t^*_{observed} = \dfrac{-1.375}{.42} = -3.27.$

h. Since $|t^*_{observed}| > t_{critical}(|-3.27| > 2.365)$, reject H_0. Conclude that the number of targets accurately tracked is significantly greater with yellow foreground on green background.

⋅ Review of Summation Notation ⋅

THIS is a brief review of some basic concepts in using summation notation. In particular, we present the concepts of simple and multiple summation notation along with some fundamental rules for working with summations. Since students in elementary statistics courses usually vary tremendously in their previous training in mathematics, this material will be more familiar to some students than to others. We recommend that you spend as much time as is necessary with this review, since mastery of these concepts is important to an understanding of the mathematical concepts and formulas presented throughout the textbook and proofs presented in footnotes.

In most research one or more variables are selected for study and scores on these variables are collected on several subjects. Thus, the researcher typically wants to describe a set of scores or make inferences based on a group of scores rather than on single scores. In computing statistics for these scores, then, it is useful to have some common symbols or notation to represent groups of scores and arithmetic operations on them.

COMMON MATHEMATICAL NOTATION

The capital letter X is often used to represent scores on a particular variable. (If one or more variables are collected in a study, the capital letters Y and Z are often used to denote these variables.) For example, suppose a researcher collected the scores for seven students on a measure of mathematical achievement—the McCormick Arithmetic Test (see Table R-1). The capital letter X can be used to denote the variable mathematical achievement, as measured by the McCormick Arithmetic Test. The seven scores represent specific values of X earned by each of the seven students. In order to distinguish one score from another, each value of X is customarily given a subscript corresponding to the identification number of the subject who received that score. Therefore, the scores in Table R-1 can be denoted from X_1 to X_7 (see the third column).

In general, if there are N scores, the subscripts will range from 1 to N. Often, it is useful to refer to any single score in a distribution of X's. This single score is denoted in this textbook by the subscript p and is referred to as the pth score in the distribution—X_p (where p refers to persons). Note that X_p refers to the score of any unidentified person p, and it does not denote a particular person's score.

◆　　◆　　◆　　◆　　◆

Simple Summation Notation

In order to compute many of the statistics in this book, it is necessary to sum all or a portion of the scores collected. The symbol Σ (an oversize Greek capital letter sigma) is used to denote the operation of summing or adding up a group of numbers. Thus, ΣX means the sum of all the values of X. In the example data in Table R-1, $\Sigma X = 48 + 35 + 50 + 19 + 43 + 47 + 21 = 263$.

As noted above, it is sometimes necessary to sum only a portion of scores collected. The summation sign can be modified as follows to indicate more specifically the values that are to be added:

$$\sum_{p=1}^{N} X.$$

The small notations above and below the summation sign are referred to as the "limits of the summation." This symbol is read as the "sum of X from $p = 1$ to N." It means that the values of X_1 to X_N should be added:

$$\sum_{p=1}^{N} X = X_1 + X_2 + X_3 + \cdots + X_N.$$

This notation can be used to indicate that only a portion of scores within a group are to be summed. For example, $\sum_{p=3}^{6} X$ indicates that the sum of X_3, X_4, X_5, and X_6 should be taken. In the example data in Table R-1,

$$\sum_{p=5}^{N} = X_5 + X_6 + X_7$$
$$= 43 + 47 + 21$$
$$= 111.$$

◆　　◆　　◆　　◆　　◆

Multiple Summation Notation

In many research studies, data are available on more than one group of subjects. For example, subjects may be randomly assigned to a control or experimental group. The respective treatments are administered, and subjects in all groups are given a posttest upon completion of the treatment. Scores on the dependent variable are available on subjects in each group.

As an example, suppose a researcher studying verbal learning is investigating the type of strategies that produce the greatest learning of a list of words.

Table R-1 ◆ Scores of students on the McCormick Arithmetic Test

Student	Test score (X)	Score notation
1	48	X_1
2	35	X_2
3	50	X_3
4	19	X_4
5	43	X_5
6	47	X_6
7	21	X_7

She randomly assigns five college sophomores to one of three conditions. In one condition, subjects are presented with a list of ten words (to keep the example data 10 or less) and instructed to learn the words by constructing a story using the list of words (meaningful strategy). In another condition, subjects are presented with the same list of words and instructed to learn the words by repeating them over and over (rote strategy). In the third condition, subjects are presented with the same list of words, but are not instructed to use any particular strategy in learning the words (control group). At the end of the session, subjects are asked to recall as many of the words as they can remember. The data from this hypothetical experiment are presented in Table R-2.

In research designs such as the one described above, it is often necessary to specify particular scores within a specific group. In this case, the notation must

Table R-2 ◆ Number of words recalled (X) in hypothetical verbal-learning study

Meaningful strategy group	Rote strategy group	Control group
8	4	5
7	5	5
10	7	7
9	6	4
6	6	6

specify both the group and the subjects within the groups. Two subscripts are necessary to denote scores in such designs. By convention, any single score is denoted as X_{pi}, where p refers to the subject number and i refers to the group number. Thus X_{13} refers to subject 1 in group 3. Similarly, X_{51} refers to subject 5 in group 1. Using the data in Table R-2,

$$X_{13} = 5$$

and

$$X_{51} = 6.$$

The summation sign is also used to denote the operation of summing scores within a particular group in these more complex designs. For example, $\sum_{p=1}^{N} X_{p3}$ means that the scores of subjects 1 to N in group 3 should be added. The limits of the summation identify the subjects' scores to be added, and the second subscript for X identifies the group. In the example study described above,

$$\sum_{p=1}^{N} X_{p3} = X_{13} + X_{23} + X_{33} + X_{43} + X_{53}$$

$$= 5 + 5 + 7 + 4 + 6$$

$$= 27.$$

If the group number is specified only generally by an i, this means that the scores of the subjects identified by the limits of the summation should be summed separately within each group. Thus, $\sum_{p=1}^{n} X_{pi}$ is a direction to add each subject's scores within each group. This procedure will yield i sums. For example, using the data in Table R-2, $\sum_{p=1}^{n} X_{pi}$ is a direction to take the sum of the scores of subjects within each group. This procedure will result in three sums:

$$\sum_{p=1}^{n} X_{p1} = 8 + 7 + 10 + 9 + 6 = 40,$$

$$\sum_{p=2}^{n} X_{p2} = 4 + 5 + 7 + 6 + 6 = 28,$$

$$\sum_{p=3}^{n} X_{p3} = 5 + 5 + 7 + 4 + 6 = 27.$$

Now suppose we wished to add the sums of all subjects' scores within each group over the i groups. This operation is denoted as $\sum_{i=1}^{k} \left(\sum_{p=1}^{n} X_{pi} \right)$. This symbol directs us to add the scores of subjects 1 to N within each group

$\left(\displaystyle\sum_{p=1}^{n} X_{pi} \right)$ and then to add these sums over the k groups $\left[\displaystyle\sum_{i=1}^{k} \left(\displaystyle\sum_{p=1}^{n} X_{pi} \right) \right]$. Note that this procedure yields the total sum of all scores.

Using the example data shown in Table R-2,

$$\sum_{i=1}^{k} \left(\sum_{p=1}^{n} X_{pi} \right) = \sum_{p=1}^{n} X_{p1} + \sum_{p=1}^{n} X_{p2} + \sum_{p=1}^{n} X_{p3}$$

$$= 40 + 28 + 27$$

$$= 95.$$

There are several rules that are helpful in using the summation sign in algebraic operations. These rules concern the summation of both variables and constants. (Constants are typically denoted by lowercase a, b, or c.)

RULES OF SUMMATION

♦   ♦   ♦   ♦   ♦

The rule for the summation of a constant is that if a is a constant value over N persons, then

Summation of a Constant

$$\sum_{p=1}^{n} a_p = na.$$

This expression says that the sum of a constant taken N times is N times the constant.

This equality can be loosely demonstrated as follows:

$$\sum_{p=1}^{n} a_p = a_1 + a_2 + \cdots + a_n$$

$$= na.$$

To take a specific example, suppose $a = 2$. Then

$$\sum_{p=1}^{n=4} a_p = 2 + 2 + 2 + 2$$

$$= 4(2)$$

$$= 8.$$

This rule also applies to multiple summation notation. If a is a constant value over n persons and k groups, then $\displaystyle\sum_{i=1}^{k} \sum_{p=1}^{n} a = kna$. This expression says that the sum of a constant taken over N subjects and k groups is kn times the constant.

This equality can also be easily demonstrated:

$$\sum_{i=1}^{k} \sum_{p=1}^{n} a_{pi} = \sum_{i=1}^{k} (a_1 + a_2 + \cdots + a_n)_i$$

$$= \sum_{i=1}^{k} (na)_i$$

$$= (na)_1 + (na)_2 + \cdots + (na)_k$$

$$= k(na).$$

Suppose that $a = 4$. Then

$$\sum_{i=1}^{k=3} \sum_{p=1}^{n=5} a = 3 \times 5 \times 4 = 60.$$

Summation of a Variable Multiplied by a Constant

The rule for the summation of a variable multiplied by a constant is that if a is a constant over N persons, then

$$\sum_{p=1}^{N} aX_p = a \sum_{p=1}^{N} X_p.$$

That is, the sum of a constant times a variable equals the constant times the sum of the variable. This equality can be demonstrated as follows:

$$\sum_{p=1}^{N} aX_p = aX_1 + aX_2 + \cdots + aX_N$$

$$= a(X_1 + X_2 + \cdots + X_N)$$

(by the distributive law of multiplication)

$$= a \sum_{p=1}^{N} X_p.$$

Suppose $a = 2$. Using the hypothetical data in Table R-1, what is the value of $\sum_{p=1}^{N=7} aX_p$? Since $\sum_{p=1}^{N=7} X_p = 263$ (as computed above),

$$\sum_{p=2}^{N=7} aX_p = a \sum_{p=1}^{N=7} X_p$$

$$= 2(263)$$

$$= 526.$$

This rule can also be applied to multiple summation notation. If a is a constant value over n persons in each of k groups, then

$$\sum_{i=1}^{k} \sum_{p=1}^{n} aX = a \sum_{i=1}^{k} \sum_{p=1}^{n} X.$$

That is, the sum over subjects and groups of a constant times a variable equals the constant times the sum of the variable over persons and groups.

This equality can be shown as follows:

$$\sum_{i=1}^{k} \sum_{p=1}^{n} aX_{pi} = \sum_{i=1}^{k} (aX_1 + aX_2 + \cdots + aX_n)$$

$$= \sum_{i=1}^{k} \left[a(X_1 + X_2 + \cdots + X_n) \right]$$

$$= \sum_{i=1}^{k} \left[a \sum_{p=1}^{n} X_{pi} \right]$$

$$= a \sum_{p=1}^{n} X_{p1} + a \sum_{p=1}^{n} X_{p2} + \cdots + a \sum_{p=1}^{n} X_{pk}$$

$$= a \sum_{i=1}^{k} \sum_{p=1}^{n} X_{pi}.$$

Suppose $a = 3$. Using the hypothetical data in Table R-2, what is the value of $\sum_{i=1}^{k} \sum_{p=1}^{N} aX_{pi}$? Since $\sum_{i=1}^{k} \sum_{p=1}^{N} X_{pi} = 95$ (as computed above),

$$\sum_{i=1}^{k} \sum_{p=1}^{n} aX_{pi} = a \sum_{i=1}^{k} \sum_{p=1}^{n} X_{pi}$$

$$= 3(95)$$

$$= 285.$$

♦   ♦   ♦   ♦   ♦

The distributive rule for a summation sign is that, if addition or subtraction of variables (or constants) is the only operation to be executed before summation, then   **Distributive Rule**

$$\sum_{p=1}^{N} (X_p + Y_p) = \sum_{p=1}^{N} X_p + \sum_{p=1}^{N} Y_p.$$

Similarly,

$$\sum_{p=1}^{N} (X_p - Y_p) = \sum_{p=1}^{N} X_p - \sum_{p=1}^{N} Y_p.$$

That is, the distributive rule states that the summation can be distributed across variables (or constants) when they are added together or subtracted from one another. This equality can be shown as follows:

$$\sum_{p=1}^{N} (X_p + Y_p) = (X_1 + Y_1) + (X_2 + Y_2) + \cdots + (X_N + Y_N)$$

$$= X_1 + Y_1 + X_2 + Y_2 + \cdots + X_N + Y_N$$

$$= (X_1 + X_2 + \cdots + X_N) + (Y_1 + Y_2 + \cdots + Y_N)$$

$$= \sum_{p=1}^{N} X_p + \sum_{p=1}^{N} Y_p.$$

(A similar proof can be given for subtraction.)

The summation sign can also be distributed across constants or the sum of differences of a variable and a constant. For example, suppose $a = 5$ and $\sum_{p=1}^{N=4} X_p = 8$. Then

$$\sum_{p=2}^{N=4} (X_p + a) = \sum_{p=1}^{N=4} X_p + \sum_{p=1}^{N=4} a.$$

Since $\sum_{p=1}^{N} a = Na$, this is

$$\sum_{p=1}^{N} X_p + Na = 8 + 4(5)$$

$$= 28.$$

• Answers to Selected Chapter Exercises •

1. **a.** Time-series design
   b. Change of desk arrangement
   c. Number of times students volunteered in class discussions
   d. Sixth-grade students
   e. Reduced fear
   f. History, possibly instrumentation
   g. Selection of subjects

CHAPTER 1

3. **a.** Pretest-posttest control-group design
   b. Type of achievement training
   c. Measure of motivation in score on T.A.T.
   d. High-school students
   e. Achievement motivation
   f. None
   g. Selection of subjects, dependent variable

4. **a.** One-group, pretest-posttest design
   b. Type of achievement training
   c. Measure of motivation in score on T.A.T.
   d. High-school students
   e. Achievement motivation
   f. History, testing, instrumentation
   g. Selection of subjects, dependent variable

7. **a.** Intact group comparison
   b. Assertion training
   c. Self-estimate of assertiveness in various situations
   d. Undergraduate psychology students
   e. Assertiveness
   f. Selection, mortality
   g. Selection of subjects, selection of dependent variable

8. **a.** 2×2 factorial
   b. Preparation for the DMRT; Field independence, field independence.
   c. Scores on the DMRT
   d. N/A

        e. Learning or reasoning
        f. None
        g. None

  9. Nominal.

 10. Ordinal.

 12. Ratio.

 14. c

 15. Constant.

 16. Variable.

 19. Variable.

 20. **a.** *Use of control group.* A control group is a group of subjects whose selection and treatment is exactly the same as that of the experimental group, except that the control group does not receive the experimental manipulation.
     b. *Random assignment.* The method of assigning subjects to control and experimental groups such that each subject has an equal chance of being in either group.
     c. *Pretests.* Pretests are used to examine differences between groups and to statistically control for individual differences between subjects.

CHAPTER 3   **2.**

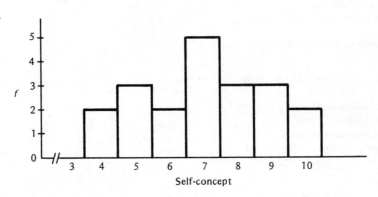

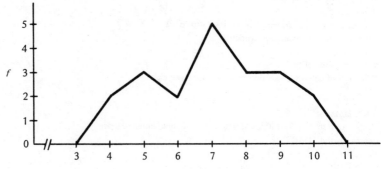

5.

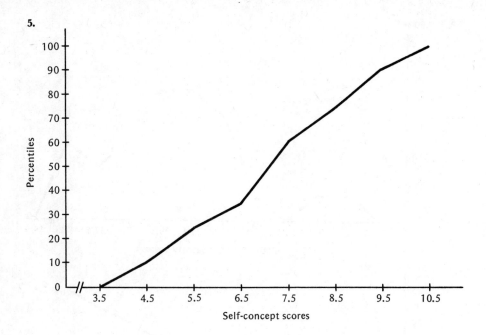

6.

		6.		**8.**		**9.**	**10.**	
					Upper			
Class		Exact		Rel.	exact	Cum.	Cum.	Cum.
interval	f	limits	Midpoint	f	limit	f	prop.	%
40–43	3	39.5 − 43.5	41.5	.12	43.5	25	1.00	100
36–39	2	35.5 − 39.5	37.5	.08	39.5	22	.88	88
32–35	3	31.5 − 35.5	33.5	.12	35.5	20	.80	80
28–31	5	27.5 − 31.5	29.5	.20	31.5	17	.68	68
24–27	5	23.5 − 27.5	25.5	.20	27.5	12	.48	48
20–23	4	19.5 − 23.5	21.5	.16	23.5	7	.28	28
16–19	1	15.5 − 19.5	17.5	.04	19.5	3	.12	12
12–15	0	11.5 − 15.5	13.5	.00	15.5	2	.08	8
8–11	1	7.5 − 11.5	9.5	.04	11.5	2	.08	8
4– 7	1	3.5 − 7.5	5.5	.04	7.5	1	.04	4
Σ	25	—	—	1.00	—	—	—	—

8.

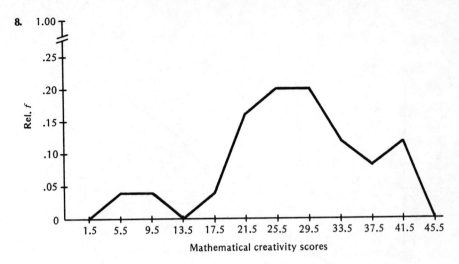

9.

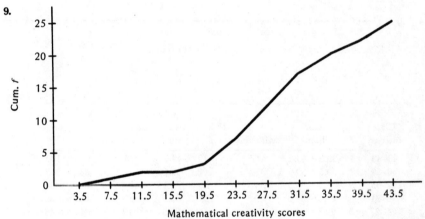

10.

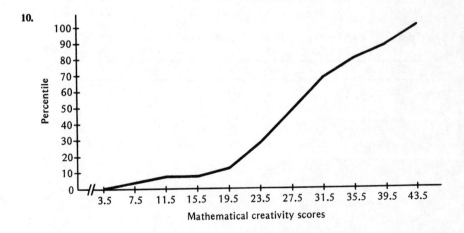

11. 18, 85.

12. 33.83, 22.75.

14. 4, 11, 18, 25, 32, 39, 46.

16. Bimodal.

18. Negatively skewed.

21. The point falling exactly halfway between the two score values indicating the upper boundary of one interval and the lower boundary of the other interval.

24. Provides a means for comparing frequencies based on different group sizes.

25. Number of cases falling below the upper exact limit of that value or interval.

CHAPTER 4

2. Hi I, words: 6.17.
    Hi I, pictures: 15.
    Lo I, words: 13.
    Lo I, pictures: 9.5.
    Conclusion: Imagery appears to facilitate memory of picture pairs more than word pairs. Mode and median are quite similar in each group.

4. Word task:

$$\frac{10(7.4) + 9(13.33)}{19} = \frac{74 + 119.97}{19} = 10.21.$$

Picture task:

$$\frac{9(15.2) + 10(9.2)}{19} = \frac{136.8 + 92}{19} = 12.04.$$

Conclusion: Overall performance was better when picture pairs were used compared with word pairs.

5. The mean is the most appropriate measure for all groups *except* the Lo I word group, since scores appear approximately symmetrically distributed. The median best describes the Lo I word group because the distribution is negatively skewed (i.e., one extremely low score).

7. Hi I, words: 2.88.
    Hi I, pictures: 2.17.
    Lo I, words: 1.56.
    Lo I, pictures: 2.00.

10. Hi I, words: $2.84^2 = 8.07$.
     Lo I, words: $3.46^2 = 11.97$.
     Hi I, pictures: $3.03^2 = 9.18$.
     Lo I, pictures: $2.70^2 = 7.29$.

11. Measures of central tendency describe the *location* of a distribution on a scale of score values, by indicating a score value that represents the center of the distribution. Measures of variability describe the *spread* or range of scores.

13. With grouped data, the mode may vary depending on number and size of class intervals used. For example, the mode might change if class intervals of two score values rather than three had been used.

14. The mode is a poor representation of "flat" distributions in which frequencies for class intervals or score values containing the majority of cases are nearly the same.

16. Median (since distribution is asymmetric or contains a few extreme scores).

18. Because the mean represents the point in the distribution at which the algebraic sum of the difference of each score from the mean is zero. This analogy implies that the mean will be sensitive to extreme scores.

20.

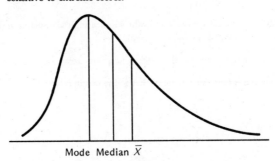

Mode Median $\overline{X}$

22. The range does not reflect the pattern of variation in the distribution. It is also an unstable estimate, since it is influenced by the two most extreme scores in the distribution.

24. $\overline{X} = 21.67$.

CHAPTER 5

1. 50 percent.

3. Approximately 68 percent.

5. The *magnitude* of z score tells the distance the observed score lies from the mean in standard-deviation units. The *sign* of the z score indicates whether the observed score lies above or below the mean.

7. a. $z = 1.00$, proportion $= .3413$.
   d. $z = -.10$, proportion $= .0398$.

8. a. $z = 0$, proportion $= .5000$.
   c. $z = -1.25$, proportion $= .8944$.

9. a. $z = -1.00$, proportion $= .1587$.
   c. $z = .80$, proportion $= .7881$.

10. a. $z_1 = -.50$, $z_2 = .50$, proportion $= .3830$.
    b. $z_1 = -1.25$, $z_2 = -.75$, proportion $= .1210$.
    c. $z_1 = .25$, $z_2 = 1.00$, proportion $= .2426$.

12. $z \approx -.53$. So $X = 447$.

13. Verbal: $z = 1.60$, 95 percent.
    Quantitative: $z = .90$, 82 percent.
    Psychology: $z = -.35$, 36 percent.

14. Final (since $z_{midterm} = -1.00$ and $z_{final} = -.67$).
    Final: approximately 75 percent.

16. Must assume that the test scores are normally distributed.

17. Hyde did better than Jekyll on the midterm since $z_{Hyde} = -.75$ and $z_{Jekyll} = -1.00$. Hyde also did better than Jekyll on the final since $z_{Hyde} = 1.20$ and $z_{Jekyll} = -.67$.

19. IV.

21. III.

23. Maximum value of z.

24.

Grade	z	X
A	1.28	94.20
C	-0.53	67.05
F	Below -1.29	Below 55.80

CHAPTER 6

2.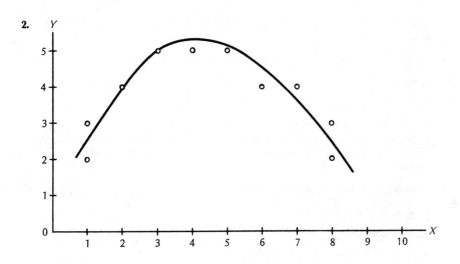

3. Low scores on anxiety (X) tend to be associated with low scores on complex problem-solving (Y); moderate scores on X tend to be associated with high scores on Y; high scores on X tend to be associated with low scores on Y.

6. Low scores on the dogmatism scale are associated with higher ratings of student teaching performance; high scores on the dogmatism scale are associated with low ratings of student teaching performance.

8. Relationship becomes curvilinear.

10. Linear.

12. $X = 35$, $Y = 80$.

14. B, D.

15. Curvilinear.

16. *I.*

18. *A, C.*

CHAPTER 7

2. r_{XY} appropriate, since relationship is linear.

3. r_{XY} calculated on ranks gives r_S.

4. $r = .65$.

6. 42 percent.

7. $r_{XY} = .25$.

9. Since 6 percent of the variance in creative thinking is accounted for by IQ, one could conclude that there is a very small amount of overlap in the competencies measured by the two tests.

11. Less than 1 percent (0.16 percent) of the variance in creative performance is accounted for by IQ.

13. No. Causality cannot be inferred from a single correlation coefficient.

14 $r_S = .97$.

16. $r_S = .57$.

18. The researchers would have concluded that there is a stronger relationship between aggression and violent TV viewing than if they had included both measures of aggression. It appears that violent TV is associated with fantasy aggression and reality aggression to different degrees.

21. Moderate positive relationship ($r_{XY} \approx +.50$ to $+.70$).

23. Outliers (IV).

25. Restriction of range (I).

CHAPTER 8

1. $b_{Y \cdot X} = (.84)\dfrac{2.07}{1.58} = 1.10$.

3. $\hat{Y} = 5.6 + 1.10(3 - 3) = 5.6$.

5. $5.6 \pm 1.12 = 4.48 < \hat{Y} < 6.72$.

7. $b_{X \cdot Y} = (.84)\dfrac{1.58}{2.07} = 0.64$.

8. $3 + 0.64(7 - 5.6) = 3.90$.

10. $s_{X \cdot Y} = 1.58\sqrt{1 - .84^2} = .85$.

11. $3.90 \pm .85 \; (3.05 < \hat{X} < 4.75)$.

13. $r_{XY}^2 \times 100 = (.84)^2 \times 100 = 71$ percent, or $(b_{X \cdot Y})(b_{Y \cdot X}) \times 100 = (.64)(1.10) \times 100 = 70$ percent (difference is due to rounding error).

14. $\hat{Y} = 6.25 + (-1.46)(X - 1.63)$.

15. $6.25 + (-1.46)(2 - 1.63) = 5.71$.

17. $s_{Y \cdot X} = .99$.

20. A line with a slope of 3 means that Y *increases* by 3 units for every unit increase in X, while a line with a slope of -3 means that Y *decreases* by 3 units for every unit increase in X.

22. b.

23. 21. [When there is no correlation between X and Y, the best prediction of Y ($\hat{Y}$) that can be made for any X is the mean of Y ($\bar{Y}$).]

CHAPTER 9

1. Population refers to the indefinitely large set of observations to which researchers wish to generalize. Sample refers to a subset of these observations. Members of the sample are usually assumed to have been randomly sampled from the population.

3. Are the two groups of employees drawn from the same population or from different populations?

4. $H_0: \mu_1 = \mu_2$, $H_1: \mu_1 > \mu_2$.

6. Employees from two branches represent different populations. Population of employees from branch 1 have higher morale than population of employees from branch 2.

7. **a.** May incorrectly reject H_0 and conclude that the two groups of employees represent different populations when, in fact, they come from the same population (i.e., they actually do not differ in morale).
 b. Selection—the employees at branch 1 might have been more satisfied before the administrative change.

9. $H_0: \mu = 35$, $H_1: \mu \neq 35$.

11. Sample of recruits obtained under the new program belong to the population of recruits obtained since the abolition of the draft. They do not differ in leadership ability.

12. May incorrectly fail to reject H_0. May conclude that new recruits do belong to the general population of recruits when, in fact, they belong to a different population (i.e., new recruits actually do differ in leadership ability).

13. Are the two groups of golfers drawn from the same population or different populations?

16. Golfers in the two clinics represent the same population. They do not differ in golfing ability.

18. Selection—subjects in the two clinics may have differed prior to the study.

19. c.

20. A parameter is a descriptive measure of a characteristic of the population; a statistic is a descriptive measure of a characteristic of the sample.

21. Case I.

24. Case II.

CHAPTER 10   1. $\dfrac{50}{100} = .50.$

3. $\dfrac{1}{100} = .01.$

4. $\dfrac{2}{100} = .02.$

5. $\dfrac{8}{104} = .08.$

6. $\dfrac{52}{104} = .50.$

10. $\dfrac{22}{60} = .37.$

12. $\dfrac{40}{60} = .67.$

13. $\dfrac{50}{105} = .48.$

16. $\dfrac{22}{105} = .21.$

17.   Statistical inference is concerned with making a generalization about a population from sample data. Probability theory can be used to state *how likely* it is that this inference is correct (or incorrect).

18. $(.33)^3 = .02.$

19. $3(.33)^2(.67) = .22.$

22. $4(.25)(.75)^3 = .422.$

23. $6(.25)^2(.75)^2 = .211.$

25. $(.25)^4 = .004.$

CHAPTER 11   2.   Sampling distribution of means.

4. μ, which is, in this case, 75.

5.   Standard error of the mean. In this case,

$$\sigma_{\bar{X}} = \frac{\sigma}{\sqrt{N}} = \frac{10}{\sqrt{36}} = 1.67.$$

6.   Approximately normal.

8.   A sampling distribution of means refers to a frequency distribution of *means* based on random samples from a population. Frequency distributions discussed previously showed the frequency distribution of *scores* from a sample or population.

10. $\mu = 5,\ \sigma_{\bar{X}} = .33.$

12. $\mu = 50,\ \sigma_{\bar{X}} = .67.$

14. **a.** $z_{\overline{X}} = 3.00$, $p = .0013$.
     c. $z_{\overline{X}} = -1.00$, $p = .1587$.

15.

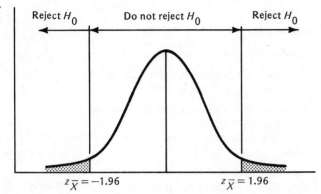

17.

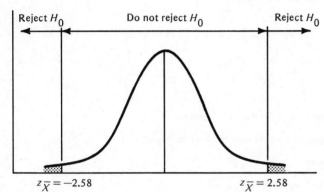

18.

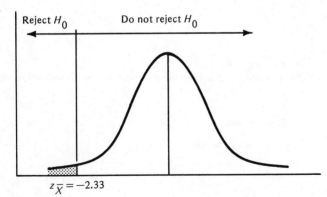

20. (2) Reject H_0 if $|z_{\bar{X}}(\text{observed})| > 1.96$. Do not reject H_0 if $|z_{\bar{X}}(\text{observed})| < 1.96$.
    (3) $z_{\bar{X}}(\text{observed}) = 2.73$, where $\sigma_{\bar{X}} = .55$.
    (5) Conclude that job satisfaction is significantly different in the Western region from other branches.

21. $CI_{.95}$: $18.42 < \mu < 20.58$

22. Reject H_0 since $CI_{.95}$ does not include μ.

23. Yes. Critical region for rejecting H_0 in two-tailed test at $\alpha = .05$ marks off same region of distribution as that outside the 95-percent confidence interval.

24. (2) Reject H_0 if $|z_{\bar{X}}(\text{observed})| > 2.33$. Do not reject H_0 if $|z_{\bar{X}}(\text{observed})| < 2.33$.
    (3) $z_{\bar{X}}(\text{observed}) = 1.75$, where $\sigma_{\bar{X}} = .57$.
    (5) Conclude that clients in the special program are not significantly higher in self-esteem than clients in general.

25. (3) $z_{\bar{X}}(\text{observed}) = -.67$ where $\sigma_{\bar{X}} = .03$.
    (5) Conclude that the chain advertising lower meat prices does not have significantly lower prices than other markets in the city.

26. (1) H_0: $\mu = 80$, H_1: $\mu \neq 80$.
    (2) Reject H_0 if $|z_{\bar{X}}(\text{observed})| > 2.58$. Do not reject H_0 if $|z_{\bar{X}}(\text{observed})| < 2.58$.
    (4) Reject H_0.

27. $CI_{.99}$: $80.57 < \mu < 87.43$.

CHAPTER 12   2. A sampling distribution of the differences between means.

4. Zero, since H_0 specifies no difference between the populations.

6. Approximately normal.

9. $\sigma_{\bar{X}_1} = .56$, $\sigma_{\bar{X}_2} = 1.11$, $\sigma_{\bar{X}_1 - \bar{X}_2} = 1.24$.

12. $z_{\bar{X}_1 - \bar{X}_2} = 2.00$; $p = .0228$.

15. $z_{\bar{X}_1 - \bar{X}_2} = -1.83$; $p = .0336$.

16. (1) H_0: $\mu_i - \mu_v = 0$, H_1: $\mu_i - \mu_v \neq 0$.
    (3) $z_{\bar{X}_i - \bar{X}_v} = 2.11$, where $\sigma_{\bar{X}_i} = \sigma_{\bar{X}_v} = .67$.
    (5) Conclude that children receiving verbal or imaginal strategies differ significantly in recall.

17. $CI_{.95}$: $.14 < \mu_i - \mu_v < 3.86$

18. Reject H_0, since $CI_{.95}$ does not include zero.

19. (3) $z_{\bar{X}_{PS} - \bar{X}_{CC}} = 3.28$, where $\sigma_{\bar{X}_{PS}} = \sigma_{\bar{X}_{CC}} = .43$.
    (4) Reject H_0.

20. $CI_{.99}$: $.43 < \mu_{PS} - \mu_{CC} < 3.57$.

22. (2) Reject H_0 if $z_{\bar{X}_1 - \bar{X}_2}(\text{observed}) < z_{\bar{X}_1 - \bar{X}_2}(\text{critical}) = -1.65$. Do not reject H_0 if $z_{\bar{X}_1 - \bar{X}_2}(\text{observed}) > z_{\bar{X}_1 - \bar{X}_2}(\text{critical}) = -1.65$.
    (3) $z_{\bar{X}_1 - \bar{X}_2}(\text{observed}) = -5.26$, where $\sigma_{\bar{X}_1} = \sigma_{\bar{X}_2} = .67$.
    (5) Conclude that provision of material rewards for an intrinsically satisfying task significantly decreases subsequent persistence in the same task.

1. **a.** Correct inferences: Researcher infers that the average motor development of premature infants is:
   (1) 70 when, in fact, $\mu = 70$; or
   (2) less than 70 when, in fact, $\mu < 70$.
   b. Incorrect inferences: Researcher infers that the average motor development of premature infants is:
   (1) 70 when, in fact, $\mu < 70$; or
   (2) less than 70 when, in fact, $\mu = 70$.

CHAPTER 13

2. Power $(1 - \beta)$.

4. Type II error (β).

7. Inverse relationship (as α increases, β decreases, and vice versa).

8. Power $= .9936$, where $\overline{X}_{\text{critical}} = 16.93$, $\sigma_{\overline{X}} = .83$, and $z_{\overline{X}}$ in H_1 is -2.49.

9. $N = 20.36 \approx 20$.

10. Power $= .9875$, where $\overline{X}_{\text{critical}} = 17.14$ and 12.86, $\sigma_{\overline{X}} = .83$, and $z_{\overline{X}}$ in H_1 is -2.24.

11. $N = 23.28 \approx 23$.

13. Power $= .9706$, where $(\overline{X}_1 - \overline{X}_2)_{\text{critical}} = 2.33$, $\sigma_{\overline{X}_1 - \overline{X}_2} = 1.414$, and $z_{\overline{X}_1 - \overline{X}_2}$ in H_1 is -1.89.

14. $n = 20.84 \approx 21$.

15. Power $= .9429$, where $(\overline{X}_1 - \overline{X}_2)_{\text{critical}} = 2.77$; $\sigma_{\overline{X}_1 - \overline{X}_2} = 1.414$; and $z_{\overline{X}_1 - \overline{X}_1}$ in H_1 is -1.58.

17. $n = 28.13 \approx 28$.

18. **b.** Select subjects from a homogeneous population (i.e., σ small).

19. Type I error.

21. Type II error.

22. No error.

2. Test for assumptions:
   (2) *Normally distributed scores.* It is not possible to determine from these scores if the shape of the distribution is normal. Previous information from other scores on this test might help to check this assumption; however the t test is not sensitive to violation of this assumption.

CHAPTER 14

3. $t_{\text{observed}} = 1.38$.

4. $t_{\text{critical}} = 2.36$.

5. Conclusions: Since $|t_{\text{observed}}| < t_{\text{critical}}$, do not reject the null hypothesis. There is insufficient evidence to conclude that the new employees differ from the previous employees.

6. $91.27 < \mu < 133.23$.

7. Yes. Since H_0 was not rejected at $\alpha = .05$, one would expect that the value of μ under H_0 would be included in the 95-percent confidence interval.

10. $t_{\text{observed}} = 6.00$.

11. $t_{critical} = 2.602$.

12. Since $t_{observed} > t_{critical}$, reject H_0. Conclude that the mean recall of subjects drawn from a population with mnemonic training is greater than that in the general population.

14. *Random sampling*. Subjects were randomly sampled.
    Normality. Information not available; t test is not sensitive.

15. $t_{observed} = -3.00$.

17. Since $|t_{observed}| > 1.711$, reject H_0. Conclude that the sample was drawn from a population with a mean below the norm of 36.

18. $26.58 < \mu < 33.42$.

19. No. A two-tailed test is analogous to the $100(1 - \alpha)$-percent confidence interval.

CHAPTER 15

2. $$t = \frac{\bar{X}_1 - \bar{X}_2}{\sqrt{\dfrac{s_1^2 + s_2^2}{n}}} = -2.99.$$

3. $t_{critical(.05, 10)} = 2.22$.

4. Since $|t_{observed}| > t_{critical}$, reject H_0. Conclude that those subjects who received training in voluntary alpha production produced alpha waves for a greater period of time than those subjects who did not receive training.

5. $CI_{.95}$: $-2.44 < \mu_1 - \mu_2 < .36$.

6. **a.** One independent variable with two levels: The training in voluntary alpha production is the independent variable, with the control group and experimental group comprising the two levels of the variable.
   c. Subjects are observed in one and only one group in the design.

8. No.

9. The U test assumes no ties for small samples. While this test is unaffected by tied scores within the same group, it is affected by tied scores between the two groups. Since subject 3 in the control group received the same score as subject 2 in the experimental group, the U test is inappropriate.

12. $$t_{observed} = \frac{2.50 - 6.67}{\sqrt{\dfrac{1.52^2 + 1.75^2}{6}}} = -4.39.$$

14. Since $|t_{observed}| > 2.228$, reject H_0. Conclude that the mean level of reported relaxation in the experimental group is greater than that in the control group.

15. $-6.29 < \mu_C - \mu_E < -2.27$.

16. H_0: The distributions of relaxation ratings in the populations of the experimental and control groups from which these groups were drawn are identical.
    H_1: The relaxation ratings of the populations of experimental and control groups from which these groups were drawn differ in their means: $\mu_C \neq \mu_E$.

17.

Group	C	C	C	C	C	E	C	E	E	E	E	E
Rating	1	1	2	3	3	4	5	6	6	7	8	9
Rank	1.5	1.5	3	4.5	4.5	6	7	8.5	8.5	10	11	12

18. $T_L = 6 + 8.5 + 8.5 + 10 + 11 + 12 = 56.$

$$U = 6(6) + \frac{6(6+1)}{2} - 56 = 1.$$

20. The null hypothesis should be rejected at $\alpha = .05$, since $U_{observed}$ is less than $U_{critical}$. The mean ratings of relaxation differ between the two groups: the experimental group, on the average, reports greater relaxation than the control group.

21. $z_U = -5.77.$

1. From the results of the ANOVA, conclusions can be drawn as to whether there is a treatment effect—that is, whether any two treatment means, or some combination of treatment means differ. In the example, there was a treatment effect due to drug dosage ($\alpha = .05$).

CHAPTER 16

2. ANOVA is preferable to multiple t tests because the probability of obtaining a Type I error can be controlled.

4. No. The planned comparisons are conducted whether or not the overall F is significant.

5. Post-hoc comparisons are appropriate when research is exploratory and so there is reason to examine any particular differences between means.

7. Error variability: Unsystematic variation in scores due to measurement error (unreliability of the dependent variable), random events which occur during the conduct of the study, or both.

8. Omega square: A statistic used to calculate the strength of association between a nominal independent variable and a dependent variable.

10. Mean square: The sum of squares divided by their appropriate degrees of freedom. The mean square may be thought of as a variance.

12. $H_0: \mu_1 = \mu_2 = \mu_3$, $H_1: \mu_i \neq \mu_i'$ for some i and i'.

13. *Independence*. Subjects were randomly assigned to treatment groups and received the treatment independently. *Normality*. ANOVA is not sensitive to violations of this assumption. *Homogeneity of variances*. With equal cell sizes, ANOVA is not sensitive to violation.

15.

Source of variation	Sums of squares	df	Mean square	F
Between groups	80.17	2	40.09	9.30[a]
Within groups	38.75	9	4.31	
Total	118.92	11		

[a]$p < .05$

17. $F_{observed} = 9.30.$

18. $\omega^2 = .58$.

19. Since $F_{observed}$ exceeds $F_{critical}$ (4.26), reject H_0. The differences between means probably did not arise by chance; conclude a treatment effect which accounts for 58 percent of the variance in the dependent variable.

20. $H_0: C = 0$, $H_1: C \neq 0$.

21.

	Cage 1	Cage 2	Cage 3
Mean	6.25	7.5	1.5
Weight	+1	+1	−2

23. $t_{observed} = 4.23$.

25. Since $t_{observed}$ exceeds $t_{critical}$ (2.92), reject H_0. Conclude that there is a significant difference between the means of the treatment groups and the control group.

26. $H_0: C = 0$, $H_1: C \neq 0$, for all comparisons.

	$\bar{X}_3 = 1.5$	$\bar{X}_1 = 6.25$	$\bar{X}_2 = 7.5$
$\bar{X}_3 = 1.5$	—	4.75[a]	6.0[a]
$\bar{X}_1 = 6.25$		—	1.25
$\bar{X}_2 = 7.5$			—

[a] $p < .05$.

$$HSD = q(.05, 9, 3)\sqrt{\frac{4.31}{4}}$$

$$= (3.95)(1.04)$$

$$= 4.10.$$

Conclude that the means of cages 2 and 3 are significantly different, as are those of cages 1 and 3. The means of cages 1 and 2 do not differ significantly.

C_1	$\bar{X}_1$	$\bar{X}_2$	$\bar{X}_3$
	6.25	7.5	1.5
Weight:	−1	−1	2

$\hat{C}_1 = -10.75$, $|t| = 4.23$, $t_{critical(.05, 9)} = 1.83$.

Since $|t_{observed}|$ exceeds $t_{critical}$, reject H_0 and conclude that $(\bar{X}_1 + \bar{X}_2)/2$ is significantly greater than $\bar{X}_3$; that is, that some type of reinforcement is significantly better than no reinforcement in training the monkeys to put garbage into the can.

CHAPTER 17

1. Information about the interaction of the variables.

2. Ordinal.

3. Disordinal.

6. Main effect for A, main effect for B, interaction of A and B.

8. When cell sizes are equal.

9. Start with the interaction effect and move upward to the main effects. If the interaction effect is significant, it means that the effects of factors A and B must be qualified, so that the main effects, in themselves, do not provide an accurate representation of the effects of the two factors combined.

10. For factor A: H_0: $\mu_1 = \mu_2$,
    $\qquad\qquad$ H_2: $\mu_1 \neq \mu_2$ or $\mu_i \neq \mu_i'$ for some i.
    For factor B: H_0: $\mu_1 = \mu_2$
    $\qquad\qquad$ H_1: $\mu_1 \neq \mu_2$ or $\mu_j \neq \mu_{j'}$ for some j.
    For interaction effect:
    $\qquad\qquad$ H_0: interaction effect $= 0$,
    $\qquad\qquad$ H_1: interaction effect $\neq 0$.

12. *Step 1.* Data summary table:

	Experimental	Control	Row mean
High	2 3 3 $\bar{X} = 2.67$	1 2 3 $\bar{X} = 2.0$	2.33
Low	6 14 10 $\bar{X} = 10.0$	4 5 4 $\bar{X} = 4.33$	7.17
Column mean	6.33	3.17	

Step 3. **a.** $\dfrac{3249}{12} = 270.75 = [1]$.
$\qquad$ **b.** $340.84 = [2]$.
$\qquad$ **c.** $300.84 = [3]$.
$\qquad$ **d.** $389.66 = [4]$.
$\qquad$ **e.** $425 = [5]$.

13. ANOVA summary table:

Source	SS	df	MS	$F_{observed}$
Self-concept (A)	70.09	1	70.09	15.86[a]
Treatment (B)	30.09	1	30.09	6.81[a]
$A \times B$	18.73	1	18.73	4.24
Within (error)	35.34	8	4.42	
Total	154.25	11		

[a]$p < .05$

15. *Main effect for A.* Since $F_{observed} > F_{critical}$, reject H_0. There is a significant difference between performance of subjects scoring high or low in self-concept. Subjects low in self-concept, on the average, gave greater shocks than did subjects high in self-concept.
    Main effect for B. Since $F_{observed} > F_{critical}$, reject H_0. There is a significant difference between performance of subjects in the experimental and control groups. Subjects in the experimental group, on the average, gave greater shocks than did subjects in the control group.
    Interaction of A and B. Since $F_{observed} < F_{critical}$, do not reject H_0. There is no significant interaction.

16. Graph of interaction effect:

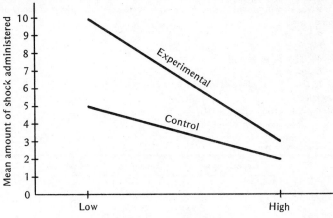

17. $\omega_A^2 = \dfrac{SS_A - (q-1)MS_W}{SS_T + MS_W} = \dfrac{70.09 - 1(4.42)}{154.43 + 4.42} = \dfrac{65.67}{158.85} = .41.$

18. The strongest effect is the main effect of Factor A (self-concept), which accounts for 41 percent of the variance. The treatment effect accounts for 16 percent. The interaction effect was not significant.

19. $H_0: C = 0, H_1: C \neq 0.$

20.

	$\bar{X}_{H,C} = 2.0$	$\bar{X}_{H,E} = 2.67$	$\bar{X}_{L,C} = 4.33$	$\bar{X}_{L,E} = 10.0$
$\bar{X}_{H,C} = 2.0$	—	.67	2.33	8.0*
$\bar{X}_{H,E} = 2.67$		—	1.66	7.33*
$\bar{X}_{L,C} = 4.33$			—	5.67*
$\bar{X}_{L,E} = 10.00$				—

24. $C_1: H_0: C = 0, H_1: C \neq 0.$
    $\hat{C}_1:$ Levels of B at A_1:

	B_1	B_2
A_1	$+1$	-1

$$\hat{C}_1 = (+1)4.25 + (-1)2.10 = 2.15,$$

$$t_{observed} = \dfrac{2.15}{\sqrt{\dfrac{2MS_W}{n}}} = \dfrac{2.15}{\sqrt{\dfrac{(2)(2.53)}{3}}} = 1.66,$$

$$t'_{critical} = \sqrt{3(F_{critical(.05, 1, 8)})} = \sqrt{3(5.32)} = 3.99.$$

Conclusion: Do not reject H_0, since $|t_{observed}|$ does not exceed $t'_{critical}$.

$\hat{C}_2$: H_0: $C = 0$, H_1: $C \neq 0$.

$\hat{C}_2$: Levels of B at A_2:

	B_1	B_2
A_2	$+1$	-1

$$\hat{C}_2 = (+1)10.0 + (-1)3.8 = 6.2,$$

$$t_{observed} = \frac{6.2}{\sqrt{\dfrac{2MS_W}{n}}} = \frac{6.2}{\sqrt{\dfrac{(2)(2.53)}{3}}} = 4.77,$$

$$t'_{critical} = \sqrt{3(5.32)} = 3.99.$$

Conclusion: Reject H_0, since $|t_{observed}| > t'_{critical}$.

CHAPTER 18

1. **a.** χ^2 compares observed frequencies with expected frequencies.
   e. A subject's response can fall in one and only one cell of the design.

3. $t_{critical}$ depends on sample size, while $\chi^2_{critical}$ depends on the number of levels of the independent variable(s).

4. χ^2 tests how closely the observed frequencies fit the theoretically expected frequencies ("goodness of fit").

6. The inconsistency between the smooth theoretical and actual sampling distribution is only serious enough to affect χ^2 at 1 *df*.

7. H_0: The observed distribution of frequencies across categories equals the expected distribution of frequencies across categories.
   H_1: The observed distribution of frequencies across categories does not equal the expected distribution of frequencies across categories.

8. **a.** *Random sampling.* Subjects were randomly selected.
   b. *Mutually exclusive categories.* Each subject could choose only one response.
   d. *Expected frequencies greater than* 5. If all opinions were equal, E for each category would be $\frac{1}{3} \times 60 = 20$.
   e. *Correction for continuity.* Does not apply in this case, since $df = 2$.

9.

Category	O	Expected proportion	E	$O - E$	$(O - E)^2$	$\dfrac{(O - E)^2}{E}$
1	28	.33	20	8	64	3.20
2	15	.33	20	-5	25	1.25
3	17	.33	20	-3	9	.45
Sum	60	1.00	60	0	$\chi^2_{obs.} = 4.90$	

11. Since $\chi^2_{observed} < \chi^2_{critical}$ (9.21), do not reject H_0. There is insufficient evidence to conclude that there is a significant difference of opinion about the idea for a television series.

12.

O	$O*$	E	$O - E$	$(O - E)^2$	$\dfrac{(O - E)^2}{E}$
28	27.5	20	7.5	56.25	2.81
12	12.5	20	-7.5	56.25	2.81
40	40	40	0		$\chi^2 = 5.62$

13. $\chi^2_{\text{critical}} = 6.63$.

15. H_0: Severity of illness and the patient's opinion of his doctor are independent in the population.

H_1: Severity of illness and the patient's opinion of his doctor are related in the population.

16. b. *Mutually exclusive categories.* Each subject could choose only one response and belong to only one type of group.

d. *No expected frequency less than 10 with 1 df.* The smallest expected frequency is 11.25.

e. *Correction for continuity.* Must be used, as $df = 1$.

17. $\chi^2 = \dfrac{N\left(|ad - bc| - \dfrac{N}{2}\right)^2}{(a + b)(c + d)(a + c)(b + d)} = \dfrac{80(|100 - 800| - 40)^2}{(30)(50)(30)(50)} = 19.47$.

18. $\chi^2_{\text{critical}(.05,\ 1)} = 3.84$.

20. Collapse: $E_{\text{rc(smallest)}} = \dfrac{24 \times 16}{111} = 3.46$. Smallest frequency must be 5 or greater to use χ^2.

21. Collapse age since it represents continuum; collapsing type of cestacea would change study since each category is important in its own right.

	Sperm whale	Blue whale	Dolphin	Orca	
1 mo–10 yr	4	12	16	18	50
> 11 yr	12	14	15	20	61
	16	26	31	38	111

$E_{\text{rc(smallest)}} = \dfrac{16 \times 50}{111} = 7.21$.

23. $\chi^2_{\text{critical}(.05,\ 3)} = 7.81$.

24. Do not reject H_0. There is insufficient evidence to conclude that there is a relationship between the age and the type of cestacea found off the coast of Baja California.

CHAPTER 19

2. When pairs of subjects are matched on a variable that is thought to affect performance in the two treatments.

3. Because in the dependent-sample t test, the scores of subjects in treatment 1 are correlated with, not independent of, the scores in treatment 2. So there are only n different subjects and only n independent observations. Thus, there are $n - 1$ degrees of freedom for the t test.

5. The difference lies in the term $-2\,r_{12}\sigma_{\bar{X}_1}\sigma_{\bar{X}_2}$. For the independent t test, scores in the two groups are expected to be unrelated, so $r_{12} = 0$ and this term drops out. For the dependent t test, scores for the same or matched subjects are expected to be correlated, so this term remains.

7. $t_{\text{critical}(.05,\ 5)} = 2.02$.

8.
Pair	X_1	X_2	D	$\bar{D}$	$D - \bar{D}$	$(D - \bar{D})^2$
1	4	2	2	3	-1	1
2	6	3	3	3	0	0
3	7	1	6	3	3	9
4	9	5	4	3	1	1
5	2	2	0	3	-3	9
6	9	6	3	3	0	0
Sum	37	19	18	18	0	20

$$s_D = \sqrt{\frac{20}{5}} = 2, \qquad s_{\bar{D}} = \frac{2}{\sqrt{6}} = .82.$$

9. $t^*_{\text{observed}} = 3/.82 = 3.66$.

11. $\text{CI}_{.95}$:

$$3 - (2.57)(.82) < \mu_1 - \mu_2 < 3 + (2.57)(.82),$$

$$5.11 < \mu_1 - \mu_2 < .89.$$

12. Over all possible samples of $\bar{X}_1 - \bar{X}_2$, the probability is .95 that a confidence interval like the one constructed will include the true difference between population means.

13. Not necessarily. A one-tailed test was conducted, while the confidence interval takes into account both tails of the sampling distribution. As it turned out, $\text{CI}_{.95}$ did not include zero. (Typically, a symmetric confidence interval would not be used with a one-tailed, asymmetric, alternative hypothesis.)

14. $H_0: \mu_1 - \mu_2 = 0,\ H_1: \mu_1 - \mu_2 \neq 0$.

15. $t_{\text{critical}(.01/2,\ 9)} = 3.25$.

16. Do not reject H_0 if $|t^*_{\text{observed}}| < 3.25$. Reject H_0 if $|t^*_{\text{observed}}| > 3.25$.

18. $t^*_{\text{observed}} = 1.84/.09 = 20.44$.

19. Reject H_0. As might be expected, food deprivation increases the mean food intake of rats.

. Miscellaneous Tables .

Table A ♦ Random numbers.[a]

---

22 17 68 65 84	68 95 23 92 35	87 02 22 57 51	61 09 43 95 06	58 24 82 03 47
19 36 27 59 46	13 79 93 37 55	39 77 32 77 09	85 52 05 30 62	47 83 51 62 74
16 77 23 02 77	09 61 87 25 21	28 06 24 25 93	16 71 13 59 78	23 05 47 47 25
78 43 76 71 61	20 44 90 32 64	97 67 63 99 61	46 38 03 93 22	69 81 21 99 21
03 28 28 26 08	73 37 32 04 05	69 30 16 09 05	88 69 58 28 99	35 07 44 75 47
93 22 53 64 39	07 10 63 76 35	87 03 04 79 88	08 13 13 85 51	55 34 57 72 69
78 76 58 54 74	92 38 70 96 92	52 06 79 79 45	82 63 18 27 44	69 66 92 19 09
23 68 35 26 00	99 53 93 61 28	52 70 05 48 34	56 65 05 61 86	90 92 10 70 80
15 39 25 70 99	93 86 52 77 65	15 33 59 05 28	22 87 26 07 47	86 96 98 29 06
58 71 96 30 24	18 46 23 34 27	85 13 99 24 44	49 18 09 79 49	74 16 32 23 02
57 35 27 33 72	24 53 63 94 09	41 10 76 47 91	44 04 95 49 66	39 60 04 59 81
48 50 86 54 48	22 06 34 72 52	82 21 15 65 20	33 29 94 71 11	15 91 29 12 03
61 96 48 95 03	07 16 39 33 66	98 56 10 56 79	77 21 30 27 12	90 49 22 23 62
36 93 89 41 26	29 70 83 63 51	99 74 20 52 36	87 09 41 15 09	98 60 16 03 03
18 87 00 42 31	57 90 12 02 07	23 47 37 17 31	54 08 01 88 63	39 41 88 92 10
88 56 53 27 59	33 35 72 67 47	77 34 55 45 70	08 18 27 38 90	16 95 86 70 75
09 72 95 84 29	49 41 31 06 70	42 38 06 45 18	64 84 73 31 65	52 53 37 97 15
12 96 88 17 31	65 19 69 02 83	60 75 86 90 68	24 64 19 35 51	56 61 87 39 12
85 94 57 24 16	92 09 84 38 76	22 00 27 69 85	29 81 94 78 70	21 94 47 90 12
38 64 43 59 98	98 77 87 68 07	91 51 67 62 44	40 98 05 93 78	23 32 65 41 18
53 44 09 42 72	00 41 86 79 79	68 47 22 00 20	35 55 31 51 51	00 83 63 22 55
40 76 66 26 84	57 99 99 90 37	36 63 32 08 58	37 40 13 68 97	87 64 81 07 83
02 17 79 18 05	12 59 52 57 02	22 07 90 47 03	28 14 11 30 79	20 69 22 40 98
95 17 82 06 53	31 51 10 96 46	92 06 88 07 77	56 11 50 81 69	40 23 72 51 39
35 76 22 42 92	96 11 83 44 80	34 68 35 48 77	33 42 40 90 60	73 96 53 97 86
26 29 13 56 41	85 47 04 66 08	34 72 57 59 13	82 43 80 46 15	38 26 61 70 04
77 80 20 75 82	72 82 32 99 90	63 95 73 76 63	89 73 44 99 05	48 67 26 43 18
46 40 66 44 52	91 36 74 43 53	30 82 13 54 00	78 45 63 98 35	55 03 36 67 68
37 56 08 18 09	77 53 84 46 47	31 91 18 95 58	24 16 74 11 53	44 10 13 85 57
61 65 61 68 66	37 27 47 39 19	84 83 70 07 48	53 21 40 06 71	95 06 79 88 54
93 43 69 64 07	34 18 04 52 35	56 27 09 24 86	61 85 53 83 45	19 90 70 99 00
21 96 60 12 99	11 20 99 45 18	48 13 93 55 34	18 37 79 49 90	65 97 38 20 46
95 20 47 97 97	27 37 83 28 71	00 06 41 41 74	45 89 09 39 84	51 67 11 52 49
97 86 21 78 73	10 65 81 92 59	58 76 17 14 97	04 76 62 16 17	17 95 70 45 80
69 92 06 34 13	59 71 74 17 32	27 55 10 24 19	23 71 82 13 74	63 52 52 01 41
04 31 17 21 56	33 73 99 19 87	26 72 39 27 67	53 77 57 68 93	60 61 97 22 61
61 06 98 03 91	87 14 77 43 96	43 00 65 98 50	45 60 33 01 07	98 99 46 50 47
85 93 85 86 88	72 87 08 62 40	16 06 10 89 20	23 21 34 74 97	76 38 03 29 63
21 74 32 47 45	73 96 07 94 52	09 65 90 77 47	25 76 16 19 33	53 05 70 53 30
15 69 53 82 80	79 96 23 53 10	65 39 07 16 29	45 33 02 43 70	02 87 40 41 45
02 89 08 04 49	20 21 14 68 86	87 63 93 95 17	11 29 01 95 80	35 14 97 35 33
87 18 15 89 79	85 43 01 72 73	08 61 74 51 69	89 74 39 82 15	94 51 33 41 67
98 83 71 94 22	59 97 50 99 52	08 52 85 08 40	87 80 61 65 31	91 51 80 32 44
10 08 58 21 66	72 68 49 29 31	89 85 84 46 06	59 73 19 85 23	65 09 29 75 63
47 90 56 10 08	88 02 84 27 83	42 29 72 23 19	66 56 45 65 79	20 71 53 20 25
22 85 61 68 90	49 64 92 85 44	16 40 12 89 88	50 14 49 81 06	01 82 77 45 12
67 80 43 79 33	12 83 11 41 16	25 58 19 68 70	77 02 54 00 52	53 43 37 15 26
27 62 50 96 72	79 44 61 40 15	14 53 40 65 39	27 31 58 50 28	11 39 03 34 25
33 78 80 87 15	38 30 06 38 21	14 47 47 07 26	54 96 87 53 32	40 36 40 96 76
13 13 92 66 99	47 24 49 57 74	32 25 43 62 17	10 97 11 69 84	99 63 22 32 98

10 27 53 96 23	71 50 54 36 23	54 31 04 82 98	04 14 12 15 09	26 78 25 47 47
28 41 50 61 88	64 85 27 20 18	83 36 36 05 56	39 71 65 09 62	94 76 62 11 89
34 21 42 57 02	59 19 18 97 48	80 30 03 30 98	05 24 67 70 07	84 97 50 87 46
61 81 77 23 23	82 82 11 54 08	53 28 70 58 96	44 07 39 55 43	42 34 43 39 28
61 15 18 13 54	16 86 20 26 88	90 74 80 55 09	14 53 90 51 17	52 01 63 01 59
91 76 21 64 64	44 91 13 32 97	75 31 62 66 54	84 80 32 75 77	56 08 25 70 29
00 97 79 08 06	37 30 28 59 85	53 56 68 53 40	01 74 39 59 73	30 19 99 85 48
36 46 18 34 94	75 20 80 27 77	78 91 69 16 00	08 43 18 73 68	67 69 61 34 25
88 98 99 60 50	65 95 79 42 94	93 62 40 89 96	43 56 47 71 66	46 76 29 67 02
04 37 59 87 21	05 02 03 24 17	47 97 81 56 51	92 34 86 01 82	55 51 33 12 91
63 62 06 34 41	94 21 78 55 09	72 76 45 16 94	29 95 81 83 83	79 88 01 97 30
78 47 23 53 90	34 41 92 45 71	09 23 70 70 07	12 38 92 79 43	14 85 11 47 23
87 68 62 15 43	53 14 36 59 25	54 47 33 70 15	59 24 48 40 35	50 03 42 99 36
47 60 92 10 77	88 59 53 11 52	66 25 69 07 04	48 68 64 71 06	61 65 70 22 12
56 88 87 59 41	65 28 04 67 53	95 79 88 37 31	50 41 06 94 76	81 83 17 16 33
02 57 45 86 67	73 43 07 34 48	44 26 87 93 29	77 09 61 67 84	06 69 44 77 75
31 54 14 13 17	48 62 11 90 60	68 12 93 64 28	46 24 79 16 76	14 60 25 51 01
28 50 16 43 36	28 97 85 58 99	67 22 52 76 23	24 70 36 54 54	59 28 61 71 96
63 29 62 66 50	02 63 45 52 38	67 63 47 54 75	83 24 78 43 20	92 63 13 47 48
45 65 58 26 51	76 96 59 38 72	86 57 45 71 46	44 67 76 14 55	44 88 01 62 12
39 65 36 63 70	77 45 85 50 51	74 13 39 35 22	30 53 36 02 95	49 34 88 73 61
73 71 98 16 04	29 18 94 51 23	76 51 94 84 86	79 93 96 38 63	08 58 25 58 94
72 20 56 20 11	72 65 71 08 86	79 57 95 13 91	97 48 72 66 48	09 71 17 24 89
75 17 26 99 76	89 37 20 70 01	77 31 61 95 46	26 97 05 73 51	53 33 18 72 87
37 48 60 82 29	81 30 15 39 14	48 38 75 93 29	06 87 37 78 48	45 56 00 84 47
68 08 02 80 72	83 71 46 30 49	89 17 95 88 29	02 39 56 03 46	97 74 06 56 17
14 23 98 61 67	70 52 85 01 50	01 84 02 78 43	10 62 98 19 41	18 83 99 47 99
49 08 96 21 44	25 27 99 41 28	07 41 08 34 66	19 42 74 39 91	41 96 53 78 72
78 37 06 08 43	63 61 62 42 29	39 68 95 10 96	09 24 23 00 62	56 12 80 73 16
37 21 34 17 68	68 96 83 23 56	32 84 60 15 31	44 73 67 34 77	91 15 79 74 58
14 29 09 34 04	87 83 07 55 07	76 58 30 83 64	87 29 25 58 84	86 50 60 00 25
58 43 28 06 36	49 52 83 51 14	47 56 91 29 34	05 87 31 06 95	12 45 57 09 09
10 43 67 29 70	80 62 80 03 42	10 80 21 38 84	90 56 35 03 09	43 12 74 49 14
44 38 88 39 54	86 97 37 44 22	00 95 01 31 76	17 16 29 56 63	38 78 94 49 81
90 69 59 19 51	85 39 52 85 13	07 28 37 07 61	11 16 36 27 03	78 86 72 04 95
41 47 10 25 62	97 05 31 03 61	20 26 36 31 62	68 69 86 95 44	84 95 48 46 45
91 94 14 63 19	75 89 11 47 11	31 56 34 19 09	79 57 92 36 59	14 93 87 81 40
80 06 54 18 66	09 18 94 06 19	98 40 07 17 81	22 45 44 84 11	24 62 20 42 31
67 72 77 63 48	84 08 31 55 58	24 33 45 77 58	80 45 67 93 82	75 70 16 08 24
59 40 24 13 27	79 26 88 86 30	01 31 60 10 39	53 58 47 70 93	85 81 56 39 38
05 90 35 89 95	01 61 16 96 94	50 78 13 69 36	37 68 53 37 31	71 26 35 03 71
44 43 80 69 98	46 68 05 14 82	90 78 50 05 62	77 79 13 57 44	59 60 10 39 66
61 81 31 96 82	00 57 25 60 59	46 72 60 18 77	55 66 12 62 11	08 99 55 64 57
42 88 07 10 05	24 98 65 63 21	47 21 61 88 32	27 80 30 21 60	10 92 35 36 12
77 94 30 05 39	28 10 99 00 27	12 73 73 99 12	49 99 57 94 82	96 88 57 17 91
78 83 19 76 16	94 11 68 84 26	23 54 20 86 85	23 86 66 99 07	36 37 34 92 09
87 76 59 61 81	43 63 64 61 61	65 76 36 95 90	18 48 27 45 68	27 23 65 30 72
91 43 05 96 47	55 78 99 95 24	37 55 85 78 78	01 48 41 19 10	35 19 54 07 73
84 97 77 72 73	09 62 06 65 72	87 12 49 03 60	41 15 20 76 27	50 47 02 29 16
87 41 60 76 83	44 88 96 07 80	83 05 83 38 96	73 70 66 81 90	30 56 10 48 59

[a]Table A is taken from Table XXXIII of Fisher and Yates, *Statistical tables for biological, agricultural and medical research*, published by Longman Group Ltd., London (previously published by Oliver and Boyd, Edinburgh), and by permission of the authors and publishers.

Table B. Proportions of Area Under the Standard Normal Curve.

(1) z	(2) area between mean and z	(3) area below z	(4) area above z	(1) z	(2) area between mean and z	(3) area below z	(4) area above z
0.00	.0000	.5000	.5000	0.60	.2257	.7257	.2743
0.01	.0040	.5040	.4960	0.61	.2291	.7291	.2709
0.02	.0080	.5080	.4920	0.62	.2324	.7324	.2676
0.03	.0120	.5120	.4880	0.63	.2357	.7357	.2643
0.04	.0160	.5160	.4840	0.64	.2389	.7389	.2611
0.05	.0199	.5199	.4801	0.65	.2422	.7422	.2578
0.06	.0239	.5239	.4761	0.66	.2454	.7454	.2546
0.07	.0279	.5279	.4721	0.67	.2486	.7486	.2514
0.08	.0319	.5319	.4681	0.68	.2517	.7517	.2483
0.09	.0359	.5359	.4641	0.69	.2549	.7549	.2451
0.10	.0398	.5398	.4602	0.70	.2580	.7580	.2420
0.11	.0438	.5438	.4562	0.71	.2611	.7611	.2389
0.12	.0478	.5478	.4522	0.72	.2642	.7642	.2358
0.13	.0517	.5517	.4483	0.73	.2673	.7673	.2327
0.14	.0557	.5557	.4443	0.74	.2704	.7704	.2296
0.15	.0596	.5596	.4404	0.75	.2734	.7734	.2266
0.16	.0636	.5636	.4364	0.76	.2764	.7764	.2236
0.17	.0675	.5675	.4325	0.77	.2794	.7794	.2206
0.18	.0714	.5714	.4286	0.78	.2823	.7823	.2177
0.19	.0753	.5753	.4247	0.79	.2852	.7852	.2148
0.20	.0793	.5793	.4207	0.80	.2881	.7881	.2119
0.21	.0832	.5832	.4168	0.81	.2910	.7910	.2090
0.22	.0871	.5871	.4129	0.82	.2939	.7939	.2061
0.23	.0910	.5910	.4090	0.83	.2967	.7967	.2033
0.24	.0948	.5948	.4052	0.84	.2995	.7995	.2005
0.25	.0987	.5987	.4013	0.85	.3023	.8023	.1977
0.26	.1026	.6026	.3974	0.86	.3051	.8051	.1949
0.27	.1064	.6064	.3936	0.87	.3078	.8078	.1922
0.28	.1103	.6103	.3897	0.88	.3106	.8106	.1894
0.29	.1141	.6141	.3859	0.89	.3133	.8133	.1867
0.30	.1179	.6179	.3821	0.90	.3159	.8159	.1841
0.31	.1217	.6217	.3783	0.91	.3186	.8186	.1814
0.32	.1255	.6255	.3745	0.92	.3212	.8212	.1788
0.33	.1293	.6293	.3707	0.93	.3238	.8238	.1762
0.34	.1331	.6331	.3669	0.94	.3264	.8264	.1736
0.35	.1368	.6368	.3632	0.95	.3289	.8289	.1711
0.36	.1406	.6406	.3594	0.96	.3315	.8315	.1685
0.37	.1443	.6443	.3557	0.97	.3340	.8340	.1660
0.38	.1480	.6480	.3520	0.98	.3365	.8365	.1635
0.39	.1517	.6517	.3483	0.99	.3389	.8389	.1611
0.40	.1554	.6554	.3446	1.00	.3413	.8413	.1587
0.41	.1591	.6591	.3409	1.01	.3438	.8438	.1562
0.42	.1628	.6628	.3372	1.02	.3461	.8461	.1539
0.43	.1664	.6664	.3336	1.03	.3485	.8485	.1515
0.44	.1700	.6700	.3300	1.04	.3508	.8508	.1492
0.45	.1736	.6736	.3264	1.05	.3531	.8531	.1469
0.46	.1772	.6772	.3228	1.06	.3554	.8554	.1446
0.47	.1808	.6808	.3192	1.07	.3577	.8577	.1423
0.48	.1844	.6844	.3156	1.08	.3599	.8599	.1401
0.49	.1879	.6879	.3121	1.09	.3621	.8621	.1379
0.50	.1915	.6915	.3085	1.10	.3643	.8643	.1357
0.51	.1950	.6950	.3050	1.11	.3665	.8665	.1335
0.52	.1985	.6985	.3015	1.12	.3686	.8686	.1314
0.53	.2019	.7019	.2981	1.13	.3708	.8708	.1292
0.54	.2054	.7054	.2946	1.14	.3729	.8729	.1271
0.55	.2088	.7088	.2912	1.15	.3749	.8749	.1251
0.56	.2123	.7123	.2877	1.16	.3770	.8770	.1230
0.57	.2157	.7157	.2843	1.17	.3790	.8790	.1210
0.58	.2190	.7190	.2810	1.18	.3810	.8810	.1190
0.59	.2224	.7224	.2776	1.19	.3830	.8830	.1170

Table B. (continued)

(1) z	(2) area between mean and z	(3) area below z	(4) area above z	(1) z	(2) area between mean and z	(3) area below z	(4) area above z
1.20	.3849	.8849	.1151	1.80	.4641	.9641	.0359
1.21	.3869	.8869	.1131	1.81	.4649	.9649	.0351
1.22	.3888	.8888	.1112	1.82	.4656	.9656	.0344
1.23	.3907	.8907	.1093	1.83	.4664	.9664	.0336
1.24	.3925	.8925	.1075	1.84	.4671	.9671	.0329
1.25	.3944	.8944	.1056	1.85	.4678	.9678	.0322
1.26	.3962	.8962	.1038	1.86	.4686	.9686	.0314
1.27	.3980	.8980	.1020	1.87	.4693	.9693	.0307
1.28	.3997	.8997	.1003	1.88	.4699	.9699	.0301
1.29	.4015	.9015	.0985	1.89	.4706	.9706	.0294
1.30	.4032	.9032	.0968	1.90	.4713	.9713	.0287
1.31	.4049	.9049	.0951	1.91	.4719	.9719	.0281
1.32	.4066	.9066	.0934	1.92	.4726	.9726	.0274
1.33	.4082	.9082	.0918	1.93	.4732	.9732	.0268
1.34	.4099	.9099	.0901	1.94	.4738	.9738	.0262
1.35	.4115	.9115	.0885	1.95	.4744	.9744	.0256
1.36	.4131	.9131	.0869	1.96	.4750	.9750	.0250
1.37	.4147	.9147	.0853	1.97	.4756	.9756	.0244
1.38	.4162	.9162	.0838	1.98	.4761	.9761	.0239
1.39	.4177	.9177	.0823	1.99	.4767	.9767	.0233
1.40	.4192	.9192	.0808	2.00	.4772	.9772	.0228
1.41	.4207	.9207	.0793	2.01	.4778	.9778	.0222
1.42	.4222	.9222	.0778	2.02	.4783	.9783	.0217
1.43	.4236	.9236	.0764	2.03	.4788	.9788	.0212
1.44	.4251	.9251	.0749	2.04	.4793	.9793	.0207
1.45	.4265	.9265	.0735	2.05	.4798	.9798	.0202
1.46	.4279	.9279	.0721	2.06	.4803	.9803	.0197
1.47	.4292	.9292	.0708	2.07	.4808	.9808	.0192
1.48	.4306	.9306	.0694	2.08	.4812	.9812	.0188
1.49	.4319	.9319	.0681	2.09	.4817	.9817	.0183
1.50	.4332	.9332	.0668	2.10	.4821	.9821	.0179
1.51	.4345	.9345	.0655	2.11	.4826	.9826	.0174
1.52	.4357	.9357	.0643	2.12	.4830	.9830	.0170
1.53	.4370	.9370	.0630	2.13	.4834	.9834	.0166
1.54	.4382	.9382	.0618	2.14	.4838	.9838	.0162
1.55	.4394	.9394	.0606	2.15	.4842	.9842	.0158
1.56	.4406	.9406	.0594	2.16	.4846	.9846	.0154
1.57	.4418	.9418	.0582	2.17	.4850	.9850	.0150
1.58	.4429	.9129	.0571	2.18	.4854	.9854	.0146
1.59	.4441	.9441	.0559	2.19	.4857	.9857	.0143
1.60	.4452	.9452	.0548	2.20	.4861	.9861	.0139
1.61	.4463	.9463	.0537	2.21	.4864	.9864	.0136
1.62	.4474	.9474	.0526	2.22	.4868	.9868	.0132
1.63	.4484	.9484	.0516	2.23	.4871	.9871	.0129
1.64	.4495	.9495	.0505	2.24	.4875	.9875	.0125
1.65	.4505	.9505	.0495	2.25	.4878	.9878	.0122
1.66	.4515	.9515	.0485	2.26	.4881	.9881	.0119
1.67	.4525	.9525	.0475	2.27	.4884	.9884	.0116
1.68	.4535	.9535	.0465	2.28	.4887	.9887	.0113
1.69	.4545	.9545	.0455	2.29	.4890	.9890	.0110
1.70	.4554	.9554	.0446	2.30	.4893	.9893	.0107
1.71	.4564	.9564	.0436	2.31	.4896	.9896	.0104
1.72	.4573	.9573	.0427	2.32	.4898	.9898	.0102
1.73	.4582	.9582	.0418	2.33	.4901	.9901	.0099
1.74	.4591	.9591	.0409	2.34	.4904	.9904	.0096
1.75	.4599	.9599	.0401	2.35	.4906	.9906	.0094
1.76	.4608	.9608	.0392	2.36	.4909	.9909	.0091
1.77	.4616	.9616	.0384	2.37	.4911	.9911	.0089
1.78	.4625	.9625	.0375	2.38	.4913	.9913	.0087
1.79	.4633	.9633	.0367	2.39	.4916	.9916	.0084

(1) z	(2) area between mean and z	(3) area below z	(4) area below z	(1) z	(2) area between mean and z	(3) area below z	(4) area above z
2.40	.4918	.9918	.0082	2.85	.4978	.9978	.0022
2.41	.4920	.9920	.0080	2.86	.4979	.9979	.0021
2.42	.4922	.9922	.0078	2.87	.4979	.9979	.0021
2.43	.4925	.9925	.0075	2.88	.4980	.9980	.0020
2.44	.4927	.9927	.0073	2.89	.4981	.9981	.0019
2.45	.4929	.9929	.0071	2.90	.4981	.9981	.0019
2.46	.4931	.9931	.0069	2.91	.4982	.9982	.0018
2.47	.4932	.9932	.0068	2.92	.4982	.9982	.0018
2.48	.4934	.9934	.0066	2.93	.4983	.9983	.0017
2.49	.4936	.9936	.0064	2.94	.4984	.9984	.0016
2.50	.4938	.9938	.0062	2.95	.4984	.9984	.0016
2.51	.4940	.9940	.0060	2.96	.4985	.9985	.0015
2.52	.4941	.9941	.0059	2.97	.4985	.9985	.0015
2.53	.4943	.9943	.0057	2.98	.4986	.9986	.0014
2.54	.4945	.9945	.0055	2.99	.4986	.9986	.0014
2.55	.4946	.9946	.0054	3.00	.4987	.9987	.0013
2.56	.4948	.9948	.0052	3.01	.4987	.9987	.0013
2.57	.4949	.9949	.0051	3.02	.4987	.9987	.0013
2.58	.4951	.9951	.0049	3.03	.4988	.9988	.0012
2.59	.4952	.9952	.0048	3.04	.4988	.9988	.0012
2.60	.4953	.9953	.0047	3.05	.4989	.9989	.0011
2.61	.4955	.9955	.0045	3.06	.4989	.9989	.0011
2.62	.4956	.9956	.0044	3.07	.4989	.9989	.0011
2.63	.4957	.9957	.0043	3.08	.4990	.9990	.0010
2.64	.4959	.9959	.0041	3.09	.4990	.9990	.0010
2.65	.4960	.9960	.0040	3.10	.4990	.9990	.0010
2.66	.4961	.9961	.0039	3.11	.4991	.9991	.0009
2.67	.4962	.9962	.0038	3.12	.4991	.9991	.0009
2.68	.4963	.9963	.0037	3.13	.4991	.9991	.0009
2.69	.4964	.9964	.0036	3.14	.4992	.9992	.0008
2.70	.4965	.9965	.0035	3.15	.4992	.9992	.0008
2.71	.4966	.9966	.0034	3.16	.4992	.9992	.0008
2.72	.4967	.9967	.0033	3.17	.4992	.9992	.0008
2.73	.4968	.9968	.0032	3.18	.4993	.9993	.0007
2.74	.4969	.9969	.0031	3.19	.4993	.9993	.0007
2.75	.4970	.9970	.0030	3.20	.4993	.9993	.0007
2.76	.4971	.9971	.0029	3.21	.4993	.9993	.0007
2.77	.4972	.9972	.0028	3.22	.4994	.9994	.0006
2.78	.4973	.9973	.0027	3.23	.4994	.9994	.0006
2.79	.4974	.9974	.0026	3.24	.4994	.9994	.0006
2.80	.4974	.9974	.0026	3.30	.4995	.9995	.0005
2.81	.4975	.9975	.0025	3.40	.4997	.9997	.0003
2.82	.4976	.9976	.0024	3.50	.4998	.9998	.0002
2.83	.4977	.9977	.0023	3.60	.4998	.9998	.0002
2.84	.4977	.9977	.0023	3.70	.4999	.9999	.0001

Table C ◆ Critical values of t[a]

For any given df, the table shows the values of t corresponding to various levels of probability. Obtained t is significant at a given level if it is equal to or *greater than* the value shown in the table.

df	Level of significance for one-tailed test					
	.10	.05	.025	.01	.005	.0005
	Level of significance for two-tailed test					
	.20	.10	.05	.02	.01	.001
1	3.078	6.314	12.706	31.821	63.657	636.619
2	1.886	2.920	4.303	6.965	9.925	31.598
3	1.638	2.353	3.182	4.541	5.841	12.941
4	1.533	2.132	2.776	3.747	4.604	8.610
5	1.476	2.015	2.571	3.365	4.032	6.859
6	1.440	1.943	2.447	3.143	3.707	5.959
7	1.415	1.895	2.365	2.998	3.499	5.405
8	1.397	1.860	2.306	2.896	3.355	5.041
9	1.383	1.833	2.262	2.821	3.250	4.781
10	1.372	1.812	2.228	2.764	3.169	4.587
11	1.363	1.796	2.201	2.718	3.106	4.437
12	1.356	1.782	2.179	2.681	3.055	4.318
13	1.350	1.771	2.160	2.650	3.012	4.221
14	1.345	1.761	2.145	2.624	2.977	4.140
15	1.341	1.753	2.131	2.602	2.947	4.073
16	1.337	1.746	2.120	2.583	2.921	4.015
17	1.333	1.740	2.110	2.567	2.898	3.965
18	1.330	1.734	2.101	2.552	2.878	3.922
19	1.328	1.729	2.093	2.539	2.861	3.883
20	1.325	1.725	2.086	2.528	2.845	3.850
21	1.323	1.721	2.080	2.518	2.831	3.819
22	1.321	1.717	2.074	2.508	2.819	3.792
23	1.319	1.714	2.069	2.500	2.807	3.767
24	1.318	1.711	2.064	2.492	2.797	3.745
25	1.316	1.708	2.060	2.485	2.787	3.725
26	1.315	1.706	2.056	2.479	2.779	3.707
27	1.314	1.703	2.052	2.473	2.771	3.690
28	1.313	1.701	2.048	2.467	2.763	3.674
29	1.311	1.699	2.045	2.462	2.756	3.659
30	1.310	1.697	2.042	2.457	2.750	3.646
40	1.303	1.684	2.021	2.423	2.704	3.551
60	1.296	1.671	2.000	2.390	2.660	3.460
120	1.289	1.658	1.980	2.358	2.617	3.373
∞	1.282	1.645	1.960	2.326	2.576	3.291

[a]Table C is taken from Table III of Fisher and Yates, *Statistical tables for biological, agricultural and medical research*, published by Longman Group Ltd., London (previously published by Oliver and Boyd, Edinburgh), and by permission of the authors and publishers.

Table D ♦ Critical values of χ^{2a} (Continued)

ν \ Q	0.995	0.990	0.975	0.950	0.900	0.750	0.500
1	392704.10^{-10}	157088.10^{-9}	982069.10^{-9}	393214.10^{-8}	0.0157908	0.1015308	0.454937
2	0.0100251	0.0201007	0.0506356	0.102587	0.210720	0.575364	1.38629
3	0.0717212	0.114832	0.215795	0.351846	0.584375	1.212534	2.36597
4	0.206990	0.297110	0.484419	0.710721	1.063623	1.92255	3.35670
5	0.411740	0.554300	0.831211	1.145476	1.61031	2.67460	4.35146
6	0.675727	0.872085	1.237347	1.63539	2.20413	3.45460	5.34812
7	0.989265	1.239043	1.68987	2.16735	2.83311	4.25485	6.34581
8	1.344419	1.646482	2.17973	2.73264	3.48954	5.07064	7.34412
9	1.734926	2.087912	2.70039	3.32511	4.16816	5.89883	8.34283
10	2.15585	2.55821	3.24697	3.94030	4.86518	6.73720	9.34182
11	2.60321	3.05347	3.81575	4.57481	5.57779	7.58412	10.3410
12	3.07382	3.57056	4.40379	5.22603	6.30380	8.43842	11.3403
13	3.56503	4.10691	5.00874	5.89186	7.04150	9.29906	12.3398
14	4.07468	4.66043	5.62872	6.57063	7.78953	10.1653	13.3393
15	4.60094	5.22935	6.26214	7.26094	8.54675	11.0365	14.3389
16	5.14224	5.81221	6.90766	7.96164	9.31223	11.9122	15.3385
17	5.69724	6.40776	7.56418	8.67176	10.0852	12.7919	16.3381
18	6.26481	7.01491	8.23075	9.39046	10.8649	13.6753	17.3379
19	6.84398	7.63273	8.90655	10.1170	11.6509	14.5620	18.3376
20	7.43386	8.26040	9.59083	10.8508	12.4426	15.4518	19.3374
21	8.03366	8.89720	10.28293	11.5913	13.2396	16.3444	20.3372
22	8.64272	9.54249	10.9823	12.3380	14.0415	17.2396	21.3370
23	9.26042	10.19567	11.6885	13.0905	14.8479	18.1373	22.3369
24	9.88623	10.8564	12.4011	13.8484	15.6587	19.0372	23.3367
25	10.5197	11.5240	13.1197	14.6114	16.4734	19.9393	24.3366
26	11.1603	12.1981	13.8439	15.3791	17.2919	20.8434	25.3364
27	11.8076	12.8786	14.5733	16.1513	18.1138	21.7494	26.3363
28	12.4613	13.5648	15.3079	16.9279	18.9392	22.6572	27.3363
29	13.1211	14.2565	16.0471	17.7083	19.7677	23.5666	28.3362
30	13.7867	14.9535	16.7908	18.4926	20.5992	24.4776	29.3360
40	20.7065	22.1643	24.4331	26.5093	29.0505	33.6603	39.3354
50	27.9907	29.7067	32.3574	34.7642	37.6886	42.9421	49.3349
60	35.5346	37.4848	40.4817	43.1879	46.4589	52.2938	59.3347
70	43.2752	45.4418	48.7576	51.7393	55.3290	61.6983	69.3344
80	51.1720	53.5400	57.1532	60.3915	64.2778	71.1445	79.3343
90	59.1963	61.7541	65.6466	69.1260	73.2912	80.6247	89.3342
100	67.3276	70.0648	74.2219	77.9295	82.3581	90.1332	99.3341
z_Q	−2.5758	−2.3263	−1.9600	−1.6449	−1.2816	−0.6745	0.0000

Table D ♦ (Continued)

ν \ Q	0.250	0.100	0.050	0.025	0.010	0.005	0.001
1	1.32330	2.70554	3.84146	5.02389	6.63490	7.87944	10.828
2	2.77259	4.60517	5.99147	7.37776	9.21034	10.5966	13.816
3	4.10835	6.25139	7.81473	9.34840	11.3449	12.8381	16.266
4	5.38527	7.77944	9.48773	11.1433	13.2767	14.8602	18.467
5	6.62568	9.23635	11.0705	12.8325	15.0863	16.7496	20.515
6	7.84080	10.6446	12.5916	14.4494	16.8119	18.5476	22.458
7	9.03715	12.0170	14.0671	16.0128	18.4753	20.2777	24.322
8	10.2188	13.3616	15.5073	17.5346	20.0902	21.9550	26.125
9	11.3887	14.6837	16.9190	19.0228	21.6660	23.5893	27.877
10	12.5489	15.9871	18.3070	20.4831	23.2093	25.1882	29.588
11	13.7007	17.2750	19.6751	21.9200	24.7250	26.7569	31.264
12	14.8454	18.5494	21.0261	23.3367	26.2170	28.2995	32.909
13	15.9839	19.8119	22.3621	24.7356	27.6883	29.8194	34.528
14	17.1170	21.0642	23.6848	26.1190	29.1413	31.3193	36.123
15	18.2451	22.3072	24.9958	27.4884	30.5779	32.8013	37.697
16	19.3688	23.5418	26.2962	28.8454	31.9999	34.2672	39.252
17	20.4887	24.7690	27.5871	30.1910	33.4087	35.7185	40.790
18	21.6049	25.9894	28.8693	31.5264	34.8053	37.1564	42.312
19	22.7178	27.2036	30.1435	32.8523	36.1908	38.5822	43.820
20	23.8277	28.4120	31.4104	34.1696	37.5662	39.9968	45.315
21	24.9348	29.6151	32.6705	35.4789	38.9321	41.4010	46.797
22	26.0393	30.8133	33.9244	36.7807	40.2894	42.7956	48.268
23	27.1413	32.0069	35.1725	38.0757	41.6384	44.1813	49.728
24	28.2412	33.1963	36.4151	39.3641	42.9798	45.5585	51.179
25	29.3389	34.3816	37.6525	40.6465	44.3141	46.9278	52.620
26	30.4345	35.5631	38.8852	41.9232	45.6417	48.2899	54.052
27	31.5284	36.7412	40.1133	43.1944	46.9630	49.6449	55.476
28	32.6205	37.9159	41.3372	44.4607	48.2782	50.9933	56.892
29	33.7109	39.0875	42.5569	45.7222	49.5879	52.3356	58.302
30	34.7998	40.2560	43.7729	46.9792	50.8922	53.6720	59.703
40	45.6160	51.8050	55.7585	59.3417	63.6907	66.7659	73.402
50	56.3336	63.1671	67.5048	71.4202	76.1539	79.4900	86.661
60	66.9814	74.3970	79.0819	83.2976	88.3794	91.9517	99.607
70	77.5766	85.5271	90.5312	95.0231	100.425	104.215	112.317
80	88.1303	96.5782	101.879	106.629	112.329	116.321	124.839
90	98.6499	107.565	113.145	118.136	124.116	128.299	137.208
100	109.141	118.498	124.342	129.561	135.807	140.169	149.449
z_Q	+0.6745	+1.2816	+1.6449	+1.9600	+2.3263	+2.5758	+3.0902

[a]Table 8 of the *Biometrika Tables for Statisticians,* Vol. 1 (3 ed.), edited by E. S. Pearson and H. O. Hartley. Reproduced here with the kind permission of E. S. Pearson and the trustees of *Biometrika.*

Table E ♦ 5% (upper values) and 1% (lower values) points for the distribution of F [a]

Degrees of Freedom in Numerator of F (df_1)

Degrees of Freedom in Denominator of F (df_2)

df_2	1	2	3	4	5	6	7	8	9	10	11	12	14	16	20	24	30	40	50	75	100	200	500	∞
1	161	200	216	225	230	234	237	239	241	242	243	244	245	246	248	249	250	251	252	253	253	254	254	254
	4052	4999	5403	5625	5764	5859	5928	5981	6022	6056	6082	6106	6142	6169	6208	6234	6258	6286	6302	6323	6334	6352	6361	6366
2	18.51	19.00	19.16	19.25	19.30	19.33	19.36	19.37	19.38	19.39	19.40	19.41	19.42	19.43	19.44	19.45	19.46	19.47	19.47	19.48	19.49	19.49	19.50	19.50
	98.49	99.01	99.17	99.25	99.30	99.33	99.34	99.36	99.38	99.40	99.41	99.42	99.43	99.44	99.45	99.46	99.47	99.48	99.48	99.49	99.49	99.49	99.50	99.50
3	10.13	9.55	9.28	9.12	9.01	8.94	8.88	8.84	8.81	8.78	8.76	8.74	8.71	8.69	8.66	8.64	8.62	8.60	8.58	8.57	8.56	8.54	8.54	8.53
	34.12	30.81	29.46	28.71	28.24	27.91	27.67	27.49	27.34	27.23	27.13	27.05	26.92	26.83	26.69	26.60	26.50	26.41	26.30	26.27	26.23	26.18	26.14	26.12
4	7.71	6.94	6.59	6.39	6.26	6.16	6.09	6.04	6.00	5.96	5.93	5.91	5.87	5.84	5.80	5.77	5.74	5.71	5.70	5.68	5.66	5.65	5.64	5.63
	21.20	18.00	16.69	15.98	15.52	15.21	14.98	14.80	14.66	14.54	14.45	14.37	14.24	14.15	14.02	13.93	13.83	13.74	13.69	13.61	13.57	13.52	13.48	13.46
5	6.61	5.79	5.41	5.19	5.05	4.95	4.88	4.82	4.78	4.74	4.70	4.68	4.64	4.60	4.56	4.53	4.50	4.46	4.44	4.42	4.40	4.38	4.37	4.36
	16.26	13.27	12.06	11.39	10.97	10.67	10.45	10.27	10.15	10.05	9.96	9.89	9.77	9.68	9.55	9.47	9.38	9.29	9.24	9.17	9.13	9.07	9.04	9.02
6	5.99	5.14	4.76	4.53	4.39	4.28	4.21	4.15	4.10	4.06	4.03	4.00	3.96	3.92	3.87	3.84	3.81	3.77	3.75	3.72	3.71	3.69	3.68	3.67
	13.74	10.92	9.78	9.15	8.75	8.47	8.26	8.10	7.98	7.87	7.79	7.72	7.60	7.52	7.39	7.31	7.23	7.14	7.09	7.02	6.99	6.94	6.90	6.88
7	5.59	4.74	4.35	4.12	3.97	3.87	3.79	3.73	3.68	3.63	3.60	3.57	3.52	3.49	3.44	3.41	3.38	3.34	3.32	3.29	3.28	3.25	3.24	3.23
	12.25	9.55	8.45	7.85	7.46	7.19	7.00	6.84	6.71	6.62	6.54	6.47	6.35	6.27	6.15	6.07	5.98	5.90	5.85	5.78	5.75	5.70	5.67	5.65
8	5.32	4.46	4.07	3.84	3.69	3.58	3.50	3.44	3.39	3.34	3.31	3.28	3.23	3.20	3.15	3.12	3.08	3.05	3.03	3.00	2.98	2.96	2.94	2.93
	11.26	8.65	7.59	7.01	6.63	6.37	6.19	6.03	5.91	5.82	5.74	5.67	5.56	5.48	5.36	5.28	5.20	5.11	5.06	5.00	4.96	4.91	4.88	4.86
9	5.12	4.26	3.86	3.63	3.48	3.37	3.29	3.23	3.18	3.13	3.10	3.07	3.02	2.98	2.93	2.90	2.86	2.82	2.80	2.77	2.76	2.73	2.72	2.71
	10.56	8.02	6.99	6.42	6.06	5.80	5.62	5.47	5.35	5.26	5.18	5.11	5.00	4.92	4.80	4.73	4.64	4.56	4.51	4.45	4.41	4.36	4.33	4.31
10	4.96	4.10	3.71	3.48	3.33	3.22	3.14	3.07	3.02	2.97	2.94	2.91	2.86	2.82	2.77	2.74	2.70	2.67	2.64	2.61	2.59	2.56	2.55	2.54
	10.04	7.56	6.55	5.99	5.64	5.39	5.21	5.06	4.95	4.85	4.78	4.71	4.60	4.52	4.41	4.33	4.25	4.17	4.12	4.05	4.01	3.96	3.93	3.91
11	4.84	3.98	3.59	3.36	3.20	3.09	3.01	2.95	2.90	2.86	2.82	2.79	2.74	2.70	2.65	2.61	2.57	2.53	2.50	2.47	2.45	2.42	2.41	2.40
	9.65	7.20	6.22	5.67	5.32	5.07	4.88	4.74	4.63	4.54	4.46	4.40	4.29	4.21	4.10	4.02	3.94	3.86	3.80	3.74	3.70	3.66	3.62	3.60
12	4.75	3.88	3.49	3.26	3.11	3.00	2.92	2.85	2.80	2.76	2.72	2.69	2.64	2.60	2.54	2.50	2.46	2.42	2.40	2.36	2.35	2.32	2.31	2.30
	9.33	6.93	5.95	5.41	5.06	4.82	4.65	4.50	4.39	4.30	4.22	4.16	4.05	3.98	3.86	3.78	3.70	3.61	3.56	3.49	3.46	3.41	3.38	3.36
13	4.67	3.80	3.41	3.18	3.02	2.92	2.84	2.77	2.72	2.67	2.63	2.60	2.55	2.51	2.46	2.42	2.38	2.34	2.32	2.28	2.26	2.24	2.22	2.21
	9.07	6.70	5.74	5.20	4.86	4.62	4.44	4.30	4.19	4.10	4.02	3.96	3.85	3.78	3.67	3.59	3.51	3.42	3.37	3.30	3.27	3.21	3.18	3.16
14	4.60	3.74	3.34	3.11	2.96	2.85	2.77	2.70	2.65	2.60	2.56	2.53	2.48	2.44	2.39	2.35	2.31	2.27	2.24	2.21	2.19	2.16	2.14	2.13
	8.86	6.51	5.56	5.03	4.69	4.46	4.28	4.14	4.03	3.94	3.86	3.80	3.70	3.62	3.51	3.43	3.34	3.26	3.21	3.14	3.11	3.06	3.02	3.00
15	4.54	3.68	3.29	3.06	2.90	2.79	2.70	2.64	2.59	2.55	2.51	2.48	2.43	2.39	2.33	2.29	2.25	2.21	2.18	2.15	2.12	2.10	2.08	2.07
	8.68	6.36	5.42	4.89	4.56	4.32	4.14	4.00	3.89	3.80	3.73	3.67	3.56	3.48	3.36	3.29	3.20	3.12	3.07	3.00	2.97	2.92	2.89	2.87

Table E ♦ (Continued)

Degrees of Freedom in Numerator of F (df_1)

Degrees of Freedom in Denominator of F (df_2)

df_2	1	2	3	4	5	6	7	8	9	10	11	12	14	16	20	24	30	40	50	75	100	200	500	∞
16	4.49	3.63	3.24	3.01	2.85	2.74	2.66	2.59	2.54	2.49	2.45	2.42	2.37	2.33	2.28	2.24	2.20	2.16	2.13	2.09	2.07	2.04	2.02	2.01
	8.53	6.23	5.29	4.77	4.44	4.20	4.03	3.89	3.78	3.69	3.61	3.55	3.45	3.37	3.25	3.18	3.10	3.01	2.96	2.89	2.86	2.80	2.77	2.75
17	4.45	3.59	3.20	2.96	2.81	2.70	2.62	2.55	2.50	2.45	2.41	2.38	2.33	2.29	2.23	2.19	2.15	2.11	2.08	2.04	2.02	1.99	1.97	1.96
	8.40	6.11	5.18	4.67	4.34	4.10	3.93	3.79	3.68	3.59	3.52	3.45	3.35	3.27	3.16	3.08	3.00	2.92	2.86	2.79	2.76	2.70	2.67	2.65
18	4.41	3.55	3.16	2.93	2.77	2.66	2.58	2.51	2.46	2.41	2.37	2.34	2.29	2.25	2.19	2.15	2.11	2.07	2.04	2.00	1.98	1.95	1.93	1.92
	8.28	6.01	5.09	4.58	4.25	4.01	3.85	3.71	3.60	3.51	3.44	3.37	3.27	3.19	3.07	3.00	2.91	2.83	2.78	2.71	2.68	2.62	2.59	2.57
19	4.38	3.52	3.13	2.90	2.74	2.63	2.55	2.48	2.43	2.38	2.34	2.31	2.26	2.21	2.15	2.11	2.07	2.02	2.00	1.96	1.94	1.91	1.90	1.88
	8.18	5.93	5.01	4.50	4.17	3.94	3.77	3.63	3.52	3.43	3.36	3.30	3.19	3.12	3.00	2.92	2.84	2.76	2.70	2.63	2.60	2.54	2.51	2.49
20	4.35	3.49	3.10	2.87	2.71	2.60	2.52	2.45	2.40	2.35	2.31	2.28	2.23	2.18	2.12	2.08	2.04	1.99	1.96	1.92	1.90	1.87	1.85	1.84
	8.10	5.85	4.94	4.43	4.10	3.87	3.71	3.56	3.45	3.37	3.30	3.23	3.13	3.05	2.94	2.86	2.77	2.69	2.63	2.56	2.53	2.47	2.44	2.42
21	4.32	3.47	3.07	2.84	2.68	2.57	2.49	2.42	2.37	2.32	2.28	2.25	2.20	2.15	2.09	2.05	2.00	1.96	1.93	1.80	1.87	1.84	1.82	1.81
	8.02	5.78	4.87	4.37	4.04	3.81	3.65	3.51	3.40	3.31	3.24	3.17	3.07	2.99	2.88	2.80	2.72	2.63	2.58	2.51	2.47	2.42	2.38	2.36
22	4.30	3.44	3.05	2.82	2.66	2.55	2.47	2.40	2.35	2.30	2.26	2.23	2.18	2.13	2.07	2.03	1.98	1.93	1.91	1.87	1.84	1.81	1.80	1.78
	7.94	5.72	4.82	4.31	3.99	3.76	3.59	3.45	3.35	3.26	3.18	3.12	3.02	2.94	2.83	2.75	2.67	2.58	2.53	2.46	2.42	2.37	2.33	2.31
23	4.28	3.42	3.03	2.80	2.64	2.53	2.45	2.38	2.32	2.28	2.24	2.20	2.14	2.10	2.04	2.00	1.96	1.91	1.88	1.84	1.82	1.79	1.77	1.76
	7.88	5.66	4.76	4.26	3.94	3.71	3.54	3.41	3.30	3.21	3.14	3.07	2.97	2.89	2.78	2.70	2.62	2.53	2.48	2.41	2.37	2.32	2.28	2.26
24	4.26	3.40	3.01	2.78	2.62	2.51	2.43	2.36	2.30	2.26	2.22	2.18	2.13	2.09	2.02	1.98	1.94	1.89	1.86	1.82	1.80	1.76	1.74	1.73
	7.82	5.61	4.72	4.22	3.90	3.67	3.50	3.36	3.25	3.17	3.09	3.03	2.93	2.85	2.74	2.66	2.58	2.49	2.44	2.36	2.33	2.27	2.23	2.21
25	4.24	3.38	2.99	2.76	2.60	2.49	2.41	2.34	2.28	2.24	2.20	2.16	2.11	2.06	2.00	1.96	1.92	1.87	1.84	1.80	1.77	1.74	1.72	1.71
	7.77	5.57	4.68	4.18	3.86	3.63	3.46	3.32	3.21	3.13	3.05	2.99	2.89	2.81	2.70	2.62	2.54	2.45	2.40	2.32	2.29	2.23	2.19	2.17
26	4.22	3.37	2.89	2.74	2.59	2.47	2.39	2.32	2.27	2.22	2.18	2.15	2.10	2.05	1.99	1.95	1.90	1.85	1.82	1.78	1.76	1.72	1.70	1.69
	7.72	5.53	4.64	4.14	3.82	3.59	3.42	3.29	3.17	3.09	3.02	2.96	2.86	2.77	2.66	2.58	2.50	2.41	2.36	2.28	2.25	2.19	2.15	2.13
27	4.21	3.35	2.96	2.73	2.57	2.46	2.37	2.30	2.25	2.20	2.16	2.13	2.08	2.03	1.97	1.93	1.88	1.84	1.80	1.76	1.74	1.71	1.68	1.67
	7.68	5.49	4.60	4.11	3.79	3.56	3.39	3.26	3.14	3.06	2.98	2.93	2.83	2.74	2.63	2.55	2.47	2.38	2.33	2.25	2.21	2.16	2.12	2.10
28	4.20	3.34	2.95	2.71	2.56	2.44	2.36	2.29	3.24	2.19	2.15	2.12	2.06	2.02	1.96	1.91	1.87	1.81	1.78	1.75	1.72	1.69	1.67	1.65
	7.64	5.45	4.57	4.07	3.76	3.53	3.36	3.23	3.11	3.03	2.95	2.90	2.80	2.71	2.60	2.52	2.44	2.35	2.30	2.22	2.18	2.13	2.09	2.06
29	4.18	3.33	2.93	2.70	2.54	2.43	2.35	2.28	2.22	2.18	2.14	2.10	2.05	2.00	1.94	1.90	1.85	1.80	1.77	1.73	1.71	1.68	1.65	1.64
	7.60	5.52	4.54	4.04	3.73	3.50	3.32	3.20	3.08	3.00	2.92	2.87	2.77	2.68	2.57	2.49	2.41	2.32	2.27	2.19	2.15	2.10	2.06	2.03
30	4.17	3.32	2.92	2.69	2.53	2.42	2.34	2.27	2.21	2.16	2.12	2.09	2.04	1.99	1.93	1.89	1.84	1.79	1.76	1.72	1.69	1.66	1.64	1.62
	7.56	5.39	4.51	4.02	3.70	3.47	3.30	3.17	3.06	2.98	2.90	2.84	2.74	2.66	2.55	2.47	2.38	2.29	2.24	2.16	2.13	2.07	2.03	2.01

Degrees of Freedom in Numerator of F (df_1)

Degrees of Freedom in Denominator of F (df_2)

df_2	1	2	3	4	5	6	7	8	9	10	11	12	14	16	20	24	30	40	50	75	100	200	500	∞
32	4.15	3.30	2.90	2.67	2.51	2.40	2.32	2.25	2.19	2.14	2.10	2.07	2.02	1.97	1.91	1.86	1.82	1.76	1.74	1.69	1.67	1.64	1.61	1.59
	7.50	5.34	4.46	3.97	3.66	3.42	3.25	3.12	3.01	2.94	2.86	2.80	2.70	2.62	2.51	2.42	2.34	2.25	2.20	2.12	2.08	2.02	1.98	1.96
34	4.13	3.28	2.88	2.65	2.49	2.38	2.30	2.23	2.17	2.12	2.08	2.05	2.00	1.95	1.89	1.84	1.80	1.74	1.71	1.67	1.64	1.61	1.59	1.57
	7.44	5.29	4.42	3.93	3.61	3.38	3.21	3.08	2.97	2.89	2.82	2.76	2.66	2.58	2.47	2.38	2.30	2.21	2.15	2.08	2.04	1.98	1.94	1.91
36	4.11	3.26	2.86	2.63	2.48	2.36	2.28	2.21	2.15	2.10	2.06	2.03	1.98	1.93	1.87	1.82	1.78	1.72	1.69	1.65	1.62	1.59	1.56	1.55
	7.39	5.25	4.38	3.89	3.58	3.35	3.18	3.04	2.94	2.86	2.78	2.72	2.62	2.54	2.43	2.35	2.26	2.17	2.12	2.04	2.00	1.94	1.90	1.87
38	4.10	3.25	2.85	2.62	2.46	2.35	2.26	2.19	2.14	2.09	2.05	2.02	1.96	1.92	1.85	1.80	1.76	1.71	1.67	1.63	1.60	1.57	1.54	1.53
	7.35	5.21	4.34	3.86	3.54	3.32	3.15	3.02	2.91	2.82	2.75	2.69	2.59	2.51	2.40	2.32	2.22	2.14	2.08	2.00	1.97	1.90	1.86	1.84
40	4.08	3.23	2.84	2.61	2.45	2.34	2.25	2.18	2.12	2.07	2.04	2.00	1.95	1.90	1.84	1.79	1.74	1.69	1.66	1.61	1.59	1.55	1.53	1.51
	7.31	5.18	4.31	3.83	3.51	3.29	3.12	2.99	2.88	2.80	2.73	2.66	2.56	2.49	2.37	2.29	2.20	2.11	2.05	1.97	1.94	1.88	1.84	1.81
42	4.07	3.22	2.83	2.59	2.44	2.32	2.24	2.17	2.11	2.06	2.02	1.99	1.94	1.89	1.82	1.78	1.73	1.68	1.64	1.60	1.57	1.54	1.51	1.49
	7.27	5.15	4.29	3.80	3.49	3.26	3.10	2.96	2.86	2.77	2.70	2.64	2.54	2.46	2.35	2.26	2.17	2.08	2.02	1.94	1.91	1.85	1.80	1.78
44	4.06	3.21	2.82	2.58	2.43	2.31	2.23	2.16	2.10	2.05	2.01	1.98	1.92	1.88	1.81	1.76	1.72	1.66	1.63	1.58	1.56	1.52	1.50	1.48
	7.24	5.12	4.26	3.78	3.46	3.24	3.07	2.94	2.84	2.75	2.68	2.62	2.52	2.44	2.32	2.24	2.15	2.06	2.00	1.92	1.88	1.82	1.78	1.75
46	4.05	3.20	2.81	2.57	2.42	2.30	2.22	2.14	2.09	2.04	2.00	1.97	1.91	1.87	1.80	1.75	1.71	1.65	1.62	1.57	1.54	1.51	1.48	1.46
	7.21	5.10	4.24	3.76	3.44	3.22	3.05	2.92	2.82	2.73	2.66	2.60	2.50	2.42	2.30	2.22	2.13	2.04	1.98	1.90	1.86	1.80	1.76	1.72
48	4.04	3.19	2.80	2.56	2.41	2.30	2.21	2.14	2.08	2.03	1.99	1.96	1.90	1.86	1.79	1.74	1.70	1.64	1.61	1.56	1.53	1.50	1.47	1.45
	7.19	5.08	4.22	3.74	3.42	3.20	3.04	2.90	2.80	2.71	2.64	2.58	2.48	2.40	2.28	2.20	2.11	2.02	1.96	1.88	1.84	1.78	1.73	1.70
50	4.03	3.18	2.79	2.56	2.40	2.29	2.20	2.13	2.07	2.02	1.98	1.95	1.90	1.85	1.78	1.74	1.69	1.63	1.60	1.55	1.52	1.48	1.46	1.44
	7.17	5.06	4.20	3.72	3.41	3.18	3.02	2.88	2.78	2.70	2.62	2.56	2.46	2.39	2.26	2.18	2.10	2.00	1.94	1.86	1.82	1.76	1.71	1.68
55	4.02	3.17	2.78	2.54	2.38	2.27	2.18	2.11	2.05	2.00	1.97	1.93	1.88	1.83	1.76	1.72	1.67	1.61	1.58	1.52	1.50	1.46	1.43	1.41
	7.12	5.01	4.16	3.68	3.37	3.15	2.98	2.85	2.75	2.66	2.59	2.53	2.43	2.35	2.23	2.15	2.06	1.96	1.90	1.82	1.78	1.71	1.66	1.64
60	4.00	3.15	2.76	2.52	2.37	2.25	2.17	2.10	2.04	1.99	1.95	1.92	1.86	1.81	1.75	1.70	1.65	1.59	1.56	1.50	1.48	1.44	1.41	1.39
	7.08	4.98	4.13	3.65	3.34	3.12	2.95	2.82	2.72	2.63	2.56	2.50	2.40	2.32	2.20	2.12	2.03	1.93	1.87	1.79	1.74	1.68	1.63	1.60
65	3.99	3.14	2.75	2.51	2.36	2.24	2.15	2.08	2.02	1.98	1.94	1.90	1.85	1.80	1.73	1.68	1.63	1.57	1.54	1.49	1.46	1.42	1.39	1.37
	7.04	4.95	4.10	3.62	3.31	3.09	2.93	2.79	2.70	2.61	2.54	2.47	2.37	2.30	2.18	2.09	2.00	1.90	1.84	1.76	1.71	1.64	1.60	1.56
70	3.98	3.13	2.74	2.50	2.35	2.23	2.14	2.07	2.01	1.97	1.93	1.89	1.84	1.79	1.72	1.67	1.62	1.56	1.53	1.47	1.45	1.40	1.37	1.35
	7.01	4.92	4.08	3.60	3.29	3.07	2.91	2.77	2.67	2.59	2.51	2.45	2.35	2.28	2.15	2.07	1.98	1.88	1.82	1.74	1.69	1.62	1.56	1.53
80	3.96	3.11	2.72	2.48	2.33	2.21	2.12	2.05	1.99	1.95	1.91	1.88	1.82	1.77	1.70	1.65	1.60	1.54	1.51	1.45	1.42	1.38	1.35	1.32
	6.96	4.88	4.04	3.56	3.25	3.04	2.87	2.74	2.64	2.55	2.48	2.41	2.32	2.24	2.11	2.03	1.94	1.84	1.78	1.70	1.65	1.57	1.52	1.49

Table E ♦ (Continued)

Degrees of Freedom in Numerator of F (df_1)

df_2	1	2	3	4	5	6	7	8	9	10	11	12	14	16	20	24	30	40	50	75	100	200	500	∞
100	3.94	3.09	2.70	2.46	2.30	2.19	2.10	2.03	1.97	1.92	1.88	1.85	1.79	1.75	1.68	1.63	1.57	1.51	1.48	1.42	1.39	1.34	1.30	1.28
	6.90	4.82	3.98	3.51	3.20	2.99	2.82	2.69	2.59	2.51	2.43	2.36	2.26	2.19	2.06	1.98	1.89	1.79	1.73	1.64	1.59	1.51	1.46	1.43
125	3.92	3.07	2.68	2.44	2.29	2.17	2.08	2.01	1.95	1.90	1.86	1.83	1.77	1.72	1.65	1.60	1.55	1.49	1.45	1.39	1.36	1.31	1.27	1.25
	6.84	4.78	3.94	3.47	3.17	2.95	2.79	2.65	2.56	2.47	2.40	2.33	2.23	2.15	2.03	1.94	1.85	1.75	1.68	1.59	1.54	1.46	1.40	1.37
150	3.91	3.06	2.67	2.43	2.27	2.16	2.07	2.00	1.94	1.89	1.85	1.82	1.76	1.71	1.64	1.59	1.54	1.47	1.44	1.37	1.34	1.29	1.25	1.22
	6.81	4.75	3.91	3.44	3.13	2.92	2.76	2.62	2.53	2.44	2.37	2.30	2.20	2.12	2.00	1.91	1.83	1.72	1.66	1.56	1.51	1.43	1.37	1.33
200	3.89	3.04	2.65	2.41	2.26	2.14	2.05	1.98	1.92	1.87	1.83	1.80	1.74	1.69	1.62	1.57	1.52	1.45	1.42	1.35	1.32	1.26	1.22	1.19
	6.76	4.71	3.38	3.41	3.11	2.90	2.73	2.60	2.50	2.41	2.34	2.28	1.17	2.09	1.97	1.88	1.79	1.69	1.62	1.53	1.48	1.39	1.33	1.28
400	3.86	3.02	2.62	2.39	2.23	2.12	2.03	1.96	1.90	1.85	1.81	1.78	1.72	1.67	1.60	1.54	1.49	1.42	1.38	1.32	1.28	1.22	1.16	1.13
	6.70	4.66	3.83	3.36	3.06	2.85	2.69	2.55	2.46	2.37	2.29	2.23	2.12	2.04	1.92	1.84	1.74	1.64	1.57	1.47	1.42	1.32	1.24	1.19
1000	3.85	3.00	2.61	2.38	2.22	2.10	2.02	1.95	1.89	1.84	1.80	1.76	1.70	1.65	1.58	1.53	1.47	1.41	1.36	1.30	1.26	1.19	1.13	1.08
	6.66	4.62	3.80	3.34	3.04	2.82	2.66	2.53	2.43	2.34	2.26	2.20	2.09	2.01	1.89	1.81	1.71	1.61	1.54	1.44	1.38	1.28	1.19	1.11
∞	3.84	2.99	2.60	2.37	2.21	2.09	2.01	1.94	1.88	1.83	1.79	1.75	1.69	1.64	1.57	1.52	1.46	1.40	1.35	1.28	1.24	1.17	1.11	1.00
	6.64	4.60	3.78	3.32	3.02	2.80	2.64	2.51	2.41	2.32	2.24	2.18	2.07	1.99	1.87	1.79	1.69	1.59	1.52	1.41	1.36	1.25	1.15	1.00

Degrees of Freedom in Denominator of F (df_2)

[a]Reprinted by permission from *Statistical Methods*, Sixth Edition, by George W. Snedecor and William G. Cochran, © 1967 by the Iowa State University Press, Ames, Iowa.

Table F ♦ Percentage points of the studentized range[a]

Error df	α	k = number of means or number of steps between ordered means									
		2	3	4	5	6	7	8	9	10	11
5	.05	3.64	4.60	5.22	5.67	6.03	6.33	6.58	6.80	6.99	7.17
	.01	5.70	6.98	7.80	8.42	8.91	9.32	9.67	9.97	10.24	10.48
6	.05	3.46	4.34	4.90	5.30	5.63	5.90	6.12	6.32	6.49	6.65
	.01	5.24	6.33	7.03	7.56	7.97	8.32	8.61	8.87	9.10	9.30
7	.05	3.34	4.16	4.68	5.06	5.36	5.61	5.82	6.00	6.16	6.30
	.01	4.95	5.92	6.54	7.01	7.37	7.68	7.94	8.17	8.37	8.55
8	.05	3.26	4.04	4.53	4.89	5.17	5.40	5.60	5.77	5.92	6.05
	.01	4.75	5.64	6.20	6.62	6.96	7.24	7.47	7.68	7.86	8.03
9	.05	3.20	3.95	4.41	4.76	5.02	5.24	5.43	5.59	5.74	5.87
	.01	4.60	5.43	5.96	6.35	6.66	6.91	7.13	7.33	7.49	7.65
10	.05	3.15	3.88	4.33	4.65	4.91	5.12	5.30	5.46	5.60	5.72
	.01	4.48	5.27	5.77	6.14	6.43	6.67	6.87	7.05	7.21	7.36
11	.05	3.11	3.82	4.26	4.57	4.82	5.03	5.20	5.35	5.49	5.61
	.01	4.39	5.15	5.62	5.97	6.25	6.48	6.67	6.84	6.99	7.13
12	.05	3.08	3.77	4.20	4.51	4.75	4.95	5.12	5.27	5.39	5.51
	.01	4.32	5.05	5.50	5.84	6.10	6.32	6.51	6.67	6.81	6.94
13	.05	3.06	3.73	4.15	4.45	4.69	4.88	5.05	5.19	5.32	5.43
	.01	4.26	4.96	5.40	5.73	5.98	6.19	6.37	6.53	6.67	6.79
14	.05	3.03	3.70	4.11	4.41	4.64	4.83	4.99	5.13	5.25	5.36
	.01	4.21	4.89	5.32	5.63	5.88	6.08	6.26	6.41	6.54	6.66
15	.05	3.01	3.67	4.08	4.37	4.59	4.78	4.94	5.08	5.20	5.31
	.01	4.17	4.84	5.25	5.56	5.80	5.99	6.16	6.31	6.44	6.55
16	.05	3.00	3.65	4.05	4.33	4.56	4.74	4.90	5.03	5.15	5.26
	.01	4.13	4.79	5.19	5.49	5.72	5.92	6.08	6.22	6.35	6.46
17	.05	2.98	3.63	4.02	4.30	4.52	4.70	4.86	4.99	5.11	5.21
	.01	4.10	4.74	5.14	5.43	5.66	5.85	6.01	6.15	6.27	6.38
18	.05	2.97	3.61	4.00	4.28	4.49	4.67	4.82	4.96	5.07	5.17
	.01	4.07	4.70	5.09	5.38	5.60	5.79	5.94	6.08	6.20	6.31
19	.05	2.96	3.59	3.98	4.25	4.47	4.65	4.79	4.92	5.04	5.14
	.01	4.05	4.67	5.05	5.33	5.55	5.73	5.89	6.02	6.14	6.25
20	.05	2.95	3.58	3.96	4.23	4.45	4.62	4.77	4.90	5.01	5.11
	.01	4.02	4.64	5.02	5.29	5.51	5.69	5.84	5.97	6.09	6.19
24	.05	2.92	3.53	3.90	4.17	4.37	4.54	4.68	4.81	4.92	5.01
	.01	3.96	4.55	4.91	5.17	5.37	5.54	5.69	5.81	5.92	6.02
30	.05	2.89	3.49	3.85	4.10	4.30	4.46	4.60	4.72	4.82	4.92
	.01	3.89	4.45	4.80	5.05	5.24	5.40	5.54	5.65	5.76	5.85
40	.05	2.86	3.44	3.79	4.04	4.23	4.39	4.52	4.63	4.73	4.82
	.01	3.82	4.37	4.70	4.93	5.11	5.26	5.39	5.50	5.60	5.69
60	.05	2.83	3.40	3.74	3.98	4.16	4.31	4.44	4.55	4.65	4.73
	.01	3.76	4.28	4.59	4.82	4.99	5.13	5.25	5.36	5.45	5.53
120	.05	2.80	3.36	3.68	3.92	4.10	4.24	4.36	4.47	4.56	4.64
	.01	3.70	4.20	4.50	4.71	4.87	5.01	5.12	5.21	5.30	5.37
∞	.05	2.77	3.31	3.63	3.86	4.03	4.17	4.29	4.39	4.47	4.55
	.01	3.64	4.12	4.40	4.60	4.76	4.88	4.99	5.08	5.16	5.23

Table F ♦ (Continued)

\(k = \) number of means or number of steps between ordered means										
12	13	14	15	16	17	18	19	20	α	Error df
7.32	7.47	7.60	7.72	7.83	7.93	8.03	8.12	8.21	.05	5
10.70	10.89	11.08	11.24	11.40	11.55	11.68	11.81	11.93	.01	
6.79	6.92	7.03	7.14	7.24	7.34	7.43	7.51	7.59	.05	6
9.48	9.65	9.81	9.95	10.08	10.21	10.32	10.43	10.54	.01	
6.43	6.55	6.66	6.76	6.85	6.94	7.02	7.10	7.17	.05	7
8.71	8.86	9.00	9.12	9.24	9.35	9.46	9.55	9.65	.01	
6.18	6.29	6.39	6.48	6.57	6.65	6.73	6.80	6.87	.05	8
8.18	8.31	8.44	8.55	8.66	8.76	8.85	8.94	9.03	.01	
5.98	6.09	6.19	6.28	6.36	6.44	6.51	6.58	6.64	.05	9
7.78	7.91	8.03	8.13	8.23	8.33	8.41	8.49	8.57	.01	
5.83	5.93	6.03	6.11	6.19	6.27	6.34	6.40	6.47	.05	10
7.49	7.60	7.71	7.81	7.91	7.99	8.08	8.15	8.23	.01	
5.71	5.81	5.90	5.98	6.06	6.13	6.20	6.27	6.33	.05	11
7.25	7.36	7.46	7.56	7.65	7.73	7.81	7.88	7.95	.01	
5.61	5.71	5.80	5.88	5.95	6.02	6.09	6.15	6.21	.05	12
7.06	7.17	7.26	7.36	7.44	7.52	7.59	7.66	7.73	.01	
5.53	5.63	5.71	5.79	5.86	5.93	5.99	6.05	6.11	.05	13
6.90	7.01	7.10	7.19	7.27	7.35	7.42	7.48	7.55	.01	
5.46	5.55	5.64	5.71	5.79	5.85	5.91	5.97	6.03	.05	14
6.77	6.87	6.96	7.05	7.13	7.20	7.27	7.33	7.39	.01	
5.40	5.49	5.57	5.65	5.72	5.78	5.85	5.90	5.96	.05	15
6.66	6.76	6.84	6.93	7.00	7.07	7.14	7.20	7.26	.01	
5.35	5.44	5.52	5.59	5.66	5.73	5.79	5.84	5.90	.05	16
6.56	6.66	6.74	6.82	6.90	6.97	7.03	7.09	7.15	.01	
5.31	5.39	5.47	5.54	5.61	5.67	5.73	5.79	5.84	.05	17
6.48	6.57	6.66	6.73	6.81	6.87	6.94	7.00	7.05	.01	
5.27	5.35	5.43	5.50	5.57	5.63	5.69	5.74	5.79	.05	18
6.41	6.50	6.58	6.65	6.73	6.79	6.85	6.91	6.97	.01	
5.23	5.31	5.39	5.46	5.53	5.59	5.65	5.70	5.75	.05	19
6.34	6.43	6.51	6.58	6.65	6.72	6.78	6.84	6.89	.01	
5.20	5.28	5.36	5.43	5.49	5.55	5.61	5.66	5.71	.05	20
6.28	6.37	6.45	6.52	6.59	6.65	6.71	6.77	6.82	.01	
5.10	5.18	5.25	5.32	5.38	5.44	5.49	5.55	5.59	.05	24
6.11	6.19	6.26	6.33	6.39	6.45	6.51	6.56	6.61	.01	
5.00	5.08	5.15	5.21	5.27	5.33	5.38	5.43	5.47	.05	30
5.93	6.01	6.08	6.14	6.20	6.26	6.31	6.36	6.41	.01	
4.90	4.98	5.04	5.11	5.16	5.22	5.27	5.31	5.36	.05	40
5.76	5.83	5.90	5.96	6.02	6.07	6.12	6.16	6.21	.01	
4.81	4.88	4.94	5.00	5.06	5.11	5.15	5.20	5.24	.05	60
5.60	5.67	5.73	5.78	5.84	5.89	5.93	5.97	6.01	.01	
4.71	4.78	4.84	4.90	4.95	5.00	5.04	5.09	5.13	.05	120
5.44	5.50	5.56	5.61	5.66	5.71	5.75	5.79	5.83	.01	
4.62	4.68	4.74	4.80	4.85	4.89	4.93	4.97	5.01	.05	∞
5.29	5.35	5.40	5.45	5.49	5.54	5.57	5.61	5.65	.01	

[a]This table is abridged from Table 29 in *Biometrika Tables for Statisticians*, Vol. 1, (2d ed.), New York: Cambridge, 1958. Edited by E. S. Pearson and H. O. Hartley. Reproduced with the kind permission of the editors and the trustees of *Biometrika*.

Table G ♦ Critical values of the Pearson product-moment correlation coefficient[a]

df = N−2	Level of significance for a directional (one-tailed) test				
	.05	.025	.01	.005	.0005
	Level of significance for a non-directional (two-tailed) test				
	.10	.05	.02	.01	.001
1	.9877	.9969	.9995	.9999	1.0000
2	.9000	.9500	.9800	.9900	.9990
3	.8054	.8783	.9343	.9587	.9912
4	.7293	.8114	.8822	.9172	.9741
5	.6694	.7545	.8329	.8745	.9507
6	.6215	.7067	.7887	.8343	.9249
7	.5822	.6664	.7498	.7977	.8982
8	.5494	.6319	.7155	.7646	.8721
9	.5214	.6021	.6851	.7348	.8471
10	.4973	.5760	.6581	.7079	.8233
11	.4762	.5529	.6339	.6835	.8010
12	.4575	.5324	.6120	.6614	.7800
13	.4409	.5139	.5923	.6411	.7603
14	.4259	.4973	.5742	.6226	.7420
15	.4124	.4821	.5577	.6055	.7246
16	.4000	.4683	.5425	.5897	.7084
17	.3887	.4555	.5285	.5751	.6932
18	.3783	.4438	.5155	.5614	.6787
19	.3687	.4329	.5034	.5487	.6652
20	.3598	.4227	.4921	.5368	.6524
25	.3233	.3809	.4451	.4869	.5974
30	.2960	.3494	.4093	.4487	.5541
35	.2746	.3246	.3810	.4182	.5189
40	.2573	.3044	.3578	.3932	.4896
45	.2428	.2875	.3384	.3721	.4648
50	.2306	.2732	.3218	.3541	.4433
60	.2108	.2500	.2948	.3248	.4078
70	.1954	.2319	.2737	.3017	.3799
80	.1829	.2172	.2565	.2830	.3568
90	.1726	.2050	.2422	.2673	.3375
100	.1638	.1946	.2301	.2540	.3211

[a]Source: Table G is taken from Table VII of Fisher and Yates, *Statistical Tables for Biological, Agricultural, and Medical Research*, published by Longman Group Ltd., London (previously published by Oliver and Boyd, Ltd., Edinburgh), and by permission of the authors and publishers.

If the observed value of r is *greater than or equal to* the tabulated value for the appropriate level of significance (columns) and degrees of freedom (rows), then reject H_0. The degrees of freedom are the number of pairs of scores minus two, or N − 2. The critical values in the table are both + and − for nondirectional (two-tailed) tests.

Table H ◆ Coefficients of correlation significant at the .05 level (upper values) and at the .01 (lower values) for varying degrees of freedom (two-tailed test)[a]

Degrees of freedom	Number of variables									t
	2	3	4	5	6	7	9	13	25	
1	.997	.999	.999	.999	1.000	1.000	1.000	1.000	1.000	12.706
	1.000	**1.000**	**1.000**	**1.000**	**1.000**	**1.000**	**1.000**	**1.000**	**1.000**	**63.657**
2	.950	.975	.983	.987	.990	.992	.994	.996	.998	4.303
	.990	**.995**	**.997**	**.998**	**.998**	**.998**	**.999**	**.999**	**1.000**	**9.925**
3	.878	.930	.950	.961	.968	.973	.979	.986	.993	3.182
	.959	**.976**	**.983**	**.987**	**.990**	**.991**	**.993**	**.995**	**.998**	**5.841**
4	.811	.881	.912	.930	.942	.950	.961	.973	.986	2.776
	.917	**.949**	**.962**	**.970**	**.975**	**.979**	**.984**	**.989**	**.994**	**4.604**
5	.754	.836	.874	.898	.914	.925	.941	.958	.978	2.571
	.874	**.917**	**.937**	**.949**	**.957**	**.963**	**.971**	**.980**	**.989**	**4.032**
6	.707	.795	.839	.867	.886	.900	.920	.943	.969	2.447
	.834	**.886**	**.911**	**.927**	**.938**	**.946**	**.957**	**.969**	**.983**	**3.707**
7	.666	.758	.807	.838	.860	.876	.900	.927	.960	2.365
	.798	**.855**	**.885**	**.904**	**.918**	**.928**	**.942**	**.958**	**.977**	**3.499**
8	.632	.726	.777	.811	.835	.854	.880	.912	.950	2.306
	.765	**.827**	**.860**	**.882**	**.898**	**.909**	**.926**	**.946**	**.970**	**3.355**
9	.602	.697	.750	.786	.812	.832	.861	.897	.941	2.262
	.735	**.800**	**.836**	**.861**	**.878**	**.891**	**.911**	**.934**	**.963**	**3.250**
10	.576	.671	.726	.763	.790	.812	.843	.882	.932	2.228
	.708	**.776**	**.814**	**.840**	**.859**	**.874**	**.895**	**.922**	**.955**	**3.169**
11	.553	.648	.703	.741	.770	.792	.826	.868	.922	2.201
	.684	**.753**	**.793**	**.821**	**.841**	**.857**	**.880**	**.910**	**.948**	**3.106**
12	.532	.627	.683	.722	.751	.774	.809	.854	.913	2.179
	.661	**.732**	**.773**	**.802**	**.824**	**.841**	**.866**	**.898**	**.940**	**3.055**
13	.514	.608	.664	.703	.733	.757	.794	.840	.904	2.160
	.641	**.712**	**.755**	**.785**	**.807**	**.825**	**.852**	**.886**	**.932**	**3.012**
14	.497	.590	.646	.686	.717	.741	.779	.828	.895	2.145
	.623	**.694**	**.737**	**.768**	**.792**	**.810**	**.838**	**.875**	**.924**	**2.977**
15	.482	.574	.630	.670	.701	.726	.765	.815	.886	2.131
	.606	**.677**	**.721**	**.752**	**.776**	**.796**	**.825**	**.864**	**.917**	**2.947**
16	.468	.559	.615	.655	.686	.712	.751	.803	.878	2.120
	.590	**.662**	**.706**	**.738**	**.762**	**.782**	**.813**	**.853**	**.909**	**2.921**
17	.456	.545	.601	.641	.673	.698	.738	.792	.869	2.110
	.575	**.647**	**.691**	**.724**	**.749**	**.769**	**.800**	**.842**	**.902**	**2.898**
18	.444	.532	.587	.628	.660	.686	.726	.781	.861	2.101
	.561	**.633**	**.678**	**.710**	**.736**	**.756**	**.789**	**.832**	**.894**	**2.878**
19	.433	.520	.575	.615	.647	.674	.714	.770	.853	2.093
	.549	**.620**	**.665**	**.698**	**.723**	**.744**	**.778**	**.822**	**.887**	**2.861**
20	.423	.509	.563	.604	.636	.662	.703	.760	.845	2.086
	.537	**.608**	**.652**	**.685**	**.712**	**.733**	**.767**	**.812**	**.880**	**2.845**
21	.413	.498	.552	.592	.624	.651	.693	.750	.837	2.080
	.526	**.596**	**.641**	**.674**	**.700**	**.722**	**.756**	**.803**	**.873**	**2.831**
22	.404	.488	.542	.582	.614	.640	.682	.740	.830	2.074
	.515	**.585**	**.630**	**.663**	**.690**	**.712**	**.746**	**.794**	**.866**	**2.819**
23	.396	.479	.532	.572	.604	.630	.673	.731	.823	2.069
	.505	**.574**	**.619**	**.652**	**.679**	**.701**	**.736**	**.785**	**.859**	**2.807**

Degrees of freedom	Number of variables									t
	2	3	4	5	6	7	9	13	25	
24	.388	.470	.523	.562	.594	.621	.663	.722	.815	2.064
	.496	.565	.609	.642	.669	.692	.727	.776	.852	2.797
25	.381	.462	.514	.553	.585	.612	.654	.714	.808	2.060
	.487	.555	.600	.633	.660	.682	.718	.768	.846	2.787
26	.374	.454	.506	.545	.576	.603	.645	.706	.802	2.056
	.478	.546	.590	.624	.651	.673	.709	.760	.839	2.779
27	.367	.446	.498	.536	.568	.594	.637	.698	.795	2.052
	.470	.538	.582	.615	.642	.664	.701	.752	.833	2.771
28	.361	.439	.490	.529	.560	.586	.629	.690	.788	2.048
	.463	.530	.573	.606	.634	.656	.692	.744	.827	2.763
29	.355	.432	.482	.521	.552	.579	.621	.682	.782	2.045
	.456	.522	.565	.598	.625	.648	.685	.737	.821	2.756
30	.349	.426	.476	.514	.545	.571	.614	.675	.776	2.042
	.449	.514	.558	.591	.618	.640	.677	.729	.815	2.750
35	.325	.397	.445	.482	.512	.538	.580	.642	.746	2.030
	.418	.481	.523	.556	.582	.605	.642	.696	.786	2.724
40	.304	.373	.419	.455	.484	.509	.551	.613	.720	2.021
	.393	.454	.494	.526	.552	.575	.612	.667	.761	2.704
45	.288	.353	.397	.432	.460	.485	.526	.587	.696	2.014
	.372	.430	.470	.501	.527	.549	.586	.640	.737	2.690
50	.273	.336	.379	.412	.440	.464	.504	.565	.674	2.008
	.354	.410	.449	.479	.504	.526	.562	.617	.715	2.678
60	.250	.308	.348	.380	.406	.429	.467	.526	.636	2.000
	.325	.377	.414	.442	.466	.488	.523	.577	.677	2.660
70	.233	.286	.324	.354	.379	.401	.438	.495	.604	1.994
	.302	.351	.386	.413	.436	.456	.491	.544	.644	2.648
80	.217	.269	.304	.332	.356	.377	.413	.469	.576	1.990
	.283	.330	.362	.389	.411	.431	.464	.516	.615	2.638
90	.205	.254	.288	.315	.338	.358	.392	.446	.552	1.987
	.267	.312	.343	.368	.390	.409	.441	.492	.590	2.632
100	.195	.241	.274	.300	.322	.341	.374	.426	.530	1.984
	.254	.297	.327	.351	.372	.390	.421	.470	.568	2.626
125	.174	.216	.246	.269	.290	.307	.338	.387	.485	1.979
	.228	.266	.294	.316	.335	.352	.381	.428	.521	2.616
150	.159	.198	.225	.247	.266	.282	.310	.356	.450	1.976
	.208	.244	.270	.290	.308	.324	.351	.395	.484	2.609
200	.138	.172	.196	.215	.231	.246	.271	.312	.398	1.972
	.181	.212	.234	.253	.269	.283	.307	.347	.430	2.601
300	.113	.141	.160	.176	.190	.202	.223	.258	.332	1.968
	.148	.174	.192	.208	.221	.233	.253	.287	.359	2.592
400	.098	.122	.139	.153	.165	.176	.194	.225	.291	1.966
	.128	.151	.167	.180	.192	.202	.220	.250	.315	2.588
500	.088	.109	.124	.137	.148	.157	.174	.202	.262	1.965
	.115	.135	.150	.162	.172	.182	.198	.225	.284	2.586
1,000	.062	.077	.088	.097	.105	.112	.124	.144	.188	1.962
	.081	.096	.106	.115	.122	.129	.141	.160	.204	2.581
∞										1.960
										2.576

[a] Adapted from Wallace, H. A., and Snedecor, G. W., *Correlation and machine calculation.* Ames, Iowa: Iowa State College, 1931, by courtesy of the authors.

Table I ◆ Conversion of a Pearson *r* into a Fisher *Z* coefficient[a]

r	*z*	*r*	*z*	*r*	*z*	*r*	*z*	*r*	*z*
.000	.000	.200	.203	.400	.424	.600	.693	.800	1.099
.005	.005	.205	.208	.405	.430	.605	.701	.805	1.113
.010	.010	.210	.213	.410	.436	.610	.709	.810	1.127
.015	.015	.215	.218	.415	.442	.615	.717	.815	1.142
.020	.020	.220	.224	.420	.448	.620	.725	.820	1.157
.025	.025	.225	.229	.425	.454	.625	.733	.825	1.172
.030	.030	.230	.234	.430	.460	.630	.741	.830	1.188
.035	.035	.235	.239	.435	.466	.635	.750	.835	1.204
.040	.040	.240	.245	.440	.472	.640	.758	.840	1.221
.045	.045	.245	.250	.445	.478	.645	.767	.845	1.238
.050	.050	.250	.255	.450	.485	.650	.775	.850	1.256
.055	.055	.255	.261	.455	.491	.655	.784	.855	1.274
.060	.060	.260	.266	.460	.497	.660	.793	.860	1.293
.065	.065	.265	.271	.465	.504	.665	.802	.865	1.313
.070	.070	.270	.277	.470	.510	.670	.811	.870	1.333
.075	.075	.275	.282	.475	.517	.675	.820	.875	1.354
.080	.080	.280	.288	.480	.523	.680	.829	.880	1.376
.085	.085	.285	.293	.485	.530	.685	.838	.885	1.398
.090	.090	.290	.299	.490	.536	.690	.848	.890	1.422
.095	.095	.295	.304	.495	.543	.695	.858	.895	1.447
.100	.100	.300	.310	.500	.549	.700	.867	.900	1.472
.105	.105	.305	.315	.505	.556	.705	.877	.905	1.499
.110	.110	.310	.321	.510	.563	.710	.887	.910	1.528
.115	.116	.315	.326	.515	.570	.715	.897	.915	1.557
.120	.121	.320	.332	.520	.576	.720	.908	.920	1.589
.125	.126	.325	.337	.525	.583	.725	.918	.925	1.623
.130	.131	.330	.343	.530	.590	.730	.929	.930	1.658
.135	.136	.335	.348	.535	.597	.735	.940	.935	1.697
.140	.141	.340	.354	.540	.604	.740	.950	.940	1.738
.145	.146	.345	.360	.545	.611	.745	.962	.945	1.783
.150	.151	.350	.365	.550	.618	.750	.973	.950	1.832
.155	.156	.355	.371	.555	.626	.755	.984	.955	1.886
.160	.161	.360	.377	.560	.633	.760	.996	.960	1.946
.165	.167	.365	.383	.565	.640	.765	1.008	.965	2.014
.170	.172	.370	.388	.570	.648	.770	1.020	.970	2.092
.175	.177	.375	.394	.575	.655	.775	1.033	.975	2.185
.180	.182	.380	.400	.580	.662	.780	1.045	.980	2.298
.185	.187	.385	.406	.585	.670	.785	1.058	.985	2.443
.190	.192	.390	.412	.590	.678	.790	1.071	.990	2.647
.195	.198	.395	.418	.595	.685	.795	1.085	.995	2.994

[a] Adapted with permission from Table V.B. of Fisher's *Statistical methods for research workers*, Edinburgh: Oliver & Boyd, 1932.

Table J ◆ Probabilities associated with values as small as observed values of U in the Mann-Whitney test $(3 \leqslant n_L \leqslant 8)^a$

$N_2 = 3$

U \ N_1	1	2	3
0	.250	.100	.050
1	.500	.200	.100
2	.750	.400	.200
3		.600	.350
4			.500
5			.650

$N_2 = 4$

U \ N_1	1	2	3	4
0	.200	.067	.028	.014
1	.400	.133	.057	.029
2	.600	.267	.114	.057
3		.400	.200	.100
4		.600	.314	.171
5			.429	.243
6			.571	.343
7				.443
8				.557

$N_2 = 5$

U \ N_1	1	2	3	4	5
0	.167	.047	.018	.008	.004
1	.333	.095	.036	.016	.008
2	.500	.190	.071	.032	.016
3	.667	.286	.125	.056	.028
4		.429	.196	.095	.048
5		.571	.286	.143	.075
6			.393	.206	.111
7			.500	.278	.155
8			.607	.365	.210
9				.452	.274
10				.548	.345
11					.421
12					.500
13					.579

$N_2 = 6$

U \ N_1	1	2	3	4	5	6
0	.143	.036	.012	.005	.002	.001
1	.286	.071	.024	.010	.004	.002
2	.428	.143	.048	.019	.009	.004
3	.571	.214	.083	.033	.015	.008
4		.321	.131	.057	.026	.013
5		.429	.190	.086	.041	.021
6		.571	.274	.129	.063	.032
7			.357	.176	.089	.047
8			.452	.238	.123	.066
9			.548	.305	.165	.090
10				.381	.214	.120
11				.457	.268	.155
12				.545	.331	.197
13					.396	.242
14					.465	.294
15					.535	.350
16						.409
17						.469
18						.531

Table J ◆ (Continued)

	$N_2 = 7$						
N_1 U	1	2	3	4	5	6	7
0	.125	.028	.008	.003	.001	.001	.000
1	.250	.056	.017	.006	.003	.001	.001
2	.375	.111	.033	.012	.005	.002	.001
3	.500	.167	.058	.021	.009	.004	.002
4	.625	.250	.092	.036	.015	.007	.003
5		.333	.133	.055	.024	.011	.006
6		.444	.192	.082	.037	.017	.009
7		.556	.258	.115	.053	.026	.013
8			.333	.158	.074	.037	.019
9			.417	.206	.101	.051	.027
10			.500	.264	.134	.069	.036
11			.583	.324	.172	.090	.049
12				.394	.216	.117	.064
13				.464	.265	.147	.082
14				.538	.319	.183	.104
15					.378	.223	.130
16					.438	.267	.159
17					.500	.314	.191
18					.562	.365	.228
19						.418	.267
20						.473	.310
21						.527	.355
22							.402
23							.451
24							.500
25							.549

					$N_2 = 8$					
N_1 \ U	1	2	3	4	5	6	7	8	t	Normal
0	.111	.022	.006	.002	.001	.000	.000	.000	3.308	.001
1	.222	.044	.012	.004	.002	.001	.000	.000	3.203	.001
2	.333	.089	.024	.008	.003	.001	.001	.000	3.098	.001
3	.444	.133	.042	.014	.005	.002	.001	.001	2.993	.001
4	.556	.200	.067	.024	.009	.004	.002	.001	2.888	.002
5		.267	.097	.036	.015	.006	.003	.001	2.783	.003
6		.356	.139	.055	.023	.010	.005	.002	2.678	.004
7		.444	.188	.077	.033	.015	.007	.003	2.573	.005
8		.556	.248	.107	.047	.021	.010	.005	2.468	.007
9			.315	.141	.064	.030	.014	.007	2.363	.009
10			.387	.184	.085	.041	.020	.010	2.258	.012
11			.461	.230	.111	.054	.027	.014	2.153	.016
12			.539	.285	.142	.071	.036	.019	2.048	.020
13				.341	.177	.091	.047	.025	1.943	.026
14				.404	.217	.114	.060	.032	1.838	.033
15				.467	.262	.141	.076	.041	1.733	.041
16				.533	.311	.172	.095	.052	1.628	.052
17					.362	.207	.116	.065	1.523	.064
18					.416	.245	.140	.080	1.418	.078
19					.472	.286	.168	.097	1.313	.094
20					.528	.331	.198	.117	1.208	.113
21						.377	.232	.139	1.102	.135
22						.426	.268	.164	.998	.159
23						.475	.306	.191	.893	.185
24						.525	.347	.221	.788	.215
25							.389	.253	.683	.247
26							.433	.287	.578	.282
27							.478	.323	.473	.318
28							.522	.360	.368	.356
29								.399	.263	.396
30								.439	.158	.437
31								.480	.052	.481
32								.520		

[a] Reproduced from H. B. Mann & D. R. Whitney. On a test of whether one of two random variables is stochastically larger than the other, *Annals of Mathematical Statistics*, 1947, 18, 52–54, with the kind permission of the authors and the publisher.

Table K ♦ Critical values of U in the Mann-Whitney test ($9 < n_L \leq 20$)[a]

Critical Values of U for a One-tailed Test at $\alpha = .001$ or for a Two-tailed Test at $\alpha = .002$

N_1 \ N_2	9	10	11	12	13	14	15	16	17	18	19	20
1												
2												
3									0	0	0	0
4		0	0	0	1	1	1	2	2	3	3	3
5	1	1	2	2	3	3	4	5	5	6	7	7
6	2	3	4	4	5	6	7	8	9	10	11	12
7	3	5	6	7	8	9	10	11	13	14	15	16
8	5	6	8	9	11	12	14	15	17	18	20	21
9	7	8	10	12	14	15	17	19	21	23	25	26
10	8	10	12	14	17	19	21	23	25	27	29	32
11	10	12	15	17	20	22	24	27	29	32	34	37
12	12	14	17	20	23	25	28	31	34	37	40	42
13	14	17	20	23	26	29	32	35	38	42	45	48
14	15	19	22	25	29	32	36	39	43	46	50	54
15	17	21	24	28	32	36	40	43	47	51	55	59
16	19	23	27	31	35	39	43	48	52	56	60	65
17	21	25	29	34	38	43	47	52	57	61	66	70
18	23	27	32	37	42	46	51	56	61	66	71	76
19	25	29	34	40	45	50	55	60	66	71	77	82
20	26	32	37	42	48	54	59	65	70	76	82	88

Critical Values of U for a One-tailed Test at α = .01 or
for a Two-tailed Test at α = .02

N_1 \ N_2	9	10	11	12	13	14	15	16	17	18	19	20
1												
2					0	0	0	0	0	0	1	1
3	1	1	1	2	2	2	3	3	4	4	4	5
4	3	3	4	5	5	6	7	7	8	9	9	10
5	5	6	7	8	9	10	11	12	13	14	15	16
6	7	8	9	11	12	13	15	16	18	19	20	22
7	9	11	12	14	16	17	19	21	23	24	26	28
8	11	13	15	17	20	22	24	26	28	30	32	34
9	14	16	18	21	23	26	28	31	33	36	38	40
10	16	19	22	24	27	30	33	36	38	41	44	47
11	18	22	25	28	31	34	37	41	44	47	50	53
12	21	24	28	31	35	38	42	46	49	53	56	60
13	23	27	31	35	39	43	47	51	55	59	63	67
14	26	30	34	38	43	47	51	56	60	65	69	73
15	28	33	37	42	47	51	56	61	66	70	75	80
16	31	36	41	46	51	56	61	66	71	76	82	87
17	33	38	44	49	55	60	66	71	77	82	88	93
18	36	41	47	53	59	65	70	76	82	88	94	100
19	38	44	50	56	63	69	75	82	88	94	101	107
20	40	47	53	60	67	73	80	87	93	100	107	114

Table K ♦ (Continued)

Critical Values of U for a One-tailed Test at α = .025 or
for a Two-tailed Test at α = .05

N_1 \ N_2	9	10	11	12	13	14	15	16	17	18	19	20
1												
2	0	0	0	1	1	1	1	1	2	2	2	2
3	2	3	3	4	4	5	5	6	6	7	7	8
4	4	5	6	7	8	9	10	11	11	12	13	13
5	7	8	9	11	12	13	14	15	17	18	19	20
6	10	11	13	14	16	17	19	21	22	24	25	27
7	12	14	16	18	20	22	24	26	28	30	32	34
8	15	17	19	22	24	26	29	31	34	36	38	41
9	17	20	23	26	28	31	34	37	39	42	45	48
10	20	23	26	29	33	36	39	42	45	48	52	55
11	23	26	30	33	37	40	44	47	51	55	58	62
12	26	29	33	37	41	45	49	53	57	61	65	69
13	28	33	37	41	45	50	54	59	63	67	72	76
14	31	36	40	45	50	55	59	64	67	74	78	83
15	34	39	44	49	54	59	64	70	75	80	85	90
16	37	42	47	53	59	64	70	75	81	86	92	98
17	39	45	51	57	63	67	75	81	87	93	99	105
18	42	48	55	61	67	74	80	86	93	99	106	112
19	45	52	58	65	72	78	85	92	99	106	113	119
20	48	55	62	69	76	83	90	98	105	112	119	127

N_1 \ N_2	9	10	11	12	13	14	15	16	17	18	19	20

Critical Values of U for a One-tailed Test at $\alpha = .05$ or for a Two-tailed Test at $\alpha = .10$

N_1 \ N_2	9	10	11	12	13	14	15	16	17	18	19	20
1											0	0
2	1	1	1	2	2	2	3	3	3	4	4	4
3	3	4	5	5	6	7	7	8	9	9	10	11
4	6	7	8	9	10	11	12	14	15	16	17	18
5	9	11	12	13	15	16	18	19	20	22	23	25
6	12	14	16	17	19	21	23	25	26	28	30	32
7	15	17	19	21	24	26	28	30	33	35	37	39
8	18	20	23	26	28	31	33	36	39	41	44	47
9	21	24	27	30	33	36	39	42	45	48	51	54
10	24	27	31	34	37	41	44	48	51	55	58	62
11	27	31	34	38	42	46	50	54	57	61	65	69
12	30	34	38	42	47	51	55	60	64	68	72	77
13	33	37	42	47	51	56	61	65	70	75	80	84
14	36	41	46	51	56	61	66	71	77	82	87	92
15	39	44	50	55	61	66	72	77	83	88	94	100
16	42	48	54	60	65	71	77	83	89	95	101	107
17	45	51	57	64	70	77	83	89	96	102	109	115
18	48	55	61	68	75	82	88	95	102	109	116	123
19	51	58	65	72	80	87	94	101	109	116	123	130
20	54	62	69	77	84	92	100	107	115	123	130	138

[a]Adapted and abridged from Tables 1, 3, 5, and 7 of D. Auble. Extended tables for the Mann-Whitney statistic. *Bulletin of the Institute of Educational Research at Indiana University*, 1953, **1**, No 2, with the kind permission of the author and the publisher.

Table L ◆ Squares and square roots[a]

N	N²	√N̄	√10N̄	N	N²	√N̄	√10N̄
1.00	1.0000	1.00000	3.16228	**1.50**	2.2500	1.22474	3.87298
1.01	1.0201	1.00499	3.17805	1.51	2.2801	1.22882	3.88587
1.02	1.0404	1.00995	3.19374	1.52	2.3104	1.23288	3.89872
1.03	1.0609	1.01489	3.20936	1.53	2.3409	1.23693	3.91152
1.04	1.0816	1.01980	3.22490	1.54	2.3716	1.24097	3.92428
1.05	1.1025	1.02470	3.24037	1.55	2.4025	1.24499	3.93700
1.06	1.1236	1.02956	3.25576	1.56	2.4336	1.24900	3.94968
1.07	1.1449	1.03441	3.27109	1.57	2.4649	1.25300	3.96232
1.08	1.1664	1.03923	3.28634	1.58	2.4964	1.25698	3.97492
1.09	1.1881	1.04403	3.30151	1.59	2.5281	1.26095	3.98748
1.10	1.2100	1.04881	3.31662	**1.60**	2.5600	1.26491	4.00000
1.11	1.2321	1.05357	3.33167	1.61	2.5921	1.26886	4.01248
1.12	1.2544	1.05830	3.34664	1.62	2.6244	1.27279	4.02492
1.13	1.2769	1.06301	3.36155	1.63	2.6569	1.27671	4.03733
1.14	1.2996	1.06771	3.37639	1.64	2.6896	1.28062	4.04969
1.15	1.3225	1.07238	3.39116	1.65	2.7225	1.28452	4.06202
1.16	1.3456	1.07703	3.40588	1.66	2.7556	1.28841	4.07431
1.17	1.3689	1.08167	3.42053	1.67	2.7889	1.29228	4.08656
1.18	1.3924	1.08628	3.43511	1.68	2.8224	1.29615	4.09878
1.19	1.4161	1.09087	3.44964	1.69	2.8561	1.30000	4.11096
1.20	1.4400	1.09545	3.46410	**1.70**	2.8900	1.30384	4.12311
1.21	1.4641	1.10000	3.47851	1.71	2.9241	1.30767	4.13521
1.22	1.4884	1.10454	3.49285	1.72	2.9584	1.31149	4.14729
1.23	1.5129	1.10905	3.50714	1.73	2.9929	1.31529	4.15933
1.24	1.5376	1.11355	3.52136	1.74	3.0276	1.31909	4.17133
1.25	1.5625	1.11803	3.53553	1.75	3.0625	1.32288	4.18330
1.26	1.5876	1.12250	3.54965	1.76	3.0976	1.32665	4.19524
1.27	1.6129	1.12694	3.56371	1.77	3.1329	1.33041	4.20714
1.28	1.6384	1.13137	3.57771	1.78	3.1684	1.33417	4.21900
1.29	1.6641	1.13578	3.59166	1.79	3.2041	1.33791	4.23084
1.30	1.6900	1.14018	3.60555	**1.80**	3.2400	1.34164	4.24264
1.31	1.7161	1.14455	3.61939	1.81	3.2761	1.34536	4.25441
1.32	1.7424	1.14891	3.63318	1.82	3.3124	1.34907	4.26615
1.33	1.7689	1.15326	3.64692	1.83	3.3489	1.35277	4.27785
1.34	1.7956	1.15758	3.66060	1.84	3.3856	1.35647	4.28952
1.35	1.8225	1.16190	3.67423	1.85	3.4225	1.36015	4.30116
1.36	1.8496	1.16619	3.68782	1.86	3.4596	1.36382	4.31277
1.37	1.8769	1.17047	3.70135	1.87	3.4969	1.36748	4.32435
1.38	1.9044	1.17473	3.71484	1.88	3.5344	1.37113	4.33590
1.39	1.9321	1.17898	3.72827	1.89	3.5721	1.37477	4.34741
1.40	1.9600	1.18322	3.74166	**1.90**	3.6100	1.37840	4.35890
1.41	1.9881	1.18743	3.75500	1.91	3.6481	1.38203	4.37035
1.42	2.0164	1.19164	3.76829	1.92	3.6864	1.38564	4.38178
1.43	2.0449	1.19583	3.78153	1.93	3.7249	1.38924	4.39318
1.44	2.0736	1.20000	3.79473	1.94	3.7636	1.39284	4.40454
1.45	2.1025	1.20416	3.80789	1.95	3.8025	1.39642	4.41588
1.46	2.1316	1.20830	3.82099	1.96	3.8416	1.40000	4.42719
1.47	2.1609	1.21244	3.83406	1.97	3.8809	1.40357	4.43847
1.48	2.1904	1.21655	3.84708	1.98	3.9204	1.40712	4.44972
1.49	2.2201	1.22066	3.86005	1.99	3.9601	1.41067	4.46094
1.50	2.2500	1.22474	3.87298	**2.00**	4.0000	1.41421	4.47214
N	N²	√N̄	√10N̄	N	N²	√N̄	√10N̄

N	N²	√N	√10N	N	N²	√N	√10N
2.00	4.0000	1.41421	4.47214	**2.50**	6.2500	1.58114	5.00000
2.01	4.0401	1.41774	4.48330	2.51	6.3001	1.58430	5.00999
2.02	4.0804	1.42127	4.49444	2.52	6.3504	1.58745	5.01996
2.03	4.1209	1.42478	4.50555	2.53	6.4009	1.59060	5.02991
2.04	4.1616	1.42829	4.51664	2.54	6.4516	1.59374	5.03984
2.05	4.2025	1.43178	4.52769	2.55	6.5025	1.59687	5.04975
2.06	4.2436	1.43527	4.53872	2.56	6.5536	1.60000	5.05964
2.07	4.2849	1.43875	4.54973	2.57	6.6049	1.60312	5.06952
2.08	4.3264	1.44222	4.56070	2.58	6.6564	1.60624	5.07937
2.09	4.3681	1.44568	4.57165	2.59	6.7081	1.60935	5.08920
2.10	4.4100	1.44914	4.58258	**2.60**	6.7600	1.61245	5.09902
2.11	4.4521	1.45258	4.59347	2.61	6.8121	1.61555	5.10882
2.12	4.4944	1.45602	4.60435	2.62	6.8644	1.61864	5.11859
2.13	4.5369	1.45945	4.61519	2.63	6.9169	1.62173	5.12835
2.14	4.5796	1.46287	4.62601	2.64	6.9696	1.62481	5.13809
2.15	4.6225	1.46629	4.63681	2.65	7.0225	1.62788	5.14782
2.16	4.6656	1.46969	4.64758	2.66	7.0756	1.63095	5.15752
2.17	4.7089	1.47309	4.65833	2.67	7.1289	1.63401	5.16720
2.18	4.7524	1.47648	4.66905	2.68	7.1824	1.63707	5.17687
2.19	4.7961	1.47986	4.67974	2.69	7.2361	1.64012	5.18652
2.20	4.8400	1.48324	4.69042	**2.70**	7.2900	1.64317	5.19615
2.21	4.8841	1.48661	4.70106	2.71	7.3441	1.64621	5.20577
2.22	4.9284	1.48997	4.71169	2.72	7.3984	1.64924	5.21536
2.23	4.9729	1.49332	4.72229	2.73	7.4529	1.65227	5.22494
2.24	5.0176	1.49666	4.73286	2.74	7.5076	1.65529	5.23450
2.25	5.0625	1.50000	4.74342	2.75	7.5625	1.65831	5.24404
2.26	5.1076	1.50333	4.75395	2.76	7.6176	1.66132	5.25357
2.27	5.1529	1.50665	4.76445	2.77	7.6729	1.66433	5.26308
2.28	5.1984	1.50997	4.77493	2.78	7.7284	1.66733	5.27257
2.29	5.2441	1.51327	4.78539	2.79	7.7841	1.67033	5.28205
2.30	5.2900	1.51658	4.79583	**2.80**	7.8400	1.67332	5.29150
2.31	5.3361	1.51987	4.80625	2.81	7.8961	1.67631	5.30094
2.32	5.3824	1.52315	4.81664	2.82	7.9524	1.67929	5.31037
2.33	5.4289	1.52643	4.82701	2.83	8.0089	1.68226	5.31977
2.34	5.4756	1.52971	4.83735	2.84	8.0656	1.68523	5.32917
2.35	5.5225	1.53297	4.84768	2.85	8.1225	1.68819	5.33854
2.36	5.5696	1.53623	4.85798	2.86	8.1796	1.69115	5.34790
2.37	5.6169	1.53948	4.86826	2.87	8.2369	1.69411	5.35724
2.38	5.6644	1.54272	4.87852	2.88	8.2944	1.69706	5.36656
2.39	5.7121	1.54596	4.88876	2.89	8.3521	1.70000	5.37587
2.40	5.7600	1.54919	4.89898	**2.90**	8.4100	1.70294	5.38516
2.41	5.8081	1.55242	4.90918	2.91	8.4681	1.70587	5.39444
2.42	5.8564	1.55563	4.91935	2.92	8.5264	1.70880	5.40370
2.43	5.9049	1.55885	4.92950	2.93	8.5849	1.71172	5.41295
2.44	5.9536	1.56205	4.93964	2.94	8.6436	1.71464	5.42218
2.45	6.0025	1.56525	4.94975	2.95	8.7025	1.71756	5.43139
2.46	6.0516	1.56844	4.95984	2.96	8.7616	1.72047	5.44059
2.47	6.1009	1.57162	4.96991	2.97	8.8209	1.72337	5.44977
2.48	6.1504	1.57480	4.97996	2.98	8.8804	1.72627	5.45894
2.49	6.2001	1.57797	4.98999	2.99	8.9401	1.72916	5.46809
2.50	6.2500	1.58114	5.00000	**3.00**	9.0000	1.73205	5.47723
N	**N²**	**√N**	**√10N**	**N**	**N²**	**√N**	**√10N**

663

Table L ♦ (Continued)

N	N²	√N̄	√10N̄	N	N²	√N̄	√10N̄
3.00	9.0000	1.73205	5.47723	**3.50**	12.2500	1.87083	5.91608
3.01	9.0601	1.73494	5.48635	3.51	12.3201	1.87350	5.92453
3.02	9.1204	1.73781	5.49545	3.52	12.3904	1.87617	5.93296
3.03	9.1809	1.74069	5.50454	3.53	12.4609	1.87883	5.94138
3.04	9.2416	1.74356	5.51362	3.54	12.5316	1.88149	5.94979
3.05	9.3025	1.74642	5.52268	3.55	12.6025	1.88414	5.95819
3.06	9.3636	1.74929	5.53173	3.56	12.6736	1.88680	5.96657
3.07	9.4249	1.75214	5.54076	3.57	12.7449	1.88944	5.97495
3.08	9.4864	1.75499	5.54977	3.58	12.8164	1.89209	5.98331
3.09	9.5481	1.75784	5.55878	3.59	12.8881	1.89473	5.99166
3.10	9.6100	1.76068	5.56776	**3.60**	12.9600	1.89737	6.00000
3.11	9.6721	1.76352	5.57674	3.61	13.0321	1.90000	6.00833
3.12	9.7344	1.76635	5.58570	3.62	13.1044	1.90263	6.01664
3.13	9.7969	1.76918	5.59464	3.63	13.1769	1.90526	6.02495
3.14	9.8596	1.77200	5.60357	3.64	13.2496	1.90788	6.03324
3.15	9.9225	1.77482	5.61249	3.65	13.3225	1.91050	6.04152
3.16	9.9856	1.77764	5.62139	3.66	13.3956	1.91311	6.04979
3.17	10.0489	1.78045	5.63028	3.67	13.4689	1.91572	6.05805
3.18	10.1124	1.78326	5.63915	3.68	13.5424	1.91833	6.06630
3.19	10.1761	1.78606	5.64801	3.69	13.6161	1.92094	6.07454
3.20	10.2400	1.78885	5.65685	**3.70**	13.6900	1.92354	6.08276
3.21	10.3041	1.79165	5.66569	3.71	13.7641	1.92614	6.09098
3.22	10.3684	1.79444	5.67450	3.72	13.8384	1.92873	6.09918
3.23	10.4329	1.79722	5.68331	3.73	13.9129	1.93132	6.10737
3.24	10.4976	1.80000	5.69210	3.74	13.9876	1.93391	6.11555
3.25	10.5625	1.80278	5.70088	3.75	14.0625	1.93649	6.12372
3.26	10.6276	1.80555	5.70964	3.76	14.1376	1.93907	6.13188
3.27	10.6929	1.80831	5.71839	3.77	14.2129	1.94165	6.14003
3.28	10.7584	1.81108	5.72713	3.78	14.2884	1.94422	6.14817
3.29	10.8241	1.81384	5.73585	3.79	14.3641	1.94679	6.15630
3.30	10.8900	1.81659	5.74456	**3.80**	14.4400	1.94936	6.16441
3.31	10.9561	1.81934	5.75326	3.81	14.5161	1.95192	6.17252
3.32	11.0224	1.82209	5.76194	3.82	14.5924	1.95448	6.18061
3.33	11.0889	1.82483	5.77062	3.83	14.6689	1.95704	6.18870
3.34	11.1556	1.82757	5.77927	3.84	14.7456	1.95959	6.19677
3.35	11.2225	1.83030	5.78792	3.85	14.8225	1.96214	6.20484
3.36	11.2896	1.83303	5.79655	3.86	14.8996	1.96469	6.21289
3.37	11.3569	1.83576	5.80517	3.87	14.9769	1.96723	6.22093
3.38	11.4244	1.83848	5.81378	3.88	15.0544	1.96977	6.22896
3.39	11.4921	1.84120	5.82237	3.89	15.1321	1.97231	6.23699
3.40	11.5600	1.84391	5.83095	**3.90**	15.2100	1.97484	6.24500
3.41	11.6281	1.84662	5.83952	3.91	15.2881	1.97737	6.25300
3.42	11.6964	1.84932	5.84808	3.92	15.3664	1.97990	6.26099
3.43	11.7649	1.85203	5.85662	3.93	15.4449	1.98242	6.26897
3.44	11.8336	1.85472	5.86515	3.94	15.5236	1.98494	6.27694
3.45	11.9025	1.85742	5.87367	3.95	15.6025	1.98746	6.28490
3.46	11.9716	1.86011	5.88218	3.96	15.6816	1.98997	6.29285
3.47	12.0409	1.86279	5.89067	3.97	15.7609	1.99249	6.30079
3.48	12.1104	1.86548	5.89915	3.98	15.8404	1.99499	6.30872
3.49	12.1801	1.86815	5.90762	3.99	15.9201	1.99750	6.31664
3.50	12.2500	1.87083	5.91608	**4.00**	16.0000	2.00000	6.32456
N	N²	√N̄	√10N̄	N	N²	√N̄	√10N̄

N	N²	√N	√10N	N	N²	√N	√10N
4.00	16.0000	2.00000	6.32456	**4.50**	20.2500	2.12132	6.70820
4.01	16.0801	2.00250	6.33246	4.51	20.3401	2.12368	6.71565
4.02	16.1604	2.00499	6.34035	4.52	20.4304	2.12603	6.72309
4.03	16.2409	2.00749	6.34823	4.53	20.5209	2.12838	6.73053
4.04	16.3216	2.00998	6.35610	4.54	20.6116	2.13073	6.73795
4.05	16.4025	2.01246	6.36396	4.55	20.7025	2.13307	6.74537
4.06	16.4836	2.01494	6.37181	4.56	20.7936	2.13542	6.75278
4.07	16.5649	2.01742	6.37966	4.57	20.8849	2.13776	6.76018
4.08	16.6464	2.01990	6.38749	4.58	20.9764	2.14009	6.76757
4.09	16.7281	2.02237	6.39531	4.59	21.0681	2.14243	6.77495
4.10	16.8100	2.02485	6.40312	**4.60**	21.1600	2.14476	6.78233
4.11	16.8921	2.02731	6.41093	4.61	21.2521	2.14709	6.78970
4.12	16.9744	2.02978	6.41872	4.62	21.3444	2.14942	6.79706
4.13	17.0569	2.03224	6.42651	4.63	21.4369	2.15174	6.80441
4.14	17.1396	2.03470	6.43428	4.64	21.5296	2.15407	6.81175
4.15	17.2225	2.03715	6.44205	4.65	21.6225	2.15639	6.81909
4.16	17.3056	2.03961	6.44981	4.66	21.7156	2.15870	6.82642
4.17	17.3889	2.04206	6.45755	4.67	21.8089	2.16102	6.83374
4.18	17.4724	2.04450	6.46529	4.68	21.9024	2.16333	5.84105
4.19	17.5561	2.04695	6.47302	4.69	21.9961	2.16564	6.84836
4.20	17.6400	2.04939	6.48074	**4.70**	22.0900	2.16795	6.85565
4.21	17.7241	2.05183	6.48845	4.71	22.1841	2.17025	6.86294
4.22	17.8084	2.05426	6.49615	4.72	22.2784	2.17256	6.87023
4.23	17.8929	2.05670	6.50384	4.73	22.3729	2.17486	6.87750
4.24	17.9776	2.05913	6.51153	4.74	22.4676	2.17715	6.88477
4.25	18.0625	2.06155	6.51920	4.75	22.5625	2.17945	6.89202
4.26	18.1476	2.06398	6.52687	4.76	22.6576	2.18174	6.89928
4.27	18.2329	2.06640	6.53452	4.77	22.7529	2.18403	6.90652
4.28	18.3184	2.06882	6.54217	4.78	22.8484	2.18632	6.91375
4.29	18.4041	2.07123	6.54981	4.79	22.9441	2.18861	6.92098
4.30	18.4900	2.07364	6.55744	**4.80**	23.0400	2.19089	6.92820
4.31	18.5761	2.07605	6.56506	4.81	23.1361	2.19317	6.93542
4.32	18.6624	2.07846	6.57267	4.82	23.2324	2.19545	6.94262
4.33	18.7489	2.08087	6.58027	4.83	23.3289	2.19773	6.94982
4.34	18.8356	2.08327	6.58787	4.84	23.4256	2.20000	6.95701
4.35	18.9225	2.08567	6.59545	4.85	23.5225	2.20227	6.96419
4.36	19.0096	2.08806	6.60303	4.86	23.6196	2.20454	6.97137
4.37	19.0969	2.09045	6.61060	4.87	23.7169	2.20681	6.97854
4.38	19.1844	2.09284	6.61816	4.88	23.8144	2.20907	6.98570
4.39	19.2721	2.09523	6.62571	4.89	23.9121	2.21133	6.99285
4.40	19.3600	2.09762	6.63325	**4.90**	24.0100	2.21359	7.00000
4.41	19.4481	2.10000	6.64078	4.91	24.1081	2.21585	7.00714
4.42	19.5364	2.10238	6.64831	4.92	24.2064	2.21811	7.01427
4.43	19.6249	2.10476	6.65582	4.93	24.3049	2.22036	7.02140
4.44	19.7136	2.10713	6.66333	4.94	24.4036	2.22261	7.02851
4.45	19.8025	2.10950	6.67083	4.95	24.5025	2.22486	7.03562
4.46	19.8916	2.11187	6.67832	4.96	24.6016	2.22711	7.04273
4.47	19.9809	2.11424	6.68581	4.97	24.7009	2.22935	7.04982
4.48	20.0704	2.11660	6.69328	4.98	24.8004	2.23159	7.05691
4.49	20.1601	2.11896	6.70075	4.99	24.9001	2.23383	7.06399
4.50	20.2500	2.12132	6.70820	**5.00**	25.0000	2.23607	7.07107
N	N²	√N	√10N	N	N²	√N	√10N

Table L ♦ (Continued)

N	N²	√N̄	√10N̄	N	N²	√N̄	√10N̄
5.00	25.0000	2.23607	7.07107	**5.50**	30.2500	2.34521	7.41620
5.01	25.1001	2.23830	7.07814	5.51	30.3601	2.34734	7.42294
5.02	25.2004	2.24054	7.08520	5.52	30.4704	2.34947	7.42967
5.03	25.3009	2.24277	7.09225	5.53	30.5809	2.35160	7.43640
5.04	25.4016	2.24499	7.09930	5.54	30.6916	2.35372	7.44312
5.05	25.5025	2.24722	7.10634	5.55	30.8025	2.35584	7.44983
5.06	25.6036	2.24944	7.11337	5.56	30.9136	2.35797	7.45654
5.07	25.7049	2.25167	7.12039	5.57	31.0249	2.36008	7.46324
5.08	25.8064	2.25389	7.12741	5.58	31.1364	2.36220	7.46994
5.09	25.9081	2.25610	7.13442	5.59	31.2481	2.36432	7.47663
5.10	26.0100	2.25832	7.14143	**5.60**	31.3600	2.36643	7.48331
5.11	26.1121	2.26053	7.14843	5.61	31.4721	2.36854	7.48999
5.12	26.2144	2.26274	7.15542	5.62	31.5844	2.37065	7.49667
5.13	26.3169	2.26495	7.16240	5.63	31.6969	2.37276	7.50333
5.14	26.4196	2.26716	7.16938	5.64	31.8096	2.37487	7.50999
5.15	26.5225	2.26936	7.17635	5.65	31.9225	2.37697	7.51665
5.16	26.6256	2.27156	7.18331	5.66	32.0356	2.37908	7.52330
5.17	26.7289	2.27376	7.19027	5.67	32.1489	2.38118	7.52994
5.18	26.8324	2.27596	7.19722	5.68	32.2624	2.38328	7.53658
5.19	26.9361	2.27816	7.20417	5.69	32.3761	2.38537	7.54321
5.20	27.0400	2.28035	7.21110	**5.70**	32.4900	2.38747	7.54983
5.21	27.1441	2.28254	7.21803	5.71	32.6041	2.38956	7.55645
5.22	27.2484	2.28473	7.22496	5.72	32.7184	2.39165	7.56307
5.23	27.3529	2.28692	7.23187	5.73	32.8329	2.39374	7.56968
5.24	27.4576	2.28910	7.23878	5.74	32.9476	2.39583	7.57628
5.25	27.5625	2.29129	7.24569	5.75	33.0625	2.39792	7.58288
5.26	27.6676	2.29347	7.25259	5.76	33.1776	2.40000	7.58947
5.27	27.7729	2.29565	7.25948	5.77	33.2929	2.40208	7.59605
5.28	27.8784	2.29783	7.26636	5.78	33.4084	2.40416	7.60263
5.29	27.9841	2.30000	7.27324	5.79	33.5241	2.40624	7.60920
5.30	28.0900	2.30217	7.28011	**5.80**	33.6400	2.40832	7.61577
5.31	28.1961	2.30434	7.28697	5.81	33.7561	2.41039	7.62234
5.32	28.3024	2.30651	7.29383	5.82	33.8724	2.41247	7.62889
5.33	28.4089	2.30868	7.30068	5.83	33.9889	2.41454	7.63544
5.34	28.5156	2.31084	7.30753	5.84	34.1056	2.41661	7.64199
5.35	28.6225	2.31301	7.31437	5.85	34.2225	2.41868	7.64853
5.36	28.7296	2.31517	7.32120	5.86	34.3396	2.42074	7.65506
5.37	28.8369	2.31733	7.32803	5.87	34.4569	2.42281	7.66159
5.38	28.9444	2.31948	7.33485	5.88	34.5744	2.42487	7.66812
5.39	29.0521	2.32164	7.34166	5.89	34.6921	2.42693	7.67463
5.40	29.1600	2.32379	7.34847	**5.90**	34.8100	2.42899	7.68115
5.41	29.2681	2.32594	7.35527	5.91	34.9281	2.43105	7.68765
5.42	29.3764	2.32809	7.36206	5.92	35.0464	2.43311	7.69415
5.43	29.4849	2.33024	7.36885	5.93	35.1649	2.43516	7.70065
5.44	29.5936	2.33238	7.37564	5.94	35.2836	2.43721	7.70714
5.45	29.7025	2.33452	7.38241	5.95	35.4025	2.43926	7.71362
5.46	29.8116	2.33666	7.38918	5.96	35.5216	2.44131	7.72010
5.47	29.9209	2.33880	7.39594	5.97	35.6409	2.44336	7.72658
5.48	30.0304	2.34094	7.40270	5.98	35.7604	2.44540	7.73305
5.49	30.1401	2.34307	7.40945	5.99	35.8801	2.44745	7.73951
5.50	30.2500	2.34521	7.41620	**6.00**	36.0000	2.44949	7.74597
N	N²	√N̄	√10N̄	N	N²	√N̄	√10N̄

N	N²	√N	√10N		N	N²	√N	√10N
6.00	36.0000	2.44949	7.74597		**6.50**	42.2500	2.54951	8.06226
6.01	36.1201	2.45153	7.75242		6.51	42.3801	2.55147	8.06846
6.02	36.2404	2.45357	7.75887		6.52	42.5104	2.55343	8.07465
6.03	36.3609	2.45561	7.76531		6.53	42.6409	2.55539	8.08084
6.04	36.4816	2.45764	7.77174		6.54	42.7716	2.55734	8.08703
6.05	36.6025	2.45967	7.77817		6.55	42.9025	2.55930	8.09321
6.06	36.7236	2.46171	7.78460		6.56	43.0336	2.56125	8.09958
6.07	36.8449	2.46374	7.79102		6.57	43.1649	2.56320	8.10555
6.08	36.9664	2.46577	7.79744		6.58	43.2964	2.56515	8.11172
6.09	37.0881	2.46779	7.80385		6.59	43.4281	2.56710	8.11788
6.10	37.2100	2.46982	7.81025		**6.60**	43.5600	2.56905	8.12404
6.11	37.3321	2.47184	7.81665		6.61	43.6921	2.57099	8.13019
6.12	37.4544	2.47386	7.82304		6.62	43.8244	2.57294	8.13634
6.13	37.5769	2.47588	7.82943		6.63	43.9569	2.57488	8.14248
6.14	37.6996	2.47790	7.83582		6.64	44.0896	2.57682	8.14862
6.15	37.8225	2.47992	7.84219		6.65	44.2225	2.57876	8.15475
6.16	37.9456	2.48193	7.84857		6.66	44.3556	2.58070	8.16088
6.17	38.0689	2.48395	7.85493		6.67	44.4889	2.58263	8.16701
6.18	38.1924	2.48596	7.86130		6.68	44.6224	2.58457	8.17313
6.19	38.3161	2.48797	7.86766		6.69	44.7561	2.58650	8.17924
6.20	38.4400	2.48998	7.87401		**6.70**	44.8900	2.58844	8.18535
6.21	38.5641	2.49199	7.88036		6.71	45.0241	2.59037	8.19146
6.22	38.6884	2.49399	7.88670		6.72	45.1584	2.59230	8.19756
6.23	38.8129	2.49600	7.89303		6.73	45.2929	2.59422	8.20366
6.24	38.9376	2.49800	7.89937		6.74	45.4276	2.59615	8.20975
6.25	39.0625	2.50000	7.90569		6.75	45.5625	2.59808	8.21584
6.26	39.1876	2.50200	7.91202		6.76	45.6976	2.60000	8.22192
6.27	39.3129	2.50400	7.91833		6.77	45.8329	2.60192	8.22800
6.28	39.4384	2.50599	7.92465		6.78	45.9684	2.60384	8.23408
6.29	39.5641	2.50799	7.93095		6.79	46.1041	2.60576	8.24015
6.30	39.6900	2.50998	7.93725		**6.80**	46.2400	2.60768	8.24621
6.31	39.8161	2.51197	7.94355		6.81	46.3761	2.60960	8.25227
6.32	39.9424	2.51396	7.94984		6.82	46.5124	2.61151	8.25833
6.33	40.0689	2.51595	7.95613		6.83	46.6489	2.61343	8.26438
6.34	40.1956	2.51794	7.96241		6.84	46.7856	2.61534	8.27043
6.35	40.3225	2.51992	7.96869		6.85	46.9225	2.61725	8.27647
6.36	40.4496	2.52190	7.97496		6.86	47.0596	2.61916	8.28251
6.37	40.5769	2.52389	7.98123		6.87	47.1969	2.62107	8.28855
6.38	40.7044	2.52587	7.98749		6.88	47.3344	2.62298	8.29458
6.39	40.8321	2.52784	7.99375		6.89	47.4721	2.62488	8.30060
6.40	40.9600	2.52982	8.00000		**6.90**	47.6100	2.62679	8.30662
6.41	41.0881	2.53180	8.00625		6.91	47.7481	2.62869	8.31264
6.42	41.2164	2.53377	8.01249		6.92	47.8864	2.63059	8.31865
6.43	41.3449	2.53574	8.01873		6.93	48.0249	2.63249	8.32466
6.44	41.4736	2.53772	8.02496		6.94	48.1636	2.63439	8.33067
6.45	41.6025	2.53969	8.03119		6.95	48.3025	2.63629	8.33667
6.46	41.7316	2.54165	8.03741		6.96	48.4416	2.63818	8.34266
6.47	41.8609	2.54362	8.04363		6.97	48.5809	2.64008	8.34865
6.48	41.9904	2.54558	8.04984		6.98	48.7204	2.64197	8.35464
6.49	42.1201	2.54755	8.05605		6.99	48.8601	2.64386	8.36062
6.50	42.2500	2.54951	8.06226		**7.00**	49.0000	2.64575	8.36660
N	**N²**	**√N**	**√10N**		**N**	**N²**	**√N**	**√10N**

Table L ♦ (Continued)

N	N²	√N̄	√10N̄	N	N²	√N̄	√10N̄
7.00	49.0000	2.64575	8.36660	**7.50**	56.2500	2.73861	8.66025
7.01	49.1401	2.64764	8.37257	7.51	56.4001	2.74044	8.66603
7.02	49.2804	2.64953	8.37854	7.52	56.5504	2.74226	8.67179
7.03	49.4209	2.65141	8.38451	7.53	56.7009	2.74408	8.67756
7.04	49.5616	2.65330	8.39047	7.54	56.8516	2.74591	8.68332
7.05	49.7025	2.65518	8.39643	7.55	57.0025	2.74773	8.68907
7.06	49.8436	2.65707	8.40238	7.56	57.1536	2.74955	8.69483
7.07	49.9849	2.65895	8.40833	7.57	57.3049	2.75136	8.70057
7.08	50.1264	2.66083	8.41427	7.58	57.4564	2.75318	8.70632
7.09	50.2681	2.66271	8.42021	7.59	57.6081	2.75500	8.71206
7.10	50.4100	2.66458	8.42615	**7.60**	57.7600	2.75681	8.71780
7.11	50.5521	2.66646	8.43208	7.61	57.9121	2.75862	8.72353
7.12	50.6944	2.66833	8.43801	7.62	58.0644	2.76043	8.72926
7.13	50.8369	2.67021	8.44393	7.63	58.2169	2.76225	8.73499
7.14	50.9796	2.67208	8.44985	7.64	58.3696	2.76405	8.74071
7.15	51.1225	2.67395	8.45577	7.65	58.5225	2.76586	8.74643
7.16	51.2656	2.67582	8.46168	7.66	58.6756	2.76767	8.75214
7.17	51.4089	2.67769	8.46759	7.67	58.8289	2.76948	8.75785
7.18	51.5524	2.67955	8.47349	7.68	58.9824	2.77128	8.76356
7.19	51.6961	2.68142	8.47939	7.69	59.1361	2.77308	8.76926
7.20	51.8400	2.68328	8.48528	**7.70**	59.2900	2.77489	8.77496
7.21	51.9841	2.68514	8.49117	7.71	59.4441	2.77669	8.78066
7.22	52.1284	2.68701	8.49706	7.72	59.5984	2.77849	8.78635
7.23	52.2729	2.68887	8.50294	7.73	59.7529	2.78029	8.79204
7.24	52.4176	2.69072	8.50882	7.74	59.9076	2.78209	8.79773
7.25	52.5625	2.69258	8.51469	7.75	60.0625	2.78388	8.80341
7.26	52.7076	2.69444	8.52056	7.76	60.2176	2.78568	8.80909
7.27	52.8529	2.69629	8.52643	7.77	60.3729	2.78747	8.81476
7.28	52.9984	2.69815	8.53229	7.78	60.5284	2.78927	8.82043
7.29	53.1441	2.70000	8.53815	7.79	60.6841	2.79106	8.82610
7.30	53.2900	2.70185	8.54400	**7.80**	60.8400	2.79285	8.83176
7.31	53.4361	2.70370	8.54985	7.81	60.9961	2.79464	8.83742
7.32	53.5824	2.70555	8.55570	7.82	61.1524	2.79643	8.84308
7.33	53.7289	2.70740	8.56154	7.83	61.3089	2.79821	8.84873
7.34	53.8756	2.70924	8.56738	7.84	61.4656	2.80000	8.85438
7.35	54.0225	2.71109	8.57321	7.85	61.6225	2.80179	8.86002
7.36	54.1696	2.71293	8.57904	7.86	61.7796	2.80357	8.86566
7.37	54.3169	2.71477	8.58487	7.87	61.9369	2.80535	8.87130
7.38	54.4644	2.71662	8.59069	7.88	62.0944	2.80713	8.87694
7.39	54.6121	2.71846	8.59651	7.89	62.2521	2.80891	8.88257
7.40	54.7600	2.72029	8.60233	**7.90**	62.4100	2.81069	8.88819
7.41	54.9081	2.72213	8.60814	7.91	62.5681	2.81247	8.89382
7.42	55.0564	2.72397	8.61394	7.92	62.7264	2.81425	8.89944
7.43	55.2049	2.72580	8.61974	7.93	62.8849	2.81603	8.90505
7.44	55.3536	2.72764	8.62554	7.94	63.0436	2.81780	8.91067
7.45	55.5025	2.72947	8.63134	7.95	63.2025	2.81957	8.91628
7.46	55.6516	2.73130	8.63713	7.96	63.3616	2.82135	8.92188
7.47	55.8009	2.73313	8.64292	7.97	63.5209	2.82312	8.92749
7.48	55.9504	2.73496	8.64870	7.98	63.6804	2.82489	8.93308
7.49	56.1001	2.73679	8.65448	7.99	63.8401	2.82666	8.93868
7.50	56.2500	2.73861	8.66025	**8.00**	64.0000	2.82843	8.94427
N	N²	√N̄	√10N̄	N	N²	√N̄	√10N̄

N	N²	√N	√10N	N	N²	√N	√10N
8.00	64.0000	2.82843	8.94427	**8.50**	72.2500	2.91548	9.21954
8.01	64.1601	2.83019	8.94986	8.51	72.4201	2.91719	9.22497
8.02	64.3204	2.83196	8.95545	8.52	72.5904	2.91890	9.23038
8.03	64.4809	2.83373	8.96103	8.53	72.7609	2.92062	9.23580
8.04	64.6416	2.83549	8.96660	8.54	72.9316	2.92233	9.24121
8.05	64.8025	2.83725	8.97218	8.55	73.1025	2.92404	9.24662
8.06	64.9636	2.83901	8.97775	8.56	73.2736	2.92575	9.25203
8.07	65.1249	2.84077	8.98332	8.57	73.4449	2.92746	9.25743
8.08	65.2864	2.84253	8.98888	8.58	73.6164	2.92916	9.26283
8.09	65.4481	2.84429	8.99444	8.59	73.7881	2.93087	9.26823
8.10	65.6100	2.84605	9.00000	**8.60**	73.9600	2.93258	9.27362
8.11	65.7721	2.84781	9.00555	8.61	74.1321	2.93428	9.27901
8.12	65.9344	2.84956	9.01110	8.62	74.3044	2.93598	9.28440
8.13	66.0969	2.85132	9.01665	8.63	74.4769	2.93769	9.28978
8.14	66.2596	2.85307	9.02219	8.64	74.6496	2.93939	9.29516
8.15	66.4225	2.85482	9.02774	8.65	74.8225	2.94109	9.30054
8.16	66.5856	2.85657	9.03327	8.66	74.9956	2.94279	9.30591
8.17	66.7489	2.85832	9.03881	8.67	75.1689	2.94449	9.31128
8.18	66.9124	2.86007	9.04434	8.68	75.3424	2.94618	9.31665
8.19	67.0761	2.86182	9.04986	8.69	75.5161	2.94788	9.32202
8.20	67.2400	2.86356	9.05539	**8.70**	75.6900	2.94958	9.32738
8.21	67.4041	2.86531	9.06091	8.71	75.8641	2.95127	9.33274
8.22	67.5684	2.86705	9.06642	8.72	76.0384	2.95296	9.33809
8.23	67.7329	2.86880	9.07193	8.73	76.2129	2.95466	9.34345
8.24	67.8976	2.87054	9.07744	8.74	76.3876	2.95635	9.34880
8.25	68.0625	2.87228	9.08295	8.75	76.5625	2.95804	9.35414
8.26	68.2276	2.87402	9.08845	8.76	76.7376	2.95973	9.35949
8.27	68.3929	2.87576	9.09395	8.77	76.9129	2.96142	9.36483
8.28	68.5584	2.87750	9.09945	8.78	77.0884	2.96311	9.37017
8.29	68.7241	2.87924	9.10494	8.79	77.2641	2.96479	9.37550
8.30	68.8900	2.88097	9.11043	**8.80**	77.4400	2.96648	9.38083
8.31	69.0561	2.88271	9.11592	8.81	77.6161	2.96816	9.38616
8.32	69.2224	2.88444	9.12140	8.82	77.7924	2.96985	9.39149
8.33	69.3889	2.88617	9.12688	8.83	77.9689	2.97153	9.39681
8.34	69.5556	2.88791	9.13236	8.84	78.1456	2.97321	9.40213
8.35	69.7225	2.88964	9.13783	8.85	78.3225	2.97489	9.40744
8.36	69.8896	2.89137	9.14330	8.86	78.4996	2.97658	9.41276
8.37	70.0569	2.89310	9.14877	8.87	78.6769	2.97825	9.41807
8.38	70.2244	2.89482	9.15423	8.88	78.8544	2.97993	9.42338
8.39	70.3921	2.89655	9.15969	8.89	79.0321	2.98161	9.42868
8.40	70.5600	2.89828	9.16515	**8.90**	79.2100	2.98329	9.43398
8.41	70.7281	2.90000	9.17061	8.91	79.3881	2.98496	9.43928
8.42	70.8964	2.90172	9.17606	8.92	79.5664	2.98664	9.44458
8.43	71.0649	2.90345	9.18150	8.93	79.7449	2.98831	9.44987
8.44	71.2336	2.90517	9.18695	8.94	79.9236	2.98998	9.45516
8.45	71.4025	2.90689	9.19239	8.95	80.1025	2.99166	9.46044
8.46	71.5716	2.90861	9.19783	8.96	80.2816	2.99333	9.46573
8.47	71.7409	2.91033	9.20326	8.97	80.4609	2.99500	9.47101
8.48	71.9104	2.91204	9.20869	8.98	80.6404	2.99666	9.47629
8.49	72.0801	2.91376	9.21412	8.99	80.8201	2.99833	9.48156
8.50	72.2500	2.91548	9.21954	**9.00**	81.0000	3.00000	9.48683
N	N²	√N	√10N	N	N²	√N	√10N

Table L ♦ (Continued)

N	N^2	$\sqrt{N}$	$\sqrt{10N}$	N	N^2	$\sqrt{N}$	$\sqrt{10N}$
9.00	81.0000	3.00000	9.48683	**9.50**	90.2500	3.08221	9.74679
9.01	81.1801	3.00167	9.49210	9.51	90.4401	3.08383	9.75192
9.02	81.3604	3.00333	9.49737	9.52	90.6304	3.08545	9.75705
9.03	81.5409	3.00500	9.50263	9.53	90.8209	3.08707	9.76217
9.04	81.7216	3.00666	9.50789	9.54	91.0116	3.08869	9.76729
9.05	81.9025	3.00832	9.51315	9.55	91.2025	3.09031	9.77241
9.06	82.0836	3.00998	9.51840	9.56	91.3936	3.09192	9.77753
9.07	82.2649	3.01164	9.52365	9.57	91.5849	3.09354	9.78264
9.08	82.4464	3.01330	9.52890	9.58	91.7764	3.09516	9.78775
9.09	82.6281	3.01496	9.53415	9.59	91.9681	3.09677	9.79285
9.10	82.8100	3.01662	9.53939	**9.60**	92.1600	3.09839	9.79796
9.11	82.9921	3.01828	9.54463	9.61	92.3521	3.10000	9.80306
9.12	83.1744	3.01993	9.54987	9.62	92.5444	3.10161	9.80816
9.13	83.3569	3.02159	9.55510	9.63	92.7369	3.10322	9.81326
9.14	83.5396	3.02324	9.56033	9.64	92.9296	3.10483	9.81835
9.15	83.7225	3.02490	9.56556	9.65	93.1225	3.10644	9.82344
9.16	83.9056	3.02655	9.57079	9.66	93.3156	3.10805	9.82853
9.17	84.0889	3.02820	9.57601	9.67	93.5089	3.10966	9.83362
9.18	84.2724	3.02985	9.58123	9.68	93.7024	3.11127	9.83870
9.19	84.4561	3.03150	9.58645	9.69	93.8961	3.11288	9.84378
9.20	84.6400	3.03315	9.59166	**9.70**	94.0900	3.11448	9.84886
9.21	84.8241	3.03480	9.59687	9.71	94.2841	3.11609	9.85393
9.22	85.0084	3.03645	9.60208	9.72	94.4784	3.11769	9.85901
9.23	85.1929	3.03809	9.60729	9.73	94.6729	3.11929	9.86408
9.24	85.3776	3.03974	9.61249	9.74	94.8676	3.12090	9.86914
9.25	85.5625	3.04138	9.61769	9.75	95.0625	3.12250	9.87421
9.26	85.7476	3.04302	9.62289	9.76	95.2576	3.12410	9.87927
9.27	85.9329	3.04467	9.62808	9.77	95.4529	3.12570	9.88433
9.28	86.1184	3.04631	9.63328	9.78	95.6484	3.12730	9.88939
9.29	86.3041	3.04795	9.63846	9.79	95.8441	3.12890	9.89444
9.30	86.4900	3.04959	9.64365	**9.80**	96.0400	3.13050	9.89949
9.31	86.6761	3.05123	9.64883	9.81	96.2361	3.13209	9.90454
9.32	86.8624	3.05287	9.65401	9.82	96.4324	3.13369	9.90959
9.33	87.0489	3.05450	9.65919	9.83	96.6289	3.13528	9.91464
9.34	87.2356	3.05614	9.66437	9.84	96.8256	3.13688	9.91968
9.35	87.4225	3.05778	9.66954	9.85	97.0225	3.13847	9.92472
9.36	87.6096	3.05941	9.67471	9.86	97.2196	3.14006	9.92975
9.37	87.7969	3.06105	9.67988	9.87	97.4169	3.14166	9.93479
9.38	87.9844	3.06268	9.68504	9.88	97.6144	3.14325	9.93982
9.39	88.1721	3.06431	9.69020	9.89	97.8121	3.14484	9.94485
9.40	88.3600	3.06594	9.69536	**9.90**	98.0100	3.14643	9.94987
9.41	88.5481	3.06757	9.70052	9.91	98.2081	3.14802	9.95490
9.42	88.7364	3.06920	9.70567	9.92	98.4064	3.14960	9.95992
9.43	88.9249	3.07083	9.71082	9.93	98.6049	3.15119	9.96494
9.44	89.1136	3.07246	9.71597	9.94	98.8036	3.15278	9.96995
9.45	89.3025	3.07409	9.72111	9.95	99.0025	3.15436	9.97497
9.46	89.4916	3.07571	9.72625	9.96	99.2016	3.15595	9.97998
9.47	89.6809	3.07734	9.73139	9.97	99.4009	3.15753	9.98499
9.48	89.8704	3.07896	9.73653	9.98	99.6004	3.15911	9.98999
9.49	90.0601	3.08058	9.74166	9.99	99.8001	3.16070	9.99500
9.50	90.2500	3.08221	9.74679	**10.00**	100.000	3.16228	10.0000
N	N^2	$\sqrt{N}$	$\sqrt{10N}$	N	N^2	$\sqrt{N}$	$\sqrt{10N}$

. References .

Applebaum, M. I., & Cramer, E. M. Some problems in the nonorthogonal analysis of variance. *Psychological Bulletin*, 1974, **81**, 335–343.

Atkinson, R. C., & Paulson, J. A. An approach to the psychology of instruction. *Psychological Bulletin*, 1972, **78**, 49–61.

Bennett, N. *Teaching styles and pupil progress*. London: Open Books, 1976.

Betz, M. A., & Gabriel, K. R. Type IV errors and analysis of simple effects. *Journal of Educational Statistics*, 1978, **3**, 121–143.

Blalock, H. M. *Causal inferences in non-experimental research*. Chapel Hill: University of North Carolina Press, 1964.

Blalock, H. M. (Ed.). *Causal models in the social sciences*. Chicago: Adline Publishing Co., 1971.

Bloom, B. S., Hasting, J. T., & Madaus, G. F. *Handbook on formative and summative evaluation of student learning*. New York: McGraw-Hill, 1971.

Bower, G. H., Clark, M. C., Lesgold, A. M., and Winzenz, D. Hierarchical retrieval schemes in recall of categorized word lists. *Journal of Verbal Learning and Verbal Behavior*, 1969, **8**, 323–343.

Bracht, G. H., & Glass, G. V. The external validity of experiments. *American Educational Research Journal*, 1968, **5**, 437–474.

Brunswik, E. Representative design and probabilistic theory in a functional psychology, *Psychological Review*, 1955, **62**, 193–217.

Campbell, D. T., & Stanley, J. C. Experimental and quasi-experimental designs for research on teaching. In Gage, N.L. (Ed.), *Handbook of research on teaching*. Chicago: Rand McNally, 1963.

Campbell, D. T., & Stanley, J. C. *Experimental and quasi-experimental designs for research*. Chicago: Rand McNally, 1966.

Cannon, W. B. *Bodily changes in pain, hunger, fear and rage* (2nd ed.). New York: Appleton, 1929.

Clarke, R. B., Coladarci, A. P., & Caffrey, J. *Statistical reasoning and procedures*. Columbus, Ohio: Charles E. Merrill Books, 1965.

Cochran, W. G. Some methods for strengthening the common χ^2 tests. *Biometrics*, 1954, **10**, 417–451.

Cochran, W. G. *Sampling techniques* (2nd ed.) New York: Wiley, 1966.

Cohen, J. *Statistical power analysis for the behavioral sciences*. New York: Academic Press, 1969.

Coleman, J. S., et al. *Equality of educational opportunity*. Washington: U.S. Government Printing Office, 1966.

Cooley, C. H. *Human nature and the social order*. New York: Scribner, 1902.

Cornfield, J., & Tukey, J. W. Average values of mean squares in factorials. *Annals of Mathematical Statistics*, 1956, **27**, 907–949.

Cronbach, L. J. Beyond the two disciplines of scientific psychology. *American Psychologist*, 1975, **30**, 116–127.

Dayton, C. M. *The design of educational experiments*. New York: McGraw-Hill, 1970.

Dixon, W. J., & Massey, F. J., Jr. *Introduction to statistical analysis* (3rd ed.). New York: McGraw-Hill, 1969.

Draper, N. R., & Smith, H. *Applied regression analysis*. New York: Wiley, 1968.

Duncan, O. D. *Introduction to structural equation models*. New York: Academic Press, 1975.

Elashoff, J. D. Analysis of covariance: A delicate instrument. *American Educational Research Journal*, 1969, 6, 383–401.

Elashoff, J. D., & Snow, R. E. *Pygmalion reconsidered*. Worthington, Ohio: Charles A. Jones Publishing Company, 1971.

Games, P. A. Type IV errors revisited. *Psychological Bulletin*, 1973, **80**, 304–307.

Games, P. A. Nesting, crossing, Type IV errors, and the role of statistical models. *American Educational Research Journal*, 1978, **15**, 253–258.

Glass, G. V., & Hakstian, A. R. Measures of association in comparative experiments: Their development and interpretation. *American Educational Research Journal*, 1969, 6, 403–414.

Glass, G. V., & Stanley, J. C. *Statistical methods in education and psychology*. Englewood Cliffs, N.J.: Prentice-Hall, 1970.

Goldman, R. D., Schmidt, D. E., Hewitt, B. N., & Fisher, R. Grading practices in different major fields. *American Educational Research Journal*, 1974, **11**, 343–357.

Guilford, J. P. *The nature of human intelligence*. New York: McGraw-Hill, 1967.

Guilford, J. P., & Fruchter, B. *Fundamental statistics in psychology and education* (5th ed.). New York: McGraw-Hill, 1973.

Hays, W. L. *Statistics for the social sciences* (2nd ed.). New York: Holt, Rinehart & Winston, 1973.

Hebble, P. W. The development of elementary school children's judgment of intent. *Child Development*, 1971, **42**, 1203–1215.

Hewitt, B. N., & Goldman, R. D. Occam's razor slices through the myth that college women overachieve. *Journal of Educational Psychology*, 1975, **67**, 325–330.

Hilgard, E. R., & Bower, G. H. *Theories of learning*. New York: Appleton-Century-Crofts, 1966.

Illich, I. *Deschooling Society*. New York: Harper and Row, 1971.

James, W. *The principles of psychology*. New York: Holt, 1890.

Jones, L. V. The nature of measurement. In Thorndike, R. L. (Ed.). *Educational Measurement* (2nd ed.). Washington: American Council of Education, 1971.

Kelley, H. H. Attribution theory in social psychology. In D. Levine (Ed.), *Nebraska symposium on motivation*, Vol. 15. Lincoln: University of Nebraska Press, 1967, 192–237.

Kerlinger, F. N., & Pedhazur, E. J. *Multiple regression in behavior research*. New York: Holt, Rinehart & Winston, 1973.

Kirk, R. E. *Experimental design: Procedures for the behavioral sciences*. Belmont, Calif.: Brooks/Cole, 1968.

Kuhn, T. S. *The structure of scientific revolutions* (2nd ed.). Foundations of the Unity of Science, Vol. 2, No. 2. Chicago: University of Chicago Press, 1970.

Levin, J. R. Determining sample size for planned and post hoc analysis of variance comparisons. *Journal of Educational Measurement*, 1975, **12**, 99–108.

Levin, J. R., & Marascuilo, L. A. Type IV errors and interactions. *Psychological Bulletin*, 1972, **78**, 368–374.

Levin, J. R., & Marascuilo, L. A. Type IV errors and games. *Psychological Bulletin*, 1973, **80**, 308–309.

London, H., & Nisbett, R. E. (Eds.) *Thought and feeling: Cognitive alteration of feeling states*. Chicago: Aldine, 1974.

Lord, F. M. A paradox in the interpretation of group comparisons. *Psychological Bulletin*, 1967, **68**, 304–305.

Majasan, J. K. College students' achievement as a function of the congruence between their beliefs and their instructor's beliefs. Unpublished doctoral dissertation, Stanford University, 1972.

Marascuilo, L. A., & Levin, J. R. Appropriate post hoc comparisons for interaction and nested hypotheses in analysis of variance designs: The elimination of Type IV errors. *American Educational Research Journal*, 1970, **7**, 397–421.

Marascuilo, L. A., & Levin, J. R. The simultaneous investigation of interaction and nested hypotheses in two-factor analysis of variance designs. *American Educational Research Journal*, 1976, **13**, 61–65.

Mead, G. H. *Mind, self and society*. Chicago: University of Chicago Press, 1934.

Miller, G. A. The magical number seven, plus or minus two: Some limits on our capacity for processing information. *Psychological Review*, 1956, **63**, 81–92.

Myers, J. L. *Fundamentals of experimental design* (3rd ed). Boston: Allyn and Bacon, 1979.

Neisser, U. *Cognition and reality*. San Francisco: Freeman, 1976.

Newell, A., & Simon, H. A. *Human problem-solving*. Englewood Cliffs, N.J.: Prentice-Hall, 1972.

Nisbitt, R. E., & Schacter, S. Cognitive manipulation of pain. *Journal of Experimental Social Psychology*, 1966, **2**, 227–236.

Piaget, J. *The moral judgment of the child* (translated by Marjorie Gabain). New York: Free Press, 1966.

Porter, A. C. Analysis strategies for some common evaluation paradigms. Paper presented at the Annual Meeting of the American Educational Research Association, 1973.

Rosenthal, R. *Experimenter effects in behavioral research*. New York: Appleton-Century-Crofts, 1966.

Rosenthal, R., & Jacobson, L. *Pygmalion in the classroom*. New York: Holt, Rinehart and Winston, 1968.

Runkel, P. J. Cognitive similarity in facilitating communication. *Sociometry*, 1956, **19**, 178–191.

Schacter, S., & Singer, J. E. Cognitive, social, and physiological determinants of emotional state. *Psychological Review*, 1962, **69**, 379–399.

Schacter, S., & Wheeler, L. Epinephrine, chlorpromazine, and amusement. *Journal of Abnormal and Social Psychology*, 1962, **65**, 121–128.

Shavelson, R. J. Teachers' decision making. In Gage, N.L. *Psychology of teaching methods* (75th Yearbook of the NSSE). Chicago: University of Chicago Press, 1976.

Shavelson, R. J., & Atwood, N. Teachers' estimates of student "states of mind." *British Journal of Teacher Education*, 1977, **3**, 131–138.

Shavelson, R. J., Cadwell, J., & Izu, I. Teachers' sensitivity to the reliability of information in making pedagogical decisions. *American Educational Research Journal*, 1977, **14**, 83–97.

Shavelson, R. J., Hubner, J. J., & Stanton, G. C. Self-concept: Validation of construct interpretations. *Review of Educational Research*, 1976, **46**, 407–441.

Siegel, S. *Nonparametric statistics for the behavioral sciences*. New York: McGraw-Hill, 1956.

Smith, M. L., & Glass, G. V. Meta-analysis of psychotherapy outcomes studies. *American Psychologist*, 1977, **32**, 752–760.

Snow, R. E. Representative and quasi-representative designs for research on teaching. *Review of Educational Research*, 1974, **44**, 265–291.

Thistlethwaite, D. L., & Campbell, D. T. Regression-discontinuity analysis: An alternative to the ex post facto experiment. *Journal of Educational Psychology*, 1969, **51**, 309–317.

Tversky, A., & Kahneman, D. Judgment under uncertainty: Heuristics and biases. *Science*, 1974, **185**, 1124–1131.

Valins, S. Cognitive effects of false heart-rate feedback. *Journal of Personality and Social Psychology*, 1966, **4**, 400–408.

Weiner, B. *Theories of motivation: From mechanism to cognition*. Chicago: Markham Publishing Co., 1972.

Weiner, B., & Peter, N. A cognitive-developmental analysis of achievement and moral judgments. *Developmental Psychology*, 1973, **9**, 290–309.

Wiley, D. E., & Harnischfeger, A. Explosion of a myth: Quantity of schooling and exposure to instruction, major educational vehicles. *Educational Researcher*, 1974, **3**, 7–11.

Winer, B. J. *Statistical principles in experimental design* (2nd ed.). New York: McGraw-Hill, 1971.

· Index ·